D0327865

See You on the High Ground

The Jared Monti Story

See You on the High Ground

The Jared Monti Story

by

Len Sandler

WWW. FIRESHIPPRESS.COM

See You on the High Ground by Len Sandler

Copyright © Dec 2014 Len Sandler

All rights reserved. No part of this book may be used or reproduced by any means without the written permission of the publisher except in the case of brief quotation embodied in critical articles and reviews.

ISBN-13: 978-1-61179-351-2 (Paperback)
ISBN -978-1-61179-352-9 (e-book)

BISAC Subject Heading:
BIO008000 Biography Military

Portrait photo courtesy of Phil Taylor
Front cover photo by Jimmy McPherson
Cover assembly by Christine Horner

Address all correspondence to:
Fireship Press, LLC
P. O. Box 68412
Tucson, AZ 85737
Or visit our website at:
www.fireshippress.com

Commentary

"A wonderful gift – both Jared and the book!" – Susan Fitzpatrick Bradbury

“Len Sandler's account and admirable telling of the Jared Monti story gains its power from the brutal facts as well as its humanity in illustrating the life of a great American Soldier." – MAJ Joe Hansen

"I've been reading this book whenever I go to the gym at work because it's the only free time I have. I'm pretty sure my coworkers think I'm nuts because I've gone from laughing at Jared's antics to crying with tears streaming down my face." – Jennifer Slage

“Wow, what a moving story!”- Doug Boren, author of *Patriot's Point*

“The book is full of laughs and tears. It is a great tribute to an amazing man and friend of mine. Thank you for writing this.” – SSG John Hawes

“Len Sandler has captured the saga of Jared Monti in such a moving and explicit way, you can't put this book down. A great story. You'll stand and salute when you're done!” – Mike Lowe, iHeart Media Program Director

“I am blown away by the stories from those of you who served with Jared. You knew a Jared I did not know. I knew he was great but I'm his mother, he was always my hero. Thank you all for sharing your stories with Len. It's helped me more than you know.” – Janet Monti

“A great read! I am forever indebted to Len Sandler, my friend and classmate.” – Jared’s father, Paul Monti

“I’m speechless. Well done, Len.” – MSG Lee Power

"Just finished reading this; great read but have the tissues close by!!!!" – Rick Wood

"I read the book and it is awesome! A must read. You will be proud and amazed!" – Rita Hammerstad

"I just finished reading it, Len. Tears of laughter and tears of joy shed throughout. You captured Jared as he was. Truly a deeply loving and caring person." – Barb Dresser

“When you have turned the final page you’ll understand a lot more about service and sacrifice, especially if, like me, you’ve never been in the military. You’ll also understand just how many people one person can touch just by being someone who is devoted to others. Jared Monti died trying to save one of his “guys” but he lives on in this book.” – Alex Ashlock, Director & Producer, WBUR & NPR Radio

Table of Contents

Table of Contents

Photographs and illustrations that accompany this book can be viewed at www.seeyouonthehighground.com

Dedication

SFC Jared Monti was not the only hero in the battle on Hill 2610. There were 15 other brave American soldiers in the patrol who refused to back down despite the overwhelming odds against them. Jared undoubtedly would have said, "Write about them. There's no need to mention me." At the very least, he would have approved of having this book dedicated to his comrades-in-arms: SSG Chris Cunningham, SSG Patrick Lybert, SGT John Hawes, SPC John Garner, SSG Chris Grzecki, SPC Sean Smith, SPC Franklin Woods, SPC Brian Gonterman, SPC Max Noble, PFC Brian Bradbury, PFC Derek James, SPC Matthew Chambers, SPC Shawn Heistand, SPC Daniel Linnihan, and SSG Josh Renken.

As John Hawes says, "Jared would have been proud to have this book dedicated to 'his boys.' He would have wanted it known that we fought together as a team."

"It would be a challenge to find a group of soldiers who better represent the legacy of the 10th Mountain Division than the soldiers who fought so bravely on top of that rocky mountain near Gowardesh, Afghanistan," proclaims 10th Mountain Division Commander Major General Stephen J. Townsend. "Although badly outnumbered and separated from their unit, those soldiers refused to accept defeat."

Special thanks are extended to Paul and the Monti family, along with Janet and the Ross family for their invaluable support and assistance. In addition, I am indebted to my wife Marilyn who has been my partner in every sense of the word for nearly 30 years. As my muse and sounding board, she was instrumental in the writing of this book. I could not have done it without her.

Foreword

By General George W. Casey, Jr. (Ret.)
Former U. S. Army Chief of Staff

I was honored when Len Sandler asked me to write the foreword to his book on Jared Monti. I was there on September 17, 2009 when President Obama presented the Medal of Honor to his parents, Paul and Janet, where I heard the President speak of Jared's actions in Afghanistan. I had met and got to know the Monti family the night before at a dinner at my quarters. I felt an immediate connection to them because I, too, was from Massachusetts and I, too, had lost a family member in combat. My father, Major General George W. Casey, commander of the Army's 1st Air Cavalry Division in Viet Nam, was killed on July 7, 1970 in a helicopter crash while en route to a hospital to visit his wounded soldiers. I was 21 and had just been commissioned a 2nd Lieutenant in the Army after graduating from Georgetown University. I had a sense of what they were dealing with.

I stayed in touch with Paul and Janet and visited Jared's grave at Bourne National Cemetery with Paul. I was struck by their stories about him, and by their obvious pride in the wonderful man he was. They had instilled in him the importance of family and the values and determination to succeed that guided his life and inspired him to inspire others. They were very proud, but grieving terribly from his loss.

On September 11th, 2001, our world changed forever. Brave Americans like Jared carried the fight to the enemy in Iraq and Afghanistan and liberated millions from tyranny and oppression. Len not only describes the incredible things Jared and his generation did to secure this country, but he also explains the incredible person Jared was. He shows how virtually everyone

Jared came in touch with throughout his civilian and military life was affected by him. Jared represents a new generation of 21st Century heroes that this country can be proud of. He also represents the best of what we seek in our Non-Commissioned Officers, and because of that he was featured in a 2009 Department of the Army video to highlight the "Year of the NCO".

Jared was one of the greatest of his generation. He epitomizes what is best about America and is a shining symbol of what makes this country great. His willingness to sacrifice to help build a better future for others and to preserve our way of life was exemplary.

Our Army today is recognized as the best Army in the world. Since September 11, 2001, it has successfully accomplished every mission given to it by our national leadership. The men and women of our armed forces are embraced by the American people and hailed as the most respected professionals in the country. I am extremely proud to have led an Army that consisted of soldiers like Jared Monti, and I believe his book will help Americans understand why young people like Jared serve, and why parents like Paul and Janet will continue to raise men and women that respect the values that make this country what it is today—the greatest nation on earth.

Preface

This Is What He Was Meant to Do

Deliberately exposing himself to machine gun and rocket-propelled grenade fire, Jared Monti sacrificed himself attempting, not once but three times, to rescue one of his squad members from the “kill zone” after his patrol came under attack by insurgents on a mountain in Afghanistan. He declared, “He’s my guy. I’m going to get him.” In doing so, Jared was able to protect the rest of the unit by drawing fire away from them and buy time for air support to arrive. After suffering a direct hit from an RPG, the 30-year-old SFC recited the Lord’s Prayer as he lay dying. His last words were, “I’ve made peace with God. Tell my family I love them.”

“I've come to the conclusion, and it's the only way I can deal with it, that it was his destiny. This is what he was meant to do,” confesses his mother Janet.

His father, my childhood friend Paul, has been unable to throw out anything of his son’s. His house is crowded with boxes of Jared’s personal belongings, and he continues to drive Jared’s Dodge Ram truck. Songwriter Connie Harrington heard a radio interview with Paul that inspired “I Drive Your Truck”, which became the #1 country song in America and was named Song of the Year at both the 2013 CMA and 2014 ACM Awards shows. “I Drive Your Truck” was given the first annual Golden Boot Award as 2014 Song of the Year.

“The actions we honor today were not a passing moment of courage. They were the culmination of a life of character and commitment,” said Barack Obama as he posthumously presented Jared with the first Medal of Honor of his presidency on September 17, 2009. Jared died a heroic death, but more importantly, lived a heroic life. This is the story of that life.

PART I

A Hero in the Making

The Monti Tree

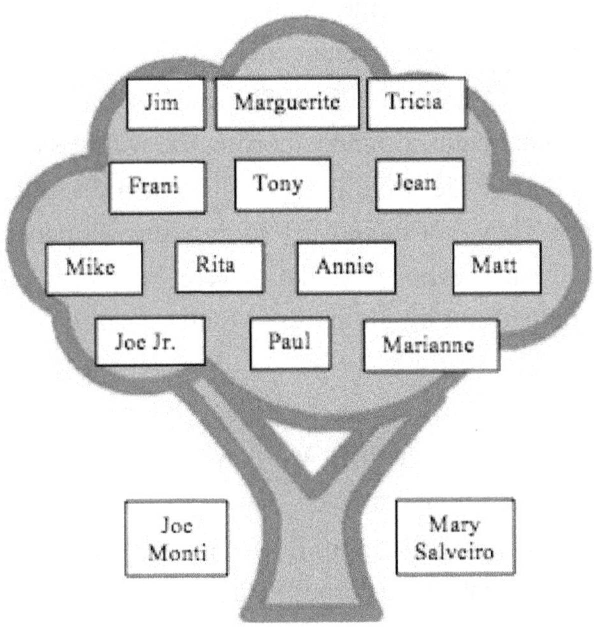

Chapter 1
The Vine & the Tomatoes

To understand who Jared Monti was, you have to understand from whom he came. The tale starts with his grandparents: Joe and Mary on his father's side, Urban and Marjorie on his mother's side.

"We didn't have a lot of money in our family, but wealth is measured in many forms," said Jared's godfather and uncle, Mike Monti. "If the term of measurement is love and laughter, we were very well off." Mike's sister Jean says simply, "My parents were an inspiration to all of us."

Mary was married to Joseph. A story doesn't get much more biblical than that. They had 13 children but actually talked about having 15. Tricia was the youngest. Their doctor said he wouldn't charge them for her delivery as long as they promised not to have any more kids. Evidently, the doctor was getting weary, even if Mary and Joe weren't. They reluctantly agreed.

Joe worked at the Fore River Shipyard in Quincy, MA as a rigger. There were signs around exhorting the workers to "Produce, produce, produce." He would say, "That's what I did. Thirteen kids' worth." They consumed 20-30 big brown paper bags of groceries a week. Fortunately, there were butchers, bakers, and others who helped out by giving the Montis quantity discounts on food.

Frani (Monti) Harring says, "Every Christmas, we'd take a picture with the whole family. Mom was always in a maternity dress carrying a different baby."

"We just had immediate family at our small wedding, but that was 85 people," recalls Rita (Monti) Hammerstad with a laugh.

"Because our family was so large, we learned to stand by each other. Family is and will always be our world. You learned togetherness and compassion. Somehow, Jared inherited a depth of compassion well beyond any of us," claims Annie (Monti) Eagles.

"Many a summer night, Joe would come home from work and say, 'Let's all go to Sunset Lake or Wollaston Beach.' Then they'd pile 15 people into the car. Don't ask me how they did that. On the way home, they'd have those same 15 in the car, all soaking wet," recalls neighbor Frank Drollett. "I remember having dinner over their house. It was like an army of people eating. They'd have a table that took up a whole wall. Then, there was another table set up like the letter 'T.' They welcomed everyone into their home. Lots of laughter, teasing, and good food. Going over the Monti's was always a special time."

Tricia (Monti) Corsini says, "If it's not chaotic, I'm lost. That's how I was brought up. That's all I know." There is an advantage to being the youngest. She admits, "I was spoiled rotten. I had lots of little mothers and fathers to take care of me. I was the baby. In fact, they still call me, 'Baby' and not 'Tricia' most of the time. Unless my mother was mad at me. Then it was 'Patricia Ann.' When I heard that, I knew I was in trouble."

Joe was proud of his children, but also proud of the tomato plants he raised in the back yard. He'd sometimes combine both thoughts by saying, "Your mother and I are the vine and you kids are our tomatoes."

He loved going dancing with Mary at the local Knights of Columbus Hall on Saturday nights. "Joe was such a good dancer. At family functions, he'd say to me, 'C'mon, Baby, let's dance,' says Marti, who is married to Tony Monti. I had a hard time keeping up with him. I'd ask him not to go too fast. Of course, he'd whisper to me how I was his favorite. He'd say that to all the daughters and daughters-in-law. He was a charmer."

When Marti and Tony had a son, they decided to name him after Joe. "I remember telling my Dad that we just had a son and he responded with, 'It's great that God blessed you with a son,'" Tony reveals. "Then I said, 'His name is Joseph. We decided to name him after you.' He got all choked up and had such a huge grin on his face. I'll never forget it. He was so proud. What better legacy is there than to name our first son after THE Joe Monti? Of course, my brother, Joe, Jr., always kidded us and said that it's great we named our son after him."

Among the ships Joe helped build at the Fore River Shipyard was the Battleship USS *Massachusetts,* which fired the first 16 inch shells of World War II at the battle of Casablanca, and the last at a Japanese steel mill at Hamamatsu. Joe was a perfect rigger in that he was just 5'2" but strong. He would get down on his hands and knees in the hold of the ship in tight crawl spaces to run electrical power lines. He snuck Mary on board once for a personal tour. She was the first woman to set foot on the USS *Massachusetts*. Fortunately, they didn't get caught. It's easy to see where Jared's mischievous side came from.

Joe worked alongside James J. Kilroy, who would write the phrase KILROY WAS HERE with indelible yellow crayon on the sections of a ship that he had inspected. He'd also draw a little cartoon of a bald-headed figure peeking over a wall with the fingers of each hand gripping the wall. Other inspectors would simply use chalk, but sometimes workers would erase the chalk so they could get double-paid for their work.

World War II sailors saw the graffiti on their ships and began to duplicate it wherever they went. Other branches of the service picked up the practice. Soon, "Kilroy was here" became a pop culture phenomenon as it appeared in unlikely places in war zones throughout the world. It became as famous as the phrase "G. I. Joe." Soldiers to this day talk about seeing building rubble in far-flung areas of war zones scrawled with that famous doodle. It was permanently engraved on the World War II Memorial in Washington, DC as a bit of nostalgia for visiting veterans.

Legend has it that German intelligence officers found the phrase on captured American equipment and brought the information to Adolph Hitler, who thought that Kilroy must be a secret code name of a high-level spy or military operation. He ordered them to find out the meaning of the name "Kilroy." Joseph Stalin is said to have seen the graffiti in a bathroom at the Potsdam Conference and asked his aides to investigate its origin.

Mary Monti never took a day off. If she was sick, she toughed it out. According to Mike, "She was a wonderful mother. The most distinctive thing about her aside from her cooking was her laugh. It was kind of a guffaw. We'd watch some comedy show on television and she'd laugh like crazy. The children got more of a kick out of that laugh than watching any show. She was a great Red Sox fan, too. She'd be the one cheering the loudest during the games on TV." Paul recalls, "She'd always watch American Bandstand. She knew all the names of all the couples who danced on the show." Frani said, "We were blessed to have the parents we did. They were so warm and caring. I'm so proud to be part of this family."

When Joe wasn't at home or working at the shipyard, he was at St. Francis of Assisi Church in Braintree. Saint Francis represented, in many ways, Joe and the values he passed down to his children and eventually to his grandchildren, including Jared. Joe didn't preach his religion to anyone. He just lived it. Others learned from his example.

It was said that Joe did everything for the church but celebrate the mass. He ushered at events, taught Sunday School, helped the Boy Scouts, painted rooms, passed the collection plate, and tallied the collections on Sundays. Joe was a Eucharistic Minister, which meant that he could assist with communion. He'd also get the vestments ready for the priest. Mary would always sit in the exact same seat in church. Pastor Reverend Richard P. Crowley used to call Joe "the real Pastor" or even "Monsignor." Mary would simply call him "Honey."

According to Tony, "Before any of us got married, we had to be careful around my Dad. Once, Marti and I were sitting too close. I remember Dad giving me that stare of his and saying, 'ANTHONY!' in a stern voice. Then he pointed to his wedding ring as if to say, 'You'd better wait until you're married.'"

"We couldn't accommodate all the families at the table at one time," admitted Mary in an interview published by the church

"Family Newspaper" in March of 1997. "So Joe and I figured a solution. We'd invite one of the kids' families to dinner and have the rest show up later in the day. They would take turns at the table." That explains why holiday dinners would start in the morning and last until late in the evening. "Sunday dinners with my parents was the greatest place you could be in the world," claims Marianne (Monti) Riley. "Nothing but laughter and good times."

On weekdays, Joe followed the same routine. He'd attend mass in the morning, come home for breakfast, and then go to work. One of his favorite sayings was, "A day's work for a day's pay." He'd sometimes take a second job at the Post Office, especially around Christmas time. He also did electrical work for people, never handing out a bill. He'd say, "Pay me what you can afford."

Marianne, the oldest daughter, recalls, "I was Little Miss Mom. Fortunately, I loved kids. I'd change their diapers, and by the time I was 10 years old I was doing a lot of the cooking to help my mother out. I can remember people saying, 'I'll bet you'll never have kids of your own.' Just the opposite was true. I couldn't wait to have kids of my own."

All of the children had jobs, starting with paper routes from the time they were old enough to carry newspapers. Nothing was ever handed to them. Just the opposite. They had to earn everything they got. They also learned about the importance of giving to others. There wasn't enough money for the kids to buy lunch at school, but they would always put part of what they earned in a red metal milk can that Mary kept for their milk money. They'd put money in another coin box for what Joseph called, "The Missions of the Church." He'd sometimes hold up the box and shake it in front of the kids and say, "Don't forget. You always have to give back. Part of what you earn has to go to the church." Joseph was once named Kiwanis' "Man of the Year". From the way his children describe him, he could have been "Man of the Year" every year.

"I'd always look forward to Christmas because I'd get to wear something new, not a hand-me-down," notes Rita. Although the kids didn't know it, their presents were left at the front door by volunteers. Joe would help the church year-round and the church would, in turn, help the family at Christmas time. He taught them that hard work pays dividends. He'd say to them, "We'll give you a roof over your heads but you have to do the rest. That's what will make you a better person." The 13 kids slept as many as three to a bed. If they wanted to go to college, they knew they'd have to find a way to pay for it. They learned a lot of humbling lessons.

Joe died of colon cancer and other assorted ailments in 1999 at age 85 on Easter Sunday. There were 1,200 people at his funeral and 200 cars in the procession. That's pretty impressive for someone who began as a shipyard worker and wound up as a meter reader for Massachusetts Electric before retiring. "I still remember getting laryngitis from saying, 'Thank you for coming' over and over again to all those at his funeral," recalls Rita.

People were standing outside in the cold waiting to get into the church. "You kept hearing them say how he was like a father to them," says Annie. "At first it bothered me. I felt like saying back to them that he was MY father, not yours. Then, I realized he was like a father to everyone. He just happened to live in our house. He was known for his compassion. He tried to instill that in all of us."

Paul fondly recalls an outing with his Dad shortly before he died. "We had a wonderful time. I took him out for a day. We drove to the shipyard, to places we had gone fishing, and to other spots that meant a lot to him. It was a day that I'll cherish forever."

"My sister Frani and I were taking care of Dad at the end," said Rita. "We had to give him doses of morphine so he wouldn't feel the pain. He couldn't talk. I remember saying to him, 'Dad, you're 85 and I'm 40. I have 45 more years to raise hell.' He held up a crooked finger and pointed it at me. I got the message. He was saying, 'You'd better be careful. I'll be watching you.' It was about 2:30 a.m. when we left my Mom and Dad alone for a short time to get some sleep, and that's when he died. When they were together. She held his hand as he died."

Mary passed away in 2001 at age 82 from complications resulting from a perforated bowel she suffered during a routine colonoscopy. "We gave her a Red Sox cap on her deathbed. She rooted for them right up to the end," said Frani. The family regrets the fact that she didn't live to see her beloved team finally, after 86 years of futility, win the World Series three years later.

Joe and Mary didn't leave much to their children except for some small mementos. Mike has the wooden spoon that his mother used to use to stir her spaghetti sauce, along with the baking pans that she received as a wedding present in 1939. There's also a bean pot, a tapestry that he displays in his living room with the words *God Bless our Family*, and a small picture that says, *It's not a sin to be rich nowadays. It's a miracle*. Mike admits, "If I had a choice of ten thousand dollars or Mom's wooden cooking spoon, I'd take the spoon. Those things are so important to us that they're written into our will. They're the things of real value. We'll pass them on to our kids."

Rita spoke of another choice. "If could choose any parents in the world, I'd take my Mom and Dad. No question about it. If we were poor, we didn't know it. We were rich in so many ways." "It was an honor to be part of our family," proclaims Jean.

According to Paul, "When a father has a child, he immediately begins thinking, 'What values should my child learn? What should I give my child to help make him or her successful in life?' You want them to be brave and courageous but you also want them to be compassionate and caring. It wasn't difficult. It was easy to choose the values to pass on. I simply followed the teachings of my father, who was a wonderful man. He didn't just do things to keep his own family going. He was always doing things for others. He lived the word 'Love.' It was his values that I tried to pass onto my children."

Chapter 2
"I'm the Richest Man in the World"

When they were dating, Joe Monti cut Mary Ann Salveiro's picture out of the high school yearbook to keep in his wallet. Paul admits, "I wondered who the sucker was on the other side of the page who had his picture carried around by my father." Later, he found out it was, by coincidence, Janet's father, Urban Allan Ross, who was in the same class in school.

Joe and Mary were married for 59 years, while Urban and Marjorie Ross were married for 41. That's precisely 100 years between them and a combined total of 24 children. While the

Montis were exclusively Italian, the Ross family was an all-American hybrid. "Ross is a 'Heinz 57' name. It's French, Welsh, German, and Scottish. It's the United Nations," jokes Janet, who was the oldest of the 11 children. She might not have had to wear hand-me-down clothes like her siblings, but she certainly had to take on more household chores than most children. "I was kept crazy busy helping out with the little ones while also going to school. I changed plenty of diapers, fed the others, and helped around the house. It wasn't easy. I had to be the responsible one," she says.

"My father Urban was loving and nurturing. He'd do anything for us. He was a forklift operator for Proctor and Gamble in Quincy. He and his brothers actually built our house in East Braintree. We learned to do without a lot of things with such a large family. I wouldn't have traded it for anything, though," Janet adds. "The biggest thing I remember about my father was his empathy. For instance, I remember when I had to get a root canal as a kid. Naturally, I was scared. I'll never forget when he said, 'I wish I could go in your place.' What could you say to that? It made me say, 'That's okay, Dad. I can do it.'"

Janet remembers, "My Dad never wanted to be a supervisor. Jared was that way, too. He never wanted to be an officer. He wanted no part of any politics. Same thing for me. I wanted to be an LPN (Licensed Practical Nurse). We all preferred hands-on work.

"The family was big and confusing with all those kids but my mother and father were great parents," Janet recollects. "We had a long picnic table we used as a dining table. Six kids on one side and five on the other. My Mom and Dad on the ends. They couldn't do enough for us." Like Mary, Marjorie didn't drive, so Urban had the responsibility of taking the children around until Janet was old enough to get her license.

The Ross children were very close, just like the Montis. Frankly, they didn't have much of a choice. "One of our traditions was back-scratching. I called it 'Gitchigatchi.' We'd line up in a straight line and we'd all scratch each other's backs. Funny that none of us ever thought of doing it in a circle. That probably would have made more sense," recalls Terri (Ross) Lindsay. It was the symbolic beginning of the children adopting the life-long practice of "having each other's backs."

"In our family, if you were called in for dinner, we knew that you'd better come running. If you weren't there on time, there might not be anything left for you. My mother would bring home two full shopping carts of food. When she walked in the door, we'd run out and say, 'Did you get anything good?' If it was Captain Crunch with Crunchberries, it wouldn't make it to the cabinet. It would be gone within minutes," recounts Terri.

"I hated canned peas," continues Terri. "They'd make me sit there until I ate them. Sometimes I'd feed them to the dog. I remember being in fourth grade and my parents said, 'We have an announcement to make, but we won't make it until Terri eats her peas.' I didn't want to do that so I blurted out, 'You're just going to tell us you're having another baby.' That was going to be Lynda, the youngest in the family. I guess I spoiled their surprise, but I didn't have to eat the peas, so it was worth it to me."

On Saturday, November 28, 1942, Urban's brother Archie was home on leave from the military and they decided to go into Boston together to celebrate. The "place to be" at the time was the Cocoanut Grove night club in the Bay Village area. However, it was uncomfortably crowded that night, so they decided to leave and go someplace else. Coincidentally, Marjorie was babysitting for a couple who went to the same night club but also left early because of the crowd. The two brothers, as well as the couple for whom Marjorie was babysitting, were given a second chance at life because of their decision.

A former speakeasy, the Cocoanut Grove suffered the most tragic nightclub fire in history that night. A total of 492 people were killed and hundreds of others injured, many with serious second and third degree burns. It's believed that more than a thousand people were crammed into the Cocoanut Grove, despite the fact that the official capacity was just 460. The resultant scandal led to a reform of safety standards and building codes.

Decorated in a South Seas tropical motif, the club's restaurant, bars, and lounges were covered with paper palm trees, cloth draperies, and flammable decorations, some of which obscured the exit signs. The main entrance was a single revolving door that quickly became jammed with people trying to escape the fire. Side doors had been locked to prevent anyone from sneaking in without paying. There were some emergency exits, but they opened inward, so that a panicked crowd pressing against them trapped patrons inside.

It wasn't the last time Urban would narrowly escape death. He served in the Army and was stationed in Italy during World War II. His parachute was stolen just before a mission. Supplies were scarce and there wasn't a spare for him. He was told, "Look, if you have to bail out, just hold on tight. You don't need a chute." He didn't think that was very safe and so he protested. He was replaced on the plane, which was subsequently shot down and all on board were killed. He was grateful to be given not just a second but a third chance at life.

That may have led to his quick action after the war was over. He had been corresponding with a woman named Marjorie Edwards, who was one of the many who volunteered to write letters to U. S. Servicemen stationed overseas. She had been given Urban's name at random. They established a rapport during their exchange of letters. This developed into romance, and they became engaged shortly after meeting for the first time in October of 1945. They were married in June of 1946. Marjorie, who was born Protestant, converted to Catholicism so she and Urban could be married in a Catholic church.

Urban suffered a mild heart attack in 1969 – the same year that daughter Lynda was born – while swimming in the water during a company outing at Lake Pearl in Wrentham, MA. The family worried about his health issues from that time forward. Despite the fact that they put a pool into their back yard when they moved from Braintree to South Weymouth, he never went into it.

"I looked at our life as controlled chaos, recalls daughter Patti (Ross) Furtney. "Always people coming and going. We didn't know anything else. It was crazy but a lot of fun. I never thought of us as poor. We had everything we needed."

Marjorie was fond of saying to people she met, "I'm the mother of 11 children," to which they'd typically respond, "You're kidding." She'd then proudly come back with, "No, I'm not."

Patti remembers, "When we used to fight, my dad would sit us in a chair and have us stare at each other. He'd make us sit there and eventually we'd start laughing. Then he'd ask if we were okay. He would remind us that if we were laughing, we couldn't be fighting. We'd say we're fine and we'd run off to play together."

"Since Janet was the oldest, she got to practice being a nurse by taking care of us when we got hurt. I can remember being in first grade and having stitches over my eye. They broke and she took me to the doctor because our parents were away," Patti says. "She used to put us up on the step stool and cut our hair, too. She was a hairdresser before becoming a nurse, so you could say we helped prepare her for that, too."

"I wanted my own bicycle for years, recalls Patti. "We only had a couple of bikes for all the kids. I had to stand up to pedal the bike I got to use. It was too small for me to sit down on it. I remember saving over $100 to buy an expensive 10-speed fancy bike I wanted. My sisters Lynda and Barbara each chose bikes that cost just $30 or $40 dollars. I was really mad. Why should they be able to get a bike and not me? My parents finally asked if I would be willing to get a bike like my sisters had. I said I would. I figured it was better than nothing. I went riding with them and learned an important lesson. It was about sharing so everyone could get something, rather than my getting the fancy, expensive bike and them getting nothing. That was the environment we grew up in. We all shared. We were all playmates. My father was always teaching us a lesson. He didn't lecture us. He taught us. You didn't want to disappoint him."

Patti remembers how her parents would sit down with each of the children and show them Urban's paycheck and go through the monthly bills with them. She says, "It made us appreciate the value of money. Unlike many kids, we grew to understand that there wasn't an unlimited supply of money. It helped you to appreciate why you might get a 'no' when you wanted to buy something."

When the Ross family moved to nearby South Weymouth before Janet's senior year, she was able to finish high school with her class in Braintree thanks to her father. Since Marjorie didn't drive, it was up to Urban to help get the children off in the morning, take Janet to school in Braintree, go to work in Quincy, and then pick her up after school. "I'll never forget what my Dad did for me. He was the kind of person who would do without so his kids could have what they needed. I knew I had to stay out of trouble because my Dad was going to pick me up. So I could never get detention. That was probably a good thing."

Urban died at age 69 in 1987 of brain and lung cancer after earlier having surgery for colon cancer. Janet cherished the final weekends she got to spend with him, and recalls how they moved Thanksgiving up to the middle of the summer that year so they could have one last family gathering before his death.

One of Urban's favorite lines was, "I'm the richest man in the world. My kids are my wealth." The grandchildren loved to pile on Urban, much to his delight. If there was anything he adored as much as his children, it was his grandchildren. "I was only 10 years old when I watched that man die," says Jared's younger brother Tim. "I didn't understand it completely but it really affected me. He was a hell of a granddad. He had a heart attack and several kinds of cancer. My grandmother took care of him while raising 11 kids. That's quite an accomplishment."

The old expression, "The apple doesn't fall far from the tree" comes to mind. But in this case, the apple named Jared came from two equally impressive strong, proud family trees called "Monti" and "Ross."

Chapter 3
"I Have a Son. I Have a Boy."

Janet Ross was a year behind Paul at Braintree High School. They got to know each other when they marched together in the Braintree Warriors Drum and Bugle Corps. With all their siblings, finding privacy was a problem as they were dating. Since Janet was the oldest, she would often babysit for her brothers and sisters. As her sister Terri recalls, "Paul was always over our house. I still remember how I'd sit on the stairs with the other kids and we'd watch them and try to listen carefully, until Janet would glance over and catch us. She'd then send us back to our rooms. She was always larger than life. I've always looked up to her." That didn't keep them from playing tricks on her. "I remember once when my brother Allan embarrassed me," says Janet with a smile. "I had a laundry chute in my room that allowed you to drop things down into the basement. Once I was sitting there with Paul when Allan went to my room and threw all my 'intimate apparel' down piece by piece."

Evidently they concluded the only way they were going to get privacy was to get married, so in 1970 they were wed by Father James Haddad, a visiting Priest at the St. Francis Church in Weymouth who had impressed Janet with his eloquent sermons.

Jared was born at Quincy Hospital on September 20, 1975. The

Monti family was living in Abington, MA at the time, but soon after moved to Raynham. Delivered via caesarean section because of his size, Jared was what Paul referred to as “one big bruiser of a baby” weighing in at 9 pounds 4½ ounces. His uncles called him “Moose.” His private baptism was performed by Father Haddad.

“I was thrilled when I was asked to be Jared’s godmother. It was like returning the favor, because Janet is my godmother,” says Terri. “I can still remember holding him at his baptism and not wanting to let him go.” Mike recalls, “I was honored to be named godfather. I’ve always looked up to Paul. We’ve always had a close relationship and I had that kind of relationship with Jared, too.”

Their new child was named “Christopher Michael” for a few hours. Paul and Janet had talked about calling him “Jared Christopher” but were hesitant because they felt it wasn’t a “modern sounding” name. According to Janet, “I was looking through old books and found the Hebrew name ‘Jared.’ I just loved it. My room-mate in the hospital said, ‘If that’s what you want to name him, you should do it.’ That made the difference. Paul came in and he agreed. I said to the hospital staff, ‘You’re going to hate me. I know we’ve already filled out the paperwork, but I want to change the baby’s name.’ So we tore up the old birth record and filled out a new one, changing the name from Christopher Michael to Jared Christopher.”

Paul left the hospital that night with what he describes as “an ear-to-ear grin” and remembers pumping his fist in celebration. He kept saying to himself, “I have a boy. I have a son.” Years later, he posted this message to Jared: “It seems like yesterday that I first saw you in Quincy Hospital. What a joy you were. A happy, smiling child who grew into an incredible man but never lost that great smile.”

Cousin Michelle said, “I remember Jared as a little baby. He was about eight years younger than I was, and I remember seeing him on Sunday afternoons at my grandparents' house eating spaghetti and getting sauce all over his face. He had a big, round 'Charlie Brown' head and was *sooo* cute and pudgy."

Raynham is a small New England town that, like so many others, was named after a town in England. With a population of just over 13,000, it's located in Bristol County 32 miles south of Boston and 22 miles northeast of Providence, Rhode Island. According to the 2010 census, the per capita income for the working-class community is $24,476. Picturesque Raynham Center is dominated by the huge First Congregational Church. Raynham carries the distinction of being the first town in the United States to be founded by a woman, Elizabeth Pole. Originally settled in 1639 as part of Taunton, it was incorporated in 1731. Raynham Park, the town's biggest attraction, featured greyhound racing until a referendum in the state election led to the banning of the practice. The track was closed on January 1, 2010.

There are two other famous historical figures who made their home in Raynham. The first was Shibodee Turrey Wurry, who, at age 16, was captured by slave traders in coastal West Africa around 1758. He was chained and placed in the hold of a slave ship named *Dove*. The ship was bound for Virginia but was damaged in a severe storm and was forced to change course and land in Rhode Island. He was purchased by John Gilmore of Raynham and given the name Toby Gilmore. John was drafted to serve in the Continental Army at the start of the Revolutionary War. As was the custom, he could avoid serving in the military if he could get someone to take his place. Legend has it that Toby volunteered in 1776 with the understanding that the act would gain him his freedom. He crossed the Delaware with General George Washington, served as his Tent Master, and spent the brutal winter of 1776 at Valley Forge. Washington presented Toby with a cannon in appreciation for his service. Fortunately, military awards are a lot smaller these days.

Private Frederick C. Anderson lived an American success story of his own. An orphan, he was placed in a South Boston workhouse called The House of Industry. At age 14, Anderson was sent on the "Orphan Train" which transported abandoned and homeless children from cities to rural areas. When the train reached Raynham, Anderson was chosen by Stilman Wilber, who put him to work on his farm. Anderson played a real-life game of Capture the Flag at the Civil War battle of Wheldon Railroad, also known as the Battle of Globe Tavern, on September 6, 1864. He wound up retrieving the battle flag of the 27th South Carolina Regiment and returning it to the Union lines. Capturing the enemy's flag was considered an act of courage since it typically involved being a focal point for enemy fire. Many of those attempting to capture an enemy flag were killed in the effort.

A member of the 18th Massachusetts Volunteer Infantry, Anderson had answered Abraham Lincoln's call for volunteers. He fought in, and somehow survived, many of the most famous Civil War battles, including Antietam, the Second Battle of Bull Run, Chancellorsville, Fredericksburg, and Gettysburg. Anderson was wounded in the siege of Petersburg but returned to witness the surrender of the Confederate Army at Appomattox. He was presented with the Medal of Honor on August 21, 1864.

Little Raynham has both produced and honored more than its share of remarkable people.

Included is Jared, who described himself this way: "I started out from a lower middle class family, from a father who worked his ass off and a mother who did the best she could for her children. I had an older sister and a younger brother. I was your average middle child. I was raised to know right from wrong. I had little money."

Jared was correct that his family was not going to get rich on his father's teacher's salary and, eventually when she went back to work after raising the children, on his mother's nurse's salary. The part he got wrong, though, was about his being "average." That may have been his humble self-image, but it's not a word that anyone who knew him used to describe him.

Paul claims Jared was "extremely adventurous" not only as an adult but as a child. When Jared was just four years old, Paul got him his first Big Wheels to ride around. Paul came home from work one day and saw that Jared had built a ramp with pieces of plywood and was doing jumps and yelling with excitement. Jared just couldn't ride the Big Wheels the safe, normal way.

Over the years there would be many trips to the emergency room. Jared tumbled off a stool as a toddler, fell out of a tree, was thrown from a truck that was going around a corner, was hit in the mouth by a baseball, etc. There were panicked calls to the Poison Control Center after Jared ate some flux that a plumber left on a paint brush, and again when he overdosed, along with his brother and sister, on some Flintstones vitamins when the bottle was left open. "When Jared was a child, he always was in some kind of trouble. He lived on the edge. I told the pediatrician that I just don't know what to do with him," says Janet. "Whatever he did, though, he always managed to get out of it."

"People might assume that I resented Jared. Nothing could be further from the truth," asserts his brother Tim. "Jared would teach me the things only an older brother could teach. He wanted me to be strong. Like if he wanted to teach me boxing, he'd put on gloves and start hitting me. He'd expect a lot out of me. In my 20's, I started to understand.

"We were different in many ways, that's for sure," continues

Tim. "Jared would choose the biggest guy at the bar and want to fight him. I wasn't like that at all. I remember once getting picked on at school by five kids who held me up against a fence. I chipped two teeth and got beat up pretty badly. Because of my brother, though, I learned to take it. I can still remember being punched and it was like they couldn't hurt me. When it was over I turned around and just flipped them off. I could do that because of Jared. He helped me to not be afraid of anything or anyone."

"He was always the superstar in sports. Whether it was soccer, baseball, basketball or anything else he tried," explains Tim. "He was amazing. I wasn't jealous of him in any way. I didn't feel that I had to try to be as good because I knew I couldn't. He taught me to have confidence in myself and do my best. We were raised by our parents to be team players. Play to the best of your ability, whether you win or lose the game."

There were many times in Jared's early life when he showed unusual compassion for others. In second grade, he saw a little girl fall down and scrape her knee. Jared ran over to pick her up and see if she was all right. That may not sound like anything exceptional, but the teacher said that in all her years she had never seen a second grader do that. The typical response would be for a youngster to stand and stare while waiting for an adult to go over to a hurt child.

"Jared was a deeply caring kid who didn't do things for fanfare or anything else," says his fourth grade teacher Chip Mansfield. "He stood out. He exuded the values that we really need to make this society and country work."

His grandmother Mary had an after-church routine on Sundays, starting with preparing her spaghetti sauce for the family dinner to come. Mary would have the meatballs in a big bowl sitting beside the stove to cool before she put them into the sauce. As she turned her back, little Jared would sneak over and steal a meatball and pop it in his mouth. When asked, he'd say, "Oh, no, I don't have a meatball." He thought he was fooling his grandmother. Of course, she was on to him all along.

You could get away with a lot of things when you came over for Sunday dinner at the Montis, which would often last until 10 or 11 p.m. with breaks for Cribbage or games with the kids out in the yard, but you had to eat the food on your plate. That was the rule. Those in the family still talk about how Jared touched a slice of blueberry pie. It was a mistake. "My grandmother had another rule that 'If you touch it, you have to eat it.' Jared made the mistake of touching the pie," says his brother Tim. Jared's eyes were bigger than his stomach that day. He told her he couldn't eat it. She gave him the look that everyone in the family dreaded and then she said sternly, "FINISH YOUR PIE!" He reluctantly complied and, sure enough, got sick at the table. From that time on, Jared could never eat blueberry pie. Of course, his aunts, uncles, and cousins would always tease him after that and say, "Jared, would you like some blueberry pie?" He'd give them a disgusted look and then they'd all break into laughter.

When he was five, Jared was playing upstairs with some of his cousins at their grandparents' house. Aunt Marianne had some loose change on the dresser in her room and told everyone that it was missing. Paul turned to Jared and asked, "Did you take that money?" Jared responded, "No, Dad, I didn't." Then Paul said, "If you did, you're going to be in big trouble." Jared was indignant. He pointed his pinkie finger at his father and sobbed, "You think I took it!" It turned out the money was under a scarf. After it was found, Jared kept saying, "You thought I took it!" The incident was used as another way to tease Jared. His aunts, uncles, and cousins would point their pinky finger at him, pretend to cry, and say, "You think I took it!" Then, once again, they'd all laugh.

"We're an Italian family. For everyone else, if they wanted to be heard, they'd have to talk the loudest," recalled Mike. "Not Jared, though. He'd have that 'cat that caught the canary' sly grin on his face. He'd be in the background with his cool, easy manner and then crack a joke or tell a story. The cousins always wanted to be around him. They really admired him. He was always leading them in games. Because there were so many cousins, they could play any sport they wanted. They could play football and easily field two full teams. He was always happy and fun-loving."

"We'd try to pull our sons Joey and Kevin away from something they were doing to go to a family get-together," reminisces Aunt Marti. "We couldn't get them to come in and get ready. But if we called out that Jared was going to be there, they'd come running. Like all the cousins, they just adored him."

"There was a girl murdered in Raynham in the early 1980's," recalls Tim. "Everyone was on high alert. A bunch of us were standing around when a red pickup truck pulled up. The guy told us to get in and he'd buy us candy. We were stupid enough to get in. It didn't take long before Jared realized that we'd better get out. So he opened the door and jumped out of the truck. We all followed. After all, Jared was the MAN. We'd all do whatever he did. Fortunately, the truck was only going 5 mph at the time. The guy didn't even stop. He just kept driving. I don't know but Jared might have saved our lives that day."

Jared was ten years old and coming home from school when he saw that a bully had thrown a little kid's bike into a small swamp off the side of the road. Jared stood up to the bully, who actually towered over him. "I saw Jared throw the bully's bike into the swamp and then tell him to go get both bikes," says Tim. Jared told the bully, "Now you see what it's like." As so often happens with bullies, he backed down immediately and complied with Jared's demands. "I was proud of my brother. He displayed a lot of character that day," recalls Tim. Jared always had a sense of fair play. From the beginning, he would defend the "little guy" who was being picked on.

Jared's Aunt Marti tell this story: "I have a twin sister named Marsha who married one of Tony's best friends. They wanted to get Tony and me together and, sure enough, we hit it off. The time came for me to meet the Monti family. There was going to be an outdoor family party at their house on Robinson Avenue in Braintree. I came from a pretty big family, since I was one of seven brothers and sisters. I figured, 'How bad can this be?' Well, I was not prepared for what was in the back yard. There were people everywhere. Tony introduced me around, but I couldn't keep straight who belonged to who or whose kid was whose. I was overwhelmed. I had to sit down because my head was spinning. Jared was just 11 years old at the time. He saw me sitting by myself. I'll never forget how he came over and said, 'You play hoops?' I said, 'Yes, I play.' He said, 'Let's go.' I couldn't believe that a kid his age would be willing to play basketball with a woman my age. That's a testament to who he was. I relaxed and started to laugh. He put me at ease. Jared and I were close from that day on."

Jared also had an affinity for animals. It started when he was young and brought a kitten home. "He wasn't sure how we'd react, so he just reached into his pocket, pulled out that kitten, and asked if he could keep it. Who could resist? He wound up calling the kitten 'Pocket.' When he went in the military, of course, we had to take care of it. It lived to be 25 years old. I think it was the world's oldest cat," jokes Janet. "He also had a big dog named J. D. that he loved. She was a Rottweiler/Doberman mix." It's no accident that J. D. stands for Jack Daniels, or that the breed characteristics of both the Rottweiler and Doberman are "courageous, fearless, obedient, loyal, energetic, intelligent, self-assured, etc." The former was Jared's favorite drink and the latter are words that many people used to describe him.

When it came time for pictures to be taken, Jared would always try to hide in the back row. He hated it, whether it was a family gathering or a Little League baseball team. He wanted to be hard to spot. He'd always hide behind the other kids. He'd often crouch down to try to make himself invisible.

"Jared just had a natural talent for sports," says Darin Souza, who has known him since childhood. "I'm convinced he could have excelled at any sport he chose." When Jared played travel soccer he would be on defense, and once he was assigned to cover another team's top player, a girl named Andrea, who was the opposing coach's daughter. Up to that point, she had been able to easily dribble the ball past every defender. She couldn't do that with Jared. He kept taking the ball away from her. She got so frustrated that she sat on top of him in the middle of a game. She was given a red card for the infraction. That's not within the rules of soccer.

"I helped Paul coach CYO basketball and I remember how some of the other kids were a full foot taller than Jared. Size never deterred him, though. He was like a waterbug the way he moved on the court. He had determination. He could dribble like crazy, was always a threat to steal the ball, and led the team in scoring," said Uncle Mike.

As a top scorer, of course, it's typical to be accused of being a "ball hog." One day, someone called him that and Jared decided to completely change his game. He went from being a shooting guard to a point guard who always thought "pass first." Jared's height was increasingly seen as a liability as he grew older. He tried out for the Junior High School basketball team three times, and was cut each time. Coach John Tartufo admired his determination and said, "Jared, I'll tell you what. You can be our team manager. You can even warm up with the team before the games, if you want."

"I can remember his first game when he was warming up in street clothes. I felt bad for him, but Jared was willing to do it. It didn't matter to him what other people might think. He just wanted to get a chance to play," recalls Janet.

After the second game, Jared had earned a team shirt. By the third game, he was actually playing during "garbage" time at the end of a game. Jared would hustle, dive for balls, and play the game as if the score were tied. Other players saw that and it was infectious. Coach Tartufo noticed that, too. Jared's playing time kept increasing. Despite the fact that he was one of the shortest boys in the school, his grit and determination made him valuable on the court. By the end of the season, Jared was one of the team's top scorers. He was a solid all-around player but was particularly known for his tenacious defense.

"I remember back when Jared finally got to play on the basketball team and it was half-time. We happened to see him out in the hallway. I gave him a thumbs-up sign for encouragement because he was playing well. He gave me the 'Oh, Ma!' look. It embarrassed him to have any attention called to him. It's a look I saw many times."

At graduation, Coach Tartufo got up to present the basketball awards. He saved Jared's for last and admitted in front of all the students, relatives, and friends in attendance, "Jared was last not because he was least. But not picking him for the team to begin with was the greatest mistake I've ever made in my coaching career."

Jared always enjoyed having a good time and didn't mind calling attention to himself if it was for self-deprecating fun. At the high school's semi-formal dance, he dressed like John Travolta in

Saturday Night Fever. "He split his pants while dancing on a table," said his friend Joe McDonough. "He was just a ball of light."

Yet Jared shied away from serious attention. Before he got his driver's license, he asked to be driven to a weight-lifting competition in Weymouth. According to Paul, "I asked him if he wanted me to stay. He said I shouldn't bother. Afterwards, he got a ride home with someone else. He never said anything about the competition. Later, I happened to find a three-foot high trophy under his bed. He had won the Under-17-Year-Old New England Weight-Lifting Championship but didn't tell anyone about it."

According to high school wrestling Coach Stan Holmes, "Jared was a terrific kid. He was always smiling, always happy. He let his actions do the talking for him. He had an outstanding work ethic. If I asked him to do a certain exercise or work at a certain wrestling maneuver, he'd always do it to the letter. Wrestling is all about repetition until something becomes automatic. Just like the military, there's a lot of discipline required. Many of the kids who wrestled for me over my 35 years of coaching went on to serve their country. Jared was a well-rounded athlete and played a number of sports. His goal was to be in the best physical condition he could. He worked hard and trained hard. Wrestlers have to be in top shape. We didn't have a weight-lifting team, so Jared entered the New England Championships on his own and wound up winning it."

When Jared saw people eating alone in the school cafeteria, he would sit with them and befriend them. He spent his life reaching out to those who were ignored or forgotten.

Jared was a talented artist. He did a lot of drawings for the Bridgewater-Raynham High School yearbook but never put his name on them. Instead, he hid it in what he drew. One of the other students working on the yearbook said, “No one will ever know it was you who did the drawings.” Jared responded, “I’ll know.” That was enough for him.

When he was 17 years old, Jared asked his parents if he could cut down one of the six-foot spruce trees that were growing in the yard. When they asked him why, he answered, “Well, some of the guys and I just want to have a Christmas of our own.” It turned out there was a single mother with three young children in town who couldn’t afford her own tree. The boys bought a stand. They brought it over her house, set the tree up, put the lights on it, decorated it, and bought presents for her and the kids. They bought them Christmas dinner. Janet and Paul didn’t find out about it until years later.

Both his parents knew their son was someone who showed unusual compassion for others. “From a very early age Jared helped those who could not help themselves,” claims Janet.

One day, Paul noticed that Jared’s bed had disappeared from his room. When he asked about it, Jared explained, “Look, Dad. One of my friends from school was thrown out of his house by his parents. He’s trying to sleep on someone’s floor now, but he’s having a tough time doing it. So, I gave him my bed. It’s okay. I can use a sleeping bag. I don’t mind sleeping on the floor.” Paul asks rhetorically, “What could you say to that?”

Those who knew him recognize that Jared was destined to serve in the military. “He was so gung-ho about it,” says Charlie Witkus. “He probably would have signed up when he was two years old if he could have.”

When Jared was a junior in high school, Paul noticed that his free weight set was missing from home. He asked Jared what happened to it and learned that he had brought it to the local Army Recruiter’s office to conduct work-out sessions with a group of his peers as part of informal pre-Basic Training. He just couldn't wait.

Jared met Charlie in formal training exercises that were offered before Boot Camp in nearby Taunton, MA. He decided he needed more preparation for his upcoming military career, so he organized some "Survival Training." He convinced Charlie and another friend, Pete Charbonneau, to take a canoe trip on the Taunton River with him.

According to Charlie, "Jared put the whole thing together. He wanted it to be bare minimal. It was just the canoe and some beer. That was it. We were going to go out all the way from Bridgewater to Fall River, but we never made it. We got to the bridge in Raynham on Route 44. We pulled up into some corn fields. Jared called it Indian Corn. It wasn't like the corn you normally eat. Sunfish from the river. It wasn't my favorite. I don't like fish. I probably had a piece but that was it. Just random stuff to eat. Jared made a stew lunch with leaves to try to soften up the corn, which never softened up. He caught himself a turtle. That I wasn't having any part of. He tried to catch some birds. We ate berries. Pete and I just sat back and pretty much laughed the whole time. For Jared, it was typical. It was his way the whole way."

After a couple of days, the boys decided they'd had enough. It was raining. They were cold, wet, and miserable. Survival Training was over. They stopped under a familiar bridge where Jared and Paul used to go fishing. Jared walked on the road and found a pay phone to sheepishly call home and ask to be picked up. Jared told his father that he was at "that bridge" on Route 44. Paul asked, "What bridge?" Jared said, "You know, Dad, *our* bridge. The one where we used to go fishing." So, Paul took them home and gave them some hot food.

Jared had lots of ideas for how to have fun around his house, such as using the patio furniture to climb onto the roof to reach his room on the second floor. Then he'd climb out the window and swing down from the gutter. Or he'd shimmy up the gutter and jump off the roof. Jared also invented a new game called Grill Toss which involved throwing the barbecue grill from person to person. Fortunately, the grill would not be lit. He also tried a variation which is called Table Toss. That involved taking the table he didn't like from the sun room of the house and tossing it around with his friends. It somehow found its way into the swamp in back of the house. It's not likely that either game will catch on. According to Charlie, "No matter what, being around him, there was always something going on. He definitely was fearless. There was nothing that scared him."

There was some road construction going on outside the family home on Center St. in Raynham. The sight of orange barrels and blinking yellow lights proved too much for Jared to resist. They were so colorful and enticing. It's only understandable that they would all wind up in his room. Janet opened his bedroom door and found them covering virtually every inch of the floor. "I suggested to him that it might be a good idea if he put them back on the road," says Janet. "He was no angel," Paul concedes.

So some of the things he did were out of line. Others were pretty typical, things any parent can identify with. For example, Jared claimed he hated bologna and refused to eat it. One morning Janet decided to make all the kids bologna sandwiches with mayonnaise, lettuce, and tomato for their school lunches. Jared came home & said "Ma, that was the best lunch ever." Janet says, "I make the mistake of telling him it was bologna. The next day I made him the same thing and, you guessed it, the sandwich came home in his lunch box. He didn't eat it. Stubborn or what?"

"You would not want to play hide and seek with Jared because you'd never be able to find him. He'd be the kind of kid who'd be in the river under water breathing through a straw," claims Paul.

"Jared was my best friend when we were growing up in Raynham," recalls Jeff Gomes. "He was naturally outgoing, athletic, and daring. He lived for sports the way that I did. We did the usual kind of stuff that kids do. I remember that there's nothing he wouldn't try to do. He was a prankster. I can remember things like shooting a BB gun at bats that were flying in the back yard. We never got any of them, of course. We put tape on a cat's tail and watched him go around in circles trying to get it off. My Mom wasn't a fan of that. We sure thought it was fun, though."

Jared thought of becoming a school teacher like his father. At one time, he thought of pursuing archaeology. He toyed with the idea of becoming a comedian, but "He wasn't really any good," Charlie Witkus says with a laugh.

Chapter 4
A Passion, Not a Job

Janet enrolled in nursing school at age 38 and worked at Carney Hospital and then St. Luke's Hospital. An Earth Science major, Paul graduated from Bridgewater State College and was a science teacher at Stoughton, MA High School for 36 years before retiring in 2005. Anyone can have a job. Both of them, however, had a passion for the work they did. When they talk about their work, it sounds just like the way Jared would later describe his Army career.

"I had worked in the business office at Carney Hospital where I submitted insurance forms and charted patients in the ER from time to time. I took out a student loan and decided to enroll in nursing school at Bristol Plymouth Regional Technical School to get my LPN Certification. I knew nursing was what I wanted to do," explains Janet. "I think it was good that the kids saw me working hard for something I cared about. I used to study all the time. I can remember studying while cooking on the stove."

Janet had found her calling. She began working as a medical/ surgical nurse. She says, "I just loved it. The best part was working with the patients. I loved teaching them about what medical terms meant. I'd always try to explain to them what was going on and why. They might be going in for surgery and many didn't know what to expect. Some of the most difficult people were my favorites. They were a challenge to me. It's funny, but the things I thought I would hate were the things I loved. The ornery patients usually just didn't understand what was happening and were frightened.

"I made it a point to know where everything was," continues Janet. "I'd be the one people would go to when they needed something. I'd do anything for a patient. If it was a pillow, blanket, or some equipment, I'd know where it was in the hospital. I'd trade with another nurse or even 'borrow' it from another floor if a patient needed it."

She worked as a floater, rotating to Surgical, Intensive Care, Maternity, Pediatrics, Emergency, etc. "The Nursery and Labor and Delivery were my favorites, and I also just loved the Operating Room. I wanted to be where the action was," explains Janet. Working the 3 p.m. to 11 p.m. shift as a floater was ideal for her, as she could get the kids off to school in the morning and Paul would be there in the late afternoon when they got home from school.

Her sister Mary says, "Janet just adores taking care of people. She's always been a very caring person. She's always been there for people. She was the perfect nurse. The area of the hospital she liked the least was Pediatrics. It would break her heart to see sick children. If she lost one of them, she'd take it very personally."

Janet's Charge Nurse happened to be Mike's wife, Duella Monti, who says, "Janet was a very devoted and conscientious nurse! She cared deeply for her patients. The only thing that frustrated her was the low staffing and not being able to spend more individual time with her patients toward the end of her career. As a Charge Nurse, I never had to worry about her doing her assignment. She went the extra mile! She was a true caregiver in every sense of the word!"

After her nursing career, Janet served as a pre-school teacher at the local YMCA. Again, she worked with a family member. This time it was Paul's sister Jean, who recalls, "Janet was compassionate and caring. She just loved those children. She was so patient and kind. That's the kind of mother she was, too. Jared, Tim and Niccole all turned out to be great kids."

As a teenager, Jared worked with after-school kids at the same YMCA as Janet. "We had kids there that came from some pretty difficult backgrounds," she recalls. "A number of them were involved with the Division of Social Services for a variety of reasons. They could be tough to deal with. They often acted out and could be aggressive. Those were the kids he was the best with. He could reach them when the other counselors could not."

One of the after-school kids was particularly tough to get through to. Nothing Jared said seemed to work. Until he let him use his Gameboy. Jared used that as a way to connect with the kid, and then he won him over by giving him the Gameboy to keep. Jared seemed to always find some way to establish a rapport with people of any age, culture, and personality.

Paul had applied to join the Marine Corps when he came out of school but was rejected because he was too short at 5'2". Paul was actually rejected for military service a second time. He worked for Procter and Gamble unloading 70 to 80 pound bags of salt from trucks. One day, he wrenched his back. One of his vertebrae was pushed up against the spinal cord. He went for his physical after having his name come up in the draft. The doctor took one look at the X-Ray and said, "You can serve your country only if America is invaded and you're our last line of defense." Fortunately, it never came to that.

Like Janet, Paul was regarded as unusually caring. Pamela Galizio Lewis referred to him in this post: "You were always such a wonderful teacher and deserve the wonderful reputation that you still have. Just thought you needed to hear that. I know I needed to say it."

Jayne Fitzgerald, a former student, claims that Paul was just as good a teacher as he is a father. She said, "Paul Monti was my High School Science teacher. What an amazing man and dedicated father."

"Thanks for being a great teacher all those (too many to mention) years ago. Once a teacher, always a teacher," wrote Teresa Marques Dolloff.

Chris Peterson posted this message to Paul: "Thanks for being such a positive influence in my life! I only remember a few of my teachers but you stick out in my mind above the rest in a good way!"

Paul had an approach that you wish every teacher had. He asserts, "I loved teaching and I loved each and every one of those kids as if they were my own. I was charged with the most important job in the world: helping kids to realize their potential. Not every one of them did. Sometimes they disappoint you. But I wanted to give all of them the opportunity."

He would tell a class on the first day that they had to turn in their homework and it would be graded. Invariably, one of the students would say, "None of the other teachers do that." Paul would always retort, "Well, I do!"

"Sure it was more work for me to grade every homework paper, but it helped provide structure and discipline," admits Paul. "That's always the key to success in any field. Whether you're a banker, musician, politician, athlete, accountant, or whatever you are. You always need structure and discipline. It helps if there's someone who expects a lot out of you."

Paul takes great satisfaction in hearing from former students who have passed the bar exam, gotten their medical degree, or accomplished something else they're proud of. Many of them have felt the need to let Paul know and thank him for being a part of it. "When they tell me of what they've done, I write or say back to them, 'I always knew you could. I always knew you would.' It's the same message for everyone."

Other teachers might have let their students just go through the motions, but Paul wouldn't consider it. That certainly rubbed off on Jared. It set an example for him. That became his approach to his job as an NCO in dealing with his soldiers and, frankly, to everything else he did. There was no such thing in the family as "just doing enough to get by."

Paul continues to get messages from former students. This one was recently written by Domenic Candeloro: "I was thinking of you and just wanted to say I may have not been the best student, even though I had the best teacher. I learned a lot from your class, and not just science but respect and honor. You're a great man and I wanted to thank you for the life lessons."

Paul was driving to the Roger Williams Zoo in Rhode Island one day when his daughter Niccole and granddaughter Carys were visiting. He was caught speeding by a State Trooper, who pulled him over to the side of the road. Paul turned to Niccole to ask her to get the registration from the glove compartment. Suddenly, the officer reached his arm into the window and extended his hand for Paul to shake. It was John Fanning, a former student. He said, "Mr. Monti! I can't believe it's you! I'd probably be in jail now if it weren't for you." John and his friend, Vinnie Noe, had been behavior problems at Stoughton High. Paul sat them both down one day and said, "You two need to go into the military and learn a little discipline." They took his advice and joined the Marines, and then both became State Troopers. "I'm so proud of where they got to from where they came from," says Paul.

There was no way Paul was going to get a ticket that day. Officer Fanning said, “Mr. Monti, you can drive as fast as you want. If anyone stops you, just have them call me at the Framingham barracks.”

Chapter 5
Welcome to Hell!

Just a junior in high school, Jared came home one day and announced, "Dad, I want to join the Army." Paul shook his head and responded, "I don't think so, Son. I want you to go to college." Jared argued, "But Dad, you can't afford to send me." Paul said, "Look, if I have to take on another job, I'll get the money for your tuition." Jared begged, "But you're already working more than one job. Please sign my papers."

Paul said what any red-blooded American Dad would say: "Talk to your mother."

"I didn't want to sign the parental permission papers, but Jared was insistent," recalls Janet. Both parents relented, and Jared joined the National Guard's Early Entry Program on March 11, 1993. Janet accompanied him as they spoke to the Army recruiter who asked, "Do you have any medical problems I should know about?" Jared and Janet looked at each other. "What?" asked the recruiter. "Broken hip," they said. "Okay, I'll disregard that," responded the recruiter. "Any other problems?" Jared and Janet looked at each other again. "What?" asked the recruiter again. "Migraine headaches which require medication," they said. "Okay, I'll disregard that," responded the recruiter.

"I'll always question whether I should have signed those

papers and let them look the other way about the medical issues," laments Janet. "He just wanted it so badly that we let him go for it. The Viet Nam war had been over for many years. Our country was at peace. It didn't seem like he'd be in danger in the foreseeable future." At the end of his senior year in high school, Jared declared, "I want to get into the regular Army. The National Guard is all right, but I want to be in the regular Army. I really like this and I want to serve my country."

Why did Jared feel compelled to join the military? He explained in a memoir, "As a child, I was star-struck by my Uncle, Michael Gerrity, who was in the Navy. I was enthralled by his words of patriotism and remember being blinded by his brilliant white uniform." Married to Janet's sister Eileen, Michael later suffered a stroke on January 25, 2014 and died at age 61. He was buried with full military honors.

Jared had always dreamed of being a pilot. Whenever they visited Eileen and Michael in Virginia Beach, he would ask his Mom to go to the Norfolk Naval Air Station and buy him U. S. Navy model planes and pictures of military aircraft. When he was young, Jared loved to talk to his grandfather Urban, who had served in the Air Force during World War II, about military aircraft. He'd draw pictures of airplanes before he visited to show them to his grandfather. Urban would sit in his "special easy chair" and talk to Jared, who would be on his lap.

Since he couldn't become a pilot because of a problem with migraine headaches, Jared decided to join the Army instead. He was hoping to fly helicopters, but again the health issue held him back. While many of his friends were on summer vacation between his junior and senior years in high school, Jared went off to Basic Training at Ft. Leonard Wood, Missouri. Located in the Missouri Ozarks, the base was opened in December, 1940, and is named in honor of General Leonard Wood. During World War II, Italian and

German POW's were interned there. Most of the Army Engineer School's operations were consolidated there in 1984.

Jared had a rude awakening. "It was 1993 and I had just turned 18 years old. It was crazy," he reported. "I boarded a plane for the first time in my life. I had never left Massachusetts before and felt I'd landed in a different world." The area around Fort Leonard Wood is rural and felt "southern" to him. He wasn't prepared for what is sometimes referred to affectionately as "Fort Lost in the Woods."

Jared described himself as a "northerner being suddenly thrust into the south." Everything was different. "The smell of the south, the style of the south, everything about the south threw me for a loop," he continued. "The heat and humidity in Missouri hit me like a ton of bricks. It was more than I'd ever had to contend with. I had never felt anything like it before. I was so overwhelmed.

"At Ft. Leonard Wood, I learned a new appreciation for life. The first five days of in-processing were fine, with learning how to march and things like that, but the day the Drill Instructors picked us up was a day I'll never forget. I saw people pass out for the first time in my life. The agonizing wait for the Drill Instructors was unbearable. They arrived in cattle trucks surrounded by dust from the unpaved roads. They called our names off, one by one, and loaded us into the trucks. Then we were greeted with, 'Welcome to Hell!' When the doors closed and the trucks jerked forward, my face got thrown into one of the duffle bags. The whole trip to Basic Training was awful."

Things didn't get better for him later. "That night the sky seemed to open up from the heavens and the thunder and lightning rained down. I lay awake all that first night wondering what the hell I had gotten myself into," he recalled. If only Jared had known what was coming. Missouri was like a vacation spot compared to

South Korea, Kosovo, and Afghanistan.

There were incidents of trainees becoming sick and even dying during Basic Training. They were all required to write a letter home saying they were being taken good care of and given plenty of fluids. How did they know what to say? They all wrote the exact same letter. The trainees were told what to say by the Drill Sergeants.

Jared and his friend Pat Spano enjoyed one of the rituals of Basic Training, learning about tear gas first-hand by entering a building with gas masks on and then doing it a second time without the gas masks. The trainees must say out loud their name, rank, and social security number the second time, so they get a good dose of the gas before the doors are opened, much to the delight of the Drill Sergeants, who stand and watch. Jared wanted to ensure that his good friend had a meaningful learning experience, so he pushed him back into the building for a third try at the gas. It was another prank that they laughed about for years.

Jared next went to Fort Sill in Oklahoma for Advanced Individual Training. Built in 1869 and designated as a National Historic Landmark, it's located about 85 miles southwest of Oklahoma City and is the only active installation among the forts on the Southern Plains built during the American Indian Wars. General Philip H. Sheridan arrived in 1868 with the 7th US Cavalry under Lieutenant Colonel George A. Custer, along with other units. The post was named in honor of General Joshua Sill, a Civil War casualty. Fort Sill is also famous as the base of operation for the Afro-American regiments commonly referred to as the "Buffalo Soldiers" of the late 1800's.

"It was at Fort Sill that I learned how to use artillery to engage the enemy in a mass formation without any form of discrimination. Every target was the same. A Soviet-style army. A mass of Soviet tanks or infantry. The same old cliché of T-72's (Soviet tanks that were produced beginning in 1970) and BRDM's (a light-armored amphibious patrol vehicle called *Boyevaya Razvedyvatelnaya Dozornaya Mashina* in Russian.) We were not ready for today's wars. We learned to kill on the line. Today it's a three-dimensional fight. We didn't learn about civilians on the battlefield or humanitarian needs throughout the world," explained Jared, who would later have a hand in updating and teaching artillery and aircraft fire training for warfare in the 21st Century.

While at Ft. Sill, Jared became friends with Chris Havran, a civilian EMT, and they kept in touch via telephone. The only problem was Jared liked to call him collect from various places around the world at the most unlikely times. "I remember one of those times, it was 2 a.m. and I dozed off during the call. I woke up a few hours later and Jared was still talking. UGLY phone bill – but hilarious, nowadays!"

"After I graduated Advanced Individual Training with my peers, I landed in a dusty field in the middle of Kansas called Fort Riley," Jared recalled. Soon he had an adventure that was to be the first of a number of occasions where he narrowly escaped death or serious injury. He and his friend, John Reardon, were admiring genuine American bison, also known as buffalo. Since he was from Massachusetts, Jared was seeing them for the first time. Evidently Jared felt compelled to connect with the iconic symbol of the Great American West. Literally. He was always a hands-on kind of guy. He noticed a small, cuddly bison calf. Like with the orange barrels and yellow blinking lights of his youth, he couldn't resist. He told John he was going to jump over the fence and pet the calf. "You're crazy," said John. It wasn't going to be the last time that someone said that to Jared.

What Jared didn't know was that not only are bison mothers very protective of their young, they travel in herds, and the entire herd is also protective of the young. Adult bison range in size from 700 to 2,200 pounds, and both sexes have horns that can grow as long as two feet. Furthermore, they can easily outrun humans, clocking in at near-racehorse speeds of up to 40 miles per hour. They are among the most fearsome animals found in U. S National Parks. Over the last 30 years, for example, three times as many bison attacks as bear attacks have been reported on humans at Yellowstone Park.

The mother bison menacingly pawed the ground as Jared approached her calf. The brave (or crazy, depending on how you look at it) soldier ignored the warning and continued to move forward. The angry herd turned on him. Suddenly realizing they were a lot bigger and faster than he was, he scrambled up a tree. And stayed there. John recognized there was no way he could help his friend. Twenty minutes went by and the herd began to lose interest in the frightened soldier. Jared called out, "I'm going to make a run for it." He slowly climbed down the tree, ran like he had never run before, and leaped over the fence to safety. Once he got there, John didn't say, "Are you okay?" or "Glad you made it out alive." Instead, he greeted him with, "You're covered in bison shit!" as he burst into laughter. While fleeing, Jared had run through massive amounts of turds, which covered his uniform. It was not an attractive sight. Or smell. Jared concluded he had experienced enough of the Old West for one day as he went "moseying" back to the barracks to clean up.

There was another incident involving Jared and John Reardon that actually did result in a serious injury. Jared was doing a reconnaissance of drinking establishments in the Fort Riley area and evidently got so involved in this important mission that he somehow lost track of the time. He managed to duck under the front gate to get into the base, but the barracks had been locked shut. He shimmied up the gutter to the second floor and began banging on the window, yelling for someone to let him in. John heard the noise outside and opened the window. There was just one problem. The window opened outward. So John knocked Jared off the roof and he tumbled two stories to the ground, breaking his wrist in a number of places.

"I messed up good. I broke my hand in an alcohol-related incident and should have been kicked out of the military," Jared confessed. "The chain of command must have found something in me, because they let me go without punishment."

At Fort Riley Jared participated in Forward Observer training and became a member of a proud society of "FISTers" – artillery soldiers in a Fire Support Team. The official MOS, or Military Occupation Specialty, is 13-F Fire Support Specialist. That doesn't refer to putting out fires. Rather, it's someone responsible for leading, supervising, and serving in an intelligence and target-processing role for Field Artillery units. It means you're an "FO," or Forward Observer, typically climbing to positions high above the enemy.

FISTers don't take the easy, flat-ground trails. It's one of the military's most important and dangerous jobs. Why would anyone want to do it? Because it's one of the military's most important and dangerous jobs. In traditional conflicts, you could say it involved working behind enemy lines. But in a place like Afghanistan, the whole country was behind enemy lines.

Jared loved to call cadence, a verse with a regular beat or rhythm that helps soldiers march in unison. He would often do it before a round of drinks at a bar. His favorite was:

"Here's to the FISTer
Deep in the grass
One round short
And it's your ass!"

This refers to the fact that a FISTer might be lurking anywhere to observe the enemy and then call for artillery and/or aircraft fire. A good FISTer is respected by the infantry as someone who can save lives. However, a FISTer who makes a mistake can cause a catastrophe. If 99 rounds are on target, but one is either long or short, it can result in death to civilians or friendly troops. There's a poster that's often seen where FISTers are found. It says, "If everything around you is exploding…It's probably us."

They often refer to themselves as Twisted FISTers, a play on the name of 1980's rock group Twisted Sister, which recorded "We're Not Gonna Take It" and "I Wanna Rock." They'll exhort each other on with cries of "Rock hard, FISTers!" and "FISTers lead the way!" They have to be smart, well-trained, and determined athletes. That's why they often say good-bye with, "See you on the high ground." They also talk about meeting together on "Fiddler's Green" when they die. Legend has it that Captain Sammy Pearson was the first to use the term at a campfire in the Medicine Bow Mountains of Wyoming. It's still used by modern cavalry units to describe the resting place of those who die in combat. Many restaurants, bars, and places associated with the U. S. Army around the world have adopted the name Fiddler's Green.

The original FISTer is thought to have been Thaddeus Lowe, who called himself Professor Lowe even though he was self-educated. Abraham Lincoln was intrigued with the idea of using balloons to survey battlefields, spot enemy troop movements, and direct artillery fire during the Civil War. He appointed Lowe as Chief Aeronaut of the experimental Union Army Balloon Corps.

The first recorded use of the approach was to direct artillery fire on an unseen encampment of Rebel troops at Falls Church, VA in 1861. Lowe was stationed in a hydrogen gas balloon and waved signal flags to Camp Advance, the firebase, as well as telegraphing results to Fort Corcoran Headquarters. Field artillery was able to successfully fire without being able to see the enemy. Lowe was bothered by the idea of firing on the Rebels early in the morning while they were still sleeping. He reported actually feeling relieved when the first round fell long and the explosion woke them. For some reason, he thought it would be fairer if they were awake for the artillery barrage. He adjusted coordinates and the Union side fired shell after shell at the Rebel encampment.

After this initial success, there were seven balloons commissioned and used in such battles as Yorktown, Seven Pines, Antietam, and Fredericksburg. However, by 1863 the novelty had worn thin. There were logistics problems, such as how to keep the balloons filled with hydrogen gas, and how to navigate them in high winds. None of the members of the Balloon Corps were in the military, so if they were captured they were treated as spies and shot. Many of those in the Army considered them nothing more than a carnival attraction. Lowe was placed under the command of Army Corps of Engineers Captain C. B. Comstock, who was incensed by the fact that this civilian was being paid more than he was. He reduced Lowe's per diem salary from $10 gold to $3 gold, which led to his resignation, and the Balloon Corps was subsequently disbanded.

After the rocky start, Forward Observers became essential to directing fire from artillery that was increasingly distant from the enemy. Satellite surveillance and drone technology have changed the landscape of modern warfare, but there'll likely always be a place for "boots on the ground" and "human eyes on the enemy."

Things did not go well for Jared at Ft. Riley. "I felt isolated in my new unit. I was an outcast. I was way too motivated. I was ready to fight for my country," he admitted. "There was a Staff Sergeant who used to ridicule me all the time. He called me 'Rambo' and poked fun at me because of my excitement at being in the military." The Sergeant would bark at Jared to give him 25 push-ups and Jared would do 30. He'd tell him to give him 50 push-ups and Jared would do 60. Since Jared had broken his wrist, he was unable to do push-ups the traditional open-hands way. He was forced to do them on his knuckles. That really incensed the Sergeant. He felt that Jared was trying to show off in front of the other troops.

"I told my room-mate that if I ever saw the Sergeant in a bar, I would kick his ass. My room-mate passed this information on to him and he showed up at my door drunk. I hit him a few times, but the incident never got out of control. Luckily, there was another NCO there with him. He did, however, have a newfound respect for me," said Jared.

Did Jared settle down? Did he learn his lesson? Did he turn into a model citizen from that point on and obey all the rules? Not at all. He was just getting started.

Jared loved mountains and spoke of going to school at the University of Colorado when he got out of the Army. Ben Barreaux tells the story of Jared breaking rules to accompany him on a trip there from Kansas. Ben says, "When we were at Ft. Riley I had a four-day pass, and he noticed me packing my car in the parking lot. He asked me where I was going, and I told him I was going to visit my sister in Colorado. Five minutes later he had his bag packed and we were on our way. He didn't have a pass and we were well past the 100-mile limit, so he was technically AWOL. We got back and no one said anything about it. Funny side note, he had never skied before. We stopped off at an end-of-season sale and we each bought a set of skis, boots and bindings. I still use those skis today."

Ben adds, "Everyone has funny stories about Jared, because that was just the way he was. The thing I remember the most about him, though, is how easily he made friends, and that once you were his friend, you knew he was always going to be there for you. It could be as little as doing something to cheer you up, or as big as getting you out of a fight. Either way, he was there, and he didn't ask for anything in return. When I knew Jared at Ft. Riley, we were still just 19-year-old kids, and that character trait was something I was always aware of, but at the time didn't fully appreciate. That's the way he lived his life. Looking out for his friends. I think if the rest of us were half as good at that as he was, the world would be a better place."

Chapter 6
Escape from the Turtle Farm

After World War II, Korea was divided by the 38th parallel as the boundary between what became The Democratic People's Republic of Korea, the official name of communist North Korea, and the Republic of Korea, commonly known as democratic South Korea. The peninsula had been under the control of Japan since 1910. The country soon became a battleground. The Korean War began on June 25, 1950, when the North Koreans crossed the 38th parallel to invade the south, and ended in 1953 when they were pushed back to that line. The United Nations, and the United States in particular, supported the Republic of Korea, while the Democratic People's Republic of Korea was supported by the Soviet Union, which provided weapons and financial aid, and by China, which committed troops to the war effort.

There was little popular support from the American public for the war. In fact, it's known as the "Forgotten War" because of the lack of attention. It was overshadowed earlier by the giant landscape of World War II and later by the controversial Viet Nam War, which garnered daily headlines and highly visible anti-war protests. Yet the neglected little Korean War proved to be quite deadly, resulting in close to 34,000 American and an estimated 1.2 million overall casualties.

On July 27, 1953, the Armistice Agreement created the DMZ, the Demilitarized Zone, which was a buffer 2.5 miles wide and 160 miles long which roughly divides the Korean Peninsula in half. It also formed the Military Demarcation Line, or MDL, which runs down the center of the DMZ. Soldiers and weapons are allowed in the DMZ and both sides patrol it, but neither side is permitted to cross over the MDL.

North Korean leaders have periodically issued bellicose threats about starting another war with South Korea in an attempt to gain notoriety and negotiate concessions. Current North Korean leader Kim Jong Un has carried on that tradition. The DMZ remains a dangerous place, even though the Cold War has long been over. It is perhaps the most heavily fortified barrier between countries in the world. President Bill Clinton famously referred to the DMZ as "the scariest place on earth." Nearly two million troops stand watch over its 151-mile length, which is crowded with guard towers, razor wire, land mines, tank-traps and heavy weaponry.

Jared was stationed at Camp Stanley, east of the city of Uijeongbu in the Gyeonggi Province. Located close to the DMZ, it began as a tent city in 1955, and the first permanent buildings were constructed in 1969.

"After months of rehabilitation and a hand that worked somewhat normally, I finally went off to a different country; and boy, what a different country it was," said Jared. He was ready to serve but wound up serving in an unanticipated way. "My first two weeks in South Korea were spent serving an Article 15 for violating pass policy," he recalled. That's the military equivalent of a civil rather than criminal court action. It involves non-judicial punishment for violating Article 15 of the Uniform Code of Military Justice. It can mean loss of pay, reduction in rank, extra duty, or confinement in a military prison.

Jared was bored at the slow-moving Headquarters, dubbed the Turtle Farm. “It was a miserable time for me at the Turtle Farm, so I wanted to spread my wings. I pulled out my Leatherman knife and proceeded to hack through the triple strand of concertina that held me within the confines of the base camp. I had a hell of a weekend in Tong Du Chon. On Monday I was read my rights and spent 14 days of labor and restriction,” he said. A pretty steep price to pay for a trip into town.

“I was sent to the 1st Battalion of the 506th Regiment for my sins,” continued Jared. “It was considered a much-dreaded assignment. But I loved it. There was no tighter band of brotherhood that existed anywhere. We were a family. Everyone knew you were in the 506th in Korea. You carried a certain persona if you were from the Regiment. We got a one-day pass from there about twice a month. The pass usually sent you to Seoul for the night. Seoul was the place where you went to really get wasted and spend your well-earned paycheck.”

At last Jared was in his element. He felt like he belonged to something special – an elite unit. This was what had he had been missing up to that point. It would cause him to continually seek out assignments that would challenge him, even if they placed him in extremely dangerous situations. It also allowed him to bond with other soldiers who felt as committed as he was. It was that special bond that caused him to keep re-enlisting and eventually cost him his life.

Janet understood completely when she said about her son, “He liked being where the action was.”

You can just picture Jared flashing that charming, sheepish, sly grin as he went on to say, “I did get in a little more trouble. I killed a pig and got caught trying to have a pig roast. That was not a very well-looked-upon practice in the Korean way of doing things. I spent a day or two in jail and had to re-enlist to foot the bill for the pig and a lawyer. Otherwise, I would have become a civilian."

Kris Kanzler remembers Jared this way: "You were my best friend and brother-in-arms. When we last saw each other a Sergeant 1st Class seemed so old to us. I sure miss the days in Alpha Company 1/506th INF as young FO team leaders and radio operators. My first experience with you was being ordered by our FIST Sergeant to find you down range and bring you back to Camp before curfew. That wouldn't be the last time we missed curfew together, either. We became instant friends and were near inseparable since. You lived life to the fullest and inspired us to do the same. Never did I ever worry about not having someone to watch my back when we got into a difficult situation, which we tended to get ourselves into frequently. Next time we meet, we will have a great big party, but this time I will bring the pig."

So Jared learned an important life lesson – "Let someone else (like Kanzler) provide the pig."

Kris offers this additional accolade: "He was someone that everyone liked and wanted to be around. Jared was truly a 'Gift from God.' I am honored to have known him."

When Jared went home on leave, he surprised his friend Jeff Gomes by showing up at his house. "He told us how we wouldn't believe what's going on there. He told us how American and South Korean troops take fire regularly. It's just not publicized." In fact, estimates are that more than 500 South Korean and 50 American soldiers have lost their lives in minor skirmishes since 1953.

Jared got in trouble once again in South Korea after breaking up a barracks fight between two enlisted men. "The smaller guy was just being pummeled by a bigger guy. Jared always stood up for the underdog. He had to break up the fight no matter what," says Janet.

He first tried to stop the altercation by getting between the two men. That didn't work, so he threw the instigator up against the wall. It was Jared who got in trouble. He was reprimanded by the Sergeant Major the following day and wound up getting another Article 15 for "Pushing an enlisted man." That's not as serious as "Hitting an enlisted man" but still is a violation of Army regulations. This time, it wound up costing him a reduction in rank from E-6 Staff Sergeant to E-5 Sergeant, along with a forfeiture of over $1,000 in pay. After the unfortunate series of incidents in his first assignment outside of the United States, Jared either calmed down, doing less "spreading his wings," or he got smarter and learned how not to get caught. Those who served with him would claim the latter.

What was the Army supposed to do with this problem child? He questioned the training he received, calling it outdated. He got drunk. He fell out of a second-story window and broke his wrist. He fought with a Sergeant. He cut through wire to go AWOL. He killed a farmer's pig. He pushed an enlisted man. He flouted the rules. He felt no remorse. He was establishing a track record. Was there any hope for this scofflaw, this rule-breaker, this rabble-rouser? On the other hand, virtually all of America's successful leaders have been called those things at one time or another. That's the same spirit that founded the country and has produced a history of innovation and responding to challenges. Jared didn't back down from anyone or anything. He wasn't going to change.

It certainly helped that Jared was now in a unit where both the level of difficulty and expectations had increased significantly. He subsequently got in a bar fight that was like something out of an old movie. It involved not just fisticuffs but two-by-four planks used as weapons. There was blood shed. This time, Jared wasn't reprimanded. On the contrary, when he and his buddies stood bruised and battered before the Sergeant in charge, they were told,

"Good way to keep in training, guys." Things had, indeed, changed. The world was looking a little different now.

On July 27, 1996, the night of the Centennial Olympic Park bombing in Atlanta, there were serious mud slides in South Korea that caused a number of deaths. Jared pulled a soldier out of a Humvee and saved his life. Janet recalls, "We were worried about Jared's safety. We tried to get information about the mud slides, but the news was dominated by the bombing." Paul and Janet were so concerned that they called Jared on the phone that night to make sure he was all right.

Chapter 7
The Full Monti

"The next step for me was Airborne School at Ft. Benning, Georgia. I figured I'd better get jump school in there since I had re-upped," reasoned Jared. So he decided to use some of that pent-up energy to begin training as a paratrooper with the 82nd Airborne Division at Fort Bragg, NC. Again, the more difficult the assignment, the more he liked it. Airborne is about as difficult as it gets. Fort Bragg, located mainly in Fayetteville, is named for Confederate General Braxton Bragg and is the home of the Army Airborne and Special Forces.

Paratroopers specialize in assault operations into denied areas. Rather than just entering a war zone by land or sea, they use the tactical advantage of evasion of fortifications by entering from the air. Originally formed as the 82nd Infantry Division on March 5, 1917, members came from all of the then-48 states. The Division was therefore nicknamed "All-American," represented by the famous "Double A" insignia.

Jump school at Ft. Benning, GA consists of three rigorous weeks of instruction and physical training led by the "Black Hats," so-named because of the distinctive black baseball caps they wear. They are always referred to as "Sergeant" no matter what rank they hold. It's similar to Basic Training where the instructors are all called, "Drill Sergeant," even if they aren't actually Sergeants. It's expected that there will be only two sentences said to a Black Hat by a jump school student during the three weeks. They are "Yes, Sergeant, Airborne!" or "No, Sergeant, Airborne!" Their favorite phrase when saying hello or good-bye to one another is, "Airborne, all the way!" Many will use the phrase for the rest of the lives.

The three intensive three weeks that Jared went through started with Ground Week, where the students learn, practice, and perfect their PLF (parachute landing fall). The so-called "Five Points of Performance" taught are: proper exit, check body position, and count; check canopy and immediately gain canopy control; keep a sharp lookout for all jumpers during your entire descent; slip/turn into the wind and prepare to land; and land with your legs and knees together. The second week focuses on jumping out of thirty-four foot towers. They learn how to exit an aircraft and practice safe landings. The students put it all together by jumping out of a real aircraft, typically a C-17, over the drop zone in the final week, known as Jump Week. Most of those who pass advance to another military school for more training; a few "wash out" and fail the program.

Upon satisfactory completion of the course, students are awarded the Army Parachutist Badge, commonly referred to as "Jump Wings". After earning his wings, Jared became one of the first enlisted soldiers in the 82nd Airborne Division selected to be trained to call in air strikes on enemy positions.

How did Jared relax on weekends when he didn't have duty? By skydiving with his military buddies. He just couldn't get enough of the adrenaline rush. His back, however, was not responding well to the constant pounding of the landings. This would lead to an abbreviated career as a paratrooper and later almost cause him to be medically discharged.

Jared was creative about administering punishment when it was warranted. SSG Mike Bower was just a Specialist when he was asked to drive to the motor pool to pick something up. He was only going 15 miles per hour, but that is considered speeding in a motor pool area. "I got yelled at by the Motor Sergeant," he recalls. "I also may or may not have said some words back to him. Okay, let's be honest, I did say something to him." Mike was asked who he reported to. By the time he got back to the FIST office just five minutes later, Jared was waiting for him. "I was greeted with a smile and told to run around the unit saying, 'Vroom. Vroom. I'm a race car.' Every time I passed by the Commander's office, I had to say, 'Sir. Vroom. Vroom. I'm a race car,' to the Commander. After a while he got tired of all the noise and said, "Okay, Monti, I think the Specialist has had enough." What did Mike learn that day? "I never drove to the motor pool again," he quips.

SSG Lance Harding relates this story about Jared's tough but caring approach. He tells of how one night he was caught drinking underage by CID on base at Ft. Bragg. The United States Army Criminal Investigation Command is usually abbreviated to CID. Harding said, "They turned me over to my chain of command. Jared, who was my first-line leader, was awoken from bed and was the first to know about it. I was one month from being 21. I'll never forget that long hard night, morning, next day, and week of discipline that Jared worked into me. He told me, 'If you're old enough to go off to battle and defend this country, you're old enough to drink.' He disciplined me for the stupidity of my getting caught, not because it was a written law. I hated Jared for that next week, but he never let word of that incident go past him, keeping me from losing my rank and money, and letting me keep the very pride that he had instilled in me. I knew he truly cared about the good of people."

Lance continues, "Jared was the first true inspiration to me. I know I'll be looking up towards the heavens today thanking him for his leadership and mentorship. I just re-enlisted for another six years, and it's people like Jared that have kept me going strong in this Army. He had all the right core values and taught them to me, not just in military terms, but in terms of a friend and person who you would want to be beside you for the rest of your life. It's just a shame I never got to speak to Jared again after I left Bragg. He made a big impact on my life and all his friends' lives!

"Monti was a long-time mentor to me. He was my first team leader and a good friend in the 82nd. Monti taught me everything I needed to know about the Army, and not just job related stuff. A large majority of his time was dedicated to me as a new Private in the 82nd Airborne. His best and most memorable lessons were the many nights of drinking together! Also, how to be easy going, don't take no shit, roll with the punches, and how to be down to earth in the fast-paced 82nd. His lessons translate into everyday life," concludes Lance.

Darin Souza, the President of Jared's senior class at Bridgewater-Raynham High School, went on to graduate from West Point and began his military career as a 2nd Lieutenant at Ft. Bragg. "I reported to the infantry officer in charge. The first thing I heard was, 'Watch that guy over there, that NCO teaching the artillery group. He knows his shit better than anyone around. Listen to him and what he has to say and you'll be okay.' It turned out to be Jared. In high school, we'd goof off and fool around. In the military, though, he was very confident, knowledgeable, and professional."

According to Darin, "I realized first-hand what Jared was all about during a huge Joint Exercise. There was a tough, hard-nosed Colonel that about a hundred of us had to stand in front of and, one at a time, brief on our mission that day. "We'd start out with 'Today my task is...' and then describe why and how we were going to do it. Everyone was uptight and nervous. It was painful. In walked Jared and the entire room changed. The Colonel yelled out one word as loud as he could, 'MONTI!' and welcomed him as if they were drinking buddies in a bar. Jared was so well-liked and well-known. The whole room just lost the sense of tension. It was obvious the Colonel knew things would go well because Jared was involved. He was like a famous brand that a company might have. He gave people confidence."

Niccole indicated that she understood her brother for the first time after she went to visit him at Fort Bragg. She said, "That gave me the clearest picture of how he was in the military. That's when I got it. I saw a totally different side of him. It was such a brotherhood. He was so close to them. And that's when I completely understood why he stayed in the military. He just loved the guys."

Jared was presented with the Saint Barbara's medal by 4-25 Artillery Battalion Commander LTC David Bushey at a Military Ball at Fort Sill. It is the highest award for accomplishment an artillery commander can give. Saint Barbara is the Patron Saint of the Artillery. When gunpowder began being used in the western world, Saint Barbara was invoked for aid against accidents resulting from explosions, since some of the early artillery pieces would blow up instead of firing their projectile.

Artillery Warrant Officer Keith Williams made the mistake that night of telling Jared he felt bad that he had not earned a Bronze Star. That was all Jared needed to hear. Keith explains what happened in this post written to Jared: "Hey, bro. Just wanted to let you know that I speak of you every week when my class talks about fire support or FO's. Got a picture of you on my desktop and tell friends about the time we were at the Saint Barbara's Ball and you were taking Bronze Star Medals off some of the officer's uniforms because I didn't get one. I will never forget you. Cobra

3-5 out!!"

According to Keith, "I had the pleasure of soldiering with Monti. He was one of the best Forward Observers the Army had. His knowledge, skill, kindness, and dedication to our nation were second to none."

Jared shared an apartment at Ft. Bragg with SGT Jeff Bolding. Both were friends with Matthew Hatfield. Jeff and Matthew went out for lunch one day and returned to the apartment afterwards. They opened the door and Jeff said, "Where's my table?" Matthew responded, "The door wasn't busted. The window's not broken. How could someone have stolen it?" They both suddenly looked at each other and called out at the same time, "JARED!" Jeff called him on the phone. Sure enough, Jared had gone to one of his soldier's houses and saw that the family was using one of those big wooden cable spools for furniture. So the $1,000 kitchen set disappeared and wound up in that soldier's home. "We'll just have to play cards someplace else," explained Jared.

Jeff recalls, "We went in on the furniture 50/50. It was my $500 that I was angry about. I told him he had no right to give away that kitchen set without asking me. It was a nice big table with 6 chairs. I was yelling and cussing. He looked me in the face and said, 'His kids were eating sitting on the floor.' I felt about 2 inches tall. What could I say? That's just the type of person Jared Monti was. The best! Jared didn't just become a hero that day on the mountain. He has been a hero ever since I have known him!"

In truth, Matthew was not an admirer of the black lacquer with gold trim kitchen set that they had bought. "It was just ugly furniture. It was horrible, so it was no big loss," he laughs.

On a bitterly cold night in North Carolina, Jeff and Jared were walking home. They passed by a homeless man who asked them for money saying, "I want to buy something to keep me warm."

Jeff responded the way most people would by walking right past him. He assumed the man would spend the money on alcohol and drugs. But Jared took off an Abercrombie & Fitch sweater he was wearing and gave it to the man. Afterwards, Jeff said, "Why would you do that?" Jared responded, "Because I'm going to go home and sleep in a warm bed, but this guy will be out there freezing." According to Jeff, "He would do stuff that maybe you didn't understand at first. Then he'd explain it to you and it made sense. He's the only person I know who literally would give you the shirt off his back."

Others, such as Brent Nedley, have told similar stories of Jared's generosity. Brent was an 18-year-old who understandably was having difficulty supporting a wife and new baby on his PFC's salary. He received a Red Cross emergency message that his father, a 64-year-old Viet Nam war veteran, had been rushed to the hospital. There was no way he could afford the cost of the $600 flight home. "Jared just told me not to worry about it. He paid for the whole thing with his credit card and even personally drove me to the airport. It meant so much to my Dad that his only son came that he cried when he saw me. He personally called Jared to thank him."

Jared's Boston accent would sometimes be picked up by his Army friends. "I learned to like one of Jared's favorite drinks – a 'Cape Coddah.' I'd always say it like Jared did," recalls Matthew. "Then one night a bartender asked me if I was from Boston. I said, 'I'm from Louisiana.' He asked, 'Why do you say Cape Coddah?' I told him that's what I thought it was. He told me that a vodka and cranberry juice drink is actually called a 'Cape Codder.' I told him I didn't know that. I've continued to say it with the Boston accent, though, in honor of Jared.

"At Fort Bragg, we procured a mason jar of real moonshine," Matthew goes on to say. "It was 110 proof. Okay, the truth is I got it shipped to me from my uncle back home. We agreed we'd share it when I got off weekend duty. It's was 3 a.m. on a Saturday night, or Sunday morning if you want to look at it that way. The phone rang. I knew it wasn't going to be anything good. Jared said, slurring his words, 'Hey, Mattie, what's up?' He was clearly drunk. I said, 'I'm on duty.' He responded, 'Mattie, are you having a good time?' I started to get mad and said again, 'I'm on duty. Hey, did you have any of the moonshine?' Jared said, 'Just a little bit.' He was calling from a pay phone in front of the Firehouse Pub. I had to go get him and drag him back to the barracks.

"There's a story that still sends chills up my spine," recalls Matthew. "Jared was quite an artist. At Fort Bragg he made a huge placard out of plywood of the FIST insignia with the gauntlet glove and lightning bolt. He affixed it to the wall. Our Battery First Sergeant actually hated it until it went missing. Then he went around saying, 'Where's my sign?' Jared had just left for another tour in South Korea, so everyone figured he must have been the one to take it or give it away. I wound up going to Fort Sill to be an instructor. We decided to decorate each of the classrooms with the logos and posters of the organizations where a FISTer might serve. One of the rooms was just going to be a generic Army black and gold room. Somehow, the FISTer placard just showed up there. I couldn't believe it. Years later, at the new Call to Fire training facility, the sign showed up again in the new building. The same sign that Jared made years before. It's like it followed me around everywhere I went."

SGT Dario Lee was assigned to the 82nd Airborne Division at Ft. Bragg and met Jared in an unusual way, although not so unusual for Jared, as many soldiers have reported. "I walked into the barracks and heard a lot of ruckus outside. I looked out the window. A Sergeant was leading a group of men on a naked run around the volleyball court. 'Oh, that's just Monti and his FISTers going streaking,' said one of the guys. Jared just looked up at me when he passed by and said matter-of-factly, 'Hi, how you doin'?' That was my introduction to SGT Monti," recalls Dario.

Jared's penchant for streaking naked around barracks areas earned him the nickname, "The Full Monti." He would do this the same way he did everything else – with that big grin of his. This grin was captured perfectly in the iconic photograph taken by SGT Jimmy McPherson which graces this book's cover. Jimmy has since retired from the Army, earned a degree in Computer Science, and works at Fort Drum as a civilian.

Dario and Jared became good friends and would often go fishing on the Cape Fear River. One day, Dario took Jared into a Wal-mart, a store Dario always refers to as "Wally World," to look for a fishing rod. Dario bought a bargain-basement variety, which caused Jared to laugh and say, "You're never going to catch a damn thing with that." Well, Dario showed him. He got a bite and what a bite it was. He claims it was a 57-pound flathead catfish. When asked how he knew it was exactly 57 pounds, Dario became defensive and said, "I could just tell it was 57 pounds by looking at it. That's what it was. It took us 45 minutes to land the sucker. It had to be that big. This isn't a fish story, anyhow. This is a goose story."

What he meant by that is that the two Americans were trapped in a boat and suddenly attacked by two Canadian geese, threatening an international incident. Dario swears they did nothing to provoke them, but geese are territorial, especially during nesting season. The gander, if he could talk, would simply explain that he was protecting the female and the nest from a perceived threat. Fortunately, the valiant American soldiers were highly trained and went immediately into fighting mode. They demonstrated their proficiency in hand-to-hand combat. Despite being surrounded by the vicious enemy, they lashed out with fishing poles and oars.

SGT Monti was able to strike a mighty blow and knocked the larger goose on the head. They waited a full five minutes to make sure the enemy from the north had been subdued. "I think you killed it," Dario finally said. "I guess I did," responded Jared. At that moment, the goose sprang back to life, started squawking, and retreated. The Americans were feeling pretty good about driving off the invaders until they turned around and noticed that the huge (according to Dario) catfish that they were ignoring was gone. It evidently had jumped into the water and swum away. So they had nothing to show for their courageous battle that day. At least they left with their dignity.

Another favorite destination of theirs was Holton Beach. "Jared just had to disobey every rule there was," recalls Dario. "I remember once there were 397 signs around saying that jumping off the pier was prohibited." We'll have to take his word for it that there were exactly that number of signs. After all, it's not a "sign story." "Jared just had to take off his clothes and jump off the pier. He couldn't resist," says Dario. Evidently, it was again like the orange cones and blinking yellow lights that Jared took from the construction site. You can just imagine Jared's eyes lighting up and his breaking into a big smile. He couldn't resist breaking rules.

Dario often thinks of Jared: "I went fishing the other day and I was sitting there thinking about the time we were on the Cape Fear River and that stupid snake swam right up beside me and scared the crap outta me, and you thought it was sooo damn funny 'cause I got scared of a little snake. Made me smile."

As happens all too frequently with paratroopers, Dario broke his back while jumping and was medically discharged. He is now a civil engineer with the National Resources Conservation Service. He fondly says of Jared, "He was the shortest badass you've ever seen in your life. My fishing buddy had a heart of gold. I never saw him without that smile of his. If he got chewed out for doing something wrong, he'd still be flashing that smile. As far as I'm concerned, there's no greater American hero."

Dan Crespo had tried out for a professional volleyball team in Brazil but failed to make the final cut. He was at a crossroads in his life when 9/11 happened. A New Jersey native, he felt the need to serve by joining the Army. After a stint at Ft. Benning, he was transferred to Ft. Bragg, where he met Jared.

Now a successful college volleyball coach for both the men's and women's team at the City College of New York, Dan claims he learned leadership and life lessons from Jared. "He changed my life. I use him as an example when I talk to my teams about working together and the importance of sacrifice. They say that we meet people every day but only a few truly make their impression on our lives. He made that kind of impression on me. Monti was always smiling. I remember his energy, his positive approach towards training regardless of how far we had to run or how senseless an exercise felt, and his 'never quit' attitude. These attributes not only defined Monti, but I like to believe I've made them my own in the best of my ability.

"We had people from so many demographics in our unit. Jared kept them together," continues Dan. "There was a camaraderie that other groups didn't have. He did it with his personality because he was a cool guy. He was always working. Every moment was a teaching moment. He had quite a following. I'm not one of those people who are easily impressed. But he had 'it.' The intangible. I can only count on one hand the number of people I've known who had that kind of charisma. He had an amazing impact on me."

Dan, however, made Jared very angry during a soccer game between American and Canadian soldiers at Ft. Bragg. The

Canadians were not related in any way to the geese that were described earlier in this chapter. "Jared gave me that smile of his and said, 'You're from Brazil. You must know how to play soccer. You can play for them because they're a couple of players short.' I told him that I'd try to do my best," recalls Dan. "I wound up scoring three goals and the Canadians won, 5-4. Jared was so pissed that he told me he was going to smoke me, and he did. He had me doing push-ups for hours after the game. He didn't let up. Actually, I didn't mind. I was the push-up king. It was in good fun. We all had a laugh over it."

"The U. S. Army has allowed me to make some friends who were powerful individuals and would have been as successful had they chosen something different. Monti is no exception and I aspire to continue those lessons," says Dan.

Elaine Harmon has always lived a life of service to others. The 77-year-old taught first grade in New Jersey for 31 years and was one of those people who would say, "I'd love my job even if they didn't pay me." She proved that after retirement when she volunteered for another 20 years as a teacher's aide. "I would always tell my first graders about soldiers, people in need, and doing things for others. I stressed respecting other people, even if they're different from you. I was teaching them the Golden Rule. With other kids, you'd ask them what they'd do if they were given a million dollars and they'd say buy a big house or do something else for themselves. When you asked my kids, I was proud of the fact they'd invariably say they'd use the money to help others."

"I had a friend who told me about how fulfilling it was being a Platoon Mom. It seemed like a natural fit for me. The idea is that you adopt a group of soldiers and watch over them. You talk to them on the phone, e-mail them, and send them things in the mail. I was assigned to an 82nd Airborne Division Platoon at Fort Bragg. That's when I started to correspond with Jared Monti. I felt there was something special about him right away. It's like he was who I wanted those first graders to grow up to be. I was always so impressed by the way he treated other people. He lived the Golden Rule."

Elaine claims she will always remember her first trip to Ft. Bragg to meet the Platoon. "Jared picked me up at the train station. I still remember the welcoming hug. It was magnetic. We were like family to each other. I had a wonderful time at Ft. Bragg. Before I left, Jared stopped by the PX (Post Exchange.) He knew I loved bears so he bought me a ten-inch Angel Bear. It looks like a regular brown bear, but it has a pink heart in the middle and angel wings. He told me I was like an angel to him. I feel the same way about him. I still have that bear. I'll always keep it. He was such a great person."

"Elaine always told me Jared was her favorite soldier," smiles Janet. "Even though one time she disappointed him when she tried to do something thoughtful and videotape the Super Bowl game for him & his unit and then send it to them. The problem was she didn't tape the commercials, and the troops were disappointed, saying the commercials were the best part."

Elaine has two daughters, one son, and four grandchildren along with her husband John to look after. "I don't get out as much as I used to, but whenever I leave the house I always wear a "Support Our Troops" shirt. Most of the time it's to go to the Post Office to mail something out to soldiers or to go the supermarket. About three-quarters of the food I buy is for them. Sometimes I'm slow, and I turn around and say to people waiting in line behind me, 'I'm sorry you have to wait, but this is for the troops.' I hope they understand there's nothing more important than that."

One of her favorite pastimes is sending out what she calls Military "Personwell" (a term she invented) Survival Kits. You can picture the smiles on the faces of those who serve their country in some far off place as they open up the contents of a typical kit, which might contain gift items and messages such as a "pack of gum to help your unit stick together, cotton ball to cushion the rough roads, mint because you're worth a mint, string for when you reach the end of your rope, candle so you can brighten someone's day, tootsie roll to help you roll with the punches, penny to remind you we each shine in our own way, hugs for when you need one, smiles for when you don't have one, yellow ribbon to let you know you'll be supported until you come home, and marbles for when you may lose yours."

How long will Elaine continue her work with soldiers? "I'll be helping those in the military as long as God keeps this body of mine moving," she asserts. "It's amazing how much these things matter to the troops. Some of them don't ever get anything from their families. It's hard for me to understand that."

Darren Hammerstad is stationed at the Jacksonville Naval Air Station as a 3rd Class Petty Officer. The son of Paul's sister, Rita (Monti) Hammerstad, he's one of Paul's godchildren. He says, "Jared is the reason why I'm in the military, no question about it."

While stationed at Fort Bragg, Jared spent a week on leave with his cousin Darren and his family. Darren was ten years old at the time and remembers their playing Manhunt, an outdoors Hide and Go Seek game at night. "He could find me right away but when I'd try to find him, he'd be behind a tree and move around. I could never find him. He'd reach out and grab me. We'd both laugh. I didn't know how he did it. I felt so good being around him. I knew I wanted to be just like him."

Jared left his red Army beret with Darren and also gave him a 10th Mountain Division T-shirt. Darren not only still has them but keeps the T-shirt neatly folded on the back of his computer chair at home. He vows that it will always stay there in the same spot with the 10th Mountain Division insignia face up. His mother Rita, posted this message to her nephew Jared:

"I am and always have been so proud of you from the first day I picked you up at Ft. Bragg and brought you to my home and listened to all your Army stories. You have touched the lives of many, including my son who has decided to join the military. He still has the uniform hat you gave him when you came to visit, and your 10th Mountain t-shirt hangs on his chair, never to be worn. You are an inspiration, a hero, and a friend."

According to Barb Dresser, "In my 72 years, I've come to realize that our lives are a journey – a journey of events and circumstances, a journey of triumphs and failures, a journey of lessons learned and taught. Along the way, we meet a myriad of people – some young, some old, some good, some evil; some stay for a long time and some are with us for only a short time. I used to call some of these events coincidences, but then there were times that were so special that it seemed like God was in it. A divine appointment is a meeting which was inspired and God-led. I believe that Jared Monti was one of those in my life."

Barb met Jared as a result of what she calls "a long, twisted and painful path." She says she "escaped" from Michigan in 1995 with her 13-year-old daughter, a dog, and two cockatiels, winding up in Easley, South Carolina. In leaving behind what she terms "a violent and abusive marriage," she lost her home, most of her belongings, family, and friends.

Shortly after arriving in South Carolina, her daughter attempted suicide, and Barb was diagnosed with PTSD. She also fell down some stairs and had to recover from a serious back injury. At the time, her son Henry was deployed overseas with the Army. "I felt very much abandoned and alone," she admits. Then she made an important choice. “I decided that I wanted to thrive, not just be a survivor,” she proclaims. “I needed to get ‘outside of myself’ and support those who were in similar circumstances. I joined a local abuse survivor group. Then I became a facilitator of that group.” She began to reach out and provide online support to veterans, particularly those in the 173rd Airborne who are known as “Sky Soldiers” and call themselves “The Herd.” Headquartered in Vicenza, Italy, they are an airborne infantry brigade combat team forming the U. S. European Command’s conventional airborne strategic response force.

She began leading a support group at Fort Bragg, NC. One of the projects she took on was helping to organize a reunion for the 173rd, and that’s when she was put in touch with Jared. “We not only became friends, but immediately bonded. Knowing I had a son in the military, he started calling me ‘Mom.’ We talked, we shared, we emailed, and we IM’d online,” she recalls.

She felt she’d be out of place at the reunion and wasn’t planning to attend. But Jared insisted saying, “Mom, you HAVE to be there! You’ve supported these guys, now’s your chance to meet some of them in person.” Still having what she called “trust issues,” she argued. Jared refused to take no for an answer. He said, “Don’t worry, Mom – we’ll look out for you!”

She relented and went to that reunion. She sat with a couple of women, not really socializing with anyone else. Jared would periodically come up to check on her, asking if she was okay. “As one of my ‘young’uns’ there at Ft. Bragg, Jared and his buds looked out for me,” she recalls fondly. “Then he asked me if I’d be willing to talk to a fellow who was alone and recently widowed. He told me he was harmless.” Barb and the “harmless” fellow got along quite well. If fact, it turned out that Jared had introduced Barb to her future husband, retired SFC James Dresser, whom she married in 2000.

She got a call from Jared, saying that "the Herd" was throwing a going-away picnic for the troops who were being deployed overseas. Jared wanted his Military Mom to be there. "I wouldn't have missed it for the world," she says. So Barb and Jim drove to Ft. Bragg. "We had a great time at that picnic – good eats, lots of beer, and lots of hugs. Since Jared was being promoted from E-5 to E-6 (Sergeant to Staff Sergeant), he drove us back to his barracks and retrieved one of his Class A uniform jackets and gave it to Jim," recalls Barb fondly. "It was at that picnic that I last saw Jared."

Chapter 8
Down by the River

Jared left for a second deployment to South Korea and was assigned to Camp Casey in Dongducheon, again close to the DMZ. According to PFC Ryan Kelley, "SSG Monti immediately made an impact on our platoon in South Korea. He was a very motivated soldier, a genuine good dude. At your first meeting with him, you get that gut feeling that you just know this guy. He was the kind of person where there was never an awkward silence. Someone you look up to when you're a young soldier. Monti had this actual 'soldier swagger' about him. He knew his shit. Whether it was FISTer, 11-B (the MOS for Infantry Soldier), vehicle identification, weapons knowledge, light movement tactics, air assault and airborne operations, or general soldiering shit." (The latter is a technical term that only those who have served in the military can understand.)

"I went down by the river one time with SSG Monti in 2002 at Camp Casey, South Korea, HHB, 1/15th FA, 2nd Platoon, 2nd Squad. Being in the Striker Platoon, as a 13-Foxtrot FO (Forward Observer), you knew you were the best of the best. Because of this, it was understood that our Platoon would be given additional duties in the field. It could be providing other units with Op4 services (playing the role of the opposing force in a training exercise),

Observer Control grading units in the field, Road Guard (first out of the gate and last in for field exercises), Field Training, Live Fire, or simulation training, to name a few. This specific time out in the field, the Striker Platoon was given the task to play Op4 against the Gun Bunnies (members of the artillery who operate mortars, cannons, etc.) It was roughly two weeks' worth of rucking (hiking or marching with a weighted pack for long distances over varied terrain) all over the northern part of South Korea in the dust bowl, moving through small villages and rice patties, then attacking the firing batteries AO (area of operations)," recalls Ryan.

The Platoon Leader was 1LT Thomas E. Kennedy, who was later killed in Kunar Province, Afghanistan, when he encountered an insurgent who detonated a suicide vest. On one particular movement, Jared's team, Radio Call Sign Striker 75, which included PFC's Steve Rush and Ryan Kelley, were to ruck 12 clicks (kilometers) to the first assault that night. They had already been in the field for a week. The team was briefed about the movement, which included a river crossing, among terrain features found in the backwoods of South Korea. SSG Craig Brown and 1LT Kennedy RECON'ed the area and picked a place for the team to cross the river. They felt it to be the slowest, shallowest point. They gave specific grid coordinates to make sure the team would cross at the approved spot.

"After the briefing, SSG Monti had us load up the Humvee with gear and supplies and wait for dusk to roll out. Often the squad leaders would come up with random shit for us to do. SSG Monti had a few 'go to' things, the most famous was the 'who has the better war face' contest. That time I won. I'm not sure if that's a good thing or bad thing. I did think about that face in March of 2003, as I was rolling over the border from Kuwait to Iraq during the invasion," recalls Ryan.

"So dusk came and we started our movement," he continues.

"Once we found an area to ditch the Humvee in the woods, we started out on our long ruck march to the river bed. SSG Monti kept things positive. I remember him saying that we only had one click to go, when we really had about 3-4 clicks straight line distance, through mountains and sometimes thick brush. Once we made it to the river bed, I called on the radio back to the TOC (Tactical Operations Center) that we were in position, and we were given the order to cross."

There was a problem, however. Jared saw the area and felt it wasn't safe. He wouldn't allow his soldiers to go in the water without his testing it first. It wasn't the last time he would choose to risk his own life rather than those of his soldiers. "Monti insisted he would go first because of the sounds we heard, and looking through our NVG's (night vision goggles), the river did look pretty rough. SSG Monti buttoned up all his gear and started into the water. He called back to us that once he got to the other side, another one of us could cross. Monti only wanted one man in the water at a time. As he got further into the water, it began to reach above his knees. As we were smoking and joking, we watched Monti disappear into the dark, raging river and not come out. SPC Steve Rush and I dropped our ruck sacks and ran down the riverbed like lifeguards. Finally SSG Monti popped out of the water and yelled, 'I dropped my fucking weapon!' Rush and I asked if he was all right. Monti said, 'Yeah, but I won't be once we call this in.'

"After getting in the water ourselves and looking for his M-4, we realized we would not find it that night," says Ryan. "Once you got in the middle of the river there was a drop off and it was over six feet deep. We called in 'Red' on the Sensitive Items Report, meaning we'd lost a weapon." As every soldier knows from the first day of Boot Camp, losing a weapon is an extremely serious offense that can result in a Court Martial leading to a less-than-honorable discharge. This was exacerbated by the fact that the weapon was lost close to the DMZ, not in a secure training area. If a South Korean thief retrieved the weapon from the water that was fished in every day and sold it to the North Koreans, the incident would cause significant embarrassment to the U. S. Army.

Ryan acknowledges, "We needed to find this weapon before anyone else did. The next day we had the Army Corp of Engineers out connecting ropes across the valley that we were to hold on to while looking in the water through goggles. After all day of searching the river we had no luck. This went on for about three days. They moved the ropes down further to see if the M-4 was pushed down the river. SSG Monti, Rush, and I kept on saying we needed to look right where he crossed, because that was where he dropped the weapon, right in the deepest spot. No luck. The commanders had the final say. The fourth day came, and CID showed up. There were rumors we had sold the brand new M-4 to some Korean fisherman. CID took each one of us away separately to interrogate us."

The local news started to speculate about what was going on with all the commotion by the river. An official statement was made, saying the Americans were on a Co-op training mission with the South Koreans. Their Navy divers, working with the fire and rescue department, were summoned. "They had little scuba jets with them. Once they came down and got geared up, they asked us where we thought the weapon was, so we told them, 'Where SSG Monti crossed.' Then the commanders told the divers they needed to look about 50 yards down river. The divers listened to the officers, since they understood rank structure. The divers would pop out of the water with nothing in hand. After about 15 minutes, one of the divers stayed under water with the jet propulsion and went right to where SSG Monti, Rush and I had told them the rifle would be. The next thing we saw was SSG Monti's M-4 being raised out of the river. The M-4 hadn't traveled but a few inches down river. This whole operation lasted about a week in the middle of the summer, when it was hot as hell. It was like a strange work vacation down by the river," recalls the soldier, who to this day ends the story with a heavy sigh of relief.

In his second South Korean deployment, Jared had a dog named Gator, named for the 6x4 John Deere M-Gator Military Utility Vehicle, an adaptation of the civilian Deere Gator Tractor. After the Army phased out the quarter-ton Jeep, the three-cylinder, 18 horsepower diesel engine Gator filled the gap for small, mobile tactical vehicles used for transporting supplies and other light-duty transportation.

Not surprisingly, he didn't receive permission to keep Gator the dog in the barracks. The Battalion Commander found out about Gator and at morning formation said to the troops, "It's come to my attention that someone may have an animal in the barracks. As you know, that's against regulations. If such an animal had the required shots, however, it is possible that it could be kept as a battalion mascot." As the Colonel made this speech, he stared directly at Jared, who was hunching down, trying to make himself as small as possible. So, Jared got the necessary vaccinations for Gator and was able to keep the dog as a mascot.

Captain Tom Greer, who served with Jared, says, "When I was in the field along the DMZ, he was right there next to me. Just as cold, just as tired, just as hungry, but with a smile on his face. He never complained and truly loved the warrior lifestyle. He was a super teammate, and we are all so much better for having his company and example. Monti arrived in Korea in the mid 90's as a young and very motivated trooper. He always looked at you with his head tilted slightly forward, eyes looking upward, and with a devilish grin as if he had just gotten away with something that his buddies nearby were trying to hold in their laughter about. He was the type of soldier that other soldiers serving hardship tours loved to have around. He made the freezing cold South Korean winters bearable with his sense of humor and positive attitude, even while digging in all night. He was pretty unique. Very focused, a great sense of humor, but always dedicated." Tom goes on to say, "He was considered an equal, which is saying a lot for a young FISTer in a rifle company of ornery infantrymen. I'm sure there isn't anyone out there that knew Jared who is surprised by his extraordinary bravery and commitment to his mates."

Bill Highsmith posted this message to Jared: "You truly are one of the greats. If I had to use one word to describe you, it would be humble. I remember in Korea one morning during a PT test, I saw you doing push-ups with a grimace on your face. Your back was so messed up you could barely walk. It didn't affect your score. You smoked me the entire PT test. It was all because you wanted to be the best, and you were."

It was on to another overseas tour of duty for Jared, to a place called Kosovo. Most Americans have no idea where Kosovo is, or even if it's a city or a country. It's actually a country bordered by Macedonia, Albania, and Montenegro, if that helps.

Like the DMZ and Afghanistan, it's a dangerous place that historically has been filled with tension and violence. They somehow never managed to send Jared to resort areas. Kosovo is ethnically divided by age-old disagreements between Albanians and Serbs. In the Kosovo War of 1999, NATO forces bombed Yugoslavia in an effort to force President Slobodan Milošević to withdraw his troops and give up control of the country. He consented, but skirmishes between Albanian guerrillas and Yugoslav forces continued for years afterwards.

Control over the country eventually passed from the United Nations to the European Union. Finally, the Republic of Kosovo declared independence on February 17, 2008. The United States recognized its independence immediately, and by 2014, 107 out of the 193 countries in the United Nations had followed suit.

In 1996, Jared was sent on a two-year deployment to Camp Bondsteel, the largest American military base in the Balkans. Although it sounds like something from a British spy movie, it's actually named after U. S. Army Staff Sergeant James L. Bondsteel, a Medal of Honor recipient from the Viet Nam War. It's located near Urosevac and is the NATO headquarters for KFOR's Multinational Brigade East. KFOR stands for the Kosovo Force, NATO's peace-keeping organization.

On Jared's first patrol, he witnessed the kind of brutality to which people in Kosovo had become accustomed. For Jared, it was his initial exposure to an active war zone. On his first day there, he saw two men walking toward him. He sensed something was wrong but could only watch to see how the scene would play out because of the restrictive rules of engagement. Suddenly, the one in front knelt down, and the man behind him aimed his weapon and shot him in the head, killing him instantly.

Shortly after that, Jared witnessed soldiers tearing down someone's farmhouse for wood to build a fire. That family was left standing and shivering in the cold, watching their home being dismantled. Again, he could only watch in horror.

In Kosovo, violence between Albanians and Serbians was common. When Jared was stationed there, he saw Muslim kids being taunted and having garbage thrown at them when they walked through the Albanian section of town on the way to school. They would wait for Jared to pick them up in his Humvee and be driven to school. Jared didn't want them have to deal with the harassment. His Aunt Tricia said, "Jared told us how he'd get up early to drive kids to school and try to get back to the base in time before his superiors woke up. Sometimes they'd find out what he did and he'd get in trouble for it. That didn't stop him, though."

Janet sent a package of new clothes to Kosovo for Jared. He said he appreciated receiving them, but the local children appreciated wearing them even more. He had given those clothes away. From that point on, Janet and other relatives realized that whatever they sent to him, he'd give away to someone he regarded as more needy.

"Jared wasn't a 'GI Joe' or 'Rambo' who was hell-bent on killing the enemy. That's not him at all. He was a humanitarian. Everywhere he went, he left people feeling respected no matter what their status," says Paul.

Using the back of a Swiss Miss hot cocoa mix label, Jared wrote the following matter-of-fact letter from Kosovo to his Aunt Annie and Uncle Rich Eagles:

> Hi guys, sorry about the paper, had nothing better to write on...Not much doing over here...There's quite a bit of shooting going on in our sector. Had a pretty good firefight the other night. The Albanians launched five rockets into a Serbian house about three houses away from the abandoned building we are staying in. Then a few grenades got chucked around. Then a huge firefight followed. Talk about a 4th of July! Wrong place to be in the middle of. Other than that, it's usually quiet.

According to Matthew Hatfield, "I was stationed with Jared in Kosovo. Our friend David Caldwell was a huge Salma Hayek fan. He had posters of her all over the place. He was obsessed with her. There was going to be a USO (United Service Organization) show with a number of celebrities. Salma was one of them. Jared set it up so that David would pick up her up in his Humvee, but he didn't tell Caldwell. He wanted him to be surprised. The problem was, it was very cold and she had an arctic jacket pulled up over her head. A Humvee has no rear-view mirror, anyhow. So, we dropped the celebrities off and I said to him, 'Did you talk to her?' David says, 'Talk to who?' I said, 'Didn't you look in the back?' He said, 'No, I wasn't paying attention.' It was a great plan, except David never realized he had been Salma Hayek's driver."

At David's wedding back in the States, Jeff Bolding put the bride's wedding ring on a cat's tail as a joke. Naturally, the cat ran off and wasn't found. Poor David couldn't catch a break. The couple had to go through with the ceremony without the ring.

"People wonder why Jared never went into the Special Forces. He was the perfect kind of guy for it," admits Matthew. "He'd say to me, 'I can't dip tobacco during the selection phase, so I'm not interested.' I could understand that, because I dipped too. It's funny that he was from Massachusetts and I was from Georgia but we really seemed to have a lot in common. His favorite song was 'Long Haired Country Boy' by Charlie Daniels. He made a huge impact on a lot of people's lives, including mine."

As early as November of 1999, when he was still stationed in Kosovo, Jared wrote to Annie and Rich Eagles about the possibility of his ending his military career:

> They are trying their hardest to keep me in. I've gotten all sorts of job offers, but I'm sticking to my guns and readying myself for the real world and college. Kinda nervous about college. I'm gonna be a pretty old freshman. Probably be the go-to guy for beer runs. I should be all right at school, though. I've got much better study habits than I had in high school. I took a few courses here in the Army and caught on pretty quickly. Now it's just a matter

> of choosing a good school. The G. I. Bill should help out quite a bit, plus I'll get some scholarship money from ROTC. That will equal out to free schooling. I still have 14 months on a decision so I'm not stressing it too bad yet.

"Jared was changed when he came back from Kosovo," recalls Paul. "He had seen man's inhumanity to man up-close. I picked him up at T. F. Green Airport in Providence, Rhode Island. He was sullen. He wasn't his usual self. I remember his saying, 'I'm hungry. I need to eat.' Just like that. He had never talked that way before. I pulled right over into a Dunkin' Donuts. I was worried about him. He came home and he spent the entire time on his leave sleeping on the couch. He slept like I've never seen before."

Jared returned to the States to join the 10th Mountain Division Headquarters at Fort Drum, which borders Watertown in upstate New York. Fort Drum provides planning and support for the mobilization and training of almost 80,000 troops annually. It was there that he was able to overcome the trauma of what he had experienced in Kosovo and ready himself for the trying times to come.

According to MSG Lee Power, "One time I was assigned to do a barracks inspection at Fort Drum. It was pretty routine until I got to Jared's room. He was working on a motorcycle and had spread parts all over his bed. He was sleeping beside the bed on a Barcalounger." There was a report that a Barcalounger was missing from the Officer's Lounge. A strange coincidence. According to Power, "That was, shall we say, not completely up to military standards." When asked if he wrote Jared up, he laughed and said in his best military-speak, "Spreading motorcycle parts out on a bed was not within the parameters of my inspection." That translates as "No one would have believed it, so it was best to ignore it." Imagine a Court Martial where everyone, including the

Presiding Officers, can't stop laughing.

Despite his penchant for mischief, Jared became well known throughout the Army as someone who was respected by those at higher levels. Lee Power claims, "Jared did things his way and accepted the consequences. He didn't have a problem telling people the truth, even if it wasn't what they wanted to hear. That's why people would seek him out. They respected his straight talk. I know I did."

At Fort Drum, a high-ranking General from Washington visited the base and pulled up in front of his unit and got out of his staff car. Immediately, a nervous but eager 2nd Lieutenant ran up and saluted him. The General, in no mood to waste his time on formalities, barked, "Put your fucking arm down, Lieutenant. I'm here to see Monti." He wanted to get down to business.

There was a reason that even Generals sought him out. "I had known him since 1998. I knew him well because of his outstanding performance," said CSM James Redmore. "He was the kind of guy who spoke his mind, and he wasn't willing to hold any punches when he felt something was going wrong, which is a positive trait in my eyes because he's the guy who applied common sense to what was going on. It was important to me to get honest feedback, and I could always count on him for that."

According to SGT John Hawes, "Jared had no problem going head-to-head with an officer when ordered to do what he called 'something stupid.' If someone was showing a lack of common sense, he'd put them in their place, no matter who they were."

Chris Grzecki concurs. "Jared was willing to stand up for his soldiers. In the Army what you get is a lot of people who are not so concerned with the guy below them as much as they are in impressing the guy above them. SFC Monti was the opposite of that. He wanted to take care of his guys. That was the basis of what made him such a great NCO. That and the fact that he knew so much about the job. From the moment you meet him, you're just in awe of him. He's the type of guy you don't want to disappoint. You want to become like him."

His soldiers knew the compassionate side of Jared. Steve Ramirez wrote this to him: "I'll always remember that when I was a Private I had poor marksmanship skills, and you saw me struggling. You were kind enough to show me different methods of achieving that 40 out of 40 expert marksmanship. Since that day, whenever I bumped into you, you always asked me how my shooting skills were."

Private Franklin Woods also first came in contact with SSG Monti out on the firing range at Fort Drum. "I was getting yelled at by the Sergeants for doing everything wrong," he admits. "One of them comes over and says, 'Calm down.' I told him I was brand new and I didn't know what I was doing. He said, 'Relax. Don't worry about it. Where are you from, Private?' I told him I was from Oklahoma. Then we started this big conversation about Kenny Rogers and 'The Gambler.' He assumed someone from Oklahoma would like that song, and he was right. I realized this guy was not your typical Sergeant. He was someone who cared about you, like a big brother," says Franklin, now a SSG himself stationed in Italy.

Jared's life consisted of a lot of little stories. Little things he did that touched people. Little things that made a difference. Many say they'll remember these little stories the rest of their lives. It turns out the little things were really pretty big things.

Chapter 9
America Under Attack

Afghanistan is an idyllic setting. It's similar to life in a Colorado ski resort, except that it's not in Colorado, there's no skiing, and there aren't any resorts. But, at least the terrain and weather conditions are similar. There are spectacular views of snow-peaked mountains and deep, sweeping valleys. Pine forests blanket the majestic mountainsides. Countless ancient high passes transect the mountains.

Roughly the size of Texas, the country touches Turkmenistan, Uzbekistan, and Tajikistan on the north, countries that are not exactly household names to Americans. To the northeast it's bordered by China, on the east and south by Pakistan, and on the west by Iran. The first part of the country's name, "Afghan" is derived from the alternate name of the founders of the country, the Pashtuns. The second part comes from the Persian word "stan" which means country or land. It is split east to west by the majestic Hindu Kush Mountains, which rise to heights that peak at Mt. Noshaq, standing at 7,492 meters or 25,480 feet. That rivals Mt. Everest in Nepal, the world's tallest mountain, which is 8,796 meters or 28,858 feet.

Afghanistan has always been one of the most desolate, dangerous, and violent regions on earth. Throughout history, it has been referred to as the "Graveyard of Empires." Military campaigns were waged there by Alexander the Great and Genghis Khan. Are the Afghanis tired of war? Frankly, they've never known anything else. Peace is a theoretical concept to them.

The country has some of the most extreme weather conditions on earth. The sheer cliffs are dangerous to navigate on foot. One slip can mean a catastrophic tumble down a mountain. The sun can be blinding in the summer, severe blizzards are common in the winter, and there is the possibility of avalanches year-round. Few of the "highways" are paved. Those that are paved are in such a state of disrepair that they are close to unusable. The rebuilding of roads destroyed by centuries of war is beyond the scope of the Afghan government. In short, there aren't many places in the world that are as inhospitable.

The thin air makes physical activity difficult. Summers are oppressively hot, with temperatures as high as 120 degrees Fahrenheit. Winters are bitterly cold, with temperatures as low as 15 degrees Fahrenheit being common. Strong winds in the mountains cause wind chills to dip well below zero. Temperatures often vary greatly, even within the same day. It's not unusual for temperature swings of as much as 50 or 60 degrees from noon to midnight.

On the other hand, Afghanistan is replete with gold, copper, coal, lithium, precious gems, and natural gas. Then, of course, there's the opium. The country is by far the biggest producer of opium in the world. In fact, it's estimated that Afghanistan is responsible for growing more opium than all other countries combined. It's also the world's largest producer of cannabis and hashish. It has been reported that as little as 25% of the billions of dollars of revenue in illicit drug sales goes to growers. The rest goes to warlords, drug traffickers, terrorist groups, and government officials. Little wonder the country has had corruption, purges, atrocities, and struggles for power throughout its history. It's business as usual with no end in sight.

There's also the influence of Islamic Fundamentalism. Nuristan Province earned the designation as the "Cradle of Jihad" in the 1980's. The Islamic term "Jihad" means "struggle." It's meant in the sense of the internal struggle "to perform religious duties" and also the external struggle "against the enemies of Islam." It's the second meaning of "Jihad" that is best known.

Leonid Brezhnev ordered the Soviet Union invasion of Afghanistan in December of 1979, following the overthrow of communist leader Nur Muhammad Taraki. It led to the American Cold War boycott of the 1980 Summer Olympic Games in Moscow, and subsequent funding and support by the United States of insurgent forces in a fight against the Soviets. Among the trained and equipped insurgents was Osama bin Laden, as well as others who would go on to become terrorists and turn against the United States. These forces were called "Mujahideen", which means "strugglers" in Arabic. They were among the world's fiercest and most cunning fighters, using advanced military tactics to consistently outflank and outmaneuver the Soviet army. They would invariably gain the most favorable high ground position in battles, place booby traps and land mines on trails, or simply fire rifle shots and then disappear into the mountains.

It's estimated that 15,000 Soviet troops were killed in Afghanistan before Mikhail Gorbachev recognized they had been soundly defeated and ordered a withdrawal in 1989. The cost ran to billions of dollars and helped bankrupt an already struggling Soviet economy. That has led many to refer to the Soviet Afghan War as "Russia's Viet Nam."

After years of bloody in-fighting, the Taliban began to emerge in Kandahar and had virtually the entire country under their control by 1998. The Taliban is an Islamic fundamentalist political movement which spread from Pakistan and officially formed the Islamic Emirate of Afghanistan with Kandahar as its capital in September of 1996. Only three countries recognized the regime – Pakistan, the United Arab Emirates, and Saudi Arabia.

The word "Taliban" comes from the Pashto and means "students". Ironically, one of their basic beliefs is that women should be subjugated and never become students. They brutally enforce strict interpretation of Sharia Law. Countless Taliban atrocities have been reported against Afghanis and Pakistanis. The United States watched with a wary eye as Afghanistan served as an operating base for the Al Qaeda terrorist organization headed by Osama bin Laden. The name "Al Qaeda" means "the base", which signified their vision of one organization leading Jihad. That vision today has been adopted by the Islamic State rebels.

The United States was forever changed the morning of September 11, 2001. Nineteen terrorists seized control of two Boeing 757 and two Boeing 767 commercial airliners that were en route from the East Coast to California. They were chosen because the hijackers knew that the jets would be fully fueled for cross-country flights.

At 8:46 a.m., American Airlines Flight 11 was flown into the North Tower of the World Trade Center, followed by United Airlines Flight 175, which hit the South Tower at 9:03 a.m. Then American Airlines Flight 77 struck the Pentagon at 9:37 a.m., and United Airlines Flight 93 crashed into a field in Shanksville, PA at 10:03 a.m. America suffered one killing blow after another. The attacks left 2,996 people dead.

With an eight and a half-hour difference between Eastern Standard Time and Afghanistan Time, it was already early evening in Afghanistan. A Kuwaiti-born cleric, 48-year-old Sulaiman Abu

Ghaith, was being driven to an unknown destination on a long, bumpy ride on barely navigable roads in a remote mountainous area of Afghanistan. He was about to meet with Osama bin Laden, who was impressed with reports of Abu Ghaith's passionate religious sermons at al Qaeda training camps and knew he was an ardent believer in Jihad.

Sulaiman Abu Ghaith, Osama bin Laden's spokesman for al Qaeda, was tried and convicted of multiple counts of conspiracy in Manhattan Federal Court on March 26, 2014. The prosecution claimed, "Abu Ghaith was a terrorist who sat alongside bin Laden celebrating the murder of nearly 3,000 innocent, men, women and children." When asked directly by Manhattan U. S. Attorney Preet Bharara if he knew about the attacks beforehand, he claimed under oath that he knew "something" might happen. When asked if he knew something big was coming, he responded, "Yes."

The meeting in the secret cave started with bin Laden saying excitedly, "Come in, sit down. Did you learn what happened? We are the ones who did it."

When bin Laden asked what he thought would happen next, Abu Ghaith declined to respond, saying that he was not a military analyst. But bin Laden pressed him for an answer. Abu Ghaith then predicted, "America will not settle until it kills you and topples the State of the Taliban."

Abu Ghaith recalled that bin Laden retorted, "You're being too pessimistic." To which he replied, "You asked my opinion and this is my opinion."

The next morning, bin Laden told him, "I want to deliver a message to the world. I want you to deliver the message." Abu Ghaith said he stayed for two to three weeks in the cave with bin Laden and others because, he claimed, "the situation was tense and the roads were dangerous."

The videos Abu Ghaith made warned that there would be more attacks on America. One of them promised "the storm of airplanes will not abate." Abu Ghaith said he used "quotes and points by Sheik Osama" to try to inspire others to join al Qaeda's cause. He claimed that these videos were religious in nature and meant to "encourage Muslims to fight oppression." He later married into bin Laden's family by wedding his daughter.

On September 23, 2014, Federal Judge Lewis Kaplan sentenced Abu Ghaith to life in prison. The defense had argued that Abu Ghaith deserved no more than 15 years behind bars because he wasn't convicted of any acts of violence. They said he "faces the harshest penalties for talk – and only talk." On the other hand, federal prosecutor John Cronin called him an "operational terrorist" and claimed he was "just as valuable, if not more so, than the person who straps on a suicide vest and detonates a bomb." Both the jury and judge wound up agreeing with him.

"When I watched the towers being hit by those planes on 9/11, I knew Jared would get involved," acknowledges Janet. "It changed everything. You could feel it in the air. Our country was going to war, and so was he."

There were several weeks of frustrating negotiations with the Taliban, who refused to extradite bin Laden. They obfuscated, saying, "We asked him and he said he had nothing to do with the attacks on America." The Americans and a coalition of allies had heard enough. They began military strikes on October 7, 2001 in what was called "Operation Enduring Freedom" to end the Taliban's ability to provide safe haven to their al Qaeda allies.

Jared's Aunt Annie has always connected Jared's service in Afghanistan with the terrorist attack on America. She maintains, "I have a friend who suffered the loss of a son on 9/11. I thought of Jared fighting the fight. I could do it comfortably because I knew that was why he was there. That's what he was doing. He was making sure our country and our people stay protected."

The United States and the United Kingdom were later joined by forces from many other nations. Throughout the protracted war, the Americans bore the brunt of the war effort, contributing the most troops and suffering the greatest number of casualties.

As Abu Ghaith predicted, the Taliban regime was driven off in a decisive 45-day military campaign. They officially relinquished power in December of 2001. The United Nations Security Council then established the ISAF, the International Security Assistance Force, in Resolution 1386, to oversee security and train the ANSF, the Afghan National Security Force. Unfortunately, the war didn't end there. Relatively few al Qaeda and Taliban were captured or killed. They instead escaped to neighboring Pakistan, or fled from the populated areas to Afghanistan's remote mountainous regions, forming an insurgency which struck back in the form of ambushes and sniper attacks. After the impressive start, the Afghan war became a quagmire dragging on for well over a decade and ultimately becoming America's longest war. The plan of turning the war effort over to the Afghan military turned out to be an agonizingly slow process.

At the height of the war, there were more than 700 military bases inside Afghanistan. About 400 of these were used by American-led forces, and the others by Afghan Security Forces.

In all, 49 nations contributed nearly 53,000 troops. It's estimated that since 2001, more than 10,000 Afghan Security troops have been killed in the war effort.

Hamid Karzai was chosen to lead the country as part of the Afghan Interim Administration. Later, in a democratic election, he would be officially elected President of what was renamed the Islamic Republic of Afghanistan.

Perfectly suited to fight in Afghanistan, the U. S. Army's 10th Mountain Division is Light Infantry specializing in combat under extreme conditions. They are well-trained students of warfare who learned from mistakes made by the Soviets. Like the infantrymen of days gone by, they fight on foot and engage in close combat. It used to be that enemy could be easily identified by the uniforms they wore. In today's wars, however, the enemy can be anywhere. It's difficult to tell who's a friend and who's a foe. Someone walking toward you can easily conceal a weapon or explosives. You have to be constantly alert and wary of everyone you meet. That takes its toll, both physically and mentally. Even if you're stationed at Headquarters, you're likely to hear gunfire throughout the course of the day. You might even have some of the gunfire directed at you.

Being a foot soldier has always been dangerous and often thankless work. They usually carry shelter and supplies on their backs. Frostbite, snow blindness, heat stroke, insect and other animal bites, trench foot, serious illness, loss of hearing after a battle, and lack of sleep are common occupational hazards. Typically, they suffer the most casualties in combat. On the other hand, members of the Army infantry, cavalry, and artillery usually form close bonds with one another. Their units are models of discipline, team-work, and co-operation. Many soldiers establish life-long relationships with their comrades-in-arms.

SGT Jarred Wesley, who served with Jared, offers this insight: "As a soldier I gained a unique perspective on interpersonal relationships, because when you serve with people from all walks of life in one of the most dangerous things you can do, you develop bonds that can't be described no matter how eloquent the words. It is a weird thing to have brothers who weren't born from the womb of your mother. It is also a weird thing to know that you have a high chance of losing your brother to a violent death every single day. To understand what it means to be a veteran is to try to fathom what it is like missing people who shared the most intense moments of your life with you."

The 71st Cavalry Regiment has a lineage that traces back to its activation in 1941 as a tank destroyer unit. The soldiers had the courage and temerity to use light armor, speed, and cunning to seek out and attack the dreaded German Panzers in World War II. They are self-described as having "an aggressive, elite spirit." By the end of World War II, the Regiment was attached to the 10th Mountain Division in Northern Italy. Subsequently, the 71st served as a mechanized cavalry reconnaissance, a heavy tank, and then an armored infantry battalion. In 2004, it was repurposed to provide reconnaissance squadrons for the famed 10th Mountain Division headquartered at Fort Drum, New York.

Jared spoke of the war effort with a hint of foreshadowing: "For those of you who have lost somebody in today's wars, I hope you understand why we are there and what it may mean to us."

Chapter 10
The Thin-Skinned Humvee

Jared began his first deployment to Afghanistan in 2003, where he was awarded the Bronze Star. According to Battery Commander and Captain Alexander J. Shrom, "SSG Monti proved himself to be an expert in his craft and a first-rate leader of soldiers in combat." Jared was caught in a deadly ambush on December 31 of that year. He not only directed fire for attack helicopters but fought off insurgents by manning the turret machine gun to protect his convoy.

He was part of a Task Force that went to a village in the Margritay Valley to search for insurgents and weapons. The twenty-vehicle convoy was departing shortly after sunset. As they approached the exit of the steep-sided mountain road, enemy forces attacked from six different ambush positions. The lead 2/3 of the convoy was able to push through the enemy fire. The trailing eight vehicles were trapped in the enemy's kill zone. There was a young Private manning the turret on the machine gun of Jared's Humvee. He froze and didn't know what to do. Jared grabbed him and pulled him down into the vehicle. He called in air support while also firing the machine gun.

An excerpt from the Bronze Star narrative written by Major Dennis Sullivan reads as follows: "Not only was he able to accurately provide the AH-1 Cobra crews the information they needed to fire on the enemy positions, he also remained in the turret of his own vehicle, though not his assigned location, and directly engaged enemy positions with the vehicle's mounted machine gun. SSG Monti's valorous actions played a critical role in maximizing enemy casualties and allowing the Task Force Soldiers and vehicles to depart the kill zone without further serious injury or damage."

It may sound that the act of shooting a machine gun from the protection of a turret is not all that dangerous. But the Humvee was "thin-skinned", which is another way of saying "unarmored". Jared had to dodge machine gun fire that was coming in one side of the turret and going out the other. A "thin-skinned" Humvee has flimsy sheet metal that can't even stop bullets from a small-caliber handgun. It doesn't provide the protection of an "armored" or "up-armored" vehicle.

The Humvee (High Mobility Multipurpose Wheeled Vehicle) began to replace the Army Jeep in the late 1970's and has gone through a number of iterations. There's a well-known story about the military campaign in Iraq. Captain Cameron Birge, who led twice-weekly convoys through Iraq's desert, was told that new armored Humvees with specially designed add-on armor kits would begin to arrive within a year. That wasn't going to help him, because his deployment was ending in six months. Like Jared, he considered himself a renegade. Earlier in the week, insurgents had dynamited a section of the road he regularly traveled. So he decided to bolt scrap steel to the back of his Humvee in the hope that it would provide him some protection. He then removed his Humvee's canvas doors and welded on slabs of metal. He spread Kevlar blankets over the seats and stacked sandbags on the floor. There were others who followed suit. The Army's failure to produce more of the armored vehicles became a hot topic among soldiers in both Iraq and Afghanistan. Then it became a political issue for lawmakers.

Jared had known his Advanced Individual Training at Fort Sill was outdated. War was going to consist of small-scale guerrilla conflicts. So when Jared first saw the "thin-skinned" Humvee, he realized it would be inadequate in a world of snipers, ambushes, and improvised explosive devices.

When the Humvee was introduced, armoring it wasn't even a consideration. The Army was preparing to fight on a battlefield where heavily armored tanks and Bradley fighting vehicles were out front, providing a line of defense for supply vehicles in the rear. Defense Department and Army officials defend their decisions, saying no one could have predicted that the military would have been involved in missions where IEDs (Improvised Explosive Devices) and RPGs (Rocket-Propelled Grenades) were the norm. In fairness, the heavier and clumsier armored Humvee was not well-suited for Afghanistan because it is too wide for small mountain roads and too large for many forms of air transport. Lack of mobility can also be a hindrance in combat situations.

The future of the Humvee mirrors the approach now being taken to modernize the entire U. S. Military. Nimble JLTVs (Joint Light Tactical Vehicles) are being designed from the ground up to ensure both adequate protection and maneuverability.

Before leaving on the mission, Jared had a brush with death when a Humvee in which he had been riding ran over an IED, killing all the soldiers inside. Jared had changed vehicles just before the bombing occurred. "Luckily, one of his nine lives had switched Humvees," Paul notes.

"It almost got to a point where he seemed invincible, because he had so many close calls," says his sister Niccole.

Jared would never mention being in combat. He'd never

discuss risking his life, having to kill people, or seeing friends get killed. He'd let others know about sharing the packages that people sent him with the Afghani children. He didn't let them know about how much it bothered him that he might go back into the same neighborhood the next day to engage in a battle where those same children might be hurt or killed as collateral damage.

After coming home on leave, Jared left a paper on his bed. He didn't mention it to anyone, but Janet happened to see it. It was the Bronze Star citation. The family was coming over to the house to see Jared. Knowing how he'd react, Janet called everyone and asked them not to mention anything about it when they arrived. She predicted correctly that Jared would want to answer the inevitable "How's it going over there?" questions with his usual "Nothing much happening", followed by one of his patented shrugs.

Jared, in fact, developed a stand-up comedy routine that he'd use with both sides of his family when he'd come home. Someone typically would ask him how things were going in Afghanistan. He'd say, "I'll explain the routine. Leave the Forward Operating Base. Climb a mountain for four and a half hours. Link up with Afghan commandos. Settle into dirt hut. Drink tea. Stare at goat. Remove goat head. Skin goat. Boil goat with potatoes. Eat goat stew. Drink follow-up tea. Pull security through the night. Drink morning tea. Do morning patrol from dirt hut. Return to dirt hut. Eat bread. Drink tea. Play horseshoes, only with rocks. Find another goat. Remove goat head. Skin goat. Drink more tea. Rinse. Wash. Repeat. Go back to Forward Operating Base. Do it all again." The family would laugh and invariably say, "Tell us again what you do."

In 2002, SGT Keith Barber returned to Fort Drum after his first deployment to Afghanistan. He invited Jared to a cook-out at his home because "Jared was one of the soldiers he really liked," according to his wife Eden. "I hit it off with him too, because he was funny and got all my jokes and loved my cooking and my Long Island ice teas." Keith and Eden had Jared over their house quite a bit until Keith was transferred to Fort Lewis, Washington, and then deployed to Iraq. They reunited in 2005 back in Fort Drum. When Keith went on his next deployment, Eden says, "I had someone to take care of, and had a true friend I could lean on in the times of missing my husband. I had someone that loved to eat, drink, and be merry." Then Jared left for his final Afghanistan deployment. "He told me something Keith always says, 'I'll be back before you know it.'"

Jared used to tell Eden he was a better man and a better soldier for having known Keith. In turn, Keith greatly admired Jared. He posted this tribute to him: "I ensure that all new FISTers are aware of the example you set about pushing ourselves to be better."

According to SPC Max Noble, "My sister had served in the military, so I knew how it could help pay for college. That was my real motivation to join. I was interested in crypto-linguistic language, so I thought about that, but wound up with a specialty as a clinical medic. I also studied Arabic, figuring I'd most likely be deployed to the Middle East. I was assigned to the 3-71 CAV at Fort Drum while waiting for our overseas assignment. The only contact I had with Jared was when he'd come into the infirmary for ibuprofen. He had a lot of aches and pains, like many of the guys who had been in combat, but it was his back that was really messed up from his Airborne days. He never complained, though."

"Very frankly, I was scared of him," admits Max. "He used to really push his soldiers. He was always doing physical training with them. I thought he was a 'tough guy' that I should stay away from. Jared was renowned for 'smoking' his soldiers, meaning he was a fanatic about physical training. It's funny how perceptions can change. I was looking at it through the eyes of a new soldier. I was really naïve. I later realized how important it was to have soldiers be as physically strong as possible. I honestly didn't understand it back then. I was so wrong about him. At the Squadron Military Ball before we were deployed, I saw the clownish side of him for the first time when he put on a "Ms. Universal" sash and crown. I realized this guy wasn't all gruff."

That evening stood out in more than one person's memory. "I'll always remember that Squadron Ball we had before we left Fort Drum for Afghanistan when 'Ms. Universal' was there with her crown and sash. Monti wound up wearing them before the night was through. He was preening for pictures. Everyone knew it was going to happen," laughs Chris Cunningham. "There was that side of him. I agree that there was also the side where he'd rigorously train his men. Not just in how to do their jobs but physically train them. Those guys could move. Other people would get hurt in climbing mountains. They'd get knee, back, and ankle injuries, but Monti's guys never did. When they had to fill in and do someone else's job, I had complete confidence that they wouldn't miss a beat."

SPC Brian Gonterman comments, "No matter what the conversation was about, he was laughing and telling jokes to the other soldiers. He was one of the guys that you can joke with, but have a serious conversation with as well. He was so easy to approach. The way he would talk to people and make people laugh made you feel like you were not deployed; you felt like a bunch of guys out camping and drinking (even though it was water)."

Jared told his father he didn't want to marry until his commitment to the Army was complete. He explained that he didn't want to leave a widow behind, because he had seen too many of his soldiers go through that. After hearing of the elaborate wedding plans of many of his cousins, he wrote jokingly in an e-mail, "I think if I ever tie the knot, it'll be at a drive-through in

Vegas."

"Niccole and I were much more aware of what was going on between our parents, who divorced in 2005," explains Tim. "We saw the tension between our parents up-close. Jared was out riding his motorcycle, and then away in the Army for so many years that he pretty much missed the family drama."

Jared thought about having children some day, and even had a name picked out. His cousin Michelle says, "Jared loved my daughter's name, Haley. He told me he always wanted to give that name to one of his own children someday. He put my daughter's picture in his Humvees and said that he wrote 'Haley' on the side of them. So, I guess instead of naming a child Haley, he ended up giving the name to his war truck."

When Jared received CARE packages from home during his deployment in Afghanistan, he would immediately give everything away to the local children. He told everyone that they needed it more than he did. "We'd send him clothing, candy, gum, little toys, etc., and then ask if he got them. He'd always say the same thing.'Yeah, I did. Thanks. But I gave it away to some kids,'" recalls his Uncle Mike.

"I'd send him silly things like a paint set, a top, crayons, a toy Easter bunny, Halloween stuff, and a ring toss. Things that would make him laugh," says Janet. "He'd always give it away. There was one thing, though, that he kept for himself. It was a lunch box in the shape of a fish. He loved to fish. That he kept because it meant something special to him. Unfortunately, it was stolen. I tried to replace it, but they'd stopped making it."

Jared had an easy manner about him that made people trust him. You knew you were dealing with a man of integrity. Little wonder that he'd be the one sent to sit, eat goat meat, and negotiate with the Afghani civilians and military. Little wonder that when he said something, they believed it. Little wonder that they referred to him as "Gift of God," the Hebrew meaning of his name, and presented him with a tribal neck scarf called a "shemagh" out of respect.

Jared called the soldiers under his command "my boys". They, in turn, would call him "grandpa" because he was several years older than most of them. His aunt, Annie Eagles, asked him if he was going to get out of the service. He responded with, "No, I've got to take care of my kids." She said, "Is there something I don't know about?" He said, "No, I mean my boys, my guys. I can't leave them behind. I've got to take care of them."

CSM James Redmore explains, "Jared believed in what the Greeks called 'Agape,' a brotherly love. That brotherly love built a cohesiveness which made the most effective war fighters we could produce. That was evident in his day-to-day duties, and his soldiers loved him for it."

"He treated every last one of them better than what they were. Doing that, they got motivated to do bigger and better things," says MSG Gary Young.

It was Jared's generous and caring side that impressed people the most. Jared once paid for one of his soldiers and his wife to go to a Military Ball. He even gave the soldier money to buy his wife a dress.

"He was one of those leaders that soldiers didn't want to disappoint," says Chris Grzecki.

"I remember having a long conversation with Jared. I was frustrated by the lack of manpower," recalls SGT Drew Gibbs. "He told me to keep the faith and things would get better. He was such an approachable guy, yet he had such a great reputation. I'm just proud that I knew him. I got back and told my men that I had a discussion with Monti, and they were so impressed. They said,

'Wow! You got to talk to HIM?'"

Jared had a way of forming a connection with his "boys." For example, while soldiers are required to shave every day, even in the field, he would let his beard grow and shave only before returning to base. In violation of the Army dress code, he also liked to leave his boots unbloused. Of course, whatever Jared did, his soldiers had to emulate. Jared had a "boonie cap" that he took to a shop in Bagram to have modified. He had the brim shortened and the webbing taken off the crown of the brim. "It absolutely drove the Command Sergeant Major crazy. Every time he would see Jared wearing it he'd make him take it off. As soon as he'd go around the corner, Jared would put it back on," remembers SGT Ron Haapala with a chuckle.

Those were small things, but people took notice of how he would bend rules. What the officers really cared about was that he was an NCO who had the unwavering loyalty of his troops. Any experienced military officers will tell you that a good NCO is invaluable. It takes a number of years to develop a good one, so they'd let Jared get away with the "small things."

One of the things he liked to do was lead his men on "creative physical training" missions. They would shimmy up the barracks gutters, climb on the roof, and compete in spontaneous competitions. The more dangerous it was, the more Jared enjoyed it. When he got caught, he'd flash that smile. According to MSG Lee Power, "That wide grin he had got him out of a lot of trouble. He had a way of charming people."

Captain Matt Jacobs observes, "The guy was fearless. He would do anything for his soldiers and they knew it. It's just the kind of guy he was."

"I remember how we used to grumble when you were put in charge of PT, because we knew how much pain we'd be in for. I am honored to have known you. I can only strive to become the man that you were," says Adam Kelley in tribute.

Jared was famous for playing tricks on new Lieutenants as a form of initiation. One of his favorites was duct taping them from head to toe. Why would officers allow such a thing? Because they know that NCOs like Jared run the day-to-day operation of the Army. An officer would have difficulty being successful without the active support of the NCOs. So letting them have a little fun is a small price to pay.

Officers weren't the only ones who were victimized by Jared's pranks. Sergeant Major Steven Brock arrived in Afghanistan on a hot summer day and was met at Kandahar Airfield by Jared. Brock told him he needed a rest room and Jared suggested that, for his convenience, he use the Porta-Potty that was adjacent to the runway. He also thoughtfully told Brock that he would be cooler if he took all his clothes off, as was the custom in Afghanistan. Brock complied and went about his business until the Porta-Potty door got blown open by a helicopter that was landing. Jared offered his sincerest apologies with a big grin saying, "Sorry, I had no idea that would happen." Brock was covered in sweat and sand, which caused Jared to point out respectfully, "You look like a big sugar cookie!" Of course, Jared felt compelled to repeat the story to everyone he saw for the next several days. Brock might have been embarrassed by the incident, but he was immediately embraced by the troops for being a good sport.

Many of the stories that his fellow soldiers tell about Jared involve "barely making gate." A soldier must be inside the front gate of a military base by morning role call in order to be considered "present." The opposite of being present is Absent without Leave, which is not a good thing in the military. Were there times when Jared was technically AWOL but, because of his charm and his close relationships with others, the absence might not have been noted? Nobody has actually said that, but nobody has denied it either.

The e-mail address he chose is revealing. It was “Renegadefo.” The “fo” stands for “Forward Observer.” It’s obvious what the “renegade” stands for. But Jared was as loyal to his men as they were to him. According to Paul, “I can’t tell you how many times I’d ask him if he was coming home for the holidays and he’d say, ‘No, Dad, I’ve got duty.’ We knew he had given away leave time again.” He would often donate his leave time to the married soldiers, especially those with children. When sent packages for things he couldn’t give away to children, like cigars, Jared would give them to his soldiers despite the fact that he would have loved to have kept them for himself.

MSG Christine Fallow remembers, “He would be the one sitting out on guard duty or whatever on Christmas Eve or Christmas day so that someone else could be at home with their family.”

“After first meeting Jared at Fort Drum, I saw him again at Naray in Afghanistan,” recounts Franklin Woods. “I saw him running the track in uniform. It was really hot and he had his full uniform on. I asked him why he didn’t have his P. T.’s (Physical Training clothing) on. He said, ‘I’ve got to stay in shape. My stuff isn’t here yet.’ I noticed he had combat boots on without any socks. I asked him about that and he said, ‘I never wear socks.’ I went away thinking, ‘This guy must have leather feet or something. Wow. What a tough guy. Caring, but tough.’”

Both sides were exhibited countless times in Jared’s later life. In Afghanistan, for example, there was a young PFC who was having a great deal of trouble with his first mountain climb. He became dehydrated and felt sick with nausea. Jared stayed with him while the rest of the squad went ahead. “How are you doing,

Private?" asked Jared. "Not so well," responded the PFC, who was obviously straining. "Let me give you a little help." Jared removed the 70-pound pack and carried it along with his own pack. He never told any of the other soldiers what happened. The young PFC worked on his physical conditioning. Even more than having Jared being willing to physically lighten his load, he appreciated the fact that no one ever found out about his first embarrassing day on the mountain.

Chapter 11
FISTers, Get the Duct Tape!

"When I drove into work on my first day in an Army unit on December 2, 2004, I had no idea the everlasting impact one man would have on my life. That was the day I met Jared Monti," recalls Steve Raveia. After graduating from Virginia Military Institute earlier that year, Steve was commissioned as a 2nd Lieutenant and attended the Field Artillery Officer Basic Course at Ft. Sill. His first assignment was at the 10th Mountain Division Headquarters at Fort Drum as the Fire Support Officer for Delta Company, 1st Battalion, 32nd Infantry Regiment, 3rd Brigade Combat Team.

Delta Company was newly-formed and didn't have an official designated work space when he arrived. They used a training classroom as the duty place for soldiers. Company Headquarters was a small room, barely enough to fit a desk and five chairs. Steve sat for about 20 minutes shuffling his feet and feeling the typical anxiety that people have on their first day of work. The Company Executive Officer came in and asked, "You the new FSO?" Steve acknowledged that he was, and he was told to sit tight because the Company Commander was out on the rifle range.

"It was not long before a Staff Sergeant with a big ol' grin on his face comes walking into the HQ area," says Steve. "He stuck out his hand and introduced himself: 'Hey Sir, I'm Staff Sergeant Monti. I hear you're my new boss.' I couldn't help but smile. Jared just had the personality that was welcoming and put you at ease."

Jared told Steve that he was assigned as the Fire Support NCO and showed Steve his new office. Then he returned to in-processing new soldiers while Steve got settled. "Jared would go on to be my right hand man," Steve says. "Even though I was his 'boss', I only had about six months of training under my belt, whereas he had almost 10 years of service, including a deployment to Afghanistan. In reality, I was going to be learning from him."

When people started to scatter for lunch, Jared returned to the HQ area and invited Steve to go out for lunch. Steve hesitated, thinking, *Oh, crap, I don't even remember where I parked, let alone knowing how to drive somewhere for food in an area I just moved to*. "Thinking that I don't want to look like a fool in front of my FSNCO, I responded with a kind 'No, thank you.' Jared quickly tapped me on the shoulder and whispered in my ear, 'Sir, you never turn down lunch from your FSNCO on the first day. Come on, I know a great hole-in-the-wall place we can go to.' He said it with the trademark grin on his face. I really knew at that moment he was somebody who truly cared for others and was going to look out for my best interests."

As they walked outside, Steve realized he still couldn't remember where he had parked his car in the snow-filled parking lot. Jared suggested they just take whichever of their cars was closest to avoid the cold. Steve mumbled a noncommittal "I don't know...." Without hesitation, Jared sensed his discomfort and volunteered to drive. "That was the first time I rode as a passenger in his now famous Dodge Ram pickup truck," says Steve. "I can't remember the place we ate, but I remember having the soup, which Jared highly recommended. We talked about where we were from and what are our interests were. After five minutes, I felt like I had known him for years. He just had something about him that instantly made you gravitate towards him."

Over the next six months, the two friends spent countless hours together. They had been informed that they would deploy to Afghanistan the following year. According to Steve, "Jared knew that training our soldiers was our number one priority. When he spoke, we all listened. He was the standard of what 'right' looks like. We all wanted to be like him, and I know I even started talking like him. What on earth is someone who was born and raised in Virginia doing saying the word 'wicked?' But, in all seriousness, I've never seen anyone train soldiers like Jared. He was able to see the good in everyone and had a keen ability to exploit it. The environment he created was one that made everyone feel that they were worth his time and were one of 'his guys'. I never once had the sense that he was ego-driven. In fact, it was the complete opposite."

Steve offers this example: "I remember sitting in a Delta Company weekly training meeting. Jared spoke up to the Commander about a really elaborate training event that I had planned. The only problem was I hadn't planned it, Jared had. It was all his idea, but he publicly gave me the credit. I tried to give him credit, and he down-played his involvement. After the meeting I reminded him that it was his idea all along. His response was a simple, 'Sir, it's my job to make you look good!' The translation to me was that he wants me to succeed. I'll never forget his doing that. Taking care of others was one of his biggest attributes. He wanted me to be successful more than anyone I had ever encountered outside my family."

The duo oversaw the Supply, Medic, Chemical, and Artillery soldiers. "One day one of them told us that a training course he was going to take started at 8 a.m., so he would not be able to attend physical training that morning. Jared found out it was actually at a later start time and he had lied to get out of PT," remembers Steve. "Jared called him into our office and told him that he was disappointed in him and that he had lost his trust. He never once even raised his voice. He told the soldier that the road to earning that trust back started here and now. Then he told him to apologize to me for lying. When the soldier turned around toward me, I saw that tears were streaming down his cheeks. It wasn't that Jared belittled him and called him names. It was simply that the soldier knew he'd let Jared down. That caused him sorrow. I remember that event mainly because it speaks a lot about who Jared was. He was so respected that the sheer thought of disappointing him was emotional. He also took the high road in dealing with the situation. He gave the soldier a second chance."

After an exhausting two-week training exercise that April, the troops felt burnt out. Jared asked rhetorically, "What's up with all the down faces?" and then announced, "What we need is a naked man!" He stripped off his uniform and ran around the training area shouting. Everyone in the all-male Delta Company started laughing. The "naked man" saw a very large puddle caused by the snow, which had just started to melt. He rolled around in it and splashed.

"Morale was instantly boosted. Exactly what we all needed! Afterwards, he said he may need to head back early, because he'd got a whole lot of something in places that should not have anything in," laughs Steve. "A picture that was tastefully taken of the incident hung in our office until we deployed. I still have it today. Not only was it a funny story, but it makes me remember the side of Jared that didn't take life so seriously.

"A couple of months later, Jared was transferred to 3-71 CAV. It was not easy to accept that he would be going to a different unit. I looked up to him so much that I hated to see him leave, but I knew he was going to be in a position that would benefit the

Army," says Steve. "Jared would swing by Delta Company every few weeks to check on me and offer advice. One of the fondest memories of my entire life occurred during one of his visits. I had just gotten a new soldier on the team, and Jared told him that he should listen to me and that I was 'awesome to work with'. Hearing that he thought that highly of me was my single greatest moment in the Army. There isn't a medal or rank that could top that. It was the equivalent of Ted Williams telling a kid that he is an awesome hitter in baseball."

When the 3rd Combat Brigade deployed to Afghanistan, both Delta Company and the 3-71 CAV ended up at Forward Operating Base Salerno. Jared and Steve were able to share a few breakfasts together. Jared lobbied a number of times to get Steve switched over to 3-71, but each attempt was unsuccessful. Jared's unit was about to move to a new location when they shared a good-bye. "The last thing I said to Jared was, 'If you guys aren't back by September, we'll celebrate our birthdays when we're back at Drum.' He gave me a head nod and a big grin," says Steve. "I said this while walking toward the convoy of Humvees getting ready to leave. That was the last time I would ever see or speak to Jared Monti."

Jared was an Artillery soldier "borrowed" from the 4-25 Field Artillery Battalion to serve with the 3-71 Cavalry Squadron in its deployment to Afghanistan. His role was to provide expertise for fire support of artillery and mortars, naval gunfire, attack helicopters, and Air Force or Marine Aviation CAS (close air support). Captain Joe Hansen, the senior advisor on the Battalion Fire Support Team for the 3-71 CAV, spent substantial time with Jared in training and operations, but they were not technically in a the same chain of command.

When Captain Hansen first came to Fort Drum, the Army was building new Brigades to increase the number of available rotational forces for overseas deployment. The 3-71 CAV had just been created and had completely new people, with only about six months to get ready to leave for Afghanistan. SFC Gary Hunsucker, the Battalion Fire Support NCO, was sent overseas in advance to get the Fire Support Element (FSE) infrastructure up and running.

According to Joe, "The team was young and inexperienced. SFC Hunsucker was really the only NCO leadership we had. The rest of the FSE consisted of 24 Privates fresh out of Basic Training. The NCOs are the ones that make the whole thing work. We started with nothing. Hunsucker and I requested, pressed, and griped about getting some NCO leadership, with only promises that some were coming in. My primary concern was that I needed to train those Privates fast. With the deployment coming up, it was getting interesting. That lack of NCOs, our biggest issue, went away once Jared walked through the door, thanks to LTC Joe Fenty, who went to bat hard for us on getting help."

"We learned that we had snagged Monti to go to Afghanistan with us," says Gary. "A lot of people knew him and were very happy about that, including me. He was very knowledgeable and proficient. He had already made a name for himself. He was the kind of guy who always wanted to be on the front lines and you wanted him there with you."

"I remember my first conversation with Jared. I liked him right off the bat," recalls Joe. When Joe said, "We are going to need a little help training these Privates, and damn fast," Jared responded confidently, "I'm all over it." According to Captain Hansen, "Saying he came out like a bat out of hell training those guys is an understatement. He spent every available minute on getting our Lieutenants and the Privates to where they needed to be."

"On one exercise we were conducting a 'walk and shoot' where a small fire support team walks the lane and reacts to small arms contact, calls for fire from the artillery and mortars, utilizes close air support and close attack aviation, and then gets to the other side," recalls Joe. "Getting the fire support teams comfortable on the radio and adept at utilizing artillery, CAS, and Apaches was a big priority. As it sometimes does, our resources got pulled. I was struggling a bit on getting some training together to cover the shortfall. Jared came up with the suggestion that he would play the role of the artillery, CAS, and attack aviation. I said, 'What are you talking about?' 'Just have them go through the lane, sir,' he responded.

"So the first team goes in and is progressing down the lane in patrol formation," Joe continues. "After about half a click, Jared comes over the radio and starts voicing the Battalion HQ and giving the guys instructions, pretending he is Battalion. The guys send up their reports, updating location and whatnot. They progress further down the lane and receive small arms fire. The FIST team begins to call for fire and Jared responds over the net in a different voice, simulating the gun line: 'The fire mission reporting....' I'm standing right next to him, all grins, and say, 'What about the aviation?' Jared then begins to beat against his chest with the radio right next to it and starts talking to the FIST team. 'This is NO MERCY 12 inbound on SW track to your location. I have hellfires, 2.75 rockets, and 30mm. Standing by for link up.' It was a great day of training."

Jared also liked to play "Fire Support Jeopardy" on tactics, techniques, and procedures with the troops. Like the television show, it would involve replying to an answer with a question. The loser wound up pulling duty.

Jared was adept at making ghillie suits, camouflage clothing designed to look like foliage. The suit is usually a net or cloth garment covered in strips of burlap and scraps of leaves, brush, and grass from the area in which it will be used. It can effectively break up the silhouette of the wearer and move in the wind to help blend in with its surroundings. In addition to being used in the military by snipers and forward observers, it is often used by hunters and nature photographers.

There are at least two theories for the derivation of the word. The first is the Scottish Gaelic word "gille" which means "servant" or "lad" and refers to someone who assists a hunter. The other is "Ghillie Du," the Scottish version of the British folklore hero "Green Man," a nature spirit and tree guardian who lived in the forest and was dressed in local foliage.

The most effective ghillie suits are made by hand, using netting of burlap, jute, or fishing line. Then natural materials present in the environment in which the wearers will be operating are added. They need to be carefully constructed and may take weeks for the foliage to season. It's common for a ghillie suit to be dragged behind a vehicle to give it an authentic worn, muddy look. Once on location, the wearer adds twigs, leaves, and other elements of the local foliage. Sometimes local customizations need to be changed as often as every few hours, due to wilting of grass or leaves.

At JRTC (The Joint Readiness Training Center in Ft. Polk, LA where the Air Force exercises with the Army), Jared showed his soldiers how to make ghillie suits. The FIST team he led disrupted and destroyed about 40% of the OPFOR (opposing force) by calling for fire from a position they could not find, despite repeated attempts. The Brigade Commander wanted to award Jared and his team coins for their outstanding performance. He was told Jared's general location and went to the site several times but couldn't locate him. He finally had several staff and the Battalion Commander go out to the site with him. None of them could find Jared and his team. The Brigade Commander was irritated, because the Battalion Commander didn't know where his own troops were.

When it started to get a little heated, Jared suddenly stood up in his ghillie suit about five meters away, gave everyone his big grin, and said, “Looking for me, sir?”

“I remember the times we spent at my house around the campfire in the backyard looking over maps of Afghanistan,” says Joe. “One night Jared was showing us the ‘hucklebuck’, which is where you get your hands around a person’s head and arms and they can’t move. For some reason, my wife Stephanie was selected for the demonstration. Jared applied it and said, ‘Now try to get out of it.’ Stephanie paused and then proceeded to back-kick Jared right in the groin and drop him. Jared groaned, ‘First time THAT happened.’

“We spent many a night planning for the deployment. Jared and I talked about how the key to successful operations in the Hindus was to maintain and leverage the high ground with what we were going to do with the Kill Team sniper/forward observer concept. ‘See you on the high ground’ became our mantra to each other throughout the Afghanistan deployment.” Joe adds this thought, which seems to capture his feelings perfectly in just a few words – “Great man, that Jared.”

Alika Ichinose, a graduate of Norwich University ROTC (Reserve Officers’ Training Corps), was commissioned as a 2nd Lieutenant and taught an immediate lesson by his first Platoon Sergeant. “I was talking what SSG Monti would call the ‘proverbial shit.’ I thought I was saying what I was supposed to say. It was clear to him that I needed a certain level of humbling.” So what did Jared do? He climbed on Alika’s back, wrapped his arms around his neck, kicked the back of his knees and brought him to the ground. “I’m a small Asian and he was a small Caucasian, but it was no contest,” laughs Alika. Then Jared bellowed the dreaded order that struck fear into the hearts of many Army officers: “FISTERS, GET THE DUCT TAPE!”

"In my mind, I was fighting for my life. I was desperately trying to get away," recalls Alika. "As I was struggling, more guys would jump on top of me. It was like a cartoon. I didn't even have a chance to put down my rifle. They duct-taped it right to my body. We were in this enormous circus-type tent. There were hundreds of soldiers and plenty of officers around. It became clear that no one was going to help me, though. There were far more of them than there were of us. One of the soldiers whispered in my ear, 'Just let it happen, sir.' Hey, I didn't have much of a choice. I had to let it happen."

Afterwards, some of the other Lieutenants cut Alika free. He asked one of them why they hadn't helped and got this explanation: "Ichi, if I tried to help you, I would have been duct-taped along with you. I'm not an idiot." Another said, "If the most you got was duct-taped, consider yourself lucky."

"It's typical for a new Lieutenant to be initiated in some way. So I mulled over the lesson I had just learned. SSG Monti was giving me a simple reminder that as a leader, you serve your subordinates. You're really nothing without them. It's something that he taught me every day. Monti commanded more respect than anyone I've ever seen in the Army, including all the officers. His guys would do anything for him," says Alika.

He was victimized once again by Jared. Ichi made the mistake of seeking refuge in a small lean-to tent with another new 2nd Lieutenant, Erik Jorgensen, during a driving rainstorm at Fort Drum. "There was a small gap between the tent and the ground, and suddenly I noticed seven or eight pairs of boots," he says. "When enlisted men consolidate like that, you know that something bad is going to happen. I knew Monti was around somewhere. They wouldn't have done this without his consent, or more likely his leadership. I had learned from my previous experience to look for a roll of duct tape. Sure enough, I saw it. I grabbed it and flung it into a puddle. I was hoping it would somehow screw up the adhesion of the tape. It actually did. They were able to tape our hands and feet together, but we didn't get the full-body treatment. "

Alika asked them why they would want to tape him up a second time. The soldiers said, "We were afraid you were going to help Lieutenant Jorgensen." After Alika told them there was no way he was going to be foolish enough to help his fellow Lieutenant, they said, "Okay, we won't do it to you again. We might do it to him again, though."

Even Captain Hansen was not safe from Jared's antics. Alika describes how imposing Joe is by saying, "The guy has muscles in his face." Jared told Alika and Erik that the enlisted men wanted to do something special for Joe's birthday. He said they were going to give him a chocolate brownie with matches on it standing up like candles and sing Happy Birthday to him. "Erik and I thought that was very nice of Monti," recalls Alika."We should have known better." They asked Jared if it was going to be a real chocolate brownie, and he assured them that it was. However, Jared added, "You guys probably shouldn't be there. But if you do come, it's best that you stay toward the back of the tent." They started to get suspicious and asked Jared exactly what was going to happen. He replied, "If I give you the details, you'll be culpable."

They presented the brownie with the lit matches to Captain Hansen, who was very appreciative. The Lieutenants had been warned, so they worked their way to the back of the tent. Suddenly, Jared yelled out in his best command voice – "GET HIM!" Sure enough, all the soldiers piled on top of Joe, tackling and restraining him. According to Captain Hansen, "The incident Monti pulled on me started as a pile-on by the soldiers at Monti's say-so, but ended in a stalemate that left the younger soldiers a bit petrified that hell was coming back on them." He does admit, however, "Monti showed a lot of chutzpah on that one." As the composed, highly-professional officer that he is, Joe addressed the troops after the incident saying simply, "I want to thank you all for recognizing my birthday."

Shortly thereafter, Erik woke up in his tent and said to Alika, "Hey, I can't find my boots." Alika responded, "You've got to be kidding me." However, after some searching, Alika was unable to find his boots, either. They walked around barefoot outside and saw both pairs of boots tied together high up in a tree. They had had enough of the foolishness. "We confronted Monti and told him that was it. He wasn't going to undermine our authority." Jared, however, swore that he'd had nothing to do with the prank. "If I had done it, I would tell you," he asserted. They were still suspicious when they reported to Captain Hansen for the day's activities. He asked, "Why the long faces?" They told him the sad story and how they felt they had lost their dignity. Joe then asked, "Are you sure the soldiers did it?" They gave him an incredulous look. Then he said, "Next time, maybe you won't have them pile on me."

Jared taught Alika an important lesson one day. "There was another Captain, a real meathead, who wanted me to teach a class," he recalls. "He was one of those guys who only respected you if you were very aggressive. He told me how to teach the class in detail. He wanted it taught his way, by the book." Alika refers to this as "clinging to procedure." He walked into the classroom and Jared said, "Are you all set for class? What did the Captain tell you to say?" Alika went over details and Jared said, "It's all wrong. Things don't happen by the book." Alika responded, "Look, we have a lesson plan. We have a boss. We've got to do it his way."

Jared stood impatiently with his arms folded in the back of the room while Alika taught the class. When the troops were about to be dismissed, Jared said, "Fuck that shit that the Lieutenant just told you." He proceeded to let them know what really happens in combat, and how things don't go according to the textbook. Jared explained, "We're about to be deployed to Afghanistan. I'm going to tell you what will save your life and save the life of the guy next to you." He then took over the class. "To tell you the truth, I started taking notes," says Alika. "I was learning and Jared was teaching. He had complete credibility. He had been there and done that. Hey, I wanted to survive, too, and figured maybe I'd have a family someday. I hadn't been in combat before. I needed to listen carefully to him the same as everyone else."

Afterwards, Jared went up to Alika and said, "You're really pissed at me, aren't you?" Alika replied, "Part of me has had my pride hurt. I'm supposed to be the officer. But I'll never let my pride overpower doing the right thing. Jared, if I ever give the wrong advice or say the wrong thing, please trump me. It's okay. I don't want these guys to get killed. Can I buy you lunch?" Alika went on, "From that point on, Jared and I got along famously. He was such an innovative leader. Every person he touched is better off for it."

"I also learned a lot about humility from him," continues Alika. "I learned to listen to those who know their stuff, regardless of rank. I became a better man and a better leader because of him. He did things a typical leader wouldn't. It came naturally to him. There was a spark in this man."

The lessons that Jared taught him obviously helped 2nd Lieutenant Ichi. He has now attained the rank of Major with less than ten years of military service. Proving that he took the lesson about modesty to heart, he claims, "That has nothing to do with me. It's just that the Army has needed a lot of officers. It's based on their needs." No one should believe that for a second.

Chapter 12
Nothing More

Randy Robinson's first assignment in the Army in 2005 was as a PFC with an infantry division, but he volunteered to serve with the 3rd Squadron 71st CAV in Fort Drum, when it was preparing for deployment to Afghanistan. "I saw an opportunity that seemed like an adventure," he says. Things started off well for him. "I remember Monti bought a bunch of tickets for us to go into Watertown, New York and see a band called Dropkick Murphys that was big in Boston. I knew their music and was just about doing back flips because we'd be going to see them. I told myself that I kind of liked this Sergeant," he says.

"When he did physical training, though, I didn't like him so much. He was really tough on us," admits Randy. "We'd go on long runs all the time, particularly on a Friday and a Monday. On Fridays he'd say we had to prepare for the weekend, and then on Mondays we'd have to work off the effects of the weekend. We'd run all day. What he was doing was teaching us to how to breathe. We'd have to suck in air. It was getting us ready for the mountains in Afghanistan. It paid off. Monti's soldiers were always the best-conditioned.

"Unfortunately, I was having pre-deployment anxiety attacks. I was really nervous about the prospect of being in combat. Jared was always the kind of guy you could talk to, so I was willing to share that with him," says Randy. "He told me that combat is just controlled chaos. The worst thing about it is that it's loud. He told me that people shoot at you and then you shoot back at them. They might be running around at the same time, so they'd be unlikely to hit anything. Bullets are being sprayed around; but, he said, they're just little things about the size of the tip of your pinkie finger. He told me to keep my head down and I'd be fine. Afterwards, he'd kind of be looking out for me, asking me how I was doing. His confidence made me feel better.

"I still couldn't shake the jittery feeling, though. My heart was skipping beats. I was throwing up. I couldn't breathe. I was drinking heavily. Jared set me up for a doctor's appointment and personally drove me to it. He wanted to be sure that I'd be all right. I was told there was nothing wrong with my heart, and the doctor gave me some relaxation techniques to use. Jared looked out for me from that point on. He'd always come up to me and say, 'Randy, how are you doing?' I really appreciated that when we were alone he'd call me by my first name. It was like a sign that he cared about me. It was more than just business."

"After we got to Afghanistan, I downed a whole bottle of tequila one night," Randy confesses. "I was out of control. I called one of the Sergeants a douchebag. I got in a grappling match with another guy and hurt him. I hit another guy. I really messed up. Monti came into the barracks and grabbed me. I'll never forget the look on his face. It was like staring into the eye of the tiger. No one wanted to let Monti down, including me. He could just give you a look that said, 'You've got to be kidding me.' He wouldn't have to say anything. You'd break your own heart if you disappointed him. He had me doing push-ups and other exercises for hours. I'll never forget standing in front of the Commanding Officer the next morning with Monti at my side. He asked what happened. Monti told the CO, 'I've taken care of it, sir. It's an internal matter. I'll continue to work with the Private to teach him proper conduct.' The CO saluted and said, 'All right. You're both dismissed.' That was it. Monti had my back. I knew I had messed up big-time. That was the first and only time I got in trouble with Monti. I wasn't going to let him down again after that.

"I was the driver of a Humvee Jared was riding in when we went down a narrow road. We hit a rock that was jutting out from the wall, causing the wheel to climb the wall and tip the truck over. I spun the wheel and hammered down on the gas, hoping to go nose-down, but it was too late. We flipped 2 3/4 times down the side of the hill approximately 12-15 feet and landed driver side down in the bottom of a dry river bed. The vehicle was totaled. Just like you'd expect with Monti, he jumped right out and checked on everyone. I was hurt pretty bad. Initially I thought I was paralyzed, but after 15-20 seconds my legs kicked and the pain started. Monti and a medic pulled me out and helped me to a stretcher to be evaluated. I suffered two herniated discs, two bulging discs, six compression fractures in my vertebrae, torn muscles in my arm and back, nerve damage, permanent blunt force arthritis, and traumatic brain injury. It took about six months for the tingling in my hands to stop. What did they do for me at the hospital? They told me to take Motrin. I still have nightmares about the accident," says Randy. It's not surprising that the prescribed medical treatment did not produce very positive results.

Jared seemed to take things in stride that would be crises for other people. After the accident, he wrote a casual e-mail home saying, "My driver, Private Randy Robinson, decided to drive us off a cliff and roll the Humvee. I pulled out of the turret just in time. We destroyed the vehicle. We're fine. Just bumps and bruises. I figured I'd get in trouble, but nobody really seems to care." His concern was not about being almost killed in the rollover. It was about getting in trouble.

"Jared never rode with me again after the rollover, by the way. Six days after returning to Fort Drum, I bought a car and, wouldn't you know it, hit a deer on the ride home and totaled the car. I bought another one about a month later," laughs Randy.

"I'll never forget the parties Jared led with his big crooked smile and a pinch of dip in his lip. We'd 'welcome' new recruits to the platoon by shaving eyebrows, drawing on their faces with permanent markers, or duct-taping them to poles while we partied in their rooms. In the field, we'd initiate new officers with a couple of rolls of duct tape, or teach new guys how to koalafy (hang upside down for a predetermined amount of time). I repressed a lot of the bad stuff that happened in Afghanistan, but I sure remember all the funny stuff that Monti did."

"I was just 21 years old. I frankly joined the Army figuring I'd put in four years and use it to build my resume. Jared was like a mentor to me. He'd always be fooling around and cracking jokes, but he taught me some serious stuff about the world being bigger than my little bubble. He made me care about what I was doing. He taught me about commitment. He'd always say that it's what you do for others that defines who you are. That's how he lived his life."

There's a beautiful song called "Nothing More" that was not, but could have been, written about Jared. It seems to fit him perfectly, in virtually the same words that Randy used to quote him. It was recorded in 2013 by The Alternate Routes, a band formed by Tim Warren and Eric Donnelly, who met while attending Fairfield University in Connecticut. They released the song in 2013 in tribute to the 20 children and 6 adults who tragically lost their lives in the Sandy Hook Elementary School shooting. It was written for Newtown Kindness, a non-profit organization dedicated to encouraging acts of kindness. The song was featured in the Christmas episode of *NCIS* on December 17, 2013 and was a part of the 2014 Winter Olympics Opening Ceremony in Sochi, Russia. The band also played it on *The Late Late Show* with Craig Ferguson in March of 2014. The song can be downloaded at https://itunes.apple.com/us/album/nothing-more-feat.lily-costner/id719763916?i=719763964&ign-mpt=uo%3D4. A portion of the proceeds goes to Newtown Kindness.

After hearing Jared's story, the band members wrote in an e-mail, "We are honored that you would consider using the words of our song in a book about Jared. He sounds like an amazing man with an incredible story."

Nothing More

To be humble, to be kind,
It is the giving of the peace in your mind.
To a stranger, To a friend
To give in such a way that has no end.

We are Love
We are One
We are how we treat each other when the day is done.
We are Peace
We are War
We are how we treat each other and Nothing More.

To be bold, to be brave,
It is the thinking that the heart can still be saved
And the darkness can come quick;
The Danger's in the Anger and the hanging on to it.

We are Love

We are One
We are how we treat each other when the day is done.
We are Peace
We are War
We are how we treat each other and Nothing More.

Tell me what it is that you see,
A world that's filled with endless possibilities?
Heroes don't look they used to, they look like you do.

We are Love
We are One
We are how we treat each other when the day is done.
We are Peace
We are War
We are how we treat each other and Nothing More.

(Reprinted with permission)

Chapter 13
When It's Your Time, It's Your Time

Jared suffered serious injuries throughout his life. The first had been when he was just 14 years old. He was playing soccer when the femur bone in his leg popped out of the socket. It was forced in by his next step, and that broke off another section of bone in his hip.

Prior to being deployed, Jared was told by a doctor in Okinawa that he had to be medically discharged due to bulging and herniated discs resulting from repeated parachute jumps. Jared argued until the doctor relented and agreed not to mention the injury in the medical report. The doctor warned him, though, "If I get one report of your not being able to do your job, that's it. You're out!" Needless to say, the doctor never got such a report.

Jared was insistent that his troops take at least one correspondence course at all times to stay in top shape mentally, and also be in top shape physically. Many of them talk about being made to run around the various bases where they were stationed until they were ready to drop from exhaustion. Then they had to run some more. Mike Bower tells of the day Jared had his soldiers run from 7:30 a.m. to 9 a.m. and then told them to fall out for breakfast chow. They welcomed the chance to rest, but it wasn't a very long rest. "He told everyone to fall out and go eat. About three seconds later, he told us to fall back in, and we ran until around 11:30 a.m. That sucked, but it's what we did."

When leading a long march, Jared would exhort them on by saying, "There's only one click to go. You can do it. Come on. No time to rest." Ryan Kelley, who went on to become an NCO, says, "You were my Team Chief, my mentor, and my friend. I remember you told us on a long movement 'only one click left.' Then 12 clicks later we made it. I used that on my soldiers and it works."

SSG Brendan Kearns says, in describing Jared, "He was dedicated to his soldiers. He led by example. He didn't have to be out there every day cleaning things up or putting everything back together, but he was. I can remember when the FIRES section was tasked to do HA (humanitarian assistance) and organize, inventory, and distribute supplies. Jared was out there with the wood and the hammer building shelves, hoping they were straight. Sometimes they were and sometimes they weren't. He could just have told other people to do that. But, he was, 'No, this is what we're going to do today' and he was out front. He led from out front every time."

Trish Larsen admitted in this posting to Jared, "When I think about Afghanistan it is hard not to think of you. That is impossible, in fact. You were such a good leader. You are an inspiration. The last time I saw you I would have never dreamed I would never see you again. You were driving a Gator in FOB (Forward Operating Base) Salerno and I screamed because I was so excited to see you. You gave me such good advice. You helped me in so many ways through the hard times in the Army. It is not every day that you can say that you talked about the Steve Miller Band with an actual hero. I was your favorite mechanic. It is an honor to say that I worked for such a great Sergeant!"

Captain Joe Hansen recalls, "In Afghanistan, we participated in numerous shuras (open meetings between tribal elders, government officials, and others) on council carpets with Afghani leaders, some of whom had fought the Russians as Mujahedeen. Many Afghanis had and would fight alongside Jared and his FIST team in the near future. Some of the Pashtuns sat in council and became tolerable neighbors, some of them became trusted and loyal friends, and some would unfortunately meet us again in the mountains of Kunar and Nuristan as regrettable rivals for the future of Afghanistan.

"Many of the Afghanis Jared trained and fought alongside became brothers, believing in the mission to provide the Afghanis better options for a country that had known only war for so many years," continues Joe. "The time he spent with me in the shura councils ennobled his efforts to seek other options for mediation or cooperation amongst disparate tribal members. However, if need be he would fight, and when he fought from the high ground, he brought hell with him." Jared exemplified the expression, "No better friend, no worse enemy."

Just nine days before the patrol left for its reconnaissance mission on Hill 2610, Jared wrote a detailed e-mail to his Aunt Terri and Uncle Rich. Jon Krakauer spent two weeks traveling with Jared in Afghanistan as part of the research for his book, *Where Men Win Glory: The Odyssey of Pat Tillman,* which was published on July 27, 2010.

Jared's e-mail read in part:

> Been really busy, climbing lots of mountains, operating between 8-10,000 feet with Afghani Special Forces and Recon elements. Took a famous author named Jon Krakauer out on a mission with me. He's writing a book about the war in Afghanistan. He said it would be done in 2-4 years. He was a pretty cool guy and I had read a

> couple of his books. *Into Thin Air* probably being his most famous book. He's also summited Everest four times so he's a badass at climbing, especially for being 52. He took a liking to me so he gave me his address and email to keep in touch and ensure I get a copy of the book.

According to Joe Hansen, "Jared and I had ongoing discussions over the most effective means to try to bring stability to the district of Naray. In May of 2006, we introduced Jon Krakauer to some of the local national Afghanis in the area. The people in the valley were for the most part good folks. They welcomed Americans, and day-to-day interactions were often quite pleasant, as well as educational for both sides. One night after dinner, some of us were sitting in the small mud house (a 'qalʿah') with a man named Mahbub Shah, who made tea and flattened bread (Na'an) for us. The chairs were issue cots that had been set up, and we sat for what must have been several hours drinking tea and eating bread. Jon Krakauer talked about his book that had come out, called *Three Cups of Deceit,* and a proverb that says, "The first time you share tea with an Afghani, you are a stranger. The second time you take tea, you are an honored guest. The third time you share a cup of tea, you become family."

The Americans started to pack up, as they had an early mission in the morning. Jared's parting comment was, "*Three* cups? What about three *hundred* cups of tea?"

As he did from time to time, Jared also wrote in email to his aunt and uncle about the possibility of his getting out of the military:

> Time is really flying. I have a big decision ahead right

> now. I'm half-way from retirement but not sure whether or not to do the long haul. It's a lot of years to throw away if I get out and I'm still having fun over here. Not doing bad physically for an old man, as my soldiers call me, either. I've lost about twenty pounds since I've been over here but I'm getting really lean and moving well with my sniper section. I've got some great kids on my team and they've impressed me so far on their first combat tour. As for needing anything, we're pretty much taken care of. We are getting all the hygiene stuff that we need and we have a mess hall up and running on base. Up in the mountains, it's MREs and goat meat with occasional beans and rice the Afghani forces scrape up.

In the e-mail, Jared also talked about the loss of LTC Joe Fenty, who had been killed in a tragic Chinook helicopter accident along with nine other American soldiers several weeks before, on May 5. The CH-47 crashed while attempting to land in night time military operations east of Asadabad in the Kunar Province. Married for 20 years, Joe's wife Kristen had given birth to a daughter less than a month before the accident. Jared wrote:

> The scenery up here is really beautiful. We even have packs of monkeys running around. The only unfortunate thing here is that al Qaeda is starting to pick up the fight as the glaciers melt and passes begin to open. This could be such a nice country to visit if we could stamp out the terrorists. But me and my boys are doing our best. My Mom probably told you I lost a good friend a couple of weeks ago but I figure when it's your time, it's your time.

> We had a service over here for him and I got to be in the rifle squad for the 21-gun salute. It was pretty sad. His wife just had their first child, a little girl, and he never got to see her.

Finally Jared wrote that he wasn't sure when he'd be going home:

> It seems like the whole Ross family will be down south before we know it. I'm glad my Mom has some family around to help. She said she picked up Nana and spent some time with her. How's the rest of the family doing? Hopefully, I'll get down there to pay a visit. I'm not sure of when I'm going home or when I'll get some leave. Hopefully, the weather will be nice when I do. Well, that's all for now. I'll write back soon. Love you guys and thanks for thinking of me.

Terry Flood recalls, "I saw Jared in Bagram, Afghanistan one week prior to his leaving on the mission on Hill 2610. We gave each other some good-natured ribbing about hiding out from the war by going to Bagram. We were both stationed at Combat Outposts and were just refitting and getting supplies. True combat arms soldiers hate the metropolis that is Bagram. We said our goodbyes and agreed we'd hang out stateside once the deployment ended. Jared wouldn't want any attention. He's probably laughing now and saying, 'All I want is an ice cold drink from the Pewter Mug in Fort Drum, New York to be named after me, and maybe a Harley.' His actions inspire me daily, both as a soldier and human being. He wasn't the biggest, strongest, or fastest, but he had that one intangible that separate great men from good men –HEART!"

One of the more interesting backstories of those who were part of Jared's patrol on the mountain belongs to SPC John Garner. John's friend and future brother-in-law, Joey St. Lucas, lead singer of the rock band The Strikers, got him a job at the Guitar Center in San Marcos, CA. One day a woman came in and asked if they carried a real leopard skin case for a Gibson guitar. "No, Ma'am," John said. "I'm pretty sure everything we have is animal print." Just to make sure, John typed "Leopard Skin Guitar Cases" into his computer. Surprisingly, it turned out that they did carry them, and there was one in stock. John told her that he'd go upstairs in the storage room to look for it and, if it was there, he'd find it. She smiled and said, "You're so nice. Such a gentleman."

When he brought down the guitar case, she almost cried. She said she just wanted to be a mom who got her son something cool. She told John her son was in a band and she thought they were pretty good. John asked her the name of the band. She said, "They're called Guns 'n Roses, and his name is 'Slash.'" What was John's response? In his words, he says, "I shit myself and then I shit myself again, and then one more time."

John looked at her credit card and saw the name Ola Hudson. He immediately recognized her as the person who had designed clothing for John Lennon and David Bowie. This time, John mentioned something about urination. His pants were undoubtedly in desperate need of being changed at that point.

Shortly thereafter, John sold a guitar to Joe Walsh of the Eagles, and then a keyboard to Tom Delong of Blink 182. "I despised selling musical equipment for a commission, and I secretly sold everything at a discount. I didn't tell anyone. It was my secret. Unfortunately, it showed up in my paychecks," he confesses.

Around that time, a group of musicians contacted John, asking if they could record a few songs that he had written. The recording engineer was a former skateboarder in a group of kids known as The Lords of Dog Town, which eventually was the name of a 2005 cult film classic. The movie is dedicated to the memory of comedian Mitch Hedberg, who appears in it but died before the film was released.

Bill Medley, half of The Righteous Brothers duo, heard one of those songs and approached John to ask if his daughter, McKenna, also a singer, could record it. “She did, and she sang it beautifully,” says John.

“I hadn’t really made money from music. My songs were played on the radio in San Diego. I really wrote songs for myself,” admits John. “Then 9/11 happened, and that affected me much more than a check from a song. So I joined the Army.”

The 3-71 CAV had just been created, and John joined by a quirk of fate. He was supposed to be assigned to a regular infantry unit. “Staff Sergeant Siercks and Chris Cunningham happened to ask me what my Physical Training score was. They were impressed enough to ask if I was ready to do recon. They gave me 30 seconds to jump on their truck. They gave me a chance. It’s the quickest I’ve ever run. I had found a home with the 3-71,” says John.

Chapter 14
Not One of the Glorious Days

The U. S. Army's 10th Mountain Division has "Climb to Glory" as its proud motto. However, June 21, 2006 was not one of the glorious days.

Three days earlier, Paul's phone rang back in Raynham, MA at 7:30 a.m. He picked it up and heard his son Jared, the soldier with the big, wide grin, exclaiming, "Hey, Pop, how you doing? Happy Father's Day." Paul told him that there couldn't be a better Father's Day gift than hearing from him. They talked for a while, and then Jared said, "Dad, I have to go now. We're leaving on a mission." Those would be Jared's last words to his father. At the end of every telephone conversation Paul would say, "Be safe. Keep your head down," to his son. "For some reason, I forgot to do it that time," he admits. "I realized it as soon as I put the phone down. It still bothers me to this day that I didn't say it."

In the spring of 2006, the 3rd Squadron, 71st Calvary, 10th Mountain Division had travelled by convoy from FOB Salerno in the Khost Province of Afghanistan to establish FOB Naray in the Nuristan Province of northeast Afghanistan. The two-week trek took place over 250 miles of dangerous dirt trails and mountain passes. It took the soldiers into an area that had historically been a safe haven for insurgent and anti-governmental elements operating in the Hindu Kush mountains and the Afghan-Pakistan FATA (Federally Administered Tribal Areas) cross-over points. "We moved into unknown terrain," recalls Lieutenant Colonel and Squadron Operations Officer Jeffrey Abbott.

After being transported by convoy to a mortar firing position at the Gowardesh Bridge, located south of the village of Baz-Gal, sixteen American soldiers embarked on an exhausting climb, moving mostly in the mornings and evenings. They hiked for three days up an uncharted mountain known only as Hill 2610. The military designates mountains based on how many meters above sea level they are. So, Hill 2610 was 2,610 meters or 8,562 feet high. If topographical features have the same height, they are further designated by their compass location.

The patrol members were wearing body armor and carrying packs that ranged in weight from 70 to 110 pounds in 100-degree heat. The thin air and stifling heat sapped their strength. They rested during the heat of the day. Navigating the rugged terrain was particularly challenging during the evenings, when night vision goggles were required. They were on constant alert for Taliban snipers and "toe-poppers", small land mines still scattered around the countryside from the Soviet invasion of decades ago.

Jared was instrumental in forming "Kill" Teams comprised of three Snipers and three Forward Observers to provide precision fire. He wanted to work with the Kill Teams himself but was kept busy with other responsibilities. He was a renowned mountain climber and was often chosen to lead Squadron soldiers up to Observation Posts, along with performing other duties, including being the Forward Observer Platoon Sergeant and Fires NCO for the Squadron. A cavalry squadron is typically less than 1,000 soldiers, equivalent to an infantry battalion. These were just a few of Jared's many job titles. He'd often be involved in negotiations with the Afghanistan military or civilians because he had earned the trust of both. For his part, he just wanted to “stay busy”.

SGT John Hawes and Cunningham learned they would finally get their wish: Jared would be going along on the reconnaissance assignment. Hawes would get a chance to work with Jared on a Kill Team. The 22-year-old Hawes came from the small town of Brookfield, NY (population of 2,500), which is in Madison County, not far from Syracuse. There is only one school in the town, the Brookfield Central School, which John attended from kindergarten through high school. He said, “Monti was going to be the Team Leader taking charge of the Forward Observer stuff due to his greater experience and rank, and I would be Assistant Team Leader taking charge of the Sniper stuff. I looked forward to it. I knew I would do whatever Monti asked of me.”

The patrol consisted of one squad headed by Jared and the other by SSG Chris Cunningham. Jared and Chris were savvy and experienced combat veterans, both having served multiple tours of duty in Afghanistan. They were considered among the best Non-Commissioned Officers in the theater of operation. Another small town product, the 26-year-old Cunningham called Whitingham, Vermont home. With a population of 1,300, it is located about 60 miles northeast of Albany, New York. An Airborne Ranger, Cunningham was Patrol Leader, the NCO who was over-all in charge. “Cunningham wanted the ‘A’ team for the patrol, the best of the best. He needed people who knew what they were doing and could be counted on,” says SPC Franklin Woods.

Hawes and Jared would frequently play the board game Risk and the computer game Pocket Tanks. Jared was known for being an outstanding Pocket Tanks player. The two friends challenged each other often and frequently ended up tied, or with Jared having a slight edge. Jared was frustrated, though, that he couldn’t seem to beat John at Risk. Any time Jared beat him at Pocket Tanks, Hawes would rub it in that he couldn’t beat him at Risk. Jared would respond with his patented wide smile, "Not yet, but I eventually will."

According to John, "Monti was always full of helpful information on how to do things in the Army and talked of how much the Army has changed and how things used to be back when he was a Private. I learned a great deal from Monti on being a good NCO, leader, and friend. I saw that Monti was greatly respected by all his men. He was firm but not all-controlling. If Monti said to do something, you didn't question it. You just did it. He had the knowledge and experience and would never point you in the wrong direction or give you bad advice. He wanted you to be successful just as much as himself. Monti shared his knowledge and experience with anyone who was interested in listening. He always had a great way of cracking jokes and putting a humorous twist on serious subjects to keep everything interesting. He had a positive attitude and a contagious smile. You couldn't help but to be happy around him and enjoy his company."

John adds, "In the Army there are NCOs you respect simply because of their rank, and there are others you respect because of the person, regardless of rank. Monti was the latter type. I e-mailed my wife and told her how excited I was that I was finally going with Monti on a mission. She had never met him but knew how much I respected the man."

SGT Ron Haapala waited with Jared for word to come down as to when the mission would begin. Like so many other soldiers, he speaks both of his friendship with Jared and his respect for him: "We were smoking cigars. We had a great conversation about all the things we were going to do when we got back home. I have a lake house and I like to fish. Monti was always out there fishing, so we were talking about his buying a lake house maybe on the same lake. He was my friend and someone I respected. Generally, artillery soldiers, helicopter pilots, and forward observers follow their own Standard Operating Procedures. Sometimes they don't mesh. He was one of the few who wanted us to work together. He put in the effort to understand what everyone else did in every situation to make the call for fire process a lot smoother."

There would be a number of firsts on this mission. It was the first time the Kill Teams operated as part of such a large force; the first time the Kill Teams had their own dedicated medic, Specialist Max Noble, along with them; and the first time any American operated in this remote area of Afghanistan. Soldiers can be superstitious, and firsts usually aren't regarded as good omens.

Hawes acknowledges, "Being a first on so many things, something just didn't sit right with us about this mission. We pushed our worries to the side. We told ourselves that everything had worked out well for us up till that point so there was no need to worry about this one. We convinced ourselves it would just be another 'Walk in the Park' like other missions."

The day before they were to embark, Jared asked John Hawes if he smoked cigars. It was no secret that Jared enjoyed fine cigars. John didn't like cigars and, in fact, grew up hating any kind of smoking. He told Jared that if he did smoke he would want to smoke with someone like him. Then Jared said that maybe after this mission's success they could each have a cigar to celebrate.

Ideally, as a FISTer, Jared would call for fire on the enemy force and a sniper like Hawes would shoot at the enemy from a distance without putting themselves in any real danger. John had sniped an insurgent on an earlier mission, earning the Squadron its first enemy KIA (Killed in Action); and shortly afterwards Jared had called for fire on three insurgents, completing the first confirmed fire mission in the Squadron. According to John, "I don't enjoy killing and neither did Monti, but in a weird twisted way we shared this bond of having been there and successfully completed the jobs we were trained to do, and we respected each other for it."

"I belonged to a medical platoon and was trained to be a clinical medic. I worked in an aid station and was assigned to accompany the patrol on the Hill 2610 mission," explains Max Noble, who was 25 years old at the time. "It's usually a bad sign if a patrol asks for a medic to accompany them, because it means the mission is considered dangerous. I heard stories about the Kill Teams that Jared had set up. I knew of his stature. I knew of their mystique and the legends surrounding them. They were the top, most hard-core soldiers, the guys who get the tough things done.

"I didn't find out specifically who was going on the mission until the night before," continues Max. "That's when Jared dropped by, and I guess he felt like he needed someone to talk to. A lot of times it's easier to talk to a medic rather than someone in your chain of command, either above you or below you. He was somber. He wanted to talk about his mortality. It was a very existential and philosophical discussion. I saw a vulnerable side of him. He was talking about how everyone's time is going to come. You can't do anything about it. You just don't know when it is. He said, 'You're given a lifetime which is short for some and long for others. You just have to do your best however long that lifetime is.' I sensed that the magnitude of this mission was weighing on him. He really opened up to me. I mostly listened."

As the patrol began the climb, Hawes learned more and more about Jared's personal life as he spoke about his girlfriend back home, his Harley Davidson motorcycle, Boston, beer, cigars, and fishing off the coast. They even made plans to go fishing together back in Massachusetts. John loved fishing but had never fished off the coast like Jared had and looked forward to being able to do that.

Jared described how he used to help out and work on one particular boat back home. He said the clients that fished off the boat were normally high-class, wealthy men, and he got a kick out of just being an average guy on the boat. He described how he was close friends with the boat's captain and would get to go out for free fishing with him when he came home on leave from the Army.

"Jared also talked about how much he liked baseball. I don't particularly like it, but being from New York I had to bust on Monti about the Yankees and Red Sox," Hawes admits. "Of course he fiercely defended the Red Sox, and I defended the Yankees, even though I really didn't care about them. It was just another thing to pick on each other about and get a good laugh. I felt comfortable and secure around him, knowing inside that if things got bad and hit the fan, Monti was the guy you wanted around to do the job right and help you out."

One of the members of the patrol, SSG Josh Renken, remembers Jared kidding around on the trek, telling them how he wanted his funeral to be like the Vikings – a boat pushed into the sea and set on fire with a flaming arrow. "Jared was trying to keep everyone happy, cracking jokes, giving people a hard time, just to keep the mood up, because we had no food, no water," Josh confesses. "We were hurting."

SGT Chris Grzecki says, "When we reached our destination to set up our Observation Post on a ridge we were trying to see if anyone had any water left. All of a sudden Jared passed his canteen around for everyone to drink. I couldn't believe it. He'd hardly drunk any of his own water. This guy was like superhuman. I didn't understand how he could have that much water left. That was his reputation. He's was the go-to, everything guy. He always had the answer. He always kept his cool."

The patrol stopped at a plateau on the mountain to begin

observing and reporting on the activities of insurgents who were holding up in the Gremen Valley. Of particular interest were the actions taking place at HIG Commander Hadji Usman's summer residence, which was a suspected training facility. HIG (Hizb-i-Islami Gulbuddin) is an Islamic political party that originally fought against the Soviet army and was funded by the U. S. Now its ties were to both the Taliban and al Qaeda.

This was to be the initial phase of Operation Gowardesh Thrust, the full air assault planned by the Third Brigade. If they could destroy some of the infiltration routes from neighboring Pakistan, it would result in an important strategic victory. There was bad news, though. Jared received a radio communication that troops and helicopters were being diverted to another front and the larger mission would be delayed by several days. Since they were out of supplies, the team requested a drop by helicopter as soon as possible. It's a risk to do that when hostile forces may see it, but they knew they were going to be there for a while. They didn't have a choice.

Two "speedballs" were dropped on the other side of the ridge. One was filled with water and the other with MREs (Meals, Ready-to-Eat). The plan was to then send soldiers on a hike to pick up the packages. A speedball is an LCLA (Low Cost, Low Altitude) aerial delivery system that was employed throughout Afghanistan. It was completely disposable. The parachutes were made of sandbag material and the risers out of swing set plastic rope. The cost was less than $100 each. There was no need to backhaul items for reuse. A soldier in the drop zone would simply cut the lashings, take the supplies, and leave the rest of the material behind.

Originally the intent was to have the patrol re-supplied in conjunction with the squadron's main drive into the area. That way, there would have been significant helicopter traffic and little chance that the patrol's position would be compromised. But it was decided back at 3-71 CAV Headquarters that a single UH-60 Black Hawk helicopter would make the speedball drop about 2:30 p.m., since the patrol was critically short of supplies.

Cunningham explains, "There was bad communication between the helicopter and those of us on the mountain. The copter exposed our position. It flew over the enemy and then it flew right over us."

About an hour later, two women in burqas were spotted on the trail walking toward the patrol. They appeared innocent enough, as they were carrying bags of wheat. They gave a hand signal, asking for permission to pass by. "We had a dilemma," admits Grzecki. "They saw us and where we were positioned. We decided against detaining them. We waved them on. We'll never know if they were innocents or insurgent informants."

"I felt relieved that we didn't harm them. In warfare you have to make some tough decisions. But even if there was just a slight chance they weren't informants, I thought the right thing to do would be to let them go," admits Specialist Noble. "Shortly after that, the others went to pick up the supplies and I stayed behind to keep watch through the spotting scope. At that point, I hadn't had any food, water, or sleep for a whole day. The truth is, I figured I'd just be going along on the mission for the ride. I thought the biggest threat would be toe-poppers. I was freaking oblivious. What did I know? I hadn't been in combat before. I thought the big building in the valley was just some elder's home. I didn't realize that they were training insurgents there. I suddenly saw one of them looking up at us through binoculars and said to Hawes when he returned, 'We're being watched.'"

John knew what that grim news meant. Their position was definitely revealed and their cover blown. They were in trouble.

According to Hawes, "Regular Afghanis don't have binoculars. There's no purpose for them. Bird watching is not popular in Afghanistan."

"It was the worst-case scenario," says Captain Ross Berkoff, the squadron's Intelligence Officer, who was monitoring the botched supply drop from the Command Post. "We stirred up a hornet's nest."

The Americans had two options. They could pack up and move, or they could stay and fight. The idea of hurrying down the mountain was dismissed because they would have been in a bad strategic position with the Taliban looking down on them. They would be easy targets to be picked off one by one. Their best option was to hold their position, seek cover, and fight.

The mountain air was clear and still. Visibility was, unfortunately, not a problem. This was the first day of summer, the longest day of the year, and there were still a good couple of hours of daylight left. Those next few hours turned out to be anything but good, however. The Americans took up defensive positions and nervously awaited their fate. It was 6:45 p.m. when the attack came.

A group of patrol members had started to eat the MREs that had been picked up from the air drop. SSG Patrick Lybert opened his and found some Charms candy inside. That's considered a bad omen by soldiers. Charms are individually wrapped, assorted fruit-flavored hard square candies that come ten pieces to a pack and are made by a company called Groovy Candies. You might think they'd be regarded as good luck because of their name. It's the opposite, though. In the same way, you might think saying, "Good luck" to a dancer or actor before a performance is the right thing to do, but as most people know, saying "Break a leg" is considered more appropriate, so as not to jinx them. There's reverse logic involved. "Lybert wanted to get rid of the Charms, but no one would take them. We started throwing them around and playing hot potato. He wound up being stuck with them," recalls Noble.

The senior NCOs were huddled together discussing the need to double the guard shift in order to increase security when they were interrupted by the scream of an RPG flying over their heads. A rocket-propelled grenade is a ferocious shoulder-fired weapon that shoots a missile about a foot and a half long. It is designed to bring down a helicopter or disable a tank within a range of 500 meters. It can easily tear a person apart. "My first thought was, Who's the dumb ass who set off one of the Claymore mines that we had placed around our perimeter?" says Chris Grzecki.

According to Grzecki, "The first RPG was followed almost immediately by the most intense burst of fire I've ever witnessed." An estimated 50 to 60 Taliban soldiers began shooting with automatic weapons. Chris thought to himself, "Oh, shit, we're in for it now." The Americans dove behind rocks for cover as bullets and RPGs impacted all around them. They quickly began to return fire.

"Since my guard shift was up, I had fallen asleep using my first aid bag as a pillow. I remember waking up to what I thought was heavy rain. The dirt was kicking up all around me. Someone yelled that we were being shot at. I realized it wasn't rain. It was bullets. I jumped up and didn't have a weapon, body armor on, or my first aid bag. Later, I retrieved my bag and saw that it was full of bullet holes," recounts Max Noble.

"I remember opening my MRE and seeing meat loaf with gravy. I asked Matt Chambers if he wanted to trade with me," recalls Woods. "At that moment I heard the explosion, and the battle was on. It was in slow motion, like in the movies. It felt like the longest second, longest minute, longest hour of my life. I took cover behind a little 8-inch wide tree. I didn't even have a weapon at first. Lybert called out, 'Grab your fucking M-4 and shoot. You're exposed. Get out of there. Get behind cover.'"

The fighting got very intense very quickly. Hawes says, "It was, right from the beginning, an incredibly heavy assault with gunfire just pouring down on us. It completely pinned us down." The incessant noise was described by the patrol members as being like "thousands of rifles crackling." Jared spoke into the radio handset, carefully gave his call sign, and cleared the network to call for fire. "This is Chaos 3-5! Requesting artillery and air support now! We're under attack, heavily outnumbered, and at risk of being overrun." He then gave the co-ordinates for the American response, adding the words, "Danger Close." That indicated the enemy was in close proximity, so strikes would have to be precise or there would be the possibility of a "Killed by Friendly Fire" accident. Relief in the way of indirect fire was going to come immediately from 120 mm mortars and 105 mm howitzers from positions at the Gowardesh Bridge. The soldiers in the patrol knew the air support was going to take a while to get there. They had to stand their ground.

"I've been through a lot of fire fights and some pretty serious contact with the enemy, but this was more intense than anything I'd ever experienced," admits Cunningham.

"I was on the other end of the phone with Monti and there was no panic at all. He was doing what he was trained to do. I asked if he had eyes on the enemy," recalls SFC Gary Hunsucker. "Are you kidding?" responded Jared, "If I raise my head, I'll get it blown off."

"He then laughed," recalls Hunsucker. "We talked about how we were going to handle the situation based on where they were and where the enemy likely was. He was a pro. We were both doing our job, doing what we were paid to do. Our trust was so strong. I knew he'd give me the information we needed. He knew we'd give him the support they needed. We worked so well together we could pretty much read each other's thoughts."

Lieutenant Colonel Jeffrey Abbott, who was monitoring the situation from the Command Post, explains, "The enemy had one goal in mind. To overrun and kill everybody in the patrol."

"RPGs came in fast and furiously, skipping off rocks and exploding in the trees above our heads," recalls Cunningham, "There was so much machine gun fire that trees were being split by the bullets all around us and the branches were catching shrapnel like catcher's mitts. Everything started falling all around us. It's like violence was everywhere, enveloping us."

During the initial assault and just minutes after discovering the Charms in his MRE, 28-year-old Patrick Lybert of Ladysmith, Wisconsin was hit in the head by machine gun fire and blood spurted from his left ear. He was killed instantly. PFC Derek James remembers, "Lybert was behind a large rock but kept popping his head up to see where the insurgents were. Then, all of a sudden, he just stopped." Patrick was scheduled to go home on leave several weeks later, and he was planning to become officially engaged. He was going to finish his deployment, get married, and become caretaker for his 19-year-old brother, who had Asperger's Syndrome.

According to Derek, "An RPG exploded close to my location and I was wounded in the right arm. Immediately after that I was shot in the back with small arms fire. I thought, 'Shit, I'm going to die. We're all going to die.' We were taking so much fire we couldn't make out where the mortars landed. It was coming in so close that you could hear it right over your head, just like whizzing through. The enemy was so close you could hear them talking in

Arabic. You could hear them reloading their weapons."

Jared pulled the pin on a grenade and threw it right into the middle of a group of attackers. It was a perfect toss. Except it didn't go off. It was a dud. A terrible time for a weapons malfunction. But it did cause them to pull back.

"I was worried about my back injury because I couldn't see it. For all I knew, half my back could have been gone," confesses Derek, who at 18 years old was the youngest and least experienced of the platoon members. He was just a year out of high school.

Grzecki reached out and pulled James back to cover. "I checked him. I saw that he was moving and alert. Chambers, who's an EMT (Emergency Medical Technician), quickly patched him up. Derek went back to returning fire. He was just awesome. He went back to fighting as a member of the team, even though he had been hit twice."

Those who have been in battle understand the gripping anxiety that heightens the senses and rushes adrenalin through the body. General William Westmoreland, who served as commander of the troops in the Viet Nam war and subsequently as Army Chief of Staff, explained it simply as, "War is fear cloaked in courage."

Grzecki was unable to reach out to grab his M-16 rifle that was just a foot away due to the intense machine gun fire. "I had a choice of either diving to my left and trying for my weapon or diving to my right and seeking cover," he remembers. "I knew I couldn't do both. I chose to seek cover."

Specialist John Garner says, "Two bullets flew by my face. I reached out for my weapon, and when my hand touched it, it got shot right out of my hand." Amazingly, he was uninjured. The bullets hit the stock of his rifle but missed him. Over the deafening noise, John called out to Specialist Daniel Linnihan to reach under Lybert's body and throw him his rifle.

SPC Sean Smith looked at his watch on his wrist, as if to record his time of death. Even today he admits, "I don't know why I did that. I instantly forgot what the time was anyhow. Less than a year earlier, I had been in Basic Training and was called into the Senior Drill Instructor's office one evening. Before I entered, I tried as hard as I could to remember what I could have fucked up to get in trouble and to mentally prepare myself for the ass-chewing I thought I was about to receive. When I walked into the office, there he was: my father, who had been stationed in Iraq, who I hadn't seen in over a year. It was the last thing on earth I expected. He gave me a gift of a watch. So I really don't know whether I looked at the watch to record when 'my time' was going to be, or because I was trying to connect with my Dad. He retired out of the Army's 1st Squadron Special Forces, or Delta Force as it's called, as a Master Sergeant. I always dreamed of being just like him – tall, strong, and proud to wear that uniform – emulating everything that I thought he was. Maybe I was just looking for the strength to fight, or some sort of guidance, like, 'What do I do now, Dad?'"

Sean then said to Grzecki, "Move your foot. It's going to get shot." Chris recalls, "I could feel the dirt around it getting kicked up. I moved my foot and there was an outline of bullets around where it had been." SPC Brian Gonterman admits, "All I could think about is them coming over the stone wall and killing all of us."

SPC Shawn Heistand and PFC Brian Bradbury were together when the enemy first opened fire. Both hit the ground and began to return fire. However, they recognized that their fire was drawing enemy attention to their dangerously exposed position. Shawn urged Brian to seek cover by falling back to the large rocks. Brian was directly behind him as they sprinted. Shawn made it safely, but Brian was hit by an RPG about twenty meters or 66 feet from the

American position. His left arm was partially severed from his shoulder as he fell into a shallow depression which afforded him virtually no protection.

Members of the patrol saw that 22-year-old Bradbury from St. Joseph, Missouri was in serious trouble. Despite losing use of an arm, the PFC was somehow able to continue firing his M249 automatic weapon with the other arm until his ammunition ran out. As the SAW (Squad Automatic Weapon) gunner, Brian had already won the respect of the team by being the smallest man carrying the heaviest weapon without ever complaining. He won additional respect that day on the mountain.

James acknowledges, "Bradbury was out there in the death zone." Renken adds, "He was slowly slipping away." Someone had to do something fast. SSG Cunningham volunteered to try to rescue him. Jared refused, because Brian was from his squad. He insisted, "That's my guy. I'm going to get him."

"We all heard that Monti was going to try to get Bradbury out of the kill zone. SGT Hawes gave me his 9 mm pistol and 203 Grenade Launcher to fire a 40mm grenade to help provide cover. I launched a grenade and we all coordinated the best we could. I began returning fire with the pistol while Hawes threw grenades," remembers Gonterman.

John says, "Jared knew what he was going to have to go through. He had to do it. He knew what he was going into and it was just a mad wall of hell. As soon as he recognized that Bradbury was out there exposed and the enemy was getting close and we had to get to Bradbury, he did it without hesitation." Jared gave Grzecki his radio set and said simply, "You're Chaos 3-5 now!" And then he ran. "Monti was hunched over and moving pretty fast," says Cunningham.

With Bradbury in "no man's land", the enemy was focusing on

him. Jared knew that if he ran out to try to get him, it would draw fire away from not only Brian but from the rest of the patrol. When soldiers on the mountain would later speak of Jared having saved their lives, they were referring to the fact that he literally "put himself out there" not only for Brian but for all of them. Help would be coming in the form of air support, but no one knew how long it would take. The patrol had to hold out as long as it could. Jared was able to buy them the one thing they critically needed – time.

"I was talking to Jared on the phone, and then suddenly there was silence. Another voice came on and he identified himself as Chaos 3-5. I knew something was wrong. It wasn't Jared anymore," recalls Hunsucker.

"He just threw the radio at me," says Grzecki. "There was no plan. I didn't know what Jared had already called in. I just wanted to keep up what he had started. Neither John Garner nor I had body armor on. He did an incredibly brave thing by physically shielding me with his body to protect me from enemy fire while I tried to work the radio and grab the map to plot grids. It's crazy to put yourself at risk like that, but John did it." During the trek up the mountain, Garner had been the first in line taking the point position. He obviously was willing to put himself in danger.

Gzecki started to go through a mental check list of what needed to be done. "I knew we had a serious fight on our hands. I didn't want to be 'that guy' in a friendly fire incident who gets everyone killed. The key was to put that ordnance close enough to kill the enemy but not us. We were seriously outnumbered. It was our only chance."

"After Monti threw his radio to Grzecki, he didn't miss a beat. Chris was just amazing," praises Cunningham."In effect, Jared said to him, 'You're me now.' You know what? He was. It's a testimony to Grzecki, but also to how well Jared trained his guys. Every one of them could step in and be just as effective as him."

As the patrol provided covering fire, Jared left the protection of the stone wall to check on Lybert to make sure that he was in fact dead, and then ran straight for Bradbury. Cunningham says, "Because of the intensity of the fire, one meter was like a mile." Jared got to within three feet of Brian. He was agonizingly just out of reach when he ran into a hail of Taliban machine gun fire and had to turn back.

The enemy was using all its firepower on Jared. He didn't quit. He tried a second time and could manage just a couple of steps before being driven back by the torrent of bullets. He still didn't quit. He was not going to let Bradbury stay out there, wounded and exposed. He was going to try a third time. "That was Jared. He never gave up on anything, no matter what it was," says Paul.

He said to the members of his patrol, "I've gotta get him! I'm going to go again!" Jared called for more cover fire. He coordinated with Hawes to fire 40mm grenades from his M203 launcher onto the enemy position. Timing his movement to the sound of the exploding rounds, Jared rose from his covered position and moved into the open, knowing he once again would become the focus of insurgent fire.

Cunningham calls Jared's repeated attempts, "The bravest thing I've ever seen a soldier do," and adds, "It's expected for a guy to go out there and try to rescue someone. But to go out a second time is unheard of. To go a third time? Either you're getting him or there's no coming back."

Hawes echoes Cunningham's sentiments: "What Monti did trying to save Bradbury was the most courageous, inspiring, and selfless act I have ever seen, and I'll never forget it."

SPC Gonterman recalls, "We were always trained that if

someone was injured in the kill zone to talk to them and keep them awake, but not go after them because it takes another person out of the fight. I could tell Monti was the type of guy that would go out of his way for any soldier, though, and he truly lived up to that."

The insurgents retaliated, setting the air aglow with explosives. Jared suffered a direct hit from an RPG. "The enemy was amazed that he was running again. We were shooting with everything we had to give him cover. He threw another grenade and went out a third time. But this time they had a bead on him. They were ready. They hit him with an RPG," says Cunningham."It was pretty horrible."

Hawes recalls, "Just as he was about to reach Bradbury I ran out of ammo, and as I dropped behind the rock to change magazines, I heard an RPG explode. Monti screamed that he had been hit."

The horrifying cry was like nothing they had ever heard before. According to Grzecki, "I remember thinking, I can't believe he's fooling around. Only Monti would make a joke at a time like this." After all, Jared was supposed to be invincible. Everyone knew that. "I thought he was letting out a battle cry, like something out of *Braveheart*," recalls James.

"When we realized he was really hurt, we didn't know how we could get him. It wouldn't make sense to have casualty after casualty," says Grzecki.

"My legs are gone!" Jared cried out. Actually, they were split open and embedded with shrapnel, but he had lost feeling in his legs. He also suffered wounds to the side of his body. He was bleeding profusely. Even after that, he was still in the fight. "After being hit, he warned us that they were flanking left," recalls Gonterman.

Jared tried to gather up the strength to crawl back to his unit.

He couldn't move, though, and called out, "Cunny, come get me."

"I said, 'All right. Roger that,' and told the guys to cover me. I started crawling over there, but the enemy fire was too heavy," recounts Cunningham.

Gasping for air, Jared still was able to recite The Lord's Prayer, like he had done so many times before. He began with "Our Father, Who art in heaven", and finished with "But deliver us from evil. For thine is the kingdom, and the power, and the glory for ever and ever." This time it had special meaning.

Jared's last words to the patrol were, "I've made peace with God. Tell my family I love them." He continued to bleed until he had no more blood left to spill. "It was definitely pure courage and love for his soldier," says Cunningham.

Hawes recounts, "We told Monti that he would be telling his parents himself, but he was soon quiet. Later in the fight I was the first to reach him, where I confirmed for myself that my friend was, indeed, dead. I was devastated. When he ran out to try and save Bradbury, he did it fully knowing the tremendous danger involved but did so anyway for a fellow soldier and friend. He died the most honorable and noble way a man can: trying to save someone else's life."

Ironically, the name "Monti" comes from the Italian word for "Mountain." Paul understands why Jared ran through machine gun and RPG fire three times. He says of his son, "He wasn't looking for glory. He didn't want to be a hero. But part of the soldier's creed is that you never leave anyone behind. He wouldn't. He couldn't. Jared would want to be remembered as the guy who did the right thing. Period." In terms of Jared's final words being about his family, Paul insists, "That's the most meaningful thing that there is. That he thought of us in his last moments."

According to Garner, "I might have been there with Monti

when he passed away, but I wasn't able to shed one single tear or feel it. It was a battle, a moment, and we would not lose. It is still like a dream of a friend being taken away. But we tried and I tried. We did everything we could. I know Paul Monti knows we did."

"We all started running black on ammo. I had packed a few extra magazines in my assault pack before the mission," says Gonterman. "I had to come out from the protection of the rock half-way up to get it. I was able to grab the assault pack and hand out extra ammo to SGT Hawes who asked, 'How much more do you have?' I said, 'That's it. But SGT Lybert has more on his vest.' Hawes jumped to my side, asking for cover fire. He low-crawled to Lybert's body, took his ammo and gave it to me. I passed it around to everyone else."

Would Jared have had regrets about what he did that day? His sister Niccole answers empathically, "I know he wouldn't change anything. I know he would do it again. If he could come back and he were given a choice, he would do it exactly the same. He would change nothing." According to Janet, "His boys came first. He died doing what he loved. He wouldn't have been able to live with himself if he didn't try to save Bradbury."

"Jared knew the chances of his surviving were low," asserts Grzecki. "It didn't stop him." Captain Joe Hansen says, "He was a soldier who committed himself to something. We all continually asked ourselves if we could have done the same." Sergeant Major of the Army Kenneth Preston offers, "It was his sense of responsibility there on the battlefield that drove him to risk his life. He was bound and determined to get that soldier back to safety, no matter what."

"There were fifty things that went wrong on the mountain," muses Paul. Certainly at the top of the list were the botched supply drop and the grenade that failed to explode. The Apache attack helicopters arrived shortly after Jared died. If he had just stopped after two tries at rescuing Bradbury, he probably would be alive today.

"At this point, someone called for everyone to get down and get low because the bombs were about to be dropped danger close to us. That's the moment I was able to catch my breath. Before I had been going through the motions that kick in with training," says Gonterman. "I looked up just after the first bomb was dropped and saw some sort of shrapnel cutting through the tree near me. We then had to find where it was dropped to adjust fire. The bomb landed on my side of the mountain and I looked to try to see the smoke from where it landed the best I could without getting hit."

It turned out to be a precision strike, right on target. Attack helicopters swarmed like angry bees. Mortars continued to be lobbed in from the Gowardesh Bridge. Ordnance filled the air. Twenty-two Taliban were killed and the rest driven off.

Renken describes the terrifying attack this way: "Trees are falling over, you can hear the shrapnel whizzing over your head. Your teeth are rattling, about to fall right out of your head."

War stories in real life often have tragic endings. This one did. "I remember hearing the flight medic they dropped down say, 'Hey, don't worry. I am gonna get you guys out of here,'" recalls Smith. The medic was 28-year-old SSG Heathe Craig from Severn, Maryland, from the 159th Air Ambulance Medical Company. Earlier, he had been on a computer Skyping with his wife Judy, his 11-month-old daughter Leona, and four-year-old son Jonas, who were at off-base housing in Wiesbaden, Germany. Heathe had to cut the session short because he got word that he was needed on the emergency rescue mission.

The badly wounded Derek James was lifted out of the battle zone first and secured by straps in the helicopter. Bradbury had a tourniquet applied by Noble and was given morphine. He was too badly hurt to hold on to the cable, so Heathe rode it with him until the unthinkable happened.

"Bradbury was hurt pretty bad. He was leaning back and catching wind," recalls Woods. "He and Craig started to swing back and forth. The cable was oscillating uncontrollably. Then I saw it snap. I said, 'Oh, shit. It broke. It broke." Both Bradbury and Craig plummeted to their deaths. They dropped 100 feet onto bare rocks.

Smith will forever be haunted by the sound. "I heard a thump, like a ship anchor dropped to the ground," he says. "The steel cable snapped, and that killed Bradbury. It also killed the flight medic that had just told us we would be OK."

Judy Craig later posted this message to Brian's family: "I am very sorry for your loss. I know that Heathe tried everything to save Brian's life. I wish there would have been a better outcome for the both of us."

After hearing of the cable breaking, Captain Berkoff stood in front of the field hospital with surgeons waiting inside to operate on Bradbury and thought, *Could anything possibly go right today?* "I was really pissed when I found out about the cable," admits Hunsucker. "I had never heard of one breaking before. No one else had, either."

James was successfully flown to the aid station and recovered from his wounds. He was back in action just two months later. The surviving members of the patrol nervously remained in position for the rest of the night. "We'd call for fire every time a twig snapped or an insect landed on our shoulders," Smith says. "Things were lighting up all night long."

As the sun began to bake the mountain air the next morning, they went out to search for Taliban bodies and leftover equipment.

The ground was covered with blood trails. "It looked like a nuke had hit," Sean claims. "All the trees were cut in half. Branches were all over." There was an eerie stillness on the battlefield accompanied by the stench of death and gunpowder.

"I called in the names of our killed in action along with the last four digits of their roster numbers. They kept asking me to say it again. They asked me five times," recalls Grzecki. "They couldn't believe that such an iconic guy had been killed. Jared was a larger than life personality, someone everyone knew and looked up to." Now he was lying on that mountain, his body covered by a poncho.

"I replay the events of that night in my head, trying to think if there was anything else that I could have done to save my friend. I'm afraid I will never know," confesses Hawes. "I am lucky to have shared many personal moments with Monti in the last days of his life, and I cherish those moments."

Two more speedballs, one with ammunition and the other with batteries and other supplies, were dropped during the night. "SSG Cunningham called over the radio to ask what the plan was for the next morning," recounts Gonterman. "I walked around and realized that there were still bodies left behind. I asked Garner why the bodies were still on the mountain if they evacuated them the previous night. That's when I learned about the cable snapping and that the helicopters were going to come back."

"SSG Cunny told me he needed help getting the bodies consolidated. He and I lined up the four of them so they'd be ready for the helicopters to pick up. A few months later, I asked him why he wanted me and not someone else to help him. It ate at me," confesses Woods. Cunningham told him, "Because I knew you could handle it. I knew you'd be strong enough."

Medevac helicopters returned and dropped four 17-pound rigid plastic Olive Drab Green "Skedco" stretchers for the bodies to be loaded and hoisted.

We know the fate of the four Americans who lost their lives that night. Fallen soldiers have to be in heaven. They've already been through hell.

Cunningham asked the surviving members of the patrol if they wanted to walk down right away or wait to be evacuated by helicopters. They unanimously agreed to walk down. Smith realized he had lost his flak jacket, so they searched around for it. "I found it covering SGT Lybert. I carefully removed it and will never forget just staring at his lifeless body while waiting for the Medevac copter. Once the four casualties were safely on board, we quickly gathered what little stuff we had left and began our descent down the mountain," recalls Gonterman.

Cunningham wanted the patrol to move as quickly as possible down to the Gowardesh bridge. "If there were going to be insurgents coming after us, I knew they would have the high ground advantage," he says. "I can't tell you what a relief it was to have our bombers fly over, tip their wings to us, and watch them drop their payload on the enemy positions in the valley. They made that mountain shake. What a welcomed show of force!" Bombs weighing as much as 2,000 pounds were dropped on the enemy compound. "A little bit of retribution for what happened the previous night," says Paul.

"When the bombers came, I knew we were going to make it out," admits Woods. "The knot in my stomach untied. I wasn't worried that we were going to be hit again. It was a good feeling. When we got to the bottom of the mountain, some guys from Bravo Company met us and asked if we wanted Humvee rides to the Gowardesh Bridge. We were exhausted but said, 'No, thanks.' We were going to finish this together. We wanted to take it on in. Complete the job walking back together."

Garner offers this tribute to Jared: "Most won't know or understand the significance of what you did that day in Gowardesh. The few of us men that were there are the ones who will carry the truth. I saw your true colors when you went to get Bradbury, your soldier. You died trying to save him and us. Your selflessness has inspired me ever since. We said our goodbyes on the mountain and then we brought you home."

SSG Renken knew Jared's death would have a profound impact. He said, "We'll go home and tell stories about him to our families. We'll tell of the bravery we've seen. We can only hope to be half as good as he was."

During the battle, Jared was simultaneously calling for fire, directing his troops, and firing his rifle. "We listened as Chaos 3-5 called round after round on a seemingly endless enemy," recalls SSG Matthew Wolfganger. "I knew it was bad from what they were saying, but it didn't really go through my mind that my friends were out there and could actually be hurt. But at the end of it, they said they had wounded and soldiers killed in action. When the team returned, they gave us the details of what happened."

He adds, "Monti had not only devastated the enemy with a mix of coolness and precision but he had also made the ultimate sacrifice. He had given his life to save one of his own. He was a real hard-nosed NCO. He really demanded a lot out of his guys, but in the end we loved him for it, because he took us from soldiers who were kinda just going through the motions doing our jobs to guys who were passionate about what we were doing. He brought the best out of us. We wanted to be the best because of him. He absolutely loved what he did, and he loved us, his soldiers."

"We kept shooting artillery rounds all night long to let the enemy know we were still there. I heard there were casualties, but I didn't know who they were. I was worrying about doing my job, which was trying to get the rest of the guys home safely. You've got to stay focused on the mission. I was worried about mortars, artillery, rotary wings, and resupply," says Hunsucker. "Later I found out that Monti was killed. Guys were in shock. I was in shock. The soldiers just loved him. He was everything to his guys and to any soldier he came in contact with."

Upon hearing the news, SGT Jeremy Keeler noted, "Today the Army lost a great FISTer, a great NCO, and a truly dedicated soldier. The world lost a great human being."

By coincidence, John Krakauer left to return to the United States the day that Jared was killed. The Dedication to Pat Tillman's book simply states: "In memory of Jared C. Monti, killed in action on June 21, 2006, near Gowardesh, Afghanistan."

The following posting to the legacy.com "Jared Monti Guest Book" by Stephanie Bradbury meant a great deal to Paul and Janet. In it she refers to the two young daughters, Jasmine and Jailynn, whom Brian left behind:

> This is PFC Brian Bradbury's wife. I felt that I needed to thank you for Sgt. Monti's action that day on the mountain. I recently got a letter from Brian's section leader. He stated that Sgt. Monti ran through machine gun fire and rockets to try and pull Brian back to them. I wanted you to know that I am forever indebted to you. Sgt. Monti gave his life trying to save my husband. That is the ultimate sacrifice. It shows a kind of brotherhood that can only be dreamed about over here. Your son was a courageous man and will be remembered forever. One day I will tell my girls about Sgt. Monti and what he did on the mountain.

Paul concludes, “Jared always gave things away to other people. In the end, he gave away his life.”

Part II

The Aftermath

Chapter 15
No One Had an Answer

The crawl moving across the bottom of the CNN News television screen the morning of June 21, 2006, announced that four U. S. Army soldiers had been killed in a ground battle and helicopter accident in Afghanistan. That caught the eye of Patti (Ross) Furtney, whose first thought was about her nephew Jared. She quickly dismissed it, saying, "What are the odds?" As she was showering, she thought about the poor families that were about to get terrible news that day. Little did she know hers would be one of them.

Paul's doorbell rang at 9:45 p.m. while he was relaxing on his couch watching *America's Got Talent*. He wondered who could be calling on him at that time of night. He got up and went to the back door. There was no one there. He looked out and saw a vehicle in the driveway and two men in military dress uniforms walking to the front door. No one uses the front door of Paul's house. Everyone who knows him uses the back door. He realized immediately why they were there. He'd had too many nightmares about that black car pulling into the driveway not to understand. They didn't need to tell him. He cried out, "Not my son! Not my boy!"

Paul got the news that every military parent dreads. Jared had been killed on a mountain in far-off Afghanistan. There was a Casualty Officer along with a Chaplain. "They were talking but I couldn't hear them," he admits. "I was numb. They had a stack of paperwork and they kept asking me to sign things. I didn't know what I was signing. It was a blur. I've talked to other Gold Star families and they've had the same kind of experience when they were given the awful news."

Paul called his ex-wife Janet on the phone in North Carolina, but Niccole, who was three years older than Jared, answered. Paul told her he had to talk to her mother. Niccole could tell the call wasn't about her birthday, which she had just finished celebrating with her friends from work. "I just had a sinking feeling. I knew it was something bad. I knew that before I picked up the phone," said Niccole. Paul said simply, "I need to talk to your mother." Niccole asked, "What's wrong, Dad?" Paul admits, "I guess I was rude to her because I just repeated, 'I have to talk to your mother!' I didn't know what else to do. I didn't want to tell Niccole and then have her be the one to tell Janet. So Niccole finally put Janet on the phone. She just started screaming."

"We were celebrating Niccole's birthday. I can never forgive myself for partying while my son was dying," laments Janet, who had always referred to her children as her "Three Little Chickadees." Now, one of them was gone. "It was the worst night of my life," she recalls, "I was very angry with God. It's Jared walking through the back door unexpectedly, having leave without telling us, and just surprising us. It's his coming up behind me and putting his arms around my shoulders. Those are the things that are gone. Those are the things I'll never get back."

"It's not right for anyone to have to lose a child. It's not the natural order of things. The pain never goes away. It's not the way things are supposed to happen," confesses Paul.

The news immediately affected Niccole who says, "I was in shock. I didn't know what to do. I always knew the potential was there for something bad to happen to Jared. I just never thought it would really happen. I didn't sleep for days. Finally, I fell asleep exhausted on the couch. My Mom and I both felt like being alone but we were alone together. We stayed on separate sides of the house. It was awful."

One relative after another received the word of Jared's death. "Paul called me at 10:50 p.m. It was the worst call I ever received. I tried to hold it together over the phone with him," confessed his sister Marianne (Monti) Riley. "It was such a helpless feeling because I was living in Florida. I broke down later. That's how I always was. As the oldest sister, I'd always try to hold it together with the others. Then I'd allow myself to fall apart in private."

Paul's brother Mike, Jared's godfather, was the first to arrive at his house. He and his wife Duella had been at a Tom Petty concert with an associate from work and his wife. They took a limousine to have a memorable night out. It did turn out to be memorable, but not in a good way. When they got out of the show, Mike's cell phone rang. It was Paul. "All he could say to me was, 'Jared is dead.' I replied, 'You've got to be kidding.' Paul responded with, 'Why would I kid about something like that? Jared is dead.' I didn't know what to say other than, 'I'll get there as soon as I can.' I was in shock," recalls Mike. Because of the crowd at the Comcast Center in Mansfield, MA, it took an hour and a half for them to get out of the parking lot. "It was the longest hour and a half of my life," he admits. "When I got there, we hugged each other and just sat there on the front porch. I didn't know what to do or say, and neither did he." After a while, people started coming and they kept coming. Soon the driveway was full of cars. "I have no idea when I went to bed that night or even if I went to bed that night," admits Paul.

Paul's sister Tricia was already asleep. "The phone rang and my first thought was that something was wrong with one of my five kids. I knew a call that late couldn't be anything good. Paul said, 'He's gone. Jared's dead.' All I could say back was, 'I love you, Paul.' Then I just had to get to the house in Raynham as fast as I could. It was a surreal feeling, like a bad dream. I kept hoping it wasn't real. When I got to his house, I knew it was real."

Jared's younger brother Tim recalls, "It was a day I'll never forget. My Dad called and dropped the bomb on me. I hung up the phone and broke down. I had a million questions. How did my brother die? Did he suffer? Who else was involved? How could this have happened? I drove over my Dad's house and the first person I saw was my Uncle Joe. I just hugged him and cried into his chest. I couldn't stop. I remember his shirt was soaked with my tears."

According to Tim, "Jared was my brother, my hero, and my best friend. He was a constant source of inspiration and strength to me and to everyone who knew him. I love him dearly. He's in my heart, mind and soul every second of every day."

"We spent days and weeks just hugging Paul and each other," recalls his sister Frani (Monti) Harring.

On Janet's side of the family, the reaction was the same. "It was the second day of summer vacation. My nine-year-old son Steven was an honorary bat boy for a Little League baseball team that won a championship that day. They gave him the same trophy as the team members. He was so happy. Steven and my husband Ken were celebrating at a party over at my neighbor's house. I was just relaxing at home on an old broken recliner, the kind that you have to kick hard to get it to close. I got the call from Niccole. I asked if everything was all right. She couldn't speak. I asked again if everything was all right. She was sobbing and finally was able to get out, 'It's Jared. He's been killed,'" said Aunt Patti (Ross) Furtney.

"I wanted to hug her, but she was in North Carolina and I was in Massachusetts. I asked her what I could do. She wanted me to call our side of the family, especially my mother. She said she was going to find Janet in the house and make sure she was all right. I called Ken. He was home in two minutes. The people at the party knew we had a relative in the service. He just said to them, 'It's my nephew.' He didn't have to say anything more," continues Patti. "I was standing there shaking. I had trouble talking. I couldn't remember anyone's phone number. Can you believe that? I needed a phone book to even look up my mother's number. But my eyes were so filled with tears I couldn't read the numbers. Ken had to read them to me. I called her first and she just cried out, 'Oh, no! Oh, no!' It had to have been the worst night of my life."

Marjorie Ross, the sole surviving grandparent, was 80 years old at the time, and adored Jared, her first-born grandson. She posted the following heartbreaking message to him: "My 1st grandson, with a heavy heart I write this letter. I've been reading what others have written about you and how you influenced their lives. You accomplished so much in such a short time. I am so proud of you, Jared. Grandmothers shouldn't outlive their grandchildren. LOVE YOU. MISS YOU. REMEMBER YOU ALWAYS. Bless your heart."

"I later asked Niccole what made her call me rather than any of her other uncles or aunts, recalls Patti. "She said, 'Because I knew you'd know what to do.' I replayed that call in my mind over and over again for years. It haunted me. How could I know what to do? How could anyone?"

Niccole's godmother and Janet's sister Mary reveals, "When we heard the news about Jared, we all cried and hugged each other a lot when we got to North Carolina. You just want to be around family at a time like that. We're still dealing with it. We all knew something could happen to him because he was in Afghanistan. But we just loved him so much."

"The news of Jared's death was just devastating," says his godmother Terri (Ross) Lindsay. I still think of him every day."

"We all feel that with the passing of Jared, we are not to take each other for granted," said Lynda (Ross) Koke. "We pulled together as a family as I have never seen. It taught us all that the time is now. If you want to get together, do it now, not later. That was such a tragedy to hit us, but it truly made the family that much stronger and really brought us even that much closer. I never thought it was possible to get any closer than we had already been."

The Casualty Officer and Chaplain went to Janet's home the next day. "The neighbors were wonderful. They kept bringing food. But I didn't feel like eating anything for days," Janet admits. "When they came to officially give me the news, I was next door at my neighbor's house pruning shrubs for her, just trying to keep busy. They knew where my house was because they saw the Blue Star flag in the window. I walked over to them. It was so sad. Now it's a Gold Star flag. Then I just had to wait for word as to when Jared's body would be flown to the States so we could have a funeral." The Blue Star flag is flown by parents who have a child serving in the military, while the flag with the Gold Star signifies that a child has been lost.

Despite the large size of the two families, neither had ever experienced a tragedy involving one of the children or grandchildren. This was the first, and it hit everyone hard. They all remembered Jared as the soldier in his Army beret sporting a big smile who was adored by his cousins. They asked each other why

God would take one of them. No one had an answer.

A few weeks earlier, Jared's cousin and Paul's goddaughter Michelle had been talking to her friends about her large family and boasted, "I told them I was one of a huge number of cousins and not ONE of them had been ill or gotten a disease or… I paused, and quickly said, 'died,' then knocked on wood as soon as I could. I regretted saying the words as they were coming out of my mouth."

Immediately after learning the news about Jared, Michelle felt compelled to write the following: "I loved my cousin Jared and, of course, am very proud of him. Someone said that he died a hero, fighting with his family, his buddies over there. I know I should focus on remembering that he died doing what he believed in. He was incredibly loyal to the military and a beautiful and compassionate soul. He will be greatly missed from our family, from the military I'm sure, and from this world."

Aunt Rita remarked on the similarity between Jared and his grandfather Joe in a posting: "To you, Jared, the man who will always be our HERO. We miss you more than words can say. Tears fall daily for you and our hearts will never be the same. For those who did not know you, it is a shame, for you had a heart as big as your grandfather's and compassion for all that you met. You gave the ultimate sacrifice without hesitation and will be remembered as a HERO forever. We love and miss you, my friend and nephew."

"Jared had so much of his grandfather in him. He had his compassion and loving spirit. Both would do anything to help anyone," agrees Aunt Jean. "I'm so glad Jared was part of my life. He'll always be part of my life."

"Jared was such a loving person. As a child he'd go around and carefully kiss everyone in the room," says Aunt Marianne. "As an adult, a lasting image I have of him is when his little cousins would climb over him. He'd have them hanging off his arms and his legs. I can remember saying, 'Leave Uncle Jared alone' and he'd say, 'No. No. I like it.' Then he'd flash that ear-to-ear grin of his."

"I expected his uncles and aunts to be affected by Jared's death, but it's been shocking to me to see how much he meant to his cousins," says Paul. Here's a sample of Internet messages to Jared written by some of the generation of over well over 100 cousins he inspired:

Kim Poore: "Jared, You were a family member and friend to so many. There are not words to describe the loss we have all felt, we live such sheltered lives thinking this could never happen to us. You were the best at everything you touched and continue to shine your greatness on us every day. We love you and miss you. Our hero!"

Krystin Cotone: "Jared was my older cousin and someone I admired and looked up to. When I first found out I lost my cousin it didn't seem real and at times it still doesn't. Not a day goes by that I don't think of him and remember all the good he did, not just for his country but for me as well. He was a proud man and I'm honored that he is my cousin. I love you, Jared, and I will always remember.1-4-3."

Lisa Varrasso: "How proud I am to be the cousin of such a great man. I didn't get to see you much after you graduated high school because you answered your calling – to serve your country and help others, and that is how you gave your own life, helping others. I am so proud and honored to be known as your cousin, for you are without a doubt the bravest man I know, and my 3 children will continue to know what a hero you are. There will always be an emptiness in our family that will never be filled. I love you, Jared Christopher Monti."

Leslie Currie: "Ever since we were children, I have been

PROUD to have you as my cousin. As a child, I told all my friends about the cool tricks you could do on a bicycle, and as an adult, I told them all about my handsome cousin in the Army. Today more than ever, I can say that I'm PROUD to have you as my COUSIN. It's nothing new to miss you but now there is no end. I'll cherish all the moments we spent together but always wish there were more. Perhaps someday we'll meet again and finally get to party together like we always said we would (drinks and poker was the plan, right?) Until then, know that I love you and will always be proud of you. XOXO." Leslie recalls fondly, "Jared was always checking up on us, asking us about boyfriends, making sure we were being treated right. He was very protective."

Chapter 16
Jared Comes Home

"The worst part for any Gold Star family is making the arrangements after learning of the death of their child. It was certainly that way for me," concedes Paul. A returning soldier's body is routinely autopsied at Dover Air Force Base in Delaware, where they determine things like whether the cause of death was friendly or enemy fire. The body is flown in from overseas with an Honor Guard accompanying it. It was ten days before Jared's body arrived home. It's a gut-wrenching time, because all you can do is wait. It was a dilemma for Paul. He didn't know whether to stay at home or go to Dover. His niece, Kelley Ebel, and her Marine husband Alex were living in Virginia and volunteered to go to meet the plane as representatives of the family.

After arriving in Massachusetts to make funeral arrangements, Janet planned a quiet night with Tim and Niccole at her friend's house in Raynham to ready herself for the stressful days ahead. It didn't turn out to be so quiet, though. She decided to ease the tension and unwind in a way that she had never done before. "I had a pot party with my kids. I was 58 years old and smoking marijuana for the first time in my life," laughs Janet.

"I asked my Mom if she wanted to give it a try," recalls Tim with a smile. "I told her I was going to get her high. It was the funniest thing I ever saw in my life. She said, 'What's wrong with my mouth? I'm so thirsty.' So we gave her a drink. Then she turned around and said, 'Now I'm really hungry.' She ate turkey, pizza, grapes, anything she could get her hands on. It was a way to bring people together. She had been sobbing uncontrollably for days. Now it's like the burden was lifted. Now she could process it all."

"I learned what cotton mouth and the munchies were," agrees Janet. "It was very educational. I never laughed so hard in my life. Or ate so much." Did she have any regrets about getting high? She responds, "When it was over, the kids reassured me by saying, 'Mom, you needed that!' I think they were right."

Janet does regret one thing."I still have the ashes of Jared's dog J. D. I wish I had thought to bring them with me, to bury them with Jared. I didn't think of it then. He would have liked that," she says.

Paul and Janet drove to Logan Airport to meet the plane when Jared's flag-draped coffin was brought to Boston on a commercial U. S. Airways flight. The motorcade was escorted by a Patriot Guard Riders group and several State Police cars. The airport firefighters lined up in ceremonial fashion as the casket was loaded off the plane and put into a hearse. Paul rode in the back of the hearse, holding his hand on the casket the entire time during the trip to the Prophett-Chapman Funeral Home in Bridgewater, MA. It was as if he were holding his son's hand, as he had done so many times in the past.

"It was a very solemn, horrible night, waiting for the plane with Jared's casket to arrive," recalls Janet. "The bikers were great. They were down-to-earth, considerate people. I really appreciated the fact that they were there. One of them gave me a worry stone as a gift from his mother. I rubbed it all that night and I still have it."

Niccole was deeply affected by the experience at Logan

Airport. She admits, "After that night, airports haunted me for a couple of years. I couldn't get the thought of that night out of my mind. Even listening to a plane flying in the sky bothered me. It was terrible."

"I had always looked up to Jared, but I also looked up to Niccole, says Tim of his sister. "She was so cool. She was into heavy rock music. I liked to hang around her and her friends. She always took me under her wing the same way that Jared did. The three of us got along really well."

The Patriot Guard Riders is a motorcycle group that was formed in 2005 in Mulvane, Kansas by American Legion Post 136 to shelter and protect the deceased's family against protesters from the Westboro Baptist Church, whose members claim that the deaths of American troops in Iraq and Afghanistan are divine retribution for American tolerance of homosexuality. Paul is incensed that a religious organization is involved in such protests. He later said in a vigil for fallen soldiers held at Boston Common, "I'd just like this pastor to know the grief he causes for these families of the men and women who are fighting to protect his freedom of speech and religion. And if that's not enough, he should look to God, to pray for these men and women who made their sacrifice."

PGR members physically shield mourners at funerals from the protesters by blocking their view with their motorcade or by holding up American flags. The group also drowns out protester chants by singing patriotic songs or revving their motorcycle engines. The PGR attend the funerals of members of the armed forces, firefighters, and police at the invitation of the deceased's family. The organization says it is open to anyone as long as they have "a deep respect for those who serve our country."

There were four sets of visiting hours for Jared's wake at the funeral home. People crowded 30 to 40 deep on the porch outside, and the line stretched down the sidewalk for those waiting to pay their respects to him and the family.

"It was so unreal seeing Jared's body at his wake," says Aunt Terri. "He looked like he was sleeping in his full dress uniform." According to Janet, "A Gold Star mother presented me with the symbolic figurine of a mother holding the American Flag. She wanted to be anonymous so she gave it to someone to give to me. That was my introduction to being a Gold Star parent." It's a club no one wants to join. Sadly, once you do become a member, you're a member for the rest of your life. It's a permanent appointment, like checking into a real-life, nightmarish "Hotel California".

According to Jared's 82nd Airborne Platoon Mom Elaine Harmon, "When Janet called to tell me Jared had been killed, that was the worst day of my life. After I learned of the heroic way he died, I just thought, 'That's so typically Jared.' I'll never forget walking up to his casket at his wake and staring at his body saying, 'Oh, Jared, how I wish I could change places with you.' From that time forward, I've never left my house without making sure that I'm wearing one of Jared's remembrance bracelets."

At the wake, Jared's Aunt Tricia tucked a piece of paper inside his uniform coat pocket. It was the following poem written by her twelve-year-old daughter Brianna and signed with a big heart:

Jared was the best
It's time now he takes his rest,
The Gift of God was his name
Now without him it's just not the same,
He will shine down on us from above
As we cherish our memories with love,
He had a heart of gold
And you would never doubt

Jared was the best inside and out,
No words can describe how wonderful he was
As a son, nephew, uncle, and cuz,
There will always be that empty spot in my chest
Jared was the very best.
♥Brianna

Jared's funeral mass was celebrated at 8 a.m. on July 1, 2006 at St. Ann's Church in Raynham. The procession from the funeral home was again led by a motorcade of State Police troopers and the PGR. His casket, draped in the American flag, was carried by a Military Honor Guard as police and uniformed members of the military held flags and saluted. Jared's sister Niccole offered the eulogy, her brother Tim at her side, her voice accompanied by the sound of people sobbing throughout the church:

> "Jared Monti, the boy with that sheepish grin that lit up every room he walked in. The kid who we would joke had nine lives. The kid that always got himself into a jam but somehow found a way out of it. Like the time when he was a small boy and tried to jump over a wooden fence at our first house and got his sweatshirt hood caught on a picket and dangled for hours before a neighbor finally found him. The many times when he was deployed and was being shot at by enemy fire, but somehow escaped, unharmed. I think it was why we were so shocked to learn he wasn't coming home alive. I guess his nine lives had finally run out.
>
> "I remember shortly after his death when a distraught relative called me on the phone and asked, '*Why???!!!* Why did he have to choose the military as his career? Why did he have to choose something that always put his life at risk?' Well, I am here to tell you why. Much like the

priesthood, it was his calling. Jared always felt compelled to help the underdog. Whether it was beating up the bullies at school when the smaller kids were picked on, or giving children in Kosovo rides to school in his Humvee because they were being harassed, that's just who Jared was. He chose a career where he could stand up and fight for those who are not capable of fighting for themselves.

"There are many stories of his heroism and his kind heart. He was extremely humble. He earned medals for his heroic military deeds which we didn't even know about until he passed away. He gave his Bronze Star to me one night. I didn't want to take it, but he explained to me that he really wanted me to have it. To him, it was nothing more than a sad reminder. He told me that he killed fathers, sons, and brothers to get it, and that's not something he was proud of.

"Whenever he was deployed, he would receive many CARE packages from us. We sent him food, candy, clothing, and many, many items. But instead of keeping them, he gave them to the people who were much less fortunate. He only took leave one time for a holiday. Why? Because he would give his leave to those who wanted to go home and see their children. There was the time his roommate came home and realized they no longer had a kitchen table. I remember he said his roommate was pissed. But that anger went away as soon as Jared told him he had given the table and chairs to a fellow soldier who couldn't afford to buy one, and his kids had no place to sit and eat their food.

"As many stories I could tell you about the kind things he did for others, there were lots of funny stories that would have me on the floor laughing. There is one in particular that I remember well. His platoon went on a long run in frigid weather. Not too long into that run, he realized he had to go to the bathroom. And it wasn't number one. Well, you can't exactly tell the officer in charge to stop the run because you have to go. So, he did what any other self-controlled, honorable, disciplined soldier would do. He crapped his pants. I'm not sure if you are aware of what happens when bodily discharge exits your body when it is below freezing, but it ain't cute! At some point they came to a stop and rested, and it wasn't long before the officer noticed him walking funny. So he yelled, 'Monti! What the hell is wrong with you?' And Jared yelled back in all seriousness, and I quote, 'Sir, I have shitsickles!' The officer, not quite understanding, asked 'You have *what*?' And Jared answered again, and again I quote, 'Sir, I have shitsickles! I crapped my pants over an hour ago and it's been frozen to my ass ever since!' The officer ran up to Jared and got in his face. He yelled, 'Monti! You're the toughest son of a bitch I know!'

"I could go on and on about the stories I have heard. And I am sure we will all hear many more. And as much as my heart is broken, and as much as I will miss him, I know he died doing exactly what he wanted to do. I can say that I feel truly comforted by the fact that I will see him again one day. But for now, I know I have a soldier up in Heaven watching out for me."

"I was proud of Niccole's eulogy. She did an incredible job," says Janet.

Aunt Terri, Jared's godmother, read a Bible verse, as did Mike Monti, his godfather. Rev. Michael K. McManus then gave the homily, referring to a gospel passage telling how Jesus healed a servant upon the request of a kind Roman Centurion. He likened the Centurion to Jared, describing his generosity and compassion towards others.

"He recognized the need to reach out to those most in need, to those whom everyone else ignored," Rev. McManus said, "And he paid the ultimate price by trying to save the soldiers in his care. He fulfilled the roles that God had asked of him, and he has left us far too young, but he has left us doing what he loved."

Jared's funeral marked the first time in 57 years that the Bourne National Cemetery was opened on a Saturday. Despite the fact that it was the peak traffic July 4th weekend at one of the nation's most popular vacation spots, the major highways and the bridge leading to Cape Cod were closed for the procession, which consisted of over 300 vehicles. Cars were stopped on the roads as people got out to watch. Bystanders saluted and waved as the motorcade heading to the cemetery passed them by. "None of us knew how so many people could have found out about the funeral, but somehow they did. They were waiting for us to come by," says Michelle.

"It was during the funeral that I realized the enormity of who we were burying," admits Paul's sister Tricia. Many dignitaries were there, including then-Governor Mitt Romney, who would go on to run for President against Barack Obama in the 2012 Presidential Election.

Unfortunately, representatives from the Westboro Baptist Church tried to protest at the funeral. The Patriot Guard Riders were there, though, to protect the mourners. They set up a barricade and kept the church parishioners across the street and far from the proceedings. "It was amazing to see the PGR there. They were great. They pushed the protesters away and then saluted all of us," recalls Tricia, with tears in her eyes.

Brigadier General Mark Brown conducted the ceremony at the National Cemetery in Bourne where Jared was laid to rest. Many of those attending held American flags tied with yellow ribbons. A three-shot salute was fired by the six members of the Honor Guard, and then "Taps" was played. The flag draped on the coffin was removed and carefully folded before it was presented to the family. It was put in the triangular box that is all-too-familiar to Gold Star parents.

"My heart has a huge hole in it which will never be filled. Jared was a good man with a kind and gentle heart. His good deeds, patriotism, and loving nature will live on forever," says Paul. "My son was my hero. He loved his country. He was a dedicated soldier, but he was also a very compassionate human being. He exemplified who all of us would want to have as a child. Someone who really cares, not someone out for personal glory." Army Chief of Staff General George W. Casey, Jr. later consoled Paul Monti at Jared's gravesite.

Aunt Mary (Ross) Currie recalls, "We were in awe of the funeral. It was impressive to say the least. But it was also very sad. It was so hard to believe that Jared was gone."

Massachusetts Fourth Congressional District Representative Barney Frank read into the Congressional Record, "I attended a funeral where I heard about a particularly impressive young man, SFC Jared Monti. I was struck then by the impact he had on virtually everyone who knew him, and the magnitude of our loss as a community was clear. His parents have the knowledge that I hope will be comforting at some level at some point that the rest of the world now knows what a wonderful man he was, and the pride they felt in his accomplishments has become a matter in which our whole country takes pride."

Jared's fame and visibility is a mixed blessing. While it enables Paul to do charitable work and fundraising for worthy causes, there's a loss of privacy. He describes it this way: "It's phenomenal. He'll be remembered for all time. But I've had to take my beloved son and give him to the rest of the world, and that's a little difficult for me."

Aunt Marti and Uncle Tony had a phone conversation with Jared just before he was deployed to Afghanistan. He said, "Don't worry about me. I'll be fine. I think I might come home after this tour and be a school teacher. Maybe I'll settle down and have kids like yours." According to Marti, "Jared would have been a great father. It's just heartbreaking that he never got the chance."

Just days after his death, Marti posted this message to him: "I know you know how much you were loved. At the end of our phone conversation just before you left for duty, I said I loved you and you said, 'I know, Aunt Marti, and I love you, too.' Those few words will remain in my heart and soul forever. I am so proud to have been your Aunt. You are my hero. All my love, forever and for always."

Tony also referred to that call when he wrote, "Jared, I will never forget our last conversation on the phone. But I know I'll miss that smile of yours. You are a true hero and a great nephew. I know you are in great hands where you are. Love you."

Cousin Michelle returned to Jared's gravesite several weeks after the funeral and wrote this account to him: "I had a 'picnic' at your gravesite. I brought a mat, and water, and food. But I was the only one who ate. It is pretty, where you are. The cemetery is peaceful, green, and pleasant. We remember you, all of us do. My daughter gets excited every time she sees a person in uniform. 'Look, a soldier!' she says. You even affected her in your death…I feel sadness for the end of a beautiful life, because you lived it so gracefully, and generously, and humbly, that we didn't want it to end so abruptly. But you've given us all a standard to try to live up to."

It wasn't until July 6, 2007 that Aunt Annie (Monti) Eagles was able to post this tribute: "For over a year now, I have tried to find the right words to honor Jared. There are none. There is no word big enough to reach the heights of the commitment, dedication, and honor that Jared felt for each of his family members, friends, country, and those he helped around the world. There is nothing that can adequately explain the courage and strength he displayed to those who served under him, over him, and around him. His parents have earned more respect and admiration than I could ever express, because they gave this hero the tools he used so well in his day-to-day commitment to us all, the strength of his compassion, the comfort he allowed us to feel. I was lucky enough to be his aunt, his friend, and the recipient of his efforts to keep us free and protect our rights. God Bless Jared and all that he stands for."

Chapter 17
Maybe it Happens to Everyone

Jared's family and friends heard the story about how, during the trek up the mountain, he talked about wanting a Viking funeral. So, they arranged to give him one the night before his official funeral at the Bourne Cemetery. They took an old boat, loaded it with flammables, and launched it on a lake near Taunton. It was a private gathering filled with good cheer. It was a way for them to blow off steam. It was a celebration of Jared's life.

The police were alerted in advance that there was going to be a boat set on fire as a tribute to a fallen soldier. People were smoking cigars, drinking, and laughing. According to cousin Michelle, "It felt so weird to laugh during that time, because we were in so much pain and grieving so much."

A small, old, beaten-up, white dinghy was donated. The name *SS Jared Monti* was painted on the transom. As was the custom with Viking funerals, people filled the boat with items to be taken into the afterlife. In this case, it included letters, e-mails, flowers, three bottles of Jared's favorite drink Jack Daniels, and a sandwich so he wouldn't be hungry. It was also a Viking tradition that a dog statue or carving be at the front of the funeral boat, so someone put a hot dog in Jared's.

Lighting the fire turned out to be a challenge. Charlie Witkus, along with Paul and Tim, took a second boat out and kept trying, while onlookers laughed and called out suggestions. Finally, lighter fluid did the trick and a funeral pyre was created. By the next morning, the fire had burned out, leaving only one small piece of the boat that had not been consumed. Incredibly, it was the transom with Jared's name on it. Tim retrieved it and gave it to Paul, who said, "I was in awe when I saw the wood." There wasn't a charred mark on it. Paul still keeps it upstairs in his house in Jared's closet.

"The Viking Funeral is a pretty special memory, because we gave Jared what he mentioned in passing he would have liked. We all believe that he wouldn't have wanted any of the formal attention that he continues to receive, but he probably would have appreciated that night as much as we did," comments Michelle.

"He made me laugh a lot, because he was so funny," said Cassidy Witkus, the niece of Charlie Witkus. Cassidy was at the Viking funeral but was too young to understand the significance of it. She claimed, however, that she was with Jared at his "family party." "Me and Jared were sitting on the blanket together, watching fireworks," Cassidy said with the innocence of a six-year-old. "She claims she saw him," admits her mother Melissa, "and it made me feel good to think that." Melissa herself later posted this on Jared's web site: "I thought I saw you driving the other day and for a split second, just that one moment, all was right with the world again!"

Paul maintains, "I am not the least bit superstitious. Not at all. I don't mind walking under ladders or crossing in front of black cats. I don't believe any of that stuff. But I have to start questioning myself after what happened after Jared's death."

The day after Jared's funeral, Paul was working in his garden and noticed a chrysalis on the handle of the wheelbarrow he was using. He thought it was strange that a butterfly would build a chrysalis there. When the day was over, he went in the house and left the wheelbarrow out. The next morning, he noticed the chrysalis again, but this time it was all black. "I was kind of mad at myself, because I thought I left the wheelbarrow out in the hot sun and that had killed the butterfly inside," he admits. "I went into the house. When I came back out about an hour later, on the handle of the wheelbarrow, a monarch butterfly was blowing up its wings." The monarch takes its name from King Edward III of England.

"It was as if my Jared had come back to me saying, 'Here I am, Dad. Now I can fly.' He had always wanted to fly," says Paul. What followed turned out to be much more than just a single poignant moment.

That butterfly stayed in the yard the entire summer. In fact, no matter where they went, there was the butterfly. They went down to Duxbury Beach, and there on the beach appeared a monarch butterfly. The beach is big and wide open. Not a place where you'd expect to find a butterfly. Suddenly coming across the water, though, was a monarch butterfly. Paul asked rhetorically, "What are you doing here?"

Another time, they were out on a boat in the middle of the ocean and there appeared a monarch butterfly. Paul wondered, "How can this be here?"

One of Jared's former Lieutenants, Erik Jorgensen, invited Paul to represent Jared at his wedding in Westfield, in the western part of Massachusetts. The wedding was held outside in a rose garden. When the bride and groom walked down the aisle and took their place beside the Reverend, a monarch butterfly flew around them and then around the crowd. Then it disappeared.

"Everywhere I went that summer there was a monarch butterfly. It didn't matter where it was," recalls Paul. On one occasion, he was in a rock quarry pursuing his hobby of collecting gems and minerals. It was a huge quarry, at least five football fields long and 1½ football fields wide. Nothing but rocks. No vegetation. Nothing there. And, sure enough, a Monarch butterfly appeared and flew around Paul. One of his friends went back to that quarry a week later. Paul got a call on his cell phone and his friend asked if he had lost something. He responded, "Well, come to think of it, I left one of my kneeling pads."The friend indicated he was working at the quarry when all of a sudden a monarch butterfly flew around his head and landed on a rock. He didn't pay attention to it, but then it came around again and went around a corner. He was curious as to what the butterfly was doing. He followed it to a rock and it stopped. Just below the rock was Paul's kneeling pad. It was sort of like an episode of *Lassie* when the dog leads Mom to Timmy, who'd fallen down the well. Paul replied, "Wait a minute, that's not possible." But that's how it happened.

Janell Holmes, one of Jared's high school classmates and an administrator of his Scholarship Foundation, was in a parking lot talking to someone on her cell phone about a donation. She recalls having a monarch butterfly start to fly around her head the moment the call began and then having it fly away the moment the call was over.

"We continued to have the same experiences. It happened again in another rock quarry later that summer. We went to Florida. There were monarch butterflies flying around there. It didn't matter. Everywhere we went, they were around. Maybe it's just a coincidence. Maybe it happens to everybody. I don't know. Maybe it was a sign he's out there flying," ponders Paul.

As a result of those strange experiences, Paul decided to create a butterfly garden for Jared in the backyard. His brothers and sisters gave him a granite bench engraved with Jared's name. It fit perfectly into the garden, and Paul has maintained it since.

Aunt Jean says, "We haven't lost Jared. He's still with us. My granddaughter Apryl was only 1 lb. 4 ounces when she was born in the summer of 2013. I asked him to help keep her alive. I put one of his mementos in her incubator at the hospital. She's got his spirit. She's a fighter just like him." After spending her first 100 days in the hospital, she's now doing well, topping the scales at 15 pounds. What does her bedroom look like? Jean exclaims, "We've covered it in butterflies, of course!"

There have also been instances of possible "Pennies from Heaven." Once again, Paul begins by saying, "Maybe this has happened to me my whole life and I never really noticed. I don't know. What I do know is that it seems like wherever I've gone since 2006, I've seen pennies. It started when I happened to look down on a deserted dirt trail in Washington State. I thought it was unusual. But, I've seen pennies in the most unlikely places since then."

His sister Tricia says, "Many members of the family have seen those pennies, including me. My son Nicholas had a dream recently about Jared, and when he woke he swears Jared was in his room. I'm a believer."

A year later, Niccole posted this similarly-themed message to Jared: "I miss you so much. I think about you every single day. And I know Carys still sees you, because she's always telling me that Uncle Jared was tickling her with Elmo. It breaks my heart, though, that the two of you will never have that special uncle/niece relationship I always hoped for. You would have adored her, Jared. And I know she would have adored you as well."

Niccole says, "Some people believe this stuff and some just think it's a coincidence. It doesn't matter. I know I believe it. I once asked Carys what her uncle was wearing when he was tickling her and she described his uniform in perfect detail."

"I think about Jared all the time, says Janet. "Coming home from the supermarket, on my way to the bank, everywhere I go, everything I do. It never ends. There are signs and symbols everywhere. The other day, I looked up and saw four big birds in the sky, and I immediately thought of the four fallen soldiers who died on the mountain."

When Jared was killed, Kevin asked his mother Marti if he could get a tattoo in Jared's honor. She asked Kevin to do her a favor and wait until after he graduated from high school. He had a design all planned out with Jared's initials on it. When the time came, Marti took Kevin to get that tattoo on his arm.

On March 17, 2010, a special memorial event was held to honor Jared and his family at the 69th Regiment Armory in New York City. The host of the evening, The American Fallen Soldiers Project, is a 501c3 non-profit organization that makes available at no cost to a Gold Star family an original portrait of their fallen loved one that "fully captures their appearance and personality." During the ceremony, the organization's founder and artist, Phil Taylor, presented Paul with an original portrait of Jared, and several other family members who attended were given smaller replicas. Upon receiving her portrait, Janet said, "It's like you're looking at him. It just captures him perfectly." (Jared's portrait is shown on the back cover of this book.)

After attending the ceremony for Jared, Aunt Marti asked the artist's wife, Lisa, if she could get a full-size reproduction to go along with the smaller version she had received. Six months went by, and Marti had pretty much forgotten about the request. At the same time, she had been thinking about getting a tattoo like Kevin to honor Jared. "I was 50-something years old and getting my first tattoo," says Marti. "It was going to be a little Purple Heart on my right foot. I made an appointment for a Saturday. The day before I was going to get it done, a huge box arrived. I carefully started to pull the picture out of the box, and as I did, I locked eyes with Jared. Those eyes in the portrait are just so life-like. I swear I could hear him saying, 'I know what you're doing. You're getting a tattoo for me. That's pretty cool. Thanks, Aunt Marti.' I believe he's watching over us. He knows everything we do." Marti got that tattoo and will proudly show it off on request.

In 2006, Phil Taylor, a professional artist for over 25 years, learned that a childhood friend, Captain Blake Russell, had been killed in Iraq. While attending the funeral and hearing about Blake's dedication to his soldiers, he decided to paint a portrait of his friend and give it to the Russell family. Upon seeing the painting, Captain Russell's father broke down crying and said, "I feel like you've brought him home to me." Through this painting and the unexpected gift of healing it brought the family, Phil and Lisa founded The American Fallen Soldiers Project in 2007. Since then, hundreds of portraits have been given to families of America's heroes who gave their lives in the Afghanistan and Iraq Wars. The portraits may be viewed, and donations made, at the foundation's web site, www. AmericanFallenSoldiers.com.

Acknowledging how much Jared loved mountains and, of course, that the name "Monti" comes from the Italian word for mountain, Paul decided to honor his son by climbing South Baldface Mountain in New Hampshire. The mountain is not for beginners, because there are no trails. At 3,682 feet it's a real climb. Yet it was doable for a man approaching 60 years old who was a former school teacher and did not climb on a regular basis.

"It was October, and it was freezing cold and windy. It was a tough climb for me, but I'm so glad I did it. I just had a feeling that Jared was there with me. It meant so much to me that I went and did it again the next year," says Paul.

Chapter 18
Monti's Place

Kristen, the widow of LTC Joe Fenty, killed in the helicopter crash in Afghanistan, wrote an evocative e-mail to Paul shortly after Jared's death: "My husband, too, was killed last year. He was the 3-71 Squadron Commander. He felt lucky to have Jared in his unit.... Not knowing your son, I heard his name often. He was, and still is, so well-respected.... During his leave, 3-71 CSM Del Byers came to visit me. He spoke about my husband, but he also spoke about Jared, what a great soldier, leader, and man he was, and how terribly he is missed. Your son made a lasting impression on many people. As you likely know, there is a Camp named after him and his name is spoken and written daily. Also, there is not a family from 3-71 who is not aware of his contributions and the effect his loss has had on their soldier. I do believe our soldiers are pulling strength from Jared and my husband Joseph and that they are inspired by the memory of Jared. He is a true and courageous hero."

"The day Jared was killed, my husband Keith called and told me that he saw his name on a list that came across his desk. I collapsed on the floor of my living room. I didn't know what to do. A part of me died that day. I wish heaven had a phone so I could hear Jared's voice again," says Eden Barber. Her husband Keith, now a Sergeant First Class, is on his sixth overseas deployment and plans to retire in 2015.

Matthew Hatfield says, "I'll never forget how I was at a training camp at West Point when I found out my friend had gotten killed. I learned it by e-mail. There was just an explosion of e-mails throughout the Army when word got out that Jared had died a hero. That part didn't surprise me at all. Jared never thought about how many Taliban he could kill today. He wasn't like that. It was more like, How can I do my job today?"

Matthew, now a MSG, posted this tribute to Jared: "You were my leader, my comrade, and my friend. I hope that I have become half the soldier that you were. There are many who talk the talk but so few that walk the walk. You, my dear friend, walk the walk. I know in my heart that you gave them hell. I know you did because I would have done the same. That's how you taught me to be. I will pass on the warrior spirit to my paratroopers that you passed on to me. I love you, brother."

A couple of days prior to the patrol leaving on the Hill 2610 mission, Joe Hansen was preparing to travel south to the Korengal Valley to take command of the Battery there. He talked to Jared about the things that soldiers talk about. "We were sitting on the edge of our cots, elbows on our knees, our heads hung down while we spoke," recalls Captain Hansen. "We knew what we were. What we are. What we were doing here in Afghanistan. He was proud of his boys, and I told Jared I was proud of him. Getting up, he grabbed his kit and headed out on another patrol. I told Monti to take care of himself, not knowing that I would never see him again. You never do. I can picture him still, grin and all. He responded with, 'See you on the high ground, sir.'"

Referring to the previous conversation, Joe wrote after Jared's death: "I say to you now what I could not then, that I hold you in awe. In awe of your nobility, your courage and your unfailing compassion for your men and these people of Afghanistan. It is because of men such as Jared Monti that we are who we are. Who we could be. Sergeant Monti was an American soldier, he was a leader of men and he was my brother. He was that which makes us salute when we see our nation's flag and cry when we remember. It is men such as Sergeant First Class Jared Monti that makes me proud to be an American Soldier. It has been my greatest privilege and my honor to serve alongside you, Monti. I'll see YOU on the high ground."

"That is what Jared and his memory means to me. I ensure that those who serve under me continue to remember that," concludes Joe, currently a Major and Executive Officer of the 6-37 Field Artillery at Camp Casey in South Korea.

Stephanie Hansen, Joe's wife, posted this remembrance of Jared: "There are not many days that go by that something does not remind me of this man. Things that are said, a face in the crowd of soldiers, an accent from Massachusetts, a kind-hearted fellow. I see and hear him and am sad for this world's loss still."

According to John Hawes, "Although Monti's death was tragic and unexpected, it was not in vain. His loss affected every soldier in our Squadron and made them more vigilant and aware on every future mission. Everyone in the entire unit became much more proactive and on guard. We got the jump on the enemy numerous times before they could attack us, and the Squadron became much more successful because of it. This was all due to the awareness and vigilance, and in a small way seeking revenge for Monti's death," says John, who goes on to add, "I know that I learned from Monti's courageous and selfless example that night, and try my best to tell others and teach and motivate them by his example."

Unfortunately, Jared was not going to be the only friend of

John's to give his life for his country. CPL Michael Mayne was killed in Iraq on February 23, 2009. John had been his Eagle Scout mentor and Best Man at his wedding. "Mike joined the Army largely because of me. We shared many great times together. I had e-mailed him four hours before I got the call he was killed. He never got to read it," admits John. "For myself and many of the rest of us, every day is Memorial Day."

The loss of their NCO affected everyone in the unit. "There is so much to say about you," says SPC Villaverde. "You were an awesome leader. An outstanding soldier and a mentor. I looked up to you. I still look up to you. I know you're in a better place now but I'll never forget you, man. You'll always be in my thoughts and my prayers. What you did that night will never be forgotten. We miss you. I know you're watching down on us. We'll make you proud."

"As soon as I got the news about Jared, I called our friend Charlie Witkus," said Chris Costa back in the United States. "We talked about Jared and I can tell you this, we already knew how he died. Even before the reports were in. He died trying to rescue someone. Without a shadow of a doubt I knew it and Charlie knew it. If something happened to my friend it would happen while he was trying to save someone else. I have known Jared for 25 years and he is the bravest man I ever met." Chris Costa later offered this tribute: "I lost a friend but the world gained a hero."

Charlie admits he never opened up much about his feelings when Jared died. But when his son was born, he named him after Jared. "It was so I'll never forget my friend," he confesses.

Jared's cousin, Jason Eagles, says, "When this happened, I wasn't surprised. When you go off to war, this can always happen. It can happen to anybody. At first, I would think, 'Why him?' There are thousands of soldiers out there. Then, the more I thought about it, the more it made sense. When their position started getting over-run, most people would take cover and call in the air support like he did, following protocol. No one would think twice about it. No one would call you a coward for doing that. But, for whatever reason Jared would say, 'That's not enough. There's a chance I can get out there and save this person, whereas my air support may not get here quick enough.' So, you kind of have to look at yourself as a person and ask if you'd do that same thing. No one really knows until they're in that situation. When I read the story, I said, 'Yeah, that's what he would do.' If someone was hurt, he would help you. If someone didn't feel like they belonged, he would help you. At the end of the day, he was always there for you."

Jared loved playing games that built camaraderie and emphasized team play. He was competitive, but in a friendly, fun way. Shortly after June 21, some of the forward observers and cavalry scouts set up a picnic table, a little recreation area, a horseshoe pit, and put up a sign with the words "Monti's Place". After chow, they'd go out and play. It was a quiet place to relax and have some fun. Especially after the ambush on the mountain, the soldiers in the unit became even closer and tended to stick together.

When SSG Cunningham and SGT Hawes re-enlisted for another Afghanistan tour, they chose to do the ceremony under Jared's sign next to an American flag. They were surrounded by the soldiers who had been with the patrol that day. They had a forward observer and a sniper hold up the flag. According to Hawes, "It was a way for us to honor Jared's sacrifice. He gave his life for the team, our men, and the Army. We were re-enlisting for the team, our men, and the Army. We used the flag that I carried under my body armor during the fight on the mountain. I carried it with me for the rest of my military service. That flag means a lot to me. It became sort of a tradition." A number of other members of the squadron re-enlisted in front of that flag at Monti's Place.

SSG Brendan Kearns expresses his admiration this way: "For a lot of people, the values that we live are just words. Jared Monti actually lived those words. They became a part of him. He would do whatever it took to take care of his boys and that's what happened that day. Anyone who had spent time with this guy knows they were touched by an angel who now sits on his Observation Post watching us."

MSG Lee Power said, "I was watching Armed Forces Network news in Iraq and saw the story about Jared's death. I couldn't believe it. It took the wind right out of me. All his colleagues will tell you it was a blow to them when they heard he fell. It surprised me to hear that he died, but it didn't surprise me to learn how he died.

"He was also a lot of fun to be around. He knew when to laugh and when to get serious and tighten the screws. He'd do anything to protect his soldiers. To hear he sacrificed himself came as no surprise. That's who he was every day, all day. He was so full of life, I knew just one of the enemy could never take him down. It took 50-60 Taliban all focusing fire on him to do it."

On June 23, 2006, Jared was awarded the Purple Heart, a unique medal in that it signifies just one thing – sacrifice. It means a service member was either killed or suffered a wound in action that required treatment by a medical officer. It cannot be earned by exceptional deeds or achievement. It represents the fact that blood was shed in defense of America.

Jared's Purple Heart certificate reads, "This is to certify that the President of the United States of America has awarded the Purple Heart, established by General George Washington at Newburgh, New York, August 7, 1782, to SFC Jared C. Monti, United States

Army, for wounds received in action on 21, June 2006." It is signed by the Adjutant General and the Secretary of the Army.

George Washington had hoped to have a way of recognizing meritorious actions by his soldiers. He issued an order authorizing the "Badge of Military Merit" stating it "was to be retroactive to the earliest stages of the war, and to be a permanent one." But he wound up giving heart-shaped pieces of purple cloth to only three Revolutionary War veterans, and the award was soon forgotten.

What we now know as the Purple Heart had its inception in an effort to honor the Father of our Country. On February 22, 1932, the 200th anniversary of Washington's birth, the Army introduced the modern Purple Heart, which bears his profile on its face and credits him with presenting those first awards.

The Army immediately embraced the new medal and made it retroactive, allowing World War I veterans who had been wounded in action to exchange previously received Meritorious Service Citation Certificates for the new Purple Hearts.

On December 3, 1942, President Franklin D. Roosevelt issued an Executive Order authorizing the Purple Heart to be given to sailors and Marines wounded or killed on or after December 6, 1941 so that Pearl Harbor veterans would be eligible. At the same time he restricted the Purple Heart for award only to those killed or wounded in combat. Until that time, some Purple Hearts were given for meritorious service as well as for wounds received in action. Later, President Harry Truman extended the period for retroactive award back to 1917, allowing Naval and Marine Corps veterans of World War I to be eligible.

Medal of Honor recipient 1st Lieutenant Robert Howard was wounded a total of 14 times in 54 months of duty during the Viet Nam War. He received four Bronze Stars and a record nine Purple Hearts. As with other military medals, his original purple heart is decorated with eight oak leaf clusters indicating subsequent awards. Howard wound up dying of cancer in 2009 and is buried at Arlington National Cemetery.

Jared was initially recognized with his second Bronze Star. Chris Cunningham began the Medal of Honor recommendation process to upgrade of the Bronze Star by writing an account of the terrible night on the mountain and the heroism shown by his friend. SSG Chris Cunningham, SSG Patrick Lybert, and SGT John Hawes were presented with Silver Stars; SPC John Garner, SSG Chris Grzecki, SPC Sean Smith, and SPC Matthew Chambers were awarded Bronze Stars with "Valor" devices; SPC Franklin Woods, SPC Brian Gonterman, SPC Max Noble, PFC Brian Bradbury, PFC Derek James, SPC Shawn Heistand, SPC Daniel Linnihan, and SSG Josh Renken all earned Army Commendation Medals with "Valor" devices for the their exemplary performance under fire.

"I just wish I could work with those guys forever. I've been in the military for 16 years now. I've never worked with another group like that. The best group you could possibly ask for. I'd put them up against anybody. They were at their best in the shittiest of circumstances," states Franklin Woods.

The following is from Jarred Wesley's Facebook post: "I met great guys in Afghanistan. One in particular was a down-to-earth FISTer who was an E-5 NCO. Damn good soldier and crazy as all hell, with a great sense of humor. Upon landing in Afghanistan he and his squad were attached to another unit and I didn't see him again until near the end. He then went on to another base, and I didn't see him again till years later when we were back in Afghanistan and he was with the division that was relieving us, ending my second deployment. He was there just in time to make my promotion to SGT E-5. After I was pinned, the NCO of my unit welcomed me into the NCO Corp by marching me into this crappy tent, holding me against a dusty broke refrigerator, forming a line and promptly pounding my stripes so deep into my collar bone that it took me 30 min. to remove them at the end. When it was his turn, my brother in the other division, Jared Monti, decided to do a running start superman double-punch to the rank on my collar practically breaking the bone as congratulations on my promotion. Lol. After that, my unit redeployed back stateside. About two months later, Monti was in a serious firefight in which he sacrificed his own life to save another."

He adds, "Jared was a hell of a trooper."

John Reardon, Jared's friend from the bison and broken wrist incidents at Ft. Riley, suffered a fatal heart attack in 2011. Colin Farrow, one of their mutual friends, posted this message to Jared: "Hey Buddy! Was thinking about you at John Reardon's funeral. Seems the old cliché about how only the good die young holds some water. Miss you and John both, but I know you guys are watching over us. Rock steady, Bro!"

David Caldwell posted: "Went to my second 13F graduation today. You are mentioned now in each ceremony. Look out for these guys, some of them are gonna need it. The boys from Massachusetts knew who you were before I got the chance to smoke 'em and one of the instructors who never met you told me you are his hero. You are still inspiring FISTers every day. It pains me to think of all these soldiers who will never get the honor of knowing you personally and serving under your leadership. I try to emulate you but know I fall considerably short. Wish you were here."

He also wrote to Jared's family, "Thank you, Paul, Janet and the Monti clan, for raising a true man and brother-in-arms. The world is a better place for having had him among us."

Jared's former room-mate at Fort Bragg Jeff Bolding wrote: "I think about you all the time, bro. Especially on this day, June 21. At first, I'm sad because I miss the crazy things you would do and the crazy situations you would always get into. Then I smile, because I have those memories to remind me of you. Now you are not just 'famous' to everyone that knew you, but to the world. I always thought that Jared Monti would be remembered. Now, I know you will. Airborne, all the way!"

Jared's High School wrestling coach, Stan Holmes, had this to say: "I tried to instill the idea that if you're going to do anything, you do it to the best of your ability. You sacrifice whatever you have to. Jared certainly went on to demonstrate that. He sacrificed his life to try to save someone else."

Erik Jorgensen posted this message to Jared: "It's going on a year since we got back and almost two since we lost you. I'll never forget that June day and how that's affected all of us to this very day. You're in our thoughts and we miss you greatly. God Bless. We'll see you on the high ground."

Alika Ichinose says, "It means something when a soldier is devastated by someone's death. Let me tell you, everyone was devastated by Jared's death. I remember when I was transferring to Charlie Company within the 3-71 CAV, one of the men came up to me and was very upset. He said, 'If you're leaving and SSG Monti is dead, who is going to take care of us? Who is going to watch over us?' That got to me. I'll never forget it. I learned that watching over the enlisted men is what makes you a good leader. I learned that from Jared."

Alika continues, "He didn't care about medals or personal glory. He died doing what he always promised he would do – taking care of his soldiers. Most people leave a little ripple behind. Jared's ripple was huge. It took up the whole pond."

Steve Raviea recollects, "I followed my typical routine on June

22, 2006, since I was not going on patrol that day. I would wake up, work out, hit the showers, eat breakfast, and prep for future missions. As I got to the entrance of my tent, one of the NCOs stopped me and shared the news that Jared had been killed the night before. I started to get choked up immediately. I thanked him for telling me and then slowly walked back into my tent towards my cot. I cried uncontrollably. It was hard to accept. At the time, I didn't know the story of how it happened. All I knew is the person I looked up to the most had just died.

"There are two men in this world that have had the biggest impact on my life – my father and Jared Monti. To this day I wear a remembrance bracelet with Jared's name on it. I think about him all the time. My biggest regret is I never got a chance to tell him how much he truly meant to me," Steve continued. "Each day I strive to make him proud that I was one of 'his guys', and I tell his story at every opportunity. The impact Jared had on me as a soldier and a man will last a lifetime. It was an honor to serve with him, but an even greater honor to have known him. I was just one of many that he touched, which means Jared Monti will live forever through the memories of those of us who knew him. We'll pass those memories on to future generations."

Steve went on to say, "At my first lunch with Jared at Fort Drum, I had told him that my oldest sister had just moved to the Boston area," recalls Steve. Jared wanted to know which part of Boston but I didn't recall. I never followed up and have kicked myself for not doing so ever since. It wasn't until after Jared died that I realized my sister had moved to the town of Raynham. My niece was baptized at the same church where Jared's funeral was held. It wouldn't necessarily have enhanced our relationship because we had so much in common already. We had the same birthday and the same 'O Negative' blood type, and now we learned we had family linked to the same town. What are the odds?"

According to Steve's father Daniel, "I only knew SFC Monti through my son. It would have been an honor to shake his hand and talk 'shop' with him, one Redleg to another." The term Redleg dates back to the 1800's and is used to describe members of the Army Field Artillery, who originally wore trousers with two-inch scarlet stripes running down them. Red canvas leggings were also worn by horse artillerymen. The most famous Redleg was Harry S. Truman, the 33rd President of the United States.

Steve's mother Catherine wrote, "My son had graduated from VMI, and they train you pretty well there. However, Monti had lots of experience and gave very good advice. He did not have to be so helpful, he simply did it out of kindness. I can't help but think of him and what a horrible loss it was of such a fine young man."

"Both Monti and Bradbury were friends of mine," says Randy Robinson. "I was on a mission and found out about a week later that they both had been killed on the mountain. It was like getting a punch in the gut. I still start shaking and stuttering when I try to talk about it. Bradbury was just 22 years old but had a determination, an intensity about him. I wasn't surprised to hear that he kept right on firing his weapon after he had lost an arm. As for Monti, he helped me in more ways than I thought someone could. He displayed proudly the qualities of what a man can become. I hope one day I can be as great as him."

Randy goes on to say, "Whenever I think of Jared, it motivates me to make something of myself. I always ask how I can make my life worth his sacrifice. I continually ask myself if I'm living my life in a way that would make him proud. An interesting thing I noticed about Jared was that he was the most happy and free when he was deployed. It's like he was serving an important purpose. He was revered by the Afghanis. After I heard about his death, I told the Afghan Security Forces about what happened to the man they called 'Gift of God'. They gathered together and said prayers for him. He changed their lives, too."

Randy received a medical discharge from the army and is now retired. "I got a skinned elbow and broken teeth from an IED explosion, but it's really the injuries from the rollover that affected me." Randy turned 30 in August of 2014. He has to walk with the aid of a cane, an ankle brace, and a knee brace. His lingering health issues have left him on disability and unable to work. As recently as October of 2014, he was diagnosed with scoliosis in his lower and middle back. He requires the assistance of a full-time nurse. Many people would see the bad in that situation. Randy prefers to look at it differently. "I've got a great gig. I get to stay at home and be with my kids. That's the best job there is." Randy and his wife Krystal have four children – Shane Michael is five, Aiden Taylor is four, Katelyn Marie and Ethan James are two-year-old twins.

Randy Robinson also counsels returning war veterans. "I deal with soldiers with PTSD and try to get them through tough situations. I've been able to talk to some suicidal veterans and help them turn their lives around. That is a great thing for me and fills me with joy. I also help teach soldiers going overseas what to look for when it comes to IEDs. I give advice when they'll listen. I find it incredibly rewarding." Undoubtedly, those he has counseled find it incredibly rewarding, too.

Chapter 19
"Hello, This is the President"

On July 21, 2009, Janet got a phone call from someone claiming to be a White House aide. She thought it might be a prank. The person asked how she was, and Janet replied that she was sick at home with the flu. The aide then asked if she would be available within the next half hour.

Ten minutes later, President Obama called and said, "I hear you're a little under the weather." He told her that Jared would be presented with the Medal of Honor in a White House ceremony in September. Needless to say, Janet was thrilled, asking, "Who gets a call from the President?" Niccole agrees: "I thought the President calling on the phone was the coolest thing."

Janet then contacted her mother in Virginia Beach and remembers, "She was so excited. I thought she was going to jump through the phone. My mother was just crazy about Jared." Then Janet had the pleasure of reaching out to Jared's aunts and uncles, asking them if they'd like to go to the White House to meet the President of the United States.

Barack Obama had some trouble reaching Paul to let him know the news. He was out of state on a trip with the Southeastern Massachusetts Mineral Club, one of three amateur mineralogy clubs to which he belongs. Niccole called Paul's cell phone to let him know that the White House was trying to reach him to give him some "important news", but didn't say what that was. Paul came home and sat waiting until the phone finally rang at 5:10 p.m. the next day.

"Hello, Mr. Monti? This is the President," said Barack Obama. "Yes, sir, Mr. President," Paul replied, and then carried the portable phone into the bedroom to get away from the traffic noise. The President offered his condolences. He told Paul that the Secretaries of Defense and the Army had approved Jared Monti for the Medal of Honor. The call was short and to the point. Understandably excited, Paul said, "I didn't want to miss a word. I really don't know where I was — somewhere between here and the clouds. It was very surprising to talk directly to the President."

After putting down the phone, Paul was compelled to immediately write a post to Jared on his legacy.com Guest Book:

> Well Pal, I got a call from President Barack Obama tonight and he told me that you were approved for the Medal of Honor. He said that the country was proud of you and that he himself was proud of you. And you know how very proud I am of you.
>
> You never did want any medals for your actions but you got them anyway. And now you will be receiving the highest medal of them all.
>
> I do wish it wasn't so. I want you back with me. I want to hold your children on my lap and tell them about their wonderful father. I want to go fishing with you and play cards with you and just hang with you again.
>
> I live in awe of you. I could not be any prouder. You have done me the honor of being my beloved son. The Good Lord in Heaven blessed me with you and it has been

the greatest blessing in my life.

Some day we will be together again. Until then, Son, I will keep you in my everyday thoughts and prayers. I love you more than life. See you on the high ground.– Dad 143.

The "143" is short-hand that members of the family use to represent "I love you". It's based on the number of letters in the phrase. The practice has been passed down through the generations.

The Holbrook, MA Post 137 American Legion team for which cousin Joey played was mired in a losing streak. They heard the devastating news of Jared's death and decided to dedicate their next game to his memory, on July 2, 2006, the day after Jared's funeral, against league power Canton. They wound up winning the game 13-9. The game ball was signed by the entire team and given to Joe, who has kept it as one of his prized possessions.

Three years later, Coach Bill Merrigan sent an e-mail to all of the team members saying, "I read today that President Obama called Joe's Uncle Paul to let him know that Jared would be awarded the prestigious Medal of Honor. I know how proud Joe was of his cousin. Today he is even prouder."

Word spread throughout the Army that Jared was going to be the sixth recipient of the Medal of Honor from the Iraq and Afghanistan Wars. The previous five, unfortunately, were also presented with their medals posthumously. Those who knew Jared had a reaction similar to SGT Clifford Baird, who posted, "SFC Monti was the kind of guy who would have done anything for his soldiers. He cared about them more than anything. He made sure they were trained properly and had what they needed. If they were having personal problems, he'd be there for them. If anyone deserved the Medal of Honor, it was him. Just by his actions.

Going out into the line of fire three times. He was a hero. He's one of my heroes."

Mike Bower posted: "Just wanted to stop by and congratulate you for the Medal of Honor. That day stands very clear in my head. All the FISTers huddled on top of the Hesco, listening to the mission's progress and wishing we could be up there with our brothers. You keep inspiring me, even after your passing. You truly were the best NCO a soldier could ask for. My prayers go out to your family. You're truly missed.... Every time I feel scared I just grab your bracelet and feel better. It's pretty awesome, really, knowing that you bring me comfort."

The Hesco bastion that Mike refers to is a military fortification made of wire mesh with a heavy duty fabric liner, used as a barrier against explosions or small arms fire. Two feet of barrier thickness is considered sufficient to stop rifle bullets, shell fragments and other shrapnel; four feet to provide protection against most car bombs; and five feet to stop an RPG. Originally designed to help control erosion and flooding, the Hesco barriers became a popular security device in the 1990s. They were used in 2005 for their original purpose to reinforce the levees around New Orleans after Hurricane Katrina.

Shawn Williams recalls, "It hit me like a baseball bat to the face when I saw Jared's picture on national television and they said he had been killed. All I can say is that I feel proud and honored to have known such a great man. He earned the Medal of Honor every day of his life."

Representative of the postings from families of those who were with him on Hill 2610 was this one from Diana Chambers: "My son called us today and told us you were getting the Medal of Honor. We knew this day would come. My son, Matt, was fighting with you that devastating day. We are extremely proud of you and of the men who were with you then. Thank you, Monti."

And SFC James Walker says, "Think about you a lot and are proud to tell others about a FISTer and my old friend being awarded the MOH. You are an inspiration to the young 13Fs but you were an inspiration to our FISTers long before Afghanistan and your heroic actions on that day. We would gladly request that the MOH be returned so we can have our friend...our BROTHER back!!! But it is what it is and we are all proud and honored to have known and served alongside you. I love you and miss you, Brother. You will never be forgotten. NEVER! Paul and Janet, thank you for bringing Jared into this world. Without that I would have never had a wonderful friend and a great Warrior to serve beside."

Jeremy Keeler's thoughts on the award were, "You've just received the second award you always told me you didn't want (the Purple Heart and THE Medal). I've always said you deserved it and I'm not the only one. Those of us who had the honor of serving with you know this wasn't an isolated incident. You always placed your soldiers first and did everything possible to take care of your own. That is just the man, soldier, and NCO that you were. I am grateful to have been one of those soldiers. When I get to heaven I know you will be there."

Brandon Dansfiell commented, "I heard the news today of your MOH, which is just a piece of metal compared to what you stood for. I am proud to have served with you and I will never forget you, my friend. We are all forever inspired by you as one who stood against many."

Navy SEAL Lieutenant Michael P. Murphy of Smithtown, New York was the first American to be presented with the Medal of Honor for actions during the War in Afghanistan, and was the first member of the U. S. Navy to be so recognized since the Viet Nam

War. He received the Medal of Honor posthumously from President George W. Bush on October 22, 2007.

The 29-year-old Murphy led a four-member team on a mission to kill Ahmad Shah, a high-level insurgent leader, in the vicinity of Asadabad in Kunar Province on June 27, 2005. They were discovered by anti-coalition sympathizers, who revealed their position to the Taliban, and they were subsequently ambushed by 30 to 40 of the enemy. When the primary radio communicator was killed, Murphy attempted to call for assistance, but they were in a communications "dead zone" because of the rugged terrain. Despite being shot, he fought his way into open terrain to gain a better position to transmit a call. He was once again shot, yet maintained his exposed position while calling in the location and requesting help. He returned to his position to continue fighting until he finally succumbed to his wounds.

After Murphy called for help, an MH-47 Chinook helicopter was dispatched but was hit by an RPG, killing all 16 military personnel on board. That included eight SEALs and eight Special Forces members. It was the largest loss of SEALs since the Viet Nam War. Marcus Luttrell was the lone survivor from the team of four. He wandered the mountain for several days, was found and protected by Afghani villagers, and was finally rescued. The story was told in the 2013 movie *Lone Survivor,* which starred Taylor Kitsch as Michael Murphy and Mark Wahlberg as Marcus Luttrell.

After the announcement that Jared was going to be posthumously presented with the Medal of Honor, Daniel Murphy, Lieutenant Murphy's father, posted this message: "I want to extend our sincere sympathies to Jared's family on their great loss. We share a common bond, as we both have suffered the loss of a son doing what they believed in, protecting America. Our son, Navy SEAL Lt. Michael P. Murphy, was lost in 2005 in the same theater of operation, Afghanistan. Jared also joins a very small family of special American heroes whose bravery and willingness to sacrifice for others has been recognized with The Medal of Honor, this nation's highest award for valor. We are sorry for the loss of one of America's heroes but proud of all he accomplished on behalf of us all. We look forward to Jared's name being placed in the Hall of Heroes alongside our son... two very special Americans indeed."

The other Medal of Honor recipient from the Army's 10th Division was PFC John Magrath of East Norwalk, CT, who was born, appropriately enough, on July 4 of 1924.

The 20-year-old's company was pinned down by enemy fire near Castel d'Aiano in Italy on April 14, 1945. Armed with just a rifle, he volunteered to charge headlong into a German machine gun nest. He wound up killing two of the enemy and wounding three others. Securing their weapon and carrying it through heavy fire across an open field, he single-handedly captured two more machine gun nests. He then circled behind four of the enemy and killed them as they were firing on his unit. He wasn't finished. He encountered a group of five Germans and killed two while wounding three. He volunteered again to dodge artillery and mortar fire to collect a report of casualties but was mortally wounded in the effort.

U. S. Navy Captain Thomas G. Kelley of Boston, the previous Massachusetts resident to be presented the Medal of Honor, was recognized for heroism in actions that occurred on June 15, 1969. Then-Lieutenant Kelley was in command of eight river assault boats that were engaged in extracting an Army infantry company from the Ong Muong Canal in Kien Hoa province in South Viet Nam. While under attack from a hostile enemy force, one of the boats suffered a mechanical failure which prevented its loading ramp from being raised. While repairs were being made, Kelley maneuvered his own boat to serve as a shield. He lost an eye from rocket shrapnel and received a severe head wound that left him unable to stand or speak clearly. He was able, however, to relay instructions to the convoy through one of his sailors. They managed to escape without further incident. Kelley eventually retired with the rank of Captain and served as Secretary of the Massachusetts Department of Veteran's Services from 2003 to 2011.

Jared's Aunt Mary and her husband John designed a medallion to give to relatives as a souvenir of the upcoming trip to Washington. Mary explains, "We put a picture of Jared wearing the scarf the Afghani people gave to him on one side, and the Medal of Honor insignia on the other. We had no idea that so many people would want one. We've had to keep re-ordering them. Jared brought out greatness in so many people, both in the family and in the military. He's had a lasting impact. We're glad he's got a lasting memento."

John says, "We thought of providing key chains for the family and then stumbled on the idea of a coin. We weren't aware of the military tradition of challenge coins at all. So, we ordered just 100 of them to give out to the family in DC. On the one hand, it's great that he was special to so many people. On the other hand, I feel bad, because we've kind of lost the intimacy that we wanted when it was just going to be a souvenir of the trip."

Challenge coins have long been an American military tradition. They began as a way to identify the members of a unit who would be issued a medallion which took the shape of a two-sided gold, silver, nickel, brass, or bronze coin. They were expected to be carried at all times. There are stories of World War I and II soldiers losing dog tags and official ID but being identified by their coins.

Using various methods, the challenger asks to see the coin of a soldier, sailor, or Marine, or the coins of everyone present. If the people challenged do not show coins, they are required to buy a drink for the challenger. If the challenged member produces a medallion, then the challenging member is required to pay for the drink. The most common way to begin the challenge is to slap your own coin on a bar or table. Another way to challenge is to loudly tap a coin in front of a person or group that you want to challenge.

Gradually, coins began to be produced for individuals as well as military units. For example, if you were fortunate enough to meet Generals or Admirals, they might honor you by giving you one of their coins. You could then use them to trump a coin of someone of a lower rank. The coins are usually passed to others while shaking hands. There may be competitions of various sorts where the losers must give up challenge coins to the winners.

The medallions are meant to be kept in a pocket. If they are defaced, they are considered dishonored. If the challenge coin is attached to a key ring, made into a belt buckle, or worn around the neck, it typically will no longer qualify as a challenge coin.

Imagine how popular a high-ranking Washington official such as the Secretary of Defense or Secretary of the Army is handing out coins in a room full of members of the military. Many people collect challenge coins and keep them on racks. One of the most famous pictures of challenge coins is President Bill Clinton's official portrait, which hangs in the White House. There are several racks of these coins displayed behind him on a credenza.

What trumps a Medal of Honor recipient's Challenge Coin? If every member of the military up to and including the Chairman of the Joint Chiefs of Staff, has to salute a Medal of Honor recipient, the answer is probably "Nothing!" Carrying the coin of a Medal of Honor recipient could mean never again having to pay for a drink at a bar anywhere in the world where members of the American military are present.

Being given a challenge coin with SFC Jared Monti's picture on it is quite an honor. Jared's Uncle Mike carries it with him everywhere he goes, explaining, "He's always in my heart, but always in my pocket, too."

Darren Hammerstad, like many others in the family, keeps the Medal of Honor medallion with him at all times. "It reminds me that Jared is watching over me. I'm Navy Military Police so I get in some tough situations. When I need to, I just reach into my pocket and feel that medallion. I know I'm covered. I know things will be okay."

Less than three months before his death, Jared posted this regret on his cousin Jason Eagle's wedding announcement web site: "My hat's off from across the pond...wish you two the best in life. Sorry I can't make the wedding, but I'll be there in spirit. Gallantly Forward. Chaos 3-5 out." "Gallantly Forward" is the motto of the 71st Cavalry.

Jason Eagles, understandably excited to be an expectant father, later posted this message to Jared: "You will forever be missed. This time last year we were talking about my wedding. Now I am getting ready to have my firstborn son. I cannot wait to tell him about a hero. To tell him about being a man of honor, loyalty, and passion. I can't wait to tell him about YOU."

That Medal of Honor medallion has found a way to inspire even those who never met Jared. Like many others in the family, Jason's son now carries it with him. Ben, as he was named, was asked recently to give a speech to his first grade class on Veteran's Day. Naturally, it was going to about his hero cousin. He woke up sick and normally would have missed school that day. But on this day, he admits, "I had cousin Jared's coin with me, and that gave me strength. I couldn't miss school. I had to do it for him." From all reports, the six-year-old gave a wonderful speech. There will probably be other times when he will need to seek strength from the challenge coin or some other remembrance of Jared. He won't be the only one.

Jason adds, "People will remember him forever because he'll be in the history books. If Jared had his choice, he would say, 'Remember some other soldier before you remember me.' That's just how he was. I think for that very reason, that's why he deserves to be remembered."

Chapter 20
"I Got You Guys into the White House"

When Jared was nine years old, he traveled to Washington, DC. with his family and stood outside the White House gates to pose for a photo. The family returned in September of 2009 for a whirlwind visit, only without their oldest son.

"All I could think when I found out we'd be going to Washington was, We're going to meet the President, but it's because my son died," confesses Janet.

Cousin Michelle posted this message to Jared prior to the trip: "Today is the 8th anniversary of 9/11, which led to the conflict in which you served. Next weekend would have been your 34th birthday. And this coming Thursday, your parents will accept the Medal of Honor for your work and sacrifice for our country. This week will be filled with tears and pride as we, your immediate family, cousins, aunts, uncles, and best friends from the military gather to remember and celebrate you and your life. I love you, and am forever grateful for the gifts you have bestowed on my own life, without you ever even knowing it."

Their first stop was at the Arlington National Cemetery in Arlington County, Virginia, which is located directly across the Potomac River from the Lincoln Memorial. There are between 27 and 30 funerals held there each day, for a total of 6,900 per year. It is expected that will continue until the 624-acre cemetery is full sometime before the year 2050. There are currently over 300,000 people buried there.

Among the most renowned is President John F. Kennedy, who reportedly visited the cemetery and commented, "It's so beautiful here. I wish I could stay forever." Next to him is his widow, Jackie, and not far away are the plain white wooden crosses marking the graves of his brothers – former Attorney General Robert Kennedy and one of the country's longest-serving senators, Edward Kennedy.

The Tomb of the Unknowns is one of the most popular tourist destinations at the cemetery. It originally was known as the Tomb of the Unknown Soldier, when a World War I service member was interred there during the Warren Harding Administration. It became the Tomb of the Unknowns when soldiers from World War II, the Korean War, and the Viet Nam War were later also interred. The remains of the Vietnam Unknown were disinterred in 1998 and identified as those of Air Force 1st Lieutenant Michael J. Blassie. The crypt at the Tomb of the Unknowns that contained his remains has since remained empty.

Paul and Janet had the honor of placing a wreath in Jared's name at the Tomb of the Unknowns. They were accompanied by their granddaughter Carys, who was celebrating her sixth birthday that day. Jared's Aunt Annie said, "Our whole family has been shocked to the core. Not just by Jared's death but by the impact he's had. It's been overwhelming. His story just keeps spreading. I could not be more proud. The only thing better would have been for him to live to see it all. So, we are settling for second best."

The military supplied a chocolate cake and balloons to help the family celebrate Carys' birthday. "I sucked some helium from the tank they were using to blow up the balloons and started singing

'We're off to see the Wizard' to her," says Janet. "There were members of the family, friends, and soldiers there. I don't remember if Carys thought my helium voice was funny, but everyone else in the room did."

Annie happened to mention to a security guard that they were part of Jared's family. The guard took them inside the vestibule area where the soldiers from the Army's 3rd Infantry Regiment prepare to go out for the famous Changing of the Guard Ceremony. The Sergeant in charge gave Annie's grandson Ben a poster of the ceremony.

There are four million visitors to the cemetery each year. Most of them go to the Tomb of the Unknowns. These guards are photographed constantly. You might think they are tired of having their pictures taken. They probably are. Yet they couldn't wait to be photographed with people who, for better or worse, are often known first as "part of Jared's family" before being recognized as having individual identities.

Annie posted this message to Jared: "Today your Mom, Dad, and Carys laid a wreath in your name at the Tomb of the Unknowns. Niccole and Tim were there, too. I was lucky enough to attend along with your Aunt Tricia, Aunt Jean, Krystin and Donnie. We are so filled with pride at how our country is honoring you and your heroic acts. Tomorrow we go to the White House and Friday we go to the Pentagon, all because of the selfless way you stood up to protect your fellow soldiers and your country. I love and miss you more each day."

Going to the White House proved to be a surreal experience for the Monti and Ross families. Many of the uncles, aunts, cousins, and friends came along. There were 150 guests, including all the surviving soldiers who had been with Jared on the mountain. Not everyone who wanted to was able to attend the event. Family friend Aaron Cummings drove to Washington from Taunton, MA, but was not one of those invited to the White House ceremony. "I just wanted to come down to honor Jared, to be there for the family. I just wanted to be here," he admitted.

Among those who were on hand for the ceremony in the East Room of the White House were Senator John F. Kerry and Representative Barney Frank of Massachusetts, as well as Secretary of Defense Robert M. Gates, the Chairman of the Joint Chiefs of Staff Admiral Mike Mullen, and Congressman John McHugh, who was soon to become the Secretary of the Army.

How did the surviving soldiers from the patrol feel about being in the company of such luminaries? "The truth is, I was most fired up to get back together with the team again. I felt like a little kid going to Disneyland. It was cool for us to be re-united. The nation gets a chance to hear what Jared did and I get to hang out with my buddies," admits Chris Grzecki.

"He came from a big family and it was an honor to meet his parents," says Chris Cunningham. "I can see where he got his charisma. His family raised an amazing person."

Nephew Darren Hammerstad gave Janet quite a turn that day. He claims, "I look very much like Jared, anyhow, but I was in my Navy dress whites for the Medal of Honor presentation at the White House, and his mother took one look at me and broke down and started crying. She said it was like looking at Jared."

"Going to DC was very hard for me," admits Tim. "I said to the Generals, 'Please make sure my Mom is well taken care of.' She certainly was. I was really worried about her."

The largest room in the White House, the East Room, was the setting for the Medal of Honor presentation. It's a historic place, used for gatherings such as banquets, press conferences, and receptions. It features the famous Steinway grand piano that was custom-designed for President Franklin Roosevelt in 1938 by Eric Gugler. Hanging on the wall is the iconic 8 by 5 foot Lansdowne 1797 oil painting of George Washington, which was rescued from the 1814 White House fire, along with a portrait of Martha Washington from 1878.

The official name for America's highest military honor is the Medal of Honor. It's incorrect to refer to it as the "Congressional Medal of Honor." It's presented by the President of the United States, typically in a White House ceremony, on behalf of Congress. However, the recipients are chosen exclusively by the Department of Defense. There have been close to 3,500 Medals of Honor presented since the Medal's inception during the Civil War. That number is heavily weighted to the early years, as there were no other awards or medals available to soldiers until after the Civil War. Almost half of the decorations, in fact, were presented from 1861 to 1865.

The eligibility requirement is that a member of the Armed Forces must have exhibited behavior "conspicuously by gallantry and intrepidity at the risk of life above and beyond the call of duty while engaged in an action against an enemy of the United States; while engaged in military operations involving conflict with an opposing foreign force; or while serving with friendly foreign forces engaged in an armed conflict against an opposing armed force in which the United States is not a belligerent party." There is further stipulation that "the deed performed must have been one of personal bravery or self-sacrifice so conspicuous as to clearly distinguish the individual above his or her comrades and must have involved risk of life. Incontestable proof of the performance of service is exacted and each recommendation for award of this decoration is considered on the standard of extraordinary merit."

Nearly 18% of the Medals of Honor have been presented posthumously. However, since the start of World War II, that number has jumped to 62%. There are three slightly different versions of the medal – one each for the Navy, Army, and Air Force. A Marine or Coast Guard recipient is given the Navy version.

Prior to the Civil War, there were no medals awarded for valor in combat, with the exception of the three awards presented by George Washington during the Revolutionary War. The display of medals on a uniform was looked upon with disdain by many Americans, who considered it a European tradition typically reserved for royalty. Those medals were worn because of who someone was rather than for what they did.

During the Mexican-American War in 1847, a Certificate of Merit was created to recognize those soldiers who distinguished themselves. But it was merely a voucher that could bring a small payment to the soldier, with no real recognition or actual medal involved.

The Army's Assistant Adjutant General, Lieutenant Colonel Edward Townsend, proposed a "Medal of Honor" to Commanding General Winfield Scott, famously known as "Old Fuss and Feathers" for his love of both discipline and pomp. Scott, the last Whig Party candidate for President, served in the military for more than fifty years under fourteen U. S. Presidents. He rejected the idea as being "too European". However, Secretary of the Navy Gideon liked the concept so much that he lobbied Abraham Lincoln to institute the medal to "promote the efficiency of the Navy". On December 21, 1861, President Lincoln signed the bill creating the Medal of Honor to be presented to enlisted seamen and petty officers. Commissioned officers were not eligible for it until 1915.

In 1862, the Army followed suit and established its own Medal of Honor in further legislation signed by President Lincoln. Before the war ended, the Army allowed the presentation of its Medal to enlisted men, non-commissioned and commissioned officers who distinguished themselves.

More than 2,000 Medals of Honor were presented to soldiers ranging in rank from private to general during the Civil War, many under dubious circumstances. In 1917, a review board of five retired U. S. Army generals examined the records of all those who received the medal. It resulted in the revocation of 910 Medals of Honor in what came to be known as the "Purge of 1917". It also established a hierarchy of medals called the "Pyramid of Honor", which involved the creation of "lesser awards" such as the Distinguished Service Cross, Silver Star, Bronze Star, etc. for actions that were worthy of recognition.

The Medal of Honor was subsequently accompanied by a certificate, called a "citation", detailing the actions for which it was presented. An honor roll was also established to record each recipient's name and unit. During World War I, The Medal of Honor became front-page news. For the first time, soldiers began to accept medals as an American military tradition and wear them with pride. The public welcomed the notion of its hometown heroes gaining national recognition.

Unlike other active or retired members of the military, Medal of Honor recipients have uniform privileges, meaning that they can wear their uniforms at any time and place of their choosing. If the medals are being worn, whether or not recipients are in uniform, they are expected to be saluted by those of a higher rank. Although this is not a military regulation, it is considered an obligatory sign of respect. It is regarded as improper to say the Medal of Honor was "won" or even "awarded". That connotes something that someone would receive as a prize. It's more respectful to say the Medal of Honor was "presented" or "received".

The United States Army Institute of Heraldry, located at Ft. Belvoir, Virginia, officially describes the Army version as “a gold five pointed star, each point tipped with trefoils, 1½ inches wide, surrounded by a green laurel wreath and suspended from a gold bar inscribed ‘Valor’, surmounted by an eagle. In the center of the star, Minerva’s head surrounded by the words ‘United States of America’. On each ray of the star is a green oak leaf. On the reverse is a bar engraved ‘The Congress To’ with a space for engraving the name of the recipient. The pendant and suspension bar are made of gilding metal, with the eye, jump rings, and suspension ring made of red brass. The finish on the pendant and suspension bar is hard enameled, gold plated, and rose gold plated, with polished highlights.”

Minerva is a Roman version of the Greek goddess Athena and is the sponsor of arts, trade, and defense. She is often depicted with a sacred owl symbolizing her connection with wisdom. The Medal of Honor is attached to a light blue, moire patterned silk neck ribbon featuring thirteen white stars in the form of three chevrons. It is the only neck order award that is presented to members of the armed forces. One other, the Commander’s Degree of the Legion of Merit, may be given to foreign dignitaries. The Medal of Honor certificate is signed by the Secretary of the Army and the President of the United States.

No one can be given two Medals of Honor. If someone earns more than one, the recipient wears a quarter-inch high bronze miniature letter “V” with serifs on the suspension ribbon. Nineteen members of the military, all now deceased, have earned that “V”. No one has ever been presented with three Medals of Honor.

Prior to the presentation, the immediate family was treated to a private session with Barack and Michelle Obama. It was the first time in history that a Medal of Honor pre-ceremony meeting was held in the Oval Office.

While waiting for the meeting, Carys let her mother Niccole know that she was hungry. Paul asked one of the aides if there was anything they could get for her. The aide led them into a kitchen area, where the chef asked Carys if she wanted a peanut butter and jelly sandwich. She turned down that offer, and a subsequent one of a tuna sandwich. Finally, the chef offered her a grilled cheese sandwich, and her face lit up. The chef said he would send it right up, and they rejoined the others. The family, however, was being moved from room to room. First it was the Green Room, then the Gold Room, then the Blue Room, and then the Cabinet Room. The grilled cheese sandwich was always a room behind. Carys was getting impatient.

Michelle Obama was greeting the immediate family members and said hello to little Carys, who pointed to her mouth, indicating she still hadn't gotten her sandwich. The First Lady said to the President, "This girl is hungry, Barack. She needs something to eat." The President tried to accommodate her by giving her a bag of M&Ms. They weren't ordinary M&Ms. They were official. They carried the Presidential Seal. Michelle, the mother of two, was unimpressed. She said, "That's not food, Barack. Give the girl something real to eat." So the Leader of the Free World went to the pantry that is located off the Oval Office and found some cookies. The First Lady said, "That's better, but it's still not food."

At that moment, the call came from the East Room that it was time to go there for the ceremony, and there the grilled cheese sandwich finally caught up with the six-year-old. However, a White House staffer said to her, "You can't take that into the East Room." "Oh, yes she can," insisted Michelle. The staffer, just like the President, knew better than to try to argue with the First Lady. So Carys may have been the first person allowed to eat food during a solemn Medal of Honor ceremony at the White House. It's a story she can tell for the rest of her life.

Cousin Kevin, a senior in high school, wasn't enamoured with the fancy hors d'oeuvres that had been served. It wasn't the kind of food he was used to eating. When Carys was presented with her grilled cheese sandwich, he looked over at the staffer and said, "Do you have any more of those?"

"From our humble beginnings, we went to being invited guests at the White House. There were Generals there, all kinds of high-ranking government officials, the President, and First Lady. We were just regular people. We just pictured Jared looking down with his wide grin and saying, 'Pretty good, huh? I got you guys into the White House,'" says Uncle Mike.

"He did something no amount of training can instill," the President recounted in a stirring speech as he presented his first Medal of Honor. "Jared Monti saw the danger before him. And he went out to meet it. Faced with overwhelming enemy fire, Jared could have stayed where he was, behind that wall. But that was not the kind of soldier he was."

The Medal of Honor ceremony at the White House was filmed by Jerry Gibbs, Vice President of Raynham's Cable Advisory Committee, with help from Curry College, which donated the video equipment. Gibbs is an instructor at the school and Co-Chairman of the school's Communication Department. The webcast was shown live on the Town web site. He flew to Washington along with Eric Cox of PNG Laboratories, a media-streaming company.

According to Gibbs, "This is clearly one of the most important moments in Raynham's history."

Jared thus joined an exclusive society of Medal of Honor war heroes that includes Charles Lindbergh, Douglas MacArthur, and Theodore Roosevelt. As President Obama noted, "These remarkable Americans are literally one in a million." Raynham also earned the distinction of being the only town in Massachusetts with more than one Medal of Honor recipient – SFC Jared C. Monti and Private Frederick C. Anderson. Several of the large cities, like Boston and Springfield, have more than one.

By coincidence, Congress has designated March 25 as National Medal of Honor Day. According to Janet, "Heck of a day to share my birthday with."

At the Medal of Honor ceremony, Vice Chief of Staff of the Army, General Peter W. Chiarelli, said to Janet and Paul, "What a remarkable young man you both raised together. Those values you instilled in Jared at an early age made him the very special person he was – a young man who in the face of tremendous adversity demonstrated incredible selflessness and courage."

Michelle Obama invited Carys to stay after the Medal of Honor presentation to play on the White House swing set. She told her Malia and Sasha would be home from school later and would happily take her outside. Knowing that you don't push your luck with a young child, Niccole instead chose to take Carys back to the hotel for a nap.

Most people don't know that there's an official Medal of Honor flag, but the Monti family was presented with it. The flag consists of 13 stars arranged in the same formation as in the Medal of Honor ribbon on a field of blue. It has gold fringe on three sides and, unlike most military flags, has no set proportions. The first Medal of Honor flag was presented by President George W. Bush to the family of SFC Paul Smith at a White House ceremony on April 4, 2005.

The flag was designed by retired SFC Bill Kendall to honor recipient Captain Darrell Lindsey, who was from his home town of Jefferson, Iowa. Lindsey sacrificed his own life to save the lives of his crew while participating in a bombing run over Europe in 1944.

A highly decorated veteran himself, Kendall served three tours with the Army Special Forces in Viet Nam and received the Silver Star, three Bronze Stars and three Purple Hearts.

Kendall perfectly described Jared and so many other recipients when he commented, "It takes a special type of person to do these kinds of things. Read the citations explaining the combat situation that led to the awarding of each medal, and you realize the word 'hero' doesn't quite do it. There are descriptions of running straight into enemy machine-gun fire, almost always being wounded, dragging comrades to safety, holding off a superior enemy force, etc. They'll tell you they found themselves in a rough spot and just said, 'To hell with it, I'm going to do this thing no matter the cost.' They don't even think much more about it than that. They just do it because it needs to be done."

Why did it take more than three years until Jared was presented with the Medal of Honor? Someone asking that question would obviously not be familiar with the deliberate approval process. It's comparable to trying to get a bill through Congress. The three years it took for Jared to received his Medal of Honor pales in comparison to the 103 years it took Teddy Roosevelt to posthumously receive his in 2001 by President Bill Clinton for actions in the Battle of San Juan Heights in Cuba, which took place in 1898. Teddy's Medal of Honor is on display in the Roosevelt Room of the White House along with his 1906 Nobel Peace prize.

Teddy was part of the second father and son duo to receive Medals of Honor. Teddy Roosevelt Jr. was a recipient for his actions on D-Day on June 6, 1944. The other tandem to receive the medal was Civil War hero Arthur McArthur and son Douglas McArthur for his service during World War II and the Korean War.

A former Army Captain and West Point graduate, Darin Souza explains, "I knew Jared both as a child and as a soldier. It's so painfully obvious that he deserved the Medal of Honor. The vetting process is so complex and there are so many departments and agencies involved. You have to respect that process and let it run its course."

Like any other process, it's subject to human error. The military suffered an embarrassing disclosure when Defense Secretary Chuck Hagel issued a public apology to Army Captain William D. Swenson, who received the Medal of Honor on Oct. 15, 2013 for bravery displayed on Sept. 8, 2009 in Afghanistan's Ganjgal Valley. Swenson pulled a soldier who had been shot from a kill zone and then searched for four others who had been killed. The problem was that his nomination package went missing in Afghanistan for several years. Secretary of the Army John McHugh subsequently implemented a policy that the Army's awards branch must follow-up with a soldier's chain of command every 30 days to report progress after a Medal of Honor recommendation.

Hagel, who served in the Infantry in Vietnam and has since been replaced as Defense Secretary, called for a full joint review of the awards process in March, 2014, saying that he wanted to ensure that the military "adequately recognizes all levels of combat valor." The review will determine how to honor drone operators, cyber-warfare personnel, and others who affect events on the new-age battlefield. It is expected that recommendations will be forthcoming mid-2015.

The President spoke of Jared's legacy at the presentation ceremony saying, "His name graces streets and scholarships. Across a grateful nation, it graces parks and military posts. From this day forward, it will grace the memorials to our Medal of Honor heroes. And this week, when Jared Monti would have celebrated his 34th birthday, we know that his name and legacy will live forever, and shine brightest, in the hearts of his family and friends who will love him always."

Paul admits, "I'd rather have my son back than all the medals in the world. I would give my life for his. I would give anything, because I was supposed to die before him."

"I would gladly give the Medal of Honor back in a heartbeat to have him again," echoes Janet. "If I could, I would trade places with him. I think about him every day and still have many tearful days. I miss him so very much, sometimes intolerably."

Senator John Kerry, who went on to become Secretary of State, remarked, "Courage is one of the virtues we as Americans admire most, and Jared Monti showed uncommon courage by refusing to leave behind one of his fellow soldiers."

One of the week's highlights was an Open Mike Night. The family gathered together with friends and the soldiers who were on the mountain for a group session where people were called up to a podium one at a time to relate stories about Jared. There was plenty of both laughter and tears. It was a private moment that highlighted a very public week. No members of the media were allowed. No notes were taken. "Hearing these wonderful, brave young men talking about the night they all thought they were going to die just broke your heart. They're such great guys. We loved them all. How much pain they must have been feeling," laments Frani.

Jared's former Ft. Bragg roommate Jeff Bolding wrote after the White House presentation, "I had a great time honoring my fallen brother with his family and close friends! It was a blast taking turns telling stories about Jared. If you didn't know better you would think you were in a comedy club! Jared was crazy funny and the life of the party. This weekend was no different. Jared made us all laugh till we cried AGAIN! Thanks for the memories, brother. I will miss you forever! AIRBORNE, ALL THE WAY!"

"I knew that he was humble. I knew that he liked to help people. But I never realized the magnitude of it. Ever. After he died, people started to tell me all the stories about him and that's when I began to realize what a giant this little guy was," says Paul, who claims that Jared was really 5'4", although he was officially listed at 5'6". Paul to this day is still hearing stories about Jared that are new to him.

Aunt Jean declares, "The best part of the week was meeting the soldiers, having those guys with us. They were unbelievable. I have the utmost respect for them. They're such incredible people."

The final ceremony of the whirlwind week in Washington took place on Friday, September 18, 2009. It was Jared's induction into the Hall of Heroes, a small room in the Pentagon referred to as "The Pentagon's Most Sacred Place". The family was escorted by military personnel and got to ride in golf carts around the massive Pentagon complex. His name was added to a wall listing the names of all Medal of Honor recipients from past wars.

"They loaded us into a bus and drove us by the memorial to the people who lost their lives at the Pentagon on 9/11. Up to that point, we were chatting with old friends and meeting new ones. The mood immediately changed. Everyone became quiet and somber. We realized that we were in an important place," recalls Aunt Patti.

The Pentagon Memorial, the first national 9/11 memorial, is on the southwest lawn and was dedicated in 2008. It consists of an open, public space allowing visitors access to 184 benches facing the Pentagon that pay tribute to the 125 people killed inside, including 55 military personnel, along with the 53 passengers and 6 crew on American Airlines Flight 77. The flight left Dulles Airport in Virginia for its Los Angeles destination when it was hijacked by five terrorists and flown into the Pentagon.

As the doomed flight approached, its wings knocked over light poles and its right engine smashed a power generator before it crashed into the first-floor level of the western side of the building. The fuselage front disintegrated on impact, while debris from the tail section broke through 310 feet of the three outermost rings of the Pentagon's famous five rings. The force of the airplane strike and ensuing fires caused one section of the building to collapse.

"We got off the bus and walked down a corridor, and there were Jared's enlarged baby pictures, toddler pictures, and his whole life story right in front of us," recalls Patti. "It was so unexpected. We were absolutely shocked. It just took our breath away. There wasn't a dry eye in the house."

For the 350 friends and family members in attendance, the scene epitomized the entire week of memorable events."I was not expecting this," his Aunt Marti said. "My emotions are all over the place. I don't know whether to smile or cry."

"I was interviewed by the military for a video they made about Jared that was shown at the Pentagon," recalls childhood friend Jeff Gomes. "I've never seen it. They gave me a copy of it, but it's still in the shrink-wrap. I haven't been able to open it. I'll watch it with my three kids someday when I'm ready. I'll want to teach them what a true American hero is all about."

"What a week it was. We were treated like royalty by the government," recalls Niccole.

Each family member was given a Gold Star pin, normally just presented to the immediate family, by the Department of Defense. "The week was exciting, overwhelming," agrees Aunt Mary. "We felt such pride in Jared and his accomplishments. He was a great man. We knew it. Now the world would know it."

Army Col. Joseph M. Adams filmed a documentary on Jared that was shown at the event and featured family, friends, and soldiers talking about Jared. He noted, "It's incredible to hear all these people who have known him his entire life, with the same recurring theme about his character and the kind of person he was."

Deputy Secretary of Defense William Lynn acknowledged that Paul and Janet had endured a loss few will ever know and proclaimed, "Today, every soldier, sailor, marine, airman, and civilian in the Department of Defense, more than 3 million of us, salute your son. We honor him and we will always remember him."

When presented with the Hall of Heroes award in the Pentagon auditorium, Paul acknowledged, "I accept it not just for him, but for all of the men and women who serve our country and protect our freedom and our way of life."

Cousin Katie Monti was 11 years old when Jared died; she wrote this poem, titled "Jared: War Hero and Loved by All"

I used to tell all my friends who you were; I would say it with pride
Now I say in sorrow that you died.
I know you can't be here to hold my hand
And that I understand
I still love you so dear
Even though you can't be here.
I know you can't be there, right in front of me,
But you still care and that I can see
You had a great smile
And I could see it from a mile.
You loved every child
Even if they were sweet or if they were wild.
You are someone I will always love
So let your soul fly up like a dove.

Three years later, she got to travel to Washington for the Medal of Honor presentation and the Pentagon Hall of Heroes ceremony. Like the others in attendance, Katie had mixed feelings saying, "I was really upset but tried to be as happy as I could for my family. It was a chance for them to reconnect and remember my cousin."

Katie remembers seeing Jared when he was home on leave and admits, "I looked up to him a lot. I would see him every once in a while at my Uncle's house in Raynham. He didn't talk a lot about his job because I was so young, but I would always ask him questions."

She had many of those questions answered at the White House and the Pentagon. "They talked about Jared and what he had done and how his actions were heroic. I wasn't really expecting the story that they told. It was really sad what happened to him and how it happened. I feel really proud to be related to him."

Riding in a motorcade through the historic streets of Washington, DC was another experience described by family members as "bittersweet." According to Katie, "It brought us back to when we went to the funeral. They had a motorcade then, too, and closed down all the highways and the bridge to Cape Cod."

Katie's mother Tory happened to mention to Rodney Hodo, one of the soldiers at the Pentagon's Hall of Heroes ceremony, that Katie had won a Veteran's Day essay contest and had read it at the local American Legion in Pembroke, MA. It was written five months after Jared's death. Hodo took off a Support our Troops pin that he was wearing on his uniform and gave it to Katie.

Katie later posted this message to Jared: "I wish I could sit down and talk to you one more time. You truly are a hero, not because you served our country, but because you were a great cousin. You are the person I will always look up to."

Aunt Marianne has sent 3,110 boxes of goodies to servicemen and women around the world since Jared's death. They include food items, snacks, clothing, decks of cards, batteries, etc. She heads a group that does the charitable work on behalf of the Council of Catholic Women at St. Raphael's Church in Englewood, Florida. "Everyone in our family seems to be involved in some kind of charity or community service. He inspired all of us to do something in his memory. It makes something good come out of the tragedy," says Marianne. "I'd like nothing better than to not have to send any more packages because all the soldiers have come home."

"The Arlington Cemetery, White House, and Pentagon experiences were beautiful, but I wouldn't want anyone to go through it for the reason we did," admits Aunt Rita.

Janet expressed a similar sentiment in saying, "I think it's a great honor for my son, but it's also very sad for us. Every time there's an event honoring Jared, it brings everything back again. Emotionally, it's too draining. You're crying one minute, happy the next."

The final part of the whirlwind week was a "Hang Loose Night", a reception for family and friends held at the Sheraton Crystal City Grand Ballroom, following the Hall of Heroes dedication. Jared's beloved "Nana", Marjorie Ross, was up dancing. She showed off such impressive moves for an 83-year-old woman that it was rumored she was asked to audition for Dancing with the Stars. Not only was she well enough to travel to Washington to see her grandson honored, she was exuberant about it. Marjorie, Jared's last surviving grandparent, eventually died at 85 in 2011 from complications arising from a ruptured hernia. The Ross family had a "Momapolooza" to celebrate her life. They played musical instruments and sang her favorite songs in her honor.

"What I was most concerned with the Washington trip was the

immense sense of guilt I was feeling. I survived and the Monti's son didn't," Chris Grzecki admits. "I was worried about how they'd look at us. But, they felt bad for us. Imagine that. They lost their son and they felt bad for us because of what we went through. It's a testament to that family. They're good people. They were so accepting of us. I feel like part of their family, and I know the other guys do, too. They just welcomed us in. There's so much good in these people's hearts. It's awesome."

Franklin Woods agrees. "Yes, we met high ranking officials in Washington. The highest ranking imaginable. But it meant more to us to meet Monti's family. I could see how he turned out the way he was when I met them. None of us bought anything that whole week. They wouldn't allow it. I was going to buy a drink when Jared's mother said, 'No! Put your money away.' It was like my own Mom was talking to me. I didn't dare go against her. I put my wallet right away. Going to Washington was the closure that everybody needed."

At the "Hang Loose Night" Janet was "whisked out of the room by two military officers." She had no idea what was going to happen. It turns out they also gave her another Medal of Honor in the same type of wooden and glass presentation case that had been given to Paul at the White House the day before. Typically, there is only one given, but the Army was aware of their 2005 divorce. Needless to say, she was very appreciative of the gesture.

The strong emotions didn't end in Washington for Janet. "I'll never forget the announcement they made as the plane landed on the trip home to North Carolina They asked everyone to stay in their seats. They explained that there was a mother on board whose son had just been posthumously presented with the Medal of Honor. Everyone cheered and clapped as I walked off the plane. It was a little embarrassing, to tell you the truth. I was crying and I saw that many of the passengers were, too."

The First Lady made a great impression on the family at the White House. "We were totally blown away by her genuine concern. She was wonderful," effuses Paul. She could have sat anywhere, with anyone, in the East Room to listen to the President's speech. She chose to sit with Jared's immediate family. President Obama also won their respect by asking questions about Jared, listening carefully to the answers, remembering the information, and including it a short time later along with his prepared remarks at the Medal of Honor ceremony. Many of those in attendance wondered how the President could possibly have known so much about Jared.

But Presidents and those who would be President have made some famous gaffes. He made one of the worst of his Presidency on June 23, 2011 when he spoke in front of the 10th Mountain Division soldiers at Fort Drum, NY. President Obama congratulated them on their service and unfortunately said, "I had the great honor of seeing some of you because a comrade of yours, Jared Monti, was the first person I was able to award the Medal of Honor to who actually came back and wasn't receiving it posthumously."

There was an uncomfortable silence and a lot of squirming in the room. The President was talking to Jared's people. They were his military family. Every one of them knew Jared's story. After all, he was the first Medal of Honor recipient from the division since World War II. There was an enormous display nearby showing life-size pictures of Jared and giving the details of his heroic sacrifice.

The President had confused Jared with Salvatore Giunta, of the 173rd Airborne Brigade Combat Team, who became the first living person to receive the Medal of Honor since the Vietnam War, when the President put the medal around his neck on Nov. 16, 2010.

President Obama humbled himself and called Paul and Janet

personally to say he was sorry. Both appreciated that gesture.

Paul admits, "The mistake was disconcerting at first. A White House secretary phoned to ask if I was available to speak with the President. When he got on the line, he came right out and apologized. He realized right after the speech that he had made a mistake. It was unfortunate. I'm sure he has speech writers, and someone screwed up. He apologized more than once. You know, he could have just let it go. He could have sent something to the media, he could have sent us a letter, he could have had an aide call. But he personally called and that meant a lot to me. I think the highest honor you can get from someone is a personal apology. I thought it was a wonderful thing to do."

According to Janet, "I thought it was really nice that he called both of us. Everyone makes mistakes. He's just human. I didn't understand why he was criticized so much."

Republican Party leadership and conservative pundits took advantage of the opportunity to take shots at the President, questioning his sincerity, patriotism, commitment to the troops, and everything up to and including his manhood. They called Obama "clueless" and "disrespectful." It was the lead story on many media outlets for the next several days. Fox News correspondents called it a "horrible mistake". The Palin Express blog declared with questionable grammar, "My concern is for those families and friends who see these gaffes and bring on more pain and suffering."

Paul had the final word with this post on Facebook: "President Barack Obama telephoned me personally this afternoon to apologize for his error in the speech to the 10th Mountain Division. Apology accepted."

Chapter 21
Who Does this Kind of Stuff?

The Commonwealth of Massachusetts wanted to name a bridge after Jared in tribute to him. They gave Paul some high-profile choices. When he mentioned a plain, ordinary-looking bridge on Route 44 in Raynham, they said, '*What* bridge?' The question had a familiar ring to it. Paul explained that this one had special significance, and that's why it was chosen. It was the bridge where Jared and his friends had ended their fateful "Survival Training" canoe trip years before and waited for Paul to come and take them home. The bridge was dedicated on June 12, 2011.

What would Jared's reaction have been to have a bridge named after him? According to Paul, "He was too humble to want his own bridge. He would probably want the name changed to the Veteran's Memorial Bridge." In fact, Paul is fond of saying, "If he was here, he wouldn't be here" at the dedication of a memorial or other tribute to Jared. In other words, if Jared were still alive and was invited, he probably wouldn't bother to show up. He'd prefer to have something dedicated to someone else or to soldiers in general.

Captain Marc Cleveland of the 10th Mountain Division said at the bridge dedication, "The fact that he was unwavering in the face of danger and uncertainty, audacious, and loyal to his men, these are the qualities that he will always bring to our unit. In death, just as he was in life, SFC Monti remains a leader, a teacher and a standard bearer."

The shemagh scarf that Jared wore in Afghanistan now hangs over his picture at the American Legion Post 405 in Raynham, MA, along with his full dress uniform and descriptions of his exploits. On Veteran's Day of 2010, the room was given the name, The Jared Monti Function Room. There's even a monument outside the Post dedicated to him.

Former Legion Post Commander James Banks remembers Jared as "a little tyke who used to tag along after his Dad as part of a Sunday morning softball league. Jared is one of our local sons, and we all realize the sacrifice he made; this is only a small thing we did for him to give his name recognition."

"It was heart-wrenching to go through his personal materials and decide which ones I wanted to donate to the Legion room and which to keep at home. That was the most difficult part," Paul confesses. "It means my son will be remembered into perpetuity. He will be there in people's minds and hearts long after I'm gone."

"It's gets difficult for me to talk about what happened to Jared. I've been asked by so many people over and over again. They always want me to recount that day on the mountain. I have to go over it again and again. I don't think anyone would want to do that. They always want to know how he died," explains Paul. "I think the best stories are about what he did for others and some of the goofy things he did. I still get stories today from people about Jared that make me say, Wow! Who does this kind of stuff?"

During his 12 years of military service, Jared was presented with 34 other military awards in addition to the Medal of Honor, Purple Heart, and Bronze Star. They include five Army Commendation Medals, four Army Achievement Medals, four

Good Conduct Medals, two National Defense Service Medals, two Korean Defense Service Medals, two Armed Forces Expeditionary Medals, two Kosovo Campaign Medals, two Non-Commissioned Officer Development Ribbons, two Army Service Ribbons, Overseas Service Ribbon, NATO Medal, two Afghanistan Campaign Medals, Global War on Terrorism Service Medal, Combat Action Badge, Parachutist Badge, and an Air Assault Badge.

Did Jared have the impressive collection of medals displayed in some big trophy case? Not at all. He shied away from any kind of notoriety. Some he gave to his sister the way you'd give away trinkets you won at the fair. Others he casually tossed into the sock drawer in his room. Jared never wanted to stand out. Yet stand out he has.

In addition to the bridge and the American Legion building, the following have been named after Jared: a street intersection; a playground; an annual Raynham Little League baseball Tournament; a workout center in Fort Drum, NY; two scholarships; a monument in South Carolina; a training facility in Fort Sill, Oklahoma; a combat outpost in Afghanistan; a dining facility at Kandahar Airfield; and a high school gymnasium. More monuments and dedication ceremonies are being planned.

The busy intersection in Raynham Center dedicated to Jared is called Four Corners. The street sign in his honor is at the corner of North Main, South Main, Orchard, and Pleasant streets. Jared spent many boyhood days fishing at Johnson's Pond near that spot in the center of town.

Cindy Sy Neufer posted this message to Jared about the Class of 1994's 15th reunion: "Went to the class reunion yesterday and spoke of you often. I think of you daily and I hope you know you will always be in my heart. You made a difference in so many lives. Keep smiling down on all of us whose lives you touched!"

It's easy to underestimate the impact that something as simple as a neighborhood playground can have. Someone identified only as "J. R." posted on Jared's Facebook page: "I happened upon your name for the first time about a month ago when I took my 3-year-old daughter to play at the park on King Phillip Street in Raynham. There was a memorial stone there, which briefly outlined your heroic actions in Afghanistan. I Googled your story and watched the YouTube videos about you. It really jolted me and made everything about war real for the first time. I broke down in tears. You see, Jared, I've watched countless news stories about fallen soldiers, and yet war never felt REAL to me. It always had a cinematic feel to it. I admit with regret that I've taken for granted all of the sacrifices that you and all of the brave servicemen and servicewomen make each day to ensure that America's freedom is never compromised. I promise to never make that mistake again."

The news of Jared's death had significant impact on residents of his home town. Representative of those feelings is this quote from Raynham's Senior Center Director, Joyce Rodriguez, who said, "I remember Jared as a little boy in church. I also knew Janet through an outreach group at St. Ann's. Paul helped us out last year by bringing vegetables from his garden to the Senior Center. And I feel really, really bad for his family now. They're such thoughtful people. I can't imagine the pain they're going through."

A friend, Karen Lee, posted this tribute to Jared: "Anyone who had the pleasure of meeting Jared would know he was nice, caring, down to earth, sweet, friendly to anyone and everyone he met. Never judged, never spoke an unkind word that I ever heard from his lips about anyone. Yet he was no wimp. He went in to save his men, his brothers, knowing he could lose his own life, which he did. He gave the ultimate sacrifice…Jared, you are missed so much and I am so proud to have known you…So remember not just

Jared from my amazing hometown, but every other soldier that gave the ultimate sacrifice, who has loved ones missing them."

Terri Newfield posted, "Our hometown hero didn't wear a cape, he wore dog tags." Karen DiMarzio expressed it as, "What an honor to live in a town with such a hero!" According to Michelle McGuire, "You left us too early, my friend. I think about you every day, & every time I drive by your Dad's house, I look to see if your truck is there. I don't know if some part of me hopes to one day see you walk out the door and get in your truck, but I always look. You are missed more than you know. You will never be forgotten & always in my heart."

Jared's friend Brendan Maguire declares, "I'll tell my kids about Jared's complete selflessness, where you give your life for someone else."

The Inaugural SFC Jared C. Monti Memorial Baby Shower was held on April 2, 2011 in Elsinore, California for twenty expectant military families, courtesy of Operation Showers of Appreciation and the SFC Jared C. Monti Charitable Fund. The shower was hosted by Lake Elsinore City Councilwoman Melissa Melendez and Courtney Faith Vera, a recipient of the California Commendation Medal for Meritorious Achievement for her work supporting military families. That year they surprised Jared's sister Niccole, who was having her second daughter. "We are shipping this to you!" said Courtney, as she rolled a baby stroller and diaper bag into view while Niccole and Janet participated via Skype.

Among those honored at the first baby shower were John Garner and his wife, who celebrated the birth of their first child, Jack Monti Garner. John proudly said he named his son after Jared, "because he saved my life that night on the mountain."

Although all the honors are appreciated, Paul has special affection for the building dedicated to Jared at the Fires Center of

Excellence Training Facility at Fort Sill. The state-of-the-art center houses technology to train field artillery and air defense soldiers. It has a simulation center that is like a giant interactive video game. He says, “The buildings there are all named for great American Generals. One of them is named for a lowly Sergeant – my son. That’s really something.”

At the dedication of the center’s Jared Monti Hall on August 19, 2011, CSM Byers recalled, “Monti’s efforts saved numerous lives on that rotation, and he continues to save lives through the soldiers he has trained and the leaders he mentored. His love of soldiers, ability to train and pass on his mastery of skills, and his understanding of maneuver, made him the finest forward observer, soldier, and leader I have ever known.”

MSG Power declares, “Jared was the most technically sound FISTer I’ve ever seen. He was also devoted to training his soldiers. He’d sacrifice anything for them, especially his time. If they didn’t know how to do something, he’d be willing to immediately take them out to the field and show them. That’s why I was the one who wrote up the request to have the new Call to Fire training facility at Ft. Sill named after him.”

Jimmy Phelps was excited to report, “Today I got to take my Warrant Officer Basic Course class over to the brand new SFC Jared C. Monti digital simulation facility here at Fort Sill. They are the very first group to use the facility. What a great honor for me and my guys!”

“It didn’t really hit me until I stood up to do Monti’s eulogy at the 3-71 CAV memorial service,” recalls SFC Hunsucker. “That’s when I lost it. I just remember saying that he was like mice in a wheat silo. By that I meant he was everywhere. All over the place, all the time. I talked about his legacy. I have to admit that I had trouble getting through it. They asked me if I wanted to accompany

Jared's body back to the States. I asked if someone else could do it. I didn't want to leave my guys that long. I was nervous about how they'd be."

At that service for the three fallen 10th Mountain Division soldiers, LTC Michael Howard described how the difficult phone calls he made to the families proved beneficial to him. He said, "The first words out of Mr. Monti's mouth were, 'How are my son's soldiers and friends doing?' He added that SFC Monti loved his work and his men, and he asked how his son fell. I told him he passed while trying to save the life of a comrade. Of course, his dad was not surprised. He asked me if we had gotten the men who did this, and I told him we had gotten most. He said thank you, and asked me to thank all the soldiers who were fighting for America. Then he asked me for the phone numbers of the Lybert family & Bradbury family because he intended to call them and go through the mourning process with them. These are some pretty special folks in all three families. I can't believe how strong they are in the face of the loss of their children. They're definitely serving as an example of strength for me, and I'm challenging myself every day to be as strong. After speaking to their parents, it's no surprise to me that SFC Monti, SSG Lybert, and PFC Bradbury were such superb soldiers."

The 10th Mountain Division's Command Sergeant Major James Redmore points out, "I don't think anybody ever expects to do anything extraordinary. They try to do their job every day the best they can. Jared's patrol is being overwhelmed by an enemy force. He's calmly calling in fire, which breaks up the enemy force, and he's going out to try to retrieve one of his fallen comrades. He does it once, twice, a third time. Is it extraordinary? Absolutely."

Jared's "Military Mom" Barb Dresser had this to say: "After learning of his death, I called both his Mom and Dad offering my thoughts and condolences. I then wanted to honor my surrogate son." She began what came to be known as Project Geronimo in Barnwell County, SC. Working with local organizations, they built a monument to Jared at Veteran's Memorial Park. A former 173 Airborne Brigade Sky Soldier and Viet Nam veteran who was dying of cancer provided the funds to construct the memorial. He wished to remain anonymous throughout the process and was known only as code name Geronimo."

Paul and Jared's Godmother, Terri (Ross) Lindsay, both attended the dedication of the memorial in April of 2010. Members of Jared's biological family were meeting Barb for the first time. "Barb told us to just look for the woman with the red hair. She gave me a genuine, warm hug. She spoke of Jared as if he were her son. Barb was an inspiration. The ceremony itself was just awesome," recollects Terri.

"Jared was there for me when my own son couldn't physically be," says Barb. "Ironically, Jared and my son were the same age and had the same rank. In reality, I think it was Jared who 'adopted' me. To this day, my son Henry is grateful for Jared's divine appointment in my life, and Jared's photo is proudly displayed in my home with the rest of my family photos, along with the flag that draped his memorial."

Shortly after the presentation ceremony, Barb received this e-mail from Henry in Iraq: "Oh Mom, what a story, you're making me cry here!!.... you are very fortunate to have known such a wonderful person! Thanks so much for sharing with me. I feel that I have another brother in spirit!"

According to a posting from Eddie Hair, who was instrumental in putting the dedication ceremony together, "Here in Barnwell, South Carolina, Jared's monument is forever 'standing tall and looking good.' Airborne all the way! Jared's service and sacrifice is NEVER to be forgotten."

Major General James Livingston, a retired Marine and Medal of Honor recipient himself, was a featured speaker at the memorial dedication. While serving as a Company Commander in Viet Nam, then-Captain Livingston was shot three separate times in a fierce firefight on May 2, 1968, yet refused to leave the battlefield. Even though he was unable to walk, he remained in a dangerously exposed position and supervised the removal of casualties. Only after the safety of all of his Marines was assured did he allow himself to be evacuated. As someone who knows first-hand the meaning of courage under fire, he declared in his dedication speech, "God blessed America with Jared Monti." It would be hard to say it more eloquently than that. It would be hard to find a more credible source to say it.

Army Chief of Staff Gen. George Casey, Jr. arranged through the Secretary of the Air Force to allow Janet to live Jared's dream of becoming a Navy pilot. On Nov. 10, 2010, she was invited to fly in an F-15E Strike Eagle at Seymour Johnson Air Force Base in NC. She jumped at the chance.

"I trained for the mission. I went in the day before for instructions and practice. I had to get an okay from my doctor before they let me do it. The night before the flight, I got to stay at a General's Quarters." They asked Janet what she wanted her call sign to be. She chose "Renegade" in tribute to Jared's e-mail address. She had tears in her eyes when she reported for duty and saw that all the members of the ground crew were wearing "Renegade" insignias on their uniform.

"I can't believe I'm doing this," said Janet as she boarded. "Jared is looking down on me now, saying, 'What the hell are you doing? Are you nuts?' But he'll be with me." They flew at supersonic speed. The pilot asked Janet if there was any place in particular she wanted to go. She asked if they could fly over her home in Winterville. "I loved every minute of it. I'd do it again in a heartbeat." She had told the pilot that she was hoping they could do an inverted dive like in the movie *Top Gun*, but then she got sick, as most people do on their first flight. The pilot asked if she still wanted to do the inverted dive. She replied, "Maybe not."

"She told me about who Jared was, the kind of man he was," the pilot, Colonel Patrick Doherty, said to the press shortly after their jet landed. "It was a tremendous, tremendous honor to fly her and to acknowledge her sacrifice. This is definitely a flight I'll never forget. It was special."

When Janet was presented with the photograph of her in the cockpit, she held it up to the sky saying, "See that, Jared? There's your mother!"

Jared's death was the first but, unfortunately, not the only tragedy to affect the family. Janet's sister Lynda (Ross) Koke drove her twenty-year-old daughter Courtney to her boyfriend's house the afternoon of September 10, 2011. "I also dropped her sisters off at their friends' houses and told Courtney I would drop her off last, because it would give us a bit more time to spend with each other. She was going back to Spokane in just a few more days."

Courtney was born in Spokane, Washington, and moved with her family to Massachusetts when she was five years old. She was a Taunton High School graduate and an Interior Decorating and Architectural Design student at Spokane Falls Community College. Her goal was to travel to Spain after graduation to continue her education.

"It was my understanding that she was going to a party in Foxboro that night with a bunch of friends, recalls Lynda. "As she got out of my car, we said we loved each other and I told her to have fun. I fell asleep on my couch after watching a movie with my son, and the phone rang about 10:20 p.m. I looked at the number, didn't recognize it, and ignored the call. A few minutes later, I thought I heard a car door close outside. Then the phone rang again. It was the same number as before. This time I thought it must be Courtney needing to get in the house because she had forgotten her key. So I answered the phone. It was the Boston Police Department. They asked if I was Courtney's Mom. I said that I was. They told me that Courtney had fallen through a skylight from on top of a building in Boston and was killed. I asked if this was a sick joke. They said it wasn't. I told them she wasn't in Boston, she was going to Foxboro. I just couldn't believe what I was hearing and hung up on them. I told my boyfriend what had happened and he called them back. They confirmed the story."

A friend had called Courtney to ask if they wanted to go take some pictures of the Boston skyline. They agreed, and her boyfriend knew a spot on top of a roof that gave a panoramic view of the city. They were climbing on the roof of a seven-story building at 281 Summer Street at 8:30 p.m. when "Kiki," as she was nicknamed, fell through a blind shaft to the third floor.

According to Lynda, "There were multiple buildings mortared together. She was at a higher level than other parts and was sitting on a wall. When she stood up to turn around and get down from where she was, she jumped down on what she thought was going to be a hard surface. It was actually a glass-topped, blind ventilation shaft."

A rescue team was dispatched after a call to 911, but they had a difficult time locating her in the building, even though she was still speaking as they arrived. They breached some walls in their attempt to find her. The first responders contacted someone from maintenance who knew the building. It took them another hour to finally reach her. They administered CPR, but it was too late. She had died from blunt force trauma to her head and body.

"Nothing in this world could ever prepare one for something like this. I remember running out my front door and stopping in my tracks. I went running because I was in complete shock. I wanted to jump but I realized there was nothing to jump from. They say you either have a fight or flight response when experiencing something this devastating. I definitely was looking for flight. It was in the weeks to follow that I decided to fight," she admits.

Patti remembers, "My sister Lynda called to give me the news about Courtney, but I wasn't home. I couldn't forgive myself that I wasn't there for her. We were celebrating my husband Ken's 50th birthday party. We got a text from my daughter Anna that both Lynda and my sister Mary called. I was about to call Lynda when Ken got a call from her on his cell phone. He walked in the opposite direction while he was talking. I knew something terrible had happened. I can still remember the look on his face when he told me."

Courtney's obituary noted, "She had such a vibrant spirit and made friends wherever she went. She was a talented artist and loved to dance and sing. She enjoyed hanging with her cousins and her friends and just being goofy. She loved to talk funny and had a silliness that was contagious and drew you to her. She was kind and generous and always made you smile." Like Jared's, it also said that she "will be greatly missed by her many loving aunts and uncles and had a truly special bond with her many cousins."

"Somehow I learned a lot about myself in having to cope with the awful experience with Jared. That helped me deal with Courtney's death. I can't explain why. It's like I had a new set of tools. I talked to Lynda every day on the phone for quite a while," recalls Patti.

"Our family gets together once a year to celebrate Courtney's life," says Mary. "Everyone brings a silly prop like a sombrero or witch's hat that they put in a brown paper bag. Each person chooses a bag and has to wear that prop for the night. We all laugh because that's what she would have wanted us to do. Not a day goes by that I don't think of both Jared and Courtney." One of the traditions at the annual get-together is that family members write another message to Courtney on a balloon. Then they release the balloons outside and watch them float up to the sky.

"To this day, the deaths of Jared and Courtney don't seem real. Both had such tragic things happen to them. It's still hard to comprehend," admits Terri. "Because Jared was in the military, we knew there was a possibility that he could be hurt. With Courtney, though, it was totally unexpected. I admire the way both my sisters Janet and Lynda have been able to cope. I don't know how either one has been able to do it."

Lynda posted this message to Jared on his Facebook page shortly after his death: "We may not know his reason for taking you so soon from us but, Jared, you fulfilled your purpose. You touched so many lives and gave so much of yourself to others. You have fallen doing what you were here to do."

After Courtney's fatal accident, Lynda posted a message to Jared: "Been thinking a lot about you, as I always do. You've got a lot of great people up there with you, and most recently your cousin, my daughter Courtney. She, too, like you, was taken from us way too early in life, but knowing she's up there with you does bring some peace to my sorrow. Please know, as she will never be, you too will never be forgotten and I keep you in a special place in my heart."

"The lesson for me with what happened to Jared and Courtney is to hold on to your children and love them today," concludes Niccole. "I know I appreciate my kids more because of what happened to them."

Every day, indeed, is a gift not to be wasted. That must be why it's called the present.

Chapter 22
Operation Flags for Vets

"The story of what Jared did on the mountain that day is an amazing story of valor and sacrifice. But for me this isn't about heroes. It's about a kid who grew up in Massachusetts and did the right thing, and his father who paid a dear price but turned his son's sacrifice into something really meaningful. They both did the right thing," says Alex Ashlock, who conducted the interview with Paul and his brother Matt that inspired "I Drive Your Truck."

Jared is buried in Section 11, Site 38 of the 749-acre National Cemetery in Bourne, MA, which opened in 1973 and is located 65 miles southeast of Boston. The Department of Veteran's Affairs National Cemeteries are special places reserved for special people. There are 131 of them in the United States, but the Bourne National Cemetery is the only one in Massachusetts. There are a shocking number of graves at each one. Row after row of fallen soldiers. There are about 100 burials per month that take place in Bourne.

Veterans as well as Army Reservists and members of the National Guard who die on active duty can be buried in a national cemetery. An eligible veteran must have been discharged or separated from active duty under conditions other than dishonorable. A citizen who served in the armed forces of a government allied with the United States as well as spouses and dependent minor children may also be eligible for burial in a national cemetery.

Hospital Corpsman Richard D. De Wert is the other Medal of Honor recipient buried at the Bourne National Cemetery. During the Korean War, he was attached to the 2nd Battalion 7th Marines. Originally buried in Korea, he was reinterred at the Woodlawn National Cemetery in Elmira, N. Y. and reinterred again in 1987 in Section 5 Grave 167 at the Bourne Cemetery, near his family home in Taunton, MA.

On April 5, 1951, during a battle against communist troops, he sustained a leg wound while dragging a stricken Marine from a fire-swept area to safety. De Wert refused medical treatment for himself and went back to carry a second wounded Marine out of the line of fire. He was shot in the shoulder after attempting to rescue a third Marine. He again refused treatment. While rendering assistance to a fourth Marine, he was mortally wounded.

Paul was asked by the military if he wanted Jared to be buried at Arlington National Cemetery, but with so many family members, including himself, living in close proximity to Bourne, he thought that would be a better place, similar to the thinking of De Wert's family. There was, however, a major problem with the Bourne Cemetery.

When he first visited, Paul went to place a small flag on his son's grave and was stopped. He was told that wasn't allowed. That started a process in motion for which the cemetery officials hadn't bargained.

Cemetery rules prohibited flags because the grave markers are flush with the ground. They use footstones and not headstones. Anything placed above them would supposedly make cutting the grass difficult. Paul thought that was a poor excuse. Cemetery personnel said that a flag-lined driveway leading to the burial complex was "sufficient." Paul felt something had to be done and he tried to lobby the bureaucrats to change those rules.

There is a Massachusetts State Law that requires flags to be put on every veteran's grave on Memorial Day and Veteran's Day. Yet at the Bourne National Cemetery they told Paul, "As soon as you step out of your vehicle, you're on federal land. We don't have to follow Massachusetts law."

"That didn't sit well with me," admitted Paul, "All these wonderful veterans with no American flags, not being honored." It took four and a half years of contacting veteran's groups, members of Congress, U. S. Senators, The Secretaries of the Army and the Navy, and even the Secretary of Defense to try to get things changed. Finally, thanks to the intervention of former MA Senators John Kerry and Scott Brown, cemetery officials sent Paul a letter giving permission to flag the cemetery conditionally. They said he would have to buy all the flags, place them on the graves, and remove them within four days.

Paul took on the challenge with Matt and they started a project called Operation Flags for Vets where volunteers come to the cemetery the Saturdays before Memorial Day and Veteran's Day and help place flags on the 57,000 graves there. They are later removed and put in storage.

The logistics were formidable. First there would be the purchase of the 12x18 inch flags mounted on 30 inch round wooden sticks. They wanted them to be made in the United States and managed to find a company in Georgia that produced them. But, that meant money had to be raised by donations for the initial purchase, and then subsequent purchases as the flags got damaged or worn out. They'd need to somehow get enough volunteers twice a year on holiday week-ends to plant all those flags. Then they'd have to get the same or additional volunteers to come back again and take those flags out of the ground. They'd have to find somewhere to store them.

Many people told Paul that it would take days to put in and take out 57,000 flags. They felt the cemetery officials were giving them restrictions meant to discourage them. They didn't know how they'd pay for the flags or where they would store them. Paul was determined, though. It's a trait that runs in the family. He simply said, "We'll spread the word." More than a thousand volunteers showed up, and donations poured in. There have been no corporate sponsors. Paul wanted to make the entire thing a "grass roots" effort. That first Memorial Day, the job of setting up was done in less than two hours. The cemetery officials had also decreed that the flags had to be taken down within four days. Paul agreed with all conditions except for that one. He insisted that the flags should be in for a full week. When the time came, the work of clearing was also done in less than two hours.

So American flags now fly on the graves at the National Cemetery in Bourne, Massachusetts on Memorial Day and Veterans Day of each year. Every year, the Saturday before the two holidays has been the "flags in" day and, after a full week, the Sunday after the Holidays has been the "flags out" day. Both events begin at 10 a.m. The graves are thus flagged for two weekends, which is appreciated by many of the relatives and friends of those who come to visit the graves.

Initially, the flags were stored at Bourne's Otis Air National Guard Base; now they are kept in a private warehouse in Pocasset, donated by Bill Panos of West Bridgewater.

The sea of American flags that honor the veterans is a sight to which many now look forward. "Flags represent everything that we hold dear in this country. They are reminders that a lot of people gave their lives so we can be free," says Paul. "It's about honoring the dead. These people served their country and they deserve at least a little respect."

The flag-planting and flag-removal at the cemetery has become a tradition for many volunteers. It's a real family event, where young Cub Scouts and Brownies work alongside Viet Nam and World War II veterans. After the Pledge of Allegiance, National Anthem, and some brief remarks, the volunteers fan out and go to work. Some carry screwdrivers to poke holes in the ground before planting the flags at the grave sites. They are asked to place the flags next to the middle of the footstone, about 3 to 4 inches into the ground. Some linger to look for the burial sites of relatives, loved ones, or friends. Some have quiet conversations with them.

"The wonderful thing about this is that it reaches the heart of the ordinary person that is usually silent about things, that wants to do things but can't find them," says Paul. "And here is something so simple: they can drive to a cemetery and pick up a flag and put it on the grave of a veteran they wish to honor. We have busloads of people coming in. But individual families that come down now, they've made it a tradition, and Mom and Dad and the kids and Grandma and Grandpa are all there, all putting flags on the graves. And it's just phenomenal to see people of every age, from infants in strollers to the senior citizens down there helping out, and with smiles on their faces. It's a marvelous thing."

According to Alex Ashlock, "I knew I had to go to Operation Flags for Vets, because this was the perfect example of a story from the two recent wars that deserved the kind of attention I could give it. It also started to feel very personal for me, especially after I met Paul and interviewed him at that first Operation Flags for Vets before Memorial Day, 2011. I could also tell that Paul appreciated my being there. I think the thing about this story is how one man took a horrible thing and turned it into a tradition that now attracts thousands of people to the Massachusetts National Cemetery. Paul has given all these people a chance to honor the nation's veterans, but he has also given people a chance to honor their loved ones who are buried there, just like Paul wanted to do in the first place for Jared. It makes sense that he has done this because he is a former teacher. He's still teaching."

Among those who have helped plant flags is Hill 2160 Patrol Leader Chris Cunningham, who claims, "When I first heard that flags weren't allowed at the cemetery, I thought it was crazy. It didn't make sense to me. All those veterans not being honored. Now, you step back when all the flags are planted, and you just see rolling red, white, and blue. It's beautiful. All the generations represented, including the Boy Scouts and Girl Scouts learning to respect our veterans. It's outstanding. I'm sure the cemetery officials are thinking they should have been doing this all along."

Another who has been a regular at Bourne National Cemetery to help flag the graves is Carlos Arredondo, who proudly says, "As a citizen, for me to have an opportunity to participate is an honor. I'm grateful to be able to do it. I'm part of the family."

Carlos was expecting a 44th birthday phone call from his 20-year-old son, Lance Corporal Alexander S. Arredondo, on August 25, 2004. The young Marine was on his second tour of duty in Iraq. Instead, a military van pulled up to his home. They came to inform Carlos that his son had been killed in action, but did not bring a Chaplain and spoke to him in the front yard rather than in private. Carlos became so upset that he grabbed a hammer and pounded the Marine's van. He then doused it with a five-gallon can of gasoline from his garage and ignited it with a propane torch. However, he accidentally spilled gasoline on himself and caught fire.

The Marines managed to pull him away and douse the flames,

but he was hospitalized with second and third-degree burns over much of his body. Carlos attended Alex's funeral on a stretcher with two paramedics on each side. His recovery took over a year. He was not prosecuted for destroying the van and later apologized to the Marine Corps.

Coming to the United State from Costa Rica as an undocumented immigrant, Carlos became a U. S. citizen in 2006 with the sponsorship of Senator Edward Kennedy. In doing so, he became the first parent of a slain soldier from either the Iraq or Afghanistan Wars to be granted citizenship.

His surviving son, 22-year-old Brian, committed suicide in 2011 after losing a fight with depression brought on by his brother's death. On April 15, 2013, Carlos gained national fame at the Boston Marathon bombings. In addition to being there to support the National Guard runners who were honoring Alexander, Carlos was there to support a group of suicide prevention runners who were paying tribute to Brian. He was at the finish line when the bombs exploded. At that moment, in fact, he was handling a small American flag to a member of the National Guard. Rather than running away, he ran in the direction of the blasts. "My first reaction was to run toward the injured. There was so much commotion and a lot of people running away. I was one of the first to help people and God protected me," Carlos later told reporters. He helped clear away fencing, scaffolding, and debris to allow emergency workers to get to victims and assist them.

While photographers were taking pictures and videos of the iconic "man with the cowboy hat," Carlos helped 27-year-old Jeff Baumann, who had lost both of his legs in the blast, by lifting him into a wheelchair that was there for runners too tired to walk. Carlos helped to get him to Boston University Medical Center. "Stay with me. Stay with me," Carlos kept saying to Jeff, who later underwent multiple surgeries for burns, abdominal injuries, and eventual attachment of artificial limbs below both knees. Jeff has also been an honored participant at the flag planting in Bourne.

"It really is an act of love, and it's wonderful to see the people and their reactions," Paul says of the volunteers. "They are so happy to be doing what we are doing. From the family members who have relatives interred at Bourne, to the civic organizations, to current and ex-service members, everyone appears to find some joy and satisfaction in this endeavor. There are tears and smiles and warm happy thoughts. We had an 82-year-old woman who was there last time. Her husband had been buried there for 30 years. She couldn't have been more thankful. She had to go all those years without putting a flag on his grave," says Paul.

At the other end of the age spectrum is Bob McCabe's pre-school daughter, who was touched by their experience at the cemetery. Bob posted, "I just returned from Bourne with my 2½-year-old daughter. All she kept saying was 'Look at all the flags!'"

Jen Mead also commented about the affect the experience has on her children: "Our mini people have their game faces on. Went to bed early and have their screwdrivers ready to punch holes in the earth! They loved it last year...such a powerful event!"

Mary Alice Buckley Cottle commented on what the experience meant to her: "As my two friends and I turned to leave the areas we had flagged, we were all overwhelmed by the powerful display of flags, enhanced by both the rolling land surface and the brilliance of the sun on the flags moving in the breeze. I feel selfish in saying how much my emotion benefited by being there again this year."

Michael Augustine posted, "Hey, Jared. I visited you today after helping your Dad and hundreds of volunteers take down and store the flags. You would have been impressed with the efficiency. Who knew such a diverse group of people could come together and knock something out like that."

Michael McCaffrey, who heads the Red Cross Boston Office Finance Center of Excellence, said in an e-mail that the Flags for Vets experience was "very, very impressive" and added, "My boys and I could not believe it!"

"I'm heading down to Bourne now to place flowers on my own father's grave. It used to bother my late grandmother greatly that flags were not allowed on the individual graves," said Steve Brown. "My thanks to the Monti family and all the volunteers who took part in this heartwarming gesture. The families of those who have been laid to rest there truly appreciated it."

Alex Ashlock says, "I was there again this year for Operation Flags for Vets to interview Paul. I told him that it's always an honor to speak to him. He said the same thing, and then he said, 'You changed my life.' I told him the same. Just being able to help tell his story has made me a better person than I was before. And it made me truly believe that the stories I have been trying to tell matter and can make a difference."

At the end of each Flags for Vets day, Paul goes to his son's grave to pay his respects.

Operation Flags for Vets allows everyone to make a difference, at least on Memorial Day and Veteran's Day. Imagine having a one-way conversation with a fallen vet that might go something like this: "Looks like you gave your life for your country. I don't know if anyone ever comes to visit you. I don't know if they even remember that you're buried here. But I came to honor you on this special day. I'm going to plant a flag on your grave to thank you for your service. I'll be back again. God bless you."

Chapter 23

"I Drive Your Truck"

It's the 49th annual Academy of Country Music Awards at the MGM Grand Garden Arena in Las Vegas. The date is April 6, 2014. The show is in Sunday night prime time and is being watched by 13 million people. Luke Bryan and Blake Shelton are hosting. The winner of the Song of the Year award is about to be announced. Lee Brice's "I Drive Your Truck" is up against formidable competition – Gary Allan's "Every Storm Runs Out of Rain," Miranda Lambert's "Mama's Broken Heart," Blake Shelton's "Mine Would be You," and Darius Rucker's "Wagon Wheel." But it's Lee Brice's name that's announced as the winner of the coveted award.

"I Drive Your Truck" was the third single released from the "Hard 2 Love" album on December 3, 2012. It reached #1 on the Billboard Country Music charts on April 30, 2013. It's no ordinary country song. It's not just an ode to a pickup truck. It's something special. Sales are now closing in on a million copies. Tammy Ragusa, the respected critic from *Country Music* magazine gave the song a straight "A" rating, saying, "Brice sings it like his life depends on it."

Lee reached the podium and acknowledged, "This award is not for me. This is the song of the year and it comes from the writers."

He then turned the microphone over to a teary-eyed Connie Harrington who announced, "We're so honored and grateful for the outpouring and response to this song." She closed by saying, "Thank you, Paul Monti and family, and to every person in America who knows what it's like to live the words of this song day in and day out. God bless you."

"I Drive Your Truck" also won Song of the Year at the 47th Annual Country Music Awards in Nashville on November 6, 2013. In accepting the CMA award Brice admitted, "Unbelievable song. First time I heard it, it blew my mind, changed my life." Songs that "blow your mind" and "change your life" are pretty rare. But the best ones can do just that.

Jimmy Yeary, one of the song writers along with Jessi Alexander and Connie Harrington, closed his CMA acceptance speech with, "Thank you so much, Jared, for what you did for this country, man."

The 2014 Golden Boot Award for Song of the Year has special significance because it's based on popular vote. "I Drive Your Truck" won, garnering more than 43% of the vote despite the fact that it was up against songs by powerhouses Blake Shelton, Miranda Lambert, Eric Church, Kacey Musgraves, Florida Georgia Line, and Dierks Bentley.

Janet's brother, Thomas Ross, posted, "A foot print upon the sand will be blown away in time, a Song of the Year will whisper in your ear for all time. Thank you. A tribute well deserved, and performed with love and gratitude for all to see, hear, and listen. I'm a proud uncle."

People deal with grief in different ways. Some frequently visit the gravesite of a loved one. Others never do. It's a deeply personal and individual choice. As the "I Drive Your Truck" song describes, Paul visits Jared's gravesite but really "feels him" when he jumps into Jared's black 4X4 2001 Dodge Ram 1500 and drives it. On the outside, the truck has decals for the 10th Mountain Division and 82nd Airborne Division, American flags, a bumper sticker for the Jared C. Monti Charitable Foundation, along with Go Army and Support the Troops stickers. Inside, Paul keeps his son's possessions intact. To this day, you can find small change in the ash tray, a pair of combat boots, an Old Skoal can, a Boston Red Sox cap, running shoes, and dog tags hanging from the rear view mirror. (The back cover of this book shows Jared's truck.)

Paul is trying to do something he knows he can't do – hold on to his beloved son. The truck costs more to keep up and repair than it's worth but he admits, "I want to keep the truck running as long as I can. It's him. I want to keep his DNA around me. I love driving it because it reminds me of him, even though I don't need the truck to remind me of him. I think about him every hour of every day." Paul keeps the truck in the same condition it was in when he got the terrible news of Jared's death. People have contacted Paul offering to make free upgrades to the truck. He insists, "I need to be true to Jared. This was his and he wouldn't want it to be out there flashy. Jared was a very, very humble kid." Will Paul ever clean out that truck? "I've thought of it, but I just can't bring myself to do it," he replies.

The truck's odometer is closing in on 150,000 miles. Sometimes the driver's side window refuses to close, which makes it a little uncomfortable in New England winters. Paul has replaced the engine but otherwise keeps the truck in the exact condition it was in when Jared drove it. There are even receipts and other personal papers still in the storage compartments. "The song is not about a truck. It's about holding on to something you've lost. Jared is always with me. But we're private in there. We close the windows. Just him and me. It's nice," confesses Paul. "I try to be careful with it. I know he'd yell at me if I dented it."

Paul takes the truck out almost every day but can't listen to the song when he's driving, especially on the highway, because he gets too emotional.

How did "I Drive Your Truck" come to be written? Connie Harrington was in her car when she heard a portion of an interview with Paul Monti conducted by Alex Ashlock, Producer and Director of *Here and Now*, a popular two-hour WBUR in Boston and National Public Radio live radio show, which weekly reaches an estimated 3.6 million listeners and is carried on 383 stations across the country.

Alex specializes in telling heartfelt, real-life stories about members of the military and their families. Why does he do it? He explains, "I became a student of history and started to understand what wars were all about. But by then, my Dad had died. All I knew about my Dad's war experience was that he and all of his friends went. One of them was paralyzed in France a few days after D-Day. So I decided that I would try to tell as many stories as I could about soldiers. I'm including all the services in that term. I did that in my newspaper and radio work as often as I could. I made it a point to always produce these stories for Memorial Day and Veterans Day. And it might seem like an insignificant thing, given why those days are designated as holidays, but I never take them off. I work and remember why those days are sacred. They're not about sales at Macy's."

Alex interviewed Paul and Janet before they went to Washington in 2009. He again had Paul on the show along with his brother Matt to talk about the first Operation Flags for Vets events on Memorial Day of 2011. Alex had no idea that Connie was listening and scribbling notes. "I recorded the interview that inspired 'I Drive Your Truck', but I didn't even know that inspiration had happened until nearly two years later," he says.

"I Drive Your Truck" almost didn't come to be. Connie didn't feel like listening to something about a soldier who was killed in combat. "Honestly, I tell everybody it's pretty ironic this song even got written, because I rolled my eyes and told myself I didn't want to hear that. I almost changed the station on the radio," she admits.

Connie's father spent a year and a half in as a captive in two Japanese POW camp in the Philippine Islands during World War II. He suffered from seizures and severe post-traumatic stress disorder throughout his life, often dropping to his knees in their home and calling out to his fellow 6th Ranger Battalion soldiers. "It made growing up in our house not the easiest thing," she claims. "It's a painful topic for me."

But Connie didn't change the station. "I started out half-listening and then got intrigued and started listening more closely. I was struck by the sound of Paul's voice. I keep yellow Post-It notes on my car console and I grabbed them." She then started to excitedly write down comments that Paul made without actually knowing who said them. She was crying and listening, trying not to drive off the road while she was scribbling. "It was not just the story of the truck that I connected with. Paul was actually doing the interview to ask for support for putting flags on the graves of fallen veterans at the cemetery. There was a spiritual thread running through the whole subject matter. I must not have heard the part about Jared being presented with the Medal of Honor. I didn't learn that until later," she admits.

Connie, who has co-written more than a dozen No. 1 songs in multiple genres, shared her scribbles with Jessi Alexander at a regularly scheduled songwriting session the next day. "It's more enjoyable to write with others. You bring in different viewpoints and angles. I don't know anyone in Nashville who writes by themselves," says Connie, who tried to talk about the song with Jessi but almost immediately choked up and said, "Never mind.

Let's move on." Fortunately, Jessi saw that Connie was deeply affected by something and stopped her, saying, "No, wait a minute. Tell me more about that story." "We noodled a melody and quickly exchanged ideas. We started to think that maybe this could be super special," recalls Connie.

The two made some immediate progress and even came up with some of the lines that would be in the final version of the song, including *89 cents in the ashtray*. "I don't know where that number came from," Connie says. "It was just a random thing that popped into our heads. It was important not to make it an even dollar number, because it showed that somebody spent time in that truck and knew EXACTLY how much money was in that ashtray."

They brought the beginnings of the song to Jimmy Yeary to get a "male perspective" as Connie called it, and also "because he's great with both music and lyrics." He "laid down a terrific melody" and the potent songwriting trio was on its way. "I know for sure that Jimmy came up with the line, *Half-empty bottle of Gatorade rolling on the floorboards*," says Connie. "That's something we would have never thought of."

Just a month later, "I Drive Your Truck" was born. "Sometimes a song comes out quickly and sometimes it doesn't. It comes out when it comes out," claims Connie. Coincidently, this one was born on June 21, 2011, the five-year anniversary of the day Jared lost his life. It also happened to be the birthday of Connie's father. "There were too many of these coincidences to make it accidental," muses Connie. "This was somehow just meant to be."

This song can be downloaded using the following iTunes link – https://itunes.apple.com/us/album/i-drive-your-truck/id513670724?i=513670870&ign-mpt=uo%3D4.

All the lines of the song were accurate except for the "Braves cap" part. "Many people from Nashville are Braves fans, so that's what we used in the song for the baseball cap," explains Connie. Actually Jared had a Red Sox cap in his truck. But, it did have a big "B" on it. The Atlanta Braves used to be the Boston Braves, something Connie didn't realize. How could the writers have been so attuned to Jared and what he had in that truck? Paul to this day doesn't know. He says, "I didn't go into that kind of detail during the NPR interview. How could the writers have known what was in the truck? It had to be divine intervention."

The explanation from the three writers was that they had brainstorming sessions about what a soldier that age might have in his truck. "We were just guessing," confesses Connie. For whatever reason, they somehow channeled Jared and turned out to be right on the mark.

"You feel like this song was such a gift," Connie says, "and it's facilitated healing, I think, in people. And we just wanted him to know that it was his words that touched us. I still can't talk about this song without crying. It's about acknowledgement of a loss."

Co-writer Jessi Alexander knew they had something significant. They all cried while they were writing it. Every time they'd play it for someone, they'd cry too. The writers used Connie's weeping as a barometer as to whether a line worked or not. Jimmy joked that if she didn't cry on a line, they didn't write it. "I'm an empathetic person," explains Connie. "That's both a blessing and a curse. I really felt Paul's grief."

The writers then had to find the right singer. The three credit the song's success to Lee Brice's powerful delivery. Jessi said they needed someone with "conviction and passion." They found that in Brice. Connie echoes, "He sang from the bottom of his heart, and it tore mine apart, in a good way."

"I never get tired of hearing this song. It's my favorite of all the songs I've been involved in writing," says Connie. "The songs that are the most rewarding to me are the meaningful ones. They're the ones I am most proud of. I've been surprised by how many writers have told us that we've given them hope that a serious song like this can do so well. It shows that people do care about lyrics. Words do matter."

The writers and Lee were to gather in Nashville for a #1 Celebration on May 13, 2013 at the CMA Building in Nashville, but there was someone missing. As the party approached, they started saying how they couldn't believe they hadn't found the person who inspired the song. The problem was Connie couldn't remember Paul's name. It made the search extremely difficult. She was ready to give up but told herself she'd take one last shot on the Internet. She typed in a different order of the words she had been using and, sure enough, a picture of Paul came up with the truck. "As soon as I saw it, I knew it was him," effuses Connie. "I was freaking out. It was just overwhelming, a crazy roller-coaster of emotions." Once she found Paul's name, it was then easy to go back to find that NPR interview in their archives. The two-year search was over.

Connie found Paul's phone number and called on April 29, but was disappointed when she just got his voice mail. Then she noticed a Flags for Vets request for donations that Paul's brother Matt had posted on-line that included a phone number. Connie called and asked Matt if he knew how to reach Jared's father. Paul happened to be at his brother Matt's house at the time to celebrate his 70th birthday. Matt told her the guy she wanted to speak with was standing next to him, and he handed the phone to Paul. "Connie got out about three words before she broke into tears," Paul says. She linked into Jessi and Jimmy's cell phones in conference call mode and then handed the call off to them. They had finally connected with Jared's father.

The writers introduced themselves and told Paul about the song they had written. He was familiar with the song and told them, "We feel like this song is just right out of our story." That's when they revealed to him, "Well, it IS you. It's YOUR son." They acknowledge it was a powerful moment to have Paul realize that he was the inspiration behind the song. He was so affected by the call that he had to leave his brother's party early.

Paul is certainly aware of the fact that the song could have been written about any number of other people. There are, after, all many families that keep mementos of their fallen soldiers, including trucks. Brian Bradbury's mother Rhonda Bradbury, for instance, pays homage to her son by continuing to drive his truck. Cheryl Lee Patrick, the mother of Patrick Lybert, posted this message: "I'm the Gold Star Mother of SSG Patrick L. Lybert. I had his F150 overhauled. I drive his truck windows down, tunes blaring as I drive the country roads and fishing holes where he grew up with tears streaming." Cheryl had sent Paul the link to the song shortly after it was released, not knowing that the song was about Paul.

Tim also drives a truck that used to belong to his brother Jared. It's a white with black trim 2000 Isuzu Rodeo that Jared purchased in Fayetteville when he was stationed at Fort Bragg. "It's the only thing besides some clothes of his that I have to remember him by. Of course I always think of him every time I take a drive in it. What's funny is that the song 'I Drive your Truck' tells the story of driving a brother's truck, which is kind of ironic. People have asked me many times to sell them the truck. I guess Rodeos are a hot commodity, but I'll never sell it," says Tim. "Everything still works great. I got it with about 22,000 miles on it and it's now got over 100,000 miles. It's not showy at all, just the factory base model with a standard transmission. It has Jared's battery back-up in it, and some military gear like knee pads. The glove compartment has every receipt from anything truck-related still inside."

According to Connie, Lee Brice's brother appeared in the video and Lee added the word "brother" to the lyrics "to focus the feelings he has for his brother in the song." Although Lee didn't have children at the time, he and his fiancée Sara Reeveley now have a young son, Takoda, who Brice calls affectionately "a Mini-Me, a Mini-Lee."

Paul was invited to the "Number One" party and shared the stage with Lee, the three writers, and industry executives. He was given a special commemorative plaque featuring Jared's photo. Then he was asked to tell his son's story to the packed crowd of media, industry executives, and other invited guests. Many were moved to tears. "No one had heard Paul speak before," says Connie. "We really didn't know what to expect. You could have heard a pin drop. It was so moving. Afterwards someone commented to me that he had felt like he had gone to church. It was a perfect night."

"This has been all I had ever hoped for in a song," she explains. I'm so emotionally attached to this song. It was a gift to have been a vehicle for this song and this story. I seriously doubt that I can ever top this. But I want to continue to tell stories that matter. So, I'll keep swinging for the fences."

What does Paul think of the "I Drive Your Truck" song? He points out, "To have Jared recognized nationally in this song, it's just fantastic. And it reaches Gold Star families who have lost a loved one, and other families as well, all across the country. This song has touched the hearts of many people. I've received so many emails and posts about how this song is so meaningful to them, whether they hold on to their child's truck or car or motorcycle or boots or dog tags or Barbie doll. It reaches to the heart of all people who've lost a child."

After the ACM awards, Connie e-mailed Paul, "I stood backstage and thought, Wow, this all started with some Post-it notes in my car and you. Thank you again for sharing your story. Somehow it seems to have brought acknowledgement and healing to so many. Several sweet ladies took my hand as I left the venue and with tears in their eyes. They simply said, 'Thank you.' They didn't say, but I'm quite sure they were Gold Star Mothers."

Sally Marrero, a frequent participant at Flags for Vets, wrote an email saying: "I just saw the CMAs with them acknowledging Jared!!! Absolutely touching. Hugs. You must be flooded with calls, texts, and messages, but I just wanted to let you know my son Kyle, a Marine, asked me to please thank you, and he was touched watching it as well. Also, my Dad says hello. That man sat one day in front of the television and played the song on demand over twenty times in a row and cried. The love and support you have is amazing. I know it doesn't take the place of Jared, but just know that he's always with you."

A subsequent email concerned her Dad, an Army veteran: "Hi, Mr. Monti. Hope all is well with you. My Dad passed away yesterday and his ashes will be buried at Bourne National Cemetery. I just wanted to share that with you because, well I just wanted to."

Captain Matt Jacobs posted this Facebook message to Jared: "Six months ago, I heard a country song about 'I Drive Your Truck.' The part that got stuck in my head was about 'find a field, tear it up.' That and 'burning up back roads' kept making me think about that old black Dodge of yours. It made me think about that one late night attempt to make it to Boston."

Matt was referring to an incident that occurred while they were stationed at Fort Drum in 2004. Jared and Matt decided to embark on night maneuvers to practice reconnaissance techniques as supplemental military training. It was on a Thursday night at about 2 a.m. They decided (Matt claims Jared decided) to drive to Boston in the Dodge Ram truck. Along the way, they talked trash about football, since Jared was a New England Patriots fan and Matt was so much of a Denver Broncos fan that he liked calling himself Matt "Go Broncos" Jacobs.

After fortifying themselves with beer and donuts, lots of donuts, they got to a place called Booneville, NY, which is exactly what it sounds like. They got tired of seeing nothing but open fields and red road reflectors and realized their plan might not have been well thought out. They stopped to take a short nap to sleep off the effect of the donuts and left the engine running, because it was a particularly cold night. Two State Troopers stopped by to politely let them know that the law in New York specifies that DUI applies even if the engine is idling. The car doesn't have to be in motion.

With his big grin, Jared told them they were part of America's fighting force. This time, his charm had no effect. They weren't amused. Jared and Matt were told to leave the truck where it was and were treated to a free ride in the back seat of the police car. They were taken to the closest motel and told that they were being confined to quarters until at least 06:00 hours. The "closest motel" was five miles away. So Jared and Matt had to begin the next day with a forced march back to Jared's truck. The judge allowed Jared to plea bargain the charge to avoid the DUI and remain in the Army but still fined him $600. Since he couldn't afford to pay it, he once again had to re-enlist and use his bonus for the fine.

"It seems that each time Jared got close to the time when he'd have to make a decision about whether to re-enlist or not, something happened that caused him to decide to stay in. That was just another one of those times," recalls Paul. Would his second Afghanistan tour have been his final one? We'll never know, but it would have been hard to find someone in the military who would have bet on it.

"Today, flipping through the radio on my way home, for some reason, I stop the dial on NPR and heard the explanation of how that song came about," continued Matt. "Glad to hear your truck is still on the road, brother. Can't even begin to tell you how much you're missed. I'll burn through a few donuts for you tonight. See you on the high ground."

Later, Matt proudly posted this poignant message to Jared: "My first kid was born on the 25th. I know if you were here you'd be beating down the door. I borrowed your middle name for him, didn't think you'd mind."

Chapter 24
I Drive Your Harley

There's another version of "I Drive Your Truck". It's called, "I Drive Your Harley", except it's a story, not a song, and it's about a motorcycle.

After deciding he would keep Jared's truck, Paul took his sister Tricia and her husband, Russ Corsini, to a garage where Jared's treasured black Harley Davidson was being kept. It's a vintage 1992 FXDC "Low-Rider" Harley that he always enjoyed riding and working on when he was home. Paul said to them simply, "It's yours."

Russ had never ridden a motorcycle before but was thrilled by this gift. When they take the Harley out, he's typically the driver, with Tricia holding on in the back. They both had a special relationship with Jared. They were actually closer in age to him than to Tricia's oldest siblings. "He was my nephew, but we were also best friends. Jared made you feel special. He was truly interested in the things you were interested in. Not in a phony way at all. I'd describe him as a 'genuine' person. A down-to-earth, regular guy. That's why everyone loved him. He was such a big part of the family," Russ says. "I still get teary-eyed when I ride the bike. I say, 'Hey, Jared, we're going for a ride, buddy.' Then I always talk to him while I ride. He said he felt comfort, serenity, and freedom on the bike. I feel that, too, when I ride with him. I can't really describe it in words, but when I'm riding, I feel like I have a piece of Jared with me."

Sounding much like both Paul and Tim in talking about Jared's trucks, Russ adds, "People tell me I should get it repainted, but I won't touch it. I've replaced the tires, brakes, shocks, carburetor, things like that. But I want to leave the bike just the way it is."

Tricia understands completely. "It'll always be Jared's Harley to us. We built a half-wall around it in the garage so no one would knock it over. We want it to be secure. We'll keep it forever. Jared is still listed on my cell phone. I can't delete him. I'll never delete him. I can't imagine doing that."

Tim explains, "I went camping with Tricia and Russell, which is when I realized how close they were to Jared. After only a day of camping with them, which turned into a week because we enjoyed it so much, it was very obvious how much of a bond the three shared. So, after Jared's death, I suggested to my Dad that he give the Harley to Russell. I knew not only would it honor Jared but also that he would ride it and preserve everything about it."

A year after Jared's death, an occasion Gold Star parents often refer to as an "Angelversary", Russ posted, "When your Dad gave me and Tricia your Harley, I was so honored that I would be able to have a small piece of the joy that you had riding. When we take weekend rides we know that you are riding along side of us. It makes us feel a little closer to you each time we see the bike in the garage or ride it together. I wish we had the opportunity to ride together, but I know someday we will. I treasure this gift with all my heart but wish you were here to share it with us. Love ya, man."

"You could hear Jared coming from a long way off. It's because the muffler was shot," remembers Tricia, smiling. "Our kids would get all excited when they heard his bike coming down the street. They would play Manhunt, the hide-and-seek game in the dark. Sometimes he'd bring the fake grass they use in the Military so someone could hide. Or camouflage paint. The kids always had a ball here playing with him in the back yard." When their son Ben was five years old, he announced, "Mom, I want to change my name to Jared. I want to go into the Army and be just like him."

Jared liked to ride his Harley Davidson to family events. When relatives would point out that there was no tread on the tires, he'd say, "That's okay. It's all good." They'd point out how dangerous that was, especially in bad weather. He'd respond again with either one of his favorite phrases: "That's okay" or "It's all good."

"When we got Jared's bike, we knew we wanted to do something special for him," Tricia says. "So we came up with the idea of a Bike Run in his name to raise money for military charities. It's been incredible, the outpouring from everybody to support this event. Jared was so special. He would be embarrassed by this because he was humble, but we wanted to do it anyway. None of us knew about all his medals. He never told us about them.'I'm just doing my job' is what he'd say. 'I'm doing what I'm supposed to do.'"

The problem was, they had never organized anything like a Bike Run before. "We had no idea how to do it. Rick Wood, the President of the Southeast Massachusetts Motorcyclists Survivor Fund, helped us set it up," says a thankful Russ. "He's done a lot of Bike Runs, and we couldn't have done it without him. We'll keep doing the Bike Run. It'll be the third Sunday in May, every year, no matter what." The Run is a little over 20 miles long and takes about 45 minutes. It starts at the American Legion Hall in Raynham and runs through the towns of Bridgewater and Middleboro. It passes some of the places that are named for Jared, including the bridge, intersection, playground, etc. Originally, Tricia and Russ paid for the Bike Run themselves. Now, it's grown to the point where there are 17 corporate sponsors who get their names listed in a program.

Paul was so excited after the first Bike Run that he had to post this message to Jared: "Hi Bud. WOW! What an event your Aunt Tricia and Uncle Russell put on for you. You would have been so proud. Hundreds of motorcycles all riding in your name. I led the way in your truck for a while, and Uncle Russell was close behind on your Harley. There was a great crowd and we raised a considerable sum for military charities. I would have loved to see you there on your Harley leading the parade."

Tricia claims she'll never forget the last time Jared was over at her house. "He and Russ were singing 'The Gambler' downstairs while I was laughing upstairs. It struck me that Jared would always like the songs of whoever he was with. If you liked Frank Sinatra songs, he'd sing those. If you liked Jimmy Buffett songs, he'd sing those. That's how he was. He cared what you cared about."

Russ recalls solemnly, "I remember the last thing I ever said to him when he left to go back to Afghanistan was, 'Keep your head down, Jared.'"

Chapter 25
The Wounds of War

In the summer of 2014, Derek James was excited to complete what he called "Rock and Roll School," an intensive two-month program at the Recording Workshop in Chillicothe, Ohio. The school terms it a "creative learning experience in music recording, audio engineering, and sound production." He subsequently opened his own recording studio called Fire for Effect Productions. It represented the beginning of a new life for him. The website is http://www.fireforeffectproductions.com.

According to Bob Crown, Derek's father-in-law from his first marriage, "I am forever in debt for Jared's act of heroism, because my son-in-law was one of the soldiers that he helped save that day in Afghanistan. He was the one listed as wounded during the fire fight. Heathe Craig, the soldier who put him in the chopper and died while trying to save PFC Bradbury, is also directly responsible for Derek's survival."

The wounds of war can be a lot more than just physical. There were signs that all wasn't right with the young Private after what he calls "having a chunk taken out of my arm and back" on Hill 2610. "After the ambush, Derek called me late one night. He wasn't sure I would want to speak with him," recalls Janet. No one would have blamed the 18-year-old for sitting out the battle after suffering injuries from both an RPG and machine gun fire, yet he kept on fighting. Why would he possibly think that Janet wouldn't be honored to speak with him?

"I wanted Derek and his family to know I was okay and glad that he survived. He was the first soldier I wanted to see when I went to Fort Drum for the Memorial Service. I just asked over and over again where Derek James was until I finally met him," Janet says.

It's been a long road back for Derek, who is now just 27 and still has so much of his life ahead of him. He's certainly had quite a bit happen since he was fresh out of Basic Training and Advanced Individual Training at Ft. Sill. Like Jared, he enlisted between his junior and senior years of high school. By virtue of his strong Army Aptitude and PT tests, he qualified to be a FISTer and was sent to Fort Drum to prepare for an overseas deployment to Afghanistan.

As you'd expect for someone his age, he was overwhelmed and frightened. After in-processing in Afghanistan, a kind Staff Sergeant befriended him and took him on a trip to a bazaar in Naray. "I thought it was unusual, because I was just a fresh Private (E-2), and this SSG (E-6) was trying to make me feel welcome. He showed me the gems and minerals that were for sale there. He pointed out their different characteristics and told me which would be good buys and which wouldn't. I asked him how he knew so much about the subject. He told me his father was a science teacher and amateur mineralogist. I thought that was pretty cool. SSG Monti reached out to me, like he did to so many people. He didn't have to. But he did. I'll never forget that."

After suffering the injuries on Hill 2610, Derek was hospitalized for six weeks and returned to the United States for a short leave. He was back in action in just two months. He had recovered from his physical wounds, but his mental wounds were a different story. “I was confused. I didn’t process what happened to me that night on the mountain until years later,” confesses Derek. “So I told everyone I was fine. I was so stupid. I thought asking for help would be a sign of weakness.”

So he finished his deployment and signed up for another Afghanistan tour, with two broken marriages on the personal front. “I was a mess. Panic attacks, uncontrolled anxiety, and depression. I felt I was supposed to just suck it up and do my job. I drank myself into oblivion and was guilty of substance abuse. I had all the classic PTSD symptoms. My life since that day on the mountain was one big shit storm. I couldn’t relax in any situation. I went to Washington for Monti’s Medal of Honor presentation, and even then I felt uncontrollable survivor’s guilt. Why did I live and the other guys didn’t? I met the President, the Secretary of Defense, the Secretary of the Army, etc. and I felt even more worthless, like I didn’t belong in their presence. I didn’t want to celebrate something I felt was so bad. If someone called me a hero, that really upset me. I felt like I didn’t measure up.”

Derek’s life continued to spiral out of control, until one day when things couldn’t get any worse. “That was January 17 of 2014. The day I tried to kill myself. It was seven and a half years since that night on the mountain, and I felt disgusted that I couldn’t get over it. I had hit bottom. Then I just decided to get my act together, get into rehab, and start to open up to guys who had been through the same kind of experience that I had. I’ve been clean and sober since. I haven’t told anyone outside my family the reason I decided to turn my life around. Not until today.”

Derek now enjoys spending time with Monti Cash James, his four-year-old son. “He is definitely the best thing that has ever happened to me,” he confides. “I am thankful and proud to be his Daddy. I was a lousy husband, but now I’m trying to be a good father." Derek posted a picture of his son's first day of preschool on September 4, 2014. Paul responded by writing to Monti, "Study hard and make us proud, like your namesake."

Monti Cash's middle name is for singer Johnny Cash, who had a troubled life of his own. Best-known for "I Walk the Line", "Folsom Prison Blues", and "Ring of Fire", Johnny was inducted into the Rock and Roll, Country Music, and Gospel Music Halls of Fame. Despite, or perhaps because of, his fame, he became addicted to alcohol, amphetamines, and barbiturates. He hit bottom in 1968 when he attempted suicide, but felt reborn after the experience. Shortly after, he proposed to singer June Carter at a concert in London, Ontario, Canada. She accepted with the stipulation that he go "on the wagon". He agreed, and they were married just a week later. After a relapse, the birth of his son, John Carter Cash, is said to have inspired him to finally end his dependence on drink and drugs. In a classic "dying from a broken heart" story, Johnny succumbed to complications from diabetes at age 71, less than four months after June's death.

One day little Monti will ask where his first and middle names came from, and Derek will explain. It's also likely when he's old enough to understand the courage it took for his father to say, "I don't want to live like this anymore. I need to seek help," that his son will say, "Dad, I'm proud of you."

According to Derek, "I know there are a lot of soldiers who have returned from Iraq and Afghanistan in the same shape I was in. I'd love to be able to raise awareness and encourage them to go to counseling or see a doctor. They don't have to suffer in silence."

Max Noble can identify with the issues Derek has had. He explains, "Regardless of the amount of time that has passed, those memories, emotions, and thoughts are just as present as they were during the moment of their inception. It's been eight years now.

This is the first time I've been able to even talk to anyone about my story of what happened that night on the mountain. I was in four or five firefights after that. They were like small potatoes compared to Hill 2610."

According to Sean Smith, "I accepted the fact that I was going to die that day on the mountain. You don't realize how terrifying it is. I crossed a bridge and stepped off on a mission that would change me. It changed the way I view and live my life forever. There hasn't been a day since then that the events haven't replayed over and over again in my head. I remember the violent sounds of machine gun fire and seemingly endless explosions from the RPG's. I remember the smell of the burnt powder hanging still in the air, as there was no breeze. I hear the yelling and screaming as if I was hearing it for the first time. I recall the absolute silence between artillery and mortar barrages that we called in throughout the remainder of the night. It's just strange some of the minute details that you never forget after an experience as awful and violent as that."

He continues, "I tend to get a little quieter every June, because it is a time that the memories come back harder. The details. Memories that I can't find the words to speak. So I don't. I keep it to myself. I take this time to think about the 15 other men that I was with. Most of all, I think about those that never made it back across that bridge. They have been, are now, and will continue to be on my mind and in my heart for the rest of my life."

"I'd had no real life experience. I was a kid back then," admits Franklin Woods. "I learned about the kind of person I wanted to become. Everyone should strive to be like Jared. He worried about his soldiers before he worried about himself. I've used that philosophy. I've made my guys mine. It has helped me be a better NCO and a better person. He left a hell of a legacy. At first I was reluctant to share Monti's story, but now I realize I'd rather have everyone know the greatness of him, to give him the credit he deserves. I have a whole wall at home just devoted to Jared Monti memorabilia."

According to John Hawes, "I wish things hadn't turned out the way they did. I wish I could still look forward to a fishing trip back home with him in Massachusetts. I never got to smoke that cigar with him after the mission, either. I have smoked a few cigars since his death, each one in honor of his memory and sacrifice. I no longer play Risk. The last two people I played against were PFC Bradbury and SFC Monti, both of whom died. I can't forget those final two games and how it would be the last time they had the chance to play. I think every day about that tragic night and wish I could have done more to change the outcome."

"It was an incredible group of guys. They had a collective will to survive. A will to win. I've never seen anything like it before or since. Just guys with strong individual character. Everyone held their ground. No one gave an inch," says Chris Grzecki in tribute to the patrol members.

"Grzecki used the perfect set of words," agrees Brian Gonterman. "We all feel the same way. I know I will forever be indebted to everyone who was there."

Patrol Leader Chris Cunningham says proudly, "Every one of those guys on the mountain that day performed well. They were the strong, smart, and brave. They just kept moving forward. They gave me everything I needed. It was definitely the best group I've ever worked with. Usually, there's one or two in a group that don't measure up. That wasn't the case with them. I wasn't worried. I know they'd react well to any situation. They were well trained. We were ready for anything we'd have to face. Now, it's a matter of keeping all of them alive by telling their stories and being there for each other and the families."

"As far as I'm concerned, they were all heroes, and Jared would think so, too," says Janet. "The others were not any less important than my son. My heart breaks for those that survived that night on the mountain. They have to live with the horrors they witnessed."

The rest of us can relate to what those soldiers went through if we've gone through a calamitous event. Anyone who is now over 20 years old, for example, will forever bear the psychological scars of the shared experience of 9/11. Sean Smith implored all Americans on September 11, 2014 to "Never forget those that were affected by the events of this day. It's so hard to believe that it's been that long ago, as most if not all can recall it as if it happened an hour ago. Although through tragedy and loss, it brought the people of our nation together. Black, white, brown, Democrat, Republican, gay, straight, or whatever. It brought together Americans. It made us unite and realize as a whole the capability of evil. It made us more aware of the fact that there are people who devote their whole lives to the destruction of what we as a society and people believe, love, trust and take for granted. We as Americans are in one hell of a slump now. Our focus seems to be that of a cat following a laser. All over the place."

Sean concluded, "Despite all of the deep emotions of sadness and grief that this day brings to us, and what it represents to the majority of us, it also happens to be one of the best days of my life. I am thankful that I was blessed with the birth of my second son, Wyatt James Smith, on this day. Happy birthday, my Wyatt. I love you, and Daddy is so very proud of you, son. I will be home soon and I can't wait to see your handsome face, and your brother Jessie's too." Wyatt is now five years old and Jessie is six. Sean exclaims, "They're the most amazing thing that's ever happened to me!"

Although combat can cause significant physical and

psychological damage, it can also permanently bind people together in a way that few experiences can. “This was by far the most amazing group of guys I have ever been in the presence of,” claims Chris Grzecki. “I have never seen or heard of more selflessness, heart, and will than in the guys that climbed and fought on that mountain. Everyone was strong for everyone else. It changed my life. I look at things differently. It’s taken the fear away. I’m out of the military now and don’t let little things bother me. I say, ‘What’s the worst that could happen? I made it through that night on the mountain.’ I felt privileged to be part of that team. It’s a bond that we’ll always share.”

The sacrifices made by all those willing to serve their country are inspiring. It makes the day-to-day things that many people complain about seem trivial. “My seven-year-old daughter Mia saw a Memorial Day tribute to the military on television,” reports Jared’s childhood friend Jeff Gomes. “She said, ‘Dad, I’m sad for these soldiers. I don’t know if I’ll ever be as brave as them, but I want to try to be.’ I agree with her. I hold all those guys in high regard. The character and bravery they display is staggering. What they have to go though is unbelievable.”

An unexplored area of research is the effect of combat experience on those in the family who may suffer as many mental health issues as the veterans themselves. Evidence suggests the first 90 days after a return from overseas deployment is a critical time for re-adjustment for the whole family. However, it’s also possible that a veteran can seem to be fine at first, then there can be a delayed onset of problems. Many Americans have had a relative who has served in the military, so they’re aware of the stress it puts on the family. Too many, unfortunately, have also had a relative who has been maimed or killed in action, so they’re aware of that life-long impact.

Both Paul and Janet find comfort by connecting with other

Gold Star parents. Sometimes it's to give support. Sometimes it's to get support. Paul sums up the feelings of Gold Star families when he says, "My son was supposed to give my eulogy. He was supposed to get married and give me grandchildren. Now that road is closed. When you lose your parents, you've lost your past. When you lose your child, you've lost your future." He adds, "The family is extremely proud of Jared. We also miss him an awful, awful lot. Everyone misses him. The pride is there, but pride doesn't bring him back."

"It never leaves you," maintains Janet. "You can't ever get over it. There are bad days and really bad days. You don't know if you're going to make it through. It's so personal. Some keep things to themselves. With others, I get e-mails and posts from Gold Star parents, and I listen to them express their feelings and then respond with just 'Hugs' or 'Huge Hugs.' Every Gold Star parent knows what that means. There's nothing you can say to comfort someone. Just give them 'Hugs' in whatever way you can. The greatest fear, for Gold Star Mothers & families, is that those we have lost will be forgotten. I am constantly reminded that Jared will NEVER be forgotten, because he lives on in the memories of those he served with, the stories they tell, and those who named their sons after him."

Paul looks forward to the calls, e-mails, and posts he gets from those with whom Jared served. "They continue to tell me stories about him. The funny, goofy stories. The heroic stories. If you know someone who has been lost in combat, please contact their family. Tell them the stories. It keeps the soldier, sailor, or Marine's spirit alive. It's the greatest amount of comfort you give."

Since Jared's death, Paul finds he has become much more patriotic. He'll drive his truck to Gold Star and veterans' events and display large American flags and posters of Jared. "I think when you have a child you lose in war, for the most part, the people I've met have become super patriots. I guess it's a way of justifying your child's life. They wear military clothes and T-shirts and follow a little more closely what's going on in the military."

Then there are the boxes. "You mention the boxes and every Gold Star family knows what you're talking about. The military sends you a fallen soldier's possessions. What are you supposed to do with all the stuff? Some people tell me they never even open the boxes. Some people throw everything away. Others give it to charity. There's no right or wrong. I've opened the boxes, but I can't bring myself to throw out anything of Jared's."

How many Americans have given their lives in service to their country? Nearly 2,200 died in Afghanistan since October of 2001 and nearly 4,500 in Iraq since March of 2003. The Iraq and Afghanistan Veterans of America reports that over 50,000 Americans were injured in the two theaters of operation. Non-uniformed contractors working for private employers were also lost. Estimates are that in all American Wars, the death toll for those in uniform is 1.3 million. According to the 2010 Census, that's greater than the populations of 11 states: Hawaii, Maine, New Hampshire, Rhode Island, Montana, Delaware, South Dakota, Alaska, North Dakota, Wyoming, and Vermont. That's a lot of Gold Star families.

Approximately 1.5 million members of the military have also been wounded in wars, so that would be a total of 2.8 million who have been killed or wounded. That's greater than the populations of 18 states: Utah, Kansas, Nevada, New Mexico, Nebraska, West Virginia, Idaho, and the aforementioned 11.

Unlike most clubs, the Gold Star families are not seeking to add to their ranks. Paul says empathically, "We don't want any more members in our club." When, unfortunately, there is a new member, he will often contact them by telephone. "It's hard, because you don't know what to say. You don't want to disturb them any more than they're already disturbed, but you want to give them some help, too. So you just play it by ear."

Janet posted this message on her Facebook page: "To all my sister Gold Star Mothers, you are in my thoughts and prayers every night. God bless and help us, and please, God, let there be NO more. Hugs!!"

The Blue Star Service Flag is flown by parents who have a child serving in the military. It was designed by Captain Robert Qeussner in 1917 to honor his two sons. The Gold Star Service Flag, a variation of it, was created the following year when President Woodrow Wilson authorized its use to indicate the loss of a child serving on active duty.

The small Gold Star Lapel Buttons, commonly referred to as "pins", are distributed to members of the immediate family of a fallen soldier by the Department of Defense. They are not considered "awards" but the symbols of sacrifice. During World War II, the Gold Star appeared on flags throughout America that were usually hung in windows facing the street. Gold Star Families are parents or guardians who have received the pin for the sacrifice of their loved one.

In 1947, Congress approved the use of the Gold Star Lapel Button as a way to recognize the families of service members who lose their lives in combat. These are provided to widows and widowers, children, parents, stepparents, adopted or foster parents, brothers, and sisters of members of the military who lost their lives during the two World Wars, or subsequent deployments, in support of military operations, or during an international terrorist attack.

The Lapel Button consists of a gold star on a purple circular background, bordered in gold and surrounded by gold laurel leaves. The design incorporates the gold star symbolizing loss, the laurel wreath border standing for valor, and the purple field signifying the family's grief. On the reverse is the inscription "United States of America, Act of Congress" with space for engraving the recipient's initials.

"So many times, Gold Star parents are overlooked. I don't think people understand the grief that a parent goes through who has lost a child. It's part of my life now to try to honor all the Gold Star families, because they need it and they deserve it. Everything I do is in honor of the Gold Star families. We have a very close-knit group, a thread that binds us. It's different than any thread binding anybody else," claims Paul.

Chapter 26
The Hidden Epidemic

Connie Harrington, who began the "I Drive Your Truck" song process by listening to that radio interview with Paul, has said many times, "My father died in 1945 and we buried him forty years later."

My own father was sent to London during World War II at the time the city was suffering nightly bombings by the Nazis. His company was divided into two groups, according to last name, and sent in separate troop transports across the Atlantic. The "A to M" group was torpedoed by a German submarine. There were no survivors. He was in the "N through Z" group. He may have made it to England, but he was a casualty in other ways.

I asked him many times what it was like during the London Blitzkrieg. Even at 87 years old, his mouth would open but he couldn't get any words to come out. Instead, he would just give me a blank stare. He'd be off in another world for a few seconds. At first I thought the problem was that he couldn't remember. Then I realized the real problem was that he couldn't forget. I know that I won't ever forget that vacant look. A lot of you have seen that look. Maybe some of you have given others that look.

Post-traumatic stress disorder has been around since the beginning of time. It is an anxiety disorder that typically occurs after extreme trauma involving injury or the threat of death. However, it wasn't until 1980 that it became officially accepted that the cause was a traumatic event occurring outside the individual rather than a neurosis coming from inside the person.

Stressful events can shatter people's sense of security and make them feel helpless and vulnerable. There may have been a threat to life or safety, or physical harm involved, but not necessarily so. Any situation that leaves someone feeling overwhelmed and isolated can be traumatic. The more frightened someone feels, the more likely the person is to be traumatized.

Usually after a traumatic event, the stress hormones released go back to normal levels. With PTSD, however, a person's body keeps releasing those chemicals. The general rule of thumb is that a doctor can give the PTSD diagnosis if symptoms last more than 30 days. Although usually associated with combat experience, it can occur after a car accident, a natural disaster, a robbery or assault, physical abuse, or any other violent event. The majority of people will experience some sort of trauma in their lives, but a minority of them will have it lead to PTSD.

There are often feelings of guilt associated with the event, including survivor's guilt, or survivor's syndrome, which can occur when someone is bothered by the fact that they escaped from a dangerous situation while another person or other people did not. Mild versions are often found among those who did not lose their jobs during lay-offs at work. The manifestation is a function of the seriousness of the situation and the psychological make-up of the individual.

Symptoms of PTSD include strong memories of the painful event, bad dreams, emotional numbness, guilt or worry, angry outbursts, feeling "jumpy" or "edgy", and avoiding situations that are reminders of the trauma. During World War II, these symptoms were called "combat fatigue", implying that they would just go away on their own like any kind of "tiredness." General George Patton famously slapped a soldier during World War II thinking that would be enough to "knock some sense into him." It got him relieved of his command for a year. Fortunately, it's now recognized that post traumatic stress is a lot more serious than that. A slap isn't going to cure anyone.

The trauma may cause upsetting emotions, painful memories, and result in a sense of being in constant danger. There may be an inability to connect with and relate to other people. It can take a while to return to a normal emotional state and feel safe again. In some cases, a person may be unable to return to a normal emotional state and may never feel safe again. Many homeless people, for example, are combat veterans who were unable to re-enter society.

First Lady Michelle Obama has decried the fact that so many American military veterans are literally "left out in the cold". "The idea that anyone who has worn our country's uniform spends their nights sleeping on the ground should horrify us," she declared. "The fact that right now, our country has more than 58,000 homeless veterans, well, that's a stain on the soul of this nation." Close to 100 mayors, governors, and other officials have committed to a pledge to help end veteran homelessness by the end of 2015.

Studies of the number of Iraq and Afghanistan veterans who have PTSD cite percentages that vary widely. Those who deal with the homeless, those at Veteran's Affairs hospitals, marriage counselors, and those who deal with alcoholism and drug abuse are likely to cite numbers that are higher than even the highest figures published in studies. The simple question is, "How could ANYONE come back from war unchanged?" Everyone can agree on one thing – the cost to society is significant. Most people think of the cost of war in monetary terms. It's much more than that in human terms.

There are two primary forms of treatment. The first is counseling by a psychiatrist or therapist, where a person talks about his/her feelings in a calm, accepting setting. This can be supplemented by a support group where those with similar experiences openly share them. Both can have a cathartic or releasing effect and make the events that led to the trauma seem less frightening. The other is medication to alleviate the anxiety and/or depression. Often, both forms of treatment are used concurrently. If medication is prescribed, alcohol and recreational drug use should be avoided, since they significantly worsen symptoms. Unfortunately, many veterans already have addictions to either or both.

Paul has talked to returning veterans from Afghanistan and Iraq and contends that the generally accepted numbers of those with PTSD are understated. He says, "We need people to care, and not just for the Gold Star families, but for our veterans who have served over there, who have major problems right now with PTSD. Everybody throws that term around as if it's something mysterious, and numbers come out and percentages, but the true numbers are far higher than anyone will let you know."

It used to be that soldiers stationed at headquarters were far from combat, and it took as many as 10 troops to support one on the front lines. In places like Afghanistan and Iraq, though, everyone was on the front lines. Anyone could be faced with having to dodge bullets on a daily basis. Suicide bombers and improvised explosive devices were all-too-common. So the term "combat vet" really applies to anyone who served there. "I want to help our vets coming home," says Paul. "There's a huge number of them suffering from PTSD. It's way more than is reported because most of them, the vast majority, won't ask for help. They don't understand that they need it. It's sad that we don't honor our veterans, those who keep us free. They've done so much for us. Shouldn't we be doing more for them?"

In recent years, the number of suicides of military veterans has far exceeded the total of those killed in battle. It's been the hidden secret of the Iraq and Afghanistan wars. According to the most recent statistics released by Department of Veterans Affairs, suicides were running at 22 a day, or about 8000 a year, compared to one a day or 365 a year killed in combat during the Afghanistan and Iraq War years. The situation has become so dire that in 2013 Secretary of Defense Chuck Hagel termed suicide in the military an "epidemic".

Paul says, "That's just unacceptable. If there were a flu epidemic with those kinds of numbers, it would be all over the news. They're brought up to love their fellow man and then are suddenly thrown into combat. After that, we just turn them loose in the streets. The rate of alcoholism, drug use, and divorces is incredibly high. It's not right for someone to go overseas, face death every day, come home, and then be ignored."

Why aren't there mass protests about the low priority given to veteran's care? Alex Ashcroft claims it's because too few people are paying attention. According to him, "That's because hardly anyone knows someone who is serving. It was so different than World War II. The great military historian Rick Atkinson explained the difference to me very well in an interview I did with him. He said, referring to World War II, 'Everyone had skin in the game.' In Iraq and Afghanistan, because of the all-voluntary military, only about 1 percent of the population had that skin in the game. I decided I need to find them. On *Here and Now*, I interviewed mothers whose sons were killed in Iraq. We spoke to a spouse whose husband had been on multiple deployments. The wars dragged on, and military suicide became a huge issue. I devoted a lot of time to that issue and started to meet the families of soldiers who had taken their own lives. I made it my mission to introduce listeners to these people, because they were sacrificing and the rest of us weren't. It wasn't political for me. It just seemed like the right thing to do."

When combat veterans are about to be discharged, they are put in a room and asked to raise their hands if they're having any problems. Who would want to be embarrassed in a roomful of fellow soldiers? Who would want that on a military record? Who would want to be seen as unable to "suck it up and drive on"? Paul says, "All you want is to get out. You're just looking forward to going home and having a McDonald's hamburger. When you get back to the States, you sign something saying you feel okay. That's it. Every person should get mandatory psychiatric help. It's not right. I read their posts. I talk to them. I know many of them are in trouble."

A particularly good resource where veterans talk about living with PTSD and how treatment turned their lives around is About Face, which features direct accounts from veterans who sought treatment that helped them cope with coming home from combat. There are also clinical psychologists and psychiatrists on the web site who have videos on symptoms and treatment for PTSD. (www.ptsd.va.gov/apps/AboutFace) Another useful site is provided by the Iraq and Afghanistan Veterans of America (http://iava.org/transition-home-1). It includes sections on "Starting the Transition", "Navigating the VA", "Invisible Injuries" and "In Their Words".

The Dept. of Veteran's Affairs suffered a serious setback from the disclosure of deep-seated problems in the health care system in the spring of 2014. Among the many troubling issues was the falsification of waiting times for first appointments, which were significantly longer than those being recorded. The agency has been struggling to keep up with the demand for its services with some 9 million veterans enrolled now, an increase of a million from just six years ago. The influx has come from returning Iraq and Afghanistan veterans, along with aging Viet Nam War vets, who have increasing health issues. The fact that many of its computer systems were designed in the 1980's and never updated didn't help the VA. The resulting scandal led to the ouster of VA Secretary Eric Shinseki in May of 2014.

In the largest non-government survey ever conducted of post-9/11 veterans, the Iraq and Afghanistan Veterans of America published findings in 2014 that said a staggering 47% of the respondents know at least one veteran of those wars who has attempted suicide. In addition, 40% of the respondents know someone who has died from suicide, 31% were willing to say that they have thought about taking their own life, and 53% admit to having a mental health issue.

"These veterans are America's new greatest generation and our nation's future leaders," says IAVA CEO and Founder Paul Rieckhoff. "For over a decade they've continuously had America's back. But too often, they are being ignored."

Bernie Sanders, Chairman of the Senate Committee on Veterans' Affairs and an Independent from Vermont, has championed the cause of VA reform. Senator Sanders, who is rumored to be contemplating a Presidential run in 2016, responded to those who were in no mood to spend money and expend effort on veterans: "If you think it's too expensive to take care of veterans, then don't send them to war." He is also quoted as asking this provocative question, "How is it that we can afford to allow one in four major corporations not to pay federal income taxes, but we can't afford to help our veterans?"

The week of July 28, 2014 was a good one for U. S. veterans.

On Tuesday, The Senate confirmed Robert McDonald, a former West Point graduate and Proctor & Gamble CEO, as the new Secretary of Veterans Affairs. He pledged to restore "transparency, accountability, and integrity" to the agency. The $16.3 billion Veterans Access, Choice and Accountability Act of 2014 was passed by the House of Representatives by a lopsided 420-5 vote on Wednesday. The following day it went to the Senate and was approved, 91-3. The final step was to have the President sign the legislation, which he did on August 7. It's rare that any bill receives that kind of nonpartisan support. Frankly, in recent years, it's been rare that ANY bill is agreed upon by the House, the Senate, and the President. A recent Gallup Poll reveals why Congress was forced to act in such a swift and unilateral manner. It showed that the U. S. military is held in high regard by 74 percent of Americans, while just 7 percent have such confidence in Congress. If there's one thing that pols pay attention to, it's polls.

Senator Sanders and Republican and House Veteran's Affairs Committee Chairman Jeff Miller of Florida were the architects of the landmark legislation, which authorizes the hiring of additional doctors and nurses and the opening of 27 new clinics in 18 states and Puerto Rico. It also lets patients who live more than 40 miles from a VA facility, or who have been on waiting lists for more than 30 days, to seek care from private doctors or community health centers, Defense Department health care facilities, or Indian Health Centers. The bill also authorizes the Veterans Affairs Secretary to unilaterally fire any senior executive deemed incompetent. That's a pretty unusual provision for a government organization, but one which most agree is warranted given the mismanagement at the VA.

On August 26, 2014, in his first major policy speech on veterans care since the VA scandal, President Obama announced an executive action to additionally improve care and support for veterans. The action was created in consultation with the Iraq and Afghanistan Veterans of America and included additional initiatives for raising awareness for suicide prevention, mental health research, and pilot programs to provide peer support.

"Planes and tanks and guns are a cost of war. So is taking care of the men and women who use those weapons and fight our battles," Sanders concludes.

Chapter 27
This is How Wars End

It's difficult to gauge the success of the military effort in Afghanistan. Good intentions are not important. It's good results that matter. For example, the United States and its allies initially only served an indirect role in fighting the illegal opium economy by sharing intelligence with the Afghan government, protecting Afghan poppy crop eradication forces, and helping in the coordination and the implementation of the country's anti-drug policy. Attempts at drug crop eradication negatively impacted the poorest farmers, who had no other form of employment. Understandably, that caused anger and resentment. Without alternatives, these farmers were unable to earn a living. The result was counter-productive, since many of them would then turn to, or perhaps even turn into, terrorists, nefarious drug lords, or underworld thugs. The only way to truly gain the support of the locals would have been to provide them with a viable alternative to earn a living.

Eventually, the American-led alliance of nations changed its focus in an effort to thwart the drug laboratories and drug traders, which became the targets rather than the poppy fields themselves. Still, it resulted in hurting the local farmers. Afghanistan was producing only about one metric ton per year of heroin in 2001, the year of the American invasion. Despite the approximately $2 billion that the Department of Defense spent on counter-narcotics efforts, estimates now are that the figure is up to as much as 5,500 tons per year.

The consequences of the explosion of heroin production have been felt world-wide. The abundant supply has created lower prices, making heroin the drug of choice for many. At the same time, new processing techniques have resulted in heroin that is purer and more potent. Once primarily confined to the inner cities in America, heroin overdoses are now commonplace in suburban and rural areas. In March of 2014, Eric Holder, then Attorney General, called the 45 percent increase in heroin overdose deaths between 2006 and 2010 an "urgent and growing public health crisis." Many believe when the numbers come out for more recent years, the percentage will have gone up even higher.

The processing of Afghanistan's opium into heroin traditionally took place outside of the country. Increasingly, however, Afghan drug cartels have stepped up processing in domestic heroin labs in an effort to increase profits. The recent withdrawal of U. S. troops has made stabilization efforts in Afghanistan a challenge. A stable government would not be favorable to the drug lords and terrorists who, instead, thrive on the absence of the rule of law.

Jared established strong relationships with the Afghan people. He knew relatively few were religious extremists bent on Jihad. Most respected, and got along well with, people from other religions. Jared enjoyed getting to know them and called them "nice people." He knew their primary concern, like that of other people around the world, was trying to feed their family. It's eliminating poverty and hopelessness that is vital to any effort to reduce the influence of terrorists. It's the poverty and hopelessness that leads to anger and makes people want to lash out at those who are perceived to be causing or perpetuating injustice. That's true not only in Afghanistan but in the United States. It's true everywhere around the world.

Jared's e-mails home talked about today's wars not being black or white. You're typically not fighting an organized force of uniformed soldiers representing a country. You're fighting the civilians of that country who frequently are engaged in tribal warfare or ethnic battles with each other at the same time. Sometimes soldiers come in from other countries. They'll often switch their allegiance. Perhaps they're just mercenaries who fight because there aren't any other jobs available. Because you're where some feel you don't belong, people may start shooting at you. It's quite a conundrum. What Jared knew for sure was that he was being counted on to do his job to the best of his ability. He did that, and did it well.

Once Jared was so upset he had to call Paul on the phone from Afghanistan. He said, "They've got me moving all over the place. One day I'm in the East. Next day they have me in the North. I think that maybe I might like to get out of the service, Dad. I'm tired." Jared was down to just 135 after dropping 20 pounds. He had begun to show the effects of being the "go to" guy for difficult assignments and special missions. They had him going in multiple directions at the same time.

"Look, son, you don't have far to go to retirement," said Paul, who admits, "I always wondered after that, did I say the right thing?"

Jared had also confided in his Aunt Tricia Corsini, Paul's sister, who said, "We had this conversation. He wasn't sure he was going to go in for this last round. Jared said, 'You know, even though I have this whole life that I want to move on for, those boys, I trained them and I want to go back and make sure I bring them home with me.' He had such a passion for those other soldiers and such a respect. He wanted to make sure that his training carried all the way through and that they all came home together."

It was commitment to his soldiers that drove Jared to keep re-enlisting. It was that same commitment that ultimately led him to sacrifice his life in an effort to save one of them, rather than a commitment to some great ideology. He just couldn't walk away from them.

It would nearly be a decade after the events of 9/11 before bin Laden would be brought to justice, or more accurately, before justice would be brought to bin Laden, when U. S. Navy SEAL Team Six flew into Abbotabad, Pakistan to kill him on May 2, 2011. SEAL stands for "sea, air, and land" indicating that the small, mobile, highly-efficient unit is capable of performing anywhere under any circumstances. After the success of the daring bin Laden mission, Paul posted this message to his son: "Well, Jared, they finally caught and killed that evil man who terrorized the world and you chased for so long. Death is not a thing to be celebrated, but you can have a cold one because there's one less evil man in the world."

The last of the 33,000 American "surge" troops that were sent to Afghanistan in 2010 were withdrawn in 2012. Although it sounds like something from centuries ago, 2,000 donkeys were authorized by the government to deliver ballot boxes to the remote areas of Afghanistan during the Presidential election of April, 2014. It took a full five months for results to be finalized in a democratic election with Ashraf Ghani Ahmadzai declared winner and runner-up Abdullah Abdullah given the Prime Minister's post. The American presence wound down to fewer than 10,000 troops by the end of 2014.

Did Jared and the other courageous American troops "win" the war in Afghanistan?

Not only bin Laden but many of his al Qaeda cohorts were killed. An oppressive regime that harbored terrorists was eliminated. If that's winning, then the war was won. On the other hand, there was no peace treaty, no surrender of arms, no concessions by enemy forces. If that's winning, then the war wasn't won.

It's a certainty that President George W. Bush's goal of "eliminating terrorism" hasn't been met. The entire Middle East may be in worse shape than before the "War on Terrorism" and the vaunted "Arab Spring" of demonstrations and uprisings which began in 2011.

On May 27, 2014, President Obama stated the harsh reality that, "We have to recognize that Afghanistan will not be a perfect place and it is not America's responsibility to make it one." He then announced the plan to have just a small residual force remain by the end of 2016. "Americans have recognized it is harder to end wars than it is to begin them," he concluded, "yet this is how wars end in the 21st Century."

Even-more-violent Jihadist groups such as ISIS (the Islamic State of Iraq and Syria) arose to represent perhaps even more of a threat than al Qaeda and the Taliban. ISIS claims religious authority over all the world's Muslims, and by the summer of 2014 had taken control of parts of Iraq and Syria while persecuting many from other religious sects in its path. In the final months of 2014, U. S. military efforts expanded in the form of an air war against the Islamic State in conjunction with NATO and Arab forces. President Obama declared, "America will lead a broad coalition to roll back this terrorist threat. Our objective is clear. We will degrade, and ultimately destroy, ISIL through a comprehensive and sustained counter-terrorism strategy." The Administration prefers the term "ISIL" which stands for "The Islamic State of Iraq and the Levant." The latter includes parts of

Lebanon, Jordan and other Middle Eastern countries in addition to Syria.

The Chief of Police of Afghanistan's Logar Province, General Ghulam Sakhi Roogh Lawanay, has been quoted as saying, "It is like fish. When one fish dies, another comes. The determination of these Arab fighters is high." It appears that each new species of extremist fish is more dangerous than the last.

Chapter 28
"I Thought He Would do Something Great"

On August 14, 2014, Major General Stephen Townsend, the 10th Mountain Division Commander, officially announced the end of Task Force Spartan and the 3-71 CAV in a letter to the troops saying, "Today is a bittersweet day in the history of the 10th Mountain Division. Today we say farewell to the Spartans of the 3rd Brigade Combat Team. Almost 10 years ago, our Army found itself fighting two wars and needing to expand. The Spartan Brigade was born to answer this call to war. Barely two years later, the Spartans underwent their baptism of fire, fighting a determined enemy in the mountains of eastern Afghanistan. Now, after four deployments to Afghanistan in less than 10 years, we are inactivating this gallant brigade at Fort Drum. The 3rd Brigade's legacy is marked by gallantry in action by soldiers like SFC Jared Monti, our division's second Medal of Honor recipient."

When asked what Jared has meant to his division, MG Townsend responded, "The 10th Mountain Division has a long and distinguished history dating back to 1943, when it was activated as a highly specialized unit in the Colorado Rockies. Soldiers of the division have fought in World War II, Somalia, Iraq, and Afghanistan. No soldier embodies our Division's legacy more than SFC Monti – he gallantly gave his life that night so that no soldier would be left behind."

"I thought he was special," admits Janet. "I thought he would do something great. I never imagined this, ever."

"I would like to see Jared remembered not as a hero, although he's certainly that, but for the person he was. He was a down-to-earth, wonderful guy. It's not the awards. Not the plaques. Not the buildings or the children named after him. He just made everyone around him feel good," says Paul.

"He was 100% committed to the troops," says Darin Souza. "Everyone knows the same Jared. People talk about his generosity and his dedication to others. It's not just WHAT he did on the mountain that night, it's WHY he did it. Everyone in the Army seemed to know him or know somebody who knew him. It's not like 'six degrees of Kevin Bacon' but more like '2 or 3 degrees of Jared Monti.' The expression, 'A tiger doesn't change its stripes' is usually meant in a bad way. In Jared's case, it applies in a good way. He was humble and selfless. He was consistent about it. He was always that way."

SSG Jeremy Saulnier posted this message to Paul and Janet: "I wish you could have seen your son in action. He was truly a rare person. Hardworking, honest to a fault, and cared so for his soldiers. He was one of my first bosses and set the example I try to follow now with my soldiers. I told him once that he was the best damn NCO I'd ever had. He shrugged it off with his patented, "Well, I guess…" move. But, I meant it. And I'll miss him deeply."

When Colonel Sam Whitehurst talks about welcoming new soldiers, he says, "The highlight of that discussion is always about SFC Jared Monti. He represented the best in all of us – duty, honor, selfless service and personal courage. I always ask our new soldiers to aspire to be the soldier and leader that he was, a soldier who always led from the front and never let his comrades down.

This is SFC Monti's lasting legacy."

Kelly Donnelly-Maw tells this story: "My sister was traveling recently and was in line for security at the airport. A TSA (Transportation Security Administration) agent saw that she was from Taunton and asked if that was near Raynham. She said it was, and he asked if she knew about Jared Monti. She responded that she knew the name. He told my sister the whole story and said he tries to make sure everyone he meets from Massachusetts knows about Jared. "He's a true home town hero that I can tell my kids about," enthuses Kelly.

According to Jeff Bolding, "That was me she was talking about. I work at the Northwest Arkansas Regional Airport in Bentonville. I check people's IDs, and any time I meet someone from Massachusetts I ask if they know where Raynham is and if they've heard about Jared Monti. I do that to this day and always will. Some say they know about him. Some don't, but thank me for sharing his story with them. Some tell me that I asked that question the last time they were at the airport. That doesn't bother me. I want to be sure everyone knows about my friend who received the Medal of Honor."

Caite-Nick Rose says succinctly, "You are missed by many and forgotten by no one."

Scott Archdekin wrote to Jared, "Went to Warrior Leadership Class last month and nowadays at least one person in the class gives an oral history of you and what you did. Just thought I'd let you know. You're missed greatly."

Captain Drew Shedwick admits, "I hear all the time people calling us 'heroes' and I try to tell them that I'm no hero, I'm just a guy serving his country. But you, SFC Monti, ARE the real deal. You are and will be forever a true hero to your country, the good Afghan people, and, most of all, to those soldiers you served with and saved."

Jared's friend, Charlie Witkus, feels this way: "All the time with Jared, if you ever needed something, like even a ride home from somewhere, he was there. One time we were in New Jersey and had a flat tire. I called him and he was ready to come down. I just needed money sent to me. But he was ready to jump into his car and pick me and my wife up. Everything with Jared was just trying to help someone else. If you could give the Medal of Honor to him as just a human, not just military service, he still deserved it. He was the best guy I knew and still is."

SSG David Fisher said, "He was just an outstanding young guy. He was taken way too early in his life. He made the ultimate sacrifice. No one of us will ever forget that. Anyone who knew him will never forget who he was or what he did."

Matthew Wolfanger said, "SFC Monti, I loved you, and you are responsible for the man and soldier I am today. I will pray forever to meet you in the afterlife. Chaos out."

Binster DeBinion gives Jared this message: "Miss you, brother. I am making sure all the FISTers in the new generation know what it means to be an NCO, a friend and mentor, since I learned it from being beside you. Rest easy; you are not forgotten, my friend." He also adds, "I know there is no going back for those of us that remain, but we will keep you alive in our stories and in our hearts. Decency is a hard thing to come by these days, and great leaders even more of a rarity. I doubt many people know what selfless service embodies. Jared knew exactly what it meant."

Aron Shady says, "The best memory I have of Jared was the Artillery perimeter run. I watched Jared and his team beat my other friend's team. And the best part was Jared had been out the night before partying hard like he always did. Then after finishing the race, he starts up again. He was the toughest guy I have ever known, and the most caring man as well. He was always quick to listen to a friend and offer sound advice when needed." He continues by saying, "I was deeply saddened when I learned the news of Jared's death. If you look up the word 'soldier' in the dictionary there should be a picture of Jared. Everything he did was rock solid. He truly was an outstanding friend, man, trooper, and all-around great human being."

Lance Harding offers, "Jared will be missed by me and by many of those souls he has touched. Jared was the first true inspiration to me. I knew I'd be looking up towards the heavens today thanking him for his leadership and mentorship he has shown me. I just re-enlisted for another six years, and it's people like Jared who have kept me going strong in this Army. He had all the right core values and taught them to me, not just in military terms but in terms of a friend and person who you would want to be beside you for the rest of your life. He really did this world some good. He has made a big impact on my life and all his friends' lives! He is and always will be missed."

"I felt horrible when I learned of his death. Knowing his story and his final sacrifice makes my heart heavy, and I know there is a void because there aren't that many men like Monti," says Dan Crespo.

According to Steve Pellerin, "My wife and I always think of him and have something that reminds us of him in almost every room. I just need to let out my thoughts to his friends and family that he is not being forgotten by his fellow FISTers. I can speak for every one of his friends when I say we have pushed ourselves harder to be even half the FISTer and all-around person he was. I have to thank him for saving my marriage, and for being the cool-headed one that one day (you know the day, buddy, thank you). As painful as it was to lose him, everyone needs to remember that he has improved a lot of us, both mentally and emotionally. He brought so many people together and still does to this day. This is a lot of crazy chatter talk, but it was something that Jared understood and listened to."

Sam Chewning wrote this message to Jared: "You were that person that would go to hell and back for anyone, regardless of the consequences. It doesn't surprise me that you were trying to help someone else out when the end finally came. To your family: Jared was a great person. He always said he wanted to go out with his boots on. Be proud of him."

Joseph Stone offered, "SFC Monti was a huge loss to our unit and will be sorely missed. He was a great leader, soldier, and person for all to emulate. He left his mark on the world and will not be forgotten."

Michael Ricciardi insisted, "You were one of the finest leaders I have had the honor to serve with. Words cannot express how I felt hearing this news. I will miss you greatly and was honored to be able to call you my friend. My heart goes out to your family. "

"He will forever be remembered for his actions, his personal beliefs and character. I will continue to be mentored by his lessons for years to come and I owe a great debt of thanks to him for his unwavering friendship. He is an everlasting hero and role model. I will share my memories of him with my children when I teach them about character, loyalty and the true meaning of patriotism," commented Ryan Leonard.

John Sackett offered, "We lost our friend, comrade, and Brother-in-Arms, SFC Jared C. Monti. His presence made the world a better place and his absence gives us purpose to be better persons. We miss you, Brother, and strive to carry on your legacy in all our daily lives. You continue to lead us, to inspire us to be better people."

Richie Rodriguez posted, "I was a nervous new sergeant

coming out of the National Guard. You assured me that everything was gonna be alright and I was gonna blend right in with the fellas. You kept me mentally sharp by sharing some of your knowledge with me. In my 14 years I have never met a greater role model in the Army. What an honor it was to have met you and known you."

Erin Sullivan said to Jared's parents, "I just want to express my thanks for your raising such an exceptional and wonderful son. Individuals like Jared are very rare."

"You left a greater impression on me than any other soldier that I have ever encountered in my career. You are a true hero and a patriot, and I wish so greatly that I could have been afforded the honor of standing with you on the battlefield," commented Will Wortman.

Phil Jenison said, "What an incredible man. I am so humbled to have served with you, and more importantly, to have called you a friend. Thank you, Monti, for the ultimate sacrifice for so many. He'd give anything to anyone!! And so be it that's the way he left us, GIVING IT ALL."

Jared even affected the lives of many he never met. For example, Barbara O'Neill posted this: "My utmost respect to you and your family for your brave sacrifice, and even more so being from Massachusetts and a member of the 10th Mountain Div.! We lost our son, PFC Evan O'Neill, in Afghanistan on 9/29/03. It's comforting to know my son is with a great American Hero!!!"

State Police Officer, Scott Quigley, posted this message, "I had someone in back of my State Police cruiser and he saw Jared's prayer card I carry with me. He states, 'Did you know Jared Monti? I read that guy was a badass!' I couldn't help but laugh and agree. I am a better man for having known Jared."

Then-Senator John Kerry entered this into the Congressional Record:

> Our soldiers, sailors, marines, and airmen perform acts of bravery every day. But some of those acts, like SFC Monti's on June 21, 2006, exceed even our country's highest expectations. Courage is one of the virtues we as Americans admire most. That is why the highest military decoration – and one of the oldest – our country bestows on its soldiers is the Medal of Honor. It has been awarded only to the few possessing a special brand of courage, heroism, and patriotism, Americans like SFC Monti. He was an extraordinary American and an extraordinary soldier, one of extraordinary gallantry. By his actions, he has taken his rightful place in the revered company of our country's most selfless heroes.

Janet has lived in North Carolina since her divorce from Paul in 2005. Their daughter Niccole and her husband Waldo have two daughters, Carys and Jocelyn, and also live in NC. Waldo has two sons, Bryan and Russell, along with a daughter, Brenda. She and her husband Dave have two daughters: two-year-old daughter Camden, and Arianna, who was born on July 31, 2014. That makes Niccole a step-grandmother. What was her response? She posted defiantly, "Go ahead, laugh, all of my aunts, uncles, and MOTHER and DAD!! That makes you all GREAT aunts, uncles, and grandmas and grandpas !!!! Who feels old NOW?????" All of the punctuation marks are Niccole's.

Janet started a part-time job at a day care center and recently began a course to maintain certification."I went back to school. You're never too old to learn," she says.

Jared's younger brother Tim met his girlfriend Jennifer Haeberle in an unusual 21st Century way in 2010. "I was texting with a friend and joking around, calling her a dork," Jennifer recalls. "It went to Tim by mistake. He returned the text, calling me a dork. After that, we texted back and forth every day, until he butt-dialed me and we had our first live conversation. I knew I had found someone special that day. We talked and texted every day for about a year, and I started to have feelings for him. He called me one day and said he was going to try to make things right with his ex-girlfriend, and I decided then that if I was going to keep him I needed to act right away."

Jennifer spent a week with the family and friends in the Taunton, MA area. "I loved his family. They are very kind people. I cried the whole flight home." Then, shortly thereafter, Tim showed up at her front door in Oklahoma and said, "Honey, I'm home." According to Jennifer, "He gave me my life back. I helped him deal with many things and will always be by his side. Tim always says I saved his life, but the fact is he saved mine."

Jennifer now lives with Tim in Oklahoma, along with her 14-year-old daughter Ali and an 11-year-old son Raymond. According to her, "My kids love Tim very much." Tim says, "I try to be their friend and peer. I know I can't be the disciplinarian." Jennifer is working as a Certified Medication Aide and also attending school to become an LPN. She eventually hopes to become an RN. Jennifer and Tim are engaged to be married on June 5th, 2015.

Tim is now finishing a physical therapy program at Northwest Arkansas Community College. A talented artist himself, he used to borrow his mother's nursing books and draw skulls and other body parts. "Jared blew me out of the water as a youngster, but I kept pursuing being an artist until I got better than him at it." Tim wrote this post to his brother: "Been thinking about you a lot lately, bro, and missing you more. I hope I can make you proud. I love you."

Although Paul lives alone in the house in Raynham, he claims he will never sell it. It has priceless sentimental value to him. There's the charity work, community service, and speaking engagements. Of particular importance are the visits to schools, where students invariably are captivated by Jared's story. "I think a lot of people can take a lesson from him and the way he lived his life," he maintains.

Paul has nothing to apologize for, yet he wrote this message to his son: "Your name has been splashed all over the media. I know you wouldn't want it that way, but you have inspired so many people and continue to do so. As a father, I couldn't be prouder. You are with me 24/7 and always will be. Please don't be angry with me for using you to motivate others to show their patriotism and support our troops and especially to do the right thing in life. I honor you. I love you so much and can't wait to see you again. God bless, my son, and please continue to watch over me, your family, friends, and fellow soldiers."

Paul also posted the following message to Jared: "Little did you know your actions, not only on that fateful day but throughout your life, would have such a great influence on so many." He feels compelled to "continue to spread Jared's story to all who will listen, in hopes that we can create a better world." Paul's inspiring speeches resonate with everyone from grade school children to seniors. They typically center around three simple, straightforward attributes that Jared personified:

- Always try your hardest
- Never give up
- Do the right thing.

Even with a group of Little Leaguers with short attention spans who might be waiting for the start of a baseball tournament, Paul will concisely make these points. His remarks would sound something like this: "As Jared grew, I noticed how he would never give up in sports and other activities. Ever. No matter what the score was. He always went out and tried his hardest. Nothing mattered except that he gave everything he had to whatever he was doing. I noticed how he always tried to do the right thing. Not the easiest or most acceptable thing, but the RIGHT thing."

Niccole posted this admission to Jared –"I don't know if my heart will ever truly heal. I thought I knew what a broken heart was. Now I know for sure what one is. I love and miss you so much."

"I do not believe in the word 'closure'," says Janet. "Instead, I have to try to find a way to live with my loss and move on in a way that would make my son proud, and believe me when I say it is a struggle every day. I have never been so sad, more proud and more honored to have been chosen to be the mother of SFC Jared C. Monti. I miss him more than words can express. The day I stop grieving him will be the day I die."

Anecdotes such as those in this book bring comfort to both Janet and Paul. "I'm just blown away by the stories, the impact he had on those he knew," admits Janet, while Paul says, "When I hear the stories I think I'm hearing the telling of the exploits of some noble knight in days of yore. It gives me some degree of solace and a great amount of pride."

On October 11, 2014, the Bridgewater-Raynham High School gymnasium was named after Jared. The date was picked to coincide with the class of 1994's 20th Reunion. Class President Darin Souza was instrumental in getting the School Committee to approve giving the gymnasium Jared's name. "The new high school, which opened in 2009, needed his personality. It makes the school a better place," states Souza. The old school, which is now the Junior High, has a plaque with Jared's picture and President John F. Kennedy's famous quote from his Inauguration address, "Ask not what your country can do for you, ask what you can do for your country." Souza adds, "The Raynham kids all know Jared's story. He's their hero. Not so much with the Bridgewater kids, though. The gym will help tell Jared's story."

On October 4, Paul was on a "rock hounding" trip with the Southeastern Massachusetts Mineral Club in nearby Acushnet, MA. He was looking for quartz crystals and nearly lost his life in an avalanche. A large boulder, estimated to be at least 1,000 pounds, slammed into him and knocked him over. It broke his pelvis in five places, along with one of his vertebrae and his thumb. His body was covered with lacerations and contusions. Paul considers himself fortunate to have been able to walk away. "I had my son from above looking out for me," claims Paul.

The 68-year-old emphatically said he didn't need an ambulance, and drove himself to Good Samaritan Hospital in Brockton in Jared's truck. He was transferred to Brigham & Women's Hospital in Boston, where it was determined that the surgery that would have been required to immediately fix his fractures would have been too invasive, so he was released to Spaulding Rehabilitation Center in Boston. Paul maintained that there was nothing that was going to prevent him from attending the Bridgewater-Raynham High School gymnasium dedication, scheduled for just a week after the accident. It would have been difficult to find anyone in the medical profession who believed that was possible.

Sure enough, Paul arrived at the high school in a wheel chair to speak to the audience in the school auditorium. He rose from his wheel chair and slowly, and obviously painfully, made his way to the podium with the assistance of a walker. It was an inspiring moment. Friend Bill Yetman offered this practical advice to Paul – "Switch from rocks to flowers. Softer landing when you fall."

Janet travelled from North Carolina and also spoke at the dedication, saying, "My hope is that anyone entering this gymnasium will see Jared's plaque, and it will serve as a reminder of the sacrifices made by those who have served their country, and particularly those who have given their lives."

Many other American families have, indeed, produced courageous soldiers who have willingly put themselves at risk. Our National Cemeteries are filled with those who answered the call but didn't return. Most won't have books written about them. But their contributions will be remembered. It's said that no one dies until they're forgotten. Let's make sure they live a long while.

We'll ALL see you on the high ground, Jared!

The End

The Jared C. Monti Charitable Foundation

The SFC Jared C. Monti Charitable Foundation is a 501 I (3) non-profit organization (EIN-56-2599231) that each year since 2007 has awarded scholarships to students from Bridgewater-Raynham High School and 10th Mountain Division families at Fort Drum in Jared's name. The criteria is "those who have demonstrated a financial need, academic achievement, extra-curricular activities, community service, and a bona fide connection to the military."

The Flags for Vets program is funded by the Foundation, which also supports Celebrate the Military Child by sponsoring parties for children of those in the military. Periodic contributions are given to such charities as Homes for Our Troops, The Wounded Warrior Project, The MA Military Heroes Fund, The MA Fallen Heroes Memorial, Packages to Troops, and the Fisher House Foundation.

A portion of the proceeds from the sales of this book will go to the Jared C. Monti Charitable Foundation. You can contribute on the following website – http://sfcjaredcmonti.com.

About The Author
Len Sandler

Over the past 25 years, Len Sandler has successfully developed and delivered close to 3,000 management and leadership seminars designed to help people at all levels to improve their job performance. He has conducted programs for such organizations as EMC, NASA, GEICO, General Motors, IBM, Siemens, AT&T, Disney, Lockheed-Martin, McKesson, Citigroup, Liberty Mutual, General Electric, Lucent Technologies, Fidelity Investments, Johnson & Johnson, the U. S. Navy, Hertz, Blue Cross/Blue Shield, Honeywell, Abbott Labs, Motorola, Staples, Verizon, Merck, and Oracle. Prior to that, he spent 16 years in human resources, most recently as Corp. H. R. Dir. at Computervision, a 6,000-employee company. Formerly an adjunct professor at Boston University's School of Management, he holds a B. S. in Psychology, an MBA, and a Ph. D. in Organizational Behavior. He has published numerous magazine articles and is the author of *Becoming an Extraordinary Manager: The Five Essentials for Success,* published by AMACOM in 2007.

Len lives in Westford, MA, with his wife, Marilyn. He has four children – Lori, Melinda, Scott, and Craig, along with two granddaughters, Elizabeth and Louisa.

If You Enjoyed This Book

Please post a review in locations such as Amazon, Goodreads and wherever else you can. These reviews are much more important for the author than you might think as they really help to sell their books. Reviews also assist other would be readers to make a choice so this is your opportunity to help the author. It only takes a few minutes but it makes a difference.

Thank you.

Please visit our website

FIRESHIP PRESS

www.fireshippress.com

For the Finest in
Nautical and Historical
Fiction and Nonfiction
WWW.FIRESHIPPRESS.COM

CPSIA information can be obtained
at www.ICGtesting.com
Printed in the USA
JSHW032224211022
31835JS00001B/4

9 781611 793512

Voices from the Field

Readings in Criminal Justice Research

CARL E. POPE, Ph.D.
University of Wisconsin—Milwaukee

RICK LOVELL, Ph.D.
University of Wisconsin—Milwaukee

STEPHEN G. BRANDL, Ph.D.
University of Wisconsin—Milwaukee

Australia • Canada • Mexico • Singapore • Spain • United Kingdom • United States

Executive Editor, Criminal Justice: Sabra Horne
Editorial Assistant: Ann Tsai
Marketing Manager: Jennifer Somerville
Marketing Assistant: Ken Baird
Project Editor: Jennie Redwitz
Print Buyer: Karen Hunt
Permissions Editor: Susan Walters

COPYRIGHT © 2001 Wadsworth, a division of Thomson Learning, Inc.
Thomson Learning™ is a trademark used herein under license.

Printed in Canada
1 2 3 4 5 6 03 02 01 00 99

ALL RIGHTS RESERVED. No part of this work may be reproduced, transcribed, or used in any form or by any means—graphic, electronic, or mechanical, including photocopying, recording, taping, Web distribution, or information storage and retrieval systems—without the written permission of the publisher.

For permission to use material from this text, contact us by
Web: www.thomsonrights.com
Fax: 1-800-730-2215
Phone: 1-800-730-2214

ISBN: 0534-56376-7

Production Service: Matrix Productions
Copy Editor: Jan McDearmon
Cover Designer: Bill Stanton
Cover Image: © Digital Vision Ltd.
Compositor: Omegatype Typography, Inc.
Printer/Binder: Webcom Limited

For more information, contact
Wadsworth/Thomson Learning
10 Davis Drive
Belmont, CA 94002-3098
USA
www.wadsworth.com

International Headquarters
Thomson Learning
290 Harbor Drive, 2nd Floor
Stamford, CT 06902-7477
USA

UK/Europe/Middle East
Thomson Learning
Berkshire House
168-173 High Holborn
London WC1V7AA
United Kingdom

Asia
Thomson Learning
60 Albert Street #15-01
Albert Complex
Singapore 189969

Canada
Nelson/Thomson Learning
1120 Birchmount Road
Scarborough, Ontario M1K 5G4
Canada

Contents

Preface

The purpose of this text is to provide examples of the application of research methods to criminology and criminal justice issues and to sensitize students to important issues in the application of these methods. This book is designed to be more descriptive and conceptual than technical. For example, in a primary research methods text, students may learn in an abstract way principles of measurement, scientific sampling, questionnaire construction, and research design. *Voices from the Field: Readings in Criminal Justice Research* can then be used to provide actual detailed examples of these principles in operation. In this way, students may better comprehend the research process as applied to criminal justice–related issues.

The articles included in the text were drawn primarily from respected scholarly journals in the criminal justice field (e.g., *Criminology, Justice Quarterly, Journal of Criminal Justice*). In selecting the articles to be included, we considered several factors. First, we wished to select good examples of the various methods. The studies included are well-executed research studies. Second, we wished to include articles that maximized the diversity of how the particular methods are applied and of the topics of the studies. Third, we were cognizant of the difficulty of the studies; we tried to avoid articles where the level of writing was too difficult, where the statistical methods used were too complex, or where the research designs were too complicated to be appreciated. However, we did not wish to sacrifice solid research for simplicity. There is no question that some of the studies included here are more difficult than others.

Along with articles, we provide an original introduction and conclusion section in the text and brief introductions to each methodology section. These introductions are meant to assist the reader in understanding the nature and conduct of the included studies. In addition to these introductions, commentaries written by the authors of the studies are included. These commentaries were written exclusively for inclusion in this text. In the commentaries, the authors provide a behind-the-scenes perspective on their studies, highlighting the way the study came into being and other interesting features of the research. These commentaries are offered to further assist the reader in appreciating the complexities of the research process. We trust that you will find the text to be a useful and effective learning and teaching tool.

We would like to thank those who helped us in developing this book: Bruce Berg, California State University—Long Beach; Tory Caeti, University of North Texas; Kriss Drass, University of Las Vegas—Nevada; Lois Guyon, Illinois State University; Michael Jordan, Radford University; Betsy Kreisel, Murray State University; J. Mitchell Miller, University of South Carolina; Thomas Varner, J. Sargent Reynolds Community College.

PART I

Introduction

Foundations of Criminal Justice Research

You are probably in this course because it is required in order to get your degree. But why are you interested in getting a degree? Why are you in college? Chances are, you want to develop a deeper appreciation and understanding of how things in our world work. You are rather curious about the world around you. You want to learn. Right? As a criminal justice or criminology student, you may be particularly interested in learning about issues such as why some individuals engage in serious criminal behavior while others do not, whether the threat of the death penalty deters people from engaging in certain forms of criminal behavior, whether there is a relationship between drug use and criminal behavior, or the factors that influence a police officer's decision to, say, issue a traffic citation. Of course, the list of interesting and relevant topics could go on and on.

No doubt, you already "know" some things about these issues. This knowledge may have come from various sources. As explained in Maxfield and Babbie's *Research Methods in Criminal Justice and Criminology* (1998), knowledge can be produced from, or based on, tradition (i.e., "the way it has been is the way it will always be"), authority (i.e., what is true is what "experts" say is true), our own experience (e.g., "I saw it happen this way, therefore that is the way it always is"), or scientific research. Tradition, authority, personal experience, and scientific research can provide a basis for knowledge. However, each can also lead to conclusions that are inaccurate. Scientific research, which most simply defined involves the systematic collection and analysis of data, arguably offers the best opportunity to produce accurate knowledge. In essence, the ultimate objective of scientific research is to produce, substantiate, or refute so-called facts and to ultimately attain a more accurate understanding of reality. Therefore, research can not only produce original knowledge, it can also change or alter reality, or that which we believe to be true.

To develop an understanding of a complex phenomenon, one can systematically collect and analyze data ("do research") on a particular issue or one can examine previously conducted and published research studies on an issue. As you would expect, not all research studies are similar in quality or in the believability of their findings and associated conclusions. Here again, to develop an accurate understanding of particular issues by examining previously conducted studies, one must be able to identify weaknesses and strengths in these studies. Only after considering the strengths and weaknesses of studies on a particular issue can we come to a conclusion regarding the contribution of the research in developing knowledge, or establishing the truth. The purpose of this text is to assist you in understanding how knowledge is created through the research process. Specifically, the text provides examples of published research studies and, in doing so, offers you the opportunity to examine the strengths and weaknesses of particular studies and the methods they use.

Truth and knowledge are not static; that which is believed to be true keeps changing, and with these changes the truth often becomes more complicated. Take for example the research that has examined the effect of arrest on repeat instances of domestic violence. Over the course of the past twenty years, several studies were conducted to examine the impact of various police actions on the likelihood of reducing repeat instances of domestic assault. The first of these studies was conducted by Sherman and Berk (1984) in 1981 and 1982 in Minneapolis. In this study, the police were to randomly assign offenders in eligible domestic assault incidents to three possible police actions: arrest the offender, counsel both parties, or send the offender away from the home for several hours. This random assignment process was facilitated through the police officers' use of pads of report forms that were color-coded to represent the three different police options. These color-coded forms were in random order. Whenever officers encountered an incident that could be included in the study, they were supposed to take whatever action was indicated by the report form on the top of the pad. To obtain data on repeat instances of domestic assault, the researchers attempted to contact and interview each reporting victim every two weeks for six months following the incident. The researchers also collected and analyzed criminal justice reports that identified repeat behavior of the offenders during the six-month follow-up period. In comparing the victim and official data on repeat instances across the three possible police actions, it was determined that those offenders who were assigned to the "arrest" group had the lowest frequency of repeat assaults over the six-month follow-up period. From the evidence provided in this study, then, arrest clearly seemed to be the best way of handling domestic violence incidents.

Given the importance of the issue, the Minneapolis study was replicated in five other jurisdictions: Omaha, Charlotte, Milwaukee, Colorado Springs, and Miami-Dade (see Sherman, 1992, for a discussion of each of these studies). Each study employed a slightly different methodology, used different measures of key variables (e.g., the actions that constitute "domestic violence"), and of course, was conducted in a different city with different demographic characteristics. Many of the studies produced findings that differed from what was found in Minneapolis. For example, in Omaha it was found that there was no difference between arrest and nonarrest treatments in relation to repeat incidents. In fact, in using a one-year follow-up (instead of six months as in Minneapolis) an "escalation" effect was found—the offenders who were arrested actually showed a higher rate of repeat violence. In Charlotte, a similar escalation effect was found among those who were arrested. The Colorado Springs and Miami-Dade studies produced results similar to those found in Minneapolis. In the most elaborate of the replications, Sherman and his colleagues found that in Milwaukee the effects of arrest appeared to change over time. The immediate threat to the victim was less when the offender was arrested than when warned, but a long-term escalation effect was seen after a year of the arrest. In essence, there was an initial deterrent effect but that was it. In addition, the researcher found that arrest was more of a deterrent for some (e.g., those who were employed) than for others (e.g., those who were not employed). No question, our state of knowledge has changed over the course of these studies. In the beginning we had a simple answer to the problem: arrest works best. Now the answer is more complicated: it depends.

ISSUES IN RESEARCH DESIGN

In evaluating a research study, or in conducting a research study, several issues must be considered. These include the specification of the purpose of the inquiry, the methods used to collect the data, the types of data to be collected, and two fundamental research processes: sampling and measurement. These issues are briefly discussed below.

Purposes of Scientific Inquiry

There are at least three purposes of doing research. One of the most basic purposes of conducting scientific research is to *describe* a particular phenomenon. When we have little understanding of an issue or event, the first step toward an understanding is a description. Closely related to description is *exploration* as a purpose of research. With description and exploration, the intent is to develop a beginning familiarity with the complexities of the issue at hand. An example of a study with description as the primary intent is provided by the article written by Steven Brandl (1996), "In the Line of Duty: A Descriptive Analysis of Police Assaults and Accidents," which is included in this text. Briefly, the purpose of this study was to simply describe the frequency and nature of injuries to police officers. As you will read, it was suggested that with a better understanding of the injuries sustained by police officers, one can take the next step and examine the causes of the injuries.

The third purpose of collecting systematic data is to *explain* a phenomenon. The mission of science is not only to make observations and record facts but also to provide explanations of why the observed events occurred. Hence, explanation is dependent on determining what caused a particular phenomenon to occur. Indeed, causality is a central component of science and is synonymous with explanation. Generally, in specifying a causal relationship between two variables, three conditions must be met. First, the cause must precede the effect in time (i.e., the cause *X*, or the independent variable, comes before the effect *Y*, the dependent variable). Second, there must be a correlation between the two variables (i.e., the two variables vary together; when the value of one changes, so does the value of the other). Third, the relationship between the cause and the effect cannot be as a result of some other intervening variable (i.e., the cause *X* cannot affect another variable *Z*, which in turn results in the effect *Y*). No question, this third factor is often the most difficult to establish. As a simple example, consider the relationship between the number of people who live in each city in your state and the number of animals in each city zoo in your state. In general, it may be reasonable to expect that cities with more people will also have more animals in their zoos (a correlation exists). But does the number of people in the city *influence* the number of animals in the zoo? Of course, there are problems with this causal reasoning and these problems highlight the conditions of causality that are not satisfied in this example. While there may be a correlation between the number of people and the number of animals, and although we might suppose that the number of people came before the number of animals (proper time order), what about the presence of an intervening variable? To explain the relationship, one should consider that the number of people in a city will, to some extent, influence the tax revenues available in that city, and these tax revenues may, in turn, influence the number of animals in the zoo. There are a lot of other factors that may determine the size of a zoo, but the number of people in the city, by itself, is probably not one of them.

Methods of Data Collection

In this text we divide data collection strategies into five groups with one additional group for those methodologies that cannot be easily placed into any of the other groups. They include experimental and quasi-experimental research; survey research; field research; analysis of existing records; secondary data analysis; and other methods. These groups represent the most commonly recognized methodologies for collecting data (Maxfield and Babbie, 1998). As we discuss, each of the purposes of research—to describe, explore, or explain—has implications regarding the methods used to systematically obtain the data.

Experimental Research Experimental research encompasses the most powerful designs for establishing a causal connection between independent and dependent variables. With experimental designs, subjects are randomly assigned to a treatment group (sometimes referred to as the experimental group) or a control group. The treatment group receives the experimental condition (the independent variable or the stimulus), but the control group does not. For example, if we hypothesized that participation in a discussion group would increase reading comprehension, then the experimental group would participate in a discussion group while the control group would not. Typically, experimental researchers would test both the treatment group and the control group before introducing the stimulus in order to determine their levels of reading comprehension (i.e., a pretest). This is done in order to establish a baseline measure of the variable supposed to be influenced by the treatment (reading comprehension). After the treatment group is exposed to the discussion group, both groups would again be tested (i.e., a posttest) on reading comprehension. If our hypothesis is correct, then we would expect to see improvement in the reading comprehension scores of the treatment group but not the control group.

This method is powerful in establishing causality because it contains the three characteristics of *comparison, manipulation,* and *control.* Having administered both a pre- and posttest, we are able to compare those scores at both the beginning and the end of the experiment. If we have correctly randomized our subjects into a treatment and a control group, then their pretest scores should be roughly similar. Their posttest scores, however, should be different if the stimulus has had the effect we hypothesized. In addition, we can manipulate the introduction of the stimulus by withholding it from the control group. Thus, we know who "gets it" and who does not. Finally, we have the ability to control for a variety of factors that may interfere with the course of the experiment. Potential threats to "internal validity" (the certainty that the independent variable is actually responsible for changes in the dependent variable) are handled by our ability to compare, manipulate, and control the research groups and the stimulus to which the experimental group is exposed.

True experimental designs are not without their problems. For example, true randomization of subjects to control and experimental groups is difficult to achieve in the real world. As a result, experimental designs are usually used in a laboratory-type setting (although the study by Sherman and Weisburd that is included in this text is a notable exception). Because of the "artificial" setting of many experimental studies, one may question the external validity (or generalizability) of the findings produced from the research. Simply stated, would we get the same results if the design were applied to the real-world setting? Questions of generalizability often plague experimental research studies. However, we can sometimes deal with this issue when we move our designs into a field setting.

Quasi-experimental research allows us to have more confidence in the generalizability of our findings but, as a trade-off, some degree of control over the conduct of the research study is often lost in the process. In conducting quasi-experimental research, we generally lack one or more of the features associated with true experimental designs. For example, if we move into the field and conduct our research in a prison setting, then it may be difficult, for practical or ethical reasons, to randomly assign our subjects to a treatment or a control group. Or we may not even have a control group. Thus, the need to conduct the study in a real-world setting will probably affect the type of experimental design used. Using a quasi-experimental design (no random assignment of subjects and/or no control group) will make it more difficult to establish a causal connection between the independent and dependent variables (again, issues associated with internal validity). On the other hand, we do gain something with regard to generalizability of the findings. As we shall see, there are advantages and disadvantages associated with any data collection methodology we choose.

Survey Research Survey research is the most common methodology used by social scientists. Typically, in conducting a survey research study a researcher develops a series of questions regarding some issue that he or she is interested in.

Respondents are then administered a questionnaire or interviewed regarding this issue, be it respondents' experiences, attitudes, beliefs, or behaviors. The responses to the questionnaire or interview schedule are then tabulated and analyzed. This can be a powerful technique for collecting information from a large number of subjects who may be scattered over a wide geographic area. Survey researchers may use a variety of techniques to obtain information, such as questionnaires administered on-site or through the mail, or interviews conducted over the telephone or in homes or at other places such as schools or police squad rooms. Each has its associated advantages and disadvantages, which are discussed in your text.

As an example of this method, and one that is included in this text, James Frank and his colleagues reported the results of a telephone survey conducted in the city of Detroit. The intent of the study was to describe and compare perceptions of African American residents and white residents regarding the Detroit police (Frank, Brandl, Cullen, and Stichman, 1996). Other examples of survey research are the National Crime Victim Survey (NCVS), which uses personal interviews of individuals from across the country to produce crime statistics based upon their personal experiences. Crime information is also generated by researchers who administer questionnaires to youth in order to tabulate their involvement in delinquent acts. As you may presume, a major advantage of surveys is their potential ability to generalize to larger populations (a frequent disadvantage of experimental designs), to describe the characteristics of large populations (e.g., Detroit residents' attitudes toward the police, American citizens' attitudes toward gun control), as well as to establish cause-and-effect relationships through statistical manipulations. One criticism frequently leveled against survey research is that it tells us about peoples' expressed attitudes, perceptions, beliefs, and behaviors but not necessarily what they actually think or do. Human nature is not consistent in that people do not always do what they say they do, nor say what they really think.

Field Research Field researchers study individuals or groups in their natural settings. Similar to anthropologists, who have a rich history of studying divergent cultures by living among them, social scientists may go out in the "real world" in order to get an in-depth understanding of some phenomena. In doing so, they may live with and participate with those they are studying without identifying themselves as researchers. They may gain the confidence of their subjects, identify themselves as researchers, and participate in their activities. They may just observe and interview their subjects without engaging in any participant activity. They may also engage in other activities—observing their subjects without being observed by them. The roles one can take in the field are limitless depending on the subject matter, resources available, and the imagination of the researcher. Vander Ven's article titled "Fear of Victimization and the Interactional Construction of Harassment in a Latino Neighborhood," which is included in this text, provides an example of field research. Vander Ven uses field observations to understand situations that generate fear in a Latino community.

Because there are limits on what the field researchers can realistically observe and the number of people they can study over time, it is difficult to make definitive causal statements or to generalize findings to larger groups in different settings. However, this is really not the purpose of most field research studies. Field research is best suited to explore and describe rather than to explain, and is more conducive to the generation of hypotheses than to the testing of them.

Analysis of Existing Records Data are everywhere as we begin the new millennium. Records and statistics are abundant in the form of credit information, health and death certificates, employment records, census tallies, prison counts, and crime information, and the like—not to mention the millions of bits of information found on the Internet. There really is a "data explosion," which gives researchers opportunities as well as difficulties. Because this information is available, it can be analyzed and provide answers to many questions. Records are usually prepared and maintained by a government agency for some organizational purpose and then they are made available to a researcher to analyze for some other purpose. For example, police officers complete an injury report when they are injured and these reports are then used by the police department for workers' compensation purposes. In the case of Brandl (1996), these reports were obtained and analyzed for the purpose of examining the nature, frequency, and seriousness of injuries as they occur to police officers. As another example, Pope, Stojkovic, and Feyerherm (1987) examined confinement records obtained from a local house of correction. These annual data, covering the period from 1880 through the mid-1980s, contained information on inmates' race/ethnicity, age, offense, and length of confinement. These records were originally completed by the agency and maintained for administrative purposes. In this study, these records were examined in order to identify confinement patterns over an extended period of time in the facility.

Both of these studies call attention to one of the major drawbacks of using existing records—the validity or correctness of the information contained in the record. Since none of the authors completed the original reports/records, there is no way of knowing the accuracy of the information. Thus, while this method can provide valuable information, it also raises questions regarding the validity (correctness) and reliability (consistency) of the information. Simply put, was the information contained in the report correct? Was the information consistently recorded over time or across individuals? These questions are often difficult, if not impossible, to answer. Another difficulty in analyzing existing records is that the data often cannot be made more complete, or be classified differently. With existing records, what you see is what you get. Information that is not there cannot be analyzed, nor can its form be changed once it is recorded.

Secondary Data Analysis Many research methods texts combine a discussion of the analysis of existing records with the discussion of secondary data analysis. This is not an unreasonable way of proceeding, since there are many similarities. However, we have chosen to separate each of these strategies because of their fundamental differences and the types of questions each is capable of addressing. In secondary data analysis, a researcher re-analyzes the (quantitative) data that were typically collected and analyzed by a different researcher. The purpose is to answer different questions. As we noted above, when a researcher analyzes existing records, she or he is essentially "stuck" with data at hand. In secondary data analysis, researchers are still often constrained because certain data of interest for the researcher may not have been collected by the original researcher. In addition, researchers who analyze secondary data are also constrained in that certain variables may not be measured in the most desirable way. Worden's (1990) article "A Badge and a Baccalaureate," which is included in this text, offers an interesting example of secondary data analysis. Data that were originally collected to examine the nature of police-citizen interactions and encounters were used by Worden in this study to examine the influence of police officers' level of education on officers' attitudes and performance (as measured through citizen evaluations of officers during particular contacts). No question, the major advantage of secondary data analysis is that the data have already been collected, which saves much time and money. The major disadvantage is that the researcher has to work with the data as it was collected by another researcher for a different purpose.

Other Methods The five strategies discussed above represent the most common methods used by social science researchers. However, there are variations of these methods and some distinct types that are also employed from time to time. For lack of a better label, we have chosen to group them under the category of "other." One methodological application in this category is the use of focus groups. This technique originated with marketing researchers who brought small groups of people together to discuss a particular consumer product. Information regarding product familiarity, use, and assessment would then be elicited. Focus groups were used by Pope, Lovell, Stojkovic, and Rose (1996) in their examination of juvenile processing in five Wisconsin counties. The objective of the study was to describe the differences between how minority and majority youth were processed through the juvenile justice system. First, data obtained from court case files or computer records were analyzed (analysis of existing records) in order to understand the patterns in decision making. Next, focus groups were used as a data collection strategy. Key decision makers were brought together in small groups to discuss the quantitative results. The resulting focus-group data proved to be valuable in making sense out of the other data.

Another method is content analysis, a technique used used to understand written, oral, or visual communication. If one wished to describe how good and evil are portrayed in crime novels, content analysis would be a method suited to address this issue. Relevant books would be selected in order to analyze words and their contexts. Durham et al. (1995), another study contained in this text, used content analysis to examine popular murder mysteries. Another method is simulation. Typically, simulations allow for the manipulation of some aspect of reality without venturing into the real world. We may, for example, be interested in knowing the effect on the criminal justice system of increasing the number of jury trials by 10 percent. This may be quite difficult, and perhaps unethical, to do in an actual working metropolitan court system. But we may be able to create a computer model of the criminal justice system and do just that. This simulation would help answer our question. Other methods that are illustrated with examples in this text are case studies (Mastrofski and Ritti, 1992) and combinations of methods (Schneider et al., 1996). These are all methodologies that we may be able to use to answer social science questions.

Types of Data

As discussed, the purpose of the scientific inquiry—to explore, describe, or explain—has implications for the selection of the method used to collect the data (e.g., field research is best suited to describe, experimental research is best suited to explain). In addition, the method used to collect the data determines the type of data to be collected and the nature of the analyses to be performed. In this regard, it is important to highlight the difference between quantitative data and qualitative data. Quantitative data are translated into numbers and then often entered into a computer in order to produce statistics. This process allows for statistical conclusions to be drawn about the data. With such data, the statistical relationships between and among variables can be examined. Certain methods of data collection necessitate the collection of quantitative data (e.g., experiments and surveys).

Qualitative data, on the other hand, do not involve statistical manipulations and conclusions but rather an understanding of underlying ascribed meanings of interactions, events, or other phenomena. Field research is a method that commonly involves the collection of qualitative data. Quantitative *and* qualitative data can be used to answer questions regarding our world. They are different but they are both scientific when properly analyzed and used, and of course a single study could employ the use of both.

Sampling and Measurement

Regardless of the data collection strategy used in a study, two other important issues need to be considered when evaluating research studies: sampling and measurement. If we are to have faith in the findings produced in a study and the conclusions drawn as a result of the study, we must have confidence in the sampling and measurement procedures used. Because these issues are discussed in detail in your main text, we provide a brief overview of the most important aspects to consider here.

Sampling One of the initial decisions we have to make in conducting research is who or what we are going to include as part of our data collection effort. In other words, to whom are we going to give our survey, who do we include in our experimental research, what individuals or groups do we focus on in a field setting, and what books or words do we capture in content analysis? Do we include everybody, or do we select only certain people as part of our study? Some of these questions will be answered by the particular methods that we use, while others will not. Field research, for example, by its very nature means that we can't possibly observe everyone and everything, nor can we include everyone as part of our experiment whether it be in a laboratory or a field setting. In survey research, however, it may be possible to include a large number of respondents or, conversely, to select relatively few. What we are really discussing here is the difference between a total population and a sample. If you decided to survey all students enrolled at your university on some particular issue, then we would be talking about the total population. Similarly, if you were to survey all residents of a particular city or, for that matter, all those currently residing in the United States, then we would consider these to be total populations. You should immediately grasp the difficulty in doing this and what a headache it would cause. Oftentimes we simply cannot include everyone and everything, or we may not know what the true population is. Thus, we have to decide who or what to include. The decision, especially in doing survey research, is frequently to select a sample.

In constructing a sampling plan, there are a number of choices to make, but the initial one is whether to select a probability or a nonprobability sample. In a probability sample, each unit of analysis or sample element (in survey research this would be the individuals being given the questionnaire or interviewed) must have a known, nonzero chance of being included in the sample. That is, everyone must have some chance of inclusion. If everyone has an equal chance of inclusion, then we are talking about a simple random sample. If everyone has a chance of being included, but not necessarily an equal one, then we may be talking about some type of area probability sample (refer to your text for details). For our purposes, a probability sample, especially a random one, means that we can select fewer elements than contained in the population and then generalize or make inferences to the total population. This is what we mean by the concept of generalizability, making inferences from a part to the whole.

If you had a roster of all students currently attending your university and randomly selected every tenth student, you would have drawn a probability sample, in this case a simple random one. This, in turn, would enable you to generalize back to and make statements about the entire student body. Moreover, if you sampled correctly, these statements would be relatively accurate. The importance and attractiveness of probability samples lies in the fact there are ways of determining the accuracy of our sample estimates. Your text and instructor will show you how this works. Consider another example, this time involving cooking soup (we'll do spaghetti when we discuss measurement). If you were cooking a caldron of pea soup and you wanted to determine what spices to add, what would you do? Most of us (there are always exceptions) would get a ladle and taste the soup in the caldron. We would then add spices to our satisfaction. We would not have to drink the entire caldron in order to determine what spices are needed. What we have actually done is to draw a sample of the pea soup and then make inferences back to the pot. That's what sampling is all about.

In nonprobability sampling, we seldom have the luxury of being able to generalize to the larger population. As a result, it is very difficult to assess the accuracy of our sample results. Does this mean that nonprobability samples are worthless? By no means. It just means that we can't make generalized statements. Sometimes nonprobability samples are the best that can be done. For example, if you wanted to survey inmates in a prison setting, it is rather doubtful that you would be able to draw a random sample. The warden is probably not going to line up all the inmates so that you can select every tenth one. Moreover, the warden is not going to disrupt the daily routine of the prison for the sake of research. Typically, you take what you can get and, as a result, you may have little idea how representative the inmates you selected are of the total inmate population. Similarly, if you are in a field setting on the street it will be difficult, if not impossible, to draw a probability sample. Often field researchers use a "snowball" sample, observing and talking to some people who then refer them to other people and so on. As you will read, this is the approach taken by Scott Decker in "Collective and Normative Features of Gang Violence" when trying to identify individuals who had gang affiliations. Needless to say, there is no way of knowing how representative the field sample is of some larger population. You thus lack the ability to generalize, but you can still make statements regarding your subjects.

Measurement The process of measurement involves the attempt to make some sense out of the phenomena we are trying to study. In order to measure something, you must have a basic understanding of it and a way of communicating that understanding to others. Some things that we study as social scientists have real meaning—such as gender, age, and income. Other things have no real intrinsic meaning and are simply constructs—power, alienation, religiosity, prejudice, depression, and so on. We would probably all agree that there is such a thing as prejudice or religiosity (some people being more prejudiced or religious than others), but we really can't see it, feel it, hold it, or bounce it. The first thing we must do, then, is to conceptualize these concepts. Then we must find a way to operationalize or measure them.

Gender is relatively easy since we can often observe it or perhaps have people tell us their gender in a survey. On the other hand, religiosity is not so easy since a number of dimensions are associated with this concept. Most of us would agree that religious people tend to go to church on Sundays (or every day for that matter). But there are many reasons people may attend church other than a commitment of faith. For example, going to church may provide an opportunity to socialize, to be seen, or to wear new clothes. While church attendance has something to do with religion, it is not a complete description of the concept. There may be other aspects to the measurement of religiosity. We might agree that religious people read the Bible, pray more often than not, and give money to the church. These are all indicators of the concept religiosity, and the degree to which people do or don't do these things will give meaning to the concept. If we ask such questions in a survey, what we have done is define and operationalize (or measure) the concept.

If we don't define our concepts clearly, precisely, and completely, then we introduce the possibility of error. We fail to hit the target. Let's use another cooking example—this time spaghetti. It is a fairly safe assumption that most of us have cooked spaghetti at one time or another and most of us have run into the same problem. You boil a pot of water and you put the spaghetti into it. You get a smaller pot for the sauce and begin to heat it up. You look down at the pot of spaghetti and say, hmm, that's not very much so you add some more. This may go on for a while, until you finally give up. You turn off the heat and reach for the pot of spaghetti and find you can barely pick it up. You pour the contents into a colander and find that you have a mountain of spaghetti (and very little sauce). This is an example of measurement error. You misjudged the amount of spaghetti. You don't want to do this when conducting social science research.

Before moving into the research examples contained in this text, there are two areas we need to cover at least briefly: ethical and practical considerations in conducting research.

Ethical Considerations

Most professional research organizations have standards of ethical practices that one should review and understand. But many ethical issues, like morals, are not absolute. You must apply your own reasoned judgment. The issues presented below are some that you need to consider and reflect upon. First is the principle of voluntary participation. This simply focuses on whether or not we give our subjects the opportunity to refuse to participate in our research. We surely would not want to force research on them, although in some situations we do come close to it. If we engage in field research and pose as a true participant without identifying ourselves, then we are really not giving our subjects the opportunity to "bow out." Moreover, we are not telling them that they are part of a research study. Is this ethical? In part, it may depend on the purposes of the research. Other situations are less controversial. In survey research, a cover letter typically informs respondents of the nature of the research and their right to refuse to participate. A completed questionnaire then implies voluntary participation.

Another important ethical issue in the practice of research concerns the anonymity and confidentiality of the research subjects. The bottom line is that in conducting social science research, we must guarantee our subjects' confidentiality. Even if we know who they are (as in face-to-face interviews), we must promise not to identify them. If we were conducting a study of "street hustlers," for example, it would be highly unethical to publish their names in the local newspaper, or even use their names in a research report. We must protect their identities; that is why pseudonyms are often used in published materials. The guarantee of anonymity means that we would not and could not identify our subjects. An example is a survey that is administered without respondent names or other identifiers so that there is no way to link a particular person to a particular response.

A final ethical consideration is the protection of subjects. Needless to say, we must protect our subjects from any degree of harm. We cannot beat them for the sake of science. We also need to be concerned with their psychological and emotional well-being. If we are engaged in research that may be emotionally upsetting, such as incidences of domestic violence, we need to be sensitive to the circumstances of the research subjects.

Practical Considerations

More often than not, in conducting criminal justice research we are working in the real world, dealing with real people and situations. At the same time, we may have an idealized picture of what research is all about, one that does not reflect reality. The first realization in conducting research is that things rarely go according to plan. While we might have laid out the perfect methodology on paper, it may not work that way when we actually conduct the research. Sometimes people just don't do what we want them to. In the earlier example of police response to domestic violence, the police officers did not always do what they were asked. In some instances, police officers did not follow the research protocol. They arrested the subjects when they were supposed to warn them, or they did not include an incident when they should have. To some extent, they did what they wanted to do but, luckily, not enough to jeopardize the entire research project. Also, sometimes things happen in spite of the best-laid plans. Something positive or negative may occur that was not anticipated in the original design of the study. Things do go "bump in the night."

Finally, there are two things one must keep in mind in doing research. One is that you are always subject to criticism. Anything you do can be questioned by others. Since no research design is perfect, there will always be limitations. Your job is to understand those limitations and deal with them. Second, research by its very nature can be a frustrating enterprise. You need to develop the ability to laugh when things go wrong or are beyond your control. If you don't have a sense of humor, you will probably not enjoy doing research.

It is with these understandings that we present the following studies for your consideration and analysis. The studies are organized by data collection strategy into six groups: Experimental Research and Its Variations, Survey Research,

Field Research, Analysis of Existing Records, Secondary Data Analysis, and Other Methods. Prior to each study is a commentary written by the author(s) of the study that reflects on the conduct of the study and any especially noteworthy elements of the study. These commentaries were written exclusively for inclusion in this text. They often provide a candid and "real world" perspective into the nature of the study. The text concludes with an epilogue that discusses the use of information produced from research studies.

EXAMINING THE ARTICLES

Before proceeding with your examination of the research articles, consider the following as *one* general means for structuring your assessment of the various works. These questions were proposed by David Royse (1991: 267–68) in his book *Research Methods in Social Work.* Whether you elect to use these questions, modify them, or adopt others, it is important to think systematically about the research and its presentation.

For each article, you may ask:

1. Does the introduction provide a clear notion of (a) the problem, (b) the purpose of the research, and (c) its significance?
2. Are the stated hypotheses [or research questions] reasonable? Do they appear to follow from the review of literature?
3. Is the literature review (a) relevant to the study, (b) thorough, and (c) current?
4. Is a research design stated? Do the subjects appear to have been selected without overt bias? If there is a control group, does it seem to be an appropriate group for comparison? Is the number of subjects sufficient?
5. Is there a discussion of the reliability and validity of the instruments used?
6. Is there enough information on (a) the procedures and (b) the instruments and operational definitions of the variables to allow you to replicate this study?
7. Are statistical tests present when needed? If statistical tests are used, are they the appropriate tests? [Are other forms of analysis appropriate?]
8. Are the findings discussed in terms of their implications and practical significance? Are the conclusions supported by and do they logically follow from the data that have been presented? [Has the author overgeneralized?] Has actual or potential bias been recognized?

PART II

Experimental Research and Its Variations

This part of the text contains three articles that use experimental and quasi-experimental designs to assess the impact of a treatment on a dependent variable. As noted in Part I and explained in detail in your main text, experimental research allows for conclusions about causal relationships because the elements of control, manipulation, and comparison are well reflected in such methodologies. However, not all experimental research studies are similarly designed or executed. As a result, the causal inferences offered in various experimental studies should be considered carefully.

The articles included here highlight some of the various methods and procedures that can be used in conducting experimental research. For example, MacKenzie and Shaw (1990) examine the impact of a correctional boot camp on inmates' attitudes and adjustment to prison, among other outcomes. To do so, the authors used a quasi-experimental design that consisted of a treatment group (inmates who participated in the boot camp program), a comparison group (inmates who were eligible for the program but did not participate; this group was "matched" to resemble the experimental group), and pre- and posttests of the dependent variables (e.g., prosocial attitudes, data for which were collected through self-administered questionnaires). As noted by the authors in the article and in the commentary, one of the most important features of the boot camp program and a dimension that complicated the evaluation of it was that inmates volunteered for the program and could drop out at any time. This necessitated additional comparisons between those who completed the program and those who dropped out. As discussed, this factor also complicated the conclusions that could be made about the impact of the program. The researchers found that those who successfully completed the program became more prosocial while those who were incarcerated and those who dropped out did not. Boot camps were a clear success then, right? Well, it was also found that before the program began (in the pretest), those who successfully completed the program were already more prosocial than those who dropped out and those who were incarcerated. No question, the pretest comparisons between those who completed the program and those who subsequently dropped out provided important information on which to assess the impact of the boot camp program.

The study by Leiber and Mawhorr (1995) examined the impact of a social skills training program on juvenile recidivism. To assess the impact of the program, the researchers compared the official delinquency (as determined through court records) of four groups of youth: those who completed the program, those who did not complete the program (i.e., dropouts), an equivalent sample of youth not in the program (matched to the group that completed the program on several important characteristics), and those who received traditional juvenile court services. The researchers found that the youth who completed the program were as likely to re-offend as the equivalent matched group, the group that dropped out of the program had the greatest likelihood of recidivism, and the group that received traditional services was the least likely to re-offend. However, it was also found that those who completed the program committed less serious offenses than the other three groups. The authors offer explanations for why the program was not more effective, argue the importance of other outcomes to judge the success of such a program, and offer suggestions for how the program may be improved.

Sherman and Weisburd (1995) use a true experimental design to examine the impact of increased police patrol in identified crime "hot spots" on the extent of crime (measured through UCR data) and disorder (as determined by the observations of members of the research team). The study was conducted in Minneapolis. As discussed in detail by the authors, this study sought to remedy the theoretical weaknesses of previous research that came to the conclusion that increased police presence does not impact crime (i.e., the Kansas City Preventive Patrol Experiment). In the present study, 110 eligible hot spots were identified and then randomly assigned to either the control group ($N = 55$) or the experimental group ($N = 55$). Those areas in the experimental group then received additional police patrol while those in the control area received the usual amount of patrol. The researchers compared the amount of crime that occurred prior to the initiation of the hot-spot patrols (the baseline or pretest) with the amount of crime that occurred while the hot-spot patrols were in place (posttest) for both the control and experimental areas. The amount of disorder present in the control area was compared with the amount of disorder present in the experimental area, but only while the hot-spot patrols were in place. As a result of the detailed statistical analyses performed on the data, it was found that increased police presence in hot spots had modest impacts on crime, but greater impacts on observed disorder. As explained by Sherman and Weisburd, these findings lead one to question the conclusion that the police cannot affect crime.

1

Inmate Adjustment and Change During Shock Incarceration

The Impact of Correctional Boot Camp Programs

DORIS LAYTON MACKENZIE, National Institute of Justice and Louisiana State University
JAMES W. SHAW, Louisiana State University

COMMENTARY by Doris Layton MacKenzie

When I began planning the study of the Louisiana "boot camp" prison program, there were few boot camp prisons in operation and they had received little media attention. Soon thereafter there was an explosion of the camps throughout the country. Inmates marching around and being required to do push-ups at command from drill instructors provided great visuals for the media. However, when we did the research on the Louisiana boot camp the programs were relatively new and as yet had received little media attention.

I had not heard anything about the programs until an acquaintance of mine who worked in the Louisiana Department of Corrections called me at Louisiana State University (LSU) where I was working at the time. He said, "We have a new program here at the reception and diagnostic center that you might be interested in evaluating." Later, I visited the program and decided to apply to the National Institute of Justice (NIJ) in the U.S. Department of Justice for the funding I would need to complete the evaluation. NIJ evaluated our proposal and decided to fund our research. Jim Shaw, my coauthor on this

Source: Justice Quarterly, Vol. 7 No. 1, March 1990, pp. 125-147. Reprinted by permission of the Academy of Criminal Justice Sciences.

An earlier version of was presented at the annual meeting of the American Society of Criminology, Chicago, 1988. This investigation was supported in part by grant #87-IJ-CX-0020 from the National Institute of Justice, U.S. Department of Justice to the Louisiana State University for a cooperative project with the Louisiana Department of Public Safety and Corrections (LDPSC). Opinions expressed in this paper are those of the authors and not necessarily those of the U.S. Department of Justice. Thanks are expressed to LDPSC personnel who served on the Advisory Board and who helped with data collection and to the offenders who volunteered to participate in the study.

paper, was just entering school at LSU, and I asked him if he would work with me on the research. This began our work together that ended with his tragic death in 1994.

We wanted to know whether the Louisiana boot camp was effective. Our first objective was to decide what was meant by "effective." We held focus group meetings with the staff and administrators from the program and from the Department of Corrections to obtain their help in identifying what they believed were the goals of the project. From these discussions, we identified two types of outcomes they expected from the program: (1) an impact on individual offenders (reduced recidivism, changes in attitudes), and (2) an impact on prison crowding and associated costs. They expected the program to change the offenders' behavior so that when they returned to the community they would be more apt to be involved in positive social activities, such as working or going to school, and they would be less apt to be involved in criminal activities so their recidivism rates would be reduced. They anticipated that the long-term change in behavior would be preceded by short-term changes in attitudes and beliefs. In the process of our research, we examined the impact of the program on all of these potential changes.

This paper focuses on the adjustment of the inmates to the boot camp program and changes in their attitudes and beliefs while they were in the program. In order to know whether they would have adjusted and changed in a similar way if they had gone to a traditional prison, we compared them with a group of inmates who served their sentence in a traditional prison. We were interested in various attitudes and beliefs. Some of these, such as antisocial attitudes, are particularly important because they have been found to be associated with criminal activities. That is, the more antisocial a person's attitudes the more criminally active he or she will be. If the boot camp reduces a person's antisocial attitudes, the program may have the desired long-term effect of reducing recidivism.

As we tried to design the research we faced several problems. First, a relatively small pool of offenders were available to enter the program. This occurred for several reasons. First, offenders selected for the program had to be sentenced to prison. The program was designed as an early release mechanism. That is, offenders who successfully completed the program would be released on parole earlier than if they had served their sentence in a traditional prison. So, on the one hand, offenders had to be convicted of serious enough offenses that the judge believed a prison sentence was warranted. On the other, since they would be released early, the corrections department wanted to be sure that they were appropriate candidates for early release. The legislation that was passed to permit the early release included careful identification of the characteristics of offenders who would be eligible. The requirements that candidates for the program had to be serving their first prison sentence and the sentencing judge had to recommend them for the program severely limited the number of candidates who would be eligible. Many of the judges were not aware of the program or they did not believe the program was appropriate for the offenders they sentenced.

The candidate pool was also limited because any inmate who was eligible had to volunteer to participate in the program. The candidates who would serve only a short term in the traditional prison did not volunteer because of the difficulty of the boot camp atmosphere. They would rather serve a short term in the traditional prison than to serve a slightly shorter term in the boot camp.

For our purposes, this limited pool of eligible offenders meant that it was difficult to find a reasonable comparison group. Ideally, we would have identified a large pool of eligible candidates for the boot camp. We would then ask them if they would volunteer to enter the camp and also volunteer for the research. Out of this pool of eligible volunteers, we would have randomly assigned inmates to either their traditional sentence or to the boot camp. Thus, from the start we would know that the two groups were similar and the only difference would be random. When we examined their attitudes or recidivism, we could conclude that any differences that occurred after the program were due to what had happened in either the traditional prison or the boot camp.

Random assignment was not possible because there was such a small number of eligible inmates who had received recommendations from the judge. Therefore, we had to find another way to select our comparison group. Since many of the judges did not know about the program or for some other reason did not recommend offenders for the program, we decided that we should find candidates from the offenders who were legally eligible for the program. Furthermore, we asked the classification committee to determine which of these offenders would be judged by them to be appropriate candidates for the boot camp if they had received a recommendation from the judge. So we tried to select a comparison group that was as similar as possible to the group of offenders that would be in the boot camp.

A second way to ensure that the comparison group was similar to the experimental group (e.g., the boot camp group) was to design the study so that we would know that they were similar. For this reason, we used a pretest-posttest design. We were interested in attitudes and beliefs and how they changed while the offenders were in the boot camp. If the comparison group we selected is the same as the boot camp group, they should score similarly to the experimental group on the outcomes of interest. For example, the mean antisocial attitude score of the comparison group should be similar to the mean antisocial attitude score of the experimental group in the pretest. If the boot camp successfully reduces the antisocial attitudes of the experimental group, then in the posttest the mean for this group should be lower (less antisocial) than the mean for the comparison group. From this perspective, we would expect the experimental group to change from pretest to posttest. They would become less antisocial. The comparison group would not change. Then we can conclude that most likely it was the boot camp that led to this change. This is the reason that, in the paper, we very carefully examine and compare the changes in attitudes and adjustment of the comparison group and the experimental group. The pretest-posttest design allows us to eliminate many alternative explanations (for example, that the groups differed before the program) for our results.

Another problem we had with this research is attrition or dropouts from the boot camp. Since the boot camp program was a rigorous and demanding program, many offenders dropped out before they completed the program.

This gave us problems with the statistical analysis. If we analyzed the research without the dropouts in the data, we might have a problem with our conclusions. Possibly all those who dropped out of the boot camp were the ones with the most antisocial attitudes. If this were true, then when we compared the mean change we would see a change only because the most antisocial individuals dropped out of the program and not because the boot camp program actually changed the participants. In the paper, we carefully examine the attitudes and beliefs of the dropouts so we can find out if our results are a reflection of change due to the boot camp program or just because those with certain types of attitudes and beliefs drop out of the program.

From this beginning, the boot camp research in Louisiana, I became recognized as a national expert in the area of boot camp research. In part, this was because I began the study when boot camps were new and few other people had completed research on the topic. After completing this study I completed a multisite study of boot camps for adults in eight different states. At present, I am director of a national study of juvenile boot camps. So that inauspicious phone call asking if I might want to look at Louisiana's new program led to a long-term involvement in boot camp research. People ask me if I think boot camps are a fad and when the fad will end. Yes, it is a fad, but for many years—since the early Elmira reformatory, we had returned to a military model of correctional program. What we need to know is what advantages or disadvantages come with this model and how to interface this model with rehabilitation and treatment to successfully change offenders.

ABSTRACT The prison adjustment, expectations, and attitudes of offenders participating in a shock incarceration program were compared to offenders who dropped out of the program and to a comparable group of offenders serving their sentence in a regular prison. There was some evidence that before beginning the program, dropouts from shock incarceration had less prosocial attitudes than those who continued in the program. Shock incarceration offenders differed from those in the regular prison in their adjustment to prison, in their attitudes, and in the changes in these over time. In comparison to regular prison inmates, they were more positive about their prison experience, about their ability to make positive changes in their lives, and in general prosocial attitudes. It was concluded that those who continued voluntarily in the program showed evidence of positive change during shock incarceration. Future research should examine whether these changes are related to performance during parole.

"Shock incarceration" is an alternative to a standard prison sentence, in which offenders spend a short time in prison in a "boot camp" atmosphere. The common element in various shock incarceration programs is the short period served in prison in an environment emphasizing discipline, military drills, and physical training. The specific components, such as the length of stay, counseling and educational programs, release decision making, and follow-up surveillance, vary widely among jurisdictions with shock incarceration programs (MacKenzie and Ballow 1989; Parent 1988; MacKenzie, Gould, Riechers, and Shaw 1989; U.S. General Accounting Office 1988). Although the specific components vary, the goals of the programs show some consistency. The major goal is a reduction in overcrowding in prisons. A second goal is to change offenders; the major change desired is a reduction in criminal behavior.

Shock incarceration is similar to previously developed shock probation programs in that it involves a relatively short period in prison preceding a period of community supervision (MacKenzie et al. 1989; Parent 1989; Vito 1984). In contrast to offenders receiving shock probation, offenders in these programs spend their time in prison in a "boot camp" atmosphere. Furthermore, during their time in prison the shock incarceration inmates are not mixed with the general-population inmates; they participate in programs designed specifically for them.

The first shock incarceration programs began in the early 1980s in Georgia and Oklahoma. By 1987 approximately 40 percent of the state correctional jurisdictions either had programs, were developing programs, or were seriously considering programs (MacKenzie and Ballow 1989; Parent 1988, 1989). The popularity of these programs appears to be the result of several forces. Foremost is the serious prison overcrowding now occurring in most states. The shorter period in prison for those entering shock incarceration programs gives hope for a reduction in the numbers of offenders in prison. Another reason for the general acceptance of these programs is the expectation that future criminal behavior will be reduced for those experiencing shock incarceration. Some people believe that this change will occur because of the punishment and retributive aspects of shock incarceration. Others believe that the programs bring positive benefits which will lead to a reduction in offending. From the latter perspective it is assumed that the offender will change as a result of experiences during shock incarceration, and that this change will be demonstrated by fewer criminal activities upon release.

The study reported here is part of a larger study conducted in Louisiana which is examining changes, at both the system and the individual level, that can be attributed to shock incarceration. This paper examines the changes that occur in offenders participating in the shock incarceration program during their time in prison and compares these offenders to a similar group of offenders who are serving their sentences in a regular prison. We anticipate that before any changes occur in behavior upon release, internal changes will take place during incarceration. If shock incarceration is to influence later behavior and to be an improvement over regular prison, the changes during incarceration for those in the programs should be different from changes for those serving regular sentences. A follow-up to this study will examine the performance of these offenders after they are released on parole.

LOUISIANA'S SHOCK INCARCERATION PROGRAM

Shock incarceration programs differ widely; therefore any evaluation of a program must begin with a description of the specific program under examination. The Louisiana Department of Public Safety and Corrections' (LDPSC) Intensive Motivational Program of Alternative Correctional Treatment (IMPACT) is a two-phase shock incarceration program begun in 1987 (LDPSC 1987). In the first phase, offenders are incarcerated for 90 to 180 days in a rigorous boot-camp atmosphere. After this period they are placed under intensive parole supervision for the second phase.

Those eligible for the program must be first felony offenders, must have sentences of seven years or less, and must be recommended by the Division of Probation and Parole, the sentencing court, and a designee of the LDPSC. Offenders are sentenced to a regular prison term and then may be recommended for the program. They must volunteer; they may decide at any time to withdraw from the program. They also may be removed from the program for insufficient progress or for misbehavior. An offender who leaves the program must serve his or her sentence in the regular prison until eligible for parole. Successful completion of the program reduces the amount of time the offender spends in prison; this condition is assumed to be a strong incentive for completing the program.

Along with military training, drill, and physical exercise, the incarceration phase of IMPACT involves treatment programs such as ventilation therapy, reeducative therapy, substance abuse education, and prerelease education. The staff, who are primarily responsible for the offenders, are called "drill instructors." They are expected to act as models, counselors, and agents of behavior change through positive reinforcement and support (MacKenzie et al. 1989). Offenders are required to move gradually through stages in the program until they are judged to be ready for graduation, after which they are released to intensive parole supervision.

Louisiana's shock incarceration program is similar to those currently in operation in 10 other state jurisdictions (MacKenzie and Ballow 1989). As is true of other programs, offenders spend 90 to 180 days in the program; the program is considered to be an alternative to a longer period in prison; and the atmosphere is modeled after a military boot camp. Participating offenders do not mix with the general population, although almost all programs are located at facilities that house general-population inmates. In almost all of the state programs, as in the Louisiana program, the participants are nonviolent offenders (nine of the 11 states, including Louisiana) serving time on their first felony conviction (10 out of 11).

Placement authority and release supervision differ among state programs. Most important for the present study, however, is the fact that programs differ in whether offenders enter the programs voluntarily and/or are permitted to drop out voluntarily. In five of the 11 states with programs, including Louisiana, offenders must volunteer to participate. Four other programs are similar to Louisiana's in permitting offenders to drop out of the program voluntarily. Perhaps the largest difference among programs is the amount of time spent in rehabilitation activities (such as education, counseling, and treatment) in comparison to military drill, physical exercise, and work. Louisiana's IMPACT program is among the top three of the 11 state programs in time spent each day in rehabilitation activities; offenders spend more time in rehabilitation activities in Louisiana than in most other programs.

There are several reasons why offenders who are eligible for the shock incarceration program in Louisiana may not enter the program. They may not volunteer or they may not be recommended, and they may not be recommended for various reasons. The judge may not believe the program is appropriate for the offender, or may not think of the program during sentencing because it is a relatively new sentencing option. In any case, IMPACT-eligible offenders are low-risk cases in the prison population. Those who are not recommended for IMPACT are sent frequently to the youthful offenders' prison in the Louisiana prison system, but other assignments and transfers are common. During their time in prison they are required to work (they are sentenced to hard labor); most often this work is field labor on a prison farm. These offenders are in demand at facilities throughout the state because they are appropriate candidates for trustee positions in the maximum-security prisons. They are mixed with other general-population inmates; unless they are being punished, they are housed in dormitories. Their sentence is indeterminate; the parole board determines the release date.

Offenders who enter the IMPACT program and complete it successfully appear before the parole board after approximately 120 days in the program. This hearing takes place before the date at which they would have been eligible for parole if they were serving time on a regular prison sentence. The parole board has final authority regarding release, but in all cases to date, offenders who completed the program successfully have been paroled. Offenders who do not complete the program, whether they drop out voluntarily or are dismissed for some other reason, are sent to the regular prison system to serve out their time. In almost all cases such offenders are required to serve more time in prison before they are eligible for parole than if they had completed the shock program. Thus the IMPACT program provides an offender with both a shorter period of incarceration and a more certain date of release than would occur in the regular prison.

THEORETICAL CONSIDERATIONS

Inmates in prison and those in shock incarceration programs display several differences, which might be hypothesized to affect their adjustment and reactions to the experience. Previous research with prison inmates suggests that prison adjustment might be characterized by four major factors: anxiety, prisonization, misbehavior, and passivity (MacKenzie, Goodstein, and Blouin 1987). Differences between shock incarceration inmates and others might be expected in the first three of these factors.

For example, there is evidence that offenders in prison experience a higher level of stress early in their imprisonment than later (Sapsford 1978; Zamble and Porporino 1988). Shock incarceration programs are modeled after military boot camps and are assumed to be demanding both physically and emotionally. Therefore we anticipate that offenders in shock incarceration programs will experience higher levels of stress early during their incarceration than offenders serving their time in a regular prison environment. This distress should be reflected in higher levels of reported anxiety for those in shock incarceration; for both groups, anxiety should decline with increased time in prison.

Increased conflicts with other offenders is another variable that may be associated with stress. In previous research, offenders reported a lower level of conflicts with others (MacKenzie and Goodstein 1986) and fewer angry episodes (Zamble and Porporino 1988) early in their confinement than they reported three or four months later. In these studies, the level of conflicts and angry episodes remained the same for the next year or two of incarceration. Because of the consistency in reports of conflicts with others from three months to two years, MacKenzie and Goodstein (1986) concluded that the uncertainty of the early period in prison may inhibit the normal level of conflicts for this population in this situation.

Because the behavior of offenders in the shock incarceration programs is controlled carefully, offenders are not expected to have higher levels of conflict with others than those reported by regular prison inmates. In contrast, those serving regular prison sentences are expected to have lower levels of conflict early in their time in prison but to exhibit an increase in conflicts with increased time in prison.

We also expect that a change in attitudes toward the prison and the staff will be associated with length of time in prison for the shock incarceration inmates. Early in the program we anticipate that these offenders will be extremely negative toward the staff and the program. Later we expect them to become more positive about the program; this change should be reflected in their attitudes about prison and about their experiences. Such a change would be in direct contrast to findings from previous studies of prisonization, in which offenders became more prisonized with increased time in prison (Goodstein and Wright 1989).

This change to positive attitudes reflects a general trend towards more prosocial attitudes that we expect to find in the shock inmates. Not only are the offenders expected to become more positive towards the program; they also are expected to become generally more positive in their attitudes towards other people and toward society in general. There are several reasons for expecting a positive change in the offenders who remain in the shock program. First, in the programs like Louisiana's, in which participation is voluntary, offenders have worked to complete a difficult regimen. Thus, in some sense, we might expect that they have come to believe in the program.

In addition, some components of the program might be expected to bring about this change. For one, the program may take advantage of the disruption and stress experienced early in incarceration. Zamble and Porporino (1988) argue that offenders may be particularly vulnerable and susceptible to outside influences at this time. In fact, during the early period of their time in prison, when they reported high levels of emotional discomfort, the offenders in the Zamble and Porporino study expressed a desire to change their lives and to take advantage of new opportunities. In the regular prisons this desire for change, like the symptoms of stress, declined with time. Programs such as shock incarceration, which begin early in the offender's career in prison, may take advantage of this opportunity to change the offender.

The type of change, of course, will depend upon the components of the program (MacKenzie et al. 1989; Parent 1988). As mentioned, however, a goal of the shock incarceration programs appears to be an effort to induce a positive change in the participants' attitudes. One factor that seems to be related to successful adjustment outside prison is an increase in prosocial attitudes (Cullen and Gendreau 1989). A change toward more prosocial attitudes may be particularly important if the changes that occur during shock incarceration are to be continued after release and are associated with a reduction in recidivism.

METHODS

Subjects

Two groups of subjects, a shock group and an incarcerated group, were examined in the present study. We collected information for the study from inmate records and self-report data. Self-report information from the samples was collected at three points: Time 1, immediately upon entrance to the diagnostic center (before beginning IMPACT for the shock sample); Time 2, two weeks later (approximately Week 2 of IMPACT for the shock sample and after transfer out of the diagnostic center to a prison for the incarcerated sample); and Time 3, approximately 85 days later (near the end of the IMPACT program for the shock sample and in a regular prison for the incarcerated sample). At the last testing offenders in the incarcerated sample, who were in various prisons throughout the state, were brought to several central locations for testing.

Shock Sample All 90 offenders entering IMPACT from October 25, 1987 to February 28, 1988 who volunteered to participate in the study were included in the shock sample. (All offenders asked were willing to participate in the study.) Before the end of the IMPACT program 50 percent of the offenders dropped out of the program (dropouts). A total of 86 inmates were tested before entering IMPACT; 40 inmates were tested before entry and again after 85 days in the program. Offenders were included in the analysis for this report only as long as they remained in the program.

Incarcerated Sample Forty inmates who were legally eligible for IMPACT but who had received regular prison sentences were asked to participate in the study. Two (5%) of these refused to participate; another did not participate because he was being punished. The remaining 37 inmates made up the incarcerated sample. Questionnaires were administered to the incarcerated offenders at the diagnostic center at Time 1 and in one of the state prisons at Time 2 and Time 3, if they were being held in a state prison. Nine offenders (24%) were not included in all testings because either they were paroled (11%), were being punished (5%), had medical problems (5%), or had been transferred to a community corrections center (3%). A total of 28 subjects in the incarcerated sample were tested at both Time 1 and Time 3; a total of 20 in the incarcerated sample were tested at both Time 2 and Time 3.[1] Because the small number of women admitted to the IMPACT program prohibited statistical comparisons, we chose only men for the incarcerated sample.

Procedure

From March until April 1988, we reviewed records of all offenders entering the LDPSC diagnostic and reception center to designate the incarcerated sample. We included in the sample those who were legally eligible for IMPACT but who had not received the legally required recommendations from any or all three reviewers (see program description above).

Information on demographics, present sentence and crime, and prior criminal justice system experience for both samples was collected from LDPSC inmate records. The demographic information included race, sex, age, IQ, and highest grade completed in school. Variables related to the present sentence were sentence length, sentence type (probation violation versus new criminal conviction), and current offense type (e.g., burglary, drugs) of the crime carrying the longest sentence. To categorize prior experience with the criminal justice system we used records showing prior criminal history (yes or no), prior incarcerations (yes or no), and age of first arrest.

The self-report data collected for this study were part of a larger questionnaire administered at the three time points. Most of the questions were tape recorded by a professional radio broadcaster as a public service.[2] For the present study, at Time 1 the questionnaire included the Jesness personality scales and the expectations toward IMPACT scales; at Time 2 it included the attitudes toward prison/IMPACT scales and anxiety, conflicts, and aggressiveness scales. The Jesness scales and the scales measuring attitudes toward prison/IMPACT, anxiety, conflicts, and aggressiveness were administered again at Time 3. Each of these instruments is described below.

[1]Fewer were tested at Time 2 because they were being transferred to various locations throughout the state. At Time 3, offenders were brought by LDPSC to several central locations for testing.

[2]Special thanks are extended to Dave Prince and radio station WJBO, Baton Rouge, for their help in recording questions used in this study.

Instruments

Expectations About IMPACT[3,4] We wrote 15 Likert-type items (strongly agree to strongly disagree) to reflect general expectations about the IMPACT program. We formed two additive scales from these items based on the results of a factor analysis using a varimax rotation. Examination of the eigenvalues and a Scree plot indicated two factors: 1) beneficial expectations and 2) easy time. Items loading above .40 on each factor were used to form the two additive scales.

The beneficial expectations scale (nine items) reflected expectations that IMPACT would benefit the respondent. A high score on this scale indicates high expectations of obtaining positive benefits from the IMPACT program. The coefficient alpha for this scale was .78; the interitem correlation was .28.

Items on the easy time scale reflected expectations that electing to enter IMPACT would result in an easier sentence, whether this was because it was safer, shorter, or in general simply easier. A high score on this scale indicates a belief that IMPACT is an easy way to do time. Coefficient alpha and the mean interitem correlation for this scale were .64 and .22 respectively.

Adjustment to Prison We used three scales to measure adjustment to prison: state-trait anxiety, conflicts with others, and aggressiveness. Anxiety was used to indicate the degree of distress experienced by the offenders. Conflicts and aggressiveness were used to reflect adjustment to prison. There is some indication that conflicts, like anxiety, reflect stress and distress in the offender populations (MacKenzie and Goodstein 1986; MacKenzie et al. 1989).

Anxiety was measured with the state version of the state-trait anxiety inventory (Spielberger, Gorsuch, and Lushene 1970), a 20-item Likert-type scale with four response choices (not at all to very much so). A high score indicates a high level of reported anxiety.

The conflicts with others scale indicates the frequency and amount of conflict between the respondent and other prisoners in the past three months. This is a Guttman scale developed by Shoemaker and Hillery (1980) and used previously with prison inmates (Goodstein and Hepburn 1985; MacKenzie and Goodstein 1986; MacKenzie et al. 1989). Offenders were asked to state how often in the past week they had been in certain conflict situations with another prisoner. The first situation was a discussion in which some disagreement occurred. The items became progressively more serious until the final one: a situation in which weapons were used or where someone was killed. After each

---

[3]Data from all offenders who completed the expectations about *IMPACT* items and the adjustment to prison items at the first administration were used in the factor analyses. Changes in factor scores are strongly possible if a larger data set is used. In addition, the data from samples compared later on the scales were included in the formation of the factors. Therefore the data analysis using these scales must be considered exploratory at this time.

[4]No data from dropouts were included in the analyses of changes from Time 2 to Time 3 because most of those who dropped out did so before Time 2 data collection.

statement three response choices were offered (never, once or twice, and daily or almost daily). A high score indicates a high level of conflicts.

We measured aggressiveness with a nine-item Likert-type scale containing five response choices (strongly agree to strongly disagree) which had been identified in factor analyses in previous research with prisonization items (Goodstein and MacKenzie 1984). Items in this scale are similar to those contained in many prisonization scales (Goodstein and Wright 1989). A high score indicates high aggressiveness in interactions with others (e.g., "You can't let someone push you around because if you do you'll get pushed around from then on" or "You can't really expect people to think much of you if you're willing to back away from trouble").

Attitudes Toward Program At Time 2 and Time 3, Likert-type items (strongly agree to strongly disagree) developed by the researchers were given to the inmate volunteers. These items included the previously described expectations about IMPACT. The additional items were written to be general enough to refer to either the prison or the IMPACT experience. For items that included the words "IMPACT" or "in IMPACT" the words were changed to read "prison" or "in here" for the incarcerated sample. Factor analyses of these items for Time 2 indicated three scales (eigenvalues and Scree plots): victimization, personal change, and staff and program attitudes. Items loading above .40 on any factor were used as items in each scale except when an item loaded below .5 on one factor and above .5 on another; in that case it was omitted from the factor on which it loaded lower. The eight items in the victimization scale refer to fear of getting hurt, safety, and the stress of prison life. The coefficient alpha and the mean interitem correlations for this scale were .76 and .29 respectively.

Eight items loaded above .40 on the personal change factor. A high score on this scale means that the offender expects the prison or IMPACT experience to change him in a positive manner. For this scale the coefficient alpha was .85 and the mean interitem correlation was .42.

The third attitude toward prison/IMPACT scale reflected general staff and program attitudes (11 items). A high score on this scale indicated positive attitudes toward the program (prison or IMPACT) and toward the staff in particular. Coefficient alpha was .82 and the mean interitem correlation was .34 for this scale.

Prosocial Attitudes We used the Jesness Inventory to measure the offenders' prosocial attitudes (Jesness 1983; Jesness and Wedge 1985). A total of 155 true-false Jesness items make up 11 personality scales: social maladjustment, value orientation, immaturity, autism, alienation, manifest aggression, withdrawal, social anxiety, repression, denial, and asocial attitudes. These scales were developed by Jesness to be used with adolescents, but subsequent research has found that they can be used successfully with adults as well. The scales were designed as indexes to measure tendencies predictive of social and personality problems, and particularly to distinguish delinquents from others in a wide variety of settings.

They were intended specifically to be valid measures of short-term changes in attitudes. In the present research we used the items to calculate simple additive scales scored so that high values were more prosocial. The items making up each scale are described in Jesness (1983).

Although all 11 of the Jesness scales were administered, of particular interest to this study were the four scales that are most indicative of antisocial attitudes: social maladjustment, alienation, manifest aggression, and asocial attitudes. The social maladjustment scale is made up of 65 items that reflect attitudes associated with "inadequate socialization, as defined by the extent to which individuals share the attitudes of persons who do not meet environmental demands in socially approved ways" (Jesness 1983:3). The 26 items in the alienation scale reflect attitudes of distrust toward others, especially toward authority. The manifest aggression scale contains 31 items which reflect "an awareness of unpleasant feelings, especially of anger and frustration; a tendency to react readily with these emotions; and an obvious discomfort concerning the presence and control of these feelings" (Jesness 1983:4).

The fourth scale of interest, the asocial attitudes scale, is formed from the 31 items that are given additional weight in Jesness's asocial index. Jesness's work suggests that these items are particularly important in reflecting antisocial attitudes. The items also appear to have face validity for antisocial attitudes. For these items the coefficient alpha was .79 and the mean interitem correlation was .11.

RESULTS

The shock offenders who completed the program were compared with those who dropped out of the program and with the incarcerated to examine whether those who remained in IMPACT were different from the other groups at the first testing.

For the demographic variables there were no significant differences between dropouts and shock offenders or between the incarcerated and shock offenders in race (32% white, 68% black), sex (97.5% male), IQ (M = 78.1, SD = 13.3), or age (M = 23.9, SD = 4.4). There were no differences between shock offenders (M = 10.8, SD = 1.5) and the incarcerated (M = 10.1, SD = 1.7) in education, but there was a borderline difference between the shock group and the dropouts (M = 10.1, SD = 1.8, $t_{82.0} = 1.92, p < .06$) in education.

Approximately the same number of persons in each group entered as probation violators as entered with new criminal convictions (31.9% probation violators). The majority of the entrants entered with convictions of burglary (45%), drug-related offenses (25.4%), or theft (13%) for the crime carrying the longest sentence; this finding was similar for all three groups. There were no differences between shock offenders (M = 49.8, SD = 19.6) and the incarcerated (M = 43.0, SD = 18.2), but the dropouts had significantly shorter sentences than the shock group (M = 41.1, SD = 13.6, $t_{75} = 2.37, p < .05$).

There were no differences between dropouts and shock offenders or between the incarcerated and the shock offenders in prior history (17.4% had no previous experience with the criminal justice system); nor were there differences in the number who had been incarcerated previously (70.1% had never been in jail or prison before) or in age at first arrest (M = 19.5, SD = 3.3).

In summary, overall the three groups were very similar in demographic and sentence characteristics and in prior experiences with the criminal justice system. Probably the most notable difference is that those who dropped out of IMPACT had significantly shorter sentences than those who remained in IMPACT.

Expectations About IMPACT

In order to examine whether the dropouts and the shock groups differed before entry in their expectations about the IMPACT program, we compared the groups on the two expectation scales. We found no significant differences between the groups on the easy time scale (M = 18.7, SD = 4.4), but on the beneficial expectations scale there was a borderline difference ($t_{84} = 1.79$, $p < .10$). In comparison to the shock group (M = 37.9, SD = 4.8), the dropouts (M = 35.8, SD = 5.8) expected the experience to be less beneficial.

Analyses of Adjustment to Prison

The comparison of the incarcerated offenders to the shock offenders showed that at the beginning of their time in prison (or IMPACT) shock offenders were somewhat more anxious, had somewhat less aggressive attitudes, and reported more conflicts with others than did the incarcerated offenders. After approximately three months the shock offenders were similar to the incarcerated in the level of anxiety reported, but they had less aggressive attitudes and reported more conflicts. Over the three months both groups reported an increase in the level of conflicts with others. The aggressive attitudes of the group declined slightly from Time 2 to Time 3 but the attitudes of the incarcerated group did not change.

We conducted the analyses for the above-reported results using MANOVA repeated-measures analyses run separately for each scale. The three adjustment variables were time as the repeated measure (Time 2 and Time 3), group (incarcerated versus shock), and the interaction (see Tables 1 and 2). These analyses are described below.

The analysis with anxiety as the dependent variable revealed a significant interaction of time with sample, but neither of the main effects was significant (see Table 1 and Table 2). Follow-up univariate F-tests comparing the groups for level of anxiety at each time period revealed only a borderline difference between the groups at Time 2 ($F_{1,57} = 2.73$, $p < .104$). The IMPACT group tended to be more anxious at this time. There were no differences between groups at Time 3. T-tests of the mean difference between Time 2 and Time 3 for each group showed no significant change in anxiety for either group.

The interaction of time and group was not significant for conflicts, the main effect of group was significant, and the main effect of time was borderline in significance, ($F_{1,56} = 3.35$, $p < .10$). The shock group reported more conflicts

Table 1. Mean Scores on Adjustment to Prison Scales and Program Attitude Scales for the Shock and the Incarcerated Samples at Two Time Periods

	SHOCK		INCARCERATED	
	Time 2 M(SD)	Time 3 M(SD)	Time 2 M(SD)	Time 3 M(SD)
Adjustment to Prison				
Anxiety[a]	50.6(9.6)	48.1(9.2)	46.2(10.0)	49.8(11.1)
Conflicts[b]	8.8(2.0)	9.3(1.9)	7.6(1.5)	8.2(2.2)
Aggressiveness[ab]	26.8(5.8)	28.3(5.2)	23.6(6.5)	21.7(4.5)
Program Attitudes				
Victimization[b]	20.7(5.8)	17.7(4.4)	19.7(4.6)	22.6(6.1)
Personal change[ab]	13.8(4.4)	11.9(3.7)	16.1(6.2)	19.1(8.0)
Staff & program[ab]	22.9(6.4)	20.8(4.4)	29.9(8.0)	33.6(8.6)

Note: High scores on aggressiveness mean low levels of aggressiveness.

[a]Interaction of time × sample significant at $p < .05$

[b]Sample main effect significant at $p < .05$

Table 2. Results of Separate MANOVA Repeated-Measures Analyses with Group (Shock vs. Incarcerated), Time, and the Interaction for Program Attitude Scales and Adjustment to Prison Scales

Dependent Variable	GROUP		TIME		INTERACTION	
	MS	F(df)	MS	F(df)	MS	F(df)
Adjustment to Prison						
Anxiety	48.7	.35(1,57)^{NS}	9.0	.18(1,57)^{NS}	246.3	4.8 (1,57)*
Conflicts	36.5	6.6 (1,56)*	6.6	3.4 (1,56)^{NS}	.13	.07(1,56)^{NS}
Aggressive-ness	630.5	13.8 (1,58)***	1.2	.08(1,58)^{NS}	77.7	5.1 (1,58)*
Program Attitudes						
Victimiza-tion	97.6	2.6 (1,58)^{NS}	.005	.00(1,58)^{NS}	227.7	13.7 (1,58)***
Personal change	576.8	14.2 (1,58)***	8.2	.58(1,58)^{NS}	161.0	11.4 (1,58)**
Staff & Program	2531.0	42.6 (1,57)***	15.2	.60(1,57)^{NS}	219.2	8.7 (1,57)**

*$p < .05$, **$p < .01$, ***$p < .001$

than the incarcerated group; for both groups, the reported conflicts tended to increase with time in prison.

The analysis with aggressiveness as the dependent variable showed a significant interaction between time and group and a significant main effect of group, but there was no main effect of time. Overall the shock offenders had less aggressive attitudes than the incarcerated. Follow-up tests to examine the significant interaction revealed that the difference in aggressive attitudes between the groups was borderline in significance at Time 2 ($F_{1,58} = 3.64, p = .061$) and significant at Time 3 ($F_{1,58} = 23.32, p < .001$). The test of the mean difference between Time 2 and Time 3 for each group showed a borderline significant change in aggressiveness for the shock group ($t_{39} = 1.75, p < .09$) and no significant change in aggressiveness for the incarcerated group.

Attitudes Toward the Program

The offender groups differed in their attitudes toward the program on the personal change scale and on the staff and program scale (see Table 1 and Table 2). The shock group believed more in the possibility of positive personal change while they were in the program and had a more positive attitude toward the staff and the program.

MANOVA repeated-measures analyses with time as the repeated measure (Time 2 and Time 3), group (shock versus incarcerated), and the interaction were completed separately for the three program attitude scales (see Table 1 and Table 2). These analyses are described below.

For all three program attitude scales we found an interaction between group and time. In each case the shock offenders became significantly more positive in attitudes from Time 2 to Time 3. That is, they believed they would be less victimized ($t_{40} = 3.29, p < .01$) and that they would change in a positive way as a result of their experience in the program ($t_{40} = 2.8, p < .01$); they also felt more positive about the staff and the program ($t_{40} = 2.08, p < .05$). In contrast, during the same period those in the regular prison tended to feel more victimized ($t_{19} = 1.88, p < .08$) (borderline); they believed even less that anything positive would result from their prison experience ($t_{19} = 2.17, p < .05$); and they felt somewhat more negative about the staff and the programs ($t_{19} = 1.96, p < .07$) (borderline). At Time 2 the groups did not differ on the personal change scale or on the victimization scale, but at Time 3 the shock offenders had significantly more hope for personal change ($F_{1,58} = 22.85, p < .001$) and were less fearful of being victims ($F_{1,59} = 12.66, p < .001$). The groups were significantly different in attitudes toward staff and program at both time periods, ($F_{1,57} = 13.11$, $p <.001$) and ($F_{1,57} = 58.04$, $p < .001$) respectively.

Prosocial Attitudes

Table 3 shows the scores on the 11 Jesness scales for the dropout and incarcerated samples at Time 1 (within two weeks of entering the diagnostic center). One-way ANOVA results for four of the scales (immaturity, withdrawal, social anxiety, repression) showed no significant differences in scores for the groups. For six of the scales (social maladjustment, asocial, value orientation, alienation, manifest aggression, denial), including the four scales considered in this study to be the most indicative of antisocial attitudes, there were significant differences

Table 3. Mean Scores and F Ratios on Prosocial Scales for the Shock, Dropout, and Incarcerated Groups

Scales	Dropouts	SHOCK	Incarcerated	F(df)	P <
Social maladjustment[a]	98.4	103.9	97.2	5.64(2,117)	.01
Asocial[a]	43.5	46.6	42.6	6.46(2,118)	.01
Value orientation[a]	60.3	64.2	58.9	5.77(2,119)	.01
Immaturity	74.3	74.3	74.1	NS	—
Autism[b]	46.0	47.3	45.1	3.92(2,118)	.05
Alienation[a]	39.5	41.8	38.7	5.78(2,119)	.01
Manifest aggression[a]	47.9	50.9	48.0	3.6 (2,119)	.01
Withdrawal	34.2	35.7	34.1	2.74(2,119)	.07
Social anxiety	35.5	36.0	36.2	NS	—
Repression	23.9	23.9	24.0	NS	—
Denial[a]	28.8	26.4	28.5	6.13(2,118)	.01

[a]Both dropout and incarcerated samples are significantly different from Shock at $p < .05$.

[b]The only significant difference ($p < .05$) is between Shock and Incarcerated.

between the shock group and both the dropouts and the incarcerated. In all of these cases except for the denial scale, the shock group had significantly more prosocial attitudes than the other groups but the incarcerated and the dropouts did not differ from each other. For one scale, autism, the IMPACT group differed significantly only from the incarcerated. Dropouts did not differ from either of the other groups on the autism scale.

Table 4 shows the scores on the 11 Jesness scales for the incarcerated and the shock inmates at Time 1 (taken immediately upon entering the diagnostic center) and Time 3 (approximately 85 days later). Table 5 shows the results of separate MANOVA repeated-measure analyses with time as the repeated measure (Time 1 and Time 3), group (shock versus incarcerated), and the interaction.

As shown in the tables, the samples had significantly different attitudes for seven of the 11 prosocial scales. In all but one of these scales, denial, the attitudes of the shock group were more prosocial. There was a significant main effect for time only for the alienation scale.

For four scales (asocial attitudes, alienation, value orientation, and denial) significant interactions between group and time; there was a borderline significant interaction for the social maladjustment scale ($F_{1,64} = 3.68, p < .06$). From Time 1 to Time 3 the shock group became more prosocial on asocial attitudes ($t_{39} = 2.73, p < .05$), alienation ($t_{39} = 4.98, p < .001$), value orientation ($t_{39} = 3.22, p < .01$), and social maladjustment ($t_{39} = 2.64, p < .05$). The shock group changed in the opposite direction (less prosocial) on the denial scale. In comparison, the incarcerated group showed no significant changes during this period in any of these attitudes. As shown in the previously described tests at

Table 4. Mean Scores on Prosocial Scales for Shock and Incarcerated Samples Before Entering Shock Incarceration or Prison and Approximately 85 Days Later

	SHOCK		INCARCERATION	
	Time 1 M(SD)	Time 3 M(SD)	Time 1 M(SD)	Time 3 M(SD)
Prosocial Attitudes				
Social maladjustment[c]	103.9(8.0)	106.4(8.2)	97.3(105)	96.7(10.3)
Asocial[ac]	46.6(5.2)	48.2(4.5)	42.6(6.1)	42.3(5.8)
Alienation[abc]	41.8(3.9)	44.4(3.7)	38.8(4.8)	38.9(4.2)
Manifest aggression[ac]	50.9(5.3)	50.9(4.7)	48.1(6.5)	47.6(5.3)
Value orientation[ac]	64.2(6.7)	66.6(5.4)	59.4(7.9)	59.3(7.1)
Immaturity	74.3(3.9)	75.5(3.8)	74.9(4.2)	75.3(3.2)
Autism[c]	47.3(3.5)	47.5(2.7)	44.9(3.5)	45.0(4.1)
Withdrawal	35.7(3.4)	35.7(3.1)	34.1(3.3)	34.6(3.6)
Social anxiety	36.0(3.7)	36.1(3.7)	36.2(4.2)	36.5(4.6)
Repression	23.9(3.0)	23.7(2.9)	24.5(3.3)	24.7(3.0)
Denial[ac]	26.4(3.0)	25.4(2.7)	28.3(3.9)	28.6(4.5)

[a]Interaction of time × sample significant at $p < .05$

[b]Time main effect significant at $p < .05$

[c]Sample main effect significant at $p < .05$

Table 5. Results of Separate MANOVA Repeated-Measures Analyses with Group (IMPACT vs. Incarcerated), Time, and the Interaction for the Prosocial Attitude Scales

Dependent Variable	GROUP MS	GROUP F(df)	TIME MS	TIME F(df)	INTERACTION MS	INTERACTION F(df)
Prosocial Attitudes						
Social maladjustment	2093.3	13.7(1,64)	31.9	1.56(1,64)[NS]	75.2	3.68(1,64)[NS]
Asocial	787.7	15.9(1,65)	13.2	1.88(1,65)[NS]	28.2	4.0(1,65)
Alienation	596.0	22(1,66)	61.0	9.7(1,66)	54.8	8.7(1,66)
Manifest aggression	304.5	5.9(1,65)	1.6	.24(1,65)[NS]	1.6	.24(1,65)[NS]
Value orientation	1196.3	15.3(1,65)	40.9	3.6(1,65)[NS]	52.3	4.61(1,65)
Immaturity	1.99	.10(1,65)[NS]	20.5	2.2(1,65)[NS]	5.9	.63(1,65)[NS]
Autism	192.4	10.4(1,65)	1.7	.36(1,65)[NS]	.06	.01(1,65)[NS]
Withdrawal	60.8	3.3(1,65)[NS]	1.3	.37(1,65)[NS]	1.3	.37(1,65)[NS]
Social anxiety	4.0	.14(1,65)[NS]	1.0	.25(1,65)[NS]	.20	.05(1,65)[NS]
Repression	20.0	1.37(1,65)[NS]	.10	.01(1,65)[NS]	.78	.21(1,65)[NS]
Denial	210.8	9.97(1,65)	3.7	1.2(1,65)[NS]	13.0	4.3(1,65)

Time 1, the shock group and the incarcerated group differed in scores on asocial attitudes, value orientation, alienation, denial, and social maladjustment. Univariate F-tests comparing the samples at Time 2 for the scales that had significant interactions showed that the groups also differed at Time 2 in asocial attitudes ($F_{1,64} = 20.8$, $p < .001$), value orientation ($F_{1,64} = 23.4$, $p < .001$), alienation ($F_{1,65} = 31.1$, $p < .001$), denial ($F_{1,65} = 13.0$, $p < .001$), and social maladjustment ($F_{1,64} = 18.02$, $p < .001$).

DISCUSSION

The demographic and criminal history comparisons of the dropout, incarcerated, and shock groups suggested that the groups were similar on most of these characteristics. The prosocial attitude scales, however, revealed some interesting differences in the attitudes of the groups. Those who stayed in the IMPACT program for at least 85 days differed from the incarcerated sample and from those who dropped out of IMPACT; they had more prosocial attitudes even before they entered. These scales were completed by the offenders a few days before they either were transferred to a prison or entered the IMPACT program. The differences between the incarcerated and the shock samples suggest the possibility that these groups differed before they were chosen for IMPACT. Decision makers who selected offenders for the program may have recognized subtle differences in offenders and may have given priority to those who were more prosocial. This possibility, however, does not explain why the dropouts also had less prosocial attitudes before they entered the program. They were similar to the incarcerated offenders in having more antisocial attitudes than the shock group on five of the scales. These dropouts also had been selected for the program; yet they differed in their attitudes even before they started the program. It may be that those who can complete the program must be committed to change and must believe in the program in some way that is reflected in more prosocial attitudes. Yet this difference was reflected only marginally on beneficial expectations from the program and not at all in the easy time scale.

After 85 days, when the shock offenders had remained in the program and the incarcerated offenders had been in prison, overall the shock offenders had become more prosocial. During this same period the incarcerated group had not changed. Thus they entered prison with more antisocial attitudes and their experience did not change them. The question is whether the experience of shock incarceration changed the shock offenders. They were more prosocial than the dropouts and the incarcerated before entering the program; they became even more prosocial during their time in the program. One possibility is that this change would have occurred even without any influence from the program. From this perspective these offenders were in the process of changing and would have continued to change with or without shock incarceration. Equally or more plausible is the possibility that shock incarceration acted as a catalyst to accelerate the change. If this is true, the self-selection through voluntary participation may be an important component of the program. That is, those offenders who are ready to change or who already are becoming more prosocial in their attitudes may be able to learn what is required of them in the program.

Shock incarceration programs differ in whether participation is voluntary and in whether offenders can drop out voluntarily (MacKenzie and Ballow 1989). If self-selection is an important factor, as suggested by these results, it is possible that programs which involve forced participation may not find increases in positive social attitudes, as we discovered with these offenders. This is an empirical question that might be addressed in future research.

The results of these analyses suggest strongly that the experience of those in the shock incarceration program is different from that of offenders serving their sentence in a regular prison. In comparison to the latter, the shock incarceration inmates are somewhat more anxious at the start of their time in the program, have more conflicts with others, and have less aggressive attitudes. They are approximately the same as the others in their fear of being a victim, but they are more hopeful about making positive personal changes and feel more positive about the staff and the program.

Between the time they enter the program and approximately three months later, the inmates in shock incarceration become somewhat less aggressive and are less fearful of becoming a victim. At the same time, they are more positive about the possibility of personal change and about the staff and the program. The inmates serving regular sentences also change in aggression, possibility of personal change, and attitudes toward staff and program, but their change is exactly the opposite of the shock inmates. Those in the regular prison believe less that their experiences will lead to positive personal changes; they have become somewhat more negative in their attitudes towards the staff and the program and in their fear of victimization.

Overall, then, if we leave aside for the moment the subject of conflicts with others, the experience of the shock inmates appears to be constructive. At least they are leaving prison with stronger positive feelings about their experiences. In comparison, those leaving the regular prison appear to have developed more negative attitudes toward their experience in prison. This difference between the groups may show an important difference between shock incarceration and other programs involving a short period of incarceration. If the offenders were locked up and mixed with the general population, they might develop more negative attitudes during their time in prison. In contrast, shock incarceration, a program that separates participants from others in a program involving them fully from morning to night and that emphasizes discipline and self-change, may result in a more constructive experience and in positive change.

One question that arises from this study is whether the offenders' positive attitudes about their experiences and their more positive social attitudes result from the boot camp atmosphere, the rehabilitative emphasis of the Louisiana program (see MacKenzie et al. 1989), or some combination of the two. If the changes at least in part are a function of the rehabilitative focus in the Louisiana program, then shock incarceration programs which are less rehabilitative may have a different effect on the participants' attitudes (MacKenzie and Ballow 1989; Parent 1989).

The shock incarceration program also gives offenders certainty about release and about the ability to earn early release by participating. To the extent that these factors influence their prosocial values and their general attitudes about their experience, this influence might explain in part the difference between the shock offenders and those serving time in the regular prison.

Another important issue is the higher stress that the shock inmates appear to experience early during the program. Rather than interpreting this as a disadvantage, as Zamble and Porporino (1988) propose, we believe that this actually may facilitate the other changes that occur. Thus one successful aspect of shock incarceration may be that the program begins while offenders are in a period of emotional distress, when they are susceptible to change.

The prison adjustment of the incarcerated inmates was measured when they first moved from the diagnostic center to a prison and again approximately three months later, when they were still in the regular prison. Between these two points their level of anxiety increased. This finding was in contrast to Zamble and Porporino's (1988) finding of a decrease in anxiety with increased time in prison. These inmates' concomitant negative changes toward their prison experience may demonstrate a difficult situation that becomes progressively worse early in the prison stay, particularly for these nonviolent, first-felony offenders.

Surprisingly, the shock offenders reported more conflicts with others than did the regular prisoners. Both groups reported more conflicts over time, but the shock inmates continued to have more conflicts than the incarcerated. The one similarity between the two groups in their adjustment to prison and their attitudes toward their experience is the tendency toward an increase in conflicts with others over the three-month period.

The level of conflicts varied from disagreements between the responder and other prisoners once or twice in a one-week period to "discussions in which some anger occurred." Thus these conflicts are relatively minor. It may be that because of the tension created by the strict atmosphere of the IMPACT program, more disagreements occur between inmates (Parent 1989). The initial newness of the situation for both groups may inhibit some of the conflicts early in incarceration (MacKenzie and Goodstein 1986).

The results of this research can be interpreted tentatively as showing positive changes for offenders who participate in shock incarceration. Those who complete shock incarceration have more positive attitudes in regard to their experience in prison, toward society in general, and toward their ability to make positive personal change. This is not the experience of those who spend their time in a regular prison, as has been shown in previous research and with the incarcerated in this research (Goodstein and Wright 1989). If more prosocial attitudes are associated with more positive adjustment in the community, as previous research has shown, it would appear that the shock offenders are leaving prison with a much better chance of being successful on parole (Cullen and Gendreau 1989; Gendreau and Ross 1987). That subject, of course, will be our focus in future research with these samples.

REFERENCES

Cullen, F. and P. Gendreau (1989) "The Effectiveness of Correctional Rehabilitation: Reconsidering the 'Nothing Works' Debate." In L. I. Goodstein and D. L. MacKenzie (eds.), *The American Press: Issues in Research and Policy.* New York: Plenum, pp. 23–44.

Gendreau, P. and R. R. Ross (1987) "Revivification of Rehabilitation: Evidence from the 1980s." *Justice Quarterly* 4:349–407.

Goodstein, L. I. and J. Hepburn (1985) *Determinate Sentencing and Imprisonment: A Failure of Reform.* Cincinnati, OH: Anderson.

Goodstein, L. I. and D. L. MacKenzie (1984) "Racial Differences in Adjustment Patterns of Prison Inmates: Prisonization, Conflict, Stress and Control." In D. E. Georges-Abeyie (ed.), *The Criminal Justice System and Blacks.* New York: Clark Boardman, pp. 271–306.

Goodstein, L. I. and K. Wright (1989) "Inmate Adjustment to Prison." In L. I. Goodstein and D. L. MacKenzie (eds.), *The American Prison: Issues in Research and Policy.* New York: Plenum, pp. 229–251.

Jesness, C. F. (1983) *The Jesness Inventory.* Revised edition. Palo Alto: Consulting Psychologists Press.

Jesness, C. F. and R. F. Wedge (1995) *Jesness Inventory Classification System.* Palo Alto: Consulting Psychologists Press.

Louisiana Department of Public Safety and Corrections (1987) *IMPACT: Purposes, Policies and Procedures.* Baton Rouge: Unpublished manuscript.

MacKenzie, D. L. and D. B. Ballow (1989) "Shock Incarceration Programs in State Correctional Jurisdictions—An Update." *NIJ Reports.* Washington, DC: National Institute of Justice, U.S. Department of Justice.

MacKenzie, D. L. and L. I. Goodstein (1986) "Stress and Control Beliefs of Prisoners: A Test of Three Models of Control-Limited Environments." *Journal of Applied Social Psychology* 16: 209–28.

MacKenzie, D. L., L. I. Goodstein, and D. S. Blouin (1987) "Personal Control and Prisoner Adjustment: An Empirical Test of a Proposed Model." *Journal of Research in Crime and Delinquency* 24: 49–68.

MacKenzie, D. L., L. A. Gould, L. M. Riechers, and J. W. Shaw (1989) "Shock Incarceration: Rehabilitation or Retribution?" *Journal of Offender Counseling, Services & Rehabilitation* 14:25–40.

Parent, D. (1988) "Shock Incarceration Programs." Presented to the winter conference, American Correctional Association, Phoenix.

(1989). "Shock Incarceration: An Overview of Existing Programs." *National Institute of Justice Issues and Practice Report.* Washington, DC: U.S. Department of Justice.

Sapsford, R. J. (1978) "Life-Sentence Prisoners: Psychological Changes during Sentence." *British Journal of Criminology* 18:128–45.

Shoemaker, D. J. and G. A. Hillery Jr. (1980) "Violence and Commitment in Custodial Settings." *Criminology* 18:94–102.

Spielberger, C. D., R. L. Gorsuch, and R. E. Lushene (1970) *Manual for the State-Trait Anxiety Inventory.* Palo Alto: Consulting Psychologists Press.

U.S. General Accounting Office (1988) *Prison Boot Camps: Too Early to Measure Effectiveness.* Washington, DC: U.S. General Accounting Office.

Vito, G. F. (1984) "Developments in Shock Probation: A Review of Research Findings and Policy Implications." *Federal Probation* 48:22–27.

Zamble, E. and F. J. Porporino (1988) *Coping, Behavior, and Adaptation in Prison Inmates.* New York: Springer-Verlag.

DISCUSSION QUESTIONS

1. What was the "treatment" (or independent variable) in the study? Describe how the program operated. What were the most important dependent variables in the study? How were they measured?
2. Why might one expect that the "treatment" would influence the dependent variables? In other words, what is the "theory" that links *X* with *Y*?
3. As discussed in the author's commentary and in the article, what were some of the most significant problems encountered in conducting the study?
4. In interpreting the results of the study and in making causal inferences about the effects of *X* on *Y*, why were the pretests (of the experimental group and control group) so important?

2

Evaluating the Use of Social Skills Training and Employment with Delinquent Youth

MICHAEL J. LEIBER, University of Northern Iowa
TINA L. MAWHORR, University of Northern Iowa

COMMENTARY

In the fall of 1992, we were asked by Juvenile Court Services and Area VII to evaluate the effectiveness of the Second Chance program. Before agreeing to conduct the evaluation, we examined materials to familiarize ourselves with the program's administrative procedures, goals, and objectives. One of the first difficulties in conducting the research was the identification of the theory guiding the program. While materials supplied were descriptive of the goals and objectives of the program, there was little information that explained why and how the particular program was to impart change in the attitudes and behavior of the participants. We made several attempts to contact the company that developed and marketed the curriculum, but no additional information was provided. Consequently, we studied the curriculum and relied upon the general body of literature on social skills and job training to introduce the study.

We met several times with representatives from each agency for the purpose of obtaining information about the program and what the agencies expected and hoped for from the evaluation study. Juvenile Court Services and Area VII requested that the study examine whether or not the delinquent behavior of youth who participated in the Second Chance Program was reduced. They also stated that the study was to be completed within a one-year time frame. The information derived from the research would be used to request funds for the continuation of the program.

It was clear that the agencies felt that the outcome of the evaluation would show Second Chance in a positive light (i.e., the evaluation would reveal that youths committed fewer crimes after participating in the program).

Source: Journal of Criminal Justice, Vol. 23, No. 2, pp. 127–141. Copyright © 1995, with permission from Elsevier Science.

We recommended that the evaluation include outcome variables other than a single measure of recidivism. For example, one of the goals of the program was to improve the quality of youth's interpersonal relationships. Some outcome measure that would compare the quality of relationships before and after would be an indicator of the extent to which the program had succeeded in accomplishing this goal. The agencies, however, insisted on expediting the study and resolved to remain focused solely on recidivism as the outcome variable. We agreed to conduct the evaluation with the admonition that by limiting the study to a focus on recidivism, the overall effectiveness of the program in rehabilitating troubled youth would not be entirely evident.

Funding for the study was not available from either agency. Students who volunteered to Juvenile Court Services, however, were available to aid in the undertaking of the study. In addition, the agencies agreed to allow the authors to have complete control over the research and the resulting data for the purpose of publication.

Because of the time restraints, the desire by the agencies to examine recidivism, and no funds, a research strategy was developed that relied on official records. Recidivism was operationalized as a referral to juvenile court and/or an arrest as an adult. The theoretical perspectives inherent in the Second Chance program were not tested (which alleviated our frustration of obtaining original documentation of the underlying program theory). The extent to which the program changed the social skills level of the youth, his or her relationship with his or her parents, or the youth's involvement in school were left unexamined. Similarly, we were unable to examine the quality of the youth's employment experience.

To compensate for these shortcomings, the research was planned to maximize the use of official records to study re-offending among youth participating in the treatment intervention. This was accomplished by employing four comparison groups and multiple dependent variables. Using four comparison groups allowed us not only to assess whether the treatment intervention group evidenced less official offending than the other three groups and, in particular, the equivalent matched group but also to determine (1) how youth who complete the program differ from the noncompletion group and (2) how those participating in Second Chance differ from youth involved in traditional juvenile court services.

The findings support the use of multiple comparison groups and multiple dependent variables when conducting an evaluation of the effectiveness of treatment services. First, we were able to determine that a large number of youth did not complete the Second Chance program and that these youth were the most troubled. Second, we discovered that few differences existed among the sampled populations in terms of the extent, pattern, and factors associated with official offending. The results, however, also revealed that youth who completed the Second Chance program committed less serious crimes than the other three comparison groups. Thus, a focus only on the extent of offending would ignore the success Second Chance had in reducing the severity of offending.

Both Juvenile Court Services and Area VII were receptive to the findings of the research. As a result of the study, changes in the program occurred that we believe will enable the treatment intervention to be even more successful (e.g., the hiring of minority personnel). Despite the contributions of our research, future evaluation studies could benefit from using both self-report surveys and official records and by broadening the measure of success beyond the limited indicator of recidivism to include process variables such as social skills, school performance, and family and peer relationships. In addition, the use of quantitative techniques in conjunction with qualitative strategies (e.g., open-ended interviews, observation) could enhance efforts to evaluate and understand the effects and outcomes of treatment programs.

ABSTRACT The objective of the present research was to assess the success of a program in reducing official delinquent behavior among youth identified as one step away from the state training school or waiver to adult court. The Second Chance program represents a rehabilitative strategy that uses social skills training, preemployment training, and job placement opportunities to reduce recidivism. Utilizing multiple comparison groups and a one-year follow-up period, evidence of a reduction in official delinquent and criminal offending was not found. Offenses committed by the Second Chance group were less serious, however. Implications and recommendations for future research are discussed.

Developing and implementing strategies that reduce or eliminate youthful offenders' rule-breaking behavior by providing treatment has been the historic mission of the juvenile justice system (Waegel, 1989:195). Although public sentiment has waned with regard to the desirability of rehabilitation as a correctional goal for the juvenile justice system (Bishop, Frazier, and Henretta, 1989; McGarrell, 1993), the search for effective rehabilitative programs still abounds today. The Second Chance program is one such effort that attempts to reestablish a positive relationship between delinquent youth and society by providing young offenders with social skills training (SST), preemployment training, and job placement services.

The two main goals of Second Chance are (1) to help a particular group of adjudicated delinquents become more proficient in a number of important skills, such as values clarification, communication skills, overcoming conflict, and improving relationships; and (2) to expose troubled youths to legitimate employment opportunities that would otherwise have been unavailable to them. These two intervention strategies are an attempt to improve the youths' relationships with conventional society and, in turn, reduce the likelihood that they will become reinvolved in the juvenile justice system. The juveniles involved in Second Chance have been identified as more troubled than other youths on probation and, in some cases, may be only one step away from the state training school or waiver to adult court. The objective of the present study is to evaluate the success of the Second Chance program in reducing official recidivism for those participating in the treatment effort. The theoretical and empirical evidence regarding social skills training and employment opportunities as they relate to the prevention of delinquency are discussed first.

BACKGROUND

Social Skills Training

According to Henderson and Hollin (1986:92), "there is no unitary definition of social skills," and training varies from program to program. In general, the term *social skills* is used to refer to the "abilities necessary for effective interpersonal functioning" (Wise et al., 1991:233). Social skills are generally assessed by the appropriateness and effectiveness of the individual's behavior in relations with others (McGuire and Priestley, 1985:80). Effective communication essentially involves the ability to convey information to other people about one's needs and intentions, and similarly, to understand the message being sent by other people (Hollin, 1992).

Interest in using social skills training (SST) with delinquents lies in the proposal that some forms of problematic behavior may be explicable in terms of a *lack* or *breakdown* of social skills among individuals who exhibit maladaptive or delinquent behavior; that some individuals engage in antisocial behavior because they lack the skills necessary for prosocial behavior (Sarason, 1968; McFall, 1976; Spence, 1981; McGuire and Priestley, 1985; Henderson and Hollin, 1986). The view that delinquents are socially unskilled is theoretically supported by early perceptions of the delinquent peer group and juvenile gangs as a group of social misfits who are unable to interact with their peers (e.g., Glueck and Glueck, 1950; Short and Strodtbeck, 1965). Short and Strodtbeck (1965), for example, argued that delinquent gang boys were lacking in interpersonal skills and, in general, were socially disabled.

While there is current debate regarding the *quality* of delinquent peer relationships (e.g., see Giordano, Cernkovich, and Pugh, 1986; Henggeler, 1989; Kandel and Davies, 1991; Agnew, 1991) the idea that adolescents involved in delinquent activity lack essential interpersonal skills has not often been examined by delinquency researchers. The issue, however, has been given considerably more attention in the psychological literature. The assumption that delinquent youths are deficient in their abilities to interact with others in socially appropriate ways is primarily supported "by findings in longitudinal studies that antisocial adolescents tend to have been rejected by their peers . . . and that rejected children exhibit inappropriate hostile behavior toward their peers" (Tremblay et al., 1991:149; see also Hartup, 1983; Parker and Asher, 1987; Simons et al., 1991). Aggressive and noncompliant children have also been characterized as "disruptive and off task" (Simons et al., 1991:467). The consequences of these behaviors are rejection by teachers and academic failure (Simons et al., 1991). In addition, some research suggests that, without appropriate intervention, children may not be able to outgrow their social skills deficits (Howing et al., 1990:460).

Strategies developed to help individuals with social skills deficits are often based on Bandura's (1977, 1986) social learning theory (Wise et al., 1991; McGuire and Priestley, 1985) which argues that social skills deficits are the result of an individual's failure to learn normal ways of interacting with others. The process of overcoming social skills deficits is viewed, then, as similar to overcoming the failure of learning to read or write (McGuire and Priestley, 1985; Henderson and Hollin, 1986). Thus, it is assumed that it is possible to eliminate or rectify problem behavior by teaching individuals more socially acceptable/appropriate ways of interacting with others (McGuire and Priestley, 1985:81).

There is considerable evidence to support the view that social skills training can be an effective means of reducing problematic behavior (Zaragoza, Vaughn, and McIntosh, 1991). For example, McGuire and Priestley (1985:82–95) provide a review of studies in which SST programs have been used as a strategy to reduce law violating behavior. These studies suggest that social skills training programs can effectively improve the general social performance of offender groups, help offenders learn to cope better in a number of respects with different degrees of proximity to actual offending, and influence their attitudes in a similar way (McGuire and Priestley, 1985:95; cf., Hollin, 1992).

Employment and Delinquency

The provision of job opportunities as a method of preventing and correcting delinquency is both implied and directly suggested by a number of theoretical positions (Bazemore, 1991:32). For example, strain theories suggest that lower-class youths become involved in delinquent behavior out of anger and frustration of being unable to obtain material success (the American Dream) through legitimate avenues (i.e., education and work which are more readily available to middle- and upper-class youths; Farnworth and Leiber, 1989; Leiber et al., 1994). Cloward and Ohlin's (1960) version of strain theory, in particular, emphasizes that lower-class youths participate in criminal activity as a result of blocked occupational opportunities. According to this theoretical perspective, employment initiatives are of great importance in the attempt to prevent adolescent delinquent involvement.

Greenberg (1977) also suggests that the critical factor in producing delinquency is the exclusion of juveniles from the adult world of work, although his perspective is not limited to lower-class youths. Greenberg (1977) argues that the organization of adolescent life in contemporary society produces motivation for delinquent conduct (see also Friday and Hage, 1976). The link between work and delinquency is explained through two mechanisms. First, adolescence is a time characterized by an increasing distance from parents and a greater concern with peer acceptance and popularity. As a result, teenagers become preoccupied with activities that enable them to assert their independence (e.g., driving around in cars, going to rock concerts), and markers of status which help establish their place in the peer culture (e.g., audio-visual equipment and clothes). Participation in these activities and the acquisition of these material possessions, however, can become expensive. Because of the growing distance between parents and child, the youth may be unwilling to ask for financial assistance to meet these needs (e.g., they may want to conceal their activities from their parents). In addition, some parents may be unable or unwilling to provide the money to finance these highly valued possessions and activities. Compulsory education laws and laws restricting child labor also severely limit part-time employment for adolescents. As a result of these circumstances, youths may choose to engage in delinquent activities to meet their unfulfilled financial needs. Thus, an underlying assumption of treatment efforts that involve employment is the provision of legitimate opportunities to reduce strain and, in turn, delinquency.

Bazemore (1991:32) has also identified control theory (Briar and Piliavin, 1965; Hirschi, 1969) as "the most pertinent theoretical approach to understanding the connection between work and delinquency . . ." According to control theory, employment should lead to a reduction in delinquency because it strengthens the youth's bond to legitimate institutions or develops a stake in conformity which gives the youth something to lose by further participation in delinquent activities (Bazemore, 1991:32).

Although the relationship between employment and reduced delinquency seems to be fairly well grounded in theory, the actual implementation and usefulness of employment programs for delinquent youths remains questionable (Lundman, 1993; Gottfredson and Hirschi, 1990; Finckenauer, 1984). For example, Bazemore (1991) argues that this theoretical relationship is based on an idealized work experience which would involve opportunities for associations and interactions with positive adult role models. Most youths, however, are segregated from adults because young people have jobs such as those in the fast food industry which are not conducive to the development of conventional bonds (Waldinger and Baily, 1985; William T. Grant Foundation, 1988).

Nevertheless, the use of work experience/employment programs as a strategy for dealing with youthful offenders remains appealing due to the fact that it is an active rather than a passive approach (Bazemore, 1991). Both standard probation and more treatment/services approaches are passive in that youthful offenders can avoid further involvement in the juvenile justice system by simply becoming passive targets of monitoring and surveillance (probation/parole) and avoiding behaviors identified in probation/parole contracts such as drinking or missing curfew. Youths also become the passive recipients of treatment. These youths can avoid official sanctions simply by attending required counseling or other required meetings. In contrast, the work experience/employment approach gives priority to an active, performance-based agenda which facilitates and demands positive, constructive actions by juvenile offenders on probation and parole (Bazemore, 1991).

The use of social skills training techniques and employment initiatives with delinquents has strong theoretical support. The results of empirical research, however, have not consistently shown these interventions to be effective in lowering rates of recidivism among youthful offenders. Therefore, questions have arisen concerning the value of these rehabilitative efforts in reducing youthful offender rulebreaking (Bazemore, 1991; Gottfredson and Hirschi, 1990; Hollin, 1992). Some researchers, however, remain cautiously optimistic (McGuire and Priestley, 1985; Zaragoza, Vaughn, and McIntosh, 1991; Hollin, 1992).

THE SECOND CHANCE PROGRAM

The Second Chance program represents a partnership venture between the First Judicial District Juvenile Court Services (JCS) and a regional job training program called Area VII Job Training (referred to as JTPA by juvenile court officials). JTPA is a federally funded employment and training program which prepares economically disadvantaged and long-term unemployed individuals to enter the labor force. JTPA also has a separate summer youth program which serves economical disadvantaged youths by offering remediation, career education, and work experience. The Second Chance program combines competency-based skill development provided by JCS with the services offered by JTPA as a means of meeting the needs of high-risk youths involved in the juvenile court system. The case management for Second Chance youths is conducted jointly by a JTPA employment/training specialist and a JCS probation officer.

The skill development component offered by JCS involves sixteen weekly group meetings designed to improve self-esteem and a number of important social skills such as values clarification, communication skills, overcoming conflict, and improving relationships. The curriculum for Second Chance is based on a program produced by the National Corrective Training Institute (1989) called the *NCTI Youth Crossroads Program*. Each juvenile participant is given a workbook covering sixteen lessons which include the following areas: acceptance of self and others, control over one's life, alcohol and drugs, manners and appearance, career possibilities, budgeting an income, identification of good and bad relationships, intimacy, identification of wants versus needs, identification of privileges versus rights, budgeting time, and overcoming conflict. The workbook contains questions on each of these topics, and the topics are discussed at the weekly group meetings. Homework assignments also accompany each lesson.

The program facilitator from JCS is responsible for monitoring each juvenile's case. This involves maintaining contact with parents and other agencies working with the youth and his/her family (e.g., counseling agencies or family social workers). Parents are required to monitor and verify completion of weekly assignments and goals set by youths. In addition, school personnel are routinely contacted regarding school attendance and performance for those youths who have been identified as having difficulties in school or are at risk of dropping out.

The preemployment training is also provided by JCS. Youths are given instruction in skills necessary to obtain and maintain employment. Specific skills include: how to conduct an independent job search, how to apply for a job, interviewing techniques, and good work habits. Information on community resources and subsidized employment are also provided.

Actual work sites are operated through JTPA. Youths are assisted in finding a job through the Tryout Employment and Work Experience programs. JTPA provides the costs for training and the wages of the youth for the first 130 hours of employment. If the youth performs his/her job satisfactorily, the agency is expected to, and most often does, retain the employee after the 130-hour period. During the tryout employment period, the employer is required to submit biweekly reports to the JTPA employment/training specialist.

There is a conscious effort on the part of JCS and JTPA to match the youths' interests with employment opportunities. Younger Second Chance participants have obtained work experience by volunteering at a number of organizations such as the humane society, Boy's/Girl's Club of America, and the local recreation center. Older participants have been employed at a variety of jobs which include fast food restaurants, hotels, and the local recycling center. By being attentive to the interests of the youths, the program attempts to provide participants positive work experiences that lead to continued employment, a greater sense of accomplishment, and higher levels of self-esteem.

THE PRESENT RESEARCH

The objective of the current study is to evaluate the implementation of the Second Chance program in a midwestern county in the state of Iowa. Of particular interest was the extent to which the treatment effort resulted in the reduction of official delinquency among already troubled youths (e.g., repeat offenders, poor academic records).

Comparison Groups

The design of the present study is not a true experiment (Cook and Campbell, 1979). Youths were referred to the Second Chance program by juvenile court staff. Five different groups participated in the program beginning in the late fall of 1990 through June 1992 with each session lasting sixteen weeks. Of those referred to these five sessions, fifty-seven completed the program and are identified as the "Second Chance Completion" group. Not all of the youths referred, however, completed the full sixteen weeks of treatment ($N = 28$). Some were dismissed due to delinquent and/or probation violations or a failure to attend scheduled weekly meetings. It may be that there are certain factors associated with these youths that are related to their failure to complete the Second Chance program. In order to identify any such characteristics, this group of program dropouts was included in the analysis and is identified as the "Second Chance Noncompletion" group.

Two other comparison groups were also used in the study: an equivalent matched sample and those who received traditional juvenile court services (e.g., probation, participation in diversion). The equivalent matched group was selected from a data set collected from a previous study examining juvenile court decisionmaking in the same county during the years 1980–1991 (Leiber, 1992). Of the 2,030 cases from that data set, fifty-six youths were matched with delinquents who completed the Second Chance program. This comparison group was matched with the Second Chance Completion group on race, the number of prior court referrals, and the severity of the last offense leading to the referral. Youths selected for the "Equivalent Matched" group were under juvenile court supervision during the years 1987–1990.

The group of youths receiving traditional juvenile court services was randomly selected from all youths referred to juvenile court during the same time frames as those entering the Second Chance program ($N = 85$). This group is referred to as the "Random Juvenile Court Services" group. Juvenile court personnel involved in referring youth to Second Chance had an intuitive sense that the referral group consisted of more troubled youths than the average adjudicated youths placed on probation. The Random Juvenile Court Services group, therefore, was used to establish the degree to which juvenile court officers were correct in their beliefs. That is, this comparison group was included in the analysis to determine the extent youths referred to Second Chance differed from those receiving standard juvenile court services.

Information on demographics and past and current legal status for each of the four groups was obtained through an examination of juvenile and adult court records. Adult court records were checked for official recidivism for those youths who turned eighteen years old since dismissal from juvenile court services. Finally, a twelve-month or one-year follow-up period was used to assess the extent and pattern of official recidivism. The twelve-month period begins for all youths once they were dismissed from the supervision of the juvenile court.

Characteristics of Comparison Groups

Table 1 presents information for each of the groups on a number of background variables generally found to be associated with recidivism (Greenwood and Turner, 1993). There are statistically significant differences between some of the groups for some of the variables. No significant differences exist between youths completing Second Chance and the equivalent matched group.

The Second Chance Noncompletion group stands out from the other three groups. These youths are much more likely to be African American, evidence school problems characterized by failure to attend, and have a greater prior history of offending. Youths who did not complete Second Chance were also less likely than those completing the Second Chance program and the equivalent matched group to have been charged with a felony for the offense leading to their last referral.

At the other end of the spectrum are the youths making up the Random Juvenile Court Services group. These youths appear to have less serious academic

Table 1. Descriptive Statistics for Youth Differentiated by Comparison Groups

	SECOND CHANCE NON-COMPLETION (*N* = 28)		SECOND CHANCE COMPLETION (*N* = 57)		EQUIVALENT MATCH (*N* = 56)		RANDOM JUVENILE COURT SERVICES (*N* = 85)	
Variable	*N*	%[a]	*N*	%	*N*	%	*N*	%
Background								
Sex								
Male	21	75	50	88	45	80	61	72
Female	7	25	7	12	11	20	24	28
Race[b]								
Caucasian	13	46	38	67	40	71	68	80
African American	15	54	19	33	16	29	17	20
Age								
x	15.96		15.8		15.7		15.7	
Range	11–17		9–18		9–18		9–18	
SD	1.4		1.4		1.8		1.8	
Education								
x	8.4		9.0		8.7		9.0	
Range	0–10		6–12		4–12		1–12	
SD	1.9		1.2		1.7		2.2	
School status[b]								
Attending	19	68	46	81	39	70	81	95
School problems	3	11	7	12	17	30	3	4
Nonattending	6	21	4	7			1	1
Family status								
Married	8	29	26	46	22	39	35	41
One parent	20	71	31	54	34	61	50	59
Prior offense history								
Number of priors[b]								
x	4.9		2.8		2.2		1.8	
Range	1–15		1–10		0–8		1–9	
SD	3.3		1.8		1.8		1.5	
Last offense type[b]								
Theft	10	33	19	33	17	29	16	19
Dis. conduct	4	14	5	9	6	11	18	21
Burglary	3	11	13	23	16	29	4	5
Agg. assault	1	4			1	2		
Simple assault	5	18	9	16	4	7	12	14
Criminal trespass			3	5	1	2	4	5
Resisting arrest			1	2	1	2		
Failure to appear in court	2	5					1	1
Robbery			2	4				

(continued)

Table 1. (Continued)

	SECOND CHANCE NON-COMPLETION (N = 28)		SECOND CHANCE COMPLETION (N = 57)		EQUIVALENT MATCH (N = 56)		RANDOM JUVENILE COURT SERVICES (N = 85)	
Variable	*N*	%[a]	*N*	%	*N*	%	*N*	%
Prior offense history *(cont.)*								
Last offense type[b] *(cont.)*								
Carrying concealed weapon							1	1
Drug offense	1	4	1	2	4	7	25	29
Harassment	1	4					1	1
Rape/sexual assault			2	4				
Prostitution					1	2		
Arson			1	2	1	2		
Forgery	1	4			4	7		
Traffic violation			1	2			3	4
Severity of last offense[b]								
Simple mis.	13	43	23	40	21	38	68	80
Serious mis.	4	14	6	11	7	12	9	10
Agg. mis.	5	17	5	9	6	11	1	1
Felony	7	25	23	40	22	39	7	8
Severity of past offense[b]								
No adjudication	11	39	25	44	28	50	75	88
Adjudication	17	61	32	56	28	50	10	12

[a]Due to rounding, the percentage may not add up to 100.

[b]Tests by chi-square or ANOVA indicate groups are significantly different, $p < .01$.

and legal problems. The Second Chance Completion group and the Equivalent Matched group fall in between the other two sample groups in terms of the severity of past problematic behavior. Thus, juvenile court personnel are referring youths to the Second Chance program who are more problematic than the typical youth referred for juvenile court services. The Second Chance program does not appear to be able to retain the most troublesome youths, however.

RESULTS

Recidivism is defined here as the presence of an official referral to juvenile or adult court once dismissed from juvenile court services. The goal of this study is to assess whether individuals who completed the Second Chance program evidence a lower rate of recidivism than the Equivalent Matched group or the Random Juvenile Court Services group. In addition, the Second Chance

Noncompletion group is included to discern any differential characteristics and delinquent behavior patterns that may help explain why these youths did not make it through the program.

Recidivism

The breakdown of youths in each group who were arrested at least once during a one-year follow-up is shown in Table 2. Contrary to expectations, an examination of the bivariate comparisons suggests that youths who received the treatment intervention are as likely to be involved in official offending as the equivalent matched sample (37 percent compared to 29 percent). The Second Chance Noncompletion group appears to have the greatest likelihood of recidivism and the group consisting of youths who received traditional juvenile court services the least.

Statistically significant differences do not exist between the four groups in the type of crimes committed since dismissal from juvenile court supervision. A significant association, however, is present between youths completing the Second Chance program and the severity of the offense. The data indicate that youths who complete the Second Chance program tend to become reinvolved in the juvenile court for less serious crimes than the youths representing the various comparison groups. For example, 70 percent of the youths completing the Second Chance program were charged with a simple misdemeanor compared to 44 percent of the Second Chance Noncompletion group, 42 percent of the Equivalent Matched group, and 50 percent of the Random Juvenile Court Services group.

Previous research indicates that a small number of offenders are responsible for a large proportion of official offenses (Wolfgang, Figlio, and Sellin, 1972). Table 3 presents a breakdown of the number of youths who are referred for multiple offenses to determine the extent to which this phenomenon is occurring and whether the patterns differ by the study groups. The results indicate that youths who completed the Second Chance program were referred less often for multiple crimes during the one-year follow-up period than the other three groups. These differences, however, are not statistically significant.

While youths in the Second Chance program are more likely to engage in crime than are adolescents in the comparison groups during the follow-up period, it is possible that the intervention effort may have extended the length of time before the youths became reinvolved with the juvenile court. A survival analysis on the length of time between release from juvenile court supervision and subsequent arrest was conducted to address this assumption. Survival analysis considers the rate at which failures occur within specified time intervals and is especially of interest when intervention may at least postpone recidivism (Greenwood and Turner, 1993). The survival curves for each of the four groups are presented in Figure 1.

It is apparent that few differences exist in the survival estimates between the youths who completed Second Chance and the Equivalent Matched group. A similar pattern is also evident for the Random Juvenile Court Services group.

Table 2. Extent of Recidivism for Youth Differentiated by Comparison Groups (Twelve Month Official Record Follow-Up)

	SECOND CHANCE NONCOMPLETION (*N* = 28)		SECOND CHANCE COMPLETION (*N* = 57)		EQUIVALENT MATCH (*N* = 56)		RANDOM JUVENILE COURT SERVICES (*N* = 85)	
Variable	*N*	%[a]	*N*	%	*N*	%	*N*	%
Crime[b]								
No	12	43	37	63	40	71	68	80
Yes	16	57	20	37	16	29	17	20
Type of crime								
Theft	8	50	9	45	5	36[c]	3	19[c]
Burglary					3	21	2	12
Dis. conduct	4	25	5	25	2	14	2	12
Criminal trespass			3	15			2	12
Resisting arrest					2	14		
Fraud					1	7		
Drug offense	2	10	2	10			3	19
Simple assault	1	6	1	5	1	25	1	6
Agg. assault	1	6					1	6
Traffic violation							2	12
Severity of offense[b]								
Simple mis.	7	44	14	70	5	42[c]	8	50[c]
Serious mis.	3	19	1	5	1	8	2	12
Agg. mis.	2	12	2	10	2	17	1	6
Felony	4	25	3	15	4	33	5	31

[a]Due to rounding, the percentage may not add up to 100.

[b]Tests by chi-square or ANOVA indicate groups are significantly different, $p < .01$.

[c]Totals will not add up to number of delinquencies/crimes. Information was missing from 1–4 cases.

Table 3. Multiple Frequency of Recidivism of Youth, Differentiated by Comparison Groups (Twelve Month Official Record Follow-Up)

	SECOND CHANCE NONCOMPLETION (*N* = 28)		SECOND CHANCE COMPLETION (*N* = 57)		EQUIVALENT MATCH (*N* = 56)		RANDOM JUVENILE COURT SERVICES (*N* = 85)	
Number of Crimes[a]	*N*	%[a]	*N*	%	*N*	%	*N*	%
1	4	25	10	50	2	12	6	36
2	4	25	5	25	3	19	4	23
3 or more	8	50	5	25	11	69	7	41

[a]Chi-square is not significant.

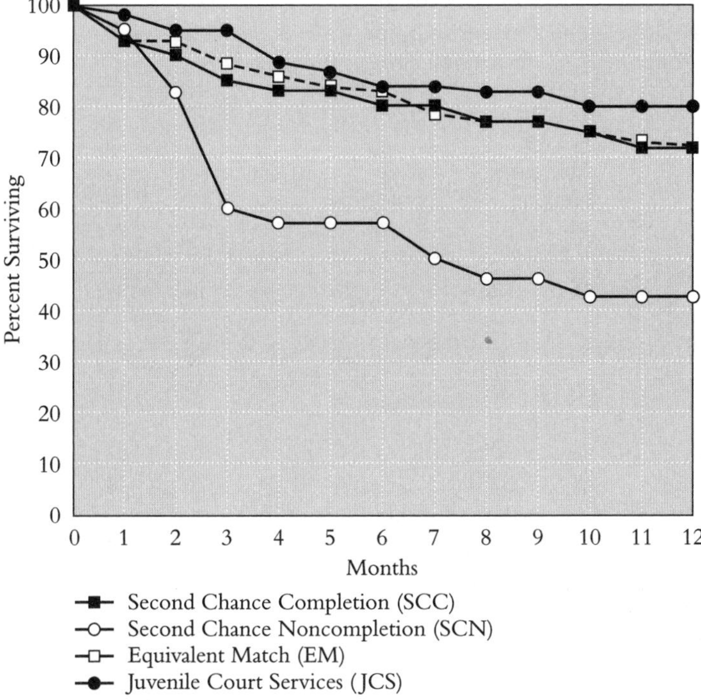

FIGURE 1. Youth's Survival Estimates During One-Year Follow-Up: Time to First Arrest

The Second Chance Noncompletion group experienced the most dramatic drop in surviving. The difference is not statistically significant.[1]

Factors Associated with Official Recidivism

In this section of the analysis, descriptive statistics are employed to determine which factors are associated with further official recidivism following release from juvenile court services. Table 4 compares juveniles who have officially recidivated with those who have not for each of the four study groups. Overall, there appears to be very few factors that distinguish those who have an official record of recidivism from those who do not. For the Second Chance Noncompletion group, there are not any statistically significant differences.

[1]An examination of pretreatment official delinquency for the Second Chance group who completed the program and the equivalent matched sample failed to provide indications of differences in patterns of offending to account for the observed findings. For example, the length of time between offenses previous to inclusion in the time frame of the study for the two groups paralleled each other. Similarly, there was no evidence that differences in the disposition or outcome for the referral during the postrelease period confounded the results. Youths in all four groups most often (87 percent) received community probation for their first referral since being released from juvenile court supervision.

Table 4. Characteristics of Youth Who Had Official Juvenile Court Contact Within Twelve Months Compared to Those Who Did Not, Differentiated by Comparison Groups (Percent)[a]

	SECOND CHANCE NONCOMPLETION ($N = 28$) CONTACT		SECOND CHANCE COMPLETION ($N = 57$) CONTACT		EQUIVALENT MATCH ($N = 56$) CONTACT		RANDOM JUVENILE COURT SERVICES ($N = 85$) CONTACT	
Variable	**Yes**	**No**	**Yes**	**No**	**Yes**	**No**	**Yes**	**No**
Sex								
Male	81	63	90	88	81	88	88	66[c]
Female	19	37	10	12	19	12	12	44
Race[b]								
Caucasian	50	50	45	76[c]	69	80	82	83
African American	50	50	55	24	31	20	18	17
Age								
x	15.63	16.51	15.85	15.91	16.38	15.44	15.53	15.81
Education								
x	8.00	9.25	8.90	9.15	8.94	8.72	8.76	9.17
School status								
Attending	69	63	75	88	56	72	94	95
School problems	6	13	15	9	44	28	6	3
Nonattending	25	24	10	3				2
Family status								
Married	31	25	25	55	44	40	24	47
One parent	69	75	75	45	56	60	76	53
Number of priors[b]								
x	4.00	6.13	3.25	2.64	2.44	1.76[c]	2.06	1.76
Last offense type[b]								
Theft	25	37	30	30	13	29	29	14
Dis. conduct	19		5	9	19	8	24	21
Burglary	6	24	20	24	19	44	12	3
Agg. assault						4		
Simple assault	25	13	20	15	13	8	6	12
Criminal trespass				9	6			5
Resisting arrest			5		6			
Failure to appear in court	6							
Robbery			5	3				
Carrying concealed weapon							6	
Drug offense	6	13		3	6	8	18	42
Harassment	6							
Rape/sexual assault			5	3				
Prostitution					6			

Table 4. (Continued)

	SECOND CHANCE NONCOMPLETION ($N = 28$) CONTACT		SECOND CHANCE COMPLETION ($N = 57$) CONTACT		EQUIVALENT MATCH ($N = 56$) CONTACT		RANDOM JUVENILE COURT SERVICES ($N = 85$) CONTACT	
Variable	**Yes**	**No**	**Yes**	**No**	**Yes**	**No**	**Yes**	**No**
Last offense type[b] *(cont.)*								
Arson				3		4		
Forgery		13			12	4		
Traffic violation			10				6	3
Severity of last offense[b]								
Simple mis.	50	38	60	30	38	32	71	85
Serious mis.	25		5	12	12	8	12	10
Agg. mis.	13	24		15	12	16		2
Felony	12	38	35	42	38	44	18	3
Severity of past offense[b]								
No adjudication	38	71	55	33[c]	44	56	77	93[c]
Adjudication	62	29	45	67	56	44	23	7

[a]Due to rounding, the percentage may not add up to 100.
[b]Comparisons across groups with chi-square or ANOVA yield significant differences at $p < .10$ for race and priors, $p < .01$ for school status.
[c]Comparisons within each individual group with chi-square and ANOVA yield significant differences at $p < .10$, except for Random Juvenile Court Services group and severity of last disposition, $p < .01$.

For the Second Chance Completion group, however, there are two factors that are significantly different. First, Caucasian youths comprise a much larger percentage of those who did not recidivate (76 percent). Second, a greater percentage of those who did not recidivate also had a referral for their last offense that resulted in an adjudication (67 percent). That is, among youths who completed the Second Chance program, individuals who had been adjudicated delinquent for the previous offense were less likely to recidivate during the follow-up period.

The search for factors associated with recidivism for the two comparison groups resulted in the identification of three statistically significant relationships. For the Equivalent Matched group, youths who did not have subsequent contact with the juvenile court exhibited fewer prior contacts with the juvenile court than youths who had officially recidivated. For the Random Juvenile Court Services group, females were less likely than males to have become reinvolved with the juvenile court system. In this group of youths, individuals who were not adjudicated for their previous offense were less likely to have become reinvolved with juvenile court services.

DISCUSSION

For many juvenile justice agencies around the country, funding for innovative delinquency prevention programs is reserved for efforts that promise to reduce the case load handled by an already overburdened juvenile justice system. This, without question, usually means that success is defined by a reduction in the number of youths who reappear in the juvenile or adult system. The findings of the present study indicate that youths who completed Second Chance were not less likely to become reinvolved in official court action than youths with similar backgrounds. On the basis of this criterion, the Second Chance program could be seen at first as a disappointment. Youths completing the Second Chance program, however, were more likely to be charged with less serious offenses than youths from other comparison groups. This is an encouraging result given the more costly and repressive alternative sanctions that might otherwise be used to deal with these high-risk youths. Thus, the implementation of the Second Chance program is not a complete failure. In fact, the results provide a starting point from which to further develop the treatment effort and to maximize its effectiveness in working with serious and repeat offenders.

Another reason for optimism regarding the Second Chance program is the number of characteristics it has in common with successful intervention programs. Characteristics identified through meta-analysis include: targeting of medium to high-risk offenders; a multimodal, structured, and focused treatment approach; a cognitive component which focuses on attitudes, values, and beliefs that support antisocial behavior; and community-based intervention. The Second Chance program has each of these characteristics.

Four characteristics that underlie successful rehabilitative interventions, however, are absent from the Second Chance program: family involvement, treatment integrity, cultural sensitivity, and follow-up care and monitoring. The absence of these attributes may help explain why the treatment effort was not totally effective in reducing recidivism among adolescents. First, effective programs target the family as well as the offending youth (Hollin, 1992). Families of the youths who participate in the Second Chance program are minimally involved. The Second Chance program requires parents to attend an orientation and verify homework accomplishments. The family clearly is not the primary target of this intervention, however. Given that Second Chance participants who recidivate tend to come from single parent families, greater emphasis on family involvement may be warranted.

The second characteristic missing from the Second Chance program is high treatment integrity. Treatment integrity refers to the use of trained staff who are involved in all the operational phases of the treatment program (Hollin, 1992:131). When this study was conducted, two Caucasian female facilitators had been responsible for the inception of the program as well as for obtaining funding and serving as program facilitators. These facilitators, however, are juvenile court officers (probation officers) who have been through limited training provided by the company from which the curricular package was purchased. A number of programs have shown that probation officers can be equipped with the skills necessary to be effective behavior therapists (e.g., Wood, Green, and Bry, 1982; as cited in Hollin, 1992:141). Still, the treatment integrity of the Second Chance program is questionable.

In a recent meta-analysis of rehabilitative efforts, Andrews et al. (1990a:372) argue that "the effectiveness of correctional treatment is dependent upon what is delivered to whom in particular settings." Currently, Second Chance is serving the needs of youths who appear more troubled than the typical youth receiving juvenile court services. The program is most successful with relatively less serious offenders, in particular Caucasian youths. Less success, however, is evident with the more serious official offender who tends to have more problems in school, comes from single parent families, and is African American. It may be that the current curriculum and its implementation are not sensitive to variations in the social and life situations of these populations.

For example, Spencer, Swanson, and Cunningham (1991) note that a lack of school achievement among African American youths may be due to cultural insensitivity in traditional approaches to education. Indeed, educational approaches may "require transformation to arrive at a culturally responsive pedagogy with the potential to enhance the academic outcomes and competence of minority youth" (Spencer, Swanson, and Cunningham, 1991:377). Perhaps the Second Chance program suffers from the same cultural insensitivity. It also may be necessary to implement a curriculum that considers the ability (or inability) of delinquent minority youths to cope with structural factors that interact with minority status and enhance their ability to avoid future involvement in delinquent activity.

An additional concern is the lack of cultural diversity among treatment staff, particularly in light of the racial makeup of the youths not completing the program. Since the completion of the evaluation, however, an African American male probation officer has replaced one Caucasian female probation officer. Follow-up research is needed to assess the impact of this change on the retention of minority youths and the overall implementation of the program.

Last, the Second Chance program seeks to improve the adolescent's ability to succeed in the job market and conventional society by first providing training in prosocial ways of interacting with others. At the end of the sixteen weekly sessions, youths are no longer under the supervision of the juvenile court. Youths find themselves in their original environment (from which delinquent behaviors were acquired and supported) without follow-up care that would reinforce and encourage the utilization of newly aquired modes of social interaction. Because delinquent acts tend to occur in groups (Elliott, Huizinga, and Ageton, 1985), the lack of some form of continued monitoring and reinforcement of prosocial values and behaviors can be detrimental to the overall treatment effort. For some youths, then, sixteen weeks of instruction may not provide the inner resources and overt activities (e.g., jobs) that enable them to resist peer pressure and participation in illegal activities.

There appear to be a number of additional avenues for future research that, if pursued, might help explain the present findings as well as enhance the ability of the Second Chance program to significantly reduce official recidivism.

For example, in a review of the literature on the use of SST with delinquents, Hollin (1992) concluded that social skills training programs are effective when assessed by measures of discrete skill performance, behavior (sociometric teacher and parent) ratings, changes in cognition, and institutional performance. Unfortunately, the present study did not systematically examine other behavioral and cognitive measures to determine the effects of the program on the attitudinal and general social performances of the youths.

There are indications that the attitudes of at least some youths have been altered. A preliminary analysis of the first two groups of Second Chance youths conducted by JCS in 1991 provides positive feedback from parents, school officials, and employers, albeit in anecdotal form (Area VII Job Training Service, 1991). For example, JCS notes that parents reported improvements in their children's self-confidence, communication, and respect for parental rules (Area VII Job Training Service, 1991). The report also indicates that school officials and staff had contacted JCS to report the "complete turnaround" of one youth who had completed the program, and a noticeable improvement in self-esteem and classroom participation in another (Area VII Job Training Service, 1991:16). Employers were also cited as impressed with the participants' positive attitudes, interest, and effort. Further encouragement for the potential of the program comes from the statements of the youths themselves. Evaluations completed by the youths for the first two groups were "very positive" (Area VII Job Training Service, 1991:17). Youths felt that the program was more beneficial than standard probation because "it helps you with a lot of problems" and "it helps you with ways to deal with peer pressure and finding a job" (Area VII Job Training Service, 1991:17). Unfortunately, this information is merely a handful of positive (probably biased) observations that were used to secure continuation funding for the program. In order to understand the effectiveness of the social skills component, future research must monitor these behavioral and attitudinal changes in a more systematic manner.[2] This is an important avenue for future research because programmatic effects may not evidence themselves in the form of an immediate reduction in criminal activity. Participation in the program, however, may positively impact the adolescent a number of years later by providing him/her with the skills necessary to maintain a law-abiding lifestyle as an adult.

The employment component is another aspect of the Second Chance program that should be more closely examined. Bazemore (1991:35) argues that a number of youthful offender employment programs have been preoccupied with molding the various work activities to fit the needs of the employees rather than providing a work experience that is beneficial and meaningful for the youths themselves. Such an approach assumes a general incompetence of young offenders which perpetuates the perception of delinquents as " 'prob-

[2]An assessment of the behavioral and attitudinal variables was not of primary importance to JCS officials in the original evaluation of the Second Chance program. Given that a great deal of energy and effort has been expended on Second Chance, however, the researchers are currently in the process of assessing the effectiveness of the program in meeting outcome variables other than recidivism.

lem' clients who require help or control . . . " (Bazemore, 1991:39). This evaluation does not examine the degree to which the work performed by the youths may be classified as beneficial and meaningful. Although JTPA attempts to match a juvenile's interest with available work opportunities, questions concerning the type of employment and the degree to which the employment experience is conducive to the development of conventional bonds remain unanswered. The forming of a conventional bond is central to the theoretical relationship between employment and reduced delinquency (Hirschi, 1969). Future research should assess the concordance between theory, job training, and the actual employment experience of youths participating in the Second Chance program.

Although Second Chance may currently be considered a failure in terms of official recidivism, there is reason to be optimistic concerning the ability of the program to help troubled youths. The alternatives to Second Chance would be an elevation of sanctions for youths in need of more than straight probation (e.g., placing the youths in the state training school or waiving them to adult court). The main effects of such strategies on recidivism, however, have been equally "slight and inconsistent" (Andrews et al., 1990a:373) and, generally, more costly.

ACKNOWLEDGMENT

We would like to thank Jane Patton and Kathy Thompson for their helpful comments and suggestions. The content of the article is the sole responsibility of the authors.

REFERENCES

Agnew, R. (1991). The interactive effects of peer variables on delinquency. *Criminology* 29:47–71.

Andrews, D. A., Zinger, I., Hoge, R. D., Bonta, R. D., Gendreau, P., and Cullen, F. T. (1990a). Does correctional treatment work? A clinically relevant and psychologically informed meta-analysis. *Criminology* 28:369–404.

Area VII Job Training Service. (1991). *Second chance youth offender program: A work force investment program.* A report submitted to the Department of Economic Development, Des Moines, IA.

Bandura, A. (1977). *A social learning theory.* Englewood Cliffs, NJ: Prentice Hall.

Bandura, A. (1986). *Social foundations of thought and action: A social cognitive theory.* Englewood Cliffs, NJ: Prentice Hall.

Bazemore, G. (1991). New concepts and alternative practice in community supervision of juvenile offenders: Rediscovering work experience and competency development. *Journal of Crime and Justice* 14:27–52.

Bishop, D., Frazier, C., and Henretta, J. (1989). Prosecutorial reform: Case study of a questionable reform. *Crime and Delinquency* 35:179–201.

Briar, S., and Piliavin, I. (1965). Delinquency, situational inducements, and commitments to conformity. *Social Problems* 13:35–45.

Cloward, R. A., and Ohlin, L. E. (1960). *Delinquency and opportunity.* Glencoe, IL: Free Press.

Cook, T., and Campbell, D. (1979). *Quasi-experimentation.* Boston: Houghton Mifflin.

Elliott, D., Huizinga, D., and Ageton, S. (1985). *Explaining delinquency and drug use.* Beverly Hills, CA: Sage Publications.

Farnworth, M., and Leiber, M. J. (1989). Strain theory revisited: Economic goals, educational means, and delinquency. *American Sociological Review* 54:263–74.

Finckenauer, J. O. (1984). *Juvenile delinquency and corrections: The gap between theory and practice.* Orlando, FL: Academic Press.

Friday, P., and Hage, J. (1976). Youth crime in postindustrial societies: An integrated perspective. *Criminology* 14:347–68.

Giordano, P. C., Cernkovich, S. A., and Pugh, M. D. (1986). Friendships and delinquency. *American Journal of Sociology* 91:1170–202.

Glueck, S., and Glueck, E. (1950). *Unraveling juvenile delinquency.* Cambridge, MA: Harvard University Press.

Gottfredson, M., and Hirschi, T. (1990). *A general theory of crime.* Palo Alto, CA: Stanford University Press.

Greenberg, D. (1977). Delinquency and the age structure of society. *Contemporary Crises* 1:66–86.

Greenwood, P. W., and Turner, S. (1993). Evaluation of the Paint Creek Youth Center: A residential program for serious delinquents. *Criminology* 31:263–80.

Hartup, W. W. (1983). *Carmichaels manual of child psychology.* New York: Wiley.

Henderson, M., and Hollin, C. (1986). Social skills training and delinquency. In *Handbook of social skills training, Vol. 1: Applications across the life span,* ed. C. R. Hollin and P. Trower. Oxford, UK: Pergamon Press.

Henggeler, S. W. (1989). *Delinquency in adolescence.* Newbury Park, CA: Sage Publications.

Hirschi, T. (1969). *Causes of delinquency.* Berkeley, CA: University of California Press.

Hollin, C. R. (1992). *Criminal behaviour: A psychological approach to explanation and prevention.* Washington, DC: The Falmer Press.

Howing, P. T., Wodarski, J. S., Kurtz, P. D., and Gaudin, J. M., Jr. (1990). The empirical base for the implementation of social skills training with maltreated children. *Social Work* 35:460–67.

Kandel, D., and Davies, M. (1991). Friendship networks, intimacy, and illicit drug use in young adulthood: A comparison of two competing theories. *Criminology* 29:441–69.

Leiber, M. J. (1992). *Juvenile justice decision making in Iowa: An analysis of the influences of race on case processing in three counties.* Prepared for The State Juvenile Justice Advisory Council of Iowa & The Division of Criminal and Juvenile Justice Planning.

Leiber, M. J., Farnworth, M., Jamieson, K., and Nalla, M. (1994). Bridging the gender gap in criminology: Liberation and gender-specific strain effects on delinquency. *Sociological Inquiry* 64:56–68.

Lundman, R. J. (1993). *Prevention and control of juvenile delinquency* (2nd ed.). New York: Oxford University Press.

McFall, R. M. (1976). *Behavior training: A skill-acquisition approach to clinical problems.* Morristown, NJ: General Learning Press.

McGarrell, E. (1993). Trends in racial disproportionality in juvenile court processing: 1985–1989. *Crime and Delinquency* 39:29.

McGuire, J., and Priestley, P. (1985). *Offending behavior: Skills and stratagems for going straight.* New York: St. Martin's Press.

National Corrective Training Institute. (1989). *NCTI youth crossroads program.* Phoenix, AZ: National Corrective Training Institute.

Parker, J. G., and Asher, S. R. (1997). Peer relations and later personal adjustment: Are low-accepted children at risk? *Psychological Bulletin* 102:357–89.

Sarason, J. G. (1968). Verbal learning, modeling, and juvenile delinquency. *American Psychologist* 23:254–66.

Short, J. F., Jr., and Strodtbeck, F. (1965). *Group process and gang delinquency.* Chicago: University of Chicago Press.

Simons, R. L., Whitbeck, L. B., Conger, R. D., and Melby, J. N. (1991). The effect of social skills, values, peers, and depression on adolescent substance use. *Journal of Early Adolescence* 11:466–81.

Spence. S. H. (1981). Differences in social skills performance between institutionalized juvenile male offenders and a comparable group of boys without offense records. *British Journal of Clinical Psychology* 20:163–71.

Spencer, M. B., Swanson, D. P., and Cunningham, M. (1991). Ethnicity, ethnic identity, and competence formation: Adolescent transition and cultural transformation. *Journal of Negro Education* 60:366–87.

Tremblay, R. E., McCord, J., Boileau, H., Charlebois, P., Gagnon, C., Le Blanc, M., and Larivee, S. (1991). Can disruptive boys be helped to become competent? *Psychiatry* 54:148–61.

Waegel, W. B. (1989). *Delinquency and juvenile control: A sociological perspective.* Englewood Cliffs. NJ: Prentice Hall.

Waldinger, R., and Bailey, T. (1985). The youth employment problem in the world city. *Social Policy* 16:1.

William T. Grant Foundation. (1988). Youth and America's future: William T. Grant Foundation Commission on work, family and citizenship. *Youth Policy* 10(12):5.

Wise, K. L., Bundy, K. A., Bundy, E. A., and Wise, L. (1991). Social skills training for young adolescents. *Adolescence* 26:233–41.

Wolfgang, M., Figlio, R., and Sellin, T. (1972). *Delinquency in a birth cohort.* Chicago: University of Chicago Press.

Wood, G., Green, L., and Bry, B. H. (1982). The input of behavioral training upon the knowledge and effectiveness of juvenile probation officers and volunteers. *Journal of Community Psychology* 10:133–41.

Zaragoza, N., Vaughn, S., and McIntosh, R. (1991). Social skills interventions and children with behavior problems: A review. *Behavioral Disorders* 16:260–75.

DISCUSSION QUESTIONS

1. What was the source of the data for the study? What are the most important limitations or potential problems with these data?
2. Describe the design of the study. What comparisons were made in order to draw conclusions about the effects of the social skills program?
3. What were the findings of the study?
4. According to the authors, how could a study that examined the effects of such a program be improved from what is described here?

3

General Deterrent Effects of Police Patrol in Crime "Hot Spots"

A Randomized, Controlled Trial

LAWRENCE W. SHERMAN, University of Maryland
DAVID WEISBURD, Hebrew University

COMMENTARY

The Minneapolis study was initiated because of core methodological and theoretical problems that had been raised in the research programs of the two principal investigators. One of us (Lawrence Sherman) was completing a study of crime at street addresses in Minneapolis, which suggested that crime was concentrated in small hot spots, often represented as an address or cluster of addresses. This was contrary to the conventional view of crime as located in larger units such as "bad neighborhoods." The other (David Weisburd) had just completed a study of community policing in New York, which raised the question of whether traditional evaluation techniques were often not fit to the interventions of the police. That study suggested that police interventions were

Source: Justice Quarterly, Vol. 12, No. 4, December 1995, pp. 625–648. © 1995. Reprinted by permission of the Academy of Criminal Justice Sciences.

This research was supported in part by National Institute of Justice Grant 88-IJ-CXOOO9 to the Crime Control Institute. Points of view or opinions expressed in this article do not necessarily represent the official position of the U.S. Department of Justice. We wish to thank Michael E. Buerger, Dennis P. Rogan, Patrick R. Gartin, Anne E. Beatty, Ellen G. Cohn, Joel Garner, Kinley Larntz, Anthony Petrosino, Lisa Maher, Joanne Oreskovich, Robert Velke, former Minneapolis Police Chiefs Anthony V. Bouza and John Laux, former Deputy Chiefs Douglas Smith and David Dobrotka, Inspectors Sherman Otto, Ted Faul, Ted Trahan, and Bill Jones, and the entire patrol force of the MPD.

Please address all correspondence to Lawrence W. Sherman, Department of Criminology and Criminal Justice, University of Maryland, 2220 LeFrak Hall, College Park, MD 20742; E-mail wsherman@bss2.umd.edu.

Revised version of a paper presented to the Academy of Criminal Justice Sciences, Denver, in March of 1990, and the American Society of Criminology, Baltimore, November of 1990.

being brought into the "small worlds" of specific problems, while evaluation strategies were often focused on the "large worlds" of beats or neighborhoods.

As in many research projects our collaboration was somewhat accidental. We were brought together because Professor Sherman had received an invitation as a distinguished visiting professor at the School of Criminal Justice, where Professor Weisburd was a faculty member. After a lunch or two, we believed that our observations on the concentration of crime at hot spots, and failure to develop evaluation strategies fit to the "small worlds" of policing, provided a context for reassessing one of the main findings in empirical criminology: that preventive police patrol was ineffective (the finding was most powerfully represented in the Kansas City Preventive Patrol Experiment). We decided to ask whether such patrol would be found more effective if it focused on hot spots of crime, and if we paid careful attention to evaluation at that level of analysis.

In asking this question, we decided at the outset to use the strongest research design possible, and to overcome some methodological objections to the prior studies. Accordingly, we proposed a randomized experimental design. Such designs have very high internal validity, meaning that when an effect is found it is highly likely to result from the treatment (defined in this case as higher levels of preventive patrol at a hot spot). We also sought to ensure that our study had a high level of statistical power. In the Kansas City Preventive Patrol Experiment this was seen as a major flaw. The statistical power of many comparisons examined in that study was low, meaning that even if an effect for preventive patrol existed it would have been difficult to identify it in the context of the research. We paid a good deal of attention to this issue in our research, identifying the number of cases, for example, included on the basis of statistical power computations.

Another methodological advance developed from our need to identify hot spots of crime. This was the first major evaluation study to rely on computer mapping to identify clusters of high-crime addresses. We began with the assumption that high-crime addresses clustered together and thus we could not simply select addresses isolated from one another for experimental and control units. Because of this, we sought to use computer mapping programs that were more often used by geographers than criminologists to identify the spacial positions of specific addresses. We encountered significant problems in this process that were later to be overcome by crime-mapping researchers. However, the choice of computer mapping as a method for defining discrete hot spots was to be followed in a series of other important studies.

Of course, designing a study and carrying it out are two different problems. This study, like many other experimental studies, would not have been possible without the commitment of practitioners concerned with the questions we raised. In particular, Chief Anthony Bouza facilitated the implementation of our experimental design. For the term of the experiment, random patrol by police officers was dictated by the needs of the experiment. While today there are many innovative police chiefs around the country willing to experiment with programs and tactics, Chief Bouza was one of the first of this innovative group. His support developed from his understanding of the importance of the questions raised, and the need to make compromises in police management to gain solid answers to such questions. Without Chief Bouza's support the experimental allocation of police officers would have been impossible.

But even with Chief Bouza's support, it was a major effort to ensure that the experiment was implemented as designed. We needed to ensure that the police spent much greater periods of time at experimental hot spots than at control hot spots. Prior experimental studies had shown that experiments are often not implemented as designed. We decided at the outset that we would need a method of auditing whether the police were indeed following the design. We used observations at the hot spots by researchers to ensure treatment integrity. In the end, thousands of such observations were conducted—a major research task. However, it turned out to be worthwhile, because it allowed us to ensure that treatment was being delivered as designed.

There are many lessons to be drawn from our research, just as we drew lessons from earlier studies in our design. Perhaps most important is that the researcher should set his or her goals as high as possible. Many had told us that an experimental study of this type would be impossible, both because of what it required from the police and because of the significant research resources necessary to implement it. While we had to work very hard to develop and implement the study, we were able to overcome major barriers. In particular, we found a police practitioner with the vision to see the importance of the study and funders (in particular, the National Institute of Justice and its director at the time, James K. Stewart) willing to support it.

ABSTRACT Many criminologists doubt that the dosage of uniformed police patrol causes any measurable difference in crime. This article reports a one-year randomized trial in Minneapolis of increases in patrol dosage at 55 of 110 crime "hot spots," monitored by 7,542 hours of systematic observations. The experimental group received, on average, twice as much observed patrol presence, although the ratio displayed wide seasonal fluctuation. Reductions in total crime calls ranged from 6 percent to 13 percent. Observed disorder was only half as prevalent in experimental as in control hot spots. We conclude that substantial increases in police patrol presence can indeed cause modest reductions in crime and more impressive reductions in disorder within high crime locations.

In 1974 the Kansas City Preventive Patrol Experiment (Kelling et al. 1974a) shook the theoretical foundations of American policing. The year-long study found that experimentally manipulated variations in the dosage of police patrol across 15 patrol beats had virtually no statistically significant effects on street crime. Then-Kansas City Police Chief Joseph McNamara concluded that "routine preventive patrol in marked police cars has little value in preventing crime or making citizens feel safe."

This finding has dominated police thinking about patrol strategies for more than two decades. Despite contradictory evidence from studies employing equally rigorous research designs (Chaiken 1978; Press 1971; Schnelle et al. 1977; Sherman 1990), the Kansas City finding remains the most influential test of the general deterrent effects of patrol on crime. It has convinced many distinguished scholars that no matter how it is deployed, police presence does not deter. Klockars (1983:130), for example, concludes that "it makes about as much sense to have police patrol routinely in cars to fight crime as it does to have firemen patrol routinely in fire trucks to fight fire." Skolnick and Bayley (1986:4) conclude that "random motor patrolling neither reduces crime nor improves chances of catching suspects." Gottfredson and Hirschi (1990:270) conclude that "no evidence exists that augmentation of police forces or equipment, differential patrol strategies, or differential intensities of surveillance have an effect on crime rates." Even Felson (1994:10–11), a rational choice theorist, interprets the Kansas City findings as evidence that "patrol has no impact on crime rates" because the low density of modern metropolitan areas makes police presence a "drop in the bucket."

The Kansas City experiment does not justify such strong conclusions. Years of debate have revealed substantial statistical, measurement, and conceptual problems in its design. The *statistical* problem is the bias, found in most area-level designs, toward the null hypothesis; the weak statistical power of such designs makes it very difficult to find an effect of patrol (or any other intervention) even when such an effect may be present (Fienberg et al. 1976). The *measurement* problem lies in determining exactly how much dosage was delivered in each of the experimental conditions, which the Kansas City study did not do. Both of these issues point up Felson's conceptual problem of dosage levels: the premise that large patrol beats or neighborhoods are the appropriate unit for allocating and testing the impact of patrol, which dilutes available dosage too much to make a reasonable impact likely (Farrington 1982).

In this article we explore those problems and a research solution: the use of very small clusters of high-crime addresses ("hot spots") as the unit of analysis instead of patrol beats or neighborhoods. We then present the research design and the results of a test of the general deterrent effects of patrol in hot spots.[1]

RESEARCH DESIGN ISSUES IN PATROL AND CRIME

Statistical Bias Towards the Null Hypothesis

The major statistical limitation in all experiments in patrol beat or neighborhood-level crime reduction is lack of power (Freiman et al 1978; Sherman 1986:362–64; Zimring 1978:162–63). This problem has three dimensions, each of which creates

[1]The use of "general" refers to potential offenders, in contrast to "specific" deterrence of future crime by persons who have been punished in the past. We do not imply that general deterrence of crime in hot spots necessarily deters crime "generally" throughout the city beyond the hot spot location; we treat that issue as empirical rather than conceptual.

a bias against demonstrating any impact of policing (or other interventions) on crime. One statistical power issue is the low frequency of *crimes* in most neighborhoods. A second is the number of *citizens* who must be interviewed in each community to permit reliable estimates of changes in the victimization rate of that community. The third is the number of *communities* included in community-level tests of policing strategies.

Most patrol beat-sized neighborhoods in most cities suffer relatively few serious crimes each year. To provide a reliable estimate of the prevalence of most types of crime through victimization surveys, large samples must be drawn for each area. The expense entailed in drawing these samples is so great that it limits the number of areas which can be studied at reasonable cost. Measures of reported crime are less expensive to collect, but they also provide low base rates. One robbery (or less) per month, for example, is a common rate for many patrol beats, as it was in the San Diego Field Interrogation Experiment in beats of 7,000 to 14,000 residents (Boydstun 1975:16, 32). That rarity creates a bias toward the null hypothesis for any crime-specific statistical tests of the impact of interventions. Kelling et al (1974b:96), for example, found that a 300 percent increase in reported robberies in the less heavily patrolled areas was not statistically significant because the large relative difference reflected an absolute difference of less than one outside robbery per month. The observed difference in robbery in Kansas City might have been significant with a sample size of hundreds of patrol beats. Few cities of over 250,000, however, have even 50 patrol beats, let alone hundreds.

Measuring and Varying Patrol Dosage Levels

A substantive bias toward the null hypothesis in the Kansas City design may have been created by insufficient differences in patrol dosage. Larson (1975) argued that five factors created as much visible patrol presence in the unpatrolled beats as would normal patrol dosage (but see Pate and Kelling 1975): 1) travel into and out of the beats to answer calls for service, 2) the operation of other (nonpatrol) units in marked cars, 3) greater use of sirens and lights, 4) more frequent responses by two units, and 5) more police-initiated contacts. This does not necessarily discount the failure of the areas with increased dosage to show more crime reduction than those with normal dosage (Zimring 1978:143). Yet it raises a key question: How certain can we be of the exact dosage of visible police presence delivered in any of the 15 beats?

If we assume that the dosage levels in Kansas City actually may have varied very little, that point alone may explain why the Kansas City results differ from those of most other quasi-experimental patrol deterrence studies. In the 1966 study of New York City police, a reported 40 percent increase in patrol car presence reduced target crimes (Press 1971). In the New York City subway study, an increase of almost 300 percent in police staffing apparently caused an initial deterrent effect (Chaiken 1978). In Nashville, a 400 percent increase in police-recorded patrol time in four target areas was associated with significant reductions in total crime (Schnelle et al 1977). Large increases in dosage thus may be essential if any effect on crime is to be observed. The Kansas City design called for substantial increases, but could not measure the dosage reliably. In the absence of carefully measured levels of patrol dosage, it is almost impossible to interpret the Kansas preventive patrol experiment.

The measurement and the control of dosage are closely related. Where dosage levels cannot be measured, it is difficult to advise police supervisors on whether proper levels are being delivered. It is also impossible to develop a precise dosage-response curve from multiple experiments, an essential condition for building theory. Thus the basic issues in measuring police patrol dosage must be carefully considered.

Patrol dosage can be measured from the perspective of either the police or the criminal. The police perspective on their own whereabouts can be measured through police logs or notes of independent observers riding in patrol cars. The potential criminal's perspective on police whereabouts can be measured by independent observers stationed in public places. To estimate with any precision the odds that police will pass any particular location, one would require repeated observations from a large sample of all possible observation posts within patrol car beats. The need to sample both space and time could make the gathering of such estimates even more costly per unit of analysis than personal victimization surveys—as long as the unit of analysis remained the entire low-density patrol beat rather than the small parts of each beat where crime is concentrated.

Moreover, spreading observations over entire patrol beats would dilute the power of the observation sample to produce a reliable estimate of police presence in any given place—just as spreading patrol itself dilutes the potential deterrent threat of police presence in any one place. This point raises the more general question of the appropriate unit of analysis for patrol experiments and operations, which should guide the methods of measurement.

The Unit of Analysis: Patrol Beats or Hot Spots?

The premise of organizing patrol by beats is that crime could happen anywhere and that the entire beat must be patrolled. Computer-age data, however, have given new support to Henry Fielding's ([1751] 1977) eighteenth century proposal that police pay special attention to a small number of locations at high risk of crime. If only 3 percent of the addresses in a city produce more than half of all the requests for police response, if no police cars are dispatched to 40 percent of the addresses and intersections in a city over one year, and, if among the 60 percent with any requests, the majority (31%) register only one request per year (Sherman, Gartin, and Buerger, 1989), then concentrating police in a few locations makes more sense than spreading them evenly throughout a beat (Sherman and Weisburd 1995).

The main argument against directing extra resources to the hot spots is that it would simply displace crime problems from one address to another without achieving any overall or lasting reduction in crime. The premise of this argument is that a fixed supply of criminals is seeking outlets for the fixed number of crimes they are predestined to commit. Although that argument may fit some public drug markets (Sherman 1990; but see Green 1995; Weisburd and Green 1995), it does not fit all crime or even all vice. One carefully studied prostitution market was closed by a police crackdown (and road closing) with no apparent displacement (Matthews 1986). There is no evidence that displacement is certain across all crime categories (Cornish and Clarke 1987); the most thorough study of displacement from increased patrol (Press 1971) found that the estimate of displaced crime was less than the reduction of crime in the experimental precinct (see also Barr and Pease 1990).

In any case, displacement is merely a rival theory explaining *why* crime declines at a specific hot spot, *if* it declines. The first step is to see whether crime can be reduced at those spots at all, with a research design capable of giving a fair answer to that question.

The geographic concentration of many crimes and many calls to police about crime provides a solution to all three dimensions of the statistical power problem discussed above. First, each "hot spot" cluster of visually connected addresses offers ample numbers of calls and crimes for statistical analysis of changes at that location. Second, any city contains far more hot spots than patrol beats, so there is no difficulty in constructing a large sample of hot spot locations. Third, concentrating patrol dosage in a hot spot could create a substantial increase in patrol dosage in a very small world, and would make systematic observation an economically viable way of measuring patrol dosage levels. Although this solution does not make victimization interviews more economical, it makes feasible an even more direct measure of the most frequent kinds of crime: systematic observation, which also can measure patrol presence. The design presented below demonstrates how this solution can be operationalized, and shows the resulting statistical power.

EXPERIMENTAL DESIGN

Selection of City

We designed the experiment in collaboration with the Minneapolis Police Department, where the pattern of hot spots across all offenses had first been demonstrated (Sherman et al 1989). The experiment was endorsed by a vote of the City Council upon the Mayor's recommendation, despite the predicted effect of minimizing patrols in outlying Council members' areas and concentrating police presence in the inner core of the city, where hot spots of crime were more prevalent. The experiment also required the cooperation of the entire patrol force; this was facilitated by a recent change in case law, which gave the Chief of Police more control over the four patrol precinct commanders. Police cooperation was also pursued through briefings, pizza parties, and t-shirts bearing the project's logo ("Minneapolis Hot Spot Cop").

Selection of Hot Spots

We defined hot spots operationally as small clusters of addresses with frequent "hard" crime calls as well as substantial "soft" crime calls for service (Reiss 1985).[2] We then limited the boundaries of each spot conceptually as easily visible from an epicenter (Sherman et al 1989). This definition failed to solve the problem of crimes occurring at rear entrances to addresses listed in the dispatch data, but the "noise" from this problem should not threaten an internally valid comparison between two randomized groups of hot spots, both of which suffer that noise problem to roughly the same extent.

The selection procedure began with a data file on all dispatched calls for police service citywide for the most recent year before the beginning of the selection analysis (June 6, 1987 through June 5, 1988; this is described below as the "selection year," as distinct from the "baseline" year preceding the starting date of the experiment). In the selection year we identified 5,538 addresses and intersections with more than three calls to police about incidents that we defined as "hard crime." We then employed a computer mapping program, MAPINFO, to locate most of the addresses, so that inspection of the computer printouts for each map grid could reveal what appeared to be visually connected clusters of these addresses.[3] Using this technique, we identified and mapped 420 address clusters with 20 or more hard crime calls (see Buerger, Cohn, and Petrosino 1995).

All 420 of these clusters were visually inspected by field staff members. The inspections had three principal goals. One goal was to reconfigure the boundaries suggested by the computer map to make them consistent with the definition based on visual contact. The second was to determine whether the type of premises at each address was eligible. To limit the sample to places where crime occurred in public and could reasonably be deterred by police presence, we excluded all residential and most commercial buildings of more than four stories (including two hotels), almost all parking garages and department stores, indoor malls, public schools, office buildings, residential social service institutions (such as homeless shelters), hospitals, police stations, and fire stations. We also excluded parks because almost all were too large to meet the visual contact criterion. Finally, we excluded a few known "magnet phone" locations, at which events occurring elsewhere were routinely reported.

The third goal of the inspection was to determine the visual proximity *between* the cluster and the possible contamination of each site by patrol car presence in the closest neighboring site. The two independent field workers,

[2]Examples of "hard crime" calls are holdup alarms, burglary, shooting, stabbing, auto theft, theft from autos, assault, and rape. Examples of "soft crime" calls are audible break-in alarms, disturbances, drunks, noise, unwanted persons at businesses, vandalism, prowlers, fights, and person down.

[3]Some difficulty developed in this process because different definitions of places were used by the City of Minneapolis and by MAPINFO. We were able to reconcile most of these differences, usually by hand-plotting addresses on the computer map, but some 5 percent of the "hot" addresses were left out of our mapping analysis.

Michael E. Buerger and Ellen G. Cohn, examined each site and drew what appeared to be logical boundaries. Their separate versions of boundaries for the final hot spots initially randomized achieved 75 percent agreement. Their reconfigurations followed these general principles:

1. No hot spot is larger than one standard linear street block (although a few exceptions were allowed on the basis of visual sightings on very short blocks).
2. No hot spot extends for more than one half block from either side of an intersection.
3. No hot spot is within one standard linear block of another hot spot (again we made a few exceptions).

The site visits produced a provisional list of 321 maps, with some overlap which we narrowed to a final list of 268 reconfigured clusters (with the ineligible locations excluded).[4] We marked the 268 on a map to make final eliminations based on proximity. Using memoranda about the layout of each site and its proximity to nearby clusters, the principal investigators created a new list of eligible clusters, all of which were required to generate at least 20 hard crime calls in the selection year. This list was also informed by the "soft crime" totals for the selection year (with a minimum of 20), and by an element crucial to the statistical power of the analysis: the percentage change (positive or negative) in the total calls for hard and soft crime from the year ending May 1987 to the year ending May 1988. High variance from year to year could have attenuated the treatment effects, so clusters with greater than 150 percent increases or 75 percent decreases in hard crime calls from one year to the next were excluded from the possible sample. The greatest decrease included in the final sample was 66 percent.

After we made exclusions for variance and the most severe cases of proximity, only 155 hot spots were left. We eliminated four more on the grounds of new data on proximity; one was eliminated because it had become dormant in recent months. At our request, the surviving 150 were randomized by an independent statistician into three treatment groups, which we presented to a planning committee of the Minneapolis Police Department. The committee concluded that the department could not handle 100 target hot spots with adequate dosage to provide a reliable test of the theory, and asked us to reduce the experimental group to 50. The final agreement called for 55 hot spots assigned to extra patrol; thus 110 sights had to be selected for randomization.

We derived the final selection of the 110 sites from the 150 previously identified sites, primarily by taking the top-ranked hot spots in order of volume of hard crime calls. The final 110 were rerandomized by University of Minnesota

[4]Secondary analysts of these data should know that the numbering system for the hot spots in the raw data reflects the surviving members of the provisional list of 365, not the final list of 110.

statistician Kinley Larntz, despite concerns that about 10 of the clusters would not appear "hot" enough to patrol officers. In the final 110 clusters, the mean number of hard and soft crime calls for service at the active addresses was 182.9 in the selection year, with a minimum of 56 and a maximum of 628.

Characteristics of Hot Spots

The typical hot spot in the final sample of 110 was a group of attached two- and three-story buildings clustered around an epicenter, usually a street corner. Addresses included in the cluster extended in all four directions but only as far as the eye could see from sidewalk corners. These intersections often consisted of a mix of commercial services, usually including food and drink, generally open until late at night. Exceptions to this pattern included low-rise multifamily housing developments and convenience stores. Bus stops and pay telephones were common features of hot spots, as was intensive street lighting.

"Hot" Times

The calls at the 110 spots were concentrated between 7:00 P.M. and 3:00 A.M. We determined this by summing the calls over the selection year by each hour of the day, for both the experimental and the control group. The 7-to-3 window for the experimental group accounted for 51.9 percent of the crime calls; for the control group, this window accounted for 50.5 percent. The 11:00 A.M. to 7:00 P.M. period registered the next highest concentrations, with 32 percent of the experimental group's calls and 33.6 percent of those for the control group. The 3:00 A.M. to 11:00 A.M. period, with the exception of a few sites, registered the fewest calls, with only 16.3 percent of the experimental group's calls and 15.8 percent of the control group's. Thus the experiment was restricted to the period from 11 A.M. to 3 A.M.

Hot Spot Sample Sizes

The sample sizes include several dimensions: the numbers of hot spot clusters, the addresses used to select the clusters, the total number of addresses within those boundaries, numbers of calls for all reasons at those addresses, and the numbers of calls about hard and soft crimes dispatched to those addresses.

The experiment randomly assigned 110 address clusters to treatment and control groups. These clusters contained a total of 677 specific "selection" addresses and intersections (320 experimental group addresses and 357 control), with a mean of six addresses per site. When all of the addresses included within the boundaries of each hot spot are considered (not only those addresses with three or more calls, as in the selection data cited above), the total was 1,663 (a mean of 15 addresses per spot): 832 addresses in the experimental group and 831 in the control.

During the *baseline* year before the experiment began, these "all-inclusive" clusters produced a total of 19,322 calls for all reasons in the experimental group and 19,693 in the control, or a mean of 355 calls per hot spot. This total constituted 10.8 percent of the 364,365 calls dispatched for all reasons citywide in the one-year baseline period, December 1, 1987 to November 30, 1988. Adjustment for nontraffic calls produced virtually identical proportions.

Treatments

This experiment tests a theory of intensified but intermittent patrol, not a theory of constant, security guard-style presence. The experimental patrol treatment approximates a crackdown-backoff pattern; a police car was not present at the target address clusters at all times. Cars left to answer calls and then returned unexpectedly. They stayed at one spot for as long as an hour or more, or for only a few minutes. Both one-officer and two-officer units were used; foot patrol presence was measured separately. Both officers and observers were given maps of the hot spot boundaries; the addresses generating the most police calls were highlighted in red.

What the officers did while present at the sites varied widely by officer. During an inspection visit at our invitation, George Kelling (1990, personal communication) observed that some were reading newspapers or sunning themselves while sitting on the patrol car, while others were engaging citizens in friendly interaction in community-policing style. The experiment was clearly no test of the content of police presence, only of the amount. To gain police cooperation in achieving the dosage goals, we did not presume to restrict the officers' discretion in *how* to police a hot spot, but only in *how much*.

Random Assignment

The final sample of 110 address clusters was assigned randomly to two groups of 55 by the independent statistician, who used a computerized pseudo-random number generator to allocate the clusters equally to two groups. The allocation was performed in five statistical "blocks," based on natural cutting points within the distribution of hard crime call frequencies. This decision was intended to increase statistical power by minimizing the differences in variance between the groups. Although blocking results in a loss of degrees of freedom in analysis of experimental effects, it produces a gain over simple randomization by maximizing the equivalence of the groups. Further, a comparison of randomization by pairs with randomization in five blocks showed little difference in statistical power.

Dosage

After extensive debate, the police department committed itself to (but never fully achieved) a goal of three hours a day of patrol presence at each of the 55 target hot spots. The dosage, based on the above analysis of "hot times," was to be divided evenly between the 11–7 and the 7–3 time periods, and was to be provided seven days a week. To enhance the power of the experiment (Weisburd 1993), our goal (which was largely achieved) was to keep dosage levels as consistent as possible. We encouraged this by giving patrol managers weekly reports on the dosage levels reported by officers in their official logs. These reports were supplemented by a monthly report on the amount of dosage recorded by our field observers. When some spots appeared in the logs to be receiving more dosage than others, we asked patrol supervisors to assign less time at those spots and to order more time at the locations receiving less logged dosage.

The independent observations by our field staff of 16 observers and three supervisors were limited to the 100 most active control and experimental spots; the five "coolest" spots in each treatment group were eliminated from the observations to maximize measurement of the places producing the largest volume of crime. The observations covered a total of 75 hours per hot spot over the course of the year. All observations were made between 7:00 P.M. and 3:00 A.M. The 7,542-hour sample thus constituted 2.6 percent of all hours on that period over 365 days times 100 locations (292,000 hours).

The observation sample was divided equally into 13 periods of 28 days each for each hot spot. Observations were conducted in a total of 6,465 blocks of 70 minutes each. Each of the 13 28-day periods contained 497 observation blocks, or about five per hot spot. A total of 3,232 observation blocks were conducted for the 50 experimental hot spots, and 3,233 for the 50 observed controls.

Observers were trained to use a systematic observation instrument that employed separate sections for observations of uniformed officers and of crime and disorder. Both sections were structured chronologically so that each entry had a start and a finish time, as did the entire observation period. Entries registering official presence included "drive-throughs" and longer stays of police in cars and on foot, private security guards, fire truck and ambulance personnel, and whether and how long police left their cars or entered buildings. Observations of crime and disorder included an array of both criminal offenses and offenses against conventional civility, as noted below.

Outcome Measures

We collected two primary outcome measures: calls about crime and observed disorders. The hot spots were selected on the basis of telephone calls about criminal activity reported by the public—as distinct from dispatchers' records of events reported by police officers over the radio, which also can generate a "call" record. Therefore citizen calls should be treated as the primary outcome measure. Calls about "soft" and "hard" crime were counted for the full 24-hour day, not only the 16 hours in which the experiment was operational, for two reasons. One was theoretical, based on our conception of general deterrence as including "residual" effects even when police patrols are not present (Sherman 1990). The other reason was statistical: we included the full 24 hours in order to increase the power of the test by using higher base rates of crime calls in each hot spot.

The other outcome measure was a more direct measure of crime than citizen calls, although it necessarily lacked baseline data for sample selection. Systematic observation data on crime and disorder in the evening observation hours coded each incident of fights, drug sales, apparent solicitation for prostitution, playing of loud music or shouting, rummaging through garbage cans, urinating, and other offensive "signs of crime" (Skogan 1990). The data even included two minor assaults on an observer sitting in a parked car.[5]

We planned to analyze the police call data by comparing Time 1/Time 2 differences between the two groups, and to analyze the observations at Time 2 only. Time 1 is the 12 months preceding the experiment; Time 2 is the 12 months of the experiment (December 1, 1988 through November 31, 1989).

Analysis of Statistical Power

The statistical power of a test "is the probability that it will lead to a rejection of the null hypothesis" (Cohen 1977:4), or the odds of detecting a statistically significant result in an experiment (at each significance level) given a true difference between experimental and control groups. We computed the power of our incidence measure using the selection-year data for the final 110 hot spots with a one-tailed 10 percent test. We used a one-tailed test because of our strong hypothesis that patrol presence reduces crime. We chose a 10 percent significance level because police executives are more interested in size of an effect than in the exact odds that the effect is due to chance. On the basis of tables provided by Cohen (1977), and assuming a standard deviation of 33.5 percent for total crime and a 10 percent significance level, we estimated that we had an 85 percent chance of gaining a significant finding in our experiment if the true impact of the treatment was about 15 percent. This level of power exceeds the .80 threshold suggested by Cohen (1977) for powerful experimental designs.

Summary of the Design

We designed this experiment to test the hypothesis that substantial increases in police patrol in high-crime hot spots could reduce crime reported and observed in those spots. We selected the hot spots on the basis of calls for service and visual proximity. The independent variable was assigned at random to half of a group of 110 hot spots constituting a universe of all address clusters meeting certain minimal levels of "hard" and "soft" crimes, as well as stability over two years in calls for police service for those types of incidents. We measured the independent variable by police logs and by independent observation of the 50 most active hot spots in each group of 55. The dependent variable was measured by police calls for service and by independently observed incidents of crime and disorder.

For 6 1/2 months, the design was implemented as planned. What happened then to modify the design produced results generally consistent with the hypothesis, even while it reduced the intended statistical power by cutting the anticipated experimental period almost in half.

---

[5]This issue is important for systematic observation of hot spots. Observers were instructed to always observe hot spots from inside an auto, and to leave if they ever felt there was any question about their safety. Both assaults were committed through an open window while the (same) observer was smoking a cigarette. Aside from these assaults, the risk to the observers appeared quite low, but this situation could be different in a city with "hotter" hot spots.

RESULTS

Independent Variable: Observed Differences in Dosage

From December 1, 1988 to November 30, 1989, the observers counted 34,416 police unit-minutes in the 50 observed experimental hot spots and 14,765 unit-minutes in the 50 observed control hot spots, a pooled ratio of 2.3 to 1. The difference in mean police presence per hot spot was slightly lower at 1.99 to 1, with $\bar{X}$ = .149 police unit-minutes per minute of observation in the 50 observed experimental hot spots and $\bar{X}$ = .0748 police-unit minutes per minute of observation in the 50 control hot spots. A "unit-minute" refers to the number of minutes each police unit spent in each location; "units" include one-officer marked cars, two-officer marked cars, and one- or two-officer foot patrols. Whenever a police unit entered the boundaries of the hot spot, the observer started the clock counting for the minutes of that unit's presence. The count ended when either the unit or the observer left the hot spot. The minutes present for each unit sometimes overlapped, so that unit-minutes divided by observation minutes cannot be taken as a prevalence measure of any police presence at all.

Compliance with the experimental protocol can be estimated by analyzing the ratio of unit-minutes to all observed minutes in each of the 100 observed hot spots. Using a criterion of one unit-minute of observed police presence for every 10 minutes of observations as the threshold for defining an "experimental" case, we find five hot spots assigned to the experimental group which failed to receive that level of dosage and four hot spots assigned to the control group which did receive that amount. Thus the "misassignment" or "crossover" rate in traditional experimental terms is 9 percent, or 9 out of the 100 observed cases. This rate is moderate for randomized trials generally, and better than the rate in most police experiments (see Dennis 1988; Weinstein and Levin 1989). Otherwise the hot spots received highly similar within-group dosage levels: 46 of the 50 experimental hot spots received 1.3 to 1.7 minutes of patrol per 10 minutes of observation, and 40 of the controls received either .7 or .8 police minutes per 10 observed minutes.

The Summer Design Breakdown

Although the mean unit-minutes across hot spots within treatment groups were relatively homogeneous, the pooled ratio between experimental and control unit-minutes varied widely by calendar month. The ratio began at 2.6 to 1 in December and fell in January to 2 to 1, where it remained until March. At that time it rose to 6 to 1 and then fell to about 2.5 to 1 in April through June. The ratio then plummeted to 1.2 to 1 in August, and rose in September to a plateau of 2.8 to 1, and remained at that level for the rest of the experiment (see Figure 1). The police logs reflect the same pattern, declining from an average of just under three hours per day in the experimental hot spots from February through May to only two hours in July and August, and rising again in the autumn. Although the observed police unit-minutes ratio exceeded 2 to 1 for every month

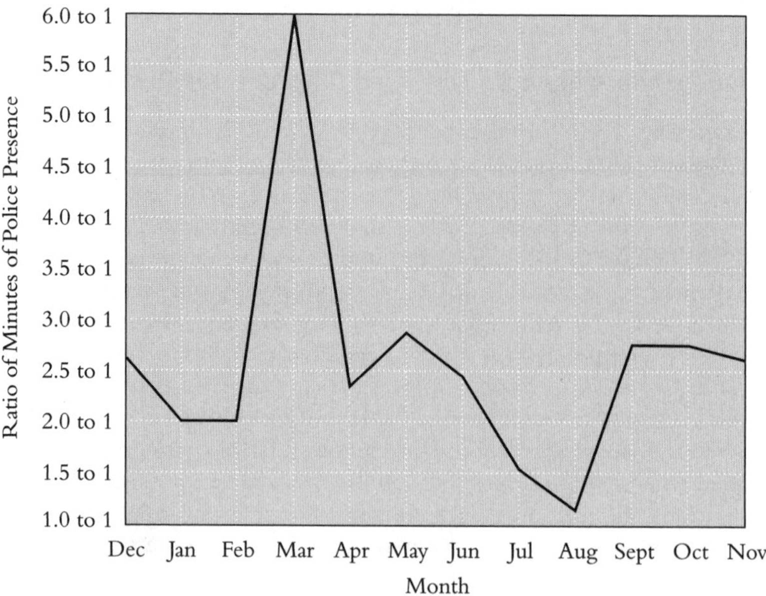

FIGURE 1. Ratio of Experimental to Control Minutes of Observed Police Presence, by Month

except August, the disruption of the experiment during the summer peak in call load (and vacation time) for police complicates the interpretation of any differences in outcomes over the entire one-year period, leaving only 6.5 months of a fully implemented design.

Dependent Variable 1: Differences in Calls About Crime

The virtual disappearance of a difference in patrol dosage between experimental and control groups in the summer months raises several options for analysis. These options are further complicated by an outcome measurement problem caused by the introduction of a new computer-aided dispatch (CAD) system from October through November 10, 1989. During that period, errors and missing data made the calls about crime an unreliable indicator. One option—perhaps the simplest—is to analyze the period from December 1 through June 15, when the police logs show the most consistent and most uninterrupted implementation of the experiment throughout the 16-hour target zone. Another option is to cut off analysis at July 31, before the only month in which observational data show virtually no difference in dosage (a period in which the overall ratio is 2.5 to 1). A third option is to analyze the full year, despite the six weeks of CAD measurement problems in October and November. A fourth option is to analyze the full year minus the period of suspect CAD data.

We find the July 31 cutoff to be the most appropriate test of the hypothesis because that date is the last date on which the experiment was minimally

Table 1. Crime Calls by Time Period and Treatment Group

	HARD CRIME		SOFT CRIME		TOTAL CRIME	
Time Period	**Experi-mental**	**Con-trol**	**Experi-mental**	**Con-trol**	**Experi-mental**	**Con-trol**
June 15						
Baseline year	1,469	1,394	3,544	3,590	5,013	4,984
Experimental year	1,377	1,374	3,919	4,542	5,296	5,916
Absolute change	–92	–20	375	952	283	932
1-Tailed P value	.27		.047*		.054*	
July 31						
Baseline year	1,893	1,798	4,638	4,693	6,531	6,491
Experimental year	1,776	1,793	5,155	5,909	6,931	7,702
Absolute change	–117	–5	517	1,216	400	1,211
1-Tailed P value	.20		.046*		.049*	
November 30[a]						
Baseline year	2,533	2,432	6,523	6,644	9,056	9,076
Experimental year	2,455	2,419	7,116	8,049	9,571	10,468
Absolute change	–78	–13	593	1,405	515	1,392
1-Tailed P value	.33		.046*		.058*	
November 30[b]						
Baseline year	2,873	2,741	7,396	7,664	10,269	10,405
Experimental year	2,754	2,700	8,163	9,016	10,917	11,716
Absolute change	–119	–41	767	1,352	648	1,311
1-Tailed P value	.31		.155		.159	

*$p < .10$

[a]Excludes period from 10/1 to 11/10.

[b]Includes period from 10/1 to 11/10/89.

implemented as planned. Because others may disagree, however, we present the data for all four of the time periods defined above.[6]

Table 1 presents the raw data for differences in hard, soft, and total citizen calls about crime for each of the four periods, as well as the significance levels for the mean Time 1 to Time 2 differences per hot spot between treatment and control groups as calculated from a mixed model ANOVA test taking randomization block into account. It shows that total crime calls and calls about soft crime increased from the baseline to the experimental year in both treatment

[6]We used a mixed-model analysis of variance, taking into account the effects of randomization block and treatment group as well as the interaction between block and treatment group. Each significant finding was subjected to tests for stability. We examined the effects of removing and including blocks of cases, of transforming the distributions of events, and of results obtained by using less powerful rank-ordering techniques, including the nonparametric combined independent Mann-Whitney rank order test. All tests produced the same results in the call analysis.

and control groups, while calls about hard crime decreased in both groups from the baseline to the experimental year. Thus the analysis centers on the *differences of differences* between the baseline and the experimental years, comparing experimental with control hot spots.

Figure 2 shows that the predicted effect, on total crime calls, of the reduced difference in patrol dosage appears in August, on schedule. At that time the experimental group fails for the first time to show a more favorable absolute difference, in calls from the same period in the prior year, than the control group. In every month before August, when the experimental group received far more police presence than the control group, the Time-1-to-Time-2 change in total calls had been more favorable for the experimental group. The August violation of that pattern disappeared in September but returned in October, when the data on calls became questionable. The violation of the predicted difference disappeared again in November, when the new CAD system was thought to be reliably established.

Table 2 presents the absolute baseline-experimental percentage differences and the difference of those differences between experimental and control hot spots as computed by a mixed-model analysis of variance using the five-block design. The effect of increasing patrol is greater on total and soft crime calls than on hard crime. Soft crime effects are strong in every period except the full year including the CAD changeover errors; they range in magnitude of relative percentage differences (experimental group baseline to experimental year percentage change minus control group baseline to experimental year percentage change) from 7 percent for the full year to 16 percent for the period ending June 15. The effects for total crime calls are similar but attenuated because the soft crime calls account for most of the total crime calls.[7]

The concept of percentage difference is presented conservatively; we compare absolute percentage changes rather than the percentage difference of percentage differences. That is, even for the full year we could say that the increase in soft crime calls was 75 percent greater in the control group than in the

[7]Whether these differences are a function of a displacement of citizens' calls onto the officers already present at hot spots is an interesting question; it reveals the failure of this design to eliminate the problem of interpreting the effects of police presence on citizens' propensity to call police, given a reason to do so. Adding in the police-generated calls made at the hot spot addresses is one proposed solution, for which we thank Professor Carl Klockars. We find this solution unsatisfactory, however, because it cannot distinguish events that citizens report to police at the scene (and would have called 911 to report, had no police been there) from events that police call in about (such as car checks), and about which citizens would never have called 911. Because of the small number of minutes when police are present, even in the experimental hot spots, any displacement of citizens' calls seems likely to be minimal, whereas the generation of police-initiated calls while they are assigned to the hot spots, as we know from direct observation in the police cars, is quite substantial. As predicted by both interpretations of this indicator, the addition of police-generated crime calls to the citizen-generated calls creates no significant differences between treatment groups in any of the time periods or crime types (data is not displayed). The addition of an hour per day of patrol presence accounts at most for one-eighth of the 50 percent of calls generated between 7 P.M. and 3 A.M. or 6.25 percent of all calls. Thus the maximum displacement of citizens' calls from 911 to police would seem to be less than half of the measured crime reduction of 13 percent or more relative to the control trend.

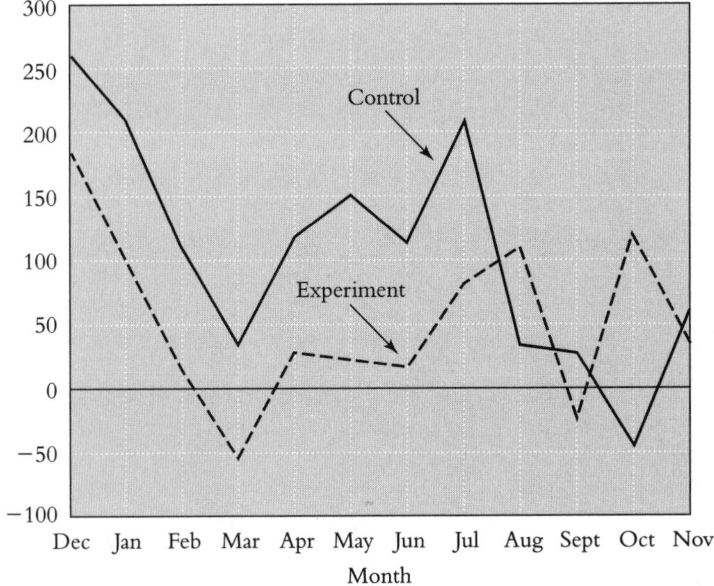

FIGURE 2. Absolute Differences from Baseline to Experimental Year in Total Crime Calls by Month and Treatment Group

Table 2. Percentage Changes of Crime Calls from Baseline to Experimental Year, by Time Period, Treatment Group, and Significance Levels of Mixed-Model ANOVA Tests

	HARD CRIME			SOFT CRIME			TOTAL CRIME		
Time Period	Exp.	Control	Difference	Exp.	Control	Difference	Exp.	Control	Difference
June 15 Percent change	–6.3	–1.4	–4.9	10.6	26.5	–15.9	5.6	18.7	–13.1
July 31 Percent change	–6.2	–.3	–5.9	11.1	25.9	–14.8	6.1	18.7	–12.6
November 30[a] Percent change	–3.1	–.5	–2.6	9.1	21.1	–12.0	5.7	15.3	–9.6
November 30[b] Percent change	–4.1	–1.5	–2.6	10.4	17.6	–7.2	6.3	12.6	–6.3

[a]Excludes period from 10/1 to 11/10.

[b]Includes period from 10/1 to 11/10.

experimental group (17.6 percent divided by 10.4 percent). By subtracting the percentage differences rather than dividing them, we focus the analysis on the magnitude of crime differences associated with more patrol rather than on its proportionate effect.

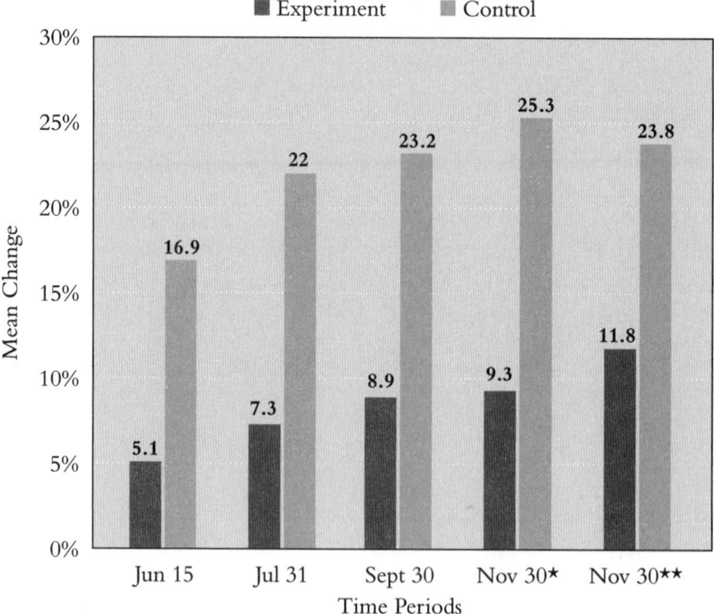

FIGURE 3. Percentage Change from Baseline to Experimental Year in Total Crime Calls Per Hot Spot by Treatment Group and Period

Figure 3 reports and illustrates the mean Time 1/Time 2 differences in calls for the experimental and the control groups, using different cutoff dates for the experiment. It is clear that no matter what cutoff date is selected, the increase in citizen calls in the 55 control hot spots is substantially greater than in the 55 experimental hot spots. The absolute size of the difference at any one hot spot is quite modest, however—about one fewer crime call per month.

Dependent Variable 2: Differences in Observed Crime and Disorder

The disorder analysis shows the most striking differences between the experimental and the control groups of any analyses. Table 3 displays the percentage of minutes of observations in different time periods in which disorderly public conduct was observed, by treatment group.[8] For the entire experimental period, we find a significant relative difference of 25 percent less disorder in the experimental than in the control group. For the two periods in which the experiment

[8]Because more than one disorder could have occurred simultaneously, Table 3 actually represents a ratio between observed minutes of all disorders and minutes of observations.

Table 3. Minutes of Disorder Observed in Experimental and Control Groups Compared with ANOVA Tests Controlled for Blocking

Period and Group	Minutes of Disorder	Minutes of Observations	Mean Ratio Per Hot Spot
Entire Year			
Experimental	5,855	225,991	.026
Control	8,623	226,295	.038
1-Tailed P value			.022*
Until 6/15/89			
Experimental	2,267	121,363	.019
Control	4,493	122,736	.037
1-Tailed P value			.006*
Until 7/31/89			
Experimental	3,545	148,617	.024
Control	5,915	149,889	.040
1-Tailed P value			.007*

*$p < .10$

had the greatest integrity (ending June 15 or July 31), the effect was even stronger: half as much disorder was observed in the experimental group as in the control. The absolute difference of only 2 percent of all observed minutes versus 4 percent reflects a difference, in odds of encountering a disorder, between 1 in 50 and 1 in 25. For a resident or user of any cluster of addresses, this difference is noticeable and substantial.

This large relative difference is not due simply to a deterrent effect on disorder while police are present. Only 6 percent (209 of 3,513) of observed disorder events began while police were present across the entire observed sample. Koper (1995) reports significant differences in observed disorders between experimental and control groups when police are *not* present—up to 65 percent less criminal disorder in the experimentals.

An analysis of 13 specific types of disorder for the entire year shows that the greatest effects (in which ratios of control disorder incidents to experimental disorder incidents exceeded 1.5 to 1) were on the categories of person down (on the ground), drug activity, vandalism, solicitation for prostitution, and assault. We found no difference, however, in observations of persons apparently drunk or drugged, the largest single category of disorder (but perhaps the one theoretically least deterrable by police presence).

Table 3 displays the difference between experimental and control groups in observed disorder ratios. One-tailed P values are derived from ANOVA tests taking into account the five blocks used for the original random assignment of all 110 hot spots, only 100 of which were observed. All ten unobserved spots (five experimentals and five controls) were in the same randomization block because the blocks were stratified by volume of hard crime calls. That block is fortunately the largest, with 58 hot spots, of which observations on ten (17%) are missing. The analysis simply treats those cases as missing data. No matter what time period we examine, these experimental year treatment group differences in observed disorder ratios are highly unlikely to be due to chance sampling fluctuations.[9]

CONCLUSIONS

These results show clear, if modest, general deterrent effects of substantial increases in police presence in crime hot spots. Just as police strikes reveal major increases in crime due to major reductions in police presence (Makinen and Takala 1980; Russell 1975), our findings show that the difference in crime is proportionate to the difference in police. If urban police agencies decided to assign even higher priority to hot spot patrols, the magnitude of the crime reductions might be even greater.

This conclusion, however, presents two problems. One is that the effects of police on crime in hot spots may be attenuated by displacement of that crime to other locations. Absent any test of that interpretation, we cannot rule out the claim that more police will push crime around rather than preventing it. Yet in light of the strong conclusions drawn about the Kansas City Preventive Patrol Experiment (Kelling et al 1974), even these results falsify the claim that patrol has no effect on crime at all.

Although we cannot conclude that these findings show a general deterrent effect of police presence throughout the community, we can claim evidence of place-specific "micro-deterrence." Even if police patrol pushes the crime elsewhere, it has been generally deterred by police presence in that location. The concept of deterrence is based on a rational calculation of risks and benefits. The prevention of crime and disorder in experimental hot spots, even when police are not there, is consistent with the hypotheses of apprehension and punishment in that place. This may be the same mechanism that causes displacement to a location where the fear of punishment is less, but it also fits the micro-general deterrence model precisely.

A second, different problem in recommending more hot spot patrols is that police may find directed patrol distasteful. The deterrent findings suggest that the more the time police stay in a hot spot, the less opportunity they will have to exercise police powers. This is good for the community but can be boring for the police. Rather than preventing crime by keeping hot spots cool, most police would prefer to catch criminals after crime has already occurred and the harm has been done. Prevention lacks glamour; apprehensions offer the excitement of the chase. A substantial change to a community policing philosophy could make hot spot patrols more interesting, especially if police leave their cars

[9]The P values in Table 3 are derived from an ANOVA design in which the effects of treatment group and block are included. The interaction between treatment type and block is not statistically significant, and is excluded from the model.

and talk to frequent users of the hot spots. But historically the resistance to such a change has been formidable.

More detailed analysis suggests how to minimize police resistance without a major philosophical change. The greatest deterrent effect may be produced not by police staying in the same hot spot for extended periods, but by police roving from hot spot to hot spot, staying in each for only a limited time. In this issue, Koper (1995) reports a curvilinear effect of the duration of police presence in hot spots on the amount of time that elapses until the first disorder or crime event is observed after police leave. The optimal length of a hot spot patrol appears to be about 12 minutes. This should be well within the police boredom threshold, allowing them to move on to the next hot spot to see who might be causing trouble upon their arrival.

This experiment remains unreplicated, and may be limited in external validity to the time and place where it was conducted. We urge caution in generalizing its results to other settings. At the same time, we conclude that the experiment offers a more powerful and more externally valid test of the patrol deterrence hypothesis than the Kansas City experiment. At the very least, it is time for criminologists to stop saying "there is no evidence" that police patrol can affect crime.

REFERENCES

Barr, R. and K. Pease (1990). "Crime Placement, Displacement, and Deflection." In M. Tonry and N. Morris (eds.) *Crime and Justice,* Vol. 12, pp. 227–318. Chicago: University of Chicago Press.

Boydstun, J. (1975). *San Diego Field Interrogation: Final Report.* Washington, DC: Police Foundation.

Buerger, M. E., E. G. Cohn, and A. J. Petrosino (1995). "Defining the Hot Spots of Crime: Operationalizing Theoretical Concepts for Field Research." In D. A. Weisburd and J. E. Eck (eds.), *Crime and Place: Crime Prevention Studies,* Vol. 4. Monsey, NY: Criminal Justice Press.

Chaiken, J. (1978). "What is Known About Deterrent Effects of Police Activities." pp. 109–36. In J. Cromer, ed., *Preventing Crime.* Beverly Hills, California: Sage.

Chaiken, J., M. W. Lawless, and K. A. Stevenson (1974). "The Impact of Police Activity on Subway Crime." *Urban Analysis* 3:173–205.

Cohen, J. (1977). *Statistical Power Analysis for the Behavioral Sciences.* NY: Academic Press.

Cornish, D. B. and R. V. Clarke, eds. (1986). *The Reasoning Criminal: Rational Choice Perspectives on Offending.* New York: Springer-Verlag.

—— (1987). "Understanding Crime Displacement: An Application of Rational Choice Theory." *Criminology* 25:933–47.

Dennis, M. L. (1988). "Implementing Randomized Field Experiments: An Analysis of Criminal and Civil Justice Research." Doctoral dissertation, Northwestern University, Department of Psychology.

Farrington. D. P. (1982). "Randomized Experiments on Crime and Justice." In M. Tonry and N. Morris (eds.), *Crime and Justice: An Annual Review of Research,* Vol. 4, pp. 257–308. Chicago: University of Chicago Press.

Felson, M. (1994). *Crime and Everyday Life.* Thousand Oaks, CA: Pine Forge Press.

Fielding, H. ([1751] 1977). *An Enquiry into the Causes of the Late Increase of Robbers.* Montclair, NJ: Patterson-Smith.

Fienberg, S., K. Larntz, and A. J. Reiss Jr. (1976). "Redesigning the Kansas City Preventive Patrol Experiment." *Evaluation* 3:124–31.

Freiman, J. A., T. C. Chalmers, H. Smith Jr., and R. R. Kuebler (1978). "The Importance of Beta, the Type II Error and Sample Size in the Design and Interpretation of the Randomized Controlled Trial: A survey of 71 'Negative' Trials." *New England Journal of Medicine* 299:690–4.

Gottfredson, M. and T. Hirschi (1990). *A General Theory of Crime.* Stanford: Stanford University Press.

Green, L. (1995). "Cleaning Up Drug Hot Spots in Oakland, California: The Displacement and Diffusion Effects." *Justice Quarterly.*

Kelling, G., A. M. Pate, D. Dieckman, and C. Brown (1974a). *The Kansas City Preventive Patrol Experiment: Technical Report.* Washington, DC: Police Foundation.

—— (1974b). *The Kansas City Preventive Patrol Experiment: Technical Report.* Washington, DC: Police Foundation.

Klockars, C., ed. (1983). *Thinking about Police.* New York: McGraw-Hill.

Koper, C. (1995). "Just Enough Police Presence: Reducing Crime and Disorderly Behavior by Optimizing Patrol Time in Crime Hot Spots." *Justice Quarterly.*

Larson, R. C. (1975). "What Happened to Patrol Operations in Kansas City?" *Journal of Criminal Justice* 3:267–97.

Makinen, T. and H. Takala (1980). "The 1976 Police Strike in Finland." *Scandinavian Studies in Criminology* 7:87–106.

Matthews, R. (1986). *Policing Prostitution: A Multi-Agency Approach.* London: Middlesex Polytechnic Centre for Criminology.

McNamara, J. (1974). "Foreword" In Kelling, et al, 1974a.

Pate, A. M. and G. L. Kelling (1975). "A Response to 'What Happened to Patrol Operations in Kansas City?' " *Journal of Criminal Justice* 3:299–330.

Press, S. J. (1971). *Some Effects of an Increase in Police Manpower in the 20th Precinct of New York.* New York: New York City RAND Institute.

Reiss, A. J., Jr. (1985). *Policing a City's Central District: The Oakland Story.* Washington, DC: National Institute of Justice.

Russell, F. (1975). *A City in Terror: 1919—The Boston Police Strike.* New York: Viking.

Schnelle, J. F., R. E. Kirchner Jr., J. D. Casey, P. H. Uselton Jr., and M. P. McNees (1977). "Patrol Evaluation Research: A Multiple-Baseline Analysis of Saturation Police Patrolling during Day and Night Hours." *Journal of Applied Behavior Analysis* 10:33–40.

Sherman, L. W. and D. Weisburd (1995). "Does Patrol Prevent Crime? The Minneapolis Hot Spots Experiment" In Koicki Miyazawa and Setsuo Miyazawa (eds.), *Crime Presentation In The Urban Community.* Boston: Kluwer.

Sherman, L. W. (1986). "Policing Communities: What Works?" In A. J. Reiss Jr. and M. Tonry (eds.), *Communities and Crime,* pp. 343–86. Chicago: University of Chicago Press.

—— (1990). "Police Crackdowns: Initial and Residual Deterrence." In M. Tonry and N. Morris (eds.), *Crime and Justice,* Vol. 12, pp. 1–48. Chicago: University of Chicago Press.

Sherman, L. W., P. R. Gartin, and M. E. Buerger (1989). "Hot Spots of Predatory Crime: Routine Activities and the Criminology of Place." *Criminology* 27:27–55.

Skogan, W. (1990). *Disorder and Decline.* New York: Free Press.

Skolnick, J. and D. Bayley (1986). *The New Blue Line.* New York: Free Press.

Weinstein, G. S. and B. Levin (1989). "Effect of Crossover on the Statistical Power of Randomized Studies." *Annals of Thoracic Surgery* 48:490–5.

Weisburd D. A., with Anthony Petrosino and Gail Mason (1993). "Design Sensitivity in Criminal Justice Experiments: Reassessing the Relationship between Sample Size and Statistical Power." In M. Tonry and N. Morris (eds.), *Crime and Justice,* Vol. 17, pp. 337–89. Chicago: University of Chicago Press.

Weisburd, D. A. and L. Green (1995). "Measuring Immediate Spatial Displacement: Methodological Issues and Problems." In D. Weisburd and J.E. Eck (eds.), *Crime and Place: Crime Prevention Studies,* Vol. 4. Monsey, NY: Criminal Justice Press.

Zimring, F. (1978). "Policy Experiments in General Deterrence, 1970–75." In A. Blumstein, J. Cohen, and D. Nagin (eds.), *Deterrence and Incapacitation: Estimating the Effects of Criminal Sanctions on Crime Rates,* pp. 140–73. Washington, DC: National Academy of Sciences.

DISCUSSION QUESTIONS

1. Briefly, as described by the authors, what were the weaknesses of previous research that the authors addressed in this study?
2. What was the control group and how was it selected? What purpose did the control group serve in the study?
3. As discussed by the authors, why was it so important to have those in the study agency (e.g., the police chief, police officers) committed to the study? What might have happened if they were not as committed as they were?
4. What did the authors conclude from this study?

PART III

Survey Research

The three articles included in this part illustrate the use of survey methods. As discussed in Part I, survey research usually involves the collection of data from a large group of subjects through the use of questionnaires (self-administered or mail) or interviews (face-to-face or telephone). Interviews as a survey research method are generally more structured than those in field research. This type of research is versatile in its purpose; survey research studies have been conducted in order to explore, describe, or explain particular phenomena. Typically, survey research studies produce quantitative data and these data are analyzed to examine statistical relationships among variables. Survey research studies are sometimes criticized because of the artificiality of the survey instruments and the potential for errors to be introduced into the data because of factors unique to the method (e.g., question wording and order, nonresponse bias; see your text for the details).

The articles included here reflect much of the diversity of the method. Each study focused on a different type of respondent and population, had a different purpose, used a different survey method to collect the data, and used different procedures in the analyses of the data. For instance, Frank et al. (1996) were interested in describing the differences between white and African American residents' attitudes toward the police. As discussed in the authors' commentary and the article, most of the previous research that has examined this issue has found that racial minorities (namely African American) have more negative attitudes toward the police than the racial majority (namely white). But what happens if this relationship is examined in a city where African Americans are the majority and white individuals are the minority? To answer this question, the authors analyzed data collected through phone interviews with 560 residents of Detroit, a city where whites represent a minority. Structured, close-ended questions regarding the respondents' race and other characteristics along with questions about attitudes toward the police were asked of all respondents.

In comparing African Americans with white respondents on attitudes toward the police, it was found that African American respondents held much more favorable attitudes toward the police than white respondents. Additional statistical analyses showed that race had a strong influence on the attitudes held. These findings suggest that attitudes toward the police are in large part a function of the racial makeup of the city in which respondents live. In Detroit, white residents are the minority, and their collective attitudes toward the police appear to reflect the traditional minority viewpoint. As discussed in the article, these findings may have important implications regarding police efforts to improve citizens' attitudes toward the police.

The article by Singer et al. (1993) sought to examine the relationship between preference for music, particularly heavy metal music, and delinquency among high school youth. Much has been written in the media about the assumed linkage between the negative messages offered in various types of music (e.g., rap) and the corresponding destructive acts of the individuals who "consume" this music. To examine this issue, the researchers conducted face-to-face structured interviews with 705 high school youth in a largely white, affluent, suburban community. The researchers asked respondents questions about parental supervision and attachment, their school performance, delinquency of their friends, their own delinquency, and their preference of music, and then sought to examine relationships among these variables. Among the findings of the researchers was that the youth who preferred heavy metal music reported significantly more delinquency than other youth, and that youth who preferred heavy metal music and scored low in parental supervision had especially high rates of delinquency. So does listening to heavy metal music cause delinquency? Not necessarily. The article explains why.

In the last article in this part, Decker and Rosenfeld (1995) describe the behavioral adaptations used by arrestees to protect against the threat of HIV exposure. A purposive sample of 959 respondents who were arrested and detained in jail in St. Louis were interviewed. In conducting the face-to-face interviews, the researchers asked open- and close-ended questions about drug use, sexual behaviors, and methods used by the respondents to ensure safe sex. As seen in the article, the open-ended questions allowed for a qualitative dimension in the analysis of the data. The researchers found that respondents reported a variety of precautionary adaptations but most reflect serious misinformation, myth, and folk belief (e.g., wash with gasoline after intercourse, the earwax test, etc.). This study provides a familiarity with the sort of preventive measures used by this high-risk segment of the population. As noted by the authors, the findings of the study call attention to the need for alternative interventions in reducing risky sexual behaviors among this group, and the authors provide suggestions regarding these interventions.

4

Reassessing the Impact of Race on Citizens' Attitudes Toward the Police

A Research Note

JAMES FRANK, University of Cincinnati
STEVEN G. BRANDL, University of Wisconsin—Milwaukee
FRANCIS T. CULLEN, University of Cincinnati
AMY STICHMAN, University of Cincinnati

COMMENTARY

The data for this article were collected as part of a larger project funded by the National Institute of Justice (NIJ) that focused on the effectiveness of narcotics enforcement (primarily crackdowns) in four neighborhoods in the city of Detroit. While the findings of the article you are about to read are based on data collected through telephone interviews of citizens who resided in the four target neighborhoods, the larger project involved the gathering of data from four other sources: (1) observations of narcotics enforcement teams in the neighborhoods in order to document the nature of the intervention, (2) official police department reports of narcotics-related arrests, charges, and seizures of property, (3) interviews with narcotics officers regarding their perceptions of the effectiveness of crackdowns on reducing drug buying and selling, and (4) interviews with arrested offenders concerning their perceptions of the risk of arrest for drug offenses.

The focus on the effectiveness of the police crackdown strategy and the need to collect data that could provide information on the content and impact of the intervention influenced how the sample of citizens was selected.

Source: Justice Quarterly, Vol. 13 No. 2, June 1996, pp. 321-334. © 1996. Reprinted by permission of the Academy of Criminal Justice Sciences.

This research was particularly supported by Grant 89-DD-CX-0049 from the National Institute of Justice. Points of view are those of the authors and do not necessarily represent the position of the U.S. Department of Justice. The authors are grateful for the comments and suggestions of the anonymous *JQ* referees.

Namely, citizens who were likely to have viewed or otherwise acquired information about the crackdown were the focus of the sample selection method. In order to increase the possibility that citizens who met these information criteria were included in the sample, a stratified (by city block) random sample selection method was used. Using a reverse telephone directory (listings by streets instead of by name), two households and four alternate households were randomly selected from each block in the study neighborhoods. When households were contacted, the interviewers (who worked in the Survey Research Center at Michigan State University) asked to speak with someone 18 years old or over who had lived at that address for at least the past six months.

The idea for the present article emerged after we examined the frequencies and distributions of the responses to the attitude questions listed in the survey. It appeared that there were substantial differences in the attitude responses of the different racial demographic groups in the sample. The data seemed to show that white people had more negative attitudes toward the police than African Americans. This pattern is just the opposite of what has been found in virtually all other studies that have examined the relationship between citizens' attitudes toward the police and race. These unusual findings instigated much discussion among ourselves as to why this might be the case in these data. There is little reason to believe that these data are biased or just simply wrong. Accordingly, we concluded that perhaps the findings are best explained by the fact that in Detroit, white people are a minority. Maybe minorities, either black or white, tend to express more negative attitudes toward the police than the majority. In this case, maybe whites have adopted the attitudes previously held by African Americans. We explore and discuss these issues in the following article.

ABSTRACT This paper reassesses the relationship between race and attitudes toward the police. Using data obtained through a telephone interview survey of 560 residents of Detroit, the study contradicts previous research by finding that blacks hold more favorable attitudes toward the police than do whites. To explain these findings, we argue that as the social context of cities changes, so might the relationship between race and citizens' attitudes toward the police.

Research has shown consistently that nonwhites—especially African-Americans—express less favorable attitudes toward the police than do whites (e.g., Bayley and Mendelsohn 1968; Boggs and Gallier 1965; Bordua and Tifft 1971; Erez 1984; Hindelang 1974; Jacob 1971; Parks 1984; Percy 1980; Reasons and Wirth 1975; Scaglion and Condon 1980). Since most of these studies on attitudes toward the police were conducted, however, considerable changes have occurred in policing and in the social context in which urban police agencies operate. In particular, many urban communities are represented increasingly by African-Americans and members of other racial minority groups. Before the 1960s, all major cities were led by white mayors and had predominantly white political machinery. Since the late 1960s, however, several cities have experienced what Eisinger (1980) calls an "ethnoracial political transition." According to Eisinger, this process refers to "the acquisition of formal executive office in a political jurisdiction by a member of a previously subordinate ethnic group that is now backed politically by a new, potentially durable working majority composed largely of or dominated by members of that group" (1980:5). Critical to such a transition are two factors: a new, growing black majority and a popularly elected black mayor. The simultaneous presence of these two ingredients translates into a "black political takeover."

At least as a partial cause of this transition and certainly as an accelerator, the once-dominant group tends to migrate from the city (i.e., "white flight") (Eisinger 1980; Wurdock 1981). Consequently the population demographics of cities that have undergone this transition are now quite different than they were just 10 years ago, and certainly 20 years ago; minority-group members now account for a far greater proportion of the population (Farley 1970; Massey and Denton 1988).[1] In addition, during this period of change for city populations, the representation of minority officers in police agencies has increased in large urban police departments that serve substantial minority populations.[2]

These changes are particularly apparent in Detroit, the site of this study. As shown in Table 1, the racial composition of Detroit was relatively constant until

[1]Listed below, for example, are the black population estimates for 1965 and 1990 for selected cities that serve a substantial minority population. The 1965 estimates are taken from the Center for Research in Marketing, as reported by the National Advisory Commission on Civil Disorders (1968) and represent percent nonwhite population. The 1990 estimates are taken from U.S. Census data and represent percent black population. The increased representation of blacks in the city populations is evident.

City	1965	1990
Detroit	39%	75%
Washington, DC	63%	66%
Atlanta	38%	67%
Chicago	27%	39%
Memphis	38%	55%
New Orleans	41%	62%
Baltimore	41%	59%

[2]Listed below are estimates of the representation of black officers in 1967 and 1992 for the same cities as listed above. The 1967 estimates are taken from the National Advisory Commission on Civil Disorders (1968) and represent percentages of nonwhite officers. The 1992 estimates are taken from the U.S. Department of Justice (1992) LEMAS study and represent percentages of black officers. Again, the increased representation of black officers is quite apparent.

City	1967	1992
Detroit	5%	48%
Washington, DC	21%	75%
Atlanta	10%	64%
Chicago	17%	24%
Memphis	5%	32%
New Orleans	4%	39%
Baltimore	7%	26%

Table 1. Black Population, Detroit

Year	Total Population	Black Population	% Black Population
1940	1,623,452	149,119	9.2
1950	1,849,568	298,875	16.2
1960	1,670,144	482,223	28.8
1970	1,514,063	672,605	43.6
1980	1,203,339	758,939	63.1
1990	1,027,974	778,456	75.7

Source: U.S. Bureau of Census, 1940–1990.

the 1960s, when the proportion of blacks in the population increased substantially and the representation of whites decreased. Between 1960 and 1980, the number of whites living in the city declined from 1,187,921 to 444,730 (71 percent to 37 percent of the population), while the African-American population increased from 482,223 to 758,939 (29 percent to 63 percent of the population). By 1990 more than three-fourths of the city's population was African-American; less than one-fourth was white.

These dramatic population changes made possible the popular election of African-Americans to positions in Detroit's state and city government (Rich 1989). In 1973, Coleman Young was elected the city's first African-American mayor, but he won only 2 percent of the votes in white precincts (Eisinger 1980); a black political takeover was in progress.

During his campaign for office, Young promised to reform the police department and to increase minority representation on the police force (which, in 1973, was 15 percent African-American). Once in office, he actively recruited black officers, instituted a policy requiring the promotion of an African-American for every white officer promoted, and vigorously enforced other affirmative action programs within the department (Hawkins and Thomas 1991; Rich 1989). In 1976 Mayor Young appointed Detroit's first African-American police chief.

When Coleman Young took office, the relationship between the police department and the African American community was hostile. The 1967 riots had reinforced each group's deeply rooted negative attitudes toward the other (Rich 1989). In the early 1970s, the city was plagued by a rate of civilian killings (mostly African-Americans) by the police which exceeded that of any other American city (Rich 1989). The mayor immediately sought to enact programs restricting the use of force by the police department (Hawkins and Thomas 1991). In addition, he set up police ministations throughout the city in an attempt to break down communication barriers between the police and community members.

The changes in the representation of African-Americans in the city population, in the police department, and in city politics may have influenced black residents' attitudes in several ways. First, increases in the visibility of black officers may have lessened the perception that minority communities are policed by "alien intruders" or an "occupying army" (Decker and Smith 1980; Wilson 1972). Second, the African-American community may have become large enough to justify changes in police policies that were demanded by this now-powerful constituency. Third, the black mayor may have been more responsive to the preferences of a growing African-American community, and policing concerns may have found a more receptive audience with the African-American police chief and African-American officers (Saltzstein 1989). While feelings of alienation among African-Americans may have declined with such contextual changes, such feelings among whites may have increased correspondingly. If respondents live in a city with a predominantly African-American population, a police force composed of a near majority of African-American officers, and a government represented by African-Americans, including the offices of mayor and police chief, will black and white citizens' attitudes toward the police differ from the typical findings of existing research?

In this paper we report the results of analyses that address this question. Specifically, we compare the attitudes of black and white respondents on several issues and find that in Detroit blacks hold more favorable attitudes toward the police than do whites. We suggest that insofar as these findings are generalizable, the changing social context of cities may require a reexamination of the relationship between race and citizens' attitudes toward the police.

METHOD

Sample

Data for the study were drawn from a survey that we conducted as part of a larger study focusing on narcotics enforcement in four areas in the City of Detroit.[3] We used a cluster sampling procedure to ensure that each block within the selected areas was represented. Households were selected randomly from each blockface and then were contacted by telephone. Interviewers asked to speak with someone age 18 or older who had lived in the home for at least six months. If no eligible respondent was at home, a return call was scheduled; this process was repeated until a refusal was received or numerous contacts had been attempted without success. The interviews were conducted in April 1991; the response rate was 74 percent ($N = 560$).

Table 2 shows the demographic composition of the sample and, on the basis of 1990 census data, the four areas from which the sample was drawn. These areas are similar to the city overall in race, gender, age, and other demographic characteristics. Like Detroit in general, the four areas are predominantly black and poor. The areas are located in the far east side, the northeast side, the far west

[3]The larger study consisted of a three-wave panel survey of the same population. For the present study we use data only from the third wave.

Table 2. Demographic Characteristics of Sample and Sample Areas

	SAMPLE							
	Blacks		Whites		Total		4 Areas Total	
Totals (*N*)	339		187		526		65,084[a]	
Gender	339		187		526		65,085	
Male	90	(26.5)	65	(34.8)	155	(29.5)	30,348	(46.6)
Female	249	(73.5)	122	(65.2)	371	(70.5)	34,737	(53.4)
Age	329		185		514		41,932[b]	
18–24	43	(13.1)	16	(8.6)	59	(11.5)	8,026	(19.1)
25–44	145	(44.1)	58	(31.4)	203	(39.5)	19,726	(47.0)
45–64	88	(26.7)	53	(28.7)	141	(27.4)	8,871	(21.2)
65+	53	(16.1)	58	(31.4)	111	(21.6)	5,309	(12.7)
Income	303		175		478			
$0–8,000	53	(17.5)	23	(13.1)	76	(15.9)		
$8,001–15,000	74	(24.4)	45	(25.7)	119	(24.9)	$15,318[c]	
$15,001–25,000	53	(17.5)	44	(25.1)	97	(20.3)		
Over $25,000	123	(40.6)	63	(36.0)	186	(38.9)		
Education	338		187		525		33,092[d]	
Elementary	29	(8.6)	16	(8.6)	45	(8.6)	4,276	(12.9)
Some high school	67	(19.8)	40	(21.4)	107	(20.4)	10,382	(31.4)
High school graduate	103	(30.5)	76	(40.6)	179	(34.1)	9,026	(27.3)
Some college	105	(31.1)	35	(18.7)	140	(26.7)	6,109	(18.5)
College graduate	34	(10.1)	20	(10.7)	54	(10.3)	3,299	(10.0)

Notes: Percentages are in parentheses.

Native Americans (*N* = 8), Asian-Americans (*N* = 3), Mexican-Americans (*N* = 4), others (*N* = 14), and missing data are excluded from sample tallies.

[a]Subgroup populations: African-American = 48,316 (74%); white = 13,530 (21%); other = 3,238 (5%).

[b]*N* = 41,932 because persons age 0–17 are not included in census data.

[c]Median income reported.

[d]*N* = 33,092 because only persons age 25 or older are included in the census data for the education measure.

side, and the south central area of the city. Each is predominantly residential; three of the four areas have business districts.

The representation of blacks and of whites in the sample is similar except for age and education: whites tend to be older (especially over 65) and less highly educated (especially see the difference in the proportion with "some college"). Table 2 also shows that the sample is more white, more female, older, wealthier, and better educated than the sample areas. Because the purpose of this study is to examine the influence of race on citizens' attitudes toward the police (and to control for other demographic characteristics in the process), the fact that this sample is not truly representative of the sample population most likely does not bias the results of this study. Most important is the fact that whites are a distinct minority in the city and in the four selected target areas.

Measures

In the present study we examine three attitudes toward the police: (1) global attitudes; (2) attitudes toward the job the police are doing in maintaining order on the streets and sidewalks; and (3) attitudes toward the job the police are doing in controlling the sale and use of drugs. In keeping with previous research (e.g., Brandl et al. 1994), we measured global attitudes by asking citizens "In general, how satisfied are you with the police? Are you very satisfied, somewhat satisfied, somewhat dissatisfied, or very dissatisfied?" This question was prefaced with the statement "Now let's talk about the police in your neighborhood." The other two attitude questions explored citizens' evaluations of the agency's performance of more specific police functions. In the question on drug-related attitudes, respondents were asked to evaluate the job "the police are doing controlling the street sale and use of illegal drugs in your neighborhood." We operationalized the third attitude by asking respondents "How good a job are the police doing to keep order on the streets and sidewalks in your neighborhood?" For each question the response options were "poor," "fair," "good," "very good," and "no opinion."

To create an overall scale, we factor-analyzed the three attitude items with the expectation that they were undimensional and tapped citizens' attitudes toward the police. Principal-components analysis confirmed this expectation.[4] We then used these three items to create the overall police attitude scale (Cronbach's alpha = .843). Scale scores, which we computed with factor scale coefficients, ranged from 2.28 to 9.13; higher scores indicated more favorable attitudes toward the police.

The multivariate analyses also included several items that potentially could confound the relationship between race and attitudes toward the police. First, research suggests that previous crime victimizations influence citizens' attitudes in this respect (Koenig 1980; Smith and Hawkins 1973). Individuals presumably hold the police responsible for crimes committed against them; thus the victimization experience tends to affect attitudes negatively. Kleinman and David (1973) suggest that blacks are more likely than whites to become victims of crime and that this fact helps to explain blacks' less positive attitudes. Accordingly we included as a control variable the number of victimizations the respondent had suffered during the past year.[5]

Second, citizens' experiences with the police have been shown to influence evaluations of overall police performance (Dean 1980; Parks 1984; Scaglion and Condon 1980; Zamble and Annesley 1987; also Mastrofski 1981). Existing research has concluded that the respondent's race appears to influence both the nature and the type of encounters with the police (Erez 1984; Hahn 1971;

---

[4]This analysis produced one significant factor with an eigenvalue of 2.283. All of the remaining factors had eigenvalues below .426.

[5]We measured crime victimization using four items that respondents answered either "yes" (if victimized) or "no" (if not victimized) during the past year. The items covered the typical property crimes (burglary and robbery) and one personal crime (assault). We scored the measure by totaling the number of offenses for which the person had been victimized.

Jacob 1971; Skogan 1991).[6] Research also has shown, however, that similar types of contacts do not necessarily elicit similar assessments and that global attitudes are more of an influence on these specific assessments than a consequence (Brandl et al. 1994). Nevertheless, as control variables in the analyses we used items measuring evaluations of the police in four types of experiences: calls for information, requests for assistance, situations in which the person was stopped by a police officer, and contact with police after being victimized. Respondents who had experienced one or more of these types of police-citizen contact during the six months preceding the interview were asked for their assessments of the police during that contact (e.g., "How satisfied were you with the way you were treated? Were you very satisfied, somewhat satisfied, somewhat dissatisfied, or very dissatisfied?"). In accordance with previous research (Dean 1980; Mastrofski 1981), we created a separate independent variable for each positive and each negative evaluation of a contact.[7]

Finally, we included demographic variables as controls: respondent's age, educational level, family income, and gender.[8]

Analysis

First we examine mean item scores and actual distributions to determine whether significant differences exist between white and African-American respondents' attitudes. Second, to examine the impact of race on attitudes, we estimate a series of regression equations, using the overall attitude scale and the individual attitude measures as dependent variables.

---

[6]Previous research found that African-Americans and Spanish-speaking Americans were more likely than whites to be involved in police-initiated interactions, that the experiences or interactions often involved a threat of sanctions by the police, and that these experiences were generally more intrusive in that they quite often included searches of the involved citizens (Erez 1984; Hahn 1971; Jacob 1971; Skogan 1991). Furthermore, officers' behavior during these encounters was often perceived by citizens as "abusive" in that citizen were more likely to report being pushed by the police and being called derogatory names (Erez 1984; Hahn 1971). For these reasons, researchers have assumed that negative contacts between African-Americans and the police were partially responsible for their less favorable attitudes. Yet when experiences with the police were examined in the present study, African-Americans (48 percent $N = 206$) were more likely than whites (26 percent $N = 137$) to state that they were "very satisfied" with police performance during the contact, and less likely to report that they were "very dissatisfied" (29 percent for African-Americans, 43 percent for whites). In any case, contact with the police is used as a control variable in this study.

[7]Each type of experience appears in the models as two variables that represent either negative or positive evaluations of each experience. If the person had a positive experience, we used the following codes: 2 = very satisfied, 1 = somewhat satisfied, 0 = no positive experience or no evaluation. Similarly, if the respondent reported a negative evaluation, we coded the response as 2 = very dissatisfied, 1 = somewhat dissatisfied, 0 = no negative experience or no evaluation. Because these evaluations are used as control variables, any observed effects of the respondents' race would be independent of citizens' evaluations.

[8]We used the following coding scheme for these variables: Age remains in its raw form; Education (1 = less than high school, 2 = some high school, 3 = completed high school, 4 = some college, 5 = completed college, 6 = some advanced college); Family Income (1 = 0–$8,000, 2 = $8,000–$15,000, 3 = $15,000–$25,000, 4 = more than $25,000); Gender (1 = male, 2 = female).

Table 3. Attitudes Toward the Police, by Respondent's Race

	RESPONDENT'S RACE			
Attitude Measures	**African-American**		**White**	
Global Satisfaction				
1 = Very dissatisfied	39	(11.7)	41	(22.5)
2 = Somewhat dissatisfied	55	(16.5)	45	(24.7)
3 = Somewhat satisfied	152	(45.5)	62	(34.1)
4 = Very satisfied	88	(26.3)	34	(18.7)
	N = 334		*N* = 182	
African-American mean = 2.87				
White mean = 2.49				
t-value = 4.19 *p* = .000				
Keeping Order on the Street				
1 = Poor	55	(16.8)	45	(25.0)
2 = Fair	110	(33.6)	70	(38.9)
3 = Good	94	(28.7)	44	(24.4)
4 = Very good	68	(20.8)	21	(11.7)
	N = 327		*N* = 180	
African-American mean = 2.54				
White mean = 2.22				
t-value = 3.40 *p* = .001				
Controlling the Sale and Use of Drugs				
1 = Poor	64	(19.9)	61	(36.3)
2 = Fair	107	(33.3)	55	(32.7)
3 = Good	88	(27.4)	39	(23.2)
4 = Very good	62	(19.3)	13	(7.7)
	N = 321		*N* = 168	
African-American mean = 2.46				
White mean = 2.02				
t-value = 4.70 *p* = .000				

Note: Percentages are in parentheses.

RESULTS

Attitudes by Race

Table 3 displays the distribution of responses to the three attitudinal measures by race. The mean level of satisfaction expressed by African-Americans is significantly higher than that expressed by whites for all three attitudinal measures (global satisfaction, $t = 4.06$, $p = .000$; keeping order, $t = 3.40$, $p = .001$; controlling drugs, $t = 4.70$, $p = .000$).

The mean scores for African-Americans and whites fall between "somewhat satisfied" and "somewhat dissatisfied" or between "fair" and "good," and thus indicate rather similar (but still statistically significant) neutral attitudes. The distribution of scores, however, particularly those at the extreme, shows more variance. For the global measure, African-Americans were more likely than whites to select "very satisfied" (26 percent versus 19 percent; whites were much more likely than African-Americans to select "very dissatisfied" (23 percent versus 12 percent). Similarly, for "keeping order," African-Americans were more likely than whites to select "very good" (21 percent versus 12 percent) and less likely than whites to select "poor" (17 percent versus 25 percent). The same pattern is evident for "controlling drugs": African-Americans were more likely than whites to state "very good" (19 percent versus 8 percent) and less likely to state "poor" (20 percent versus 36 percent).

Regression Analyses

To assess the influence of respondent's race on attitudes towards the police, we estimate four regression equations. The dependent variable in the first equation is the overall attitude scale. In each of the remaining equations, the dependent variable is one of the three attitude measures. The independent variable of primary interest is respondent's race, which is coded to make a positive coefficient indicate that African-Americans express more favorable attitudes (0 = white, 1 = African-American).

The remaining independent variables are included as controls. Our intention in these analyses is to control for variables that may confound the relationship between race and attitudes towards the police. Accordingly we include respondent's demographic characteristics (age, gender, family income, and education; see Decker 1981), along with citizens' incident-specific assessments of police performance (previous requests for information, requests for assistance, police-initiated stops, and contact after a victimization) and number of victimizations (see Dean 1980; Scaglion and Condon 1980; Skogan 1991).

Table 4 contains the results of these analyses. When the overall attitude scale is used as the dependent variable, the respondent's race has a statistically significant effect on attitudes toward the police: being African-American increases satisfaction with the police.

Table 4 displays similar findings for the influence of the respondent's race on each of the attitude items that we used to create the scale. The respondent's race is statistically significant and exerts a positive effect on global satisfaction with the police, on attitudes toward how well police are keeping order, and on evaluations of police performance concerning the sale and use of drugs.

The standardized regression coefficients for respondent's race also reveal that this variable exerts substantial influence in each of the four equations. For the attitude scale and the drug-related attitude, the magnitude of the beta for race is second largest of the included variables; for the "keeping order" attitude, race is the third most influential variable in the model (see Table 4). Respondent's race also exerts the third largest influence on citizens' global attitudes.

Table 4. OLS Regression Estimates of Attitude Measures

Independent Variables	Attitude Scale	Global Attitude	Keeping Order Attitude	Drug-Related Attitude
Race	.682*** (.18)	.284*** (.15)	.288*** (.15)	.349*** (.18)
Demographics				
Gender	.049 (.01)	–.033 (–.02)	–.017 (–.01)	.041 (.02)
Income	.073 (.04)	.006 (.01)	.065 (.07)	.029 (.03)
Education	.154 (.09)	.092* (.11)	.063 (.07)	.034 (.04)
Age	.020*** (.17)	.009*** (.17)	.010*** (.17)	.007* (.12)
Victimization				
Number of Victims	–.277* (–.10)	–.132* (–.09)	–.070 (–.05)	–.162* (–.11)
Evaluation of Experiences				
Pos. Information	.029 (.01)	.002 (.01)	.016 (.01)	.022 (.01)
Neg. Information	–.690*** (–.24)	–.398*** (–.28)	–.250*** (–.17)	–.273*** (–.18)
Pos. Assistance	.386* (.11)	.231** (.13)	.188** (.11)	.053 (.03)
Neg. Assistance	–.276 (–.07)	–.176 (–.08)	–.112 (–.05)	–.063 (–.03)
Pos. Stop	–.088 (–.02)	.018 (.01)	–.122 (–.05)	.014 (.01)
Neg. Stop	–.281 (–.05)	–.085 (–.03)	–.117 (–.04)	–.186 (–.06)
Pos. Victimization	.097 (.01)	–.101 (–.03)	–.081 (–.02)	.308 (.09)
Neg. Victimization	–.877* (–.11)	–.472** (–.12)	–.363 (–.09)	–.349 (–.08)
Adjusted R^2	.185	.205	.109	.118
N	445	471	464	445

Note: Entries are unstandardized coefficients with standardized coefficients in parentheses.

* = $p < .05$; ** = $p < .01$; *** = $p < .001$ (all two-tailed tests).

CONCLUSION

Contrary to prior research, we found that African-Americans not only held more favorable attitudes toward the police than did whites, but also were consistently more likely than whites to select the most favorable response category and less likely to choose the most negative option (see Furstenberg and Wellford 1973; Thomas and Hyman 1977). Intensity of attitudes is a significant feature because stronger attitudes are more likely to be recalled by an individual and may predispose him or her to act in a certain manner (Schuman and Presser 1981; Zanna, Olson, and Fazio 1980). Furthermore, important attitudes typically are more extreme than unimportant ones (Borgida and Howard-Pitney 1983); people who consider attitudes or the objects of attitudes unimportant tend to select the middle response options (Krosnick and Schuman 1988).

In attempting to explain these findings, once again we must highlight the respondents' context. In Detroit, African-Americans are a substantial majority of the population; the city has had a black mayor since 1973, and a significant number of major municipal government officeholders are black; nearly 50 percent of the police force is black, as are the chief and a substantial number of administrators in the department. When these factors are considered together, it seems plausible that they influence the traditional source of African-American attitudes. That is, negative attitudes toward the police are part of a larger belief system that includes negative attitudes toward authority exercised by a government composed of individuals who belong to a different racial or ethnic group. In Detroit, the people who perform the police function are not alien to African-Americans; instead they represent an indigenous force.

As control and power shifted in the city and as the institutional character of the city changed from white-dominated to black-dominated, citizens' attitudes toward the police might have changed correspondingly. Because whites are now a minority in the city, it is quite possible that they hold attitudes previously reserved for "minority"-group members. The whites who are unable or unwilling to leave the city, or who are otherwise trapped, may resist the perceived exploitation of "their city" by the new black majority. Perhaps one form of resistance to this exploitation and alienation is the sentiment toward the police, a visible representation of black power.

Some empirical evidence, albeit rather limited, exists to suggest that attitudes toward the police have changed along racial lines in Detroit. In a study conducted by Arthur Kornhauser in 1951 (Kornhauser 1952), at a time before the black political takeover, 42 percent of all African-Americans surveyed said that the police department was "not good" or "definitely bad." Only 11 percent of African-Americans said the police department was "very good." In comparison, 48 percent of the overall sample (blacks and whites) rated the police department as "very good," and 40 percent rated it "fairly good" (score distributions for whites only were not provided). Thus there is some evidence suggesting that since 1951, African-American sentiments toward the police in Detroit have improved considerably.

The findings and associated arguments of this study are merely suggestive because we were unable to vary the respondents' social context. Therefore we could not directly examine the impact of the social context on attitudes toward the police. A multijurisdictional study including other cities that have experienced an "ethnoracial political transition" (e.g., Atlanta, Washington, DC), or a longitudinal study focusing on cities that have not experienced such a transition, would permit a more rigorous test of the influence of social context on attitudes toward the police.

REFERENCES

Bayley, D. and H. Mendelsohn. 1968. *Minorities and the Police: Confrontation in America.* New York: Free Press.

Boggs, S. L. and S. F. Galliher. 1965. "Evaluating the Police: A Comparison of Black Street and Household Respondents." *Social Problems* 13:393–406.

Bordua, D. J. and L. L. Tifft. 1971. "Citizen Interview, Organizational Feedback, and Police-Community Relations Decisions." *Law and Society Review* 6:155–82.

Borgida, E. B. and B. Howard-Pitney. 1983. "Personal Involvement and the Robustness of Personal Salience Effects." *Journal of Personality and Social Psychology* 45:460–70.

Brandl, S. G., J. Frank, R. W. Worden, and T. S. Bynum. 1994. "Global and Specific Attitudes toward the Police: Disentangling the Relationship." *Justice Quarterly* 11:119–34.

Dean, D. 1980. "Citizen Ratings of the Police: The Difference Police Contact Makes." *Law and Policy Quarterly* 2:445–71.

Decker, S. 1981. "Citizen Attitudes toward the Police: A Review of Past Findings and Suggestions for Future Policy." *Journal of Police Science and Administration* 9:80–87.

Decker, S. and R. L. Smith. 1980. "Police Minority Recruitment: A Note on Its Effectiveness in Improving Black Evaluations of the Police." *Journal of Criminal Justice* 8:387–93.

Eisinger, P. K. 1980. *The Politics of Displacement.* New York: Academic Press.

Erez, E. 1984. "Self-Defined Desert and Citizen's Assessment of the Police." *Journal of Criminal Law and Criminology* 75:1276–99.

Farley, R. 1970. "The Changing Distribution of Negroes within Metropolitan Areas: The Emergence of Black Suburbs." *American Journal of Sociology* 75:512–29.

Furstenberg, F. and C. F. Wellford. 1973. "Calling the Police: The Evaluation of Police Service." *Law and Society Review* 8:393–406.

Hahn, R. 1971. "Ghetto Assessments of Police Protection Authority." *Law and Society Review* 6:183–94.

Hawkins, H. and R. Thomas. 1991. "White Policing of Black Populations: A History of Race and Social Control in America." Pp. 65–86 in *Out of Order? Policing Black People,* edited by E. Cashmore and E. McLaughlin. New York: Routledge.

Hindelang, M. J. 1974. "Public Opinion Regarding Crime, Criminal Justice and Related Topics." *Journal of Research in Crime and Delinquency* 11:101–16.

Jacob, H. 1971. "Black and White Perceptions of Justice in the City." *Law and Society Review* 5:69–89.

Kleinman, P. and D. David. 1973. "Victimization and Perception of Crime in a Ghetto Community." *Criminology* 11:307–43.

Koenig, D. J. 1980. "The Effect of Crime Victimization and Judicial or Police Contacts on Public Attitudes toward the Local Police." *Journal of Police Science and Administration* 8:243–49.

Krosnick, J. A. and H. Schuman. 1988. "Attitude Intensity, Importance, and Certainty and Susceptibility to Response Effects." *Journal of Personality and Social Psychology* 54:940–52.

Massey, D. S. and N. A. Denton. 1988. "Suburbanization and Segregation in U.S. Metropolitan Areas." *American Journal of Sociology* 94:592–626.

Mastrofski, S. 1981. "Surveying Clients to Assess Police Performance." *Evaluation Review* 5:397–408.

National Advisory Commission. 1968. *Report.* Washington, DC: U.S. Government Printing Office.

Parks, R. B. 1984. "Linking Objective and Subjective Measures of Performance." *Public Administration Review* 44:118–27.

Percy, S. L. 1980. "Response Time and Citizen Evaluation of Police." *Journal of Police Science and Administration* 8:75–86.

Reasons, C. E. and B. A. Wirth. 1975. "Police Community Relations Units: A National Survey." *Journal of Social Issues* 31:27–33.

Rich, W. C. 1989. *Coleman Young and Detroit Politics.* Detroit: Wayne State University Press.

Saltzstein, G. H. 1989. "Black Mayors and Police Policies." *Journal of Politics* 51:525–44.

Scaglion, R. and R. G. Condon. 1980. "Determinants of Attitudes toward City Police." *Criminology* 17:485–94.

Schuman, H. and B. Gruenberg. 1972. "Dissatisfaction with City Services: Is Race an Important Factor?" Pp. 369–92 in *People and Politics in Urban Society,* edited by H. Hahn. Beverly Hills: Sage.

Schuman, H. and S. Presser. 1981. *Questions and Answers in Attitude Surveys.* New York: Academic Press.

Skogan, W. 1991. "The Impact of Routine Encounters with the Police." Presented at the annual meetings of the American Society of Criminology, San Francisco.

Smith, P. E. and R. O. Hawkins. 1973. "Victimization, Types of Citizen-Police Contacts and Attitudes toward the Police." *Law and Society Review* 8:135–52.

Thomas, C. W. and J. Hyman. 1977. "Perceptions of Crime, Fear of Victimization and Public Perceptions of Police Performance." *Journal of Police Science and Administration* 5:305–17.

U.S. Bureau of the Census. *Census of the Population.* 1940, 1950, 1960, 1970, 1980, 1990. Washington, DC: U.S. Government Printing Office.

U.S. Department of Justice, Bureau of Justice Statistics. 1992. *Law Enforcement Management and Administrative Statistics, 1990.* Computer file. Ann Arbor: Inter-University Consortium for Political and Social Research.

Wilson, J. Q. 1972. "The Police in the Ghetto." Pp. 51–90 in *The Police and the Community,* edited by B. I. Garmire, J. Rubin, and J. Q. Wilson. Baltimore: Johns Hopkins University Press.

Wurdock, C. J. 1981. "Neighborhood Racial Transition: A Study of the Role of White Flight." *Urban Affairs Quarterly* 17:75–89.

Zamble, E. and P. Annesley. 1987. "Some Determinants of Public Attitudes toward the Police." *Journal of Police Science and Administration* 15:285–90.

Zanna, M. P., J. W. Olson, and R. H. Fazio. 1980. "Attitude-Behavior Consistency: An Individual Difference Perspective." *Journal of Personality and Social Psychology* 38:432–40.

DISCUSSION QUESTIONS

1. What was the purpose of the study? What were the primary issues under examination?
2. Briefly summarize the sampling procedure. How were subjects selected for the study?
3. What additional data would have been useful to support and strengthen the conclusions of the study?
4. As discussed by the authors, what are the implications of the study?

5

Heavy Metal Music Preference, Delinquent Friends, Social Control, and Delinquency

SIMON I. SINGER
MURRAY LEVINE
SUSYAN JOU

COMMENTARY by Simon Singer

I first had the idea to look at the relationship between delinquency and music preference after reading a *New Yorker* article in 1986 about Los Angeles suburban gangs. Within that excellent article by the journalist William Barich (1986), I saw a clearly articulated hypothesis. I didn't need to go much further than that to develop a theory about the possible effects of music on delinquency.

It so happened that the next year I was asked if I wished to do a "needs assessment" for a large suburban community. There was New York State agency money available to conduct a survey for which I was given discretion as to how to define the proposed assessment. I wanted not only to meet the agency's goal of evaluating the concerns and interests of the town's youth, but also to assess the extent to which youth were involved in a variety of delinquent behaviors.

The idea of linking music preference to self-reported delinquency through the survey technique came about when we needed to figure out an incentive that would lead to the participation of youth in the survey. We received a good deal on music coupons from a major retail record store in the area. To close the deal with the record store, we asked that the store cashiers record the actual music that was purchased on the returned incentive coupon. The survey also asked music preference, and we felt that along with actual music purchase

Source: Journal of Research in Crime and Delinquency, Vol. 30, No. 3, August 1993, pp. 317-329.
© 1993 Sage Publications, Inc. Reprinted by permission of Sage Publications, Inc.

This article is a substantial revision of a paper originally presented at the 1990 annual meetings of the American Society of Criminology, Baltimore. We thank Robert Agnew, Michael Farrell, and Lionel Lewis for their helpful comments on earlier versions of this article. Direct correspondences to Simon I. Singer, Department of Sociology, SUNY–Buffalo, Buffalo, NY 14260.

would provide an unobtrusive measure that would make the article a little more convincing.

The first step in the analysis showed that the main effect of heavy metal preference after controlling for other important variables was significant. It was. However, we hypothesized interaction effects based not only on what Barich proposed but also on the excellent work of Keith Roe (1985). Roe's study pointed to the need for the use of multivariate techniques of analysis to tease out the possible relationship between music preference and attachments to school and parents. This we were able to do using the techniques that Aiken and West (1991) recommended in their book on testing interactions with multiple regression. We found it quite useful to present the interaction effects as they suggest by showing how the mean level of delinquency changed at each level of interaction.

Although the article started out with a simple idea, it is important that it be considered in the broader context of subcultural theories of delinquency and crime. More is needed than just expressed attitudes and values to uncover the various subcultures that are hypothesized to contribute to high rates of delinquency. The indirect indicators of subcultural affiliation are the measures that can best further our understanding of delinquency and crime. Subcultural theory can profit more from looking at the representations of culture in the form of its various artifacts, which include not only music but styles of dress and behavior.

We would like to see more research that takes into account what goes on in the daily lives of youth. Not only do schools classify youth, but youth classify themselves and they seem to do so with regard to music preference. How strongly they identify with various forms of music is a critical part of how they see themselves. Part of what is heard is heard for its entertainment value alone, and would bear little significance except for the fact that it is associated with other factors that attract youth to a particular kind of music. The fact that we were able to show that the relationship between heavy metal and delinquency is not direct would support those who argue that youth should feel free to hear any kind of music they want. Music alone is not enough to make someone delinquent according to our data.

More research is needed on the cultural artifacts of our society and the delinquent conduct of its youth. Such data are not easy to obtain and require us to think creatively about their measurement and analysis. It is important to go beyond any simple explanation for delinquent behavior, and to apply the advanced methodological tools of criminological research to understanding the complex causes of delinquency and crime.

ABSTRACT The authors examined the relationship between a preference for heavy metal music among a large sample of suburban high school youth ($N = 715$) and delinquency, controlling for parental and school-related variables, as well as delinquent associations. They found support for the hypothesis that heavy metal has an effect on delinquency when parental control is low. However, they found no support for the hypothesized interaction between a preference for heavy metal and delinquent peers. Contrary to expectations, those students with better school marks and a preference for heavy metal music had higher amounts of self-reported delinquency.

The sounds of "heavy metal" lay along the fringe of contemporary musical preferences. Heavy metal is distinguished from lighter forms of rock and roll by the extremely loud clashing of electrical steel guitars and by lyrics with an imagery of violence. According to Gross's (1990) detailed review, heavy metal music expresses a culture of power, violence, and fatalism. He notes Mötley Crüe's song "Live Wire," which calls women whores, speaks of smashing women's faces, and going for the jugular.[1] Gross further relates a Judas Priest's hit album "Defenders of the Faith," which warns that " 'rising from the darkness where Hell hath no mercy and the screams of vengeance echo on forever, only those who keep the faith shall escape the wrath of the Metallian' "* (p. 123). Furthermore, Gross's nonrepresentative sampling of heavy metal music also includes the unpublished lyrics " 'Blessed are the wicked, cursed are the weak,' " and " 'Your God is dead and now you die, Satan rules at last' " (p. 124).

Heavy metal, as a cultural artifact, is not just communicated in lyrical form. It is also contained in distinct patterns of dress. For instance, some fans display a runic lightning bolt, borrowed from the heavy metal group AC/DC's album covers, Nazi Schutz Staffel and swastika designs, skeletons and death heads (Gross 1990, p. 125). Moreover, some of the behavior of heavy metal performers communicates particular norms of conduct. As part of their performance, heavy metal stars, at times, will dramatize bizarre forms of behavior. A widely publicized example is when Ozzy Osbourne allegedly bit the head of a bat in the middle of a concert and then received rabies shots afterwards (Barich 1986). Although the act of biting a bat might be purely theatrical, it can be considered entertainment only by particular segments of society.

Similarly, there are actual acts of violence reported among heavy metal fans. In numerous concert tours, heavy metal means heavy security, particularly in the wake of high rates of arrest and physical injuries among those attending the concerts (Montgomery 1992). The security precautions that are required at heavy metal concerts are surely much greater than those required at the philharmonic or ballet. It seems obvious that a proportion of youth present at heavy metal concerts is different in their personal taste and behavior from youth attending the symphony. Moreover, parental concern about heavy metal has led to attempts to require parental permission to purchase certain types of music that are considered offensive (see Arnett 1991).

---

*"Defenders of the Faith" by G. Tipton/R. Halford/K. Downing. © 1984 EMI April Music Inc./Crewglen Ltd./Ebonytree Ltd./Geargate Ltd. All Rights Controlled and Administered by EMI April Music Inc. All Rights Reserved/International Copyright Secured/Used by Permission.

HEAVY METAL AND DELINQUENCY

Although each generation seems to complain about the music of its youth, we know little about the relationship between popular forms of youth culture and deviant forms of behavior (Newman 1990). There are several possible ways to view the possible effects of heavy metal on delinquency. First, there are those who advocate some form of music censorship based on the argument that heavy metal is directly related to delinquent behavior. Like the viewing of violent television shows and movies, exposure to heavy metal is believed to introduce and reinforce deviant values and behaviors. This view of heavy metal ignores the possible effects of other important determinants of delinquency.

Indeed, a recent analysis by Arnett (1991) found that heavy metal listeners are already alienated youth whose reckless behavior is little affected by their music preference. Arnett (1991) further reported that youth listened to heavy metal when they were angry, and the music had the effect of making them less angry (p. 93). If anger is associated with delinquent behavior (Agnew 1985), then heavy metal music should produce a lower rate of delinquent behavior. Indeed, Arnett concludes that, contrary to what might be suggested by those who wish to ban heavy metal music, "it would seem more appropriate to advocate subscribing to heavy metal music for adolescents who show evidence of a propensity for aggression" (1991, p. 94). Thus a preference for heavy metal may even reduce delinquent behavior.

In contrast to viewing the delinquent behavior of youth as either heightened or suppressed by their preference for heavy metal, a more complex model would consider the effects of music in interaction with other indicators of delinquency. Heavy metal may be related to delinquent behavior in interaction with social control and peer group affiliations. The influence of social control and culture is emphasized in Barich's analysis of violent delinquency among suburban youth. Based on the interviews with Los Angeles suburban gang members and gang workers, Barich (1986) suggests that heavy metal lyrics increase the likelihood of delinquent behavior among naive youth and youth low in parental attachment and control.

> An intelligent kid might be able to react to heavy metal as theater, but a dull or confused kid took its messages seriously. If a kid had no parental guidance, no filter between him and the music, its anthems, however bizarre, burned into his brain with all the power of gospel. (Barich 1986, p. 102)

Thus Barich's hypothesized interaction between music and delinquency stresses that contemporary forms of youth culture affect the emerging pattern of suburban delinquency, but only among youth low in parental attachment and control. Those youth who are weak in intelligence, according to Barich, are more likely to take the words of heavy metal music seriously in justifying their delinquent behavior.

The specific and interactive effects of culture on delinquency are further specified in the research literature on subcultures and delinquency. Subcultural theory stresses that deviant values and norms are supported in the context of adolescent groups. In Matza's (1964) view, the dynamic aspects of a subculture are more important than the static vision of subcultures presented in theories that are directed towards explaining lower-class delinquency (Cohen 1955; Cloward and Ohlin 1960). Rather than refer to a "delinquent subculture," he repeatedly emphasizes a "subculture of delinquency" in which peer group interactions lead to the common acceptance of delinquent behavior. According to Matza (1964), delinquency becomes "public within the confines of more or less provincial groupings" (p. 33).

This group orientation to subcultures of delinquency is extended in the work of Schwendinger and Schwendinger (1985). They relate modern-day "consumption patterns" to contemporary adolescent subcultures. For example, they identify White street-corner youth as "punkers" and "heavy metalers." Groups of punkers and heavy metalers develop collective relationships that facilitate group decisions and acceptable forms of delinquent behavior (Schwendinger and Schwendinger 1985, p. 304).

Similarly, Willis's (1978) ethnographic study of British youth views music as a means of integrating adolescents into a common culture. Within this general youth culture, subgroups are united by their taste for particular forms of music (Willis 1990). Roe's (1985) longitudinal survey data also show that music is a vehicle for the expression of adolescent group values and identity (p. 361). According to Roe, allegiance to particular youth groups is defined by clothing, hair styles, attitudes, models of behavior, and musical preferences.

Thus a subcultural perspective leads us to suggest that patterns of delinquent peer group involvement vary by heavy metal preference. Heavy metal music should have no effect on the delinquent behavior of youth who are isolated from other delinquent youth. In the words of Sutherland's theory of differential association, "the principal part of the learning of criminal behavior occurs within intimate personal groups" (Shoemaker 1990, p. 152). Therefore, heavy metal music should increase delinquent peer identification and delinquent behavior.

HYPOTHESES

We can summarize the above discussion on the relationship between heavy metal and delinquency in terms of the following hypotheses:

1. A preference for heavy metal leads to higher rates of delinquency among youth, independent of other important indicators of delinquent behavior.

This hypothesis reflects the direct-effects model by predicting that heavy metal increases the likelihood of delinquency independent of delinquent peers, parental, and school controls. It is the hypothesis that is supported by those who favor censoring or restricting access by attaching warning labels to heavy metal music. The direct-effects model is contrary to Arnett's (1991) suggestion that heavy metal actually reduces delinquency by providing an outlet for reducing adolescent frustration and anger.

2. A preference for heavy metal leads to higher rates of delinquency among youth low in intelligence and social control.

This hypothesis reflects the suggested interactive effects of heavy metal on delinquency based on Barich's (1986) observations of suburban delinquent gangs. It stresses that heavy metal is likely to have an effect on delinquent behavior only for youth weak in parental control and low in intelligence.

3. A preference for heavy metal leads to higher rates of delinquency among youth with delinquent friends.

This may be termed the subcultural model because it suggests that delinquent peer associations are organized around music preferences. The hypothesis further suggests that a preference for heavy metal creates more delinquent conduct because of increased delinquent associations. This hypothesis stems from the literature on subcultures of adolescents and their music preferences (Roe 1985; Schwendinger and Schwendinger 1985; Willis 1978).

METHOD

The Sample

In spring 1987, we collected data on the delinquent conduct of 705 suburban high school youth. The community from which we drew our sample is largely affluent.[2] Of the population, 95% was classified as White. It should also be stressed that the vast majority of heavy metal fans are White and that they are not confined to particular urban or suburban parts of the United States (Gross 1990).

We sampled 1,475 youth in public and private high schools from school board lists. After receiving the consent of the sampled youth and their parents, we were able to complete interviews with 705 youth during noninstructional school time. The youth were administered the survey in groups of about 30 students.

Based on the demographic characteristics provided by the school districts and Bureau of Census, we are confident that the survey sample is representative of the town's senior high school population. The distribution of grade and age in our sample is within 2% of the distribution in the total high school population. The percentage of boys and girls in the survey is within 1% of the township population.

Parental and School-Related Control Measures

We measured parental attachments and supervision as reported by youth. Supervision was measured by the combined responses to the questions: "Does your (mother) (father) know who you are with when you are away from home?" The response categories were *usually, sometimes,* or *never* (3, 2, 1, respectively). Attachments were measured by questions assessing the youth's perception of parental trust and identification. We combined responses to the questions: "Does your (mother) (father) trust you?" and "Do you share your thoughts and feelings with your (mother) (father)?" The alpha for the parental attachment scale is .65.

School performance was measured according to self-reported marks (A = 5, F = 0). Our measure of the importance of school to youth was based on combined responses to three questions: "How important is it to you (a) to do well in school, (b) to have high grades, and (c) to complete high school?" (5 = *important,* 1 = *not important*). The alpha for the school importance scale is .69.

Delinquent Peers and Heavy Metal Preference

We measured delinquent associations by responses to the statement: "My friends rarely get into trouble." Responses were coded on a 5-point scale (5 = *agree,* 1 = *disagree*).

Our measure of preference for heavy metal music was based on responses to the question: "Who is your favorite musical group?" These groups were classified into categories based on a consensus among several knowledgeable individuals, consisting of a graduate student, the vice president of a large chain of retail record stores, and several of his staff.[3] Music preference data were coded soon after the survey was administered.

Nearly half of all youth (48%) said they preferred musical groups falling into the rock-pop category (e.g., Bon Jovi, Genesis, U2, Phil Collins). An additional 19% preferred "vintage or classic rock" (e.g., The Who, Rush, The Grateful Dead). Less than 1% said they preferred classical music. About 7% preferred heavy metal groups. The heavy metal category included such groups as Iron Maiden, Mötley Crüe, Metallica, and AC/DC.[4]

Stated music preference predicted the type of music youth purchased. As an incentive for completing the survey, each youth was provided with a coupon redeemable for a tape or a record in a local chain of stores.[5] When the youth purchased the record, the cashier coded the album or tape cassette the youth selected into specific music categories and placed these on the coupons, which were returned to us. Among the youth who said they preferred heavy metal, about half actually purchased a heavy metal album. If preferences were randomly related to purchases, we would expect only 7% to have purchased a heavy metal album. We use musical preference because we have more complete data than if we relied on actual purchases. We assume that preference is related to actual behavior, although it is quite possible that our heavy metal measure does not tap the extent to which youth actually listen to heavy metal music.

In the following analysis, youth who listed a heavy metal group as their favorite were coded into a heavy metal preference category (1 = heavy metal preference, 0 = others).

Delinquency

Our dependent variable, delinquency, was measured by asking youth to indicate if during the past year they had committed the following offenses: stolen anything by shoplifting or other ways (worth less than $5, between $5 and $50, over $50); purposely damaged or destroyed property that did not belong to them;

physically injured (not accidentally) or beaten someone up. We asked each youth to estimate how often he or she did each act in the past year on a 4-point scale (0–3), consisting of *never, once* or *twice,* 3 to 11 times, and 12 or more times. The sum of points on these five items provided the measurement of delinquency. The alpha coefficient is .68.

ANALYSIS

Youth who preferred heavy metal reported significantly more delinquency than other youth (for youth preferring heavy metal music, $x = 2.5$, $SD = .41$, $n = 46$; for youth preferring non-heavy metal music, $x = 1.3$, $SD = .07$, $n = 659$, $F = 2.4$ $p < .01$). Among those who preferred heavy metal, 83% reported that they had committed an act of delinquency within the last year, compared to 58% of those who preferred other kinds of music.

To test for interactions, we standardized the continuous predictor variables (Aiken and West 1991; Jaccard, Turrisi, and Wan 1990). By standardizing the predictor variables, the problem of multicollinearity in testing interactions is substantially reduced. For example, the highest correlation coefficient between the standardized variables (including interaction terms) is .39, which is substantially less than the correlations for unstandardized interaction terms. We checked the pattern of interactions by regressing delinquency on the raw scores separately for youth preferring heavy metal and non-heavy metal music. The pattern and size of coefficients produced virtually identical estimates, so we feel confident in presenting the unstandardized coefficients based on standardized values.

Also, we examined the pattern of interactions in separate analyses, controlling for gender and age and type of offense, and found that the results do not differ significantly. Higher order interactions are not presented here to simplify the analysis, but they are available upon request. Furthermore, our hypothesized relationships are not specific to gender or age characteristics.

Table 1 presents the unstandardized regression coefficients and their corresponding significant levels for regression models with and without interactions. In the main effects model without interactions, the significant predictors of delinquency are school marks, school importance, delinquent friends, and heavy metal preference. Once these variables are entered into the equation, the importance of parental attachment and parental supervision is reduced to below the .05 level of significance. The direction of the estimated effects is in the expected direction; that is, in these data low social control and delinquent associations are directly related to delinquency. Although the effect of heavy metal preference is significant in the expected direction, it is not as strong as the effects of delinquent friends and school importance. Yet the heavy metal preference variable makes a unique and significant contribution to the variance in self-reported delinquency.

Next we consider, in Table 1, main effects with interactions. When interaction effects are entered, the main effects of heavy metal preference and school marks on delinquency are above the .05 level of significance. Among the two-

Table 1. Delinquency Regressed on Social Control, Delinquent Peer, and Heavy Metal Preference Variables, With and Without Interaction Terms

Variable	Main Effects	With Interactions
Parental Attachment	–.03	–.08
Parental Supervision	–.10	–.06
School Marks	–.15*	–.14
School Importance	–.25**	–.27**
Delinquent Friends	.57**	.55**
Heavy Metal Preference	.13*	.16
Parental Attachment × Metal		.07
Parental Supervision × Metal		–.23**
School Marks × Metal		.22**
School Importance × Metal		.05
Delinquent Friends × Metal		.07
Adjusted R^2	.19	.22

Note: Standardized effects are shown.

*$p < .01$; **$p < .05$.

way interactions with heavy metal preference, only parental supervision and school marks are significant in their effects on delinquency. The two-way interaction for heavy metal preference and parental supervision is in the expected direction. But the interactive effect of school marks with heavy metal on delinquency is opposite from what was hypothesized. Moreover, contrary to expectations, the interaction between delinquent friends and heavy metal is not significant. This suggests that the effects of delinquent peers on delinquency are the same for those youth who prefer heavy metal and youth preferring other kinds of music.

Table 2 displays the standardized effects of heavy metal preference on delinquency for one standard deviation above and below the mean. In interpreting the coefficients in Table 1, recall that all variables are standardized, with a mean of zero and a standard deviation of one. The coefficients for the "main effects" refer to the effect of each variable on delinquency when all other variables are set at zero or their mean value. When all other variables are set at their mean, heavy metal preference has a standardized effect of .16 on delinquency. The coefficient for the interaction between heavy metal and parental supervision is –.23. This means that for every standard deviation increase in parental supervision, the effect of heavy metal preference on delinquency decreases by –.23. When parental supervision and all other independent variables are at their mean, the effect of heavy metal on delinquency is .16. When parental supervision is one standard deviation above its mean, the effect of heavy metal preference on delinquency decreases to –.07 (.16 + –.23). Conversely, when parental control is one standard deviation below its mean, the effect of heavy metal on delinquency increases to .39 (.16 + .23).

Table 2. Effect of Heavy Metal on Delinquency When Parental Supervision and School Marks Are Set at Various Levels

Parental supervision	
Mean – one *SD*	.39
Mean	.16
Mean + one *SD*	–.07
School marks	
Mean – one *SD*	–.06
Mean	.16
Mean + one *SD*	.38

Although the above pattern of effects for the interaction between parental supervision and heavy metal preference is in the expected direction, this is not the case for school marks. When the variable school marks is one standard deviation above its mean, the effect of heavy metal on delinquency increases to .38. Among youth who prefer heavy metal, it is not the less intelligent ones who are reporting the most delinquent acts. Rather, youth who prefer heavy metal and have higher rates of delinquency appear to achieve relatively better grades in school.

SUMMARY

The results of this analysis provide mixed support for the hypothesized interactive effects of heavy metal preference. We found support for the main effects of heavy metal preference on delinquency controlling for other important indicators. In partial support of Barich's observation on the relationship between heavy metal and delinquency, we found support for that part of our hypothesis that dealt with parental supervision. Youth who preferred heavy metal music and were low in parental supervision had higher rates of delinquency. However, this was not the case for parental attachment. Moreover, contrary to Barich's point about intelligence, our data suggest that the rate of delinquency among youth preferring heavy metal was not inversely related to school marks.

We also found little support for our subcultural hypothesis in that the effects of delinquent peers were not significantly different for youth by music preference. The effect of delinquent peers is significant and youth preferring heavy metal music may fall into a delinquent subculture, but it cannot be distinguished with these data from other subcultures that revolve around the cultural artifacts and delinquent behavior of friends.

CONCLUSION

We may have identified an element that relates an aspect of the tastes or styles of contemporary youth to their delinquent behavior. But with the available data we are unable to determine exactly how the varying elements of youth culture are related to music preferences. Parenthetically, in comparison to other youth in our sample, the few youth who preferred classical music have the lowest mean delinquency score. However, classical music oriented youth consist of a much smaller number of youth ($n = 7$) precluding any detailed analysis. There seems, however, to be some variation in the music preference of youth and their delinquent behavior.

Our multivariate analysis reveals that the direct effects of heavy metal preference are relatively small, and that it is important to consider its interaction with measures of social control. The interactive effect of parental supervision was particularly significant. Our finding that the effects of school marks for youth preferring heavy metal on delinquency were in the opposite direction from that of youth preferring non-heavy metal music requires a more complex explanation. It is possible that heavy metal may attract intelligent youth whose rebellion takes the form of heavy metal music and delinquent behavior. Or, it may be that the better grades reflect a different academic track for more delinquent youth who prefer heavy metal.

Thus future research on delinquency should further consider the manner in which popular forms of youth culture relate to delinquency. With regard to heavy metal, we have neglected to survey such symbols of heavy metal as displayed in articles of clothing and jewelry. Questions about how youth see themselves and others falling into particular adolescent subgroups, such as "punks" and "head bangers," might have more closely specified the nature of delinquent peer group associations.

Future research might also further explore the degree to which youth who said that their favorite music group is what we classified as heavy metal actually identify with the lyrics or the styles of particular heavy metal songs and groups. Obviously, not everyone who listens to heavy metal or wears a runic lighting bolt can be considered a committed heavy metal fan, or even part of a heavy metal subculture. However, music should be viewed as one of the many contemporary cultural artifacts that can provide insight into youth subcultures and their relationship to delinquency.

In a critique of prior empirical tests of subcultural theory based exclusively on surveyed norms and values, Fine and Kleinman (1979) stressed the importance of looking at the interactive and dynamic aspects of subcultures. Similarly, Messner (1983, p. 106) has made this point in arguing that sociological research on homicide should look into music preference to further understand high homicide rates in the South, controlling for the structural characteristics of southern metropolitan areas. More recently, Stack and Gundlach (1992) reported a relationship between country music and suicide with aggregate level data. And, with individual-level survey data, Hagan (1991) has considered the importance of subcultures of delinquency as predictors of status attainment.

Our research is consistent with that of others which has considered the importance of culture in explaining behavior. The more interactive and dynamic aspects of culture need to be examined through a variety of analytical techniques. Although the present research considered only the quantity of delinquent acts, much of the subcultural literature would suggest considering youth subcultures in the context of types of delinquent acts. The effects of heavy metal preference may be greater for drug offenses rather than the common forms of delinquency measured in this article. In either case, culture and subculture should not be ignored in attempts to understand the more dynamic aspects of youth and their delinquent behavior.

Finally, we wish to emphasize the correlational nature of our data and that the findings cannot be used to support music censorship as a means of preventing delinquency. Longitudinal research designs are needed to examine further the causal effects of music on delinquency. Moreover, our data is confined to music preference so we were unable to estimate the possible effects of actually listening to heavy metal music on delinquency. However, the findings do stress the importance of looking at how aspects of culture may influence delinquent behavior.

NOTES

1. Originally we had quoted directly from the Mötley Crüe song. But at the time of publication permission was denied by representatives of Mötley Crüe. Thus we paraphrase the song that Gross quotes. However, this illustrates part of the difficulty in publishing research on popular forms of culture.

2. Parents of youth surveyed were asked to indicate their occupational class. Fathers are largely in occupational positions of employers or managers (73%). The remaining proportion are equally divided among employee and self-employed occupational positions. The proportion of unemployed fathers in the survey is 6%.

3. The following music groups were classified as "heavy metal": AC/DC, Black Sabbath, Deep Purple, Dokken, Iron Maiden, Judas Priest, Mahles, Metallica, Mötley Crüe, Primitive Urges, Scorpions.

4. We realize that there is some debate as to classification of heavy metal groups. Such groups can be delineated further into lighter forms of heavy metal (e.g., Bon Jovi) and heavy heavy metal (e.g., Metallica). We prefer to confine our analysis to what might be considered as heavy heavy metal. Also, current popular heavy metal groups, such as Megadeath, Nuclear Assault, Suicidal Tendencies, and Motorhead may not have been popular at the time of the survey, which was conducted in 1987.

5. Recall the survey was completed in 1987, before the popularity of compact discs.

REFERENCES

Agnew, Robert. 1985. "A Revised Strain Theory of Delinquency." *Social Forces* 64:151–66.

Aiken, Leona S. and Stephen G. West. 1991. *Multiple Regression: Testing and Interpreting Interactions.* Newbury Park, CA: Sage.

Arnett, Jeffrey. 1991. "Adolescents and Heavy Metal Music: From the Mouths of Metalheads." *Youth & Society* 23:76–98.

Barich, William. 1986. "A Reporter at Large: The Crazy Life." *The New Yorker,* November 3, pp. 97–130.

Cloward, Richard and Lloyd E. Ohlin. 1960. *Delinquency and Opportunity: A Theory of Delinquent Gangs.* New York: Free Press.

Cohen, Albert K. 1955. *Delinquent Boys.* New York: Free Press.

Fine, Gary A. and Sheryl Kleinman. 1979. "Rethinking Subculture: An Interactionist Analysis." *American Journal of Sociology* 85:1–20.

Gross, Robert L. 1990. "Heavy Metal Music: A New Subculture in American Society." *Journal of Popular Culture* 24:119–30.

Hagan, John. 1991. "Destiny and Drift: Subcultural Preferences, Status Attainments, and the Risks and Rewards of Youth." *American Sociological Review* 56:567–82.

Jaccard, James, Robert Turrisi, and Choi E. Wan. 1990. *Interactive Effects in Multiple Regression.* Newbury Park, CA: Sage.

Matza, David. 1964. *Delinquency and Drift.* New York: Wiley.

Messner, Stephen F. 1983. "Regional and Racial Effects on the Urban Homicide Rate: The Subculture of Violence Revisited." *American Journal of Sociology* 88:997–1007.

Montgomery, David. 1992. "Injuries, Arrests Vie with Music at Heavy-Metal Fest." *The Buffalo News,* July 26, sec. C1, C4.

Newman, Graeme R. 1990. "Popular Culture and Criminal Justice: A Preliminary Analysis." *Journal of Criminal Justice* 18:261–74.

Roe, Keith. 1985. "Swedish Youth and Music: Listening Patterns and Motivations." *Communication Research* 12:353–62.

Schwendinger, Herman and Julia S. Schwendinger. 1985. *Adolescent Subcultures and Delinquency.* New York: Praeger.

Shoemaker, D. J. 1990. *Theories of Delinquency: An Examination of Explanations of Delinquent Behavior.* 2nd ed. New York: Oxford.

Stack, Steven and Jim Gundlach. 1992. "The Effects of Country Music on Suicide." *Social Forces* 71:211–18.

Willis, Paul. 1978. *Profane Culture.* London: Routledge.

——. 1990. *Common Culture.* England: Open University.

DISCUSSION QUESTIONS

1. What was the purpose of the study? What was the primary question that the authors wished to address in the study?
2. As discussed by the authors, why might one suspect that preference for certain forms of music might be related to delinquency?
3. Describe the data collection process. How were the data that were analyzed in the study collected?
4. According to the authors, does listening to heavy metal music lead to, or cause, delinquency? Why or why not?

6

"My Wife Is Married and So Is My Girlfriend"

Adaptations to the Threat of AIDS in an Arrestee Population

SCOTT H. DECKER
RICHARD ROSENFELD

COMMENTARY

This was an unusual piece of research for two criminologists, especially two criminologists with a strong quantitative orientation. However, research opportunities often emerge in unexpected ways and unexpected locations. The senior author on the paper (Decker) had been the project director for the Drug Use Forecasting (DUF) project in St. Louis since 1988. Each quarter, DUF collected interview and urinalysis data from approximately 225 adult males, 100 adult females, and 100 juvenile males who have been arrested and booked for a crime. The data we report on in this study were drawn from nearly 1,000 interviews with arrestees in late 1990 and 1991.

Both of us had conducted interviews as part of the DUF program. Despite staying up late after working our "real" job and putting up with the hassle of the holdover, it was important to participate in the interviews. We gained a good deal of insight into the measurement issues we were both so concerned about. Trying to pin down arrestees about the specifics of their sexual behavior was not always straightforward. The terminology often was difficult to translate into the neat academic categories we sought to apply to the sexual behavior and attitudes of our subjects.

The sexual behavior of arrestees was a sidelight to our larger interests in the relationships among drug use, crime, and violence. However, one item on the

Source: Crime and Delinquency, Vol. 41, No. 1, January 1995, pp. 37-53. © 1995 Sage Publications, Inc. Reprinted by permission of Sage Publications, Inc.

Scott H. Decker: Professor, Criminology and Criminal Justice, Center for Metropolitan Studies, University of Missouri–St. Louis. Richard Rosenfeld: Associate Professor, Criminology and Criminal Justice, Center for Metropolitan Studies, University of Missouri–St. Louis.

DUF questionnaire, which asked the arrestees to indicate the number of sex partners they had in the past year, piqued our interest. If self-reports are to be believed, arrestees are quite an active group. This finding, combined with our experiences with a group of local researchers who were investigating the use of clean needles and condoms among street people, caused us to look at the DUF sample as a possible source of information about how the threat of HIV, the virus that causes AIDS, altered sexual practices among arrestees. Arrestees are a worthwhile population to study in this regard. They are risk takers in many respects, and their frequent movement in and out of the "shallow-end" of the criminal justice system brings them into contact, including intimate contact, with a broad segment of the population.

We developed and pretested a questionnaire that included an open-ended item asking about the respondent's single most preferred or frequent safe-sex practice. Our interviewer debriefing sessions were fascinating, to say the least, and brought to light some of the research issues explored in this paper. Early in December 1990, Decker was approached by the most senior interviewer on the team who said she had to talk to him about a response given by a young arrestee. This savvy interviewer reported that she was told about the use of earwax to prevent the spread of HIV. She said her initial response was that the subject was trying to pull her leg, not an uncommon practice among arrestees in the holdover, especially those faced with researchers from the local university. She was sure that this street-smart young black male was trying to "get over" on her, tell her a tale in a convincing fashion. Decker advised her to record his response and to flag the interview so that we could go back to examine its validity. Imagine our surprise when we heard a similar response from individuals housed in different cells, arrested on different nights, and during different months of interviewing.

Being prepared to respond to the unexpected is an important tool in the researcher's kit. Unexpected responses often provide important insights into the behavior we wish to understand, and underscore the significance of allowing research subjects to frame responses in their own words. We would never have thought to include "use earwax test" or "wash with gasoline" in a fixed-choice questionnaire on safe-sex practices.

But our method of open-ended interviewing did more than simply produce odd or exotic tales from the urban underground. In fact, the semistructured qualitative interview often yields the opposite result, leading the researcher to discover the normal and customary functions of what, on the surface, appear to be exceptional or even bizarre behaviors. Arrestees may use unusual and ineffective strategies to protect themselves from HIV and AIDS, but their needs and desires in doing so are quite commonly felt. Most people have a strong need to believe that their intimate partners are clean, upstanding, and faithful individuals. Many people, including, we suspect, many readers of this volume, use one or another marker of a person's social status as a guide to their moral and sexual behavior. In these ways, "we" are not so different from "them," and arrestees are not the only population in need of reliable, accurate, and sensitive information and guidance regarding safe sex.

True, the qualitative field interview often yields the unexpected finding, and that is one of its most useful assets as a research method. But an equally important reason for letting research subjects speak for themselves, and listening carefully to what they have to say, is to discover the taken-for-granted understandings, needs, and wants that are shared by the researcher and the researched, the criminal and the conformist. Perhaps that is the most valuable unexpected result of qualitative interviewing in criminal justice research.

ABSTRACT A study of behavioral adaptations by a sample of arrestees to the safe-sex campaign documents a high level of risk for HIV, even among those who practice safe sex. Subjects described their preferred safe-sex practices in confidential interviews. The modal response for both males and females was "none." Large proportions of the sample reported adaptations of questionable effectiveness. Those reporting the officially prescribed safe-sex behaviors often practice a permissive form of safe sex. The results underscore the need for AIDS counseling for arrestees who believe that strict safe-sex practices place intolerable restraints on forming and sustaining sexual relationships.

The public health campaign to reduce the spread of HIV has focused on promoting safe sex and reducing unsafe intravenous drug use. Sexual contact remains the primary means of transmission of HIV and may serve as a gateway from high-risk populations, such as persons who inject drugs and have large numbers of sex partners, to other groups at lower risk. Persons arrested for crimes are at elevated risk for HIV. Therefore, it is important to document the extent to which this population has received the safe-sex message, whether the message received was the one intended, and how safe-sex information is put into practice. The present study addresses these questions, with particular emphasis on behavioral adaptations to the safe-sex campaign, using data from a study of arrestees in St. Louis.

BACKGROUND

Criminal justice populations are at high risk for transmission of and infection by HIV (Decker and Rosenfeld 1992; Inciardi 1990; McBride, Chitwood, Page, McCoy, and Inciardi 1990). Their risk is elevated for several reasons. As a group, they are risk-takers; the very act that led to their arrest is evidence of their willingness to experiment with unconventional behaviors, including illicit drug use (cf. Iguchi et al. 1992, p. 859). Evidence for illicit drug use is quite strong: Three quarters of arrestees test positive for one or more illicit substances in some cities (National Institute of Justice 1992). Substantial proportions of arrestees also report injecting drugs and sharing needles, despite knowledge of the risk for HIV associated with these practices. Drug-using arrestees have more sex partners than those who do not use drugs (Buffum 1988; Decker and Rosenfeld 1992; Huebert and James 1992). However, only limited information exists on the sex partners of intravenous drug users (Liebman, Mulia, and McIlvaine 1992). Although the main sources of HIV risk for arrestees are unsafe drug use, unsafe sex, and their combination, incarceration itself has been shown to contribute to risk, apart from its connection with these known risk factors. One study attributes this additional risk among offenders to "social membership in higher-risk cohorts of offenders and ex-offenders" (Iguchi et al. 1992, p. 859). Whatever the case, arrestees are clearly an appropriate and important population for studying the behavioral adaptations resulting from the public health campaign for safe sex.

Arrests generate huge numbers of new recruits and recidivists for criminal justice processing each year. An estimated 14 million arrests were made in the United States in 1991 (Federal Bureau of Investigation 1992). The St. Louis police alone made over 36,000 arrests in the same year. The vast majority of persons who have been arrested are detained for very short periods of time, usually a few hours. The Annual Survey of Jails (Bureau of Justice Statistics 1992) estimated over 20 million admissions and releases from the nation's jails in 1991 (10.2 million admissions and 9.9 million releases). The continuous movement of large numbers of arrestees back and forth from jails to the community, their high values (in the aggregate) on known HIV risk indicators, their frequency of contact with other high-risk populations (e.g., IV drug users and prostitutes), and lifestyles generally less structured by the routines of work and family combine to make them a critical challenge for an effective public health campaign to prevent HIV and AIDS.

From an intervention standpoint, arrestees have one advantage over other high-risk populations: Most of them are detained, if only for a few hours, in highly controlled settings where information can be communicated to them. At the same time, their lower levels of education and literacy are obstacles to effective implementation of public health messages. Among other things, lack of formal education may make arrestees more vulnerable to folk beliefs and other misconceptions about sexually transmitted diseases, including AIDS.

Educational deficits or literacy barriers do not explain fully why persons at risk for HIV resist effective behavioral changes. Intravenous drug users, for example, show a high degree of awareness of HIV risk in general but tend to minimize their own risk. Further, some research suggests that sexually active IVDUs attribute greater risk for HIV infection to their drug use than to their sexual behavior (Sibthorpe 1992, p. 257). Other researchers argue that there are "inherent difficulties" in changing the sexual practices of IVDUs (Huebert and James 1992). Although the reasons remain poorly understood, they include a dislike of condoms, skepticism about the efficacy of condoms, and a belief that infected persons can be detected by external, nonmedical signs such as poor hygiene, behavioral deviance, and low social status (Hartgers, Krijnen, van den Hoek, Coutinho, and van der Pligt 1992; Sibthorpe 1992). As a result, large numbers of IVDUs persist in unsafe activity, in spite of knowledge of possible risk to themselves and to others (Huebert and James 1992; Liebman et al. 1992).

In addition, drug users resist safe-sex practices for the same reasons others do. Most people are reluctant to engage in behavior that conveys a lack of trust in or respect for their intimate partners. No matter how well its instrumental effectiveness is understood, safe sex has expressive consequences that limit its use. "Condom use," in the words of one researcher, "is a symbolic act of great significance" (Sibthorpe 1992, p. 266). Adopting such practices as regular condom use threatens—or is perceived to threaten—primary sexual relationships. Prior research documents low levels of condom use among persons at elevated risk for HIV. However, use of condoms varies with the degree of intimacy in sexual relationships. The greater the emotional distance between partners, the more likely condoms are used (Booth and Watters 1992; Huebert and James 1992; Sibthorpe. 1992). People at high risk for HIV have no less of an interest than others in initiating and sustaining intimate sexual relationships, yet they have a much greater need to minimize the cost of risky sex. Our findings suggest that the use of ineffective safe-sex measures by people at risk for HIV, as well as their failure to use effective measures, results from the need to reconcile these powerful and conflicting desires.

METHOD AND DATA

Data for this study were collected as part of the Drug Use Forecasting (DUF) program sponsored by the National Institute of Justice. DUF interviews adult male and female arrestees four times each year in the police holdover facilities of 24 cities regarding their drug use, sex partners, and needle use. A urine test is administered to screen for recent use of a wide range of illicit drugs. Interviews and urine tests are voluntary and confidential, and rates of participation in most cities exceed 90% (National Institute of Justice 1992).

During the fourth quarter of 1990 and the first two quarters of 1991, we added items to interviews in the St. Louis DUF site to elicit information regarding subjects' knowledge of safe-sex practices, self-reported exposure to HIV, test experience for HIV and AIDS, condom use, and other steps to protect against HIV when having sex. Respondents were asked to describe their single most frequent or preferred safe-sex practice. Responses to this open-ended item were collapsed into nine separate categories. When multiple responses were provided, which occurred in roughly 10% of the interviews, only the one first mentioned was coded. Respondents were encouraged to elaborate on the techniques they used to protect themselves from sexually transmitted HIV infection. Interviewers were instructed to record in writing the resulting qualitative information as completely as possible during and immediately following each interview. Tape recorders were not used.

During the three quarters of data collection, 959 interviews were completed. With one exception, the resulting sample is representative of the arrestee population in large cities throughout the nation. Of the sample, 8 out of 10 arrestees are male. The mean age of the sample is 26.6 (SD = 9.3). Fewer than one third (32%) of the sampled arrestees had completed high school or had obtained a GED. The racial composition of St. Louis arrestees, however, differs from that of other large cities. Of our sample, 83% are Black, 16% are White, and the remaining 1% are Asian or Hispanic. In contrast, Blacks comprised 55% of persons arrested in the 100 largest cities in 1990 (computed from Kasarda 1993).

Consistent with the DUF sampling protocol, only males charged with felonies or misdemeanors were included in the sample; females charged with ordinance and traffic violations as well as felonies and misdemeanors were interviewed. Nonetheless, the sex, age, and race composition of the sample is highly representative of the St. Louis arrestee population as a whole (Decker 1992; St. Louis Metropolitan Police Department 1991; see Chaiken and Chaiken 1993, for a general discussion of the representativeness of the DUF samples). In addition, a separate study of St. Louis arrestees charged with traffic and minor criminal offenses shows levels and patterns of illicit drug use similar to those found in the DUF surveys (Rosenfeld and Reichard 1993). The results from the present study, therefore, may be generalized to the St. Louis arrestee population with some confidence. More caution should be exercised in extending our findings to other large cities, especially those with lower proportions of African American arrestees.

RESULTS

We first asked arrestees about their perceived exposure to AIDS. The results coincide with those of earlier studies that show that arrestees are at elevated risk for HIV infection compared to the general population (Decker and Rosenfeld 1992; Inciardi 1991; Magura, Rosenblum, and Joseph 1991). Just over one fifth of the sample (21%) thought they had been exposed to AIDS in some form, and 2% indicated they had sex with someone they thought had AIDS.

The modal response to the open-ended item on precautions taken to prevent HIV exposure was "none" (29%) (see Figure 1). Three of the response categories (using a condom, having only one partner, and being celibate) correspond to recommended safe-sex practices (Koop 1988). However, taken together, responses in these three categories represent only 24% of the entire sample of arrestees. Females were more than twice as likely as males to report that having only one partner is their preferred precaution. Males and females do not differ appreciably in their use of the other two recommended safe-sex practices. Substantial fractions of the sample depend on personal knowledge (15%) or asking their partner if they are "clean" (13%). Males were more than twice as likely as females to report these behaviors. Another sizable percentage of arrestees (16%) indicated that they or their partner are tested regularly for HIV. Females are somewhat more likely than males to employ this adaptation.

Two small but notable groups reported more innovative, but not more effective, ways of protecting themselves. Of the sample, 3% indicated that they and their partner always wash before having sex, and 1% responded that they use

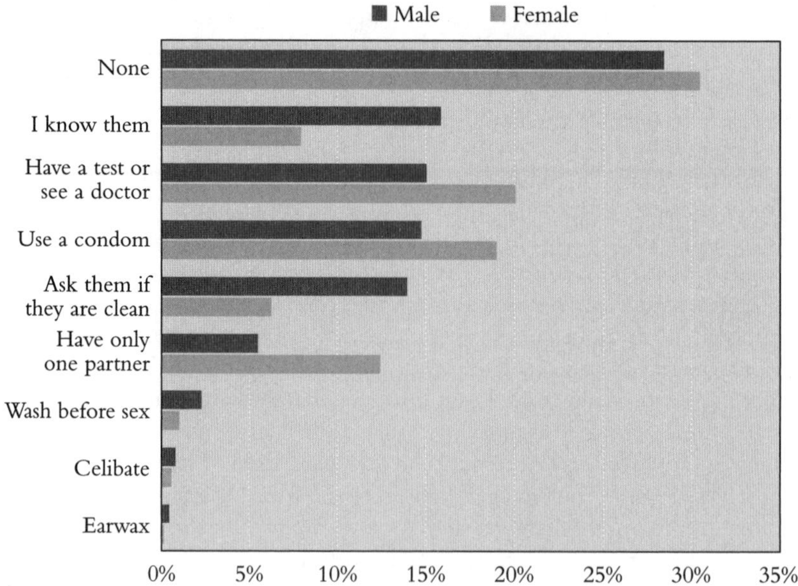

FIGURE 1. Preferred Safe-Sex Practices Among St. Louis Arrestees (*N* = 959)

earwax to determine whether their (female) partner is infected. As described by these arrestees, this procedure involves inserting earwax from their own ear into their partner's vagina. If she jumps or startles, then she is "dirty" and should be avoided. The earwax technique for safe sex is a folk practice that evidently is not limited to St. Louis arrestees. Sixth graders on Chicago's West Side report using the same procedure to detect sexually transmitted diseases (Tetzeli 1992). Other arrestees disclosed that they make their (female) partner drink orange juice and wait for her to urinate. If it burns, this is a sign of infection. Wish, O'Neil, and Baldau (1990) report a number of similar adaptive behaviors by arrestees in response to exposure to HIV through needle use. Such adaptations reflect folk beliefs about safe-sex practices to protect oneself from HIV infection.

Figure 1 documents the relative frequency of several behavioral adaptations to the threat of HIV in a high-risk population. However, considerable variation exists within these broad behavioral categories as well as across them. We have organized the diversity of responses contained in the same or closely related categories along three basic dimensions of variability: (a) relational closure, (b) technical assistance, and (c) personal and social typification.

Relational Closure: Abstention, Marriage, and Monogamy

Many people protect themselves from HIV as well as other sexually transmitted diseases by restricting their sexual relationships to a single partner or by abstaining from sexual activity. Abstention is the most effective safe-sex practice. Although some arrestees reported that the threat of AIDS has led them to abstain from intercourse, celibates are rare in our sample (see Figure 1). Further, it should not be assumed that all of the celibates abstain all of the time. Several respondents appear to use abstention as they might use other safe-sex practices, as a specific and temporary protection strategy, rather than a general and long-term change in lifestyle. The comment of one such conditional celibate is telling in its ambiguity, leaving the door open to the possibility of sexual activity under special conditions: "Generally, I don't mess with anyone."

A larger group of respondents believes that monogamy protects them from HIV infection. Here again, however, there is considerable variation in how monogamy is defined and practiced. For some arrestees, marriage confirms the belief that their partner is free of HIV. The straightforward comment of one arrestee is typical of this subgroup: "I only have sex with my wife, and we're both monogamous." Another indicated that she does not "have to take no steps; I just have sex with one person." A third woman reported:

> I make sure my man stays at home and that there is no fooling around. Besides, he has been my partner since before AIDS.

However, others who depend on the marital status of their partner follow a somewhat different line of reasoning, such as the man who proclaimed:

> There is no reason to have any questions. My wife is married and so is my girlfriend.

These comments reflect the sentiments of another arrestee who said that he was not worried about AIDS because the woman he was sleeping with "was married," though not to him. Clearly, the meaning and practice of monogamy vary among those arrestees who reported monogamy as their preferred safe-sex practice. Some arrestees, primarily females, practice a strong form of monogamy that maximizes sexual exclusivity and relational closure, whereas others, mainly males, practice a weaker and riskier one-sided monogamy that frees people to pursue multiple "monogamous" relationships. As such partially closed relationships multiply, or as partners change over time, the already diminished protection such relationships provide against HIV is reduced even further.

Technical Assistance: Testing and Condoms

Many respondents told us that they or their partners routinely undergo testing for HIV. One indicated that as a person who regularly donates blood, he is tested quite often. Another arrestee, who was recently married, had a blood test for that purpose and reported that both he and his partner were "clean." A third disclosed that his wife was pregnant and was tested at the clinic every week. Several respondents, who insist that their partners are tested, accompany them to the clinic to insure that the test is actually performed. The strength of the language used to describe this practice underscores its importance to respondents who rely on testing as their primary mode of protection, but also reveals some uncertainty about how often tests should be performed. Some said that they would "take her" themselves or that they "make them get tested." Others were reluctant to depend on a single test: "Just hope that they don't have AIDS, and he gets tested every so often" and "Get tested before sex and wait for several months and get tested again."

Condom use is the most publicized form of safe sex for sexually active people. However, consistent with previous research on high-risk populations, the use of condoms to protect against HIV infection is not a widespread practice among arrestees. Nineteen percent of the females and 15% of the males reported condom use as their primary safe-sex practice. Most respondents who use condoms view this practice as the only effective means of protection. As one put it: "There are no steps that I know of. I just use a condom." "Don't worry," said one man, "the rubber protects your stuff." According to another: "Put a rubber on. You can't catch AIDS with no rubber."

Not all respondents whose preferred mode of protection is condom use appear as certain of its efficacy. Some call attention to the ever-present possibility of human weakness and error. One man observed, for example, that he tries to always "use a condom. But being a man, if the urge hits, I don't think about AIDS." Others appear more concerned with technical problems, such as the number of condoms necessary to provide maximum protection. A number of arrestees reported that they use several condoms at a time. One woman said "Not by asking, that won't do it. Using condoms is best, sometimes use two or three condoms at once." Another advised: "Use a condom, maybe more than one at a time."

The qualifiers in these statements ("sometimes," "maybe") reveal the same uncertainty about the technical requirements for maximum protection already noted with respect to testing. Respondents who rely on technical assistance to protect themselves seem unsure about how much assistance is enough. Further, these qualified accounts reflect the conditional nature of condom use. Under what circumstances would someone from a high-risk population, whose preferred safe-sex practice is condom use, use more or fewer condoms—or none at all? Unfortunately, we do not have the data to answer this question directly. On one hand, it is reasonable to suppose that condom use is infrequent in spontaneous encounters with strangers. On the other hand, we have evidence that persons are more likely to rely on condoms for protection when sexual partners or settings seem especially risky, or when little information exists on which to base assessments of risk. In such cases, many of our respondents try to find out all they can about potential partners to establish the probable risk posed by having sex with them. This information is then interpreted in terms of commonly held beliefs regarding the individual and social correlates of risk for AIDS.

Judging by Appearances: Assessing Risk Through Individual and Social Typification

An appreciable fraction of arrestees in our sample, especially males, inquire about their partner's behavior before having sex. When asked what steps he took to make certain a potential partner is not infected, one respondent indicated, "All I do is ask, ask how many people she went to bed with in the last month [and] whether or not they use drugs." The use of drugs is a topic of concern for many of those who depend on this method. One respondent said, "Ask some questions . . . ever shot drugs . . . ever been with anyone who shot drugs." Another declared simply, "I don't go to bed with drug addicts." Many arrestees recognize the shortcomings inherent in relying exclusively on self-reports for evidence of incriminating behavior. One result is simply to suspend disbelief. One respondent who questions his partners before having sex with them said he essentially wants to know, "Hey baby, you aren't going to bury me, are you?" Others expressed similar concerns about the reliability of self-reports. An arrestee who asks questions before sex reported, "I hope they be truthful and tell the truth." Another said that he "asked questions and prayed" before sex.

The effectiveness of asking questions as a safe-sex strategy depends on the types of questions asked, as well as the truthfulness of the responses. The questions asked by our respondents are not based on "epidemiologically derived categories of risk" (Sibthorpe 1992, p. 266). Rather, they derive from individual and social typifications of questionable diagnostic utility. The perceived image of persons with AIDS plays heavily in the determination of what sort of people represent a risk for infection. In addition to asking questions, respondents also reported that they observe their partners for signs of ill health. Like respondents' questions, these observations are based more on social than on medical criteria. These criteria include "looking at a person to see if they're skinny," looking for "spots on the back," observing the vaginal area, and making sure that the partner "smells appropriate." Such observational techniques and evaluative criteria are not confined to men. Some women reported that they, as one put it, "squeezed" their partner's penis before having intercourse to see if it "leaked," an indication of "having something." This is a technique commonly practiced by prostitutes.

Just as respondents search their partners' bodies for signs of sickness, they also use physical attractiveness and signs of cleanliness as a basis for determining that a person is free from infection. Several respondents told us they "wouldn't mess with just anyone" or that they were "particular" about their sex partners. For example, a male arrestee described the procedure he used: "I don't worry about it, I am particular about people. She has to be pretty and look nice." This technique is similar to that of the arrestee who reported that he went with a "clean girl" and that "you can tell a clean girl."

Cleanliness is employed as a literal means of protection by 3% of the sample, again mainly by males. Several men reported that they make their partner take a bath or shower before having sex. A few of these respondents added that they watch to verify that their partner does indeed bathe. One respondent explained that he uses this procedure only with women he has never had sex with before. He also reported, however, that when necessary he "made them douche as well." Those who reported that they wash as a protection against infection generally do so with their partner (or they instruct their partner to wash) prior to intercourse. However, some wash after having sex, including two males who indicated that they wash their penis with gasoline after intercourse.

In addition to inquiring about past behavior and making judgments based on physical appearance, arrestees also make decisions about risk for HIV based on assessments of character. This approach is illustrated most directly by the comment of a male arrestee who stated simply that he "looked at the person's character." Some respondents use general signs of physical comportment and demeanor as characterological guides, such as "watching how a female carries herself to see if she's possibly infected." Others use occupational status as a way to judge risk, including one woman who said she is protected because she "goes out with a city employee." Other social statuses also serve as selection criteria for safe sex. A male arrestee said that he is safe because he "knew the person well, she's a housewife and a mother, a church-going woman." For these respondents, the city employee, housewife, mother, and churchgoer are redeeming roles that do not correspond with the stereotypical image of persons who present a risk for HIV infection.

A number of respondents asserted that knowledge of their partner, that is, the knowledge of a specific individual as opposed to a certain *type* of person, is their primary means of protection. For many respondents, this personal knowledge inheres in the marital relationship and presupposes a high degree of trust between partners. This was not always the case, however. For example, one respondent, who questions his partner to assess risk, also uses a "backup" method. He searches "through women's personal information, her purse, and ask questions . . . look at Medicaid card." Others felt the best way to get to know their partner was not to rush into sexual relationships. As one female arrestee put it,

> Yeah, I think about it, but I don't pick just anybody. Don't rush, wait a while to see if they are clean.

Other arrestees reported,

> Try to know something about their background, how many men do they have sex with.
>
> I don't deal with anyone that I haven't known for a few years.
>
> Get to know him, you can then know who he's been with. I'm picky.
>
> Get to know her before having sex, see if she's healthy, go to her house and check her things out.

Both male and female respondents indicated that avoiding sexual contact with strangers is a good way to protect against HIV infection. Thus waiting a period of time before having intercourse is viewed by many arrestees as a reliable means of establishing a person's character and is, therefore, an effective way to evaluate risk.

DISCUSSION

This study demonstrates that many—perhaps most—arrestees in the city of St. Louis engage in a variety of sex practices that place them at risk for contracting HIV. We cannot be more precise about the prevalence estimate because we do not know what proportion of arrestees who reported no safe-sex practices, the modal response for both males and females, engage in risky behavior.

Certainly this fraction must be greater than zero, but even if attention is restricted to those arrestees who report that they do practice safe sex, the general finding holds. Large proportions of arrestees who practice safe sex use methods of questionable effectiveness. This result most likely reflects a best-case scenario, because respondents were asked to retrospectively reconstruct past behavior. Such reconstructions are generally more rational than the behavior itself; undoubtedly they understate, to some degree, the impulsivity that often accompanies sexual behavior, and many respondents may be reluctant to honestly report heavily stigmatized or potentially harmful behaviors.

Our major findings regarding safe-sex practices among arrestees are disturbing but are not unexpected. Almost one third of the sample reported taking no steps to protect themselves from HIV infection. Equally unsettling, however, is the prevalence of misinformation and myths regarding the prevention of disease associated with sexual activity. As reported elsewhere (Decker and Rosenfeld 1992; Wish et al. 1990), arrestees have heard the message regarding the kinds of sexual and drug-using practices that increase risk for HIV and AIDS. The problem for most of them is not that they reject the safe-sex message or that they are oblivious to the dangers of risky sex. The problem lies in the application of the message in their day-to-day behavior. This study suggests that, in a high-risk population, the safe-sex message assumes a variety of forms between its pronouncement and implementation.

For example, many arrestees view monogamy or marriage as effective means of remaining free of infection, the latter presumably because it raises the probability of the former. This view is widely held in the general population as well, and clearly it is better than nothing as a guideline for safe sex. However, as illustrated by those respondents who use marriage to gauge the safety of *both* their marriage partner *and* their girlfriend(s), the protection afforded by sexually closed relationships is diminished greatly under the conditions of one-sided monogamy documented in this study (cf. Sibthorpe 1992, pp. 263–4). The same is true of the identification of health risks with "certain kinds of people." The use of social and personal typifications to make judgments about risk is not unique to the AIDS crisis; it is common to many infectious diseases, especially sexually transmitted diseases. Nor are these devices and the social assumptions underlying them found exclusively among arrestees or other high-risk groups. Social status and moral evaluations of cleanliness also guide mate selection in the general population. Again, such devices probably do provide some useful information and are better than taking no protective steps. However, they are far from adequate for persons at risk for HIV infection.

A somewhat different logic holds for the persistence of folk beliefs, such as the ear wax and orange juice tales we heard from some of our respondents, which lack any presumptive validity. These legends persist in spite of strong evidence of their ineffectiveness and are very likely to be concentrated among the poorly educated. Yet, they also arise from the dilemma facing all persons who weigh the benefits and costs of entering or remaining in a sexual relationship: reconciling the risk to themselves of infection with the risk to their relationships of taking effective precautions against infection (cf. Sidthorpe 1992, pp. 256–7).

Sexual relationships are driven by strong needs and desires. The burden of persuasion is usually on the reasons against pursuing them. In our culture and most others, this is especially true of males, who must be deterred from sex more often than compelled to pursue it. These considerations apply to populations at high risk for HIV, as well as to those at lower risk. We assume that the perceived benefits of sexual relationships are roughly equal (and high) for the two populations. What distinguishes high- and low-risk persons are the costs of sex. By definition, people at higher risk have higher costs that place them in a difficult position in their sexual relationships. On the one hand, they have a very real interest in knowing their risk of contracting disease in any given relationship. Yet, because they do not necessarily devalue sex, even though it poses risks, they have an interest in minimizing these risks. These dual needs for and against knowing the risk status of a given partner, encounter, or relationship provide fertile cognitive soil for the kind of magical thinking about sex reflected in the folk remedies used by some of our respondents.

This dilemma also helps to explain the risk-reduction behaviors reported by many more arrestees that appear less far-fetched than the earwax test, but not much more effective. It helps to account both for the exceptionally scrupulous search for clues to a partner's health status, reported mainly by males—such as observing while a partner showers or rummaging through her purse for documentary proof of a clean bill of health—*and* for the strong presumption of health underlying both male and female respondents' belief in the myth of personal purification through bathing or social purification through regular employment, church attendance, or marriage.

Persons at risk for HIV have a strong need to know their partner's health status; some with an interest in sexual relationships have a strong need not to know too much. At the extreme, this conflict nurtures magical thinking and baseless folk remedies. More often, however, it produces a kind of fuzzy logic for calculating the costs and benefits of putatively risky sex. Persons who place a high value on the benefits do not need to drive the costs to zero, but only to the point that the expected risk becomes tolerable. In this context, the use of risk management criteria such as employment or marital status, or one-way monogamy makes some sense. If risk does not have to be eliminated but only reduced to the point at which a relationship's perceived benefits equal or exceed its costs, some people will prefer regular employment over regular condom use as a means of decreasing risk without unduly threatening a relationship.[1]

In their exacting emphasis on the risk of disease, officially prescribed safe-sex practices threaten primary sexual relationships, because they reverse the burden of proof by requiring people to show, before proceeding, that a relationship is safe (cf. Huebert and James 1992). The safest sex practice, celibacy, obviously is also the most threatening to sexual relationships and, for just this reason, is not an option for most people. Moreover, many of our respondents find the remaining official options—strict monogamy or strict condom use—too constraining or threatening. Therefore, these strict standards of conduct are interpreted on the basis of a fuzzy logic that in effect converts safe sex to tolerably safe sex.

The official safe-sex message, specifically strict condom use, is much more consistent with the instrumental norms of secondary sexual relationships than with the expressive requirements of primary relationships. When sex is defined as a commodity or service in an economic exchange, partners attend more openly and scrupulously to the risk of disease. A more rigorous enforcement of safe-sex standards can be expected in relationships where there is little intimacy or trust to jeopardize. This explains in part why, adjusting for frequency of sexual contact, prostitutes report greater use of condoms than do other women, and it is probably the main reason why prostitutes are more likely to require their customers than their boyfriends to wear a condom (Booth and Watters 1992; Huebert and James 1992).

A general proposition follows from these considerations: The more impersonal and calculating the relationship, the stronger the adherence of partners—buyers and sellers alike—to official standards of safe sex. This does not mean that sex workers or their clientele are at lower risk than others for sexually transmitted HIV infection—they are not (Des Jarlais et al. 1987; Hartgers et al. 1992). In any event, the sexual relationships of most people, including most arrestees, are not like those of sex workers. Most relationships are based on norms of personal intimacy and trust. Therefore, successful HIV and AIDS intervention with arrestees must attend to the expressive requirements of primary sexual relationships.

CONCLUSION

The impact of these findings is considerable given the high volume of arrests in St. Louis, the similarity of St. Louis arrest patterns to those of other cities with substantial African American populations, the frequent movement of arrestees back and forth from jail to the community, and the high degree of sexual contact between IV drug users and nonusers found in previous research (Liebman et al. 1992). That one in five members of the sample thought they had been exposed to HIV underscores the importance of paying greater attention to the behaviors of arrestees that place them at risk both for transmitting and contracting HIV. In sum, large numbers of people move in and out of big city jails each day who either take no precautions against the sexual transmission of HIV or falsely assume that the precautions they take are effective.

The prospects for successful intervention in the arrestee population are not good. Some success has been achieved by the gay community in spreading and implementing the message about protective behaviors (Friedman et al. 1987). A marked reduction in unsafe sex practices has been observed among gay men and has been attributed to their ability to organize, communicate, and design effective interventions (Ekstrand and Coates 1990). In contrast, arrestees are unlikely to organize; by definition, they are a disorganized population lacking permanence, stability, or hierarchy. The term *arrestee* refers to an analytical category that is seldom used even by criminal justice practitioners. It does not signify membership in meaningful communities or groups with common interests to advance or defend. Even if arrestees were capable of organizing on their own behalf, they have few assets from which to draw in mounting effective campaigns to reduce HIV risk. Finally, arrestees generally lack access to preventive health care, and many people with a high probability for arrest are resistant to public health messages because of a generalized reluctance to trust or believe authority (Hammett 1988; Inciardi 1990).

Owing to their heterogeneity, as well as to the factors already mentioned, a single approach to prevention is not likely to be effective with arrestees. Multiple networks should be used to disseminate safe-sex information. Access to this high-risk population generally occurs only when they are under legal supervision. This argues that effective interventions must be located in booking facilities and jails (cf. Siegal et al. 1994). Although arrestees can be accessed relatively easily, designing effective programs will be difficult. After all, most members of our sample recognize that HIV is a risk to which their lifestyle exposes them. The challenge is to convey information about safe-sex practices that is relevant to arrestees' sexual relationships and is perceived as nonthreatening.

Straightforward messages about safe-sex practices must be provided to every arrestee, regardless of how short their stay in custody. In addition, every arrestee should leave the lock-up or jail with a packet of safe-sex information and condoms. Those arrested for sex crimes (prostitution, patronizing a prostitute, sexual assault) should be specifically targeted for safe-sex counseling and follow-up. Part of the response to this group, then, involves expanding access beyond confinement and into the streets. Probation and parole officers, community groups, and the police should be enlisted in spreading and reinforcing the message of safe sex in the arrestee population. Beyond these standard recommendations, however, arrestees also should have access to individualized counseling, in jail and in the community, that recognizes their desire to initiate and sustain primary sexual relationships and considers the risk of HIV in the context of the risk to relationships of practicing safe sex.[2] There are no easy ways to reconcile the conflicting interests inherent in the application of strict standards of safe sex to primary sexual relationships, although the gay male community provides an important model. The costs of comprehensive "relationship-based" counseling may be high, and these recommendations will only add to the burdens of an already overloaded criminal justice system. However, the risk behaviors of arrestees are significant enough to warrant such levels of response.

NOTES

1. On "diligence" in partner selection as a safe-sex substitute for condom use, see Sibthorpe (1992, p. 264). Melnick et al. (1993) also found greater care in partner selection to be a common response to the AIDS epidemic among young, urban heterosexuals.

2. See Booth and Watters (1992) on the importance of individualized approaches for persons with different HIV risk factors.

REFERENCES

Booth, Robert and John K. Watters. 1992. "A Factor Analytic Approach to Modeling AIDS Risk Behaviors Among Heterosexual Injection Drug Users." *Journal of Drug Issues* 22:807–22.

Buffum, John. 1988. "Substance Abuse and High-Risk Sexual Behavior: Drugs and Sex—The Dark Side." *Journal of Psychoactive Drugs* 20:165–8.

Bureau of Justice Statistics. 1992. *Jail Inmates 1991.* USGPO #1993-342-471:80007. Washington, DC: U.S. Government Printing Office.

Chaiken, Jan and Marcia Chaiken. 1993. *Understanding the Drug Use Forecasting (DUF) Sample of Arrestees.* Lincoln, MA: LINC.

Des Jarlais, Donald C., Eric Wish, Samuel R. Friedman, Rand L. Stoneburner, Stanley R. Yankovitz, Donna Mildvan, Wafaa El-Sadr, Elizabeth Brady, and Mary Cuadrado. 1987. "Intravenous Drug Use and the Heterosexual Transmission of the Human Immunodeficiency Virus: Current Trends in New York City." *New York State Journal of Medicine* 87:283–6.

Decker, Scott H. 1992. *Drug Use Forecasting in St. Louis: A Three Year Report.* St. Louis, MO: University of Missouri–St. Louis.

Decker, Scott H. and Richard Rosenfeld. 1992. "Intravenous Drug Use and the AIDS Epidemic: Findings From a 20-City Sample of Arrestees." *Crime & Delinquency* 38:492–509.

Ekstrand, Maria L. and Thomas J. Coates. 1990. "Maintenance of Safer Sexual Behaviors and Predictors of Risky Sex: The San Francisco Men's Health Study." *American Journal of Public Health* 80:973–7.

Federal Bureau of Investigation. 1992. *Uniform Crime Reports 1991.* USGPO #1993-342-498/94321. Washington, DC: U.S. Government Printing Office.

Friedman, Samuel R., Don C. Des Jarlais, Jo L. Southeran, Jonathan Garber, Henry Cohen, and Donald Smith. 1987. "AIDS and Self-Organization Among Intravenous Drug Users." *International Journal of the Addictions* 22:201–19.

Hammett, Theodore M. 1988. *AIDS in Correctional Facilities: Issues and Options.* Washington, DC: U.S. Department of Justice.

Hartgers, Christina, Pieta Krijnen, Johanna A. R. van den Hoek, Roal Coutinho, and Joop van der Pligt. 1992. "HIV Risk Behavior and Beliefs of HIV-Seropositive Drug Users." *Journal of Drug Issues* 22:833–47.

Huebert, Kathy and Darlene James. 1992. "High-Risk Behaviors for Transmission of HIV Among Clients in Treatment for Substance Abuse." *Journal of Drug Issues* 22:885–901.

Iguchi, Martin Y., Jerome J. Platt, John French, Robert C. Baxter, Harvey Kushner, Victor M. Lidz, Donald A. Bux, Mitchell Rosen, and Harvey Musikoff. 1992. "Correlates of HIV Seropositivity Among Injection Drug Users Not in Treatment." *Journal of Drug Issues* 22:849–66.

Inciardi, James A. 1990. "AIDS and Drug Use: Implications for Criminal Justice Policy." Pp. 303–28, in *Drugs, Crime and the Criminal Justice System,* edited by R. Weisheit. Cincinnati, OH: Anderson.

____. 1991. "Prostitution, IV Drug Use and Sex-for-Crack Exchanges Among Serious Delinquents: Risks for HIV Infection." *Criminology* 29:221–35.

Kasarda, John. 1993. *Urban Underclass Database: An Overview and Machine-Readable File Documentation.* New York: Social Science Research Council.

Koop, C. Everett. 1988. *Surgeon General's Report on Acquired Immune Deficiency Syndrome.* Washington, DC: U.S. Government Printing Office.

Liebman, Jon, Nina Mulia, and Deborah McIlvaine. 1992. "Risk Behavior for HIV Infection of Intravenous Drug Users and Their Sexual Partners Recruited From Street Settings in Philadelphia." *Journal of Drug Issues* 22:867–84.

Magura, Stephen, Andrew Rosenblum, and Herman Joseph. 1991. "AIDS Risk Among Intravenous Drug-Using Offenders." *Crime & Delinquency* 37:86–100.

McBride, Duane C., Dale D. Chitwood, Bryan J. Page, Clyde B. McCoy, and James A. Inciardi. 1990. "AIDS, IV Drug Use, and the Federal Agenda." Pp. 267–82 in *Handbook of Drug Control in the United States,* edited by J. Inciardi. New York: Greenwood.

Melnick, Sandra L., Robert W. Jeffery, Gregory L. Burke, David T. Gilbertson, Laura L. Perkins, Stephen Sidney, Heather E. McCreath, Lynne E. Wagenknecht, and Stephen B. Hulley. 1993. "Changes in Sexual Behavior by Young Urban Heterosexual Adults in Response to the AIDS Epidemic." *Public Health Reports* 108:582–8.

National Institute of Justice. 1992. *Drug Use Forecasting 1991 Annual Report.* Washington, DC: U.S. Department of Justice.

Rosenfeld, Richard and Chris A. Reichard. 1993. "Gender, Race, Sex, and Cocaine Use: Some Unexpected Findings From a Study of Traffic and Minor Criminal Offenders." Paper presented at the meeting of the Midwestern Criminal Justice Association, Chicago, October.

Sibthorpe, Beverly. 1992. "The Social Construction of Sexual Relationships as a Determinant of HIV Risk Perception and Condom Use Among Injection Drug Users." *Medical Anthropology Quarterly* 6:255–70.

Siegal, Harvey A., Jichuan Wang, Mary Ann Forney, Russel S. Falck, Robert G. Carlson, and Duane C. McBride. 1994. "Incarceration and HIV Risk Behaviors Among Injection Drug Users: A Midwestern Case Study." *Journal of Crime and Justice* 17:85–101.

St. Louis Metropolitan Police Department. 1991. *Annual Report 1990–91.* St. Louis, MO: St. Louis Metropolitan Police Department.

Tetzeli, Rick. 1992. "Most Dangerous and Endangered." *Fortune,* August, pp. 78–81.

Wish, Eric, Joyce O'Neil, and Virginia Baldau. 1990. "Lost Opportunity to Combat AIDS: Drug Abusers in the Criminal Justice System." Pp. 187–209 in *AIDS and Intravenous Drug Use: Future Directions for Community-Based Prevention Research* (NIDA Research Monograph 93), edited by C. Leukefeld. R. Battjes, and Z. Amsel. Rockville, MD: National Institute on Drug Abuse.

DISCUSSION QUESTIONS

1. What was the data collection and sampling procedure used in this study?
2. Given the sampling and data collection procedure and the associated discussions of the authors, what do you think are the most significant limitations of the study?
3. In conducting their study, the authors discovered some surprising results. What were these results, and what was it about the data collection process that allowed these findings to be uncovered?
4. As discussed by the authors, what are the major implications of the study? Now that we know some things about the issues under examination, what should be done about them?

PART IV

Field Research

This part provides examples of approaches using field methods. As explained in Part I, field researchers study individuals or groups in their natural settings. According to Taylor (1994: 208), "Field research refers to a series of techniques where the researcher has direct and sustained social interaction with participants in a particular setting." Babbie (1998: 23) observes: "Field research is especially appropriate to the study of those attitudes and behaviors best understood within their natural settings, as opposed to the somewhat artificial settings of experiments and surveys." Earlier, Smith (1975: 232) noted three broad types of field strategies:

1. *Participant observation,* which includes observing and participating in "real world" events, interviewing participants during the events, and maintaining stable relationships in the group
2. *Informant interviewing,* where the researcher interviews an informant about other people or about events not currently happening
3. *Enumerations and samples,* which includes surveys and observations that can be repeated and easily counted, involving little participation

According to Smith, field methods are flexible and adaptable to exploration or reformulation of emerging theoretical concerns. But this flexibility also can make field research more conducive to hypothesis generation than to hypothesis testing. Among the many advantages of field methods, note the following: the researcher can reformulate the problem as the work progresses; the impressions of a field-worker often are more reliable for classifying subjects than other methods; difficult-to-quantify variables may be captured better through fieldwork; and fieldwork may produce data that is rich in detail and specificity.

Decker, "Collective and Normative Features of Gang Violence," combined field contacts and interviews of gang members with observations. The author's explanation of the methodology is instructive, and the analysis provides excellent insight. As Decker observes, as a researcher he was not prepared for just how great the violence would be nor for the personal nature of such violence. As with other persons in other endeavors (e.g., emergency room physicians), researchers confronted with difficult or disturbing events must find ways of maintaining marginality and handling the personal effects. This article represents fieldwork broadly conceived, with a distinctly quantitative bent. It does not necessarily fit the usual image of fieldwork; nonetheless, it may be said to fit under the umbrella.

Schmid and Jones, "Ambivalent Actions," used Jones as a true participant-observer in a prison setting. Jones was, in fact, a prisoner serving a sentence, and may be classified as an *indigenous researcher,* a technique frequently used in field research. Schmid, on the outside, assisted in guiding the research, providing a sociological context and suggesting theoretical concepts, questions, methods, and procedures. The authors had to deal with a primary difficulty of participant observation—maintaining marginality. They succeeded in providing informative insights and a grounded approach to understanding the importance of *ambivalence* in the prison experiences of inmates.

Vander Ven, "Fear of Victimization and the Interactional Construction of Harassment in a Latino Neighborhood," employed participant observation, "drawing upon theoretical insights to address some of the neglected dimensions of public fear and how it is played out in social interaction." This article shows the importance of obtaining information from an ethnographic perspective, examining issues that quantitative approaches do not reach. The author discusses the issues of gaining acceptance and minimizing observer effects, providing crucial insight on doing fieldwork.

7

Fear of Victimization and the Interactional Construction of Harassment in a Latino Neighborhood

THOMAS M. VANDER VEN

COMMENTARY

The title of this article, "Fear of Victimization and the Interactional Construction of Harassment in a Latino Neighborhood," seems so bloated and overly formal to me now. It does not do justice to the more reckless spirit of the research. When I began the study, I was an enthusiastic graduate student who saw a great opportunity to study crime in my own neighborhood. And I had a pretty full experience in "Chronic Town"; at times, I was simultaneously scared, entertained, and astonished by what I saw there. On other occasions, I was merely bored, just waiting for something to happen. As a personal learning experience, I cannot overstate what the study did for me.

The first lesson I learned was that ethnographic research is difficult, very difficult. This was a surprise to me because at that point in my graduate training, I was most fearful of being victimized by statistics courses. I could not imagine doing a quantitative study. I just didn't have the skills yet (a great statistics professor later cured me of most of my fear). But field research seemed, well, easier. I figured I would just hit the streets, make contacts, observe behavior, and make interpretations. But then a strange thing happened. Once I got on the street corner, I had no idea what to look for. I had no questionnaire, no survey instrument, and no recording device to capture my observations. Unlike survey research where you are dealing with a fixed, controlled set of observations, the measurement of street life was much more slippery. Variables were literally flying at me at times. It was hard to be systematic and thoughtful, for

Source: Journal of Contemporary Ethnography, Vol. 27, No. 3, October 1998, pp. 374-398.
©1998 Sage Publications, Inc. Reprinted by permission of Sage Publications, Inc.

Author's Note: I would like to extend my appreciation to Mark Colvin, Francis T. Cullen, and the anonymous reviewers for their valuable comments on earlier versions of this article.

example, when observing an interaction involving four police officers, an angry store owner, a hard-to-restrain drunk man, several skateboarders, and a vocal group of onlookers. I had to measure these empirical projectiles with my senses, my memory, and later, with a pen and paper. After a night on the corner, I would go home and speed-write my field notes in an attempt to record as many of my observations as possible. I'm sure that there is much that I failed to capture and much that I forgot.

Standing on the corner was usually fun; trying to make sense of it all was, in the beginning, difficult and frustrating. This point leads me to my second lesson learned: criminological theory should be used to guide research and to sensitize the observer, but should not put undue constraints on the data collection. One reason that my earliest attempts to capture street life were so difficult was that I was trying to make sense of the data within the context of one particular theoretical orientation. That perspective, social disorganization theory (Shaw and McKay, 1942), sees urban crime as symptomatic of the breakdown in collective morality and informal social controls attributable to neighborhood traits such as poverty, heterogeneity, housing turnover, and family disruption. Gerald Suttles (1968), who argued that crime-ridden urban centers should be seen as differentially organized rather than socially disorganized, challenged this influential theory. Although Suttles's Chicago slum neighborhood was, indeed, a high-crime area, he suggested that it was intricately organized and was guided by informal controls just as in any other community. It was in the context of this theoretical debate that I began my research.

My frustrations began as I started to filter all of my observations through the social disorganization/differential organization debate. After I watched a man urinate in public, for example, I'd wonder, "Is that social disorganization? Differential organization? Or what?" All of my early observations were seen from this particular perspective and my field notes reflect this preoccupation. I soon started to feel that I was trying to wedge my neighborhood into the social disorganization debate, but wasn't getting anywhere. I had forgotten to keep my eyes wide open for other kinds of behavioral patterns. But then the patterns sort of "came to me." I witnessed several interactions where a scared pedestrian acted in ways that seemed to evoke harassment. Men who were treated like "scary" characters sometimes responded by scaring people. This scenario reminded me of labeling theory. Labeling theory suggests that treating people like criminals has the unintended consequence of making them more criminal. I had the labeling perspective in my theoretical tool belt and used it to make sense of these behavioral patterns I had witnessed and those I was yet to observe. The point of all this is that research should always be theory-driven, but a researcher should not lean too much on any one particular perspective. Theory should be a lens for seeing, not a set of blinders.

ABSTRACT The study of fear of crime has been dominated by survey researchers and quantitative analysis. However, very little is known about the kinds of social situations that generate fear, the ways in which people manage fear during social interaction, and the manner in which feared individuals respond to another's show of vulnerability. The author attends to these issues with data collected during observational research in an urban Latino community. Based on one particular setting, he discovered that the fearful and the feared often worked together to produce confrontational episodes. Driven by past harassment and ethnic prejudice, and influenced by media accounts of local violence, many pedestrians displayed obvious fear to the men who congregated in a commercial district. The author found that fearful behavior often resulted in harassment because it implicitly labeled men as dangerous. Men who sensed another's fear often reacted by behaving in a threatening manner.

Fear of criminal victimization routinely touches a large proportion of Americans. That fear may usually lie dormant within individuals as a reasonable understanding that the world can be a dangerous place: "The predators are out there and they may soon find us." Sometimes, however, we actually cross paths with someone whom we perceive to be a threat to our safety. When one individual fears another, it is an emotionally powerful, physically transforming experience; often, both the fearful and the feared are moved to interact in extraordinary ways.

Little attention, however, has been paid to the interactional dynamics of the fear-driven encounter. The dominant approach employed by fear-of-crime researchers has been to measure the intrapersonal levels of fear found in survey respondents. Over the past two decades, investigators have generated a large body of findings regarding the relationship between social status and fear. This research has demonstrated that fear is highest among the elderly, women, urban dwellers, nonwhites, and the poor (see Liska, Sanchirico, and Reed 1988; St. John and Heald-Moore 1996; Warr 1984, 1985; Yin 1982, 1985).

Other investigators have examined the manner in which fear of crime affects the lives of individuals. Research on the human consequences of fear of crime have mainly focused on the extent to which fear drives people to avoid certain situations or areas perceived to be dangerous (e.g., Liska, Sanchirico, and Reed 1988; Skogan and Maxfield 1981) or the ways in which people develop protective measures to guard against victimization (e.g., Bankston and Thompson 1989; Wright 1991). The fearful individual has been largely seen as one who, to a greater or lesser extent, avoids undesirable social interaction or devises protective strategies to lower the probability of victimization.

But avoiding undesirable interaction is not always possible. In the real world, pedestrians are often confronted with situations and people that seem dangerous. The fear that sometimes results when strangers meet in public places can have a variety of consequences. The fearful pedestrian may choose to simply exit the interaction or to employ some sort of strategic behavior to reduce feelings of vulnerability. A recent ethnographic account of pedestrian behavior, in fact, demonstrates that strangers will often actively collaborate to restore order after a violation of personal space has taken place (Wolfinger 1995). Often, however, interaction between strangers is much more problematic.

Negotiating public spaces is particularly problematic when pedestrians encounter social types who represent a potential threat or danger. Survey research shows that the majority of residents in major cities do, indeed, routinely encounter people whom they perceive to be dangerous (Kelling and Coles 1994). A widespread belief in the existence of a dangerous class of city dwellers, who are responsible for most of the crime and disorder in our urban centers, dates back to the nineteenth century (Monkkonen 1988). Public disorder as a social problem continues to play a prominent role in contemporary critiques of city life. Some of the city streets of our nation are often portrayed as virtually unnavigable due to the presence of "aggressive panhandlers, disheveled vagrants, and rude teenagers" (e.g., Kelling and Coles 1996, xiv).

As history has shown, however, men do not need to display any overt signs of aggression or criminality to signal danger to their audiences. The mere presence of gatherings of black or Latino males may be regarded as a symbol of public disorder (Anderson 1990; Bourgois 1990). The need to control these threatening populations has been a recurrent concern among city planners and policy makers. The Greaser Law of 1856, for example, was an antivagrancy statute meant to restrict Mexican immigrants to labor camps and to keep them off the public streets (Shorris 1992). More recently, legislators have worked to resurrect loitering laws by drafting order-maintenance legislation that targets specific public behaviors such as begging, lying down, obstructing pedestrian traffic, or threatening or intimidating pedestrians (Kelling and Coles 1996).

For many black and Latino men, the awareness that their mere presence represents potential danger to others may be a common experience. For these men, that recognition may have a variety of consequences. One effect of being publicly treated as dangerous is that a temporary yet compelling label may be affixed by the fearful onto the feared. Labeling theorists have argued that formal reactions to deviant behavior have the unanticipated consequence of creating the very behavior they were meant to prevent (Lilly, Cullen, and Ball 1995). Labels are compelling forces because they are not only affixed to behavior, but they also attach themselves to the identities of those so labeled. According to this perspective, treating a man as a dangerous type may increase the probability that he will behave dangerously. The feared individual may, out of frustration and resentment, behave in accordance with the label, if only to "fulfill the prophecy" of those who display fear (Anderson 1990).

Similarly, treating a man as if he might be dangerous may serve to confirm his already formed perception of himself as a street predator or "badass." As Katz (1988) has argued, the badass identity must be continually reaffirmed through structured action. He must be able to "adjust the public self sensitively to situationally contingent expectations" (p. 81). It is likely, then, that expressing obvious fear to such individuals may communicate a set of expectations that the badass is more than willing to meet; frightening people is rewarding because it transcends common morality, because it reinforces reputation, and because it is fun (Katz 1988).

In the present study, I draw upon the above theoretical insights to address some of the neglected dimensions of public fear and how it is played out in social interaction. Based on my ethnographic research in a predominantly Latino urban neighborhood, I will discuss some of the forms that fearful behavior takes. I will argue that when one pedestrian fears another, the fearful pedestrian sometimes communicates feelings of vulnerability by using overt avoidance techniques or by acting demonstratively cautious. When actors communicate fear through pure avoidance or demonstrative caution, the feared individual may respond by acting in a threatening or dangerous manner. One of the hidden costs of fear, then, is that it may be self-fulfilling. I will not argue that fearful people are to blame for their own victimization. Frightened people do not create predators through simply communicating fear; instead, the propensity for public harassment is not so much created by fearful behavior as it is activated by it.

In the pages that follow, I will discuss my method of research and describe the neighborhood where the observations took place. The neighborhood context must be understood because public fear was particularly high in this community due to its high crime rate and its reputation for being a dangerous place and due to ethnic prejudice and ethnic conflict. Next, I will discuss three general types of fearful behavior—pure avoidance, demonstrative caution, and assertive interaction—and describe the process through which fear-driven confrontations unfold.

METHODS

The neighborhood where I conducted my research, hereafter referred to as Chronic Town, is a predominantly Latino community located in a large suburb near Washington, D.C. I lived near Chronic Town and had informally observed public behavior there while grocery shopping at the local market. I became interested in the almost constant presence of groups of Spanish-speaking immigrant men who congregated in the parking lot of the grocery market. At first, the activities of the corner congregators seemed innocuous to me. Generally, I would see ten to fifteen men sitting or standing around having a conversation. At the same time, I knew that Chronic Town had a reputation for being a high-crime area where public drunkenness and disorderly behavior were common. Many of my neighbors had warned me against traveling in Chronic Town at night. I also was aware of the frequent presence of local police in the neighborhood. Something was going on at the market that had people worried. I wanted to find out what that something was.

As I began my research, I had a few general objectives. I wanted to know what brought the men to the market parking lot and what they hoped to accomplish when they got there. Furthermore, I was interested in the conflict between the social congregators and the store owners, police officers, and community members who apparently found certain street-corner behaviors objectionable. Fear of crime and how it is played out during interaction was not specifically on my mind as I planned my research. However, during the ten months that I observed street-corner behavior in Chronic Town, I witnessed a number of incidents that appeared to form a pattern. Although I did not initially look for the social relational manifestations of fear, I became sensitive to this dimension of street life as I was frequently presented with examples of it. I watched public behavior as I stood alone or with the corner congregators in the market parking lot. I hung out at the market on a semiregular basis, usually two or three evenings a week after I got off work. I also frequently spent my lunch hour at the corner. Most of the interactions that I will describe involved corner congregators and community members who were shopping in or just passing through Chronic Town during daylight hours. Because Chronic Town was generally seen as a dangerous place, it was rare for anyone other than the corner regulars to spend time in the commercial district at night. As a result, my observations are restricted to those encounters that occurred before nightfall, when pedestrian traffic was high.

I was able to gain the acceptance of the corner regulars through my role as a youth baseball coach to the sons, brothers, and nephews of some of the men who hung out at the market. I had already gained the respect of these men who had come to trust me with their children. These men introduced me to their friends and, soon, I became known to all as "the guy who's writing a book about us." More than 80 percent of Chronic Town's residents had immigrated to the United States from Central America in the past ten years. As a white male with an extremely limited Spanish vocabulary, I was clearly an outsider. Nevertheless, I became friendly with several of the corner regulars who spoke English rather well. Any language barrier that might have existed is not of particular concern for the purposes of this report since I will primarily concern myself with the nonverbal exchanges that occurred between corner regulars and outsiders who passed through Chronic Town.

I generally observed these interactions from some distance (e.g., across the street) so as to minimize observer effects. On the other hand, my presence as a researcher undoubtedly had some effect on the interactions that I will describe. For example, at times I was perceived to be an outsider by the street corner regulars who did not know me; as a result, I experienced confrontation firsthand. Many of my insights into the process of fear-driven interaction were made possible by my own fear and the responses it brought. Furthermore, as I established an identity on the corner, I was able to see how being known insulates one against fear of victimization. Since my status on the corner evolved over time, I am able to discuss public interaction from the vantage point of an outsider as well as an accepted member of the corner congregation. As an active participant in the street life of Chronic Town, my own experiences on the corner are an important part of the data that I will discuss. Over the course of my research I became, as Anderson (1990) once described himself, my own informant.

Soon after I began my research, I became particularly interested in the exchanges between the Latino Chronic Towners and the mostly white, professional pedestrians who came to Chronic Town from the nearby federal government office buildings where they worked. Federal workers came to Chronic Town to do their banking in one of the local bank branches, shop at the market, or to eat at one of the highly regarded restaurants in the area. I recognized an outsider by his or her clothing, ethnic appearance, and apparent class status. Since Chronic Town was overwhelmingly Latino and working class, I generally assumed that white—male or female—pedestrians wearing business attire were passing through and, thus, thought of them as outsiders. I sometimes stopped and interviewed outsiders to search for beliefs, biases, and attitudes about the Chronic Town community. I used this information to understand the general fears that existed toward Chronic Town and to imagine what people were feeling as they negotiated the corner congregation. Of course, I had my own set of fears. I will discuss the fear and discomfort I felt during the course of the research and some of the consequences of my fearful behavior.

The exchanges that I will report were undoubtedly influenced by the different ethnic identities of interactants and the structural inequality that separated Chronic Towners from most passersby. I will argue that ethnic prejudice and cultural stereotypes did, in fact, cause some outsiders to automatically fear the male Central American immigrants they encountered. As Anderson (1990) noted, it is common for whites to affect a strategic mood or posture (e.g., facial scowling) to ward off the dangerous racial "types" whom they anticipate meeting in an urban area. While I am prepared to address the effects of ethnic prejudice, I will not attempt to discuss any Latino cultural idiosyncrasies that might have contributed to the development of these encounters. I will not try to guess, for example, what it is about being Salvadoran and male that causes an individual to harass another or to react to another's fear in a unique way. Ethnic conflict, however, was clearly a factor here. Since the Central American immigrant population is expected to dramatically increase in the coming decade and new ethnic communities will expand, it is important that we study the interactional dynamics between these ethnic newcomers and native-born Americans as they navigate public spaces (Edmonston and Passel 1994).

Conflict between female pedestrians and neighborhood men was common in Chronic Town. I often witnessed Latino males in groups harass passing women, and I had several white females (including one local police officer) and one African American woman tell me that the immigrant men who inhabited Chronic Town were especially likely to hit on them, whistle at them, honk a car horn, or otherwise harass them. Clearly, there was a gendered dimension to many of the confrontations I observed. Gardner (1988, 1990, 1995) has written extensively on the behavioral strategies employed by women when they are harassed by men in public. Drawing from personal observation and intensive interviews, Gardner details the ways in which women use presentational strategies to avoid harassment and the management styles they use when harassment does occur. Like Gardner, I became aware that women are subject to a greater risk for harassment in public places. I did not observe any major qualitative differences, however, in the way female and male outsiders displayed fear or responded to threatening situations. While women were more likely to be harassed by the congregating men in Chronic Town, the ways in which they dealt with anticipated or actual confrontation (e.g., avoidance, demonstrative caution, assertive interaction) were similar to the behavioral strategies employed by fearful men.

CRIME, NEIGHBORHOOD REPUTATION, AND IDENTIFYING DANGER IN CHRONIC TOWN

A Dangerous Place?

I was able to obtain crime data pertaining to Chronic Town and several of the neighboring communities from the local police department. I obtained arrest data and figures on calls for police service for the three years spanning from 1990 through 1992. The data on calls for police service were helpful in comparing neighborhoods and peoples' relative perceptions about crime and disorder in their communities. While I was at least informally aware that Chronic Town had a reputation as a dangerous place, I wanted to examine police data to find out if Chronic Town had earned this reputation by having a relatively high rate of violent crime. Furthermore, if Chronic Town was a truly dangerous place, even for those just passing through, we should expect to find instances of public violence where the offender and victim were strangers. I feel confident relying on official reports to discuss the relative risks of violence by community, since crimes involving personal victimization, especially between strangers, tend to have a high rate of report (Schneider and Wiersema 1990). I also was interested in the kinds of behavior that most commonly resulted in calls for police service to Chronic Town.

At the time of my research, Chronic Town had a reputation for being a crime-ridden neighborhood characterized by vagrancy, disorderly behavior, and much public drunkenness. An examination of local crime data suggests that the neighborhood had earned this reputation. In the year before I started my research, Chronic Town generated more calls for police service than any other neighborhood in the county. About 40 percent of those calls for service involved reports of crimes against the public order. (The local police identified public disorder crimes as public drunkenness, disorderly conduct, vandalism, suspicious activity, and trespassing.) Furthermore, in the same year, Chronic Town generated more calls for violent acts than any other neighborhood in the county. The majority of these calls involved domestic violence and assaults that occurred within the residential area of Chronic Town. Because the neighborhood generated more calls for violent acts than any other nearby community, one might conclude that Chronic Town is a relatively dangerous place. On the other hand, except for one well-publicized case, I could not find any examples of random violence perpetrated against a passerby by a Chronic Towner. Both the crime data and my own observation told me that the most common kind of Chronic Town violence took the form of a family argument that escalated into violence or a drunken fistfight between two neighborhood men.

In the year before my corner observation began, Jack Carpenter (all names in the article have been changed), an elderly man who lived on the fringes of Chronic Town, was shot and killed as he was taking a shortcut through the neighborhood with an armload of newly bought Christmas packages. The local police believed that the man was murdered after he resisted a robbery attempt. Several witnesses reported seeing a group of Latino men fleeing the scene. The local media exploited the case for its emotional power: an elderly man, Christmas presents, a final courageous act of resistance, and several immigrant men cowardly escaping the murder scene. The case certainly enhanced Chronic Town's reputation as a dangerous place.

Although this incident was the only local murder that occurred in recent years in Chronic Town, locals saw the murder as business as usual in the neighborhood rather than as the isolated incident it actually was. "Those people [Chronic Towners] are animals," one white, male pedestrian told me. "They'll kill you as soon as they'll look at you." Although the man exaggerated, Chronic Town could be a scary place. I arrived at the corner one day soon after a particularly bloody fistfight had taken place in the market parking lot. The opponents were two men vying for the interests of a young woman who frequented the corner market scene. I was told by one of my contacts that the woman, Carly, had apparently admitted to having sex with both men, individuals whom I knew to be good friends before her admission. Most fights that I saw or heard about had similar origins. Friends or drinking acquaintances frequently fought over a particularly injurious personal insult or some other sign of disrespect. For example, one man, Notorio, hit one of his friends over the head with a full-quart beer bottle because his friend had laughed at him in front of several newcomers to the corner. Notorio told me that he regretted hurting his friend but felt that others would have lost respect for him had he not done it.

Public fistfights were not uncommon, but usually took place very late at night when pedestrian traffic was low. Outsiders to Chronic Town were not likely to be in the neighborhood at this time. It is unlikely that the federal workers who walked through Chronic Town during the day would have ever witnessed violence there firsthand. In fact, those pedestrians who did report a fear of being personally victimized were most likely to cite the crime beat of the local newspaper as their source for information. What many people seemed to fear most was drunken men and their drunken behaviors: staggering, shouting, harassing passersby, and vomiting and urinating in public.

Public urination, in fact, was fairly common during the months that I observed corner behavior. Although not necessarily a physical threat, it could be startling to see men urinating outside. Although men were usually discreet—relieving themselves behind a dumpster for instance—often, they were not. One corner regular, Mike from Paraguay, urinated so openly in front of oncoming Market Street traffic one afternoon that it appeared as if he had found a unique way to hail a cab. This type of behavior may have signaled to outsiders that the most basic social controls had broken down. Although public urination is not violence, public incivilities like this represent a fundamental disorder in a community that threatens people's sense of security and raises feelings of vulnerability (Ferraro 1995; Lagrange, Ferraro, and Supancic 1992; Lewis and Salem 1988; Skogan 1990; Wilson and Kelling 1989). Given Chronic Town's reputation, it is no wonder that people employed behavioral strategies to improve their chances for survival in what they perceived to be a dangerous place. Whether

Chronic Town is in fact a place to be feared is not the question being addressed here. Instead, I seek to describe the situations in which strangers work together to create a potentially dangerous confrontation. Armed with their fears, pedestrians come into contact with people who seem to be potential predators and modify their behavior to maximize survival. Next, I will discuss the visual cues that people use to decide which strangers are dangerous. Since pedestrians are generally confronted by people with whom they are unfamiliar, they must quickly identify others by use of what Lofland (1973) calls "appearential ordering." That is, to be safe, one must recognize a dangerous other by his or her immediately perceptible characteristics and demeanor.

Who Is Dangerous?

I relied on interviews with passing outsiders and residents of a nearby condominium community (the Lyndon) to find out what the criteria were for identifying a dangerous person. The mostly white residents of the Lyndon and the neighboring condominium communities generally feared the young Latino males of Chronic Town. Franz, the desk clerk at the Lyndon, felt that the immigrant population was made up of "murderers, junkies and bums." He argued that most of the Central American immigrants had fled the law in their own countries of origin to continue their criminal ways in America. Franz would only shop at the market early in the morning before the usual congregators arrived. For him, identifying dangerous men was unproblematic: Latinos were inherently dangerous and should be avoided at all costs.

Other locals had a more complicated system of appearential ordering. Nathan, an elderly Lyndonite, was able to rank the potential risk of a Chronic Town stranger according to age and clothing. According to him, the male immigrant population was simultaneously murderous and hardworking. He felt safe around the older Chronic Towners who wore symbols of work: paint-splattered clothing, construction helmets, work boots. He described such men as quiet, hardworking, respectable individuals. The men he feared were the younger types who wore "flashy" jewelry and hung around the corner instead of getting jobs. In short, a dangerous man was young, ostentatiously dressed, and unemployed. He claimed he knew of several elderly people who had been attacked by these types late at night in Chronic Town. Rachel, a white woman who lives in Chronic Town, used behavioral cues to assess the dangerousness of corner congregators. In general, she felt that the corner men were "harmless." She believed that their outdoor socializing was simply a part of their culture and misunderstood by intolerant people. The men she avoided were those who appeared to be drunk. She steered clear of those who drank in public, staggered, or were inappropriately loud. It was only when they got drunk, she said, that they "got mean."

Many of my Latino informants also differentiated between the "good" and "bad" elements of Chronic Town street life. Benny, a middle-aged Salvadoran immigrant, told me that many of the older men who congregated at the market were solid citizens who were simply exercising a cultural tradition. According to

Benny, standing outside and talking to one's friends after work is "what Spanish people do." There was a certain type of street-corner man for whom Benny held disdain. To Benny, the "nasty people" were those men who were clearly intoxicated and hanging around the market during the day, when they should be working, and late at night, when they should be sleeping. He told me that he pointed these men out to his young sons as examples of "what not to be."

Whether or not a man held a steady job and supported his family was a common way to separate the decent corner men from the untrustworthy. One of my corner associates, Andujar, often warned me to steer clear of certain market regulars. One day I was talking to Notorio, who had a well-earned reputation as a heavy drinker and troublemaker, when I felt a tugging at my sleeve. It was Andujar, who whispered, "Don't believe a word that bum says." Andujar was openly critical of men like Notorio who were chronically drunk and unemployed. Although he did not appear to fear such men, he believed that they were not to be trusted. He felt that their inability to hold a job or to meet familial obligations indicated that they were not "ready to be men yet."

Because the corner market congregation had a reputation for disorderly behavior, especially the harassment of passing women, many people I interviewed entered the neighborhood with a preconceived notion of its dangerousness. By simple association, men who gathered there were seen as potential predators. As Lofland (1973) points out, modern city dwellers often use location rather than appearance to identify strangers. In her words, "In the modern city, a man is where he stands" (p. 42). Standing on the corner, then, was often enough to stimulate fear and the behavioral survival strategies that accompanied that fear. Next, I will discuss the interaction between pedestrians and Chronic Town regulars and the way they worked jointly to construct dangerous situations.

BEHAVIORAL STRATEGIES OF THE FEARFUL AND THE INTERACTIONAL CONSEQUENCES

The objective here is to discuss some of the ways that citizens work together to create conflict and tension during face-to-face interaction. None of the confrontational episodes I describe escalated into outright violence or physical attacks of any kind. Most commonly, frightened pedestrians worked with a stranger to create a situation out of which harassment grew. My discussion of the effects of certain behavioral strategies is not intended to be the framework for a guide to urban survival. I will argue that certain presentational styles can provoke others, while other strategies work to diffuse a potential confrontation. However, I will not propose a behavioral formula for public safety. The following accounts of public behavior will demonstrate some of the hidden costs of fear of strangers and its consequences.

Pure Avoidance

I experienced firsthand how outsider behavior that reflects the fear of victimization can facilitate a confrontational episode. It was a spring day, long after the Carpenter murder, but the incident still haunted me as I walked through Chronic Town. I was walking home from a subway terminal when I noticed three young Latino males standing at a Market Street bus stop about twenty yards ahead. The men were shouting at passing cars and playfully shoving each other toward the oncoming traffic. Feeling suddenly vulnerable, I switched into a survival mode and crossed the street to avoid passing what I felt was a potentially dangerous group. One of the men recognized that I chose to wade through heavy traffic rather than come any closer to his party, and he alerted his friends to my behavior. My actions, I believe, had implicitly labeled the men as dangerous, and they enthusiastically accommodated my typification by following me across the street. I reached the other side a few steps ahead of the men and did an immediate about-face, back toward a service station that I knew to be located a few blocks away.

The men followed closely behind me, singing the lyrics to a graphically sexual song into the back of my head (the lyrics did not even rhyme, but that was the least of my worries). It was broad daylight in a heavily trafficked area near a large mall outside of Chronic Town. They trailed me the remaining block to the service station and stood outside, seemingly amused, as I pretended to talk to the station manager about the status of a car repair. Eventually, the men got bored and left. After a few minutes, I took an alternative route home. No harm was done nor do I believe any harm would have been done had I walked past them in the first place. I believe that the men merely saw an opportunity to capitalize, for their own entertainment, on my obvious fear. In this case, instead of avoiding a perilous situation, I created one. Actions like mine may be well advised in some situations, but I became aware that obvious avoidance tactics can express to the avoided that they represent a potential danger—a potential that they may be delighted to fulfill.

After several months of research, I became a familiar face around the corner market. Not only did I lose most of my fear of these men, but I came to feel a sense of security in their presence. At one point, about midway through the observation period, I saw a group of young Latino men near the corner who displayed some of the symbols of gang membership: they wore matching blue bandannas tied low on their foreheads, and many had pagers attached to their hips. The greatest fear that I ever felt on the corner was having to navigate my way through this group. The young men glared at me and made no attempt to let me pass. A year earlier, this experience might have sent me sprinting out of Chronic Town, never to return. By this point, however, I had a group of friends at the corner who I felt were looking out for me. In fact, when I finally did make it past this intimidating group, I settled about ten yards away from them where a friend, Andujar, and a group of his coworkers were lounging under a tree. I felt strongly that being in the presence of certain men on the corner communicated to others that I was okay. Having my own identity on the corner and being socially connected is what insulated me most from the fear of personal victimization.

Demonstrative Caution

Demonstrative caution is an obvious safety strategy when one feels threatened by his or her environment. Obvious displays of fear or discomfort can communicate several things to a public audience. First, people who behave fearfully in public can signal to others that they have something to hide (e.g., valuables, cash, jewelry) and therefore make good targets (Merry 1981). Second, I believe that overly cautious performances trigger a temporary labeling process whereby an individual who is treated as dangerous momentarily accommodates that label by enacting it. We can expect those whom we treat as predators, then, to behave like predators. This is not to say that the label *dangerous* communicated by fearful pedestrians becomes attached to the identity of feared individuals. In fact, it may be that feared individuals often already see themselves as dangerous and that when another affixes the label *dangerous* in public, it activates that dimension of the identity.

Many pedestrians seemed especially uncomfortable when making bank transactions at automated teller machines (ATMs). In fact, for several weeks after the Carpenter murder, I personally rushed my own ATM transactions while looking over my shoulder all the while. ATM paranoia seems reasonable enough given the circumstances surrounding the process of requesting and receiving money from a machine. The process itself seems to be a perfect formula for victimization when one considers the logistics: the ATM client orders large sums of cash from a machine with his or her back to the street, rendering him or her unable to watch for any potential predators who might be lurking nearby. If outsiders brought a fear of strangers with them into Chronic Town, operating an ATM would only compound their feelings of vulnerability.

Demonstrative caution at the ATM was most pronounced when ATM clients operated the machine while others waited behind them in line. Feeling vulnerable, the client would communicate his or her fear to others through nonverbal expressions. For example, one well-dressed, middle-aged, white man approached an ATM just across the street from the market. He quickly surveyed the area and, deciding momentarily that it was safe to proceed, he slipped his card into the machine and made his request. While the machine processed his request, two young Latino men lined up behind him. He quickly wheeled around to face them and self-consciously nodded to them in greeting. The man looked more than uncomfortable; he was clearly scared. When he turned back to face the machine, the two men behind him looked at one another and, as if in silent agreement, they drew closer to him, clearly violating the unwritten rules of ATM etiquette (from my own observation, ATM clients generally give the person making a transaction at least one arm's length of space and do not appear to be looking over the operator's shoulder). The man's extreme reaction to the mere presence of the Latino men had communicated his fear to them and in the process identified the men as "people to be feared."

They responded to his label by purposely closing the physical space that separated them from the ATM operator, thus escalating a benign ATM transaction into a perilous experience. The man looked over his shoulder repeatedly in the next several seconds before the machine finally dispensed his money. He jerked out his card, folded and stuffed his money in his pocket, and rushed away from the scene. The two men laughed and seemed pleased with their performance as he disappeared around the corner. This scene demonstrates the conflict that arises out of behavior that communicates from one to another that the other is an imposing, potentially dangerous individual. In this case, being implicitly labeled as such generated a subtly aggressive response. The men did not appear to have plans to rob the ATM client but made sport of intimidating him further when he expressed his assessment of them as dangerous men.

Some outsiders who came to shop at the market demonstrated fear of victimization by making obvious attempts to guard their property. For instance, it was common for women, especially the elderly, to tightly clutch their purses with both hands while weaving through the corner congregation. The gathering of immigrant men under a large tree on the east side of the market signaled danger to many of the market shoppers who parked their cars in the lot. On one occasion, a man pulled into a parking space, got out of his car, and strode up to the store entrance. Before he reached the front, however, he stopped, turned around, and scanned the group of men lounging in the grass under the tree near his car. He apparently saw the group as representing a threat because he returned to his car, rolled up the driver's side window and locked the door. When he finished securing his vehicle, the man returned to the market and entered it for a period of about ten minutes.

This behavior made an impression on some of the men gathered under the tree that day. While the man was in the store, several of the men arose from the grass and began to examine the car. One young immigrant male, Felix, decided that the man's car would make a nice place to sit. He lifted himself onto the trunk and rested his feet on the rear bumper. Soon after, the car owner returned. I have no doubt that he noticed Felix perched on the back of his car and that several of the other men were standing conspicuously near the driver's side awaiting his return. However, the man did not react in any noticeable way. He shifted his grocery bag, produced his car keys, and let himself into his car without even acknowledging the stowaway on the rear end of the vehicle. Felix moved as the man started his car and the others all stood and watched him as he pulled away.

Again, I saw this bit of demonstrative caution as an informal, if merely temporary, labeling exercise. The man's actions served as an invitation to the congregating men to confirm the *dangerous* label that he had conferred on them. Felix in particular seemed to feel that he was issued a challenge. By sitting on the car, Felix was able to simultaneously embrace his dangerousness and foil the car owner's unsophisticated attempt to be safe. The result was not dramatic. Although there was no physical confrontation between the men, an important thing was accomplished: if the man had never experienced or witnessed victimization in Chronic Town before, he had now. Surely, Felix's not-so-subtle claim of the man's car qualified as an aggressive move made by an young immigrant male. The car owner's fear of a certain segment of the local population had been confirmed.

Assertive Interaction

Assertive interaction involves the use of a confident, forthright presentational style when interacting with individuals perceived to be potentially dangerous. Instead of using an avoidance technique or demonstrative protective measure, the assertive actor pursues interaction with a dangerous type, sometimes even initiating the interaction, to disarm a feared stranger. A good illustration of this phenomenon was reported by Merry (1981) in her urban ethnography of a high-crime neighborhood.

> George suggests going up to someone who looks as if he is going to rob you and saying "Hello, how are you doing". . . . Even if the robber is not conned into thinking he is known, he may pause for a minute, and not finish the robbery. . . . George thinks that it is most important to treat the criminal like a person, to smile at him and not be afraid of him. (p. 175)

During my experience in Chronic Town, I witnessed the use of several variations on this strategy.

Early one evening, an unfamiliar Latino male approached me on the corner. He possessed several of the traits that suggest intoxication: red eyes, slurred speech, disheveled clothing. He put his hand on my shoulder and asked me if I had a light for his cigarette. This made me nervous. I suppose it had to do with his drunkenness and his forward manner. It was unusual for any of the men I knew on the corner to make any sort of physical contact when we interacted. Even handshakes were rare, much less a hand on the shoulder. I stammered something about not having any matches while I made a mock search of my pants pockets. The drunken man did not move. He did not answer me. He just stood there smiling as if it was just a matter of time before I admitted to owning matches, or a lighter, or some other form of fire, and shared it with him. I had learned by this time that showing my fear was not going to get me anywhere. I chose to meet the demands of the situation by denying my fear and going out of my way to interact with this man. One way of doing this was to be assertive about helping him get what he needed. I told him to wait for a minute while I went to get him some matches. When I returned minutes later with several matchbooks obtained from a nearby convenience store, the man was waiting. He was clearly surprised that I had returned and thanked me repeatedly for the matches. If this man meant me any harm (or even meant only to scare me), I successfully disarmed him by pursuing interaction with him rather than avoiding him or treating him like a dangerous fellow.

Many women who passed through Chronic Town reported instances of harassment by the groups of men who congregated at the corner. I personally witnessed this several times. For example, I once stood with Felix and a group of men in front of the market when a young woman walked by pushing a shopping cart. Felix stood out from the group, positioned himself conspicuously, and stared at the woman. When she did not immediately look up, Felix made a shrill whistling sound in her direction. When she looked up and found Felix smiling at her, she responded by grimacing in a way that suggested she had a horrible taste in her mouth. The men congregated there laughed at Felix. Her simple critique of his behavior had put an end to the harassment. Past research suggests that disarming a harassing male is usually much more problematic than this (see Gardner 1988, 1990, 1995). However, this woman's direct, negative response to Felix was clearly effective, while a purely avoidant response may have served to perpetuate and even escalate the harassment.

Another woman I knew, Helen, had a way of anticipating harassment and heading it off before it began. Helen worked near Chronic Town and did her shopping at the market a few times a week. She said that she was not afraid to shop at the market but admitted feeling uncomfortable when groups of men stared at her or called out to her in Spanish. "I know they don't want anything off me," she said. "They're just showing off." She reported being hit on repeatedly at the bus stop. This made her nervous at times, but she chose to handle it by dealing directly with the men. She told me that one man had asked her for her phone number. "I told him, 'No Sir, why don't you give me your phone number?' He didn't want to do that. They didn't bother me after that." Helen had effectively turned the tables on the man who, she felt, was more interested in impressing the men who stood nearby watching than in actually securing a date with her. Like me, Helen was somewhat of a regular at the corner since she shopped so frequently at the market. Her frequent presence at the market and her direct interaction with some of the men allowed her to develop an identity in Chronic Town. She was regarded as someone who would not stand for harassment. Furthermore, she had spent enough time in Chronic Town to decide that the men who gathered at the market were harmless. What most reduced her fear, and mine, was a feeling that she was traveling in familiar territory among familiar faces. We felt less vulnerable because the men at the corner were people we knew, not strangers.

CONCLUSION

Fear of strangers has negative consequences for both the fearful and the feared. I have suggested some of the ways in which presentational strategies that betray a fear and mistrust of others result in friction between pedestrians as they encounter each other in public. Fear can serve a self-fulfilling function; it can stimulate conflict that serves to validate prejudices, legitimize fear, and drive members of a community further apart. The outsiders who walked into Chronic Town with a preconceived notion of the local men as potential predators were often unwilling partners in their own harassment. Undoubtedly, avoidant and cautious behavioral strategies are in some cases well chosen. In the case of Chronic Town, however, fear of strangers was often the result of ethnic stereotypes and prejudices. Many of the outsiders with whom I spoke discussed the Central American immigrant population in terms of its general propensity for violence without ever having experienced or witnessed any acts of aggression by any of the men in the neighborhood or elsewhere. Pedestrians were not so much frightened of individual men as they were of social types, specifically, young Latino males. This is not to say that fearful behavior made dangerous men out of innocent ones. Some of the men who perpetrated the harassment may have even been looking for a reason to behave in a threatening manner. Scaring pedestrians may confirm an already developed badass identity (Katz 1988). Still, treating the badass as a dangerous man will almost surely trigger behavior in support of that identity.

I have argued throughout this discussion that fearful behavior can be seen as a form of temporary labeling: those treated as dangerous may respond by behaving in a corresponding fashion. These labels may be highly temporary or simply serve as an invitation to harass a clearly vulnerable individual. However, demonstrative public fear may also have long-term consequences for those individuals who are routinely assumed to be predators as they interact with others in the community. When it did appear that certain Chronic Towners realized that others feared them, the men seemed to take it lightly. As I have described, some of the men seemed amused by the fear they evoked in others and even exploited that fear in the form of recreational harassment. However, over time, public safety strategies may carry a hidden cost for the identities of those men who are consistently labeled as being dangerous. Theorists in the labeling tradition argue that official negative responses (e.g., arrest, incarceration) to behavior are criminogenic because they affix themselves not only to the behavior but to the identity of those so labeled (Becker 1963; Lemert 1951). This perspective may be useful in understanding how caution and avoidance affect the self-concept of people who are negatively labeled during face-to-face interaction. It has been suggested elsewhere that members of socially devalued racial and ethnic groups internalize the negative evaluations that they receive in public, which may result in a negative evaluation of the self (Feagin 1991) or a feeling of discontent about one's identity (Hurtado, Gurin, and Peng 1994). It would be valuable to explore the social psychological impact of the immediately impinging labels that arise out of public demonstrations of fear. This issue may be especially salient for the study of ethnic groups that are perceived as threatening to the public order, such as those Latino immigrants who have already arrived in America and those who are soon to follow.

I have tried to avoid suggesting that people should merely adjust their public behavior to avoid victimization. I would not advise, for example, that pedestrians confront their fear of strangers by aggressively interacting with every stranger who appears as if he or she might be dangerous. During the ten months that I studied interaction in Chronic Town, I continually battled with my own fears and feelings of vulnerability. Over time, what weakened my own fear was the fact that I got to know the men who frequented the market parking lot. The unfamiliar faces I encountered in the beginning became, in time, familiar. Many of the men who at first represented a threat to me became friendly acquaintances. Not only did I come to know the men who made up the corner congregation, but they came to know me. Fear of strangers becomes less relevant when the people who populate one's neighborhood or community are no longer strangers. As Lofland (1995) has pointed out, given the ever-increasing prevalence of nonintimate interaction, this is no easy task. Weak ties to the community, then, promote fear, cautious presentational strategies, and the public confrontations that legitimize fear. In my experience, those who were most frightened of Chronic Town were those least socially connected to it. I recognize that most people do not have the luxury of conducting face-to-face research with the members of their communities. While my research afforded me a unique opportunity, I was able to see that public safety is not simply a matter of effective presentational style. In the end, becoming known and becoming familiar with the members of one's community may be the best safety strategy of all.

REFERENCES

Anderson, E. 1990. *Streetwise: Race, class and change in an urban community.* Chicago: University of Chicago Press.

Bankston, W. B., and C. Y. Thompson. 1989. Carrying firearms for protection: A causal model. *Sociological Inquiry* 59:75–87.

Becker, H. S. 1963. *Outsiders.* New York: Free Press.

Bourgois, P. 1995. *In Search of respect: Selling crack in El Barrio.* Cambridge, UK: Cambridge University Press.

Edmonston, B., and J. S. Passel. 1994. Ethnic demography: U.S. immigration and ethnic variations. In *Immigration and ethnicity: The integration of America's newest arrivals,* edited by B. Edmonston and J. Passel, 1–30. Washington, DC: Urban Institute Press.

Feagin, J. R. 1991. The continuing significance of race: Antiblack discrimination in public places. *American Sociological Review* 56:101–16.

Ferraro, K. F. 1995. *Fear of crime: Interpreting victimization risk.* Albany, NY: State University of New York Press.

Gardner, C. B. 1988. Access information: Public lies and private peril. *Social Problems* 35:384–97.

———. 1990. Safe conduct: Women, crime, and self in public places. *Social Problems* 37:311–28.

———. 1995. *Passing by: Gender and public harassment.* Berkeley: University of California Press.

Hurtado. A., P. Gurin, and T. Peng. 1994. Social identities—a framework for studying the adaptations of immigrants and ethnics: The adaptations of Mexicans in the United States. *Social Problems* 41:129–51.

Katz, J. 1988. *Seductions of crime.* New York: Basic Books.

Kelling, G. L., and C. M. Coles. 1994. Disorder and the court. *Public Interest* 116:57–74.

———. 1996. *Fixing broken windows: Restoring order and reducing crime in our communities.* New York: Free Press.

Lagrange, R. L., K. F. Ferraro, and M. Supancic. 1992. Perceived risk and fear of crime: Role of social and physical incivilities. *Journal of Research in Crime and Delinquency* 29:311–34.

Lemert, E. M. 1951. *Social pathology.* New York: McGraw-Hill.

Lewis, D. A., and G. Salem. 1988. *Fear of crime: Incivility and the production of a social problem.* New Brunswick, NJ: Transaction Books.

Lilly, J. R., F. T. Cullen, and R. A. Ball. 1995. *Criminological theory: Context and consequences.* 2d ed. Thousand Oaks, CA: Sage.

Liska, A. E., A. Sanchirico, and M. D. Reed. 1988. Fear of crime and constrained behavior: Specifying and estimating a reciprocal effects model. *Social Forces* 66:827–37.

Lofland, L. H. 1973. *A world of strangers: Order and action in urban public space.* New York: Basic Books.

———. 1995. Social interaction: Continuities and complexities in the study of nonintimate sociality. In *Sociological perspectives on social psychology,* edited by K. Cook, G. Fine, and J. House, 176–201. Boston: Allyn & Bacon.

Merry, S. E. 1981. *Urban danger: Life in a neighborhood of strangers.* Philadelphia: University of Temple Press.

Monkkonen, E. H. 1988. *America becomes urban: The development of U.S. cities and towns 1780–1980.* Berkeley: University of California Press.

Schneider, V. W., and B. Wiersema. 1990. Limits and use of the uniform crime reports. In *Measuring crime: Large-scale, long-range efforts,* edited by D. MacKenzie, P. Baunach. and R. Roberg, 21–48. Albany: State University of New York Press.

Shorris, E. 1992. *Latinos: A biography of the people.* New York: Norton.

Skogan, W. G. 1990. *Disorder and decline: Crime and the spiral of decay in American neighborhoods.* New York: Free Press.

Skogan, W. G., and M. G. Maxfield. 1981. *Coping with crime.* Beverly Hills, CA: Sage.

St. John, C., and T. Heald-Moore. 1996. Age, racial prejudice, and fear of criminal victimization in public settings. *Sociological Focus* 29:15–31.

Warr, M. 1984. Fear of victimization: Why are women and the elderly more afraid? *Social Science Quarterly* 65:681–702.

———. 1985. Fear of rape among urban women. *Social Problems* 32:238–50.

Wilson, J. Q., and G. L. Kelling. 1989. Making neighborhoods safe. *Atlantic Monthly* 263:46–52.

Wolfinger, N. H. 1995. Passing moments: Some social dynamics of pedestrian interaction. *Journal of Contemporary Ethnography* 24:323–40.

Wright, J. D. 1991. Guns and crime. In *Criminology: A contemporary handbook,* edited by J. Sheley, 441–57. Belmont, CA: Wadsworth.

Yin, P. 1982. Fear of crime as a problem for the elderly. *Social Problems* 30:240–45.

———. 1985. *Victimization and the aged.* New York: Charles C Thomas.

THOMAS M. VANDER VEN is a doctoral candidate at the University of Cincinnati. His dissertation examines the impact of maternal working conditions on delinquency. He is also performing a qualitative investigation of the targeting process in a family preservation program and continuing his research in the area of fear of crime.

DISCUSSION QUESTIONS

1. Explain Vander Ven's comment that "criminological theory should be used to guide research and to sensitize the observer, but should not put undue constraints on the data collection."
2. How did the researcher gain acceptance? Minimize observer effects?
3. In what ways, if at all, did the researcher reformulate the questions or issues of interest as the study progressed?
4. Describe Vander Ven's approach to analysis of the data.

8

Collective and Normative Features of Gang Violence

SCOTT H. DECKER, University of Missouri-St. Louis

COMMENTARY

This research was conducted on the streets of St. Louis, a city with extremely high rates of homicide, robbery, and gun assault. The research was conducted among gang members, a group notable for their high levels of violent offending and victimization. Approaching gang members requires considerable negotiating skills to ensure the participation of potential subjects, as well as caution on the part of the researcher. I was able to bridge this gap with the assistance of Dietrich Smith, a veteran of the streets. In 1979, Dietrich had been shot eleven times by the brother of an offender Dietrich testified against. He was paralyzed as a consequence of his victimization. Ironically, being in a wheelchair allowed him to break down many barriers that may have impeded an individual without a "disability." Dietrich was seen as nonthreatening as he wheeled himself down the block or onto the street.

One of the difficult things about qualitative work is analyzing the data. Most students presume that quantitative data analysis (better known as statistics) is the most difficult task faced by researchers. However, deciding what to do with thousands of pages of transcribed interviews can make even the most devoted qualitative researcher long for statistical tests. I chose to use one of the many qualitative software packages on the market, GOFER. This software allowed me to identify categories, and pull together all of the comments made by gang members regarding specific topics. In this way, the software worked as a data reduction tool, providing a rough analogy to statistical measures of central tendency and measures of association.

Source: Justice Quarterly, Vol. 13 No. 2, June 1996, pp. 243-264. © 1996. Reprinted by permission of the Academy of Criminal Justice Sciences.

The research on which this paper is based was supported by Grant 90CL/1076 from the Department of Health and Human Services, Administration of Children and Families. All opinions expressed here are those of the author and are not necessarily shared by the funding agency.

One of the reasons we are interested in understanding gangs is because of the high level of violence associated with gang membership. However, as a researcher, I was not prepared for just how great the violence would be nor for the effect the personal nature of such violence would have on me. This was somewhat surprising; after all, I was working with a colleague who had been paralyzed as a consequence of violence. As our study progressed, a number of members of our sample were killed. When the following article was submitted for publication, nine of the ninety-nine gang members in our sample had been killed. In the six-month time period during which the manuscript was reviewed, two more were killed. Since the publication of the article in 1996, five more members of our sample have been killed, two have been sent to prison for life, and one is in a wheelchair.

A related component of the gang study attempted to learn about gangs from the families of gang members, especially the mothers. This led me to attend several meetings of the group Families Advocating Safe Streets (FASS), formed by a mother whose oldest son was murdered, and youngest son was convicted of second-degree murder in avenging his brother's death. Such meetings serve as poignant reminders of the tragedies criminal violence produces. Researchers must be attuned to these aspects of crime and victimization or they will miss significant issues associated with the lives of their subjects.

ABSTRACT Gang members engage in a considerable amount of violence. Based on a three-year field study of active gang members in St. Louis, this paper examines five activities in which gang members use violence. Retaliatory gang violence is highlighted for its role in generating additional violence and contributing to the growth of gangs. We pay particular attention to the normative aspects of gang violence. In addition, gang violence is interpreted from the perspective of collective behavior.

In 1927 Frederic Thrasher observed that gangs shared many of the properties of mobs, crowds, and other collectives, and engaged in many forms of collective behavior. Despite the prominent role of his work in gang research, few attempts have been made to link the behavior of gangs to theories of collective behavior. This omission is noteworthy because, despite disagreements about most other criteria—turf, symbols, organizational structure, permanence, criminality—all gang researchers include "group" as a part of their definition of gangs. Gang members are individuals with diverse motives, behaviors, and socialization experiences. Their *group* membership, behavior, and values, however, make them interesting to criminologists who study gangs.

In this paper we explore the mechanisms and processes that result in the spread and escalation of gang violence. In particular, we focus on contagion as an aspect of collective behavior that produces expressive gang violence. Collective behavior explanations provide insights into gang processes, particularly the escalation of violence, the spread of gangs from one community to another, and increases in gang membership in specific communities.

GANG VIOLENCE

Violence is integral to life in the gang, as Klein and Maxson (1989) observed, and gang members engage in more violence than other youths. Thrasher (1927) noted that gangs developed through strife and flourish on conflict. According to Klein (1971:85), violence is a "predominant 'myth system'" among gang members and is constantly present.

Our analysis of gang violence focuses on the role of *threat,* actual or perceived, in explaining the functions and consequences of gang violence. We define threat as the potential for transgressions against or physical harm to the gang, represented by the acts or presence of a rival group. Threats of violence are important because they have consequences for future violence. Threat plays a role in the origin and growth of gangs, their daily activities, and their belief systems. In a sense, it helps to define them to rival gangs, to the community, and to social institutions.

Katz (1988) argues that gangs are set apart from other groups by their ability to create "dread," a direct consequence of involvement in and willingness to use violence. Dread elevates these individuals to street elites through community members' perceptions of gang members as violent. In many neighborhoods, groups form for protection against the threat of outside groups (Suttles 1972). Sometimes these groups are established along ethnic lines, though territorial concerns often guide their formation. Sanders (1993), in a 10-year study of gangs in San Diego, argued that the mix of conventional values with underclass values—spiced by the realities of street culture—was a volatile combination. Hagedorn (1988) found that conflicts between the police and young men "hanging out" on the corner led to more formalized structures, and ultimately to gangs. Both Suttles (1972:98) and Sullivan (1989) underscored the natural progression from a neighborhood group to a gang, particularly in the face of "adversarial relations" with outside groups. The emergence of many splinter gangs can be traced to the escalation of violence within larger gangs, and to the corresponding threat that the larger gang comes to represent to certain territorial or age-graded subgroups. Sullivan (1989) documented the expressive character of most gang violence, and described the role of fighting in the evolution of cliques into street gangs. Because this occurs at a young age, the use of group violence attains a normative character.

Threat also may contribute to the growth of gangs. This mechanism works in two ways: through building cohesiveness and through contagion. Threats of physical violence increase the solidarity or cohesiveness of gangs within neighborhoods as well as across neighborhoods. Klein (1971) identified the source of cohesion in gangs as primarily external—the result of intergang conflict; Hagedorn (1988) also made this observation. According to Klein, cohesion within the gang grows in proportion to the perceived threat represented by rival gangs. Padilla (1992) reported a similar finding, noting that threat maintains gang boundaries by strengthening the ties among gang members and increasing their commitment to each other, thus enabling them to overcome any initial reluctance about staying in the gang and ultimately engaging in violence. Thus the threat of a gang in a geographically proximate neighborhood increases the solidarity of the gang, motivates more young men to join their neighborhood gang (see Vigil 1988), and enables them to engage in acts of violence that they might not have committed otherwise.

The growth of gangs and gang violence contains elements of what Loftin (1984) calls "contagion." In this context, contagion refers to subsequent acts of violence caused by an initial act; such acts typically take the form of retaliation. Violence—or its threat—is the mechanism that spreads gangs from one neighborhood to another, as well as contributing to their growth. From Loftin's perspective, the concept of contagion can be used to explain the rapid growth, or the "spikes," that occur in violent crime. He argues that three conditions must be present if contagion is to occur: (1) a spatial concentration of assaultive violence, (2) a reciprocal nature to assaultive violence, and (3) escalations in assaultive violence. These conditions apply to our use of the concept of threat in explaining gangs. Gangs have a strong spatial structure; they claim particular turf as their own and are committed to its "defense" against outsiders. The specter of a rival gang "invading" their turf and violating its sanctity is likely to evoke a violent response, leading to the spatial clustering of violence.

The reciprocal nature of gang violence explains in part how gangs form initially, as well as how they increase in size and strength. Klein and Maxson (1989:223) demonstrated that fear of retaliation was three times more likely to characterize gang homicides than other homicides involving juveniles. The perceived need to engage in retaliatory violence also helps to explain the increasing sophistication of weapons used by gang members. As Horowitz (1983) observed, gang members arm themselves in the belief that their rivals have guns; they seek to increase the sophistication of their weaponry in the hope that they will not find themselves in a shootout with less firepower than their rival. This process was documented by Block and Block (1993) in their explanation of the increase in street gang homicides in Chicago.

The threat of attack by a group of organized youths from another neighborhood is part of the gang "myth" or belief system, and helps to create the need for protection as well as to generate unity in a previously unorganized group of neighborhood youths. The origin and spread of such beliefs explain, among other things, the viability of the gang. Threat performs an additional function: it enhances the mythic nature of violence in the gang by increasing the talk about violence and preparedness for violent engagements.

The threat of violence also "enables" gang members to engage in violent acts (especially retaliatory violence) that they might not have chosen under other circumstances. The need to respond effectively to rival gang violence escalates weaponry and increases the "tension" that often precedes violent encounters between gangs. Many gang members reported to Padilla (1992) that they joined their gang out of fear of violence at the hands of rival gangs. The concern that a rival gang is considering an attack often compels a peremptory strike (particularly drive-by shootings) from the gang that considers itself under threat.

Loftin's (1984) third element of contagion, rapid escalation of assaultive violence, explains the sudden peaks in gang violence. These peaks can be explained in part by the retaliatory nature of gang violence (Decker and Van Winkle 1996), a finding in the data from Chicago gangs (Block and Block 1993).

Threat has an additional function, however. As gangs and gang members engage in acts of violence and create "dread" (Katz 1988:135), they are viewed as threatening by other (gang and non-gang) groups and individuals. Also, over time, the threats that gang members face and pose isolate them from legitimate social institutions such as schools, families, and the labor market. This isolation, in turn, prevents them from engaging in the very activities and relationships that might reintegrate them into legitimate roles and reduce their criminal involvement. It weakens their ties to the socialization power and the controlling norms of such mainstream institutions, and frees them to commit acts of violence.

COLLECTIVE BEHAVIOR

Collective behavior and social organizations such as gangs share many common elements, including group behavior, collective processes, and group structure. Thus it is productive to view collective behavior on a continuum with social organizations rather than regarding them as separate topics of study. Thrasher (1927) observed that collective behavior processes operated within the gang, and could be used to account for the emergence of collective violence. Such processes included games, fights, meetings, and defining common enemies. His theoretical formulation, and the supporting distinctions between gangs and other forms of social organizations (e.g., groups, mobs, crowds, publics),[1] make clear the role that he perceived for collective behavior explanations of gang activity.

We adopt our definition of collective behavior from McPhail (1991), who identified three elements of collective behavior: (1) group, (2) behavior, and (3) common actions that vary on one or more dimensions such as purpose, organization, or duration. McPhail observed that gang violence is a form of collective behavior because it emerges from a group process involving common actions that have a defined purpose. This view of collective behavior is agnostic with regard to motives; that is, such behavior may have either well-defined instrumental goals or more expressive goals. Most research has characterized gang motives as expressive, but Sanchez-Jankowski (1991) argued for a more instrumental orientation. On the basis of his 10-year observation of gangs in three cities, he described gangs as "formal-rational" organizations; he contended

[1]The chart (Thrasher 1927:70) depicting these distinctions is a classic, and provides considerable insight into the level of organization in gangs today. This chart has received little attention from criminologists, however.

that gangs have rules, roles, and goals, and function as highly differentiated and purposive social organizations. Sanchez-Jankowski's research, especially with regard to gang violence, stands alone in its conclusions.

Ironically, the view of gangs as a form of collective behavior may be explicated most fully not in original research on gangs, but in Pfautz's (1961) reconceptualization of Yablonsky's (1959) research on violent gangs. Yablonsky described the gang as a near-group, and attributed much of its violent behavior to the leadership of members who were emotionally disturbed and lacked effective controls against participating in violence. Pfautz argued that it is more productive to view gang violence as the outcome of collective behavior; he noted that some forms of collective behavior are more likely to emerge in the face of a weakened social structure.[2] In reviewing the gang literature, Pfautz observed that gangs lack structure, goals, and techniques. Therefore they act on the basis of what he identified as "associational characteristics," the strength of membership ties or bonds. According to this view, violent behavior by gangs is an expressive response to objective social circumstances (poverty, racism, and other pressures of the underclass) rather than a symbolic expression of "manhood," "low self-esteem," or lack of group solidarity. Gang violence, however, is not a purposive attempt to alter social structure. It emerges as a collective response by members of the underclass to organize around neighborhood affiliations.

Short (1974) attempted to develop theoretical links between several aspects of gang behavior and collective behavior. By observing that gangs emerge out of typical adolescent activities—activities that lack organization, involve groups ripe for collective action, and entail only weakly held group goals—he argued that they originate in collective behavior. Conflict between gangs is particularly important to this process because such disputes help to establish boundaries between groups and reinforce the ties between members. Short agreed with Pfautz that most gang delinquency is expressive, especially gang violence, which frequently reflects the gang's attempt to enforce its particular definition of a situation on another gang. The gang's collective liability for wrong done to rival members expands the pool of potential victims and increases the threats of retaliatory violence. These characteristics underscore the utility of collective behavior approaches in accounting for gang violence.

DATA AND METHODS

This paper is based on the results of a three-year study of gangs conducted in St. Louis between 1990 and 1993. Our work is consistent with other research (Hagedorn, 1988, 1991; Moore 1978; Padilla 1992; Vigil 1988) that used field techniques to understand gang members' perspective. We agree with Hagedorn

[2]This argument is consistent with contemporary arguments that link the reemergence of gangs in the 1980s to the growth of the urban underclass. In this context see Hagedorn (1988), Jackson (1992), Moore (1978), and Vigil (1988).

(1991) that one can understand this perspective most fully by contacting gang members directly in their communities. We contacted gang members directly on the street and conducted interviews at a neutral site.[3] This procedure was consistent with our goal of learning about gang activities in the words and terms used by gang members to describe them. Our working definition of a gang includes age-graded peer groups that exhibit permanence, engage in criminal activity, and have symbolic representations of membership. Field contacts with active gang members were made by a street ethnographer, an ex-offender himself, who had built a reputation as "solid" on the street through his work with the community and previous fieldwork. The street ethnographer had been shot several years earlier, and now used a wheelchair. The combination of his reputation in the community and his experience in contacting and interviewing active offenders enhanced the validity of the responses. Using snowball sampling procedures (Biernacki and Waldorf 1981; Wright et al. 1992), the research team made initial field contacts with gang members, verified membership, and built the sample to include more subjects.

Our sampling strategy was designed to interview members from a variety of gangs and to gain a broader perspective into gang activity. Like most field studies, the pace of our study was often erratic; in some months we held several interviews, while in others we had none. Individuals who met our criteria, acknowledged gang membership, and agreed to an interview were included in our sample. We verified membership through information from previous subjects, our own observations, or both. The field ethnographer played a key role in this process by comparing responses from the interview to street conversations. Our final sample of 99 active gang members was the outcome of more than 500 field contacts initiated with gang members. Members of the final sample were selected on the basis of extensive involvement in the gang and their willingness to participate in the study.

A semistructured questionnaire, based on a number of unstructured interviews conducted before the beginning of the study, was used to guide the interviews. We promised confidentiality to each subject, and did not record their real names. Interviews were conducted by six members of the research team; each was familiar with the gang literature, was knowledgeable about gangs in St. Louis, and had conducted several practice interviews. Each interview was tape-recorded and transcribed for analysis. Interviews generally lasted two hours; they asked for information about joining the gang, the nature of gang organization, illegal activities (especially violence), legal activities, links to other gangs, and ties to traditional institutions. A specific set of questions addressed the ties

[3]Each gang member was transported to and from the interview site, usually an office at the university, by the fieldworker. This trip offered the opportunity to speak informally about gang and nongang matters. It also provided the chance to discuss the nature of the interview, both before and after it was administered. The field ethnographer and the interviewer compared notes, particularly in cases where a subject displayed "excessive" bravado, to ensure that responses reflected the ethnographer's knowledge of the subject, based on his own contacts and observations.

between gang members and their families. We also observed a number of gang activities and individual gang members in the field. We spoke regularly with these individuals and recorded notes to supplement the interviews.

We interviewed individuals from several gangs. According to our interviews and observations, gangs in St. Louis appear to have strong ties to their neighborhood but also claim affiliation with a larger gang that extends well beyond neighborhood boundaries. The bond between gang members and their own subgroup within the gang, however, was usually stronger than the attachment to the larger gang. This finding is consistent with our observations that gangs in St. Louis were organized rather loosely. Few gangs whose members we interviewed had identifiable leaders, roles, or rules.[4] Most of our subjects identified themselves as "regular" members, though 10 individuals told us they were either leaders or "OGs" (original gangsters). We observed little variation between their responses and those of regular members.

We interviewed 99 active gang members representing 29 different gangs. Sixteen of these gangs, accounting for 67 of our 99 subjects, were affiliated with the Crips. Gang members affiliated with the Bloods accounted for the remainder of our sample, and included 13 gangs and 32 members. Field techniques cannot provide a representative sample, but our subjects varied considerably in age, gang affiliation, and activities, thus assuring that we received information from a variety of gang members. As a result, it was unlikely that our respondents revealed information about only a narrow segment of gang activity.

Although our data were collected over a three-year period, they are not longitudinal in the sense that they followed a single individual or group of individuals over time. We were sensitive to the dynamic nature of gangs in St. Louis during our study period, and incorporated those concerns into questions about how the gang had changed over time. In addition, we compared responses recorded early in the study with those of subjects interviewed in the later stages. Finally, near the end of our study, we recontacted several individuals whom we had interviewed in the early phases of the project. We noted any changes in gang violence that occurred during the course of the study.

We identified six different "constellations" of gangs in our sample, four with the Crip designation and two groups of Bloods. We use the term *constellation* to refer to a larger gang that may be composed of many gang subgroups. For example, the Genevive Thrush Posse is affiliated with the Rolling Sixties, a larger gang of Crips. We found no important differences between these constellations on any of the dimensions of violence we examined. This finding adds credence to the claim that members of our sample knew about a wide range of activities within their gang.

Ages for members of our sample ranged from 13 to 29, with an average age of 17. The majority were black (96%) and male (93%). On average, the gang

[4]In these respects, St. Louis gangs resemble those in Los Angeles (Klein 1971; Klein, Maxson, and Cunningham 1991; Vigil 1988), Milwaukee (Hagedorn 1988), Chicago (Block and Block 1993; Short and Strodtbeck 1974), and San Diego (Sanders 1993).

members we interviewed had been active members for three years. More than three-quarters of our subjects told us that their gang existed before they joined; the average age of gangs in our sample was six years. An average of 213 gang members were involved in the larger gang; subgroups ranged from six to ten members. Ninety percent of our sample reported that they had participated in violent crime; 70% reported that they had committed a property crime. Thus it is not surprising that our subjects also had extensive experience with the criminal justice system: 80 percent reported an arrest, and the average number of arrests was eight.

COLLECTIVE VIOLENCE PROCESSES WITHIN THE GANG

Gang violence includes a number of acts and is most likely to involve assaults and the use of weapons. Although the motives for these acts are diverse, much gang violence (as discussed above) is retaliatory. This quality is evident in the disproportionate number of assaults and shootings committed in response to the acts of other gangs. This finding is similar to those of other gang researchers including Hagedorn (1988), Klein and Maxson (1989), Maxson, Gordon, and Klein (1985), Moore (1978), Sanders (1993), and Vigil (1988). Initial interviews made clear that a number of violent acts were committed by gang members outside the gang. It would be inappropriate to classify these acts as gang-related, even though they were committed by gang members. Our classification of gang violence included only those acts committed by gang members which were organized by gang members and motivated by gang concerns, especially revenge, retaliation, reputation, and representation of membership. This classification corresponds to the more restrictive of the two definitions applied by Maxson and Klein (1990).

The centrality of violence to gang life was illustrated by counts of the times a topic was mentioned during an interview.[5] Except for drugs (which were mentioned more than 2,000 times), our subjects mentioned violence more often than any other topic. They referred to violence 1,681 times, including hundreds of references to specific acts such as killing or murder (246), assault (148), and robbery (71). As further evidence of the importance of violence, nine of our 99 subjects have been killed since the study began in 1990; several showed us bullet wounds during the interview.[6] As stated earlier, this group had extensive arrest histories: 80 percent had been arrested at least once, the mean number of arrests per subject was eight, and one-third reported that their most recent arrest was for assault or weapons violations.

[5]These counts were derived from GOFER, the qualitative software package used for organizing much of the analysis of the transcribed interviews.

[6]Since this manuscript was first submitted to JQ in November 1994, two more members of our sample have been killed, raising the total to 11.

Other incidents also illustrate the salience of violence in the lives of gang members. One day three gang members were sitting on their front porch, waiting for the field ethnographer to pick up one of them for an interview. As he drove up their street, he heard shots and saw the three subjects being shot in a drive-by. Their wounds were superficial, but this incident underscored the daily potential for violence as well as our ability to observe it firsthand. During the course of our research, several gang members offered to demonstrate their ability to use violence, typically by inviting us to accompany them on a drive-by shooting or to drop them off in rival territory and watch them shoot a rival gang member. We declined all such invitations, but they are not uncommon in field research (Wright and Decker 1994). On a few occasions during interviews, gang members displayed a firearm when asked whether they possessed a gun. Most subjects reported beginning their life in the gang with a violent encounter; usually they were "beaten in" by members of the gang they were joining. The process of leaving the gang was also described in violent terms: by being "beaten out," leaving through fear of violence, suffering serious injury, or death.[7]

The research reported here attempts to provide a framework for understanding the peaks and valleys of gang violence. As Short and Strodtbeck (1974) observed, efforts to understand gang violence must focus both on process variables (such as interactions) and on situational characteristics (such as neighborhood structure, age, race, and sex). For these reasons we concentrate on stages in the gang process that illustrate important aspects of gang violence, and we examine such violence in the context of five spheres of gang activity: (1) the role of violence in defining life in the gang, (2) the role of violence in the process of joining the gang, (3) the use of violence by the gang, (4) staging grounds for violence, and (5) gang members' recommendations for ending their gang.

The Role of Violence in Defining Life in the Gang

A fundamental way to demonstrate the centrality of violence to life in the gang is to examine how gang members defined a gang. Most answers to this question included some mention of violence. Our subjects were able to distinguish between violence within the gang and that which was unrelated to the gang.[8]

INT: What is a gang to you?

007: A gang is, I don't know, just a gang where people hang out together and get into fights. A lot of members of your group will help you fight.

---

[7]Despite these claims, a sample of 24 ex-gang members gave little evidence that their exit from the gang was accompanied by violence. The claim that one can exit the gang only through violence may reflect the mythic character of violence identified by Klein (1971). The threat of violence toward those interested in leaving the gang discourages such actions and reinforces the cohesion between members.

[8]Quotes are used to illustrate major substantive categories of the collective and normative features of gang behavior. INT denotes the interviewer; the number (e.g., 007) is the subject's identification number.

INT: So if you just got into a fight with another girl because you didn't like her?

007: Then it would be a one-on-one fight, but then like if somebody else jump in, then somebody would come from my side.

INT: Why do you call the group you belong to a gang?

047: Violence, I guess. There is more violence than a family. With a gang it's like fighting all the time, killing, shooting.

INT: What kind of things do members of your organization do together?

085: We have drive-bys, shootings, go to parties, we even go to the mall. Most of the things we do together is dealing with fighting.

Most often the violence was protective, reflecting the belief that belonging to a gang at least would reduce the chance of being attacked.

INT: Are you claiming a gang now?

046: I'm cool with a gang, real cool.

INT: What does that mean to be cool?

046: You don't got to worry about nobody jumping you. You don't got to worry about getting beat up.

Other subjects found the violence in their gang an attractive feature of membership. These individuals were attracted not so much by protection as by the opportunity to engage in violence.

INT: Why did you start to call that group a gang?

009: It's good to be in a gang cause there's a lot of violence and stuff.

INT: So the reason you call it a gang is basically why?

101: Because I beat up on folks and shoot them. The last person I shot I was in jail for five years.

INT: What's good about being in a gang?

101: You can get to fight whoever you want and shoot whoever you want. To me, it's kind of fun. Then again, it's not . . . because you have to go to jail for that shit. But other than that, being down for who you want to be with, it's kind of fun.

INT: What's the most important reason to be in the gang?

057: Beating Crabs.[9] If it wasn't for beating Crabs, I don't think I would be in a gang right now.

Whether for protection or for the opportunity to engage in violence, the members of our sample attached considerable importance to the role of violence in their definition of a gang. Many of the comments evoke what Klein

[9]This is a derogatory term used by Blood gang members to refer to Crips.

(1971) termed "mythic violence"—discussions of violent activities between gangs that reinforce the ties of membership and maintain boundaries between neighborhood gangs and those in "rival" neighborhoods. In this sense, violence is a central feature of the normative system of the gang; it is the defining feature and the central value of gang life.

Violence in Joining the Gang

Most gangs require an initiation process that includes participation in violent activities. This ritual fulfills a number of important functions. First, it determines whether a prospective member is tough enough to endure the level of violence he or she will face as a gang member. Equally important, the gang must learn how tough a potential member is because they may have to count on this individual for support in fights or shootings. The initiation serves other purposes as well. Most important, it increases solidarity among gang members by engaging them in a collective ritual. The initiation reminds active members of their earlier status, and gives the new member something in common with other gang members. In addition, a violent initiation provides a rehearsal for a prospective member for life in the gang. In short, it demonstrates the centrality of violence to gang life.

Three-quarters of our subjects were initiated into their gangs through the process known as "beating in." This ritual took many forms; in its most common version a prospective gang member walked between lines of gang members or stood inside a circle of gang members who beat the initiate with their fists.

> **020:** I had to stand in a circle and there was about ten of them. Out of these ten there was just me standing in the circle. I had to take six to the chest by all ten of them. Or I can try to go to the weakest one and get out. If you don't get out, they are going to keep beating you. I said "I will take the circle."

One leader, who reported that he had been in charge of several initiations, described the typical form:

> **001:** They had to get jumped on.
>
> **INT:** How many guys jump on em?
>
> **001:** Ten.
>
> **INT:** And then how long do they go?
>
> **001:** Until I tell em to stop.
>
> **INT:** When do you tell em to stop?
>
> **001:** I just let em beat em for bout two or three minutes to see if they can take a punishment.

The initiation also communicates information about the gang and its activities.

> **099:** I fought about four people at one time.
>
> **INT:** Fought who?

099: I fought some old Gs.

INT: How long did you have to fight them?

099: It seemed like forever.

INT: So they beat you down or you beat them down?

099: It went both ways because I knocked that one motherfucker out.

INT: So that was your initiation?

099: Yeah. And then they sat down and blessed me and told me the sixteen laws and all that. But now in the new process there is a seventeenth and eighteenth law.

Other gang members reported that they had the choice of either being beaten in or "going on a mission." On a mission, a prospective member had to engage in an act of violence, usually against a rival gang member on rival turf. Initiates often were required to confront a rival gang member face-to-face.

041: You have to fly your colors through enemy territory. Some step to you; you have to take care of them by yourself; you don't get no help.

084: To be a Crip, you have to put your blue rag on your head and wear all blue and go in a Blood neighborhood—that is the hardest of all of them—and walk through the Blood neighborhood and fight Bloods. If you come out without getting killed, that's the way you get initiated.

Every gang member we interviewed reported that his or her initiation involved participating in some form of violence. This violence was rarely directed against members of other gangs; most often it took place within the gang. Then, in each successive initiation, recently initiated members participated in "beating in" new members. Such violence always has a group context and a normative purpose: to reinforce the ties between members while reminding them that violence lies at the core of life in the gang.

The Use of Gang Violence

To understand gang violence more clearly, it is critical to know when such violence is used. In the four following situations, gang members did not regard themselves as initiating violence; rather, because its purpose was to respond to the violent activities of a rival gang. Retaliatory violence corresponds to the concept of contagion (Loftin 1984) as well as to the principle of crime as social control (Black 1983). According to this view, gang violence is an attempt to enact private justice for wrongs committed against the gang, one of its members, or a symbol of the gang. These wrongs may be actual or perceived; often the perceived threat of impending violence is as powerful a motivator as violence itself.

This view of gang violence helps to explain the rapid escalation of intergang hostilities that lead to assaults, drive-by shootings, or murders between gangs. Such actions reflect the collective behavior processes at work, in which acts of violence against the gang serve as the catalyst that brings together subgroups within the gang and unites them against a common enemy. Such violent events are rare, but are important in gang culture. Collective violence is one of the few activities involving the majority of gang members, including fringe members. The precipitation of such activities pulls fringe members into the gang and increases cohesion.

When Violence Comes to the Gang We asked gang members when they used violence. Typically they claimed that violence was seldom initiated by the gang itself, but was a response to "trouble" that was "brought" to them. In these instances, the object of violence was loosely defined and was rarely identified; it represented a symbolic enemy against whom violence would be used. These statements, however, indicate an attempt to provide justifications for gang violence.

INT: How often do gang members use violence?

005: When trouble comes to them.

INT: When do you guys use violence?

018: When people start bringing violence to us. They bring it to us and set it up. We take it from there.

INT: When do members of the gang use violence?

037: When somebody approaches us. We don't go out looking for trouble. We let trouble come to us.

INT: When do you guys use violence?

042: Only when it's called for. We don't start trouble. That's the secret of our success.

The view of gang members passively sitting back and waiting for violence to come to them is inconsistent with much of what we know about gang life. After all, many gang members reported that they joined the gang expressly for the opportunity to engage in violence; many lived in neighborhoods where acts of violence occurred several times each day; and most had engaged in violence before joining the gang. Even so, unprovoked violence against another gang is difficult to justify; retaliatory actions against parties that wronged them can be justified more easily. Also, such actions are consistent with the view of the gang as a legitimate social organization serving the legitimate purpose of protecting its members—a central value in the gang's normative structure.

Retaliation A number of gang members told us that they used violence to even the score with a specific group or individual. Unlike the subjects above, who reported generalized responses, these individuals identified a specific target for their violence: someone who had committed a violent act against them or their gang in the past.

002: I had on a blue rag and he say what's up cuz, what's up blood, and I say uh, what's up cuz, just like that, and then me and him got to arguin' and everything, and teachers would stop it, and then me and him met up one day when nobody was round. We got to fightin. Naw, cause I told Ron, my cousin, my cousin and em came up to the school and beat em up. And the next day when he seen me, he gonna ask me where my cousin and em at. I say I don't need my cousin and em for you. They just came up there cause they heard you was a Blood. And they whooped em. Then me and him had a fight the next day, yeah. And then I had to fight some other dudes that was his friends and I beat em up. Then he brought some boys up to the school and they, uh, pulled out a gun on me and I ran up in the school. And then I brought my boys up the next day and we beat on em.

INT: What happened yesterday?

039: This dude had beat up one of our friends. He was cool with one of my friends but he had beat up another one of my friends before. They came back and busted one of my friends' head. We was going to get him.

Specific examples of retaliation against rival gangs were mentioned less frequently than was general gang violence. This point underscores the important symbolic function of gang violence, a value that members must be ready to support. The idea that rival gangs will "bring violence" to the gang is an important part of the gang belief system; it is pivotal in increasing cohesion among members of otherwise loosely confederated organizations.

Graffiti A third type of gang violence occurred in response to defacing gang graffiti. Organizational symbols are important to all groups, and perhaps more so to those whose members are adolescents. The significance of graffiti to gangs has been documented by a number of observers in a variety of circumstances (Block and Block 1993; Hagedorn 1988; Moore 1978; Vigil 1988). In particular, graffiti identify gang territory, and maintaining territory is an important feature of gang activity in St. Louis and other cities. As Block and Block observed in Chicago, battles over turf often originated in attempts by rival gangs to "strike out" graffiti. Several gang members told us that attempts to paint over their graffiti by rival gangs were met with a violent response, but no gang members could recall a specific instance. Claiming to use violence in response to such insults again reflects the mythic character of gang violence; it emphasizes the symbolic importance of violence for group processes such as cohesion, boundary maintenance, and identity. Further, such responses underscore the threat represented by rivals who would encroach on gang territory to strike out gang graffiti.

INT: What does the removal of graffiti mean?

043: That's a person that we have to go kill. We put our enemies up on the wall. If there is a certain person, we "X" that out and know who to kill.

INT: What if somebody comes and paints a pitchfork or paints over your graffiti? What does that mean to your gang?

046: First time we just paint it back up there, no sweat. Next time they come do it, we go find out who did it and go paint over theirs. If they come back a third time, it's like three times you out. Obviously that means something if they keep painting over us. They telling us they ready to fight.

Territory Most gang members continued to live in the neighborhood where their gang started. Even for those who had moved away, it retained a symbolic value. Protecting gang turf is viewed as an important responsibility, which extends well beyond its symbolic importance as the site where the gang began. Our subjects' allegiance to the neighborhood was deeply embedded in the history of neighborhood friendship groups that evolved into gangs. Thus, turf protection was an important value.

When we asked gang members about defending their turf, we received some generalized responses about their willingness to use violence to do so.

INT: If someone from another gang comes to your turf, what does your gang do?

019: First try to tell him to leave.

INT: If he don't leave?

019: He'll leave one way or the other—carry him out in a Hefty bag.

INT: What was your interest in it (the gang)?

036: We started out, we didn't want nobody coming out and telling us, walking through our neighborhood cause we grew up in this hood and we was going to protect it even if it did mean us fighting every day, which we done. We fought every day. If you walked through the neighborhood and we didn't know you or you didn't know where you was going in the neighborhood, we would rush you.

In other instances, however, the responses identified an individual or an incident in which the gang used violence to protect its turf.

INT: What kind of things does the gang have to do to defend its turf?

013: Kill. That's all it is, kill.

INT: Tell me about your most recent turf defense. What happened, a guy came in?

013: A guy came in, he had the wrong colors on, he got to move out. He got his head split open with a sledgehammer, he got two ribs broken, he got his face torn up.

INT: Did he die from that?

013: I don't know. We dropped him off on the other side of town. If he did die, it was on the other side of town.

INT: If someone from another gang came to you-all turf, what happens? What do your gang do?

068: We shoot. If it's a lot, we gonna get organized and we shoot.

Staging Grounds for Violence

Gang members expect that when they go to certain locations they will be the targets of violence from other gangs or will be expected by members of their own gang to engage in violence. In some cases, large-scale violence will occur. Other encounters result only in "face-offs." These encounters highlight the role of situational characteristics in gang violence. Most often the staging grounds are public places such as a restaurant.

INT: Do they ever bring weapons to school?

011: No, cause we really don't have no trouble. We mainly fight up at the White Castle. That's where our trouble starts, at the White Castle.

In other instances, the encounters may take place at the skating rink.

INT: What kind of fights have you guys had lately?

057: Yeah, last Saturday at Skate King.

INT: Do you go there to skate or were you just hanging7

057: We used to skate a long time ago, but we just all the sudden went [crazy]. Crabs started hanging out there. Usually all Bloods up there but the Crabs started hanging out there so we had to get rid of them.

Dances are not new locations for youthful violence. Members of our sample identified them as locations that produced violent encounters between rival gangs.

INT: Do you go to dances?

017: Yeah. That's when we mostly get into the gang fights. Yeah, we go to dances.

INT: What about the last fight? What was that about?

031: That was at a dance. It was some Slobs[10] there. They was wanting to show they colors and just didn't know who they was around. They weren't really paying attention.

INT: How often do you guys use violence?

033: Only if we go out to a dance or something.

[10]This is a derogatory term used by Crip gang members to refer to Bloods.

The expectation of violence at certain locations was so strong that some members avoided going to those places.

INT: Do you go to dances or parties?

047: I don't. I stay away from house parties. Too many fights come out of there.

According to another gang member, violence at house parties had reached such a level that many hosts searched their guests for weapons.

074: Sometimes people wait until they get out of the party and start shooting. Now at these parties they have people at the door searching people, even at house parties.

In general, gang members reported that they "hung out" in small cliques or subgroups and that it was rare for the entire gang to be together. This reflects the general character of social organization in the gangs we studied. An external threat—usually from another gang—was needed to strengthen cohesion among gang members and to bring the larger gang together. Many members of our sample reported that they did not go skating, to the mall, or to dances alone or in small groups because they knew that gang violence was likely to erupt at such locations. Thus the gang went *en masse* to these locations, prepared to start or respond to violence. These expectations contributed to the eventual use of violence. In this way, the gang's belief system contributed to the likelihood of violent encounters.

Ending Gangs

When we asked for gang members' perspectives on the best way to end gangs, we expected to find a variety of recommendations targeted at fundamental causes (racism, unemployment, education) as well as more proximate solutions (detached workers, recreation centers, job training). Instead the modal response reflected the centrality of violence in the gang. Twenty-five of our 99 subjects told us that the only way to get rid of their gang would be to use violence to get rid of the members. This response was confirmed by gang members in their conversations with the field ethnographer. For many gang members, life in the gang had become synonymous with violence; for one respondent, even job offers were not sufficient to end the gang.

INT: What would be the best way to get rid of your gang, the Rolling Sixties?

033: Smoke us all.

INT: Kill you all?

033: Yeah.

INT: We couldn't give you guys jobs?

033: No, just smoke us.

Others recommended using extreme violence to get rid of their gang.

INT: What would it take to get rid of your gang?

035: Whole lot of machine guns. Kill us all. We just going to multiply anyway cause the Pee Wees gonna take over.

INT: What would be the best way to get rid of the Sixties?

042: Kill us all at once. Put them in one place and blow them up.

Violence is so central a part of gang culture that even the members' recommendations about ending gangs include elements of violence.

The Process of Gang Violence

The analysis above suggests a model that accounts for the escalation of gang violence and is consistent with the nature of gang process and normative structure: it reflects the lack of strong leadership, structure, and group goals. The key element is the collective identification of threat, a process that unites the gang and overcomes the general lack of unity by increasing cohesion. This occurred in response to threats against the gang, either real or perceived, by rival gangs. The role of mythic violence is particularly important in this context; it is the agent through which talk about violence most frequently unites gang members.

We suggest that a seven-step process accounts for the peaks and valleys of gang violence. The key to understanding violence is the nature of organization within gangs. Most gangs originate as neighborhood groups and are characterized by loose ties between their members and the larger gang. These groups generally lack effective leadership; cohesion in small cliques is stronger than the ties to the larger gang. Against this backdrop, symbolic enemies are identified when subgroups interact with other gangs near them. Threats from those groups—whether real or perceived—expand the number of participants, and may increase cohesion among members and heighten their willingness to use violence. Violence between gangs is most often the result of a mobilizing event that pushes a ready and willing group beyond the constraints against violence. Such events may include the deployment of gang members to protect or attack certain locations, to engage in actions in cars, or simply to act "loco." Violent encounters typically are short-lived and de-escalate rapidly. This de-escalation, however, may be only a respite before the next retaliation. The process moves through the following seven steps:

1. Loose bonds to the gang;
2. Collective identification of threat from a rival gang (through rumors, symbolic shows of force, cruising, and mythic violence), reinforcing the centrality of violence that expands the number of participants and increases cohesion;
3. A mobilizing event possibly, but not necessarily, violence;
4. Escalation of activity;

5. Violent event;
6. Rapid de-escalation;
7. Retaliation.

This model is generally consistent with McPhail's (1993) description of individual and collective violence. His explanation distinguishes between outcome violence and intended violence. The former is characterized by attempts to manage what McPhail calls "disturbances to self-perception." Examples would include challenges to status that are repelled with actions which do not originate with a violent intent, but result in a violence (Athens 1992; Luckenbill and Doyle 1989). Participants in intended violence, on the other hand, enter a setting or interaction with a predisposition toward violence. In its collective form, this type of violence generally involves two opposing groups, many of whose members play interchangeable roles of victim, perpetrator, and witness of violence. The collective violence of gangs described in our research fits McPhail's conceptual scheme: "Not only do purposive actors act alone to match their perceptions to their reference signals for violent individual goals, they occasionally act together with other members of their groups to achieve violent collective goals" (1993:17). McPhail points to the need to analyze the "planning preparations, rehearsal and implementation of collective violence" (1993:17). We believe that the current analysis and model of the collective behavior process of gang violence supports McPhail's model.

CONCLUSION

Gang violence, like other gang activities, reflects the gang's organizational and normative structure. Such violence, especially retaliatory violence, is an outgrowth of a collective process that reflects the loose organizational structure of gangs with diffuse goals, little allegiance among members, and few leaders.

If gangs are composed of diffuse subgroups, how is violence organized? Our answer to this question is "Not very well and not very often," because most gang violence serves important symbolic purposes within the gang. In addition, most gang violence is retaliatory, a response to violence—real or perceived—against the gang.

Gang violence serves many functions in the life of the gang. First, and most important, it produces more violence through the processes of threat and contagion. These mechanisms strongly reflect elements of collective behavior. Second, it temporarily increases the solidarity of gang members, uniting them against a common enemy by heightening their dependence on each other. When gang violence exceeds tolerable limits, a third function may be evident: the splintering of gangs into subgroups and the decision by some individuals to leave the gang.

REFERENCES

Athens, L. 1992. *The Creation of Dangerous Violent Criminals.* Urbana: University of Illinois Press.

Biernacki, P. and D. Waldorf. 1981. "Snowball Sampling: Problems and Techniques of Chain Referral Sampling." *Sociological Methods and Research* 10:141–63.

Black, D. 1983. "Crime as Social Control." *American Sociological Review* 43:34–45.

Block, C. R. and R. Block. 1993. "Street Gang Crime in Chicago." *Research in Brief* (December). Washington, DC: National Institute of Justice.

Decker, S. H. and B. Van Winkle. 1996. *Life in the Gang: Family, Friends and Violence.* New York: Cambridge University Press.

Hagedorn, J. 1988. *People and Folks.* Chicago: Lakeview Press.

———. 1991. "Back in the Field Again: Gang Research in the Nineties." Pp. 240–259, *Gangs in America,* edited by R. Huff. Newbury Park, CA: Sage.

Horowitz, R. 1983. *Honor and the American Dream.* New Brunswick, NJ: Rutgers University Press.

Jackson, P. I. 1992. "Crime, Youth Gangs and Urban Transition: The Social Dislocations of Postindustrial Development." *Justice Quarterly* 8:379–98.

Katz, J. 1988. *The Seductions of Crime.* New York: Basic Books.

Klein, M. 1971. *Street Gangs and Street Workers.* Englewood Cliffs, NJ: Prentice-Hall.

Klein, M. and C. Maxson. 1989. "Street Gang Violence." Pp. 198–234 in *Violent Crimes, Violent Criminals,* edited by N. Weiner. Beverly Hills: Sage.

Klein, M., C. Maxson, and L. Cunningham. 1991. " 'Crack,' Street Gangs, and Violence." *Criminology* 29:623–50.

Loftin, C. 1984. "Assaultive Violence as Contagious Process." *Bulletin of the New York Academy of Medicine* 62:550–55.

Luckenbill, D. and D. Doyle. 1989. "Structural Position and Violence: Developing a Cultural Explanation." *Criminology* 27:419–36.

Maxson, C., M. Klein, and M. Gordon. 1985. "Differences between Gang and Nongang Homicides." *Criminology* 21:209–22.

Maxson, C. and M. Klein. 1990. "Street Gang Violence: Twice as Great or Half as Great?" Pp. 71–102 in *Gangs in America,* edited by R. Huff. Newbury Park, CA: Sage.

McPhail, C. 1991. *The Myth of the Madding Crowd.* New York: Aldine.

———. 1993. "The Dark Side of Purpose: Individual and Collective Violence in Riots." Presidential address, Midwest Sociological Society, Chicago.

Moore, J. 1978. *Homeboys.* Philadelphia: Temple University Press.

Padilla, F. 1992. *The Gang as an American Enterprise.* New Brunswick, NJ: Rutgers University Press.

Pfautz, H. 1961. "Near-Group Theory and Collective Behavior: A Critical Reformulation." *Social Problems* 9:167–74.

Sanchez-Jankowski, M. 1991. *Islands in the Street.* Berkeley: University of California Press.

Sanders, W. 1993. *Drive-Bys and Gang Bangs: Gangs and Grounded Culture.* Chicago: Aldine.

Short, J. 1974. "Collective Behavior, Crime, and Delinquency." Pp. 403–49 in *Handbook of Criminology,* edited by D. Glaser. New York: Rand McNally.

Short, J. and F. Strodtbeck. 1974. *Group Process and Gang Delinquency.* Chicago: University of Chicago Press.

Sullivan, M. 1989. *Getting Paid: Youth Crime and Work in the Inner City.* Ithaca: Cornell University Press.

Suttles, G. 1972. *The Social Construction of Communities.* Chicago: University of Chicago Press.

Thrasher, F. 1927. *The Gang.* Chicago: University of Chicago Press.

Vigil, D. 1988. *Barrio Gangs.* Austin: University of Texas Press.

Wright, R., S. H. Decker, A. Redfern, and D. Smith. 1992. "A Snowball's Chance in Hell: Doing Field Work with Active Residential Burglars." *Journal of Research in Crime and Delinquency* 29:148–61.

Wright, R. T., and S. H. Decker. 1994. *Burglars on the Job: Streetlife Culture & Residential Burglary*. Boston: Northeastern University Press.

Yablonsky, L. 1959. "The Delinquent Gang as a Near-Group." *Social Problems* 7:108–17.

DISCUSSION QUESTIONS

1. What should a researcher do when he or she witnesses criminal behavior while conducting a study?
2. How would you gain access to some of the following populations: gangs, police officers, prisoners, car jackers?
3. Did interviewing the members of the gang in an office affect the results of the study? Why?
4. How did Decker approach analysis of the qualitative data developed in this study? Why was this approach important?

9

Ambivalent Actions

Prison Adaptation Strategies of First-Time, Short-Term Inmates

THOMAS J. SCHMID
RICHARD S. JONES

COMMENTARY

The prison setting provides researchers with specific challenges that must be considered prior to conducting a study. Silberman (1995: 4) identifies a number of problems in conducting research in corrections. First, prison inmates may be concerned about issues of confidentiality regarding their own prison misconduct. Second, some inmates are concerned that research findings might be used to justify more restrictive policies. A third problem is related to the separateness of the prison world, where cultural values and norms may be different from the world of the researcher. Zwerman and Gardner (1986) raise a different set of obstacles to prison research by noting that the research process may be impeded by the state's intrusion into the research project. Two specific concerns they address are the state's attempt to define the nature of the study and the state's demands for access to the data.

The following paper represents one strategy for addressing the above-mentioned challenges. In the early stages of the project, the research was entirely covert, meaning that neither the state nor the inmates under study were aware that the research for this project was being conducted. The state perceived Jones to be an inmate who met regularly with Schmid to take graduate courses. Other inmates perceived Jones as being a typical inmate. This allowed Jones the opportunity to perform the "complete participant" role so aptly described by Gold (1958: 217–233). The advantage of this role in participant observation is that it offers the greatest access to intimate knowledge about the group and the greatest opportunity for introspection.

Source: Journal of Contemporary Ethnography, Vol. 21 No. 4, January 1993, pp. 439-463.
© 1993 Sage Publications, Inc. Reprinted by permission of Sage Publications, Inc.

Authors' Note: We wish to thank Jim Thomas, Peter and Patricia Adler, and Charles Faupel for their helpful comments on earlier drafts of this article.

As the study progressed, Jones began having some difficulty balancing the conflicting roles of researcher and inmate. As an inmate, Jones experienced things much the same way that other inmates experienced them. It was difficult not to become emotionally involved, which could certainly prevent him from seeing alternative viewpoints or perspectives. Schmid, as the "complete observer," provided a nice balance to this study by being able to maintain a sense of detachment and prodding Jones to continue to search for alternative explanations that Jones might not have made on his own. Thus, the major strength of the methodology chosen for this study is that it is an exemplar for balancing both intimacy and objectivity.

The primary limitation of this study is that it provides only one piece of the puzzle, albeit a very rich piece, on the adaptation experiences of maximum security prisoners. The focus of this study was on the experiences of first-time inmates at one maximum security prison. We decided to focus on this particular group because it is the one that Jones had the most access to since he was also a first-time inmate. This does not mean that observations of other inmates were not made. Rather, our richest data was that which focused on the experiences of first-time inmates. While we believe that the findings from this project are applicable to other inmates (recidivists, long-term prisoners) at the institution studied, as well as to other maximum security prisons, we must leave it up to other researchers to confirm this belief.

ABSTRACT A person who is incarcerated for the first time becomes a "prisoner" but does not automatically acquire a meaningful status within the prison world. If the incarceration is short term, the person is unlikely to ever achieve a significant prison status because participation in the prison world will be inhibited by identification with the outside world. This condition of social marginality results in an ambivalence that directly shapes inmates' strategies for survival within the prison world. This article examines the effect of ambivalence on inmates' adaptation strategies. Data for the study were collected through participant observation and focused interviews with inmates at a maximum security prison for men.

"Doing time" in a maximum security prison is not simply a matter of being in prison. It is, rather, a creative process through which inmates must invent or learn a repertoire of adaptation tactics that address the varying problems they confront during particular phases of their prison careers.

There is an extensive literature on the informal organization of prison life and the socialization processes through which inmates come to participate in this informal organization. Clemmer (1958) defines prisonization as "the taking on in greater or lesser degree of the folkways, customs, and general culture of the penitentiary" (p. 279). Prisonization is thus fundamentally a process of cultural accommodation through which inmates are first initiated into and then made a part of the prison social and cultural system. Neither of the two theoretical models developed to account for inmate adaptations to imprisonment—the "deprivation model" (Goffman 1961; Sykes [1959] 1971; Sykes and Messinger 1960) or the "importation model" (Thomas 1973; Thomas and Peterson 1977)—adequately represent the multiple ambiguities faced by the sociologically distinctive category of inmates who have no prior experience with the prison world, and whose imprisonment is relatively brief.[1]

When first-time inmates are sentenced to prison they have already lost their status as free adults but have not yet achieved any meaningful status within the prison world; they are, to older inmates, "fish" (see Cardozo-Freeman 1984; Irwin 1980). They can shed this label through their increasing participation in prison life, but if they are short-term inmates as well as first-timers they are unlikely to ever achieve a significant prison status. Their participation in the prison world will continue to be inhibited by their ties to, and identification with, the outside world. Their social marginality, grounded both in place and in time, is thus parallel to that experienced by immigrants who expect to return to their country of origin within a few years' time (see Morawska 1987; Shokeid 1988) or who otherwise manage to maintain a "sojourner orientation" (Gibson 1988). Immigrant sojourners however, can typically draw on shared symbols or institutions in their transient adaptations to a new culture. New inmates, in contrast, have little in common with one another except their conventionality (Schmid and Jones 1991) and consequently have fewer collective resources available to resist assimilation into the prison culture.

In this article, we examine how first-time, short-term inmates in a maximum security prison make use of their social marginality, and the sociological ambivalence that results from it, to forge highly delimited adaptation strategies to the prison culture. After describing our methodological approach and fieldwork experiences, we briefly summarize our earlier analysis, which demonstrated that the social marginality of the first-time, short-term inmates we studied shaped their experiential orientations toward the prison world. We then analyze the relationship between ambivalence and inmates' prison strategies and discuss the extended sociological implications of our findings.

METHOD

Ordinarily, one of the most difficult steps in sociological research on prisons is gaining unrestricted access to inmates' day-to-day lives within the prison world. Our study originated with such access, when one of the authors (R. Jones) was serving a year-and-a-day sentence in a maximum security prison for men in the upper midwestern region of the United States. Through negotiations with prison officials, Jones was permitted to enroll in a graduate sociology course in field methods. What began as a directed studies course between professor and former student rapidly evolved, at Jones's suggestion, into a more comprehensive project conducted by co-researchers. At the same time, it evolved from a general observational study of prison life to an analysis of the prison experiences of first-time short-term inmates.

Jones's prison sentence, our decision to conduct the study together, and our focus on first-time, short-term inmates offered us an unusual strategy for balancing the participant observer's needs for both objective and intimate knowledge about the group or culture being studied (see Davis 1973). This balance can be particularly difficult to achieve in prison research, where suspicions about academic roles often lead researchers to cultivate alternative roles that are more acceptable or better defined (Giallombardo 1966; Jacobs 1977). The circumstances of our study enabled us to examine the prison world for a period of 10 months from the combined viewpoints of both a "complete participant" and a "complete observer" (Gold 1958).

As the "inside observer," Jones had a number of specific advantages. In his interactions with other inmates and with guards, he was not viewed as a sociologist or a student or any other kind of outsider: He was viewed as a prisoner. Moreover, he was not merely assuming the role of a prisoner to learn about the prison world—he *was* a prisoner. He literally shared the experiences of other first-time, short-term inmates, enabling him to contextualize his observations of others with a full measure of sociological introspection (Ellis 1991). Because of his prior training, which included an undergraduate degree in sociology, a university course in participant observation, and a supervised field research project, he was also prepared to document his own experiences and those of his fellow inmates.

Any researcher role closes as well as opens lines of information, and Jones's role had certain limitations as well. As a new inmate, he did not have immediate access to the entire prison world, a limitation that directly influenced our decision to focus on the experiences of first-time inmates. He was also constrained by prison interaction norms, especially those governing relations between members of different racial or ethnic groups. At the prison we studied, these norms were not entirely rigid, but they were sufficiently strong to suggest that Jones's initial observations primarily depicted the experiences of White inmates. (We were able to compensate for this racial selectivity to some extent through a second phase of our fieldwork.) Finally, the most critical question about any "auto-ethnography" (Hayano 1979, 1982) is whether researchers will be able to examine their own social world objectively. Jones expressed concerns about his objectivity early in the directed studies course; it was in response to this problem that we agreed to conduct the research together.

As the "outside" observer for the project, Schmid attempted to guide the direction of the fieldwork by placing Jones's observations in a sociological context—suggesting theoretical concepts that could be useful, additional questions that might be asked, methods that could be used to address these questions, and procedures through which we could test the validity of Jones's initial observations. Schmid also supplemented Jones's field notes with his own observations at the prison, and took a primary role in data analysis.

Our fieldwork essentially began with a journal that Jones started keeping several days before the beginning of his sentence. His early entries were predominantly personal expressions, although they included more traditional ethnographic descriptions as well. Once our research project was formally initiated, Jones restricted his journal entries to personal thoughts and impressions and chronology of his daily experiences. Using a process similar to the "diary-interview" method described by Zimmerman and Wieder (1977), these entries provided a framework for extended conversations between the researchers. Schmid's notes on these conversations were then used to derive new observational strategies and to identify potential analytic themes.

In addition to journal entries, Jones also prepared field notes on his participation in prison activities, his conversations with individual prisoners and groups of inmates, and his general observations of prison life. This procedure meant that the journal and the field notes contained different kinds of information, and it had the additional advantage of keeping the field notes more objective than they otherwise might have been. Although these general observations incorporated the experiences of hundreds of prisoners, most of the field notes were based on his repeated, often daily, contacts with about 50 inmates as well as on personal relationships established with a smaller number of inmates.

We were able to discuss our research progress through letters, occasional telephone calls, and regular meetings arranged with the cooperation of prison officials. Shortly after the beginning of the study, we settled on a communication routine that proved to be quite efficient. Jones prepared one to three field observations each week (averaging 8–10 handwritten pages) and mailed them to Schmid for annotation and suggestions. Every other week Schmid would meet with Jones in an office or testing room provided by the prison's education department. At these meetings, we would review the journal entries and observations, plan our research strategy, and piece together our emerging conceptualization of the prison world.

Following Jones's release from prison, we devoted a year to the analysis of our initial data, and then returned to the prison to conduct focused interviews. Using information provided by prison officials, we were able to identify and interview 20 additional first-time, short-term inmates.[2] The fieldwork we had already completed guided our preparation of the interview questions, which addressed inmates' changing prison imagery and adaptation tactics as they progressed through their prison careers. We decided that Jones should do the actual interviewing, on the assumption that inmates would be more willing to talk freely with someone who had only recently completed his own prison sentence. To retain the methodological advantages of having both an "inside" and "outside" observer, Schmid reviewed a tape recording of each interview so that we could continuously refine the interviewing procedures.

Our analysis of the prison experiences of first-time, short-term inmates thus draws on three primary sources of data. Our principal source is the field notes, representing 10 months of participant observation by a "complete participant" in collaboration with a "complete observer." Included in these notes are specific events and interactions, quotations from Jones's fellow inmates, and general observations of the prison world. A second source is Jones's prison journals in which he recorded his own prison experiences. We used these journals throughout our project as a form of research development, and we draw on them to illustrate portions of our analytic model. Our subsequent interviews with other inmates constitute our third source of data; these interviews allowed us to pursue a number of topics in greater depth and provided us with an independent source of data to test our initial findings.

MARGINALITY, PRISON IMAGERY, AND PRISON ADAPTATIONS

Our earlier analysis of experiential orientations to prison (Schmid and Jones 1990) demonstrated that, at the beginning of their sentences, first-time, short-term inmates defined prison from the perspective of an outsider, drawing on the shared public meanings that exist in our society about prison. By the midpoint of their sentences they had not lost their outsiders' perspective completely and still had only a marginal status within the prison world, but they nonetheless defined prison principally in terms of shared subcultural meanings learned from other inmates. This "insider's perspective," however, subsequently gave way to concluding images that again expressed an outsider's point of view. (More precisely, their concluding imagery was a reflection of their marginal involvement in both worlds; it was a synthesis of their anticipatory and midcareer images and hence a synthesis of their outsider's and insider's perspectives.) These changes in prison imagery are summarized in Table 1.

Inmates' subjective understandings of the prison world are important because they provide a basis for action (Blumer 1969). Our earlier analysis also demonstrated, in a general way, how inmates' adaptation strategies followed their shifting prison imagery (as summarized in Figure 1). For example, in response to the violence of their initial outsider's imagery, their earliest survival tactics were protective and defensive in nature. As cultural outsiders, however, new inmates also recognized their need for more information about the prison world, and virtually all of their early survival tactics served as information seeking as well as protective measures. Thus territorial caution, impression management, and their partnerships (a friendship with another prisoner recognized by other inmates and guards) guided their ventures into the cafeteria, the yard, the gym, and other unexplored areas of the prison.[3] Selective interaction with other inmates, impression management, and their partnerships helped them confront such prison experiences as parole board hearings, cell transfers, legal and illegal recreational activities, and participation in the prison economy. The barrage of often conflicting information they received through these tactics was the raw material out of which they continuously revised their prison images.[4] Although they continued to view prison with essentially an outsider's perspective, their survival tactics allowed them gradually to acquire an insider's knowledge of the prison and to modify their adaptation tactics accordingly.[5]

A common form of prison adaptation is the creation of a survival "niche" (Seymour 1977) that allows inmates some measure of activity, privacy, safety,

Table 1. Orientation and Prison Imagery

	Preprison	Prison	Postprison
Inmate perspective	Outside looking in	Inside looking in	Inside looking out
Central concerns	Violence/uncertainty	Boredom	Uncertainty
Specific problems	Survival	Endurance	Re-integration
Orientation to space	Prison as separate world	Prison as familiar territory	Prison as separate world
Orientation to time	Sentence as lost time	Killing time/time as measure of success	Sentence as lost time/using time
Supportive others	Family and friends	Partners	"Real" family and friends
Perception of sentence	Justified and unfortunate	Arbitrary and unjust	Arbitrary and unjust (intensified)
Predominant emotion	Fear	Detachment	Apprehension (about outside)

emotional feedback, structure, and freedom within the larger hostile environment of the maximum security prison (Johnson 1987; Toch 1977). Because of their inexperience, first-time inmates were particularly ill-equipped for finding such niches (Johnson 1987, 114) and new short-term inmates were further handicapped by their continuing marginality in the prison world, which restricted their ability to exert personal control (Goodstein, MacKenzie, and Shotland 1984) and inhibited their acceptance by other inmates. But short-term inmates, in contrast to those facing years of imprisonment, needed only to develop a *transient* niche in prison. The problems they faced were similar—understanding the prison status hierarchy and recognizing their place in it, learning whom to trust and whom to avoid, and determining how to evade trouble in a trouble-filled environment—but their solutions did not need to be as enduring. The men we studied were able to achieve such transient "accommodation without assimilation" (Gibson 1988) within a few months' time. To a casual observer, moreover, they soon became indistinguishable from long-term inmates, relying on such adaptive tactics as legal and illegal diversions and conscious efforts to control their thoughts about the outside world. Their relative integration into the prison world was short-lived, however, and their marginality within this world again became evident as they prepared for their departure from prison. Like more experienced inmates, their preparatory concerns included both practical problems, such as finding a job and a place to live, and existential concerns about how the outside world had changed and how the inmates themselves had changed during their time in prison (see Irwin 1970). Faced with these problems, it became increasingly apparent to inmates that most (though not all) of the adaptation tactics associated with their prison orientation were inadequate for dealing with the outside world.

Based on this general pattern, it is tempting to infer that inmates' adaptations strategies change simply because their reference group changes. In this

ANTICIPATORY IMAGE  **ANTICIPATORY SURVIVAL STRATEGY**

Outsider's perspective:
violence;
uncertainty; fear

Protective resolutions: to avoid unnecessary contacts with inmates; to avoid unnecessary contacts with guards; not to be changed in prison; to disregard questionable information; to avoid all hostilities; to engage in self-defense if hostilities arise

SURVIVAL STRATEGY

Territorial caution

Selective interaction with inmates

Impression management with inmates

Partnership with another inmate

Redefinition of prison violence as "explained" rather than random events

MIDCAREER IMAGE → **ADAPTATION STRATEGY**

Insider's perspective:
boredom

Legal and illegal diversions

Suppression of thoughts about outside world

Minimization of outside contacts

Impression management with inmates and outsiders

Partnership

CONCLUDING IMAGE → **DISSIPATION OF ADAPTATION STRATEGY**

Synthetic perspective:
revision of prison image and reformulation of outside image

Continued diversions

Decreasing impression management

Decreasing suppression of outside thoughts

Disassociation with partner

Formulation of outside plan

FIGURE 1. Prison Images and Strategies

explanation, suggested by Wheeler's (1961) finding of a curvilinear relationship between institutional career phase and conformity to staff expectations, inmates come to abandon the beliefs, values, and norms of the outside world as they acquire more information about and eventually achieve membership in the prison world. In similar fashion, they abandon the beliefs, values, and norms of the prison world when they are about to regain membership in the outside world. Our earlier analysis (Schmid and Jones 1990) challenged this explanation by focusing on inmates' continuous and active work to *interpret* the prison world. This explanation becomes even more unsatisfactory when we introduce into our analysis the ambivalence that inmates experience throughout their entire prison careers.

AMBIVALENCE AND PRISON STRATEGIES

In its most general sense, ambivalence refers to the experience of being pulled in psychologically different directions; because prison inmates *share* this experience, it becomes sociologically as well as psychologically significant. The ambivalence of first-time, short-term inmates flows directly from their transitional status between the outside social world and the prison's: It is an ambivalence grounded in the marginality of "people who have lived in two or more societies and so have become oriented to differing sets of cultural values . . . [or] of people who accept certain values held by groups of which they are not members" (Merton and Barber 1976, 11–12). Although inmates' ambivalence affects their prison imagery and strategies in various ways, its principal effect is to limit behavioral changes by inhibiting new inmates from becoming fully assimilated into prison culture.

Feelings of ambivalence characterized the thoughts, emotions, and, sometimes, the actions of the inmates throughout their entire prison careers. Their adaptations to prison expressed both the outsider's perspective they preferred and the insider's perspective they provisionally accepted. Because their strategies were guided by their imagery, their outsider's perspective was most apparent in their behavior at the beginning of their sentences, whereas their insider's perspective was most apparent during the middle part of their sentences. Their behavior during the final months of their sentences was a mixture of nonprison forms of interaction and prison adaptive tactics because their concluding imagery was a synthesis of outsider's and insider's perspectives. Yet a closer inspection of inmates evolving strategies reveals that the simultaneous influence of the outside and inside worlds was not restricted to the end of their sentences. At every stage of their prison careers, their actions were influenced by the underlying ambivalence that resulted from their marginal position in both the outside and prison social worlds. Table 2 presents the various manifestations of this ambivalence that occurred throughout the prison career.

Preprison and Early Career Experiences

Inmates' ambivalence began before they arrived at prison. Like most outsiders, they viewed prison as a world quite different from their own and had difficulty picturing themselves within that world. In the final days of their freedom, they were faced with conflicting desires: They wanted desperately to avoid their sentences—to escape or be forgotten about—but they also wanted their sentences to proceed because they knew this was inevitable. They retained an outsider's perspective but knew that they were no longer full members of the outside world.

Their ambivalent feelings continued throughout their sentences, although the form and emphasis of their ambivalence changed as they progressed through their prison careers. But even in their earliest days in prison, the dominant form of their ambivalence emerged: Their desire to insulate themselves from the surrounding prison world was countered by their desire for human sociability (see Glaser 1969, 18–21). Throughout their careers, but especially dur-

Table 2. Experiences of Ambivalence During Prison Career

	Career Experiences	Reported Ambivalence
Preprison	Conviction and sentencing Detention in county jail Transportation to prison	Desire to postpone sentence versus desire to proceed with sentence
Early months of sentence	Holding cell In-processing	Desire to insulate self versus desire for sociability
	First night in cell Orientation classes (first week) Initial correspondence and visits with outsiders	Desire to proceed with new experiences versus relief at security of close supervision during first weeks of sentence
	Transfer to another cell Assignment to caseworker First contacts with general inmate population Job or program assignment Cellblock transfer	Desire for greater mobility within prison versus fear of greater contact with inmates
Middle portion of sentence	Work/program participation Legal and illegal diversions Correspondence and visits with outsiders	Desire to discontinue outside contacts and "do your own time" versus desire to maintain outside contacts
Conclusion of sentence	Application for transfer to minimum security Transfer to minimum security Outside passes	Desire for greater freedom versus willingness to complete sentence in maximum security
	Home furloughs Transfer to reentry program Release from prison	Desire to put prison in past and return to free world versus desire to avoid existential concerns about return to free world

ing the first half of their sentences, both sides of this fundamental conflict between an outsider's detachment and an insider's participation in the prison world influenced their behavior. Of importance here is that inmates began to *act,* albeit cautiously, on their desire for contact with others during the first week of their sentences. Their initial contacts with others were quite limited, and they did not appreciably alter their images or strategies, but these contacts did indicate that their isolation did not need to be as extreme as they had anticipated. A 23-year-old inmate, convicted of narcotics sales, described his earliest encounter with another inmate:

> There was one guy that they brought in with me, and we sort of talked off and on. He was sort of scared too, and it was his first time too. He was talking to a guard; I overheard him talking to a guard. I heard him say that he was just basically scared as hell. The guard was trying to calm him down.

> We were all together in a group; we eat at the same table and everything, and I got talking to him. So I had somebody to talk to. (Interview)

During their first week in prison, in which they were housed together with other incoming inmates but segregated from the general inmate population, they were able to express their desire for contact with others through limited interaction with both guards and inmates. They learned that not all guards fit their initial stereotypes, and many new inmates encountered one or more fellow inmates with backgrounds similar to their own. They were still intimidated by the prison, particularly by those aspects of prison life that they had not yet experienced, but they began to reduce their isolation and expand their knowledge of the prison world.

The first week thus enabled new inmates, through passive observations and direct interaction, to modify (but not radically transform) both their images and their strategies. Their segregation during this week also led to yet another variant of their ambivalence: They were relieved at the protection of close supervision, but because they knew that they could not avoid facing the general inmate population indefinitely they were anxious to move on to the next phase of their sentences. Similar feelings of ambivalence resurfaced with each new experience. When they learned that they would be transferred to a different cell, and later to another cellblock entirely, they looked forward to the greater mobility these moves offered, but they feared the increased inmate contact the moves would necessitate:

> After only 2 days they moved me [to another cell]. . . . With this move came more freedom. . . . I could go out in the yard and to the dining hall for meals. I was a little apprehensive about getting out. I had made friends with one guy, so we went into the yard together. We were out for about an hour when we were approached by a black dude. He wanted to get us high. I'm sure that's not all he wanted. . . . It helps to find a friend or two; you feel safer in a crowd. (Field notes)

Their fear mirrored the violence of their prison imagery, whereas their desire to proceed reflected their acceptance that they were now prison inmates.

The evolution of inmates' prison perspectives continued and accelerated through the early months of their sentences. The survival strategies they formulated during these months, like their anticipatory survival strategies, were based on their images of prison. But increasingly their strategies led to modification of these images. This happened because their strategies continued to be influenced by the same motivational factors: (a) their concern for safety but also their recognition that their prison imagery was incomplete and (b) their ambivalence, especially their desire to proceed with new and inevitable prison experiences. The same tactics that gave them new information also reflected the opposing directions of their ambivalence. Their practice of territorial caution and their rudimentary impression management skills expressed their apprehension over contact with other prisoners and their desire for self-insulation, but these tactics also allowed them to initiate or accept limited interaction with others. Their selective interaction with other inmates and their partnership with one other inmate directly expressed their desire for sociability while providing them with a means of maintaining social and emotional distance from the majority of the inmate population.

Midcareer Experiences

Inmates' midcareer adaptation strategies, like their earlier survival strategies, were based on their prison imagery and their ambivalence. Their adaptation strategies differed from their survival strategies because their images changed and because the form and emphasis of their ambivalence changed. Their survival strategies were intended to insulate them from the violence of their anticipatory images but also to allow them to confront new prison experiences and to provide them with new information about the prison world. By midcareer their imagery was dominated by the theme of boredom rather than violence, and they no longer saw a need for more information. But boredom was only one of the problems associated with "doing time" at midcareer: Their relationships with the outside world presented them with other difficulties. As they approached an insider's perspective on the prison world, they came to share the long-term inmate's belief that preoccupation with the outside world could make their sentences more difficult:

> I was talking with [a long-term inmate] and he was telling me that he doesn't usually hang around short-timers because they are so preoccupied with time. He said it took him a long time to get over counting the days, weeks, and months, and that he doesn't really like to be reminded about it. (Field notes: conversation with middle-aged inmate convicted of murder)

Intimate relationships were likely to be questioned and might even be curtailed (see Cordilia 1983). As expressed by a 37-year-old convicted thief,

> I think it would be almost impossible to carry on a relationship, a real close relationship, being here for 2 years or a year and a half. It's literally impossible. I think that the best thing to do is to just forget about it, and if the relationship can be picked up again once you get out, that's fine. And if it can't, you have to accept that. (Interview)

Similar concerns were raised regarding all outside contacts. A 26-year-old inmate, convicted of the possession and sale of marijuana, told us,

> When they [the inmate's visitors] left I felt depressed. . . . It's a high when they come, and you get depressed when they leave. I was wondering if that's good. Maybe, I should just forget that there is an outside world—at times I thought that, maybe as a survival mechanism to forget that there are good people in the world. (Interview)

Within a few months' time, inmates' adoption of an insider's perspective thus resulted in yet another manifestation of their ambivalence: Their desire to maintain their involvement in the outside world was countered by a temptation to discontinue all outside contacts so that they could do their own time without the infringement of a world to which they no longer actively belonged.

In a matter of months, then, inmates' perspectives underwent a substantial transformation: They were now viewing the outside world from the perspective of the prison world rather than the reverse, and their adaptation strategies, accordingly, were designed to help them cope with their insider's problems of "doing time" rather than their outsider's fears.[6] Their viewpoints were only an *approximation* of an insider's perspective, however, and their insider's tactics were equivocal because they never achieved more than a marginal status within the prison world. During the middle portion of their sentences they may have been tempted to sever all outside contacts to make their time pass more easily, but they did not actually follow through on this temptation. And although the relationships they established in prison, especially their partnerships, might have seemed more important than their outside relationships, they knew that they would not have freely chosen to associate with most of these people on the outside, and they knew that they would not continue most of these relationships once they were released from prison. In this respect, the prison relationships of the men we studied were more cautious than those typically formed by long-term inmates (Cordilia 1983, 13–29; Johnson 1987, 62–63): They acknowledged that they did not fully belong to the prison world in the same sense that long-term or multiple-term inmates do, and they recognized that these other inmates did not fully accept them as members of their world. First-time, short-term inmates, in other words, never completely relinquished their outsider's perspective, even in the middle stage of their prison careers when they were most alienated from the outside world.

Concluding Experiences

Inmates' continuing ambivalence was a motivating factor in their decision to apply for a transfer to the minimum security unit in the concluding months of their sentences.[7] Their behavior, once again, embodied both directions of their ambivalence: Their outsider's perspective was apparent in the application itself, which indicated a desire for the greater privileges and outside contacts available in minimum security, whereas their insider's perspective was reflected in their emotional caution about their chances that the transfer would be approved:

> As much as I try to, it is very difficult to keep [minimum security] off my mind. I figure that if I don't think about it, it won't be as agonizing waiting for it to happen. It would be much easier if they would give a date to go, but they won't. (Journal)

If their applications were approved, their ambivalence also influenced their response to the transfer itself:

> I am looking at this transfer a little bit differently from my coming to prison and my transfer to "B" Hall. I don't want to expect too much from [minimum security] because then I won't be disappointed. Also, there is one big difference; if I don't like it out there I can always come back here. (Journal)

They were aware that their transfer marked the final phase of their prison sentences and a first step toward rejoining the outside world, but they were equally aware that they would still be in prison for some time and that they could be returned to maximum security at the whim of prison officials. Consequently, they were reluctant to admit—to themselves or others—that their transfers held great symbolic importance. They armed themselves with an insider's rationalization. If they didn't like minimum security, they could always come back. And if they should be sent back involuntarily, they were now confident of their capabilities to survive the remainder of their sentences in maximum security.

Once inmates were transferred to minimum security, they experienced yet another manifestation of their ambivalence similar to that reported by long-term inmates after they have been placed in halfway houses (Cordilia 1983, 99–100). They wanted to put their prison experiences behind them and prepare for their return to the free world, but they also wanted to avoid the existential concerns raised by this preparation and to complete their sentences by "doing their own time," just as they did when they were in maximum security:

> Doing time is not as easy as it may sound; actually, it is a rather complicated business. For one thing, you must try to keep yourself busy even though there is very little for you to do. . . . You would like to plan for the future, but it seems so far away that it doesn't really seem like it is worth thinking about. Also, thinking about the future tends to make the time drag. You also don't want to think about the past, because eventually you get around to the dumb mistake that got you in here. So, I guess it must be best to think about the present but that is so boring . . . that it can lead to depression. You don't want to think too much about the outside because it makes you realize all that you are missing, which can be somewhat depressing. But then, you don't really want to just think about the prison, because there isn't anything more depressing at all. (Journal)

In the final months and weeks of their sentences they vacillated between directly confronting questions about their futures and avoiding these questions through their continuing tactics of thought control and diversionary activities.[8]

Each of the manifestations of ambivalence itemized in Table 2 reflects inmates' marginality because each involved a conflict between an outsider's and an insider's point of view. At various stages in their careers, inmates might place more emphasis on one or the other viewpoint but they never fully resolved their feelings of ambivalence. During the middle portion of their sentences, for example, they might believe that thoughts about the outside world made their sentences more difficult (an insider's belief) and hence might consciously suppress these thoughts (an insider's tactic), but they did not generally terminate outside contacts and would be severely disappointed if their visitors or letters had ceased to arrive. Thus, even when inmates placed greatest emphasis on an insider's viewpoint, their perspectives (that is, the interdependent relationship between their images and their strategies) expressed their marginality. Similarly, when they placed most emphasis on an outsider's viewpoint, namely, at the beginning and end of their sentences, closer inspection of their perspective again reveals their marginality. Our analysis thus suggests that inmates' changing imagery and strategies did not represent a total conversion to an insider's point of view and a subsequent reversion to a more conventional point of view, as suggested in Wheeler's (1961) cyclical model of prison socialization. Rather, the inmates we studied experienced a subtler transformation in which their movement toward either an insider's or an outsider's perspective was circumscribed by their ambivalence.

DISCUSSION

Using ambivalence in any explanatory scheme can place social scientists in a precarious position. Psychological ambivalence is such a universal condition, and one that can result from such myriad causes and situations, that its use in sociological analysis inevitably leads to charges of reductionism. Moreover, as Room's (1976) critique of this concept in the alcoholism literature has demonstrated, pervasive ambivalence resulting from ambiguous cultural norms is a seductively easy but not very useful causal explanation for deviant (and other forms of) behavior. And yet the very pervasiveness of ambivalence in social life also suggests that its interactional significance cannot be ignored.

The ambivalence experienced by the inmates we studied was derived from a very specific set of circumstances: involuntary but relatively brief confinement in a total institution that was both entirely unknown and absolutely feared. Similar, if less extreme, feelings of ambivalence can emerge whenever human beings become fully immersed in highly demanding but time-limited social worlds or social situations. For example, we would expect ambivalence to characterize the behavioral adaptations of new mental patients, military recruits, ethnographic researchers, or students entering college or graduate school. The nature and effects of ambivalence will obviously be influenced by a host of other considerations: how the individuals involved define and evaluate the social world in question, whether their participation is voluntary or involuntary, whether participants share a previous culture, the extent to which they desire to maintain that culture and so on. Although acknowledging the importance of such situational variations, we nonetheless believe that our analysis of inmates' prison adaptations may help interpret the experiences of others whose ambivalence results from social marginality.

In his critique, Room (1976) specifically points to three connotations of the term "ambivalence" that result in theoretical difficulties: that it "draws attention away from the content of norms or values and places the emphasis on the fact of a conflict in values," that it implies a continuous state rather than an occasional condition, and that it suggests "an especially excited and explosive state, where irrational behavior is to be expected" (p. 1053). Although we are using ambivalence in a holistic rather than a causal model (Deising 1971), Room's comments are nonetheless helpful for our specification of how sociological ambivalence operates in the prison world.

First, for a new inmate the conflict of value systems was as important, or more important, than the content. The first-time inmates we studied were socially heterogeneous; one of the few characteristics they had in common was their belief that they were different from other inmates and hence did not "belong" in the prison world (Schmid and Jones 1991). To differing degrees they learned (but did not fully accept) the norms and values of the prison world. The prison strategies of new inmates had to acknowledge and deal with the content of prison norms and values, but it was the conflict between this value system and their outside values that resulted in their marginality.

The second connotation noted by Room (1976)—that ambivalence refers to a pervasive social condition—is a temporal one. But time itself was central to the marginality of the inmates we studied: They knew that they would be in prison for a year or two but they hoped (and later expected) to return to the outside world. Although ambivalence pervaded their entire prison careers, their role in prison, as defined by themselves and other inmates, was primarily determined by their status as short-timers. Their ambivalence was thus situational, imposed by the specific circumstances of their imprisonment.

It is the connotation of an excited, explosive state that makes ambivalence such an attractive variable in causal explanation. Yet this connotation, which derives from the use of ambivalence in the psychotherapeutic literature, is not inherent in the concept itself; citing *Hamlet,* Room (1976) notes that the term has traditionally suggested paralysis more than action (p. 1058). In our analysis, inmates' feelings of ambivalence served sometimes to motivate action (for example, to break through their initial isolation or later to apply for transfer to minimum security) and sometimes to inhibit action (not to break off ties to the outside world during the middle portion of their sentences despite a temptation to do so). At some career points, the inmates' ambivalence offered them no real choice in behavior (after orientation, inmates were transferred to another cellblock regardless of how they felt about it); at other points, they did face choices (decisions about continuing outside contacts). The principal effect of their ambivalence, however, was to circumscribe their behavior, keeping it somewhere between the more extreme perspectives of the prison outsider and the long-term inmate.

The traditional model of prison socialization suggests that inmates enter prison with conventional values, become socialized to the values of an inmate culture, and then subsequently become resocialized to the values of the outside world. Our research suggests an alternative model of the prison experiences of first-time, short-term inmates, in which their social marginality continuously shapes both their subjective understanding of the prison world and their adaptations to it, Specifically, we argue that the ambivalence that results from these inmates' transitional status limits the behavioral adaptations they make in prison and inhibits their assimilation into prison culture.

The importance of ambivalence in the prison experiences of the men we studied extended beyond its effect on their prison behavior: It also affected their identities. As we have shown elsewhere (Schmid and Jones 1991), these inmates drew a distinction between their "true" identities (i.e., their preprison identities) and the artificial "prison identities" they created and presented through impression management. This self-bifurcation was itself an expression of both directions of the inmates' ambivalence. Because their prison interactions were based almost exclusively on their shared prison role, conditions existed for a "role-person merger" (Turner 1978). Actual identity change was moderated, however, by the inmates' marginality within the prison world and their consequent ambivalence toward their temporary prison role. In this respect, ambivalence helped to shape not only inmates' adaptations to the prison world but their subsequent adaptations to the outside world. By extension, if the final measure of cultural assimilation is whether a new cultural identity emerges, understanding cultural ambivalence in specific, time-limited social worlds may have larger theoretical implications as well.

NOTES

1. Sociological research on the prison world relies heavily on information from those who actively participate in this world: Inmates who have already served many years in prison. Although long-term prisoners are undoubtedly the best source of information on the inmate social structure, many become so acclimatized to prison life that they have lost their outsider's perspective. First-time inmates, on the other hand, approach their sentences with an understanding of the prison world essentially similar to that of other outsiders, so their experiences offer an ideal vantage point for examining the effects of sudden immersion into the prison world. By further restricting our study to inmates serving relatively brief sentences (by maximum security standards) of 2 years or less, we were able to look at prison through the eyes of men who had generally been convicted of less serious offenses (again, by maximum security standards) and who were in a position to retain a stronger orientation toward the outside world than are inmates who are facing sentences of 5, 10, or an indefinite number of years.

2. Although key prison officials had been aware of our fieldwork activities, the interviews were officially sanctioned on a more formal basis. We were therefore able to collect and validate detailed descriptive data on the interview sample. These inmates ranged in age from 22 to 57 years (mean = 31 years) and had served from 2 to 14 months of their sentences (mean = 7.2 months) at the time of the interviews. They had been convicted of a variety of Index I crimes: theft (2), narcotics sales (4), fraud (1), burglary (3), aggravated robbery (4), sexual misconduct/assault (4), and terrorism/false imprisonment (2).

3. "Territorial caution" and "selective interaction" are essentially precautionary guidelines that allowed inmates to increase their understanding of the prison world while minimizing danger to themselves. A prison "partnership" is a special friendship bond between two inmates, typically based on common backgrounds and interests (including a shared uncertainty about prison life) and strengthened by the inmates' mutual exploration of a hostile prison world. Such partnerships provided now inmates with a means of interpreting and evaluating information about the prison world, an advocate with officials and other inmates, and the opportunity for interaction with relatively few impression management techniques, which for new inmates consist of all efforts, verbal and nonverbal, to present self-images judged to be appropriate for the prison world (see Goffman 1959; Schlenker 1980). The primary intended audience for new inmates' impression management was other inmates, not prison officials.

4. In keeping with their marginal position in the prison world, their interpretation of this information was partly individual and partly interactive. When alone in their cells they

analyzed conflicting information through intermittent self-dialogues that began before their arrival at prison (Schmid and Jones 1991). Their partnerships provided them with an interactive means of interpreting information. Goffman (1961) has observed that "where persons are deprived of knowledge of what is likely to happen to them, and where they are uninformed about how to make out in a situation where making out may mean psychological survival, information itself becomes a crucial good. . . . It is understandable, then, that buddies in all total institutions give mutual aid by 'wising' each other up" (p. 286). Although new prison inmates found information to be cheap, that is to say plentiful but conflicting, their partnerships served a similar "wising" function by allowing them to sort through and interpret this information. Whether alone or with their partners, inmates' refusal to accept fully any single piece of information was the guiding principle of their efforts to understand the prison world.

5. There was another essential process involved in inmates' approximation of an insider's perspective. For inmates to redefine prison as a monotonous world rather than a violent one, their uncertainty and fear about prison had to be reduced. This did in fact occur, though in an erratic manner that was punctuated regularly by such "dramatic events" as assaults, rapes, homicides, or suicides. Each dramatic event represented a setback in the declining uncertainty and fear made possible by inmates' survival tactics. Eventually, dramatic events themselves became subject to definitional change as they became "explained" as consequences of prison norm violations (see Jones and Schmid 1989; Schmid and Jones 1990).

6. This change in emphasis in the inmates' ambivalence did not result simply from the passage of time, nor was it a simple acceptance of a belief system learned from other prisoners. Rather, it emerged from their interactions with members of both their prison and outside social networks. Beginning with their early, cautious interactions with selected other prisoners, and their gradual development of partnerships with one other inmate, new inmates gradually widened their circle of prison acquaintances. Their estrangement from their outside social network also took place through a gradual process in which inmates and their families and friends, while trying to support or reassure one another, recognized that they were living in separate worlds, mutually withheld certain types of information, and eventually found that their communication was becoming increasingly constrictive.

7. Virtually all of the inmates we studied were eligible for transfer to the minimum security unit. Those inmates who did not apply or were not accepted to the unit experienced similar feelings of ambivalence and were equally cognizant that their sentences were coming to a conclusion. Our data suggest that their careers differed from those of inmates who did transfer primarily in that they were able to postpone (for weeks or months) many of the problems associated with anticipating their return to the free world. To the extent that they confronted these problems while still in prison, of course, they had to do so without benefit of the transition provided by minimum security.

8. The prison careers of first-time, short-term inmates toward the end of their minimum security residence had thus come full circle: They again found themselves about to enter an unfamiliar world and they again found it necessary to construct an image of this world and a plan of action based on their imagery. Like their anticipatory prison images, their reconstructed outside images included their fears and expectations about what lay ahead. Also like their anticipatory images, their outside images (as well as their outside plans) were incomplete and somewhat abstract. Perhaps the most important parallel, however, was that inmates again looked forward to their futures with feelings of ambivalence. Obviously, the emphasis of their ambivalence was different: Their fears about returning to the outside world did not compare with their earlier fears about entering the prison world. Nonetheless, these inmates' continuing ambivalence at the end of their prison careers was a matter of some consequence because of its implications for their reintegration into the outside world (see Schmid and Jones 1991).

REFERENCES

Blumer, H. 1969. *Symbolic interactionism: Perspective and method.* Englewood Cliffs, NJ: Prentice-Hall.

Cardozo-Freeman, I. 1984. *The joint: Language and culture in a maximum security prison.* Springfield, IL: Charles C Thomas.

Clemmer, D. 1958. *The prison community.* New York: Holt, Rinehart & Winston.

Cordilia, A. 1983. *The making of an inmate: Prison as a way of life.* Cambridge, MA: Schenkman.

Davis, F. 1973. The Martian and the convert: Ontological polarities in social research. *Urban Life* 2:333–43.

Deising, P. 1971. *Patterns of discovery in the social sciences.* Chicago: Aldine-Atherton.

Ellis, C. 1991. Sociological introspection and emotional experience. *Symbolic Interaction* 14:23–50.

Giallombardo, R. 1966. *Society of women: A study of a women's prison.* New York: Wiley.

Gibson, M. A. 1988. *Accommodation without assimilation: Sikh immigrants in an American high school.* Ithaca, NY: Cornell University Press.

Glaser, D. 1969. *The effectiveness of a prison and parole system.* New York: Bobbs-Merrill.

Gold, R. 1958. Roles in sociological field observations. *Social Forces* 36:217–23.

Goffman, E. 1959. *The presentation of self in everyday life.* Garden City, NY: Doubleday.

———. 1961. *Asylums: Essays on the social situation of mental patients and other inmates.* Garden City, NY: Doubleday.

Goodstein, L., D. L. MacKenzie, and R. L. Shotland. 1984. Personal control and inmate adjustment to prison. *Criminology* 22:343–69.

Hayano, D. 1979. Auto-ethnography: Paradigms, problems, and prospects. *Human Organization* 38:99–104.

———. 1982. *Poker faces: The life and work of professional card players.* Berkeley: University of California Press.

Irwin, J. 1970. *The felon.* Englewood Cliffs, NJ: Prentice-Hall.

———. 1980. *Prisons in turmoil.* Boston: Little, Brown.

Jacobs, J. 1977. *Stateville: The penitentiary in mass society.* Chicago: University of Chicago Press.

Johnson, R. 1987. *Hard time: Understanding and reforming the prison.* Monterey, CA: Brooks/Cole.

Jones, R. S., and T. J. Schmid. 1989. Inmates' conceptions of prison sexual assault. *Prison Journal* 69:53–61.

Merton, R. K., and E. Barber. 1976. Sociological ambivalence. In *Sociological ambivalence and other essays,* by R. K. Merton, 3–31. New York: Free Press.

Morawska, E. 1987. Sociological ambivalence: Peasant immigrant workers in America, 1880s–1930s. *Qualitative Sociology* 10:225–50.

Room, R. 1976. Ambivalence as a sociological explanation: The case of cultural explanations of alcohol problems. *American Sociological Review* 41:1047–65.

Schlenker, R. 1980. *Impression management: The self concept, social identity and interpersonal relations.* Belmont, CA: Wadsworth.

Schmid. T. J., and R. S. Jones. 1990. Experiential orientations to the prison experience: The case of first-time, short-term inmates. In *Perspectives on social problems,* edited by G. Miller and J. A. Holstein, vol. 2, 189–210. Greenwich, CT: JAI.

———. 1991. Suspended identity: Identity transformation in a maximum security prison. *Symbolic Interaction* 14:415–32.

Seymour, J. 1977. Niches in prison. In *Living in prison: The ecology of survival,* by H. Toch, 179–205. New York: Free Press.

Shokeid, M. 1988. *Children of circumstances: Israeli emigrants in New York.* Ithaca, NY: Cornell University Press.

Sykes, G. [1959] 1971. *The society of captives: A study of a maximum security prison*. Reprint. Princeton, NJ: Princeton University Press.

Sykes, G., and S. Messinger. 1960. Inmate social system. In *Theoretical studies in social organization of the prison,* by R. A. Cloward, D. R. Cressey, G. H. Grosser, R. McCleery, L. E. Ohlin, G. M. Sykes, and S. L. Messinger, 5–19. New York: Social Science Research Council.

Thomas, C. C. 1973. Prisonization or resocialization? A study of external factors associated with the impact of imprisonment. *Journal of Research in Crime and Delinquency* 10:13–21.

Thomas, C. C., and D. M. Peterson. 1977. *Prison organization and inmate subcultures.* Indianapolis: Bobbs-Merrill.

Toch, H. 1977. *Living in prison: The ecology of survival.* New York: Free Press.

Turner, R. H. 1978. The role and the person. *American Journal of Sociology* 84:1–23.

Wheeler, S. 1961. Socialization in correctional communities. *American Sociological Review* 26:697–712.

Zimmerman, D., and D. L. Wieder. 1977. The diary: Diary-interview method. *Urban Life* 5:479–98.

THOMAS J. SCHMID is Professor of Sociology at Mankato State University. He has conducted a number of ethnographic projects on constructed social worlds, with a particular emphasis on the relationship between social world membership and identity. His current research interests center on processes of culture making and cultural reflection.

RICHARD S. JONES is Assistant Professor of Sociology at Marquette University. His primary research emphasis has been on inmate socialization in men's and women's prisons. He has recently extended this interest to examine inmate expressions of the prison experience.

DISCUSSION QUESTIONS

1. What special problems exist when conducting research on incarcerated populations?
2. What problems were presented to Jones acting as an indigenous researcher in this study?
3. Describe Schmid's role as part of the research team. Why was this role important?
4. According to Schmid and Jones, what was the primary limitation of their study? How did they address this limitation?

PART V

Analysis of Existing Records

This part provides examples of approaches for analyzing existing records. As noted in Part I, typically these data are compiled and maintained by federal, state, and local agencies of government and are then made available for analysis. Numerous examples are contained in agency records, which contain information regarding criminal offending, court processing, prison confinement, and the like.

Existing records are quite useful in making descriptive statements and examining trends over time. This method, however, is not without its drawbacks. As discussed in the following articles and commentaries, often these records are not collected for research purposes and may not adequately answer the questions that researchers have in mind. Moreover, since these data are often compiled in summary or aggregate form, they cannot be manipulated by the researcher. The information presented must be taken at "face value." One cannot alter the information, nor is it usually possible to discern any errors associated with how the information was originally collected. This is especially true if the data are historical in nature. With this in mind, the three articles presented here are viable examples of this technique along with its associated strengths and weaknesses.

Crutchfield, Bridges, and Pitchford (1994) utilize state-level data on imprisonment and violent crime to address a critical issue in criminal justice—racial disparity within the justice system. In their review of the literature, they note that some previous research finds that blacks are treated more harshly than whites while other research does not. They note some important problems associated with previous research that examined arrest and imprisonment records at the national level. First, they argue that it is misleading to use national data to address this issue since it may tend to mask any racial effects. According to the authors, state-level data are more appropriate for this type of analysis.

A second concern raised by the authors is the location of much of the previous research in that it was typically collected in one or a few jurisdictions. This is an example of site selection bias, which was explored in an earlier paper by Pope and Hawkins (1993). They argued, as did Crutchfield et al. (1994), that much of the race-related research has continued to be collected within specific jurisdictions while ignoring others. The authors attempt to overcome these problems by examining state imprisonment and arrest data published by the U.S. Department of Justice and the FBI's Uniform Crime Reports (UCR). Analysis of these data leads Crutchfield and his colleagues to conclude that there are wide variations across states creating racial differences that have important implications for the justice system.

The second article, Taxman and Piquero's "On Preventing Drunk Driving Recidivism: An Examination of Rehabilitation and Punishment Approaches" (1998), utilizes data obtained from Maryland's Motor Vehicle Administration (MVA) to examine deterrent approaches to driving while intoxicated (DWI). DWI is a serious national problem that annually involves millions of dollars in property damage and loss of life, not to mention associated health risks. There has been a long and vigorous debate regarding the merits of punishment versus rehabilitation in dealing with motorists who drive while intoxicated. Research regarding the efficacy of these two approaches has not been consistent.

This article sheds additional light on the topic by examining punishment and rehabilitative approaches simultaneously rather than in isolation from one another. Given the limitations of the MVA data, the results reported here suggest that certain rehabilitative approaches are more effective than sanctions in reducing the likelihood of recidivism. The authors also note various problems associated with the study.

The final article contained in this part, written by Brandl (1994), examines police work from the standpoint of potential danger in the workplace. As noted by the author, much previous research in this area focuses on police homicides with information derived from records contained in the FBI's Uniform Crime Reports and other sources. Less attention has been given to assaults on the police and virtually none to accidents occurring in the field. In order to further examine accidents and assaults on police officers, Brandl examined injury reports compiled by a police department in a major midwestern city over a one-year period.

The article documents the nature of the incident that occurred including the type of activity the officer was engaged in and the type of injury received. While the data underscore the frequently dangerous nature of police work, they also contravene a popular misconception—that death and injury are most likely the result of homicide and assault. As demonstrated here, the routine activity of police work can be hazardous to one's health. Most injuries reported here were attributable to accidents, whether in the course of directing traffic at a busy intersection, pursuing a fleeing suspect, or assisting a citizen, or while engaged in other normal police functions.

10

Analytical and Aggregation Biases in Analyses of Imprisonment

Reconciling Discrepancies in Studies of Racial Disparity

ROBERT D. CRUTCHFIELD
GEORGE S. BRIDGES
SUSAN R. PITCHFORD

COMMENTARY

We wrote this paper because we were concerned that the analytical strategies employed by some researchers could lead to erroneous conclusions about racial differences in criminal justice processing. Major inconsistencies in the research literature alerted us to the possibility that methodological and conceptual considerations might help explain differences among study findings. Some studies reported findings suggesting that there were unwarranted (not based on legal factors) differences in how blacks and whites were treated, while at the same time other studies found that the differences were largely warranted (usually because of higher black and white arrest rates for violent crimes). We felt that two aspects of study design were important to understanding the differences among studies. The first is the level of aggregation used in analyzing racial differences in criminal justice processing. The second is the location of the research, both the actual geographic location of the courts that are studied and the stage of the criminal justice process at which racial differences are compared.

The first issue, level of aggregation, is not really a methodological consideration as we usually think of it, but rather a theoretical concern. In the United States, with the exception of the federal and military systems, criminal justice is

Source: Journal of Research in Crime and Delinquency, Vol. 31 No. 2, May 1994, pp. 166-182.
© 1994 Sage Publications, Inc. Reprinted by permission of Sage Publications, Inc.

administered by the states. So we felt that while some important studies had used data aggregated to the national level, it was more consistent with the nature of criminal law and criminal justice to study racial disparities across the states. To do otherwise, we thought and we found, could mask important variations in the differences in how black and white defendants were treated between the states. The message here is that the study of any topic must employ a research design, and in this case a level of aggregation, that is conceptually consistent with the phenomenon being studied. In the study of racial differences in imprisonment, it only makes sense to compare rates of imprisonment at the state level, not the national level.

The second issue we considered was the location of the study. In the research literature on race and punishment, many studies found racial differences in processing while others did not. Nearly all of the studies, however, were conducted in one or a few jurisdictions, usually one county or one state. Also, most of them restricted their consideration to racial differences in sentencing. Our own work suggested that differences could be observed in different jurisdictions and at different decision points in the criminal justice process. Qualitative research suggests that county and state courts develop their own "court culture," which would suggest that if there are racial differences they could show up at different decision points in different courts or jurisdictions. We found in our analysis reported here that those studies that examine multiple jurisdictions and multiple decision points in the criminal justice process offer a more complete picture of the extent and nature of racial differences in processing.

It is important to note that scholars who have conducted the research, which we reconsidered in our analysis, were often working under significant methodological constraints. For instance, it is extremely difficult to undertake very detailed studies in multiple jurisdictions. Researchers may choose to examine a few jurisdictions in depth rather than many jurisdictions superficially. Two important lessons can be drawn from these types of problems and from our work. First, we get a better sense of the phenomena we study when we read widely in a literature rather than restricting our consideration to a few pieces. That is, researchers may only be able to study a single jurisdiction, but students, by reading many of these studies, can have the benefits of multiple jurisdiction studies by reading widely. Second, and most important, in conducting studies it is imperative to match analytical and methodological strategies to the relevant theory and conceptualization of the research problem.

ABSTRACT The literature on racial disparities in criminal justice processing is unclear about whether Black defendants are treated differently from White defendants. Although some studies find no difference in treatment, others report that Blacks are treated significantly more harshly than Whites; still other studies find that Black defendants are treated more leniently. This analysis examines three methodological procedures: (1) the selection of single or multiple points in the criminal justice system for study, (2) the number of jurisdictions included in studies, and (3) the level of aggregation of jurisdictions used in studies of racial disparities. The authors conclude that some of the ambiguity reported in this literature can be traced to studies of single or few jurisdictions, single decision points in criminal justice processing, and to inappropriate aggregation.

The presence, pervasiveness, and causes of racial discrimination in the criminal justice system are subjects of continuing controversy. Prompted by disproportionately large populations of Black prisoners in state and federal correctional facilities, scholars continue to debate the causes of the disproportionality and, specifically, the factors contributing to Black imprisonment rates. Some attribute high Black imprisonment rates to differences in the legal system's treatment of White and Black defendants. Reasoning that law enforcement officials and courts punish Blacks and other minorities accused of crime more severely than Whites, these scholars explain disproportionality in terms of racial discrimination. Others, however, reject the idea that the legal system discriminates against racial minorities. Arguing that courts impose punishments mainly in relation to the seriousness of offenses, they explain disproportionality primarily in terms of racial differences in crime. They reason that courts imprison Blacks at higher rates because Blacks are more heavily involved in serious and violent offenses.

Within criminology, the latter view is perhaps more widely held. Criminologists and legal scholars from quite divergent orientations, from Wilbanks (1987) to Wilson (1987), conclude that racial differences in levels of criminal behavior explain disproportionately high rates of Black imprisonment. In drawing this conclusion, most typically cite research by Blumstein (1982), a replication and extension of Blumstein's work (Langan 1985), or complementary evidence on sentencing offered in reviews of the sentencing literature (e.g., Hagan 1974; Kleck 1981) for empirical support. Among these, however, Blumstein's work is one of the most prominent and frequently cited. In reporting that minority involvement in arrests for serious and violent crimes explains 80% of racial disproportionality in U.S. imprisonment rates, Blumstein (1982) concludes that "racial differences in arrests alone account for the bulk of racial differences in incarceration" (p. 1268). Further, Blumstein dismisses the need to remedy discrimination in the legal process based on these findings, reasoning that

> attacking discrimination in the criminal justice system to redress disproportionality is not likely to have the desired effect on prison populations. Any significant impact on the racial mix in our prisons will have to come from addressing the factors in our society that generate the life conditions that contribute to the different involvement between the races in serious person crimes. (p. 1281)

Despite wide acceptance and citation of Blumstein's findings, periodic publication of research countering his findings and conclusions has kept alive controversy over racial discrimination in imprisonment. A growing body of evidence suggests that justice is by no means guaranteed for some groups facing criminal processing (Peterson and Hagan 1984; Myers and Talarico 1987; Bridges and Crutchfield 1988; Bridges, Crutchfield, and Simpson 1987). Unlike other writers such as Christianson (1980a, 1980b), who considers disproportionately large Black prison populations to be evidence of discrimination, this work takes into account race differentials in crime rates, particularly for violent crimes, in analyzing the factors associated with racial differences in imprisonment. These studies show empirically that racial differences in crime and arrest rates contribute substantially less to racial differences in imprisonment than Blumstein's (1982) and Langan's (1985) work suggests. For example, Bridges and Crutchfield's (1988) multivariate analysis of state differences in imprisonment concludes that "racial differences at arrest for serious criminal behavior may be coupled with differential treatment (of minorities) in the legal system" (p. 717). That the conclusions reached in these studies about the relationship between crime and imprisonment differ from those of Blumstein and his colleagues suggests that a deeper understanding of racial inequality in criminal processing is needed.

Increasingly, research on racial disparities in imprisonment (e.g., Petersilia 1983; Crutchfield and Bridges 1986) reveals that conventional treatments may produce false negatives (i.e., conclusions that no disparity exists when courts do treat Blacks and Whites differently). Our concern in this article is with problems created by past research, which has frequently (a) focused on single decision-making points in the criminal justice process, usually sentencing; (b) focused on single jurisdictions; or (c) used inappropriately aggregated jurisdictions. The first two problems concern the analytical focus of prior research, whereas the third concerns the level of aggregation used; both can introduce bias into studies of racial disparities in imprisonment. Kleck's (1981) frequently cited review of studies of racial differences in sentencing is a useful starting point for an analysis of these sources of bias, not only because it is thorough and inclusive, but also because it highlights problems that emerge when scholars limit their studies to single decision points and to single jurisdictions.

PROBLEMS OF STUDYING SINGLE DECISION POINTS AND SINGLE JURISDICTIONS

One of the most comprehensive reviews of research on racial disparities in sentencing is Kleck's (1981) article summarizing 40 studies published between 1935 and 1979. In 28 of these studies, the authors examined a single jurisdiction, in some cases a city, in others a county, and in others a single state.[1] Of the 28 studies, 14 reported no evidence of racial discrimination (6 found evidence of discrimination and 8 reported mixed results). Among the 11 studies of two or more jurisdictions, 5 reported no evidence of discrimination, 2 reported discrimination, and 4 found mixed results. Presumably, the mixed results are indicative of some differential treatment under some circumstances based on the race of defendants. Two conclusions emerge from these results. First, although a plurality of the studies report no discrimination (19 of 40), there is insufficient evidence to dismiss altogether the possible existence of racial bias in sentencing. Second, most of the studies that report no evidence of discrimination focused on single jurisdictions.

Recently, Crutchfield and Bridges (1986), Kempf, Decker, and Bing (1990), and Bridges (1993) have shown that minorities and Whites experience significantly different patterns of treatment by courts and law enforcement agencies at different points in the processing of criminal cases. Within any single jurisdiction, racial differences in treatment may be pronounced at one stage (e.g., filing of charges or pretrial diversion) and small at another (e.g., conviction and sentencing). Further, the points at which differential treatment occurs actually vary across jurisdictions. Disparate treatment might occur at sentencing in one county or state, whereas elsewhere it might occur at the filing of criminal charges. Because convicted and sentenced defendants are a biased subsample of those initially at risk of punishment, and thus a subsample of those who may experience differential treatment in processing, it is necessary to correct for this sample selection bias in comparing Black and White differences in treatment in sentencing (Peterson and Hagan 1984; Crutchfield and Bridges 1986; Bridges 1993). Thus studies focusing solely on single points of decision making in criminal justice, or those that overlook the sample selection problem in studying sentencing, should not be generalized beyond those points in the system to jurisdictions dissimilar from those studied. All of the studies examined by Kleck suffer these limitations.

The second concern with Kleck's (1981) review is the matter of single jurisdictions. If differential treatment occurs at different points in the legal process in different jurisdictions, then studies of sentencing, particularly sentencing in one jurisdiction, may find no evidence of discrimination, when in fact it does exist. Conversely, researchers might find evidence of discriminatory treatment if it happens to occur at sentencing in the jurisdiction that they select as their research site. The conflicting findings on racial discrimination in sentencing may have emerged largely from many criminologists' failure to appreciate the complexity of this issue. At the same time, faulting this research as inadequate would be unfair. In some instances, examination of racial differences in treatment at single sites, and even at single decision points, may be the best strategy when, for example, detailed examination of case files is the objective. A thorough understanding of this issue requires, however, that we consider the larger body of evidence on the subject and, in drawing conclusions about the pervasiveness of racial discrimination in the legal process, make adjustments for the number of jurisdictions and decision points examined in the research.

PROBLEMS OF AGGREGATION

An alternate method, which scholars have used to address these jurisdictional issues, is to employ social aggregates in examining the criminal justice process. As mentioned above, Blumstein (1982) and Langan (1985) use statistics generated for the United States and conclude that little racial discrimination exists in criminal justice in the United States. Our concern with the work of Blumstein and Langan is their aggregation of prison statistics for the entire United States. This would not be problematic if they were studying federal courts, where one could argue that one system of criminal justice exists. At another level, however, the 50 states are 50 different legal and justice systems. To consolidate them is to mask important differences in procedure, law, history, and a host of other factors relevant to criminal justice processing and race relations.

Although our concerns about focusing on single points in the legal process and single jurisdictions can be made clear using the extant literature, illustrating the problem of inappropriate aggregation is best done with data. In the remainder of this article, we present partial replications of Blumstein (1982) and Langan (1985). The analysis builds on and significantly extends the work of Christianson (1980a, 1980b) in examining state-level differences in imprisonment rates. The Langan replication is less consistent with the original than is the Blumstein replication, but we believe that in both instances our analyses will reveal the major limitations of their work. The limitations suggest that their conclusions about racial discrimination in criminal justice are unwarranted.

THE STUDY

State-level data were collected from published sources on (a) race-specific trends in imprisonment and measures of racial disparity in imprisonment and (b) race-specific arrests for violent crimes and measures of racial disparity in arrest. These measures are comparable to the measures employed by Blumstein (1982). Although more recent data could have been employed in the analysis, these were used to ensure a high degree of comparability with those used by Blumstein. Further, it is unlikely that analyses of more recent data would yield significantly different findings or conclusions about the aggregate structure of racial disparities in imprisonment.

Imprisonment

We collected data on the racial composition of state prisons as of December 31, 1982, using the published census of state prisons sponsored by the U.S. Department of Justice (1982). Black-White imprisonment disparity was computed in a manner that reflects the comparative odds of imprisonment for the two groups. Consistent with Blumstein (1982), imprisonment rates were computed by (a) dividing the number of Blacks housed in state correctional institutions as of December 31, 1982 by the number of Blacks in each state's total population, (b) repeating the procedure for Whites; and (c) multiplying each rate by 10,000.[2] The measure of racial disparity in imprisonment in each state was computed as the overall ratio of the Black imprisonment rate to the White imprisonment rate.

Arrests for Violent Crimes

Data were also collected from the F.B.I.'s *Uniform Crime Reports* (UCR). State-by-state data were collected on crime and arrest rates. Race-specific data were collected on arrests for serious and violent crimes (i.e., F.B.I. Part I crimes) to determine whether disparities in imprisonment are strongly associated with disparities at arrest.[3] The measure of racial disparity in arrest in each state was computed as the overall ratio of the Black arrest rate for violent offenses to the White arrest rate for violent offenses. We chose to focus on arrests for violent crimes, as did Blumstein (1982), because (a) disparities in imprisonment are most frequently attributed to disproportionate minority involvement in violent crime (Hindelang 1978; Blumstein 1982) and (b) violent offenders currently are more than 50% of all persons housed in state correctional institutions.

RESULTS

The analyses initially examined the geographic variation in Black and White rates of imprisonment and the rankings of the states for each of these rates. The results were comparable to those reported by Christianson (1980a) except that ours were based on males and females, rates for Whites were included, arrest rates for violent crimes were included, and data included information from 1982, whereas Christianson's analysis was based on data from 1978. Christianson (1980a) uses rates such as these to make the case that America's prisons are disproportionately Black. Our analyses revealed that White rates of imprisonment tend to be high in southern states whereas Black imprisonment rates are relatively low. In contrast, Black imprisonment rates in some north central states are high whereas the White imprisonment rates are quite low.

Few would question that Blacks are overrepresented in prisons, but the critical question for criminologists is "why?" Some scholars consider the percentage of Black in state populations to be the expected level of imprisonment for Blacks. Thus, if 10% of a state's population was Black, it might be reasonable to expect that a state's prison population would also be 10% Black. If the percentage of the prison population that was Black was significantly larger than 10%, then some might conclude that there is evidence of racial discrimination. To justify this procedure, however, one must assume that levels of crime and arrest are essentially equal for Blacks and Whites. Other research (e.g., Hindelang 1978) has shown, however, that this is not an empirically defensible assumption. Our analyses of Black and White arrest rates clearly show that arrest rates are higher for Blacks in every state (except New Hampshire where the rates for Blacks are small and unstable) than they are for Whites.

The Black proportion of the prison population is larger than the Black proportion of the total population. Although some scholars (e.g., Christianson 1980a) conclude that the differences between the percentages are a direct reflection of discrimination, this conclusion ignores the most prominent explanation for racial disproportionality in imprisonment (i.e., that Blacks are overrepresented in prison because of higher arrest rates for those crimes most likely to result in prison sentences). Of course, it is possible to argue that Black arrest rates are simply indicative of discriminatory police practices, or that they are produced by pervasive racism in the society that leads to higher levels of crime among Blacks.

In many states, the Black and White rates of imprisonment vary together. In many others, however, the two rates diverge. When considering these rates, Christianson's conception of expected incarceration would suggest that those states with low Black incarceration rates are less discriminatory in criminal justice processing and those with high rates are more discriminatory. But if a state also has a high White incarceration rate in addition to a high Black imprisonment rate, its treatment of Blacks may not be unfair; all persons may be equally exposed to unusually severe sanctions. Similarly, a low incarceration rate does not mean fairness in processing either. Alaska has the lowest Black imprisonment rate, but it may be inflated by discriminatory practices if the crime rates among Blacks in Alaska are inordinately low.

Blumstein's (1982) and Langan's (1985) analyses correct for the failure of previous studies to consider racial differentials in criminal involvement in analyses of imprisonment disparity. Instead of using the Black percentage of the population to determine the expected Black imprisonment rate, Blumstein uses the Black arrest rate for violent crimes. Langan uses the results of the National Crime Survey (NCS) to measure differential involvement as reported by victims of crime. Racial disproportionality in imprisonment as defined by Blumstein includes a comparison of Black and White incarceration rates and a similar comparison of Black and White violent crime arrest rates. Further, Blumstein uses the following equation to define the amount of racial disproportionality in imprisonment that is accounted for by disproportionality in arrest:

$$\begin{array}{c}\text{Disproportionality} \\ \text{explained by crime}\end{array} = \frac{\begin{array}{c}\text{Ratio of expected Black-to-White incarceration} \\ \text{rates based only on arrest disproportionality}\end{array}}{\begin{array}{c}\text{Ratio of Black-to-White incarceration} \\ \text{rates actually observed}\end{array}}$$

Using 1974 and 1979 arrest and imprisonment rates for the United States, Blumstein found that disproportionality = 80.0%. He concludes that 80% of racial disproportionality in American prisons can be accounted for by the legally relevant factor of higher rates among Blacks of arrest for violent crimes. He suggests that the 20% of racial disparity that could not be accounted for by arrest rates might be produced by extralegal considerations that should not be a part of American criminal justice decision making. Langan's (1985) comparable analysis yielded similar results.

In our replication using 1982 rates, disproportionality explained by arrest = 89.5%. Following Blumstein, one could conclude that America made remarkable progress in reducing "unwarranted" disparities in recent years. The problem with Blumstein's computation, our comparable computation using 1982 data, and

Langan's analysis based on NCS data is that by aggregating state data and using rates for the United States, large regional and state variations are masked, leading to the unwarranted conclusion that racial disparities in imprisonment are caused almost completely by disproportionately high Black crime and arrest rates.

Two examples should illustrate the problems introduced by using national aggregations in these analyses. First, Blumstein's claim that 80% of racial differences in imprisonment can be accounted for by differences in arrest may hold true in one region or state, but not in others. Second, aggregation may mask state or regional differences between imprisonment and arrest ratios that cancel each other out. For example, if one state has a Black/White arrest ratio of 6:1 and an imprisonment ratio of 10:1, one would conclude that only 60% of the Black/White imprisonment difference can be accounted for by the higher incidence of Black arrest for violent crimes. For another state, a ratio of 16:1 for arrest and a 16:1 ratio of imprisonment for violent crimes would lead to the conclusion that 100% of the racial disparity in imprisonment is accounted for by the arrest differential. When the two states are combined to create aggregate ratios, such as those developed for the United States as a whole, the comparisons are 11:1 for violence arrest rates and 13:1 for imprisonment rates.[4] Aggregating would then suggest that 85% of Black/White differences in imprisonment is accounted for by the higher frequency with which Blacks are arrested. Although not technically incorrect, this procedure masks a substantively important finding. In one state, the imprisonment rates seem to be determined by the legally relevant determinants—who commits violent crime—but in the other state, 40% of that difference cannot be justified by this legal factor. As long as there is significant variation across states in crime rates, arrest rates, imprisonment rates, and the ratios created with them, combining states to measure the extent of racial disproportionality in imprisonment or to consider theoretical explanations for any differences is inappropriate.

Using Blumstein's (1982) procedure, we calculated ratios of expected to observed imprisonment for each state; these are presented in Table 1. The table displays ratios of Black to White imprisonment rates, ratios of Black to White arrest rates for violent crimes, and the percentage of the former that can be "accounted for" by the latter. In Table 1 the problem created by aggregating the data for states into a single ratio for the United States is graphically clear. The ranges of the Black to White imprisonment ratios and of the arrest ratios are quite large. The lowest imprisonment ratio is 2.8:1 for Alaska and the highest is 20.9:1 for Minnesota. The lowest Black to White ratio for arrest for violent crimes is New Hampshire's .5: 1, whereas the highest is Minnesota's 24.3:1. The relationship between the arrest and imprisonment ratios is much weaker than expected (r =.368, r^2 =. 14) given the high ratio of expected to observed imprisonment for the aggregated United States. Whereas Blumstein's and Langan's analyses suggest that little unwarranted racial disparity in imprisonment exists in the United States, our analysis suggests that in some areas, the unwarranted disparities are substantial and that the statistical relationship between arrest and imprisonment rates is quite weak.

Table 1. Racial Disparities in Imprisonment, 1982 and Racial Disparities in Arrest for Violent Crimes, 1981

State/Region	Black/White Imprisonment Disparity	Black/White Violent Crime Arrest Disparity	Percentage of Imprisonment Disparity Explained by Arrest Disparity
National	6.80	6.09	89.50
Northeast	9.01	6.29	69.83
Maine	6.23[a]	3.62	58.09
New Hampshire	3.44[a]	.52	15.13
Massachusetts	11.59	4.58	39.55
Rhode Island	12.38	7.99	64.50
Connecticut	10.16	9.67	95.19
New York	6.13	6.37	103.99
New Jersey	10.33	7.04	68.12
Pennsylvania	12.40	13.29	107.16
North Central	9.79	11.27	115.11
Ohio	8.01	6.12	76.36
Indiana	6.29	10.27	163.33
Illinois	9.67	7.04	72.76
Michigan	9.27	9.71	104.75
Wisconsin	14.97	21.63	144.48
Minnesota	20.90	24.29	116.22
Iowa	14.63	10.08	68.87
Missouri	5.53	8.29	149.97
North Dakota	6.25[a]	7.87	126.01
South Dakota	7.46[a]	15.63	209.55
Nebraska	14.99	18.07	120.55
Kansas	9.42	7.90	83.92
South	5.08	4.49	87.58
Delaware	6.92	7.55	109.13
Maryland	8.03	5.33	66.35
Virginia	5.66	4.98	87.95
West Virginia	4.69	5.89	125.39
North Carolina	4.08	3.86	94.67
South Carolina	3.22	2.93	90.88
Georgia	3.81	4.25	111.67
Florida	5.91	4.93	83.48
Kentucky	4.94	5.12	103.61
Tennessee	4.26	3.38	79.40
Alabama	4.53	2.45	54.13
Mississippi	4.24	5.05	119.31
Arkansas	5.54	5.43	97.91
Louisiana	6.06	4.14	68.32

Table 1. (Continued)

State/Region	Black/White Imprisonment Disparity	Black/White Violent Crime Arrest Disparity	Percentage of Imprisonment Disparity Explained by Arrest Disparity
South *(cont.)*			
Oklahoma	5.07	5.61	110.76
Texas	5.06	3.24	64.00
West	6.50	5.93	91.14
Idaho	10.92[a]	5.82	53.28
Wyoming	4.34[a]	6.03	138.82
Colorado	6.39	3.98	62.28
New Mexico	5.25	8.10	154.07
Arizona	7.07	5.90	83.35
Utah	14.41[a]	16.98	117.81
Nevada	4.22	7.59	179.80
Washington	9.28	3.72	40.05
Oregon	9.06	8.59	94.80
California	5.25	5.05	96.05
Alaska	2.82[a]	3.88	137.39
Hawaii	4.08[a]	4.61	112.85

[a]States with less than 25 Black inmates or fewer than 25,000 Blacks in the resident population. Data are not available for Vermont or Montana.

When disaggregated data are used rather than national data, the north central states, which have the highest imprisonment disparities, seem to imprison fewer Blacks than one would expect given Black arrest rates. The northeast, on the other hand, can only account for 69% of imprisonment disparities with arrest rates, far below the nationally aggregated figure of 90%. The range between states is even greater. Nebraska imprisons approximately half as many Blacks as "expected," whereas in New Hampshire, only 15%[5] of racial disparities in imprisonment can be accounted for by arrest rate differentials between Blacks and Whites. These results clearly show that using nationally aggregated rates of arrest and imprisonment glosses over dramatic and substantively important differences.

Langan's (1985) approach is similar to that of Blumstein (1982), except that Langan used NCS data instead of data from the UCR to compute his expected imprisonment rates. Langan calculated the probability of imprisonment for White offenders by dividing the number of Whites admitted to prison (1974, 1979, and 1982 admissions census of state prisons) by the number of White offenders (from NCS reports of victims' descriptions of their assailants). The proportion of Black offenders that would be expected to go to prison, according to Langan (1985), can be computed by "multiplying the number of black offenders (from NCS reports) by the crime-specific probability of a white offender going to prison" (p. 678). In a racially neutral criminal justice system, one would expect that the proportion of White and Black offenders going to prison would be equal. This Black expected imprisonment rate, which is based on the observed White imprisonment rate, was therefore used to compare the observed Black imprisonment rates for the United States in 1973, 1979, and 1982. Langan concludes that no significant difference existed between the expected and observed Black imprisonment rates for 1973 and that 84% and 85% of the 1979 and 1982 Black imprisonment rates can be accounted for by the higher offending levels of Blacks.

We concede that the data we are using are not the same as those used by Langan, but again, as is the case with Blumstein, we can demonstrate that aggregating data across states masks important differences. First, we should note that Langan makes a convincing case for the comparability of NCS and UCR data. Second, although he used prison admissions, we are restricted to prison populations. If Blacks tend to be held longer once incarcerated than Whites, then we will, by using prison populations, paint a more negative picture than the admissions data used by Langan. Langan's analysis is more conservative if the question is whether Blacks are disproportionately admitted to prison. In contrast, our analysis is most appropriate if the question is whether Blacks are treated differentially by the criminal justice system. It is our opinion that both issues are important, but the latter is most consistent with the questions asked by Christianson (1980a, 1980b) and Blumstein (1982).

Table 2 presents Black observed and expected imprisonment rates for the United States, four regions, and the individual states. Column 3 contains the percentage of the Black observed imprisonment rate explained by the Black expected imprisonment rate. The expected rates in this table are based on all seven of the UCR index crimes (Langan used the NCS equivalent of the index crimes). Clearly, the percentage of the national observed Black imprisonment rate that is explained by the expected rate, 66.41%, is substantially less than the approximately 84% reported by Langan. This difference is not unexpected because different data are used in this replication. The important point to be gained from this table is that, as was the case when Blumstein's analysis was disaggregated for regions and states, the national figures mask important differences. Nearly 40% of the states explain less of their observed Black imprisonment via differential Black involvement in serious crime than can be explained for the aggregated national observed Black imprisonment rate.

Table 3 duplicates Table 2 except that violent crimes (instead of all index crimes) are used to calculate expected imprisonment rates. Here the state-expected Black imprisonment rates do a better job of explaining the state-observed rates, but again, there is substantial variation in "percentage of observed Black imprisonment explained by expected" for the states. Although the aggregated national average is 89%, the states range from Hawaii's 172% to New Hampshire's 18%. About one third of the states account for less of their Black imprisonment via higher levels of violent crime arrest rates for Blacks than can be accounted for in the United States when aggregated values are used. Again, aggregating across states and focusing solely on national statistics masks important state and regional differences.

Table 2. Black Observed Imprisonment, 1982 and Black Expected Imprisonment (based on Index arrests, 1981)

State/Region	Black Imprisonment Observed	Black Imprisonment Expected	% of Black Observed Imprisonment Explained by Expected[a]
National	155,924	103,552	66.41
Northeast	26,650	16,505	61.93
Maine	15	56	39.45
New Hampshire	5	1	28.81
Massachusetts	1,329	408	30.71
Rhode Island	246	145	85.89
Connecticut	2,105	1,247	59.26
New York	13,407	9,721	72.50
New Jersey	4,455	1,974	44.30
Pennsylvania	5,088	3,003	59.03
North Central	33,813	22,900	67.73
Ohio	7,229	3,866	53.47
Indiana	2,795	2,677	95.78
Illinois	8,217	5,639	68.63
Michigan	8,515	5,715	67.12
Wisconsin	1,689	950	56.26
Minnesota	421	196	46.64
Iowa	490	168	34.31
Missouri	2,974	2,791	93.83
North Dakota	2	31	42.98
South Dakota	14	11	75.54
Nebraska	533	276	51.79
Kansas	934	609	65.16
South	81,065	54,645	67.41
Delaware	1,021	792	77.57
Maryland	6,761	3,387	50.09
Virginia	5,376	3,401	63.27
West Virginia	218	180	82.66
North Carolina	8,380	7,477	89.23
South Carolina	4,972	4,238	85.24
Georgia	7,313	6,081	83.15
Florida	11,351	7,205	63.48
Kentucky	1,171	882	75.35
Tennessee	3,346	2,519	75.28
Alabama	4,718	2,883	61.11
Mississippi	2,829	2,816	99.54
Arkansas	1,632	1,292	79.19
Louisiana	6,763	3,879	57.36
Oklahoma	1,482	1,178	79.47
Texas	13,732	6,433	46.84

Continued

Table 2. (Continued)

State/Region	Black Imprisonment Observed	Black Imprisonment Expected	% of Black Observed Imprisonment Explained by Expected[a]
West	14,396	9,502	66.00
Idaho	26	10	38.32
Wyoming	25	17	67.35
Colorado	579	282	48.69
New Mexico	160	—	—
Arizona	1,009	561	55.56
Utah	107	54	50.74
Nevada	591	615	104.14
Washington	1,106	213	19.26
Oregon	340	281	82.65
California	10,270	7,350	71.57
Alaska	139	856	0.99
Hawaii	44	34	78.00

[a]The percentage of observed imprisonment that is explained by the Black expected imprisonment was calculated prior to rounding of the expected values.

Table 3. Black Observed Imprisonment, 1982 and Black Expected Imprisonment (based on violent crime arrests, 1981)

State/Region	Black Imprisonment Observed	Black Imprisonment Expected	% of Black Observed Imprisonment Explained by Expected[a]
National	155,924	138,184	88.62
Northeast	26,650	24,482	91.86
Maine	15	10	65.65
New Hampshire	5	1	18.31
Massachusetts	1,329	496	37.33
Rhode Island	246	178	72.22
Connecticut	2,105	1,949	92.60
New York	13,407	13,459	100.39
New Jersey	4,455	2,788	62.59
Pennsylvania	5,088	5,600	110.07
North Central	33,813	33,208	98.21
Ohio	7,229	5,383	74.47
Indiana	2,795	4,504	161.13
Illinois	8,217	6,478	78.83
Michigan	8,515	8,796	103.30
Wisconsin	1,689	2,366	140.08
Minnesota	421	482	114.46

Table 3. (Continued)

State/Region	Black Imprisonment Observed	Black Imprisonment Expected	% of Black Observed Imprisonment Explained by Expected[a]
North Central *(cont.)*			
Iowa	490	324	66.23
Missouri	2,974	3,460	116.34
North Dakota	2	73	70.97
South Dakota	14	28	197.20
Nebraska	533	619	116.10
Kansas	934	834	89.30
South	81,065	67,657	83.46
Delaware	1,021	1,045	102.36
Maryland	6,761	4,293	63.50
Virginia	5,376	4,676	86.98
West Virginia	218	269	123.50
North Carolina	8,380	8,048	96.04
South Carolina	4,972	4,602	92.56
Georgia	7,313	8,148	111.41
Florida	11,351	9,713	85.57
Kentucky	1,171	1,176	100.40
Tennessee	3,346	2,916	87.14
Alabama	4,718	2,486	52.69
Mississippi	2,829	3,463	122.41
Arkansas	1,632	1,789	109.62
Louisiana	6,763	4,659	68.89
Oklahoma	1,482	1,515	102.23
Texas	13,732	8,860	64.52
West	14,396	12,765	88.67
Idaho	26	16	60.28
Wyoming	25	24	96.87
Colorado	579	349	60.35
New Mexico	160	—	—
Arizona	1,009	789	78.21
Utah	107	115	107.46
Nevada	591	835	141.23
Washington	1,106	398	35.98
Oregon	340	368	108.21
California	10,270	9,702	94.47
Alaska	139	93	66.74
Hawaii	44	76	172.43

[a]The percentage of observed imprisonment that is explained by the Black expected imprisonment was calculated prior to rounding of the expected values.

SUMMARY AND CONCLUSION

This article describes and illustrates two sources of discrepancy in studies of racial disparities in imprisonment. The first is different analytical foci of studies. Studies limited either to single decision points in the criminal justice process or to single jurisdictions are less likely to observe significant racial disparities because they may miss subtle manifestations of the disparate treatment of minorities (Crutchfield and Bridges 1986; Kempf et al. 1990; Bridges 1993). The second source is the different levels of aggregation used in research on racial discrimination in the administration of justice. Some states, and even some jurisdictions within states, deliver justice with greater equality than others. Because there is considerable variation among the states in the degree to which levels of criminal involvement among Blacks actually explain observed Black imprisonment rates, studies that aggregate across states and other jurisdictions are likely to mask this variation.

Racial patterns in imprisonment are substantively important for criminologists, and the perpetuation of unwarranted racial disparities in imprisonment is a critical matter for public policy. It is imperative that this issue be addressed carefully. Further, conclusions about the pervasiveness and causes of disparities must be drawn cautiously. The problems we have discussed have appeared in widely cited and publicized research, leading some to conclude that criminal justice in the United States is racially discriminatory, whereas others have concluded precisely the opposite—that problems in the treatment of Blacks and other minorities are minimal or nonexistent. Our analyses show that there is great variation within the United States in racial patterns of imprisonment, and that these variations probably account for the diversity of results that have been reported. The complexity of this variation must be incorporated into research designs, with researchers choosing appropriate levels of aggregation and bearing in mind the substantial differences in criminal processing that exist across jurisdictions. Similarly, consumers of research literature on racial discrimination and criminal justice must be cautious when drawing conclusions about the pervasiveness of discrimination or racial differences in treatment.

Finally, the results of this study lend support to the argument that social contexts influence how courts and law enforcement agencies impose criminal punishments (Myers and Talarico 1987). Differences in context contribute significantly to variation in the form and severity of punishments and to variation in the types of persons and groups punished for crimes. These differences may assist in explaining the pronounced variation in rates of imprisonment between Blacks and Whites exhibited in this article. By examining contextual differences and specifically the characteristics of areas and regions related to patterns of punishment, research may identify social and demographic conditions in which inequality in punishment is most likely to emerge. The differences may also reveal macrolevel processes at work in law and legal decision making. For example, they may establish how degrees of social or economic inequality within areas or regions influence inequality in law enforcement and judicial decisions. However, until scholars fully identify the nature of these macrolevel processes, analyses that ignore the varying contexts of law will contribute little to debate over inequality in the imposition of punishment. Further, the analyses will be vulnerable to biases that undermine their validity and importance to the field.

NOTES

1. We consider studies of federal courts and the U.S. Military to be multiple-jurisdiction studies. We categorized these as multiple because they are composed of very distinct, autonomously acting jurisdictions. They are different from states that include county jurisdictions because, within a state, county courts frequently operate with rules determined by central authority. If specific counties of one or more states were the subjects of research, these were also categorized as multiple jurisdictions.

2. Rates of imprisonment were calculated in this manner so as to reflect rates of admission to prison and the length of prison stay. This is appropriate for analyses of disproportionality (see Bridges and Crutchfield 1988).

3. In this context, serious and violent offenses mean the major categories of index crimes recorded by the F.B.I. in the UCR. These offenses include homicide, aggravated assault, forcible rape, robbery, burglary, larceny, motor vehicle theft, and arson.

4. This example assumes that the two states have equal or nearly equal populations.

5. We of course recognize that the rates for New Hampshire are very small and, as a consequence. are very unstable. The same point can be made by using New Hampshire's neighbor, Massachusetts, which has more individuals imprisoned and larger arrest rates. Massachusetts can account for only 40% of its racial disparity in imprisonment with racial differences in arrest for violent crimes.

REFERENCES

Blumstein, A. 1982. "On the Racial Disproportionality of the U.S. States' Prison Populations." *Journal of Criminal Law and Criminology* 73(3):1259–81.

Bridges, George S. 1993. *Racial Disproportionality in the Juvenile Justice System.* Seattle: University of Washington, Center for Law and Justice.

Bridges, George S. and Robert D. Crutchfield. 1988. "Law, Social Standing and Racial Disparities in Imprisonment." *Social Forces* 66:699–724.

Bridges, George S., Robert D. Crutchfield, and Edith E. Simpson. 1987. "Crime, Social Structure and Criminal Punishment: White and Nonwhite Rates of Imprisonment." *Social Problems* 34:345–61.

Bureau of Justice Statistics. 1982. *Prisoners in State and Federal Institutions on December 31, 1992.* Washington, DC: U.S. Department of Justice.

Christianson, Scott. 1980a. "Legal Implications of Racially Disproportionate Incarceration Rates." *Criminal Law Bulletin* 16(1):59–63.

———. 1980b. "Racial Discrimination and Prison Confinement." *Criminal Law Bulletin* 16(6):616–21.

Crutchfield, Robert D. and George S. Bridges. 1986. "Racial and Ethnic Disparities in Imprisonment: Final Report." Seattle, WA: University of Washington, Institute for Public Policy and Management.

Federal Bureau of Investigation. 1992. *Uniform Crime Reports.* Washington, DC: U.S. Department of Justice.

Hagan, J. 1974. "Extra-Legal Attributes and Criminal Sentencing: An Assessment of a Sociological Viewpoint." *Law and Society Review* 8:357–83.

Hindelang, M. J. 1978. "Race Involvement in Common Law Personal Crimes." *American Sociological Review* 43(1):93–109.

Kempf, Kimberly L., Scott H. Decker, and Robert Bing. 1990. "An Analysis of Apparent Disparities in the Handling of Black Youth: Technical Report." St. Louis, MO: University of Missouri, Department of Administration of Justice, Center for Metropolitan Studies.

Kleck, Gary. 1981. "Racial Discrimination in Criminal Sentencing: A Critical Evaluation of the Evidence With Additional Evidence on the Death Penalty." *American Sociological Review* 46:783–805.

Langan, Patrick. 1985. "Racism on Trial: New Evidence to Explain the Racial Composition of Prisons in the United States." *Journal of Criminal Law and Criminology* 76:666–83.

Myers, M. A. and S. M. Talarico. 1987. *The Social Contexts of Criminal Sentencing.* New York: Springer-Verlag.

Petersilia, J. 1983. *Racial Disparities in the Criminal Justice System.* Santa Monica, CA: RAND.

Peterson, R. D. and J. Hagan. 1984. "Changing Conceptions of Race: Towards An Account of Anomalous Findings of Sentencing Research." *American Sociological Review* 49:56–70.

Wilbanks, W. 1987. *The Myth of a Racist Criminal Justice System.* Belmont, CA: Wadsworth.

Wilson, W. J. 1987. *The Truly Disadvantaged.* Chicago: University of Chicago Press.

DISCUSSION QUESTIONS

1. What were some of the problems noted by the authors that were associated with previous research examining racial differences in criminal processing?
2. How does this study overcome these problems?
3. What were the methods and data used in this article to examine racial disparity in imprisonment?
4. What do you see as the major implications of this study?

11

On Preventing Drunk Driving Recidivism

An Examination of Rehabilitation and Punishment Approaches

FAYE S. TAXMAN, University of Maryland
ALEX PIQUERO, Temple University

COMMENTARY

When we wrote "On Preventing Drunk Driving Recidivism," we wanted to explore how rehabilitation and punishment approaches influenced future events of drunk driving recidivism. To examine this issue, one that we found had been little investigated in the extant literature, we obtained data from an existing project funded by the state of Maryland. The data included (a) participation in various types of rehabilitation programs and (b) various forms of punishment sanctions for over 3,000 offenders who were followed for a three-year period. Our survival analysis revealed that rehabilitation approaches reduced the likelihood of recidivism more so than punishment approaches for all offenders, while less formal punishment was most effective in decreasing future drunk driving recidivism among first-time offenders. This paper provided an empirical assessment of deterrence based on rehabilitation and punishment approaches.

Looking back over our research, we would probably try to do a number of things differently to further understand the research question. First, all of our rehabilitation and punishment measures were objective assessments based on official records; that is, there were no measures of the individual's perception of how they felt about being subject to certain types of rehabilitation approaches and punishment sanctions. This is important since a good deal of the rehabilitation and deterrence literatures indicate that perceptual measures are more useful than objective measures for understanding human behavior.

Source: Journal of Criminal Justice, Vol. 26, No. 2, pp. 129–143. Copyright © 1998, reprinted with permission from Elsevier Science.

Second, recent research within the recidivism domain has explored the experience and saliency associated with certain life events (such as marriage, employment, and schooling). The literature on these informal institutions of social control is fairly clear, showing that not only participation but the degree of participation in these social institutions serves as an important buffer against recidivism of many sorts of criminal and deviant acts.

Third, our data did not retain information on offenders' previous alcohol or drug use. While research shows that individuals who use alcohol and drugs are at higher risk to engage in various sorts of criminal offending, we were unable to assess how these factors would influence the probability of drunk driving recidivism, and how these factors may overwhelm the preventive effects of the successful rehabilitation approaches identified in our earlier research.

Fourth, even though we found some supportive evidence in favor of rehabilitation-type approaches for the prevention of drunk driving recidivism, our data on these measures were from court records. That is, we have no way of determining if the offenders had completed their required treatment programs. We were merely aware of whether the intent of the sentence was a rehabilitative or punishment emphasis based on the conditions of probation. The limitation is that, even though offenders were sentenced to some sort of rehabilitation-type treatment, we have no way of knowing if they completed their treatment. This is unfortunate since the literature shows that individuals who stay in treatment longer are less likely to incur bouts of recidivism for various sorts of criminal behaviors. Thus, we are unsure about the dosage amount that is necessary to achieve the recidivism reduction effects.

Fifth, our data did not provide information regarding the severity of the punishment sanctions administered. For example, we did not have information on the actual length of probation, the amount of fine paid (though we do have the amount fined), or the actual length of the license restriction. To the extent that deterrence theory is correct, we would expect that more severe sanctions (so long as they are proportionate to the benefit incurred from the offense) are related to decreased recidivism and criminal behavior.

Sixth, while we did not observe a main effect for gender on the probability of drunk driving recidivism, we did not explore the extent to which the rehabilitation and punishment variables interacted with gender to influence the probability of drunk driving recidivism. The prevention literature does suggest that females, relative to males, are responsive to certain types of punishments and rehabilitation efforts that males are not responsive to. Similar statements could be made about the race of the offender, and how certain individuals interpret the mandate of a rehabilitation- or punishment-type sanction.

Finally, these data were from one state, Maryland, and for a limited three-year time period. We do not know the extent to which data from different states, especially neighboring states and jurisdictions like Virginia and the District of Columbia, as well as data from different time periods would have altered the results of our research.

In the end, there is a lot we could have done had we access to various other measures. At the same time, the discussion of our paper raises two of the most important issues in social science research: (1) research tends to raise many more questions than it originally intended to address, and (2) there is no perfect data. While the latter is certainly no excuse for ill-conceived theoretical ideas and well-executed empirical research, one must always be cognizant of the fact that data are sometimes limited in what they can say about a particular research question. At the same time, one must not refrain from investigating difficult yet interesting research questions that are grounded in extant theory, applied with appropriate empirical tools, and have bearing for public policy. It is the integration of these three insights that makes for solid research.

ABSTRACT A major policy concern regarding the sentencing of drunk drivers is whether rehabilitation or punishment should be the dominant strategy. Essentially, rehabilitation attempts to treat the underlying alcohol problem of drunk drivers and inhibit future drunk driving, while punishment utilizes the threat of punitive legal sanctions and various types of punishments to deter drunk drivers. The relative merits of punishment and rehabilitation approaches have been studied in an isolated fashion with almost no empirical research examining the two simultaneously. Following a review of these approaches, this article examines the relative merits of the two strategies with data from a sample of offenders of driving while intoxicated (DWI) laws sentenced in the state of Maryland. The research also explores the differential effect of punishment and rehabilitation for first time offenders. For all offenders, Cox proportional hazard models indicate that rehabilitation sentences appear to reduce the likelihood of recidivism more than punishment sentences. For first time offenders, use of less formal punishment was the most effective in deterring drunk driving. The theoretical and policy implications of the results are addressed.

INTRODUCTION

In order to deter drunk drivers, public policy has been centered around two sentencing strategies: rehabilitation and punishment. The rehabilitation approach argues that offenders are in need of some sort of treatment to curb their use and abuse of alcohol through a variety of interventions. Emphasis is placed on addressing the underlying behavior of alcohol use that contributes to further drunk driving incidents and criminal offenses. The purpose of rehabilitation, then, is to change behavior by treating offenders' alcohol/drug problem. Others contend that punishment is the more appropriate response for drunk drivers because of the potential seriousness of the crime. The goal of the punishment approach is to deter the average road user from drinking and driving through the imposition of sanctions and/or the fear of punishment. Punishments may include, but may not be limited to, fines, license restrictions, liberty restrictions, and/or incarceration. Although both approaches attempt to change behavior in different ways, the end result for both is the same—to prevent drunk driving.

With regard to public policy, the relative merits of the rehabilitation and punishment approaches have not been addressed. Even though research exists on the separate effects of rehabilitation and punishment, the approaches have been studied in an isolated fashion with almost no empirical research examining the two simultaneously (Jacobs, 1989; Fagan, 1994; Nichols and Ross, 1990; Ross, 1992). As a consequence, there has been little research to guide the sentencing philosophy of drunk drivers. Following a review of the rehabilitation and punishment approaches to deter drinking and driving, this research aims to examine the virtues of the two strategies with data from a sample of offenders who were driving while intoxicated (DWI) and who were sentenced in the state of Maryland.

THE REHABILITATION APPROACH

Rehabilitation conjures up an image of a fundamental transformation in which a change occurs in an individual that makes him or her both law abiding and morally better. This approach is based on the notion that offenders will change as a result of some form of intervention. Historically, the nature and type of interventions have varied widely depending on the modality, the setting, and the orientation of the program (Anglin and Hser, 1990; Gottfredson and Barton, 1993).

Therapeutic interventions and education/awareness programs usually comprise rehabilitation approaches (Nichols, 1990). Programs tend to include simple dissemination of reading materials (Swenson et al., 1981), long-term treatment of alcohol problems (Reis, 1983), social skills and assertions training (Holden, 1983), and other forms of counseling. Due to wide variation among rehabilitation programs, researchers have repeatedly found it difficult to make general statements about the effectiveness of rehabilitation programs for drunk drivers.

The use of education and treatment for persons convicted of driving while intoxicated began in the mid-to-late 1960s with therapy, counseling, and driver improvement programs for problem drivers. Early on, there was a recognition of different types of drunk drivers (i.e., social versus problem drinkers), which lead to a rationale for diverse interventions. Yet, in practice, Argeriou, McCarty, and Blacker (1985) observe that most treatment programs treat the DWI offender as if he or she were part of a homogeneous group leaving some scholars to question the "homogeneity" assumption of offenders (Gottfredson and Hirschi, 1990).

While states have established many different types of rehabilitation programs, some of these have explicitly been used to divert drunk drivers from the criminal justice system. In one program, offenders assigned to a fourteen-day residential treatment program were significantly less likely than incarcerated individuals to be rearrested for drunk driving during the 749-day follow-up period (McCarty and Argeriou, 1988). Overall, however, the results of most drunk driver rehabilitation programs have been mixed (Mann, Vingilis, and Stewart, 1988). Some programs have demonstrated reduced recidivism (Holden, 1983; Reis, 1983) and others have shown little to no deterrent effect (Landrum et al., 1982; Nichols and Ross, 1989).[1] Furthermore, meta-analyses completed with regard to rehabilitation note that these differences often derive from poor implementation of programs, weak research designs, or atheoretical approaches to preventing crime (Andrews et al., 1990).

Results seem to differ on the offender's history of DWIs with more positive effects evidenced for first time offenders (Nichols, 1990). For repeat DWI offenders, most research suggests that education and treatment programs have little impact on DWI recidivism and no impact on alcohol-related crash involvement (Nichols and Ross, 1990; Stewart and Ellingstad, 1988), but this could be the result of limited funding for comprehensive treatment programs (Ross, 1992). While short-term DWI education-type programs may increase recidivism among more severe repeat offenders or problem drinkers (Ellingstad and Springer, 1976), longer term treatment programs are the only approaches that have demonstrated reductions in DWI recidivism among repeat offenders (Nichols, 1990; Reis, 1982).

Various scholars have found that alcohol and drug education programs combined with punishment have reduced DWI recidivism among both first time and multiple offenders. The alcohol education sentence appears to augment the punishment of having a driver's license taken away (Popkin, Stewart, and Lacey, 1988; Tashima and Peck, 1986). Also, Sadler and Perrine (1984) found that repeat offenders who received treatment and license restrictions had fewer subsequent DWI convictions than individuals who received only full license suspension (see also Tashima and Peck, 1986).

While much debate exists over rehabilitation programs, it appears that there is a need to determine whether rehabilitation is an effective approach to preventing drunk driving recidivism. Even though some scholars suggest that rehabilitation is an important element (Jacobs, 1989; Ross, 1992) and meta-analyses of treatment approaches show its potential for reducing recidivism (Andrews et al., 1990; Lipsey, 1991; Palmer, 1995), the question still remains about the relative merits of rehabilitation as a component of the prevention process for drunk drivers.[2]

THE PUNISHMENT APPROACH

During the latter half of the 1980s, a national movement ensued to consider drunk driving a serious offense, and to treat it like other serious criminal offenses (Homel, 1988). This movement was in part instigated by many grass roots organizations such as MADD and SADD; even the Presidential Commission on Drunk Driving (1983) recommended increasingly severe penalties for drunk drivers. The basic thrust of the punishment approach is grounded in deterrence theory (Beccaria, 1764). This approach hypothesizes that the imposition of swift, certain, and severe sanctions should deter offenders from committing the same crime for fear of the same or a similar punishment. The relevant research in this area has examined the effects of various types of punishment sanctions.

The deterrent effects of drinking and driving sanctions have been reviewed by various scholars (Peck, Sadler, and Perrine, 1985; Ross, 1982; Voas, 1986). In their review of punishment sanctions, Nichols and Ross (1990) found that most types of sanctions provided some evidence of reducing drinking and driving recidivism. In particular, license suspensions and license revocations provided the most consistent evidence for deterrence. The imposition of license revocations, particularly for first time offenders, appears to be an effective tool (Klein, 1989; Peck, Sadler, and Perrine, 1985; Rodgers, 1994; Ross and Gonzales, 1988; Ross, 1992). Losing the privilege to drive is a major punishment for a drunk driving conviction (Jacobs, 1989:119). Even though researchers have found that many convicted drunk drivers continue to drive after license suspensions (Peck, Sadler, and Perrine, 1985), the drivers maintain lower mileage and drive safer to decrease the likelihood of detection (Jacobs, 1989; Ross, 1992).

An examination of Minnesota's license plate impoundment law on recidivism found that when the law was administratively enforced, it had a significant impact in reducing recidivism (Rodgers, 1994). In addition, the impact appeared greatest when the violator experienced the impoundment from the arresting officer at the time of arrest instead of at a later time period. Yu's (1994) recent analysis of drunk driver recidivism in New York found no independent effect for license suspensions. At the same time, Yu found an interaction effect between license and fine sanctions. When license withdrawal was mandatory, an increase in fines significantly decreased the probability of recidivism.

While fines have been reported to be an effective deterrent in Europe (Homel, 1981; Nichols and Ross, 1989), little effort has been directed to changing the use of fines in the United States (Morris and Tonry, 1990; Ross, 1992). Fines have shown great promise in European countries where some offenders are punished by a fine of one and one-half months' salary before taxes (roughly about $1,500). In the United States, however, fines generally amount to about $250 for drunk driving offenses (Ross, 1992) and underenforcement of fine collection has undermined the fine as a credible sanction for drunk drivers (Yu, 1994).

This brief review of the literature indicates a need for an increased understanding of the relative merits of the rehabilitative and punishment sentencing options. Given these two competing philosophies, it is surprising that no empirical research has examined the utility of both simultaneously (Jacobs, 1989; Ross, 1992). Further, research suggests that these two approaches vary in their effectiveness for different types of offenders (i.e., first time or multiple offenders; Yu, 1994). This article attempts to fill a gap in the available research by examining the relative merits of punishing and rehabilitating the drunk driver. In addition, the analysis looks at how these approaches affect drunk driving recidivism for first time offenders.

SAMPLE

The current study uses data from the Motor Vehicle Administration (MVA) records for the state of Maryland. The data consist of drunk driving convictions from 1985 through 1993. Originally, there were 3,711 cases available for analysis. Forty cases, however, contained missing data. As a result, these cases were removed, leaving 3,671 cases. Each case was tracked to obtain a three-year follow-up of drunk driving convictions.

Table 1 presents a summary of the characteristics of the individuals in the study. Eighty-seven percent of the sample was comprised of males and 13 percent were females. The median age of the offender at the time of arrest was thirty years old. For over two-thirds of the sample (69 percent), the index arrest was their first DWI offense. The number of prior DWI convictions ranged from one to seven with 22 percent having one prior offense and 9 percent having two to five prior convictions. The sample is also characterized by a history of prior traffic convictions such as speeding, lane changes, and other moving violations. Nearly three-quarters (74 percent) of the offenders had a prior history of convictions for other traffic offenses. The average number of prior traffic convictions was almost four and nearly 23 percent had five or more traffic convictions. During the three-year follow-up period, a little over 13 percent ($N = 490$) of the sample was reconvicted at least once for a new drunk driving violation.

As shown in Table 2, first time offenders were more likely to receive a probation before judgment (PBJ), license restrictions, unsupervised probation, supervised probation, fines, intensive supervision, ordered to participate in Alcoholics Anonymous, alcohol education, and alcohol treatment. Multiple offenders were more likely to receive a guilty disposition and jail sentences. All reported differences were significant at $p < .05$.

The state of Maryland provides first time offenders with an advantage at sentencing. The PBJ is one of the tools available to the sentencing judge and is similar to a guilty disposition in that the judge can attach conditions to the PBJ similar to any other probationary sentence.[3] The only difference is that the conviction is stayed (expunged) if the offender successfully completes the probationary term. In addition, the PBJ does not affect the offender's automobile insurance or commercial license because it is not considered a public record. The designation of a PBJ is only accessible to criminal justice (i.e., judges) and motor vehicle administration employees. A PBJ was used with 65 percent of first time offenders and 11 percent of the multiple offenders.

Measures

Offender Characteristics

- First time offender: Coded 0 for multiple offenders and 1 for first time offenders.
- Number of traffic convictions: A continuous indicator measuring the number of previous traffic violations.

Table 1. Sample Characteristics (*N* = 3,671)

Variable	Mean	SD	Minimum	Maximum
Offender				
Age	32.58	11.55	16	76
Gender (1 = male)	.87	.34	0	1
First time offender (1 = yes)	.69	.46	0	1
Prior traffic convictions	3.66	4.35	0	32
Prior DWI convictions	.44	.78	0	7
Punishment				
Guilty disposition (1 = yes, 0 = PBJ)	.51	.50	0	1
PBJ (1 = yes, 0 = guilty)	.49	.50	0	1
License restriction (1 = yes)	.06	.24	0	1
Jail sentence (1 = yes)	.15	.36	0	1
Unsupervised probation (1 = yes)	.19	.39	0	1
Supervised probation (1 = yes)	.50	.50	0	1
Intensive supervision (1 = yes)	.40	.49	0	1
Fine (1 = yes)	.81	.39	0	1
Rehabilitation				
Abstinence (1 = yes)	.09	.29	0	1
Alcoholics Anonymous (1 = yes)	.17	.37	0	1
Alcohol education (1 = yes)	.21	.40	0	1
Alcohol treatment (1 = yes)	.34	.48	0	1
Recidivism				
Recidivism occurred (1 = yes)	.13	.34	0	1
Number of days until recidivism	1,053.50	268.75	1	3,278

- Previous DWI conviction: A continuous indicator measuring the number of previous DWI convictions.
- Age: A continuous indicator measuring the age of the offender.
- Gender: Gender of offender in the data. Coded 0 for female and 1 for male.

Rehabilitation Variables

- Alcoholics Anonymous sentence: Coded 0 if the offender did not receive an Alcoholics Anonymous sentence and 1 if the offender received an Alcoholics Anonymous requirement in the sentence.
- Abstinence sentence: Coded 0 if the judge did not order the offender to abstain from the use of alcohol and 1 if the judge ordered the offender to abstain from the use of alcohol.
- Alcohol education: Coded 0 if the offender did not receive a state certified alcohol education program in the sentence and 1 if the offender received a state certified alcohol education program in the sentence.

Table 2. Sentence Conditions for First Time and Multiple Offenders

	FIRST TIME OFFENDERS (N = 2,528)		MULTIPLE OFFENDERS (N = 1,143)	
Condition	*N*	%	*N*	%
Punishment variables				
Guilty disposition (1 = yes, 0 = PBJ)	877	35	1,013*	89
PBJ (1 = yes, 0 = guilty)	1,651	65	130*	11
License restriction (1 = yes)	178	7	42*	4
Jail sentence (1 = yes)	116	5	436*	38
Unsupervised probation (1 = yes)	575	23	113*	10
Supervised probation (1 = yes)	1,220	48	616*	54
Intensive supervision (1 = yes)	909	36	548*	48
Fine (1 = yes)	2,175	86	809*	71
Rehabilitation				
Abstinence (1 = yes)	232	9	114	10
Alcoholics Anonymous (1 = yes)	373	15	237*	21
Alcohol education (1 = yes)	647	26	109*	10
Alcohol treatment (1 = yes)	860	34	402	35
Reconviction (1 = yes)	302	12	188	16

*$p < .05$.

Notes: Guilty and PBJ are inverses of each other. The percentages shown reflect the percentage of individuals within either the first time or mulitple offender group who were in the one category of the condition displayed. For example, 877 of the 2,528 first time offenders, or 35 percent, received a guilty disposition.

- Alcohol treatment: Coded 0 if the offender did not receive alcohol treatment and 1 if the offender received any form of alcohol treatment, inpatient or outpatient (95 percent were outpatient).

Punishment Variables

- Intensive supervision: Coded 0 if the offender was not sentenced to intensive supervision and 1 if the offender was sentenced to intensive supervision.
- Fine: Coded 0 if the offender did not receive a fine and 1 if the offender received any fine.
- Jail: Coded 0 if the offender did not receive a jail sentence and 1 if the offender received a jail sentence.
- License restriction: Coded 0 if the offender did not receive a license restriction and 1 if the offender received a license restriction.
- Guilty disposition: Coded 0 if the offender received a PBJ and 1 if the offender received a guilty disposition.

- Supervised probation: Coded 0 if the offender did not receive supervised probation and 1 if the offender received supervised probation.
- Unsupervised probation: Coded 0 if the offender did not receive unsupervised probation and 1 if the offender received unsupervised probation.

Dependent Variable

- Recidivism: Conceptualized as (1) whether or not recidivism occurred within the follow-up period where recidivism is defined by a drunk driving reconviction and (2) the time until recidivism (measured in days). The first variable is referred to as the status variable. A zero on the status variable indicates that the offender was not reconvicted within the follow-up period, and a 1 indicates that the offender was reconvicted within the follow-up period. The other variable, the time variable, is measured in days and it indicates the time until the recidivism event. If individuals do not experience recidivism, then the time variable indicates the time until the case is censored. Both pieces of information are necessary and utilized within the framework of this analysis.

Method of Estimation

To examine the relative merits of the different sentencing approaches, Cox proportional hazards regression is utilized. This model is used to explain the differences based both on whether a reconviction occurred (no or yes) and the time until reconviction (number of days). Cox regression makes it easy for researchers to examine the independent effects of key predictors. As most conventional regression models do, Cox regression provides a test of the effect of each variable on the dependent variable while controlling for all other variables (Cox, 1972; Cox and Oakes, 1984).

The Cox regression technique is fairly straightforward and is the overwhelmingly favored method for doing regression analysis of survival data (Allison, 1995:183). Cox regression has a number of advantages that make it more robust than accelerated failure time methods. First, it makes no assumption about the shape of the distribution of survival times. Second, it allows for time-dependent covariates and is appropriate for both discrete-time and continuous time data. Third, it easily handles left truncation. Finally, it can stratify on categorical control variables. Because the purpose of the present article is not to make any assumptions about the distribution of the failure time process for the sample, Cox regression is utilized and it provides estimates regarding the drunk driving recidivism process.

While controlling for differences in offender characteristics, such as prior drunk driving convictions, age, sex, and prior traffic convictions, the analysis examines the relationship between various sentence characteristics and the risk of reconviction. To accomplish this, Cox regression produces relative risk (RR) estimates. By looking at the RR one can identify how certain variables affect reconviction while controlling for other pertinent variables. An RR greater than one indicates that the risk of reconviction is higher for the group being examined than for the reference group; an RR less than one indicates a lower risk of reconviction. An RR equal to one indicates that the risk of reconviction among the group being examined is equal to the risk for the reference group. This technique allows researchers to examine the independent effects of a variable (or a category within a variable) in models that include both offender characteristics and varying sentence conditions. As a result, all of the variables in the analysis contain reference groups or groups with which the observed indicators are compared against. For example, with regard to the variable gender, males are coded 1. This group, then, is compared to the reference group, 0, or females.

RESULTS: ALL OFFENDERS

Survival Analysis

Table 3 contains the results for the Cox proportional hazards regression for the full sample. Presented in this table are four statistics for each measure. The first is B, or the slope coefficient. The second is SE, or the standard error of the coefficient. The third is the Wald statistic. This statistic is akin to a traditional statistic that tests the hypothesis that B equals 0 in the population. In the current analysis, however, the Cox proportional hazards model reports a Wald statistic that follows a chi-square distribution with the degrees of freedom depending on the level of measurement of the independent variable(s), usually equal to one. When a variable has one degree of freedom, the Wald statistic is the square of the ratio of the logistic regression coefficient to its standard error. The final statistic is the RR ratio and it has already been discussed. The percentage increase or decrease in the risk of reconviction is calculated by taking the absolute value of 1 – RR.

The exogenous variables in this analysis are separated into three categories. The first category represents offender variables that include age, gender, whether or not the offender is a first time offender, and the number of prior traffic convictions. The second category consists of punishment variables, including guilty disposition, license restriction, jail sentence, unsupervised probation, supervised probation, fine, and intensive supervision. The final category contains the rehabilitation variables: abstinence, Alcoholics Anonymous, alcohol education, and alcohol treatment. Model diagnostics such as the log likelihood and the chi-square are also presented.[4]

Beginning with the offender variables, age (B = .02) has a significant, negative effect on drunk driving reconviction. This suggests that older offenders are less likely than young offenders to be reconvicted for another drunk driving offense. The relative risk ratio of .98 indicates that older individuals are 2 percent less likely to be reconvicted than are younger individuals. This is consistent with Hirschi and Gottfredson's (1983) position that all types of criminal and deviant behavior decline with time and is consistent with other work surrounding age and motor vehicle fatalities and age and accidents (Gottfredson and Hirschi,

Table 3. Cox Proportional Hazards Model: Full Sample

Variable	B	SE	Wald	Relative Risk
Offender				
Age	–.02	.00	18.94*	.98
Gender (1 = male)	.16	.15	1.06	1.17
First time offender (1 = yes)	–.21	.12	3.06**	.82
Prior traffic convictions	.03	.01	10.33**	1.03
Punishment				
Guilty disposition (1 = yes, 0 = PBJ)	.11	.11	.89	1.12
License restriction (1 = yes)	–.02	.21	.00	.98
Jail sentence (1 = yes)	.04	.14	.08	1.04
Unsupervised probation (1 = yes)	.08	.15	.31	1.09
Supervised probation (1 = yes)	.14	.11	1.86	1.16
Intensive supervision (1 = yes)	–.06	.10	.29	.95
Fine (1 = yes)	.08	.12	.41	1.08
Rehabilitation				
Abstinence (1 = yes)	.08	.15	.31	1.09
Alcoholics Anonymous (1 = yes)	.16	.13	1.59	1.18
Alcohol education (1 = yes)	–.25	.13	3.78**	.78
Alcohol treatment (1 = yes)	–.19	.10	3.45*	.83

Notes: Log-likelihood = –7918.51; χ^2 = 56.21; *df* = 15; *p* = .000

**p* < .10

**p < .05

1990). In terms of gender, males (B = 16) are significantly more likely than females to be reconvicted; however, this difference is not statistically significant. First time offenders (B = .21) are significantly less likely to be reconvicted than multiple offenders. The RR (.82) suggests that first time offenders are 28 percent less likely than multiple offenders to be reconvicted.

The final offender variable, the number of prior traffic convictions, indicates that offenders with a significant number of previous traffic convictions are more likely to be reconvicted (B = .03). As prior traffic convictions increase, so does the risk of reconviction. This finding is consistent with research suggesting that such behavior is analogous to, and can be a reasonable predictor of, criminal behavior (Gottfredson and Hirschi, 1990; Keane, Maxim, and Teevan, 1993). Thus, risky forms of driving resulting in traffic convictions may appear to serve as an adequate proxy for Gottfredson and Hirschi's notion of self-control in determining future risk of drunk driving reconviction.

Regarding the punishment variables, the results are not very supportive of this strategy. In fact, most of the punishment conditions have an RR greater than one suggesting an increase in the risk of reconviction. It also suggests that none of the punishment variables were statistically significant. The only two punishment variables that had a negative, though nonsignificant, effect on the risk of reconviction were license restrictions (B = -.02) and intensive supervision (B = -.06). Nevertheless, the effect of these two variables was quite small.

The rehabilitation variables, however, appear to be a bit more promising. Two of the four rehabilitation variables exerted significant and negative effects on the risk of reconviction. Both alcohol education (B = -.25) and alcohol treatment (B = -.19) significantly reduced the risk of reconviction. The RR ratios for these two variables were .78 and .83, respectively, indicating that those individuals who were sentenced to alcohol education were 22 percent less likely to be reconvicted than those individuals who were not sentenced to alcohol education. Similarly, those individuals sentenced to alcohol treatment were 17 percent less likely to be reconvicted than were those who were not sentenced to alcohol education. Both abstinence (B = .08) and Alcoholics Anonymous (B = .16) failed to exert an effect on drunk driving recidivism.

So far, the analysis has provided some information on the impact of sentencing strategies and offender characteristics on the likelihood of reconviction. Offender characteristics indicating high risk behavior (e.g., prior traffic convictions) are associated with higher reconviction rates while rehabilitation characteristics such as alcohol education and treatment appear to reduce the risk of reconviction. Various kinds of punishments, however, failed to deter drunk driving reconvictions.

FIRST TIME OFFENDERS

The results for the full sample suggest that first time offenders have different reconviction rates (about 12 percent) than multiple offenders (more than 16 percent) and this is consistent with other research regarding first time and multiple drunk driving offenders (Yu, 1994). The question framed for this part of the analysis is: Do the two sentencing philosophies differentially affect first time offenders? The following model analyzes the subset of first time offenders to examine the relationship among offender characteristics, sentence conditions, and the risk of reconviction. Finding effective practices for first time offenders is important because it provides an opportunity to prevent further drunk driving behavior through formal social control. If it can be determined "what works" for first time offenders, then subsequent involvement into the criminal justice system and additional depletion of scarce resources may be prevented.

Recall that in Table 2, first time offenders were significantly more likely to be sentenced to PBJ than were multiple offenders. It may be instructive, then, to examine the type of sentence characteristics given to first time offenders who were given PBJ as opposed to those who were given guilty dispositions. Table 4 summarizes the use of the PBJ and guilty disposition for first time offenders.

Some differences emerged in the disposition based on the number of prior traffic convictions of an offender. Thirty-three percent of the offenders who

Table 4. Sample Characteristics for First Time Offenders Only

	JUDGMENT OUTCOME			
	PBJ (*N* = 1,651)		GUILTY (*N* = 878)	
Variable	***N***	**%**	***N***	**%**
Offender				
Gender (1 = males; 0 = females)	1,374	83	764*	87
Prior traffic convictions	1,091	66	624*	71
Punishment				
License restriction (1 = yes)	160	10	18*	2
Jail sentence (1 = yes)	25	2	91*	10
Unsupervised probation (1 = yes)	458	28	117*	13
Supervised probation (1 = yes)	796	48	424	48
Intensive supervision (1 = yes)	621	38	288*	33
Fine (1 = yes)	1,419	85	757	86
Rehabilitation				
Abstinence (1 = yes)	157	10	75	9
Alcoholics Anonymous (1 = yes)	293	18	80*	9
Alcohol education (1 = yes)	478	29	169*	19
Alcohol treatment (1 = yes)	525	32	335*	38
Reconviction (1 = yes)	180	11	122	14

Note: The percentages shown reflect the percentage of individuals within either the PBJ or the guilty judgment outcome. For example, 180 of the 1,651 offenders who received PBJ, or 11 percent, were reconvicted.

*$p < .05$.

received a PBJ had no prior traffic convictions while 29 percent of those found guilty had no prior traffic convictions. Because judges tend to use the PBJ for offenders who exhibited less risky behavior, it appears that the PBJ is a privilege afforded to certain first time offenders. Similar to most drunk driving sentences, the courts tend to include fines in most dispositions for drunk driving cases. For offenders receiving a PBJ, 86 percent received a fine. Also, supervised probation was equally recommended for PBJ and guilty dispositions with 48 percent of the offenders receiving this condition. Unsupervised probation was more likely to be given to offenders receiving a PBJ (28 percent) compared to those with a guilty disposition (13 percent). Also, 10 percent of the guilty dispositions also involved some jail time compared to only 1 percent of the PBJ dispositions. Offenders receiving a PBJ were more likely to receive conditions including alcohol education and Alcoholics Anonymous (29 and 18 percent, respectively) than offenders given guilty dispositions (19 and 9 percent, respectively). Finally, alcohol treatment was more often given with a guilty disposition (38 percent) than a PBJ (32 percent).

Table 5. Cox Proportional Hazards Models: First Time Offenders Only

Variable	B	SE	Wald	Relative Risk
Offender				
Age	–.02	.01	8.47**	.98
Gender (1 = male)	.33	.19	3.16*	1.39
Prior traffic convictions	.04	.01	9.30**	1.04
Punishment				
Guilty disposition (1 = yes, 0 = PBJ)	.24	.13	3.57**	1.27
License restriction (1 = yes)	–.04	.25	.03	.96
Jail sentence (1 = yes)	–.33	.31	1.15	.72
Unsupervised probation (1 = yes)	.02	.18	.01	1.02
Supervised probation (1 = yes)	.04	.14	.09	1.04
Intensive supervision (1 = yes)	–.07	.13	.26	.94
Fine (1 = yes)	.14	.18	.57	1.15
Rehabilitation				
Abstinence (1 = yes)	.26	.19	1.94	1.30
Alcoholics Anonymous (1 = yes)	.15	.17	.79	1.17
Alcohol education (1 = yes)	–.23	.15	2.31	.80
Alcohol treatment (1 = yes)	–.12	.13	.79	.89

Notes: Log-likelihood = –4,658.88; $\chi^2 = 36.37$; $df = 14$; $p = .001$.

*$p < .10$.

**$p < .05$.

Survival Analysis

A Cox regression model was estimated to examine the differences in the risk of reconviction for first time offenders. The model presented in Table 5 illustrates the different offender, punishment, and rehabilitation variables for first time offenders. With a few important exceptions, these results are similar to the Cox proportional hazards models presented earlier for all offenders.

As was true for the full sample model, younger offenders (B = –.02) were significantly less likely than older offenders to be reconvicted. Similarly, those individuals with a history of prior traffic convictions (B = .04) were significantly more likely to be reconvicted. Finally, males (B = .33) were significantly more likely than females to incur another drunk driving conviction. The RR ratio suggests that first-time male offenders are 39 percent more likely than first time female offenders to be reconvicted.

Similar to the full sample estimation, only one of the punishment variables exerted a significant effect on drunk driving recidivism—guilty disposition. Offenders receiving a guilty disposition (B = .24) were 27 percent more likely to be reconvicted than were offenders given a more lenient sentence (i.e., PBJ). Conversely, individuals sentenced to PBJ were less likely to be reconvicted than those given a guilty disposition.[6] In terms of the rehabilitation variables, none were statistically significant. Unlike the full sample model, first time offenders did not appear to respond well to rehabilitation approaches.

DISCUSSION AND CONCLUSION

This study was designed to examine the relative merits of rehabilitation and punishment sentencing philosophies on preventing drunk driving reconvictions. The analysis examined three dimensions: reconviction rates, types of offenders, and different sentencing patterns. From this study, it is possible to assess the deterrent effect of current policies regarding drunk drivers in the state of Maryland. Prior to discussing the results of this study, however, a few data limitations must be noted.

First, the records obtained from the state of Maryland did not include information on offenders' previous alcohol and/or drug use. This is somewhat distressing because such information may be one of the most important factors involved in predicting recidivism. Second, most of the treatment conditions used in this study are court dispositions. Therefore, it is not entirely clear if the offenders had completed their required treatment programs. In other words, even though offenders were sentenced to some sort of treatment, it does not necessarily follow that they completed the treatment.

Similarly, the punishment variables in the present study provided little information regarding the severity of the sanctions administered. For example, the records from the state of Maryland did not contain information on the length of probation, the amount of the fine, or the length of the license restriction. To the extent that deterrence is operative for drunk drivers, it is quite conceivable that information relevant to the severity of sanctions could have a substantive impact on the results of the current study, as well as preventing drunk driving recidivism. Unfortunately, the only piece of information available in the Maryland records concerned whether or not the sanction was included in the sentence. Finally, these data were from the state of Maryland and as a result any sort of generalization to a state other than Maryland should be made with extreme caution.

These limitations notwithstanding, the results suggest that a few, though not all, forms of rehabilitation have the potential for reducing recidivism among high-risk drunk drivers suggesting the importance of targeting the offender's needs or risk factors (e.g., Andrews et al., 1990). Recall that in the full sample analysis, when treatment conditions were given to offenders, those offenders had lower reconviction rates than offenders without treatment conditions. For offenders receiving alcohol education, the risk of recidivism was 22 percent less than offenders without alcohol education while controlling for offender and sentence characteristics. Similarly, offenders with alcohol treatment had a 17 percent lower risk of recidivism than offenders without this condition.

In addition, age and prior traffic convictions were consistent predictors of recidivism. First, after peaking in offenders' early twenties, both drunk driving reconvictions and the number of prior traffic convictions declined with age. This result mimics earlier work by Hirschi and Gottfredson (1983).[5] The second finding concerned the relationship between previous traffic convictions and drunk driving recidivism. In all specifications, offenders with a history of traffic convictions were more likely than those without previous traffic convictions to be reconvicted for another drunk driving offense. These results are consistent with those obtained by Ross and his colleagues (1995:65), who found that those individuals who had a history of prior convictions of driving under the influence of alcohol and drugs (DUI) were more likely to incur a future DUI as well as refuse police breath tests.

An avenue of promising future research involves the link between prior traffic convictions and drunk driving reconvictions. To the extent that prior traffic convictions significantly predict subsequent drunk driving reconvictions, it is quite conceivable that prior traffic convictions evidence a form of "high-risk behavior." How the casual chain between traffic and drunk driving convictions unfolds, however, is not entirely clear, though according to some, the causal chain may be irrelevant because the correlates of both acts (crime and drinking and driving) may be a manifestation of a single underlying tendency (Gottfredson and Hirschi, 1990:93). Unfortunately, the present data can not partial out at which point in an offender's life drunk driving preceded prior traffic convictions or vice versa. Nevertheless, it is certainly plausible that these two distinct behaviors may be part and parcel of each other.

In the past few years, Gottfredson and Hirschi (1990; see also Hirschi and Gottfredson, 1993) have been adamant on two assertions: (1) that criminal/deviant acts have similar causes and (2) that offenders do not specialize in offending. With regard to the first point, they argue that the best predictor of deviant/criminal behavior is deviant/criminal/noncriminal-though-risky behavior. As a result, crime and its many manifestations are caused by some type of latent trait or propensity to engage in crime (e.g., low self-control). Recall that in the current analysis, one of the best predictors of a drunk driving reconviction was the number of previous traffic convictions. Because offenders are likely to engage in noncriminal acts equivalent to crime (i.e., traffic violations such as running stop signs and reckless and risky driving), they are also more likely to smoke, drink, skip school, fail to wear seat belts, and commit other crimes at considerably higher rates than noncriminals (e.g., Arneklev et al., 1993; Gottfredson and Hirschi, 1990:92; Keane, Maxim, and Teevan, 1993). The second notion is not far removed from the first. Gottfredson and Hirschi (1990:91) claim that crime and analogous behaviors stem from an underlying propensity to crime; as such, offenders engaging in one form of criminal behavior are also likely to engage in other forms of illegal behavior. In other words, offenders will be versatile in their offending patterns (Hirschi, 1969; Hindelang, Hirschi, and Weis, 1981). The present analysis appears to confirm these two assertations.

In a related manner, there is one particular avenue of drunk driving research that could extend the preliminary work here. Even though the data are limited in the sense that they do not contain information on criminal records, research has found that drunk drivers are also likely to have criminal records (Argeriou, McCarty, and Blacker, 1985; Gould and MacKenzie, 1990; McCord, 1984), as well as evidence of other problem behaviors such as drug use and delinquency (Vingilis and Adlaf, 1990). In their examination of Louisiana drivers, Gould and MacKenzie (1990:269) found that an individual with a DWI arrest was more likely than an individual in the general population to have had a prior arrest on another charge, and that the arrest was more likely to have come as a result of a violent crime against another person. Further, almost two-thirds (63 percent) of the DWI sample had at least one prior arrest compared to almost 11 percent of the general population sample of licensed drivers. Even though research has consistently shown a relationship between alcohol consumption, DWI, and criminal behavior (Gould and MacKenzie, 1990; Reiss and Roth, 1993; Wolfgang, 1958), the specific nature of the relationship has not been deeply examined. Because DWI may be indicative of a continuous pattern of criminal behavior, such findings have obvious policy implications for dealing with drunk drivers.

Finally, the results suggest that first time offenders may be more easily handled by less formal or punitive approaches than more severe sanctions. First time offenders who received a PBJ were rearrested at a lower rate than those who were given a guilty disposition. For these offenders, the PBJ sanction could be serving a function of reintegrative shaming.

Unlike stigmatization, reintegrative shaming attempts to integrate the offender back into the community of law-abiding citizens by using words or gestures of forgiveness directed to signify evil deeds (i.e., drunk driving) instead of identifying evil persons (i.e., the drunk driver) (Braithwaite, 1989). The PBJ could be serving as a public and symbolic statement against the behavior, and as a result, offenders may feel a sense of shame and be deterred from future drinking and driving. While still a form of punishment, the PBJ allows offenders to return to the community to resume their life with few restrictions placed on their behavior. Some scholars suggest that this experience of shame may deter behavior more than the threat and/or use of actual punishment (Andenaes, 1974:78). In any case, the importance of shame has served as a successful deterrent to drunk driving in other research (Grasmick and Bursik, 1990) and continued exploration appears worthwhile.

In recent years, public policy regarding drunk drivers has proceeded along two fronts. The public health community has vehemently tried to "treat" drunk drivers by dealing with the underlying problem of alcoholic addiction. At the same time, there has been a strong push in the United States to punish criminals, particularly drunk drivers, more severely than ever before (Grasmick, Bursik, and Arneklev, 1993). Given the movement in recent years toward more punitive policies, a logical question concerns whether or not citizens support current criminal justice measures to deter drinking and driving.

To this end, some research has attempted to answer this question. In their study of Ohio residents, Applegate et al. (1996) discovered that while the public endorsed a reduction of drunk driving through legal deterrence, citizens were also willing to support several socially based interventions centered around alcohol treatment. Citizens' desire for punitiveness concerned the harm (i.e., fatality) involved in the drunk driving incident as well as the number of previous arrests incurred by the offender. Further, Applegate and his colleagues (1996) also found a negative relationship between the level of intoxication and punishment suggesting that people may regard a high level of intoxication as indicating a drinking problem and a need for treatment rather than punishment. These results highlight the difficulty in assessing public opinion regarding punishment and rehabilitation (Cullen and Gilbert, 1982; Cullen, Cullen, and Wozniak, 1988; Cullen et al., 1989) and suggest caution when policies are based on supposed public support for punitive measures.

This study examined the two diverse sentencing approaches surrounding drunk drivers. Although the data suggest that some rehabilitation and reintegrative sanctions have the potential to reduce drunk driving recidivism, the data also suggest that the movement toward more punitive sanctions against drunk drivers is not advantageous. In terms of implications for public policy, the results from this research support a continued role for the education and treatment of drunk drivers and not the punishment of such offenders. This study implies the need for continuous examination of the relative merits of punishment and rehabilitation sentencing strategies, and the need for drunk driver policies that are grounded in solid empirical research.

ACKNOWLEDGMENTS

We would like to thank Ken Petronis, Charles Wellford, and Eric Wish.

NOTES

1. Logan and Gaes (1993) raise concerns that rehabilitation cannot occur while offenders are being held accountable for their behavior in a punishment setting.

2. For a discussion of meta-analysis in general, see Hedges and Olkin (1985). For a meta-analysis review regarding rehabilitation that led to vastly differing findings, see Whitehead and Lab (1989).

3. Near the end of our follow-up period (1990), the Maryland legislature mandated that all offenders receiving a PBJ should be given alcohol education as a condition of the PBJ.

4. Three other Cox proportional hazards models were also estimated. The first contained only offender variables such as prior drunk driving history, age, gender, and prior traffic convictions. The second contained the offender variables as well as punishment sentences including fines, jail sentence, and different types of probation alternatives. The third contained offender and rehabilitation variables such as alcohol education, treatment self-help (i.e., abstinence), and Alcoholics Anonymous. There were no differences between the log-likelihoods, chi-squares, and regression coefficients across the models as well as the model containing the full range of variables presented in Table 3. In other words, the substantive results concerning the coefficient estimates were identical across all three models. Because the purpose of this article is to examine the relative utility of both approaches for preventing drunk driving recidivism, only the full model is presented. Those interested in obtaining the other estimations are encouraged to write either author.

5. Various explanations, such as maturational reform, have been advanced to explain this decrease in crime. For an excellent review, readers should consult Sampson and Laub (1993).

6. At the same time, the finding that the PBJ served to prevent drunk driving recidivism may be due to judicial prediction of future behavior. For example, individuals who are deemed less likely to be reconvicted by judges may be given less punitive sanctions (i.e., PBJ). Caution, therefore, should be exercised when interpreting the reasons for the effect of the PBJ on drunk driving recidivism.

REFERENCES

Allison, P. (1995). *Survival analysis using the SAS system: A practical guide.* Cary, NC: SAS Institute.

Andenaes, J. (1974). *Punishment and deterrence.* Ann Arbor, MI: University of Michigan Press.

Andrews, D., Zinger, I., Hoge, R., Bonta, J., Gendreau, P., and Cullen, F. (1990). Does correctional treatment work? A clinically relevant and psychologically informed meta-analysis. *Criminology* 28:369–404.

Anglin, M., and Hser, Y. (1990). Treatment of drug abuse. In *Crime and justice: A review of research: Volume 13, drugs and crime,* eds. M. Tonry and J. Wilson. Chicago, IL: University of Chicago Press.

Applegate, B., Cullen, F., Link, B., Richards, P., and Lanza-Kaduce, L. (1996). Determinants of public punitiveness toward drunk driving: A factorial survey approach. *Justice Quarterly* 13:57–79.

Argeriou, M., McCarty, D., and Blacker, E. (1985). Criminality among individuals arraigned for drinking and driving in Massachusetts. *Journal of Studies on Alcohol* 46:483–85.

Arneklev, B., Grasmick, H., Tittle, C., and Bursik, R. (1993). Low self-control and imprudent behavior. *Journal of Quantitative Criminology* 9:225–47.

Beccaria. C. (1764). *On crimes and punishments.* New York, NY: MacMillan.

Braithwaite, J. (1989). *Crime, shame, and reintegration.* New York, NY: Cambridge University Press.

Cox, D. (1972). Regression models and life tables. *Journal of the Royal Statistical Society.* B34:187–200.

Cox, D., and Oakes, D. (1984). *Analysis of survival data.* London: Chapman and Hall.

Cullen, F., and Gilbert, K. (1982). *Reaffirming rehabilitation.* Cincinnati, OH: Anderson.

Cullen, F., Cullen, J., and Wozniak, J. (1988). Is rehabilitation dead? The myth of the punitive public. *Journal of Criminal Justice* 16:303–17.

Cullen, F., Skovran, S., Scott, J., and Burton, V., Jr. (1989). Public support for correctional treatment: The tenacity of rehabilitative ideology. *Criminal Justice and Behavior* 17:6–18.

Ellingstad, V., and Springer, T. (1976). Program level evaluation of ASAP diagnosis referral and rehabilitation efforts. Volume 3. In *Analysis of ASAP Rehabilitation Countermeasures Effectiveness,* NHTSA contract DOT-H5-191-3-759. Vermillion, SD: University of South Dakota, Human Factors Laboratory.

Fagan, J. (1994). Do criminal sanctions deter drug crime? In *Drugs and crime: Evaluating public policy initiatives,* eds. D. MacKenzie and C. Uchida. Beverly Hills, CA: Sage Publications.

Gottfredson, D., and Barton, W. (1993). Deinstitutionalization of juvenile offenders. *Criminology* 31:591–611.

Gottfredson, M., and Hirschi, T. (1990). *A general theory of crime.* Stanford, CA: Stanford University Press.

Gould, L., and MacKenzie, D. (1990). DWI: An isolated incident or a continuous pattern of criminal activity? In *Drugs and the Criminal Justice System,* ed. R. Weisheit. Cincinnati, OH: Anderson.

Grasmick, H., and Bursik, R., Jr. (1990). Conscience, significant others, and rational choice: Extending the deterrence model. *Law and Society Review* 24:837–61.

Grasmick, H., Bursik, R., Jr., and Arneklev, B. (1993). Reduction in drunk driving as a response to increased threats of shame, embarrassment, and legal sanctions. *Criminology* 31:41–67.

Hedges, L., and Olkin, I. (1985). *Statistical methods for meta-analysis.* Orlando, FL: Academic Press.

Hindelang, M., Hirschi, T., and Weis, J. (1981). *Measuring delinquency.* Beverly Hills, CA: Sage Publications.

Hirschi, T. (1969). *Causes of delinquency.* Berkeley, CA: University of California Press.

Hirschi, T. and Gottfredson, M. (1983). Age and explanation of crime. *American Journal of Sociology* 89:553–84.

Hirschi, T., and Gottfredson, M. (1993). Commentary: Testing the general theory of crime. *Journal of Research in Crime and Delinquency* 30:47–54.

Holden, R. (1983). Rehabilitative sanctions for drunk driving: An experimental evaluation. *Journal of Research in Crime and Delinquency* 20:55–72.

Homel, R. (1981). Penalties and the drunk-driver: A study of one thousand offenders. *Australian and New Zealand Journal of Criminology* 14:225–41.

Homel, R. (1988). *Policy and punishing the drinking driver: A study of general and specific deterrence.* New York, NY: Springer-Verlag.

Jacobs, J. (1989). *Drunk driving: An American dilemma.* Chicago, IL: University of Chicago Press.

Keane, C., Maxim, P., and Teevan, J. (1993). Drinking and driving, self-control and gender: Testing a general theory of crime. *Journal of Research in Crime and Delinquency* 30:30–46.

Klein, T. (1989). *Changes in alcohol-involved fatal crashes associated with tougher state alcohol legislation.* Contract DTNH22-88-C-07045. Washington, DC: National Highway Traffic Safety Administration.

Landrum, J., Miles, S., Neff, R., Pritchard, T., Roebuck, J., Wells-Parker, E., and Windham, G. (1982). *Mississippi DUI probation follow-up project.* Washington, DC: U.S. Department of Transportation.

Lipsey, M. (1991). *Juvenile delinquency treatment: A meta-analytic inquiry into the variability of effects.* New York, NY: Russell Sage.

Logan, C., and Gaes, G. (1993). Meta-analysis and the rehabilitation of punishment. *Justice Quarterly* 10:245–63.

Mann, R., Vingilis, E., and Stewart, K. (1988). Programs to change individual behavior: Education and rehabilitation in the prevention of drinking and driving. In *Social Control of the Drinking Driver,* eds. M. Laurence, J. Snortum, and F. Zimring. Chicago, IL: University of Chicago Press.

McCarty, D., and Argeriou, M. (1988). Rearrest following residential treatment for repeat offender drunken drivers. *Journal of Studies on Alcohol* 49:1–6.

McCord, J. (1984). Drunken drivers in longitudinal perspectives. *Journal of Studies on Alcohol* 45:316–20.

Morris, N., and Tonry, M. (1990). *Between prison and probation: Intermediate punishments in a rational sentencing system.* Oxford: Oxford University Press.

Nichols, J. (1990). Treatment versus deterrence. *Alcohol Health & Research World* 14:44–51.

Nichols, J., and Ross, H. (1989). The effectiveness of legal sanctions in dealing with drinking drivers. In *Office of the Surgeon General, Surgeon General's workshop on drunk driving: Background papers.* Rockville, MD: U.S. Department of Health and Human Services.

Nichols, J., and Ross, H. (1990). The effectiveness of legal sanctions in dealing with drinking drivers. *Alcohol, Drugs and Driving* 6:33–60.

Palmer, T. (1995). Programmatic and nonprogrammatic aspects of successful intervention. *Crime and Delinquency* 41:100–31.

Peck, R., Sadler, D., and Perrine, M. (1985). The comparative effectiveness of alcohol rehabilitation and licensing control actions for drunk driving offenders: A review of the literature. *Alcohol, Drugs, and Driving Abstracts and Reviews* 1:15–40.

Popkin, C., Stewart, J., and Lacey, J. (1988). *A follow-up evaluation of North Carolina's alcohol and drug education traffic schools and mandatory substance abuse assessments: Final report.* Chapel Hill, NC: Highway Safety Research Center, University of North Carolina.

Presidential Commission on Drunk Driving. (1983). *Final report.* Washington, DC: Presidential Commission on Drunk Driving.

Reis, R. (1982). *The traffic safety effectiveness of education programs for multiple offense drunk drivers. Technical Report,* DOT Contract HS-6-10414. Washington, DC: National Highway Traffic Safety Administration.

Reis, R. (1983). The traffic safety impact of DUI education and counseling programs. In *DWI reduction and rehabilitation programs—Successful results and the future.* Falls Church, VA: AAA Foundation for Traffic Safety.

Reiss, A., and Roth, J. (eds.). (1993). *Understanding and preventing violence.* Washington, DC: National Academy Press.

Rodgers, A. (1994). Effect of Minnesota's License Plate Impoundment Law on Recidivism of Multiple DWI Violators. *Alcohol, Drugs, and Driving* 10:127–34.

Ross, H. (1982). *Deterring the drinking driver: Legal policy and social control.* Lexington, VA: Lexington Books.

Ross, H. (1992). Are DWI sanctions effective? *Alcohol, Drugs, and Driving* 6:61–9.

Ross, H., and Gonzales, P. (1988). Effects of license revocation on drunk-driving offenders. *Accident Analysis and Prevention* 20:379–91.

Ross, H., Simon, S., Cleary, J., Lewis, R., and Stortkamp, D. (1995). Causes and consequences of implied consent test refusal. *Alcohol, Drugs, and Driving* 11:57–72.

Sadler, D., and Perrine, M. (1984). An evaluation of the California drunk-driving counter-measure system: Volume 2. In *The Long-Term Traffic Safety Impact of a Pilot Alcohol Abuse Treatment as an Alternative to License Suspensions.* Report no. 90. Sacramento, CA: California Department of Motor Vehicles.

Sampson, R., and Laub, J. (1993). *Crime in the making: Pathways and turning points through life.* Cambridge, MA: Harvard University Press.

Stewart, K., and Ellingstad, V. (1988). Rehabilitation countermeasures for drinking drivers. In *Surgeon General's workshop on drunk driving: Background papers, ed.* Department of Health and Human Services. Rockville, MD: U.S. Public Health Service.

Swenson, P., Struckman-Johnson, D., Ellingstad, V., Clay, T., and Nichols, J. (1981). Results of a longitudinal evaluation of court-mandated DWI treatment programs in Phoenix, Arizona. *Journal of Studies on Alcohol* 42:642–53.

Tashima, H., and Peck, R. (1986). An evaluation of the California drunk driving countermeasure system: Volume 3. In *An Evaluation of the Specific Deterrent Effects of Alternative Sanctions for First and Repeat DUI Offenders.* Sacramento, CA: California Department of Motor Vehicles.

Vingilis, E. and Adlaf, E. (1990). The structure of problem behavior among Ontario high school students: A confirmatory-factor analysis. *Health Education Research* 5: 151–60.

Voas, R. (1986). Evaluation of jail as a penalty for drunk driving. *Alcohol, Drugs and Driving* 2:47–70.

Whitehead, J., and Lab, S. (1989). A meta-analysis of juvenile correctional treatment. *Journal of Research in Crime and Delinquency* 26:276–95.

Wolfgang, M. (1958). *Patterns in criminal homicide.* Philadelphia: University of Pennsylvania Press.

Yu, J. (1994). Punishment celerity and severity. Testing a specific deterrence model of drunk driving recidivism. *Journal of Criminal Justice* 22:355.

DISCUSSION QUESTIONS

1. Note some of the major limitations of this study as identified by the authors.
2. What types of data did the authors use to examine drunk driving recidivism?
3. Discuss the independent and dependent variables used in this study.
4. What conclusions did the authors draw from this study?

12

In the Line of Duty

A Descriptive Analysis of Police Assaults and Accidents

STEVEN G. BRANDL, University of Wisconsin-Milwaukee

COMMENTARY

In early 1994 I received a phone call from the president of the Milwaukee Police Association (the labor union that represents police officers in the City of Milwaukee), and he asked if I would be interested in conducting research on two important issues relating to police work in Milwaukee: the workload demands of police officers working in Milwaukee and injuries to officers in Milwaukee. He explained that he wished to use the results of the research in the labor contract negotiation process in progress between the City and the Association. The Association was interested in the workload study because if it was found that Milwaukee officers had a heavier workload than officers employed in the suburban communities surrounding Milwaukee, then it could be argued that Milwaukee officers should receive greater pay (i.e., more work should equal more pay). They were interested in documenting the nature and extent of injuries to officers so arguments regarding shift assignments, disability pay, and retirement could be developed. I was interested in doing these studies, particularly the one related to officers' injuries, because I was confident that I would be able to publish an article using these data. Based on the existing research on the topic, we do not know much about nonfatal and especially accidental injuries to officers, and these data would provide an opportunity to address this research gap.

The data collection and analysis process went pretty smoothly. The variables were fairly well defined based on the categories already provided in the injury reports (with a few exceptions as noted in the article). The statistical analyses performed were not complicated, which again related to my overall purpose of developing a basic understanding of injuries as they occurred. On the basis of the analyses, I prepared a report that documented my findings. This report was then delivered to the Police Association and I testified in an arbitration hearing regarding my methodology and the findings of the study.

Source: Journal of Criminal Justice, Vol. 24, No. 3, pp. 255–264. Copyright © 1996, reprinted with permission from Elsevier Science.

At the conclusion of this process, I conducted some additional analyses, wrote a literature review on the topic of injuries to officers, and then put together the article you are about to read. I presented a previous draft of this paper at an Academy of Criminal Justice Sciences (ACJS) meeting. I then revised the paper in accord with some of the comments and suggestions I received as a result of the presentation and sent it to the *Journal of Criminal Justice* for editorial/peer review.

The most significant concern that developed as a result of the study was the overall validity of the reports that were completed to document the injuries sustained. This issue is a concern with virtually all research studies that rely on previously completed reports or records. Essentially the question is this: Is the information contained in the reports accurate? For example, with reference to this particular study, did the reported injuries occur as stated, or was a more acceptable explanation provided? Although there is little reason to believe that the reports were systematically biased, or that injuries were overrepresented or underrepresented, it is a possibility. Regardless, a researcher is largely at the mercy of the individuals who previously completed the reports when existing data or records are used as the basis for analysis. If one is interested in studying the nature and extent of injuries to officers, arguably the most straightforward way of approaching the issue is through an analysis of existing reports that document such injuries. Other methodologies (e.g., participant observation, survey) might be best suited to get at other related issues but would undoubtedly pose other difficulties.

Overall, this article casts light on an issue that has not received a lot of research attention in the past. Although not fancy, the article helps us understand the nature and frequency of injuries to officers and, as noted in the article, the study raises additional questions for future research.

ABSTRACT Common in the literature are discussions of the dangerousness of the police occupation. In particular, numerous studies have examined the circumstances surrounding the murder and assault of police officers. Relatively little is known, however, about how these dramatic events fit into the larger context of police injury incidents. This article reports the results of analyses based on 2,073 officer injury incidents (reports) gathered from a large U.S. midwestern municipal police department. Findings and implications are discussed.

INTRODUCTION

The police occupation is commonly portrayed by the media and police fiction as being dangerous, where officers are constantly confronted with the real threat of assault and murder. Although some researchers have questioned this depiction of the police occupation (Kappeler, Blumberg, and Potter, 1993), many empirical studies also have come to the conclusion that the police occupation is a dangerous one (see Fridell and Pate, 1993:589), or, at the very least, that certain tasks of the job are dangerous (Konstantin, 1984; Lester, 1984; Garner and Clemmer, 1986; Stanford and Mowry, 1990, Hirschel, Dean, and Lumb, 1994). The studies that draw conclusions about the dangers of the occupation have most often analyzed police assaults (Meyer et al., 1981; Uchida, Brooks, and Kopers, 1987; Hirschel, Dean, and Lumb, 1994) and homicides (e.g., Konstantin, 1984; Lester, 1984; Cardarelli, 1986).

The police occupation is not the only occupation to be analyzed in terms of its risks or dangers. Studies have examined the dangers of construction work (Sorock, Smith, and Goldoft, 1993), coal mining (Goodman and Garber, 1988), nursing (Feldstein et al., 1993; McDevitt, Lees, and McDiarmid, 1993), industrial work (Zohar, 1980; Hansen, 1989), and firefighting (Woodruff et al., 1993) among others. In these occupational settings, however, dangers are most commonly defined in terms of accidents.

The conceptualization of dangerousness in the police occupation in terms of the murder and assault of police officers, to the exclusion of accidents, is at least a partial function of the unique nature of police work and data accessibility. Of course, in few other occupations are assaults an occupational issue; the threat of assault and homicide differentiates the police occupation from most others. Further, assaults and homicides capture the exciting, the "blood and guts," and the "good versus evil" nature of police work. Such images are cast by the media and the police themselves and are, in turn, at least subtly reflected by empirical research. With regard to data accessibility, many studies that have analyzed the murder and assault of police officers have used data collected by the Federal Bureau of Investigation (FBI) (i.e., *Law Enforcement Officers Killed and Assaulted* reports; e.g., Konstantin, 1984; Lester, 1984; Fridell and Pate, 1993). Other researchers have collected data from police agencies that had standard reports and recording procedures to document such incidents (e.g., Uchida, Brooks, and Kopers, 1987; Hirschel, Dean, and Lumb, 1994). No doubt, such data have facilitated the development of this line of research.

The focus on the felonious acts of police assault and murder draws attention away from the potentially larger, but certainly less dramatic, issue of accidental injuries and deaths. A broader focus on officer injuries and deaths, regardless if they result from felonious or accidental incidents, is warranted for several reasons. First, from a police management perspective, officer injuries and deaths (regardless of how sustained) can have extraordinary personnel related costs, including lost wages, medical expenses, insurance claims, and productivity declines, to say nothing of the individual consequences for officers and their families. Second, as with the research on police homicide and assault, research on the more inclusive issue of police injuries and deaths may inform the development of training and policy to prevent such incidents in the future (Fyfe, 1979; Sherman, 1980; Bayley and Garofalo, 1989; Hirschel, Dean, and Lumb, 1994). Finally, if empirical conclusions about the dangerousness of the job are to be drawn, they may be most accurately formed from analyses not only of felonious injuries and deaths, but also accidental ones.

Unfortunately, relatively little is known about the nature and extent of accidental injuries and deaths of police officers and how accidental incidents compare to felonious ones. The present study begins to fill this research gap by analyzing work related injury and death incidents ($N = 2{,}073$) of police officers employed by a large municipal police agency. Specifically, the study compares accidental incidents that result in injury or death to felonious ones in terms of their frequency, seriousness, and distribution. The study provides a beginning familiarity with this important but neglected topic.

PREVIOUS RESEARCH

Much of what is known regarding the felonious assault and murder of police officers comes from FBI annual data. From the FBI data, several patterns regarding police homicide can be identified (FBI, 1992). First, in 1992[1] sixty-two officers were feloniously killed in the line of duty. From 1983 to 1992, 713 officers were killed. The trend is generally declining with less than ninety officers being killed each year since 1983. The rate of police killings also has declined from approximately three (per 10,000 officers) in 1980 to less than 1.7 in 1992. Second, most of the homicides occurred in arrest situations (crimes in progress and pursuing suspects; 42 percent) and during disturbance calls (bar fights, man with gun, family quarrels; 18 percent of all killings). Third, most of the officers killed were killed by firearms (85 percent). Fourth, most police homicides occurred between 4:00 P.M. and midnight (44 percent), fewest occurred between 12:01 A.M. and 8:00 A.M. (27 percent). Finally, approximately 65 percent of the officers killed were of the lowest rank (e.g., patrol officer, deputy sheriff), and 15 percent were detectives.

Data provided by the FBI on nonfatal felonious assaults[2] of police officers also reveal patterns, and these patterns are quite similar to those relating to incidents where police officers were killed. First, according to the FBI, in 1992 there were 81,252 reported assaults on police officers. The trend in police assaults is rather static with between 15.5 and 17.5 assaults per one hundred officers per year since 1983. Second, most assaults occurred in disturbance situations (32 percent), followed by attempting other arrests (24 percent), handling prisoners (12 percent), and traffic pursuits and stops (9 percent). Third, most assaults (81 percent) were inflicted via personal weapons (e.g., hands, feet), followed by other weapons (14 percent) and firearms (6 percent). Fourth, similar to police homicides, most assaults occurred between 4:00 P.M. and midnight (48 percent). Fewest assaults (17 percent) occurred between 8:00 A.M. and 4:00 P.M. Finally, as with homicides, patrol officers accounted for the vast majority of those assaulted (79 percent); 7 percent involved detectives or those who had special assignments, 14 percent involved officers in other positions.

Other research that has analyzed the nature and extent of felonious assaults on police officers (Hirschel, Dean, and Lumb, 1994; Meyer et al., 1981; Uchida, Brooks, and Kopers, 1987) generally supports the findings of the FBI and adds that most of the injuries that result from assaults are relatively minor—most injuries are in the form of bruises and scratches (see Meyer et al., 1981; Hirschel, Dean, and Lumb, 1994).

Research on accidental deaths and injuries of police officers is quite limited compared to that on felonious assault and murder. According to the FBI, in 1992, sixty-six law enforcement officers were killed accidentally. From 1983 to 1992, 699 officers were accidentally killed. The trend is rather inconsistent with between fifty-two (in 1991) and seventy-nine (in 1989) officers killed each year since 1983. When considering a longer time frame (1973–1991), it is apparent that the number of officers accidentally killed is increasing (see Fridell and Pate, 1993). In 1992, as in other years, most of the accidental deaths resulted from motor-vehicle accidents (automobile and motorcycle; 59 percent), followed by being struck by vehicles (17 percent), aircraft accidents (8 percent), accidental shootings (12 percent), and other incidents (5 percent). Finally, in a rather limited analysis, Lester (1981) compared rates of accidental and felonious deaths to rates of job related illnesses and injuries for police officers and found, not surprisingly, that rates of death were minuscule compared to those of illness and injury. The analyses also showed that job related fatalities, injuries, and illnesses for police officers were greater than the national averages for all workers. Unfortunately, injuries and illnesses were analyzed together, only those which resulted in lost work days were included, and the causes of the injuries, illnesses, and deaths were not specified. Neither the FBI's annual reports nor any other available research provide more detailed analyses of accidental injuries to officers.

In summary, previous research indicates that assault and homicide incidents are similar in several respects; namely, both are more likely to occur in the late afternoon and evening hours, and both are more likely to occur in situations where an arrest is made or attempted. From the research, it also is known that a relatively large percentage of assaults result in relatively minor injuries. Finally, approximately the same number of officers are feloniously killed each year as accidentally killed. Although the similarities between felonious assault and homicide incidents are known, little is known about the accidental deaths of police officers and virtually nothing is known about accidental injuries. The analyses reported in this article intend to cast light on these issues.

METHOD

Study Site

Data for this study came from injury reports filed by sworn police officers employed by a large municipal police department. At the time of the study, the police department served a population of about 600,000, of which approximately 15 percent were African American and 6 percent were Hispanic. The largest segment of the work force is employed in the manufacturing sector, and unemployment rates are consistently lower than the national average. Uniform Crime Report (UCR) data for 1991 indicate that the metropolitan area had the eleventh lowest rate of index crime among the nation's thirty-five largest metropolitan areas with 6,014.6 incidents per 100,000 persons. Personal and property crime rates are consistently lower than the U.S. metropolitan averages. In 1992 (the time of this study), the police department employed 1,960 sworn officers, of which 1,462 were police (patrol) officers and 207 were detectives.

Data Source

As mandated under worker's compensation laws and departmental policy, officers were required to complete a standard Report of Accident form upon sustaining a work related injury (via an accident or assault). The report was typically completed by the officer's supervisor at or near the time the incident occurred. The report contained data on the officers' demographic characteristics, employment information, date and time of the incident, description of the injuries, whether medical attention was sought, along with a narrative to explain the circumstances of the incident.

In a single report, several specific injuries may have been documented (e.g., an officer fell and received a sprained ankle and a laceration to the head). Therefore, each report documented one incident for a particular individual, not necessarily just one particular injury. If more than one officer was injured (or killed) as a result of the same incident (e.g., a motor-vehicle accident), a separate report documenting the particular injuries sustained would have been filed for each individual.

Data Collection

The process of selecting accident reports consisted of several steps. First, all of the reports that documented incidents that occurred between January 1, 1992 and December 31, 1993 ($N = 2,353$) were obtained from the police department. Second, these reports were reviewed and two categories of cases were eliminated. When the injured employee was a civilian (e.g., identification technician, file clerk), the report was excluded ($N = 158$). When the report identified the injured officer as being a sergeant or in another administrative position, the report was excluded ($N = 122$). The sample, therefore, includes only patrol officers and detectives. As a result of the case selection process, a total of 2,073 reports were included in the study (1,081 from 1992; 992 from 1993). For each of these 2,073 reports, a case data coding form was completed.

Variables

The data for the study were obtained from the accident reports and were transcribed as recorded by the supervisors who completed the reports. To compare assault and accidental incidents, the sample was disaggregated by the nature of the incident (i.e., assault versus accident). An incident was considered a result of an assault on an officer if the officer was directly injured by the intentional acts of the suspect (e.g., the officer was hit, kicked, bit, shot, or stabbed).[3] Accidents were of two types: (a) where the incident resulted from a completely unintended happening (e.g., from an automobile accident, while in physical training); and (b) where the incident resulted from acts of a suspect, but were not of an intentional or assaultive nature (e.g., suspect was fleeing or otherwise uncooperative). It is important to note that the report did not always explicitly state if the incident was an accident or assault (and even if it was stated, it may not have been congruent with the definitions used here). The nature of the incident was determined on the basis of the narrative description of the incident. The other variables consisted of the time of the incident (hour of day), whether medical attention was sought (yes/no), the number of days off work due to the incident/injury (raw number), the work task that resulted in the incident, and the nature of the most serious injury sustained.

The work task that resulted in the incident had the following values: controlling/arresting suspect, apprehending a fleeing suspect (on foot), conducting an investigation, motor-vehicle accident, other vehicle related (e.g., slammed hand in car door), processing prisoner (e.g., controlling prisoner in lock-up), during training, assisting citizen (e.g., first aid), during other physical activity (e.g., foot patrol), during fire rescue, during shooting incident, directing traffic (e.g., struck by vehicle, debris in eyes), performing forced entry, other incidents on police premises (e.g., slammed hand in file cabinet), and other (e.g., slip and fall where activity engaged in is unspecified).

The nature of the most serious injury sustained had the following values: puncture/abrasion/laceration, contusion, sprain/strain, other muscle pain, eye injury (other than black eye), broken bone/dislocated joint, other pain, burns, gun shot wound, knife wound, smoke/fume inhalation, contact with infectious disease, other injury, and injury resulting in death.

Contact with an infectious disease was further classified as either confirmed or unconfirmed. A contact was considered confirmed if it was stated as such in the report. A typical statement which indicated such a contact was, "It was known that subject has [disease]." The manner in which contact was made was classified as "bite," "bodily fluid," and "other." The disease to which the officer was exposed was coded (HIV/tuberculosis/hepatitis/other).

The determination of what constituted the most serious injury when more than one was identified often was not clear cut. Often, few medical details on the specific injuries were documented in the report. In some cases, it was easier to identify the more serious injury (e.g., fracture versus laceration), than in others (puncture versus contusion). When intuitively such a determination was difficult to make, the first injury listed in the report was considered most serious. It is important to note that many reports identified more than one injury, but because only one injury was recorded for purposes of this study, the number of injuries sustained is underestimated.

RESULTS

Given the purposes of the study, simple descriptive statistics are used in the analysis. Frequency distributions and crosstabulations are provided. Table 1 provides a breakdown of the variables used in the study. Several dimensions of the table are noteworthy. First, as seen in Table 1, the overwhelming majority of

Table 1. Description of Sample: Variables and Values

Variable Value	*N*	%
Nature of incident	2,073	100.0
Assault	201	9.7
Accident	1,872	92.3
Suspect-related (*N* = 751; 40.1%)		
Other accidents (*N* = 1,121; 59.9%)		
Task resulting in injury	2,068	100.0
Controlling/Arresting subject	814	39.4
Conducting investigation	295	14.3
Apprehending fleeing suspect	292	14.1
Motor vehicle accident	183	8.8
Other vehicle related	95	4.6
Other: On police premises	93	4.5
Processing prisoner	82	4.0
During training	81	3.9
Assisting citizen	37	1.8
During other physical activity	26	1.3
During fire rescue/discovery	10	.5
During shooting incident	8	.4
During forced entry	7	.3
Directing traffic	7	.3
Other	38	1.8

Variable Value	*N*	%
Nature of most serious injury	2,071	99.8
Puncture/Abrasion/Laceration	464	22.4
Infectious disease contact	408	19.7
Other muscle pain	356	17.2
Sprain/Strain	351	16.9
Contusion	299	14.4
Eye injury (other than black eye)	59	2.8
Broken bone/Dislocated joint	52	2.5
Other pain	24	1.2
Smoke/Fume inhalation	16	.8
Burns	3	.1
Gun shot wound	3	.1
Knife wound	1	.0
Death	0	.0
Other	35	1.7
Time of incident	2,066	100.0
8:01 A.M. to 4:00 P.M.	517	25.0
4:01 P.M. to 12:00 A.M.	903	43.7
12:01 A.M. to 8:00 A.M.	646	31.3
Medical attention sought	2,029	100.0
No	939	46.3
Yes	1,090	53.7
Days off work due to injury		
N = 2,068		
Mean = 1.46		
Standard deviation = 10.91		
Range = 0–285		
% of cases w/ time lost = 81.4		

Note: Missing data excluded from table; percentages may not sum to 100 due to rounding

incidents were accidents (*N* = 1,872; 92.3 percent) and most of the accidents (*N* = 1,121; 59.9 percent) did not result from the actions of suspects. Felonious assaults account for less than 10 percent of all incidents. Even if one wished to consider suspect related accidents as assaults, this more inclusive category would still account for less than 50 percent of all incidents.

Second, the largest proportion of incidents occurred as a result of controlling/arresting suspects (*N* = 814; 39.4 percent), with this category along with conducting investigations and apprehending fleeing suspects accounting for well over one-half (*N* = 1,401; 67.8 percent) of all incidents. Of course, without base line data on the frequency of these tasks, one cannot draw accurate conclusions about the dangerousness of these activities—only that these activities are associated with injury incidents.

Third, the most frequently reported injury was a puncture/abrasion/laceration (*N* = 464; 22.4 percent). Although there is unaccounted for variation in the measurement of injury seriousness, on the whole, these appear to be relatively minor injuries. It is also important to highlight that of the 2,071 incidents, there were no deaths, one knife wound, and three gun shot wounds. Interestingly, the second most frequent type of incident was contact with an infectious disease (*N* = 408; 19.7 percent). In 122 of the 408 incidents (29.9 percent), contact with an infectious disease was unconfirmed (analyses not tabled).[4] In 155 of the 408 incidents (38.0 percent), there was contact with bodily fluid, in twenty-one incidents the officer was bitten (5. 1 percent), and in the remaining 232 incidents (56.7 percent) contact was made through other means.[5]

Fourth, the largest proportion of incidents occurred between 4:01 P.M. and midnight (*N* = 903; 43.7 percent), which approximates a common afternoon or second work shift. Fewest incidents occurred on the day shift (8:01 A.M. to 4:00 P.M.; *N* = 517; 25.0 percent). Fifth, as seen in Table 1, most incidents were serious enough for the officer to seek medical attention (*N* = 1,090; 53.7 percent). Finally, it is seen that the mean number of days off work as a result of the incident was approximately 1.5, with the overwhelming majority of incidents (81.4 percent) resulting in no time lost.

Table 2 presents bivariate analyses, which allow for an examination of how the study variables compare across the different types of incidents. As seen in Table 2, most assaults and suspect related accidents occurred as a result of controlling/arresting suspects (79.1 percent and 54.5 percent, respectively), and the greatest proportion of other accidents occurred while conducting an investigation (24.5 percent). Of the 814 incidents that resulted from controlling/arresting suspects, 246 (30.2 percent) were not at all related to suspect actions. In fact, with the exception of controlling/arresting suspects and apprehending fleeing suspects, within each task it is seen that the overwhelming majority of incidents were not related to suspect actions of any form (i.e., other accidents). Even injuries resulting from shooting incidents were most often completely accidental (*N* = 5; 62.5 percent).

It is also seen that contusions were the most common type of injury in assaults (25.4 percent of all injuries), puncture/abrasion/laceration injuries in suspect related accidents (32.4 percent), and contacts with infectious diseases in other accidents (28.0 percent). Broken bones, gun shot wounds, and knife wounds (arguably the most serious injuries) accounted for 3.5 percent of assaults, 3.4 percent of suspect related accidents, and 2.1 percent of other accidents

As seen in Table 2, the greatest proportion of assaults (44.8 percent), suspect related accidents (45.5 percent), and other accidents (42.3 percent) occurred between 4:01 P.M. and midnight. The fewest assaults (11.9 percent) and suspect related accidents (15.3 percent) occurred between 8:01 A.M. and 4:00 P.M. In addition, of all the incidents that occurred between 8:01 A.M. and 4:00 P.M.,

Table 2. Descriptive Variables by Nature of Incident

		NATURE OF INCIDENT		
			ACCIDENT	
Variable	*N*	Assault	Suspect-Related	Other
Task resulting in incident	2,068	201	751	1,116
Controlling/Arresting suspect	814	159 (79.1)	409 (54.5)	246 (22.0)
Conducting investigation	295	16 (8.0)	6 (.8)	273 (24.5)
Apprehending fleeing suspect	292	2 (1.0)	290 (38.6)	0 (0.0)
Motor vehicle accident	183	8 (4.0)	21 (2.8)	154 (13.8)
Other vehicle related	95	2 (1.0)	3 (.4)	90 (8.1)
Other: On police premises	93	0 (0.0)	3 (.4)	90 (8.1)
Processing prisoner	82	11 (5.5)	11 (1.5)	60 (5.4)
During training	81	0 (0.0)	0 (0.0)	81 (7.3)
Assisting citizen	37	0 (0.0)	5 (.7)	32 (2.9)
During other physical activity	26	0 (0.0)	0 (0.0)	26 (2.3)
During fire rescue/discovery	10	0 (0.0)	0 (0.0)	10 (.9)
During shooting incident	8	3 (1.5)	0 (0.0)	5 (.4)
During forced entry	7	0 (0.0)	0 (0.0)	7 (.6)
Directing traffic	7	0 (0.0)	0 (0.0)	7 (.6)
Other	38	0 (0.0)	3 (.4)	35 (3.1)
Nature of most serious injury	2,071	201	751	1,119
Puncture/Abrasion/Laceration	464	49 (24.4)	243 (32.4)	172 (15.4)
Infectious disease contact	408	44 (21.9)	51 (6.8)	313 (28.0)
Other muscle pain	356	26 (12.9)	134 (17.8)	196 (17.5)
Sprain/Strain	351	15 (7.5)	145 (19.3)	191 (17.1)
Contusion	299	51 (25.4)	120 (16.0)	128 (11.4)
Eye injury (not black eye)	59	3 (1.5)	15 (2.0)	41 (3.7)
Broken bone/Dislocated joint	52	6 (3.0)	25 (3.3)	21 (1.9)
Other pain	24	3 (1.5)	4 (.5)	17 (1.5)
Smoke/Fume inhalation	16	0 (0.0)	5 (.7)	11 (1.0)
Burns	3	0 (0.0)	1 (.1)	2 (.2)
Gun shot wound	3	1 (.5)	0 (0.0)	2 (.2)
Knife wound	1	0 (0.0)	1 (.1)	0 (0.0)
Death	0	0 (0.0)	0 (0.0)	0 (0.0)
Other	35	3 (1.5)	7 (.9)	25 (2.2)
Time of incident	2,066	201	750	1,115
8:01 A.M. to 4:00 P.M.	517	24 (11.9)	115 (15.3)	378 (33.9)
4:01 P.M. to 12:00 A.M.	903	90 (44.8)	341 (45.5)	472 (42.3)
12:01 A.M. to 8:00 A.M.	646	87 (43.3)	294 (39.2)	265 (23.8)
Medical attention sought	2,029	201	745	1,083
No	939	75 (37.3)	323 (43.4)	541 (50.0)
Yes	1,090	126 (62.7)	422 (56.6)	542 (50.0)
Days off work due to injury	2,068	201	750	1,117
Mean days off per incident	1.464	.901	1.267	1.697
Standard deviation	10.914	4.361	5.732	13.965
Range	0–285	0–48	0–58	0–285
% of cases with no days off	81.4	86.1	82.3	80.0

Note: Missing data are excluded from the table. Entries in parentheses are column percentages.

73.1 percent were other accidents. Between 4:01 P.M. and midnight, 52.3 percent were other accidents, and between 12:01 A.M. and 8:00 A.M. only 41.0 percent were other accidents. Although the first shift appears safer than the other shifts in terms of assaults and suspect related accidents, this is not the case in terms of other accidents.

Table 2 also shows that medical attention was sought in a greater proportion of assault incidents (62.7 percent) than suspect related accidents (56.6 percent) or other accidents (50.0 percent). Of all those incidents where medical attention was sought, however, most were as a result of other accidents ($N = 542$ of 1,090; 49.7 percent), least were as a result of assaults (126 of 1,090; 11.6 percent). Finally, Table 2 shows the days off work due to injuries sustained as a result of the incident by the nature of the incident. Other accidents generally result in the greatest amount of time off work and the greatest percentage of incidents that resulted in days off (20 percent), although the differences are relatively small.

CONCLUSIONS

The dangers and risks associated with police work are traditionally conceptualized in terms of assaults and homicides of police officers. Not surprisingly then, studies that analyze police assaults and homicides often conclude that these events cause police work to be dangerous. As stated by Hirschel, Dean, and Lumb (1994:115), "The major threat to police safety is assault by those whom they must confront in law enforcement situations." This study takes a different approach by describing accidental and felonious incidents and finds that an equal, if not greater, threat to police safety is posed by accidents. This study shows that felonious incidents are relatively rare events—the overwhelming majority of incidents, regardless of the task engaged in, are not a result of assaults and, of course, do not result in deaths or serious injury. Most injury incidents are as a result of accidents and most injuries, regardless of how sustained, are relatively minor. Indeed, the most serious injuries are most often due to accidents, most medical treatment is due to accidents, and most days off are as a result of accidents.

One of the primary purposes of studies that have examined assaults and homicides of police officers is to identify high risk or dangerous activities. If these tasks can be identified, the reasoning goes, then policies can be developed and training can be provided to reduce the frequency of such incidents. For example, Hirschel, Dean, and Lumb (1994) suggest that two or more officers be dispatched to handle domestic disturbance situations (as they found assaults to occur less often when more than one officer was present), that officers be required to complete in-service training in crisis intervention and cultural awareness, and that officers be provided with more accurate and detailed information about calls for service before they are actually in the situation. According to

Konstantin (1984), police training should emphasize techniques of handling routine arrests and responding to robberies as much as methods of resolving domestic disturbances (see also Uchida, Brooks, and Kopers, 1987). Others have suggested that the root causes of violence be addressed to enhance the safety of police officers (Meyer et al., 1981). Such recommendations follow the results of the various studies.

Given the present study, it would seem appropriate to broaden the research focus to include not only assaults and homicides, but also accidents. If all the felonious incidents could be prevented through policies and training, there would still exist the majority of injury incidents—and even the most serious injuries would not be prevented. In essence, work place safety is a much larger issue than that reflected in the frequency of assaults and homicides.

Accordingly, additional research attention directed at this broader collection of incidents would be appropriate. Research that examined the risk adjusted frequency of various tasks, beyond simply those tasks associated with assaults, may have implications for training injury prevention efforts, and may further assist in improving the safety of officers' work environments. The development and evaluation of programs designed to reduce the frequency of felonious and accidental incidents could be quite valuable. Accident prevention programs have been found to be successful (Komaki, Barwick, and Scott, 1978; Komaki, Heinzmann, Lawson, 1980; Feldstein et al., 1993), but have not been tested in the work setting of police officers.

In addition, even though most injuries sustained as a result of felonious and accidental incidents seem to be relatively minor, the potential significance of the long-term cumulative effects of injuries should not be underestimated. Research designed to examine the debilitating effects of injuries over time, their impact on associated psychological and emotional outcomes (i.e., stress and burnout), and the contribution of physical ailments in explaining the well-established finding that older officers do less work (e.g., make fewer arrests) could have direct implications for issues of job design, performance evaluation, stress management, shift assignments, selection, disability, and even retirement (Campion, 1983; Hollenbeck, Ilgen, Crampton, 1992).

Finally, it would be worthwhile to explain individual variation in injury incidents. What individual and contextual factors explain distribution of such incidents? As a starting point, research could examine the relative impact of officers' background characteristics and job assignment on injury frequency. Some psychological research clearly highlights the relationship between injury frequency and worker age and experience (Bigos et al., 1986). Further, research in cognitive and organizational psychology suggests that the way in which individuals access and process information is a critical factor in the display of safe behavior in the work place (Hansen, 1989). Other research has examined the contributory role that the safety climate of the organization has on the exercise of safe behavior by its members (Zohar, 1980). Research focused on these broader issues may further understanding of the physical risks associated with police work and assist in reducing the significance of them.

NOTES

1. The year 1992 was selected for summary because it is within the time frame of the data analyzed in the present investigation. The patterns that emerge from the 1992 data are similar to other years as reported by the FBI, with exceptions noted.

2. The FBI provides a rather ambiguous definition of assault. According to the FBI (1992:1), "Law enforcement agencies report figures on assaults which resulted in serious injury or in which a weapon was used which could have caused serious injury or death. Other assaults are recorded only if they involved more than verbal abuse or minor resistance to arrest." Technically, any confrontation with an armed suspect, even if it did not result in injury to the officer, could be classified as an assault. Confrontations that involved suspects without a weapon could be classified as an assault if more than (the rather ambiguous) "minor resistance to arrest" was offered.

3. According to the state statutes of this jurisdiction, whoever intentionally causes bodily harm to a law enforcement officer is guilty of a felony. Hence, assaults on officers are referred to here as felonious assaults.

4. The incidents that involved an unconfirmed contact with an infectious disease occurred as a result of contact with bodily fluid ($N = 102$) or bites ($N = 20$). In these situations, it was unknown if the individual was a disease carrier.

5. With regard to the disease to which the officer was exposed, seventy-seven incidents (18.9 percent) involved HIV, seventy-six (18.6 percent) involved tuberculosis, seventy-one (17.4 percent) involved hepatitis, and the remaining 184 (45.1 percent) involved unknown (i.e., bodily fluid or bite contacts) or other diseases (e.g., pneumonia, chicken pox, scabies).

REFERENCES

Bayley, D. H., and Garofalo, J. (1989). The management of violence by police patrol officers. *Criminology* 27:1–23.

Bigos, S. J., Spengler, D. M., Martin, N. A., Zeh, J., Fisher, L., and Nachemson, A. (1986). Back injuries in industry: A retrospective study. *Spine* 11:252–56.

Campion, M. A. (1983). Personnel selection for physically demanding jobs: Review and recommendations. *Personnel Psychology* 36:527–50.

Cardarelli, A. P. (1986). *Cops, killers and staying alive: The murder of police officers in America.* Springfield, IL: Charles C. Thomas.

Federal Bureau of Investigation. (1992). *Law enforcement officers killed and assaulted.* Washington, DC: U.S. Government Printing Office.

Feldstein, A., Valanis, B., Vollmer, W., Stevens, N., and Overton, C. (1993). The back injury prevention project pilot study. *Journal of Occupational Medicine* 35:114–20.

Fridell, L. A., and Pate, A. M. (1993). Death on patrol: Killings of American law enforcement officers. In *Critical issues in policing,* eds. R. G. Dunham and G. P. Alpert. Prospect Heights, IL: Waveland Press.

Fyfe, J. J. (1979). Administrative interventions on police shooting discretion: An empirical examination. *Journal of Criminal Justice* 7:309–24.

Garner, J., and Clemmer, E. (1986). *Danger to police in domestic disturbances.* Washington, DC: U.S. Department of Justice.

Goodman, P. S., and Garber, S. (1988). Absenteeism and accidents in a dangerous environment: Empirical analysis of underground coal mines. *Journal of Applied Psychology* 73:81–86.

Hansen, C. (1989). A causal model of the relationship among accidents, biodata, personality, and cognitive factors. *Journal of Applied Psychology* 74:81–90.

Hirschel, J. D., Dean, C. W., and Lumb, R. C. (1994). The relative contribution of domestic violence to assault and injury of police officers. *Justice Quarterly* 11:99–117.

Hollenbeck, J. R., Ilgen, D. R., and Crampton, S. M. (1992). Lower back disability in occupational settings: A review of the literature from a human resource management view. *Personnel Psychology* 45:247–78.

Kappeler V. E., Blumberg, M., and Potter, G. W. (1993). *The mythology of crime and criminal justice.* Prospect Heights, IL: Waveland Press.

Komaci, J., Heinzmann, A. T., and Lawson, L. (1980). Effect of training and feedback: Component analysis of a behavioral safety program. *Journal of Applied Psychology* 63:261–70.

Komaki, J., Barwick, K. D., and Scott, L. R. (1978). A behavioral approach to occupational safety: Pinpointing and reinforcing safe performance in a food manufacturing plant. *Journal of Applied Psychology* 63:434–45.

Konstantin, D. (1984). Homicides of American law enforcement officers. *Justice Quarterly* 1:29–45.

Lester, D. (1981). Occupational injuries, illnesses and fatalities in police officers. *Police Chief* 48(10):43, 63.

Lester, D. (1984). The murder of police officers in American cities. *Criminal Justice and Behavior* 11:101–13.

Little, R. (1984). Cop-killing: A descriptive analysis of the problem. *Police Studies* 7:68–75.

McDevitt, J. J., Lees, P. S. J., and McDiarmid, M. A. (1993). Exposure of hospital pharmacists and nurses to antineoplastic agents. *Journal of Occupational Medicine* 35:57–60.

Meyer, C. K., Magedanz, T., Dahlin, D., and Chapman, S. (1981). A comparative assessment of assault incidents: Robbery related ambush and general police assaults. *Journal of Police Science and Administration* 9:1–18.

Meyer, C. K., Magedanz, T., Feimer, S., Chapman, S., and Pammer, W. (1986). *Ambush related assaults on police: Violence at the street level.* Springfield, IL: Charles C. Thomas.

Sherman, L. (1980). Perspectives on police and violence. *Annals* 452:1–12.

Sorock, G.S., Smith, E. O., and Goldoft, M. (1993). Fatal occupational injuries in the New Jersey construction industry, 1983 to 1989. *Journal of Occupational Medicine* 35:916–21.

Stanford, R. M., and Mowry, B. L. (1990). Domestic disturbance danger rate. *Journal of Police Science and Administration* 17:244–49.

Uchida, C. D., Brooks, L. W., and Kopers, C. S. (1987). Danger to police during domestic encounters: Assaults on Baltimore County police, 1984–86. *Criminal Justice Policy Review* 2:357–71.

Woodruff, B. A., Moyer, L. A., O'Rourke, K. M., and Margolis, H. S. (1993). Blood exposure and the risk of hepatitis B virus infection in firefighters. *Journal of Occupational Medicine* 35:1048–54.

Zohar, D. (1980). Safety climate in industrial organizations: Theoretical and applied implications. *Journal of Applied Psychology* 65:96–102.

DISCUSSION QUESTIONS

1. What types of data did the author use to examine the incidence of police assaults and accidents?
2. Why was the author concerned about the validity of the reports that were used to document injuries?
3. What kinds of problems could you foresee in obtaining existing records from a police agency? From a court? From a prison?
4. What did the author conclude from this study?

PART VI

Secondary Data Analysis

The three articles contained in this part exemplify research using secondary data analysis. This method usually involves an analysis of data that were collected for other purposes. As an example, one of the current authors (Pope, 1980) obtained information compiled by the California Bureau of Criminal Statistics on instances of burglary across six police jurisdictions. These data were originally collected to assess various approaches to burglary abatement. However, because these data linked burglary offenses to specific arrested offenders they could also be used for other purposes. In this case, the author was interested in examining patterns in burglary—are specific types of offenders associated with the commission of certain types of burglaries? Because the author had the original data in the form of magnetic computer tapes, this analysis could be and was carried out.

This is a very efficient and useful method. For one thing it saves the time, resources, and money that may be involved in collecting one's own data. Because researchers have the original data, they can manipulate it almost any way they want. They can conduct their own analysis for different purposes than originally intended. On the other hand, as the following articles and commentary point out, there are some drawbacks. While you can reanalyze the data, you are still limited to what was collected in the first place. Simply put, you can't analyze what is not there. More often than not, while secondary data are useful to examine a variety of topics, they are rarely a perfect fit.

Wells and Rankin (1995), in their article titled "Juvenile Victimization: Convergent Validation of Alternative Measures," provide a good example of the strengths and weaknesses associated with secondary data analysis. In order to examine the victimization experiences of adolescents across criminal offenses, they analyze the National Crime Victim Surveys (NCVS) along with two additional youth surveys, the National Youth Survey and Monitoring the Future, and compare the findings. These three data sources are currently archived at the InterUniversity Consortium of Political and Social Research and can be made available for a variety of research purposes. As they note, the National Crime Victim Surveys (NCVS) are the most reliable indicator of victimization experiences currently available. However, as they also note, the NCVS may not be as reliable for different population segments and crime types.

The findings reveal large discrepancies between the two alternative surveys and the NCVS with regard to youth victimization experiences and crime type. The authors then examine plausible explanations for these findings based upon the manner in which the surveys are conducted and the way data are recorded.

The second article (Barkan and Cohn, 1994) uses secondary data to address a critical issue within the justice system—the degree to which racial prejudice affects citizens' attitudes toward the death penalty. In order to examine this issue, Barkan and Cohn use data originally compiled by the National Opinion Research Center—the 1990 General Social Survey (GSS). This survey examines public attitudes toward criminal justice issues, and since it is a random sample, it can be generalized to the resident U.S. population. Their analysis suggests that whites are more supportive of the death penalty than blacks and that this is a function of racial prejudice.

Since the GSS contains a variety of attitude questions and demographic information, the effects of racial prejudice can be isolated. In their commentary, Barkan and Cohn point out the strengths and weaknesses of secondary data analysis when using the GSS. Conducting an original survey on attitudes toward the death penalty on a national level would be difficult, if not impossible, for any researcher regardless of where he or she teaches. Most university professors don't have millions of dollars in their pocket to support such research. Therein lies the value of secondary data analysis.

In the final article in this part, Worden (1990) examines a frequently debated issue—"are educated cops better cops?" Previous research in this area provides mixed findings, although it does suggest that police attitudes are not greatly affected by level of education. In this article, an additional dimension relating education to police performance is examined. As the author notes in the commentary, the original piece linking education to attitudes was rejected for publication until performance measures were added. The secondary data used to support this analysis consisted of a fairly large and comprehensive original study focusing on the delivery of police services (the Police Services Study or PSS).

Interestingly enough, the author concludes that neither police attitudes nor performance are strongly related to educational attainment. This is all the more interesting in that more and more police departments are supporting, and in some cases requiring, more advanced education for their officers, especially in supervisory positions. This article presents a rather comprehensive analysis of the PSS data and in the commentary discusses the use of multiple measures for examining police attitudes and performance.

13

Juvenile Victimization

Convergent Validation of Alternative Measurements

L. EDWARD WELLS
JOSEPH H. RANKIN

COMMENTARY

The most commonly used information about crime comes from official crime statistics collected by police departments and reported by the FBI. However, because official records often provide a biased and incomplete picture of the ordinary crime that occurs on the streets, we look for alternative data sources that may be more complete or less selective. The most important of these is the National Crime Victim Survey (NCVS), an annual survey of 60,000 households across the United States collected annually by the federal Bureau of Justice Statistics. Criminologists and political decision makers increasingly rely on the NCVS to inform them about national crime trends and to help them make well-informed policy decisions.

In this study, we were concerned that the NCVS, while a good estimate of ordinary street crimes in the general population, does not provide a very good picture of crimes occurring to younger victims—for example, adolescents, who are the most crime-vulnerable group in the population. Due to the ways the interviews in the survey are worded and administered, the NCVS seemed open to serious question for this important group of victims. And because we base serious policy decisions (about where and how to spend our crime control dollars) on these data, we need to be as informed as much as possible about their biases and weak spots.

The research question is this: How can we test for biases in our data if we don't have a clearly unbiased reference with which to compare them (since the NCVS is supposed to be the best we can do)? We adopted the strategy of

Source: Journal of Research in Crime and Delinquency, Vol. 32 No. 3, August 1995, pp. 287-307.
© 1995 Sage Publications, Inc. Reprinted by permission of Sage Publications, Inc.

An earlier version of this article was presented at the annual meeting of the American Society of Criminology in San Francisco, California, November 1991.

convergent validation to see how the results of alternative but different data sources (having different strengths and weaknesses from the NCVS) would compare with the NCVS estimates. To do this, we selected studies aimed specifically at measuring the experiences of adolescents, which used comparable national sampling procedures, and which asked comparable questions about victimization experiences. We found two data sources that met these criteria and provided good comparisons with the NCVS. We limited the years covered in each data set so that they would all refer to the same time period; we limited the data sets to the same age ranges; and we selected questions from each survey that were as similar as possible (in both question wordings and response formats). We also collected as much information as possible about how each survey was carried out and converted into statistical data, so we could be sure that the numbers from different surveys meant the same things. Where we had to make assumptions about the comparability of the different sources, we located additional research to verify and document the reasonableness of our assumptions. This also allowed us to estimate what the effects might be if our assumptions were incorrect—that is, how far off our results might be.

To provide additional convergent validation of our alternative results, we also compared them with the findings of more limited alternative studies done on special forms of victimization—for example, sexual assaults by intimates and parental abuse of children. If our alternative estimates disagreed with the NCVS but showed close agreement with our independent outside studies, then we would have much stronger confidence in the validity of our alternative data sources. Our main concern was to ensure that our measurement and coding procedures were as comparable as humanly possible to those used in the NCVS. Then if differences in the results (between the alternatives and the NCVS) were found, they could not be dismissed as technical deviations or procedural differences in how the data were handled. Rather, they must be due to the inherent features of the NCVS interview itself as a social event that inhibits or discourages adolescent reporting of victimizations.

ABSTRACT Surveys of crime victims provide a valuable supplement to official record measures of serious crime, enabling a more complete picture of street crime levels and a more dynamic view of crime as interactions between offenders and victims. Initiated in 1973, the National Crime Survey (now called the National Crime Victimization Survey [NCVS]) provides a systematic, reliable, national assessment of crime and constitutes the preferred source of data for many analytic purposes. However, this article suggests that the NCVS is not equally reliable for all types of victims and offenses. The authors compare the NCVS profile of youthful victimization with comparable patterns of events from two other national data sets (the National Youth Survey and Monitoring the Future) that focus specifically on juveniles and their experiences. These comparisons indicate that young persons are less reliably represented in the NCVS due to such factors as sampling frame of the survey, form of the questionnaire interview, and wording of questions.

PATTERNS OF JUVENILE VICTIMIZATION: COMPARING ALTERNATIVE MEASURES

To succeed as a scientific field, criminology depends critically on the ability to specify clearly what the concept of crime means and to collect data that are objective and valid measures of its occurrence. Traditionally, from the earliest studies by Quetelet to the most recent studies on criminal careers, measurement of crime has relied heavily on official records that result from the arrest and prosecution of criminal offenders. Such data are concrete and numerical (i.e., countable and quantifiable), already collected and available to research, and "officially" true. However, criminologists increasingly have recognized that such records are not simply facts of criminal events or activity, but rather products of administrative responding, organizational decision making, and official recording. Substantial amounts of crime are unrecorded by official agencies, and the amount of "hidden crime" is a complex variable that varies substantially across different types of crimes, social occasions, and sociopolitical contexts. By now, the fallibilities and limitations of official crime data have been amply described and documented (e.g., see Biderman and Reiss 1967; Jackson 1990; MacKenzie, Baunach, and Roberg 1990; O'Brien 1985; Skogan 1977, 1984), although the validity of official crime data is a methodological question still open to considerable debate (e.g., see Biderman and Lynch 1991; Gove, Hughes, and Geerken 1985).

In response, researchers have made use of a variety of alternative data collection methods—including observations, surveys, informant interviews, and unobtrusive measures—all aimed at avoiding some of the biases and problems of official records and bringing more officially hidden crime to light. Although each method of data collection has its strengths and weaknesses, the dominant alternative strategy has been the use of *victimization surveys* in which a representative sample from a target population is surveyed regarding experiences as victims of crime during a prior time interval. The logic of victimization surveys is simple: We can estimate the amount of predatory crime by counting the number of victims, and we can determine the number of victims by asking people. The utility of the approach is that many crimes have never been reported to police, yet victims can and will accurately report these in interviews (or on questionnaires) and in the process provide substantial detail about the crimes, their contexts, and their consequences. These victim reports are informative and reliable, because victimizations tend to be memorable events and because the questions do not ask respondents to report on their own deviant or illegal behaviors.

Because repeated studies have established their high reliability, measurement of conventional street crime has increasingly relied on victimization surveys. Because they require personal victims (who can be surveyed), this method does not allow measurement of vice or victimless crimes (e.g., illegal drug use, consensual sexual behavior) and is not well suited to indicate commercial, corporate, or organized crime. However, because they deal with predatory, personally victimizing offenses, which are primarily FBI *Uniform Crime Report* (UCR) Part I or

Index crimes, victimization surveys are commonly viewed as measuring real crime, which are the crimes of highest concern to the general public and to policymakers. For such reasons, victim surveys have been identified as the best alternative methodology for measuring the occurrence of crime and estimating its true incidence. This is indicated by the development of the National Crime Survey (now called the National Crime Victimization Survey—NCVS) and by increasing reliance on periodic reports of NCVS results as valid estimates of crime trends in the United States.

The National Crime (Victimization) Survey

Begun in 1973 as an official annual national survey of the general population concerning criminal victimizations, the NCVS constitutes the major alternative to the UCR (using police reports and records) for collecting systematic data on crimes of high concern in the United States. Using sophisticated multistage probability sampling procedures, the NCVS interviews approximately 60,000 households and 120,000 persons yearly. Administered by the U.S. Bureau of the Census, the NCVS interview has been developed, modified, and improved over the past 20-plus years to produce relatively reliable and unbiased data on the amount of conventional street crime occurring in the United States and on the circumstances surrounding its occurrence. The explicit focus of the NCVS is on those offenses that citizens and policymakers identify as "street crime," including data on UCR Part I crimes (but excluding arson and homicide) and on simple assaults (which constitute a Part II offense in the UCR).

The impact of the NCVS on criminological research has been noticeable. First, it has confirmed empirically that a considerable amount of crime is hidden from official records, and it provides a reasonable estimate of the magnitude of this hidden figure (Garofalo 1990; Gottfredson 1986; Skogan 1981). According to NCVS estimates, the actual amount of crime is roughly two to four times higher than official statistics would indicate, depending on the type of crime being considered. Second, NCVS analyses have revealed the common reasons behind victims not reporting crime to the police for official attention. Third, victimization data indicate that there are significant variations in the official reporting of crime across different types of offenses, victim-offender relationships, and situational factors. They show that the underreporting bias in official crime data is not a simple constant, but a complex variable that varies by socially meaningful factors. Fourth, the use of victimization surveys has drawn theoretical attention to crime as a social transaction that includes a victim as well as an offender. Thus the NCVS has provided a new means of measuring crime that escapes the familiar biases of official record data and allows for more valid estimation of criminal incidence, including the large amount of crimes that are hidden from official view.

Like any measurement method, the NCVS has shortcomings and limitations (Garofalo 1990). First, as a survey, the NCVS is subject to sampling problems—not the usual problems of small, local, or nonprobability samples, but of limitations in its sampling frame. Because the sampling unit for most national surveys (including the NCVS) is the *household,* people who are not clearly attached to stable household units are either omitted or grossly undersampled. Moreover, such persons (e.g., runaway juveniles, transients, homeless persons, institutionalized persons, or persons living in temporary or single-room occupancies) are likely to have higher than average levels of victimization, which will be missing or underrepresented in the NCVS estimates.

Also, as a questionnaire survey, the NCVS is also subject to several response biases common to almost all surveys. These include memory errors (e.g., the inability to accurately recall the frequency of an event), errors in interpretation (e.g., a misunderstanding of the exact content of questions or responses), and errors of deception (e.g., an unwillingness to report embarrassing events). The magnitude and frequency of such errors is variable across surveys, depending on question wording, the kinds of behaviors on which the questions focus, the questionnaire's format, the method by which the questionnaire is administered, and the social context of the interview. Although all surveys are subject to such errors, the NCVS actually is less susceptible because of its extensive testing and modification over the years (e.g., Turner 1981). Extensive studies and periodic modifications of survey procedures have greatly reduced these errors and their biasing effects on survey results.

A third source of concern is that the NCVS may not be equally valid for all types of crime and categories of victims, even within conventional predatory crimes of violence and theft. For example, researchers have noted an underreporting bias for incidents of sexual assault and sexual abuse, especially when the victim and offender are well acquainted (Eigenberg 1990; Kilpatrick et al. 1985; Koss, Gidycz, and Wisniewski 1987). This has resulted in the underestimation of the incidence of sexual assault, as well as an exaggerated picture of the problem of sexual violence by strangers relative to that by acquaintances and intimates. Respondents can be reluctant to report incidents of sexual abuse, because they involve very personal, embarrassing, or painful experiences (Turner 1981). Critics of rape estimates from the NCVS (e.g., Chappell 1989; Eigenberg 1990) have also noted that the NCVS did not ask direct questions about sexual victimization and other sensitive topics, ostensibly due to reluctance by the Bureau of the Census, who administers the survey. None of the screening questions explicitly asked about sexual victimization; it was asked through a general "miscellaneous assault" question at the end of the screening form: "Were you attacked in any other way?" Use of such indirect questions has magnified response difficulty for embarrassed or uncertain respondents, because it may not have been clear whether the question is asking about the kind of experiences they had.

Use of indirect, nonspecific questions resulted in interpretational problems with whether respondents will label and categorize forcible sex by an intimate as a criminal attack or a crime of rape. The NCVS's use of the word *attack* to ask about forcible sexual experiences assumed that respondents would interpret this term in its legal sense as unconsenting sexual contact. However, surveys describing sexual abuse behaviorally, rather than legalistically, have suggested otherwise. Such surveys have reported substantially higher rates of sexual assault and abuse—especially offenses by intimates, spouses, and friends—than the NCVS does (e.g., Ageton 1983; Kilpatrick et al. 1985; Koss et al. 1987).

Recently, the NCVS has been revised to address these kinds of weaknesses. The revised version provides more detailed questions and probes about victimizations, especially incidents of violence; also, the wordings have been modified to be more descriptive and specific, rather than general and legalistic. Comparative analysis of data from the new versus the old versions of the NCVS shows that expanded and more direct questioning results in increased levels of reported victimization (Bureau of Justice Statistics 1994). How far the new procedures go to address the limitations of the traditional NCVS form remains an open question not clearly answerable. However, they do represent a change toward increased validity.

Another problematic topic for the NCVS has involved domestic or family violence (Straus and Gelles 1990; Weis 1989). Validation studies have shown that the closer the relationship between the victim and offender, the less likely that the victimization would be revealed to an interviewer (Turner 1981; Koss, Dinero, and Seibel 1988). This reflects considerations similar to the measurement of sexual violence (Straus and Gelles 1990). The assaults frequently are viewed by victims as personal matters (in contrast to crime, which is a public matter) that are not comfortably disclosed to strangers, especially official interviewers from the government (Straus and Gelles 1990). The other complication is the ambiguity in labeling acts of force against family members—acts that would clearly be crimes if committed against non-family members. Being hit by a parent or spouse may not be defined by the victim as a criminal assault or "attack." Rather, it may be viewed as "harsh spanking" or "rough punishment." The recently revised NCVS questions include new questions about victimization by family members; however, they are still rather brief and vague prompts about this issue and their impact on domestic violence reporting is still not clear.

A third area of concern, which has drawn much less research attention, involves victimizations against younger persons, particularly adolescents and teenagers. Young respondents may be hesitant to talk about victimizations to an adult stranger who is also an official Bureau of the Census interviewer, particularly when most of the offenses are by either their peers (some of whom they know) or a family member (Hall and Flannery 1984). Being less conversant with legal labels and categories, young respondents also may interpret and label events differently than those intended in the NCVS questionnaire. Last, adolescents may be reluctant to reveal victimizations in which they themselves are involved in illegal activities. A number of studies report that there is substantial overlap between the experiences of being victimized and being involved in the victimization of others (e.g., Lauritsen, Sampson, and Laub 1991; McDermott 1983).

Although the NCVS problem areas of sexual abuse/assault and domestic violence have been studied and documented (as indicated previously), the third area involving younger respondents remains speculative. This is problematic, because juveniles as a group have the highest risk of victimization. According to NCVS results, the incidence of personal victimization for persons 16 to 19 years of age is two to three times higher than for persons 35 to 50 years of age

(Bureau of Justice Statistics 1980). Yet the crimes against younger victims are no less serious than crimes against adults in the degree to which they involve physical attacks, result in injuries, or require medical treatment (Whitaker and Bastian 1991). Because official record data are even less adequate for estimating crimes against younger persons (being less likely to be reported to the police), this gives additional relevance to the collection of victimization data that will be valid as well as reliable. With our increasing reliance on the NCVS to estimate and analyze crime patterns, this means that significant biases must be identified, estimated, and more fully taken into account.

VALIDATION OF NCVS ESTIMATES

The prior discussion raises several significant (and researchable) questions about victimization measurements and estimates on younger (i.e., adolescent) populations. To what extent are the NCVS data likely to yield less informative, more biased estimates of victimization for younger than for older persons? What is the magnitude and nature of the bias? Where (e.g., for what types of crimes or types of victims) is the bias most pronounced and problematic?

The most familiar method for validating any measurement is by comparing it to some independent factual standard taken to be a stable external reference point. This *criterion-related* validity is the degree to which measurements correspond directly with the given criterion event. The use of record checks and reverse-record checks are familiar examples of this strategy. However, for most crime measurements, this approach is generally limited by the lack of a clear, a priori validation criterion. An alternative strategy, where no such validity criterion exists, is to examine patterns of correlation and agreement among separate, but fallible, alternative indicators of the same phenomenon. In *convergent validation,* multiple (fallible) measures jointly serve to validate each other through consistent patterns of agreement when measuring the same phenomena and intelligible patterns of disagreement when measuring different things. Beyond simple convergence, disagreement among alternative measures also may be informative, if the discrepancies correspond to distinct differences in measurement procedures (i.e., "methods effects"). Analysis of the latter is termed *discriminant* validity.

The analyses of NCVS bias in measuring sexual victimization and domestic violence have relied on the convergent validation strategy, because there is no objective external criterion. As noted earlier, alternative studies of sexual assaults and violence within the family provide very different estimates of violent events from those provided by the NCVS, indicating dramatically higher levels of sexual and family violence than indicated by NCVS data. These discrepancies are too large and consistent across independent studies to result simply from sampling variation, including several national, random-sample surveys (e.g., Koss et al. 1988; Straus and Gelles 1990). The differences seem to be due mainly to features of the questionnaires, question content, and to their presentation within interview contexts. The social context of the NCVS interview (a formal questionnaire administered by an official interviewer from the Bureau of the Census in the household with other family members present) is not designed to elicit sensitive, potentially embarrassing or painful, personal disclosures. Thus the discrepancies in results between the NCVS and other surveys suggest fairly substantial threats to the NCVS's validity as an accurate measure of these types of victimizations.

The present study evaluates the validity of NCVS data for adolescent respondents (i.e., 13 years and older) by examining its convergence with comparable data on adolescent experiences from other surveys. In doing this, two distinct kinds of comparisons are relevant. First are the consistencies or inconsistencies in the *overall level* of victimization for this age group. Do the NCVS data consistently underestimate the amount of criminal victimization that occurs to adolescents, compared to alternative data sources? How large and explicable does the underestimation seem to be? Second are the convergence and discrepancies between the different data sources in terms of *comparative patterns* of victimizations (e.g., male versus female, White versus non-White, young versus old)? Do the NCVS data reflected show similar differentials in victimization between major social categories of victims, compared with alternative data sources? This second set of comparisons concerns whether any measurement bias in the NCVS is complex and variable rather than simple and constant. The implications of this second type of bias are more serious, suggesting that (a) there is no general statistical adjustment that can be made, and (b) the validity of all comparative analyses will be threatened.

RESEARCH METHOD

Data

Surveys that provide plausible, reliable alternative estimates of juvenile victimizations are necessary for comparison with the NCVS data set. Each survey needs to (a) be fairly large (to minimize errors of estimation from sampling variability and yield consistent estimates of statistically rare events); (b) involve a national probability sample of adolescents (between the ages of 12 and 20) so that results will be generalizable and comparable in scope to the NCVS; and (c) include standardized questions about victimization experiences with questions and response categories comparable to those used in the NCVS interview.

Using the Criminal Justice Archives at the InterUniversity Consortium of Political and Social Research, three survey data sets were identified that seemed to match the criteria listed above: the National Youth Survey (Elliott, Huizinga, and Ageton 1985), the Monitoring the Future survey (Bachman, O'Malley, and Johnston 1978), and the National Survey of Children (collected by Zill, Furstenberg, and Peterson). However, the third survey was subsequently dropped from this analysis, because victimization measurements were not parallel with the NCVS. The full range of victimization questions was asked only in the first National Survey of Children when the respondents were between 7 and 12 years of age, an age not directly covered in the NCVS (but included only by proxy). A later wave in the National Survey of Children panel (when respondents were between 17 and 22 years old) did include a measure of sexual assault victimization. However, the time frame for this item was unbounded (i.e., has this "ever happened"?) and not comparable to the 1-year restriction of the NCVS estimates and the other surveys.

The National Youth Survey is a longitudinal study of adolescent experiences and behavior that has focused particularly on drug use and other delinquent behaviors among 1,725 youths who were between the ages of 12 and 17 in 1976 (Elliott et al. 1985). It used a national probability sample to which five yearly interviews were administered between 1977 and 1981. This survey is noteworthy for its national sample, its use of delinquency and victimization questions that correspond closely to official categories, its use of follow-up probes to minimize counting trivial incidents of deviance, and its very low respondent dropout rate over the 5-year interval (see Elliott et al. 1985, for more complete information).

The Monitoring the Future survey is part of a continuing series of annual surveys of U.S. high school seniors concerning many attitudes, aspirations, and experiences (Bachman et al. 1978). It includes a national probability sample of over 16,000 persons mostly between the ages of 16 and 19. The core questions on the Monitoring the Future survey deal with drug use (reflecting its main funding source at the National Institute on Drug Abuse), but subsections of the survey (administered to different subsets of the total sample) consider a variety of issues, including illegal behaviors and victimization experiences.

Because of restrictions on the handling of hierarchical data files, we used the "person-level" data files for the 1978 NCVS. These rectangular files include all persons who reported being victimized during the prior 6 months plus a 10% sample of all persons who reported no victimizations. To achieve representative estimates of the general population, data for nonvictim respondents were weighted by a multiplicative factor of 10.

To maximize the amount of information available for analytic comparisons, we selected the 1978 surveys from each data set, because the National Youth Survey's data on victimization are most complete for this year (with a full set of victimization questions and the least amount of missing data). The specific year of data collection was less important for the other two surveys (Monitoring the Future and the NCVS), because they have been collected annually in similar form since 1976 and 1973, respectively; through 1985, the format of each survey remained basically unchanged (not counting the current ongoing revision of the NCVS).

To maintain comparability across data sets, our samples were restricted to persons between the ages of 13 and 19. For purposes of comparison, age was dichotomized: 13 to 15 and 16 to 19 years old. Our total effective sample sizes were somewhat reduced because of this restriction on age: NCVS (N = 6,108, weighted); National Youth Survey (N = 1,626); Monitoring the Future (N = 3,606).

Operational Measures

Victimization items on the National Youth Survey and the Monitoring the Future survey questionnaire are worded to correspond fairly closely to the screening questions of the NCVS. (For comparison, actual questions from all three surveys are reproduced in the appendix.) The National Youth Survey contains several separate items about particular forms of assault or theft (i.e., sexual assault, assault by a parent, and robbery) that compare closely to similar information in the NCVS. These items were analyzed separately. The other items in the National Youth Survey and Monitoring the Future were combined into summary indexes of *violent* and *personal theft* victimizations that correspond closely to the violence and theft summary indexes reported in NCVS statistics. In sum, this yields comparable summary estimates of violent victimization (including reports of assault by someone other than a parent, robbery, and rape) and personal theft (including reports of personal larceny events as reported on the NCVS) for all three surveys. In addition, for two of the surveys (National Youth Survey and NCVS) there are separate estimates of specific forms of victimization involving assaults by a parent, sexual assaults, and robbery. This specific information was not asked on the Monitoring the Future questionnaire. We are particularly interested in these latter items, because they are likely to be sensitive to differential willingness to respond.

Victimization is measured in two different ways. *Incidence* measures focus on the frequency of victimization *events* within the measurement period (i.e., how many victimizing acts occurred). *Prevalence* measures focus on the number of victims as the frequency of *persons* within the sample who were victimized at least once during the previous year (i.e., how many persons have been victims). These two measures provide clearly related yet analytically distinct forms of information. Our analysis focuses primarily on prevalence estimates for comparing the three surveys, although we also estimated and compared the incidence of juvenile victimizations.

Incidence estimates seem less informative for several reasons. First, not all surveys coded frequency of victimization in exactly the same way. The NCVS and the National Youth Survey questionnaires recorded the actual number reported by the victim respondent; in the Monitoring the Future questionnaire, frequency was coded as a five-category scale (with 0 being the smallest and 4 the largest number that could be recorded) that may truncate reports of multiple victimizations and attenuate the estimates of overall incidence in the sample. Second, the 1978 NCVS counted "series victimizations" (i.e., a continuing sequence of recurring victimization over an extended period of time) as single victimization events. In contrast, the National Youth Survey and the Monitoring the Future survey coded such series as multiple victimizations. Third, incidence estimates are more sensitive to reporting errors in the direction of exaggerated victimization. That is, one or two extreme scores (e.g., a person reporting being beaten up or robbed 50 times during the previous year because it seemed like it happened at least once a week) will have a dramatic effect on estimates of incidence. This is particularly true for more serious forms of victimization that are rare and thus reported by only a small number of respondents. One person who reports an unusually large number will greatly inflate the total for the entire sample of reported victims.

Prevalence estimates will not suffer from these problems, because each victim is counted only once. Exaggeration bias is eliminated, because a respondent who reports victimization is counted only once, regardless of how many events he or she reports during the measurement period. A few exaggerated responses will have a negligible effect on the overall estimates. For the same reason, differences due to differential coding of "series victimization" are also eliminated in prevalence measures. Thus our analysis differs from the usual NCVS analyses of victimization by giving more analytic weight to prevalence rather than incidence statistics, although both types of information are examined.

The prevalence figures computed from the NCVS overestimate "true" prevalence by a small but unknown amount. This is due to a data structure problem for the person-level data files used in this analysis—that is, the NCVS's data covered victimizations during the previous 6 months rather than the 1-year period covered in the National Youth Survey and the Monitoring the Future survey. Victim responses for the other 6 months of the year were not directly recoverable from the data—a rectangular person-level data set grouped into four separate quarterly files. Because of this file structure, we were unable to merge half-year data from the separate quarterly files to produce full-year information for the exact same respondents. We estimated annual prevalence by doubling the 6-month prevalence numbers. This procedure will inflate annual prevalence estimates slightly, because some persons with multiple victimizations spread throughout the year are in effect counted twice (as two victims). However, we estimate that the inflation is not great (less than 10% maximum), and our approximation provides a very usable ballpark comparison figure. Moreover, this approximation errs in a conservative direction, because the net effect will be to somewhat inflate the NCVS prevalence figures (which we expect to be lower than the comparable figures for the National Youth Survey and the Monitoring the Future survey).

RESULTS

Our initial question about convergence among the different survey estimates is concerned with overall levels of victimization. Do different surveys produce similar pictures of criminal victimization for adolescents in the United States? Table 1 reports prevalence estimates computed for the two summary indicators of violent victimizations and theft victimizations as well as estimates from the NCVS and National Youth Survey on three specific indicators of robbery, sexual assault, and assault by a parent.

The pattern of results in Table 1 is consistent and striking. First, the victim prevalence estimates from our alternative surveys (National Youth Survey and Monitoring the Future) are very similar in magnitude and show impressive convergence for estimates of victim prevalence. The National Youth Survey

Table 1. Comparison of Victim Prevalence Estimates[a]

	SURVEYS		
Type of Victimization	NCVS[b]	National Youth Survey	Monitoring the Future
Violent	6.6	26.7	25.8
Theft	13.7	37.7	46.1
Robbery	0.8	15.6	—
Sexual assault	0.1	2.1	—
Assault by parent	0	2.7	—

[a]Number of respondents victimized within the past year per 100 persons in the survey.

[b]NCVS = National Crime Victimization Survey.

estimates that about 27% of the youth sample was victimized by a violent act in the previous year, whereas the Monitoring the Future survey yields an estimate of around 26%. For theft victimizations, the comparable estimates are 38% (National Youth Survey) and 46% (Monitoring the Future). These estimates are surprisingly high and dramatically greater than our estimates for the NCVS sample: approximately four times higher for violence and three times higher for theft victimizations.

The comparisons for our specific offenses are even more discrepant. The prevalence estimates for robbery and sexual assault from the National Youth Survey are roughly 20 times the prevalence estimates from the NCVS: 15.6% versus 0.8% for robbery; 2.1% versus 0.1% for sexual assault (counting both boys and girls as the reference population). The prevalence of parental assault cannot be compared statistically, because *zero* respondents in the NCVS adolescent sample reported being assaulted by a parent. In contrast, 2.7% of the respondents in the National Youth Survey reported being "beaten up" by a parent within the prior year.

If we look at incidence rather than prevalence measures, the results are very similar. Table 2 reports the incidence estimates for victimizations in the three samples. Again, the estimates for the National Youth Survey and the Monitoring the Future survey have close agreement with each other but diverge greatly from the estimates from the NCVS on each of the crime categories. The alternative survey estimates are roughly eight times higher than the NCVS on violence and five to six times higher on theft. The estimated incidence of sexual assault is roughly 13 times higher on the National Youth Survey. As with prevalence, the differences are even greater for robbery (34.0 versus 1.0), as well as for assaults by parents where the estimated incidence for the National Youth Survey is 11.0 (per 100 persons), whereas the NCVS estimates the incidence to be 0.0.

The second analytical question in comparing different measures of victimization concerns the issue of differential or comparative bias. Data relevant to this question are presented in Table 3, which reports prevalence estimates for

Table 2. Comparison of Victim Incidence Estimates[a]

Type of Victimization	SURVEYS NCVS[b]	National Youth Survey	Monitoring the Future
Violent	7.0	60.0	58.0
Theft	14.6	85.0	87.0
Robbery	1.0	34.0	—
Sexual assault	0.3	4.0	—
Assault by parent	0	11.0	—

[a]Number of victimization incidents within the past year per 100 persons in the survey.

[b]NCVS = National Crime Victimization Survey.

Table 3. Comparison of Victim Prevalence Estimates[a] by Age, Race, and Sex

Type of Victimization	SURVEYS NCVS[b]	National Youth Survey	Monitoring the Future
Part A			
Age			
12–15	6.6	28.3	—
16–19	6.6	26.4	25.8
Race			
White	6.6	27.0	24.5
Black	6.8	28.0	29.0
Sex			
Female	2.1	16.5	19.6
Male	4.5	36.8	31.9
Part B			
Age			
12–15	13.5	38.6	—
16–19	13.9	37.5	46.1
Race			
White	14.4	37.3	46.1
Black	10.0	40.3	45.8
Sex			
Female	12.5	32.3	41.1
Male	15.4	43.0	51.0

[a]Number of respondents victimized within the past year per 100 persons in the survey.

[b]NCVS = National Crime Victimization Survey.

males versus females, Black versus White adolescents, and younger (13–15) versus older (16–19) adolescents. Part A of Table 3 reports on violent victimizations, and Part B contains results for nonviolent theft victimizations. These results suggest that the three surveys are in general agreement about the *relative* or differential magnitudes of victimization across basic social-demographic categories.

Despite differences in absolute levels of victimization, comparisons of age, race, and sex yield very similar patterns across the different data sources. All three surveys show the same "no-difference" pattern across age and race comparisons. The NCVS prevalence estimates are virtually identical for younger (13–15 years) and older (16–19 years) adolescents, on both violence (6.6% vs. 6.6%) and theft (13.5% vs. 13.9%). The National Youth Survey shows only trivially different age rates, with younger adolescents having marginally higher estimated prevalence than older respondents (28.3% vs. 26.4% for violence; 38.6% vs. 37.5% for theft). Such differences are well within normal sampling variations. Racial comparisons show some small differentials, but again they are within normal sampling variability and inconsistent in the direction of race differences. Comparisons by sex yield a very similar pattern of sex differences on all three surveys, in which prevalence rates for both violence and theft are higher for males than for females. The male-to-female ratio of violent victimizations is slightly over 2 (about 2.2) for both the NCVS and the National Youth Survey and slightly under 2 (1.6) for the Monitoring the Future survey. For theft victimization, the estimated male-to-female ratios are even more uniform, hovering around 1.2–1.3 for all three data sources. This pattern of close agreement for comparisons suggests that the biases that do occur in these surveys are relatively simple and general; they do not seem to involve more complex patterns of bias that are variable across different kinds of victims.

DISCUSSION

The results described in the previous section show notable disagreements and agreements among alternative data sources on juvenile victimizations. They raise some provocative questions about the uses and interpretations of NCVS data on victimization in adolescent respondents. The patterns are large enough and consistent enough that they cannot be dismissed as trivial methodological variation or mere sampling fluctuations. Several particular patterns merit serious consideration.

One is the striking degree of convergence between the National Youth Survey and the Monitoring the Future survey results. Using fairly different procedures—for example, sampling designs, modes of questionnaire administration, item wordings and formats—they nonetheless yield very similar estimates of juvenile victimization. This convergence holds across different categories of criminal offenses and applies to both prevalence and incidence estimators. This pattern provides convergent validation for these two different measures of adolescent victimization experiences.

A second striking pattern is the consistently large discrepancy in victimization levels between the NCVS and the two alternative surveys. The differences are not a fractional matter of a few percentage points but rather are multiplicative, where one set of estimates is several (or many) times larger than the alternative estimates. The victimization rates for general violence from the alternative surveys are four times larger than the corresponding rates from the NCVS. The National Youth Survey and the Monitoring the Future survey rates of nonviolent theft victims are roughly three times higher than NCVS estimates for prevalence measures and five to six times higher for incidence measures. The differentials are even larger for specific forms of violence. Estimated rates of robbery and sexual assault are 20 times higher on the National Youth Survey than for the NCVS; no comparison with Monitoring the Future rates is possible because these specific items were not asked on that survey. The differential for assaults by parents is "infinitely" larger, because according to the NCVS data, *none* of these incidents occurred, whereas the National Youth Survey data estimate that 2%–3% of the survey respondents had been assaulted by a parent in the previous year.

How can such large differences be explained? They are too large and consistent to be dismissed as normal sampling fluctuations or due to slight variations in item wording. The simplest explanation would account for them as a result of technical/procedural differences between the surveys. Lauritsen et al. (1991; Lauritsen, Laub, and Sampson 1992) parenthetically mentioned the patterns detailed in the results section, but dismissed them as due to three technical deviations (Lauritsen et al. 1991, p. 275). One was the inclusion of series victimizations as multiple victimization events on the alternative surveys (National Youth Survey and Monitoring the Future) although they are counted only as single victimizations on the NCVS. This seems plausible and is consistent with the larger discrepancies in the incidence estimates. However, it cannot explain the large (fourfold) differential on victim prevalence estimates between the NCVS and the alternative surveys, because prevalence measures count series victimization singly on all three data sets. A second reason cited was the use on the NCVS of proxy interviews for 12- and 13-year-old respondents (a procedure used until 1986), which could have led to underreporting for such interviews. However, examining age differentials in reported victimization, the results show that this effect is very slight. Also, disparities in victimization rates between the NCVS and the alternative surveys are just as large for older adolescent respondents (15 to 19 years old), where proxy interviews were not used.

The third factor cited by Lauritsen et al. (1992) involved the effects of different question formats across the surveys. Although plausible, this fades on closer examination, because the victimization items on the National Youth Survey and the Monitoring the Future survey are as different from each other as they are from the NCVS, yet they yield very similar results. In fact, there are larger differences in item response formats between the National Youth Survey and Monitoring the Future questionnaires than between the National Youth Survey and NCVS questionnaires. Inspection of the victimization items on the different surveys (see appendix) suggests that the wording differences intimated by Lauritsen et al. (1992) are too slight to explain the very large differences in the results found. Moreover, the modes of survey administration are different on the Monitoring the Future survey and the National Youth Survey (i.e., anonymous self-administered questionnaires on Monitoring the Future versus face-to-face interviews on the National Youth Survey), whereas the National Youth Survey and the NCVS are the same mode (i.e., interviews on both). Procedurally, the National Youth Survey is more like the NCVS than it is like the Monitoring the Future survey; thus "common methods factors" cannot explain the patterns.

Other technical differences might be considered. First, because alternative surveys lack the detailed follow-up interviews that provide error checks for the NCVS, the alternative data may be inflated by reports of more trivial victimizations (i.e., personal encounters that are deviant, unpleasant, and unfortunate but noncriminal). That criticism, paralleling common criticisms of self-reported delinquency surveys, is plausible for the Monitoring the Future survey but not for the National Youth Survey (which does use follow-up probes by trained interviewers to minimize this problem). Moreover, it would not be sufficient to account for the large size of the differences. Although not highly legalistic, the wording of questions on the Monitoring the Future survey and the National Youth Survey are not phrased in terms that would elicit trivial incidents or misunderstood responses.

A final consideration is that the National Youth Survey and the Monitoring the Future survey questions might be less valid because they are not completely "bounded." Unlike the NCVS, no baseline interviews or follow-up interviews were used on the National Youth Survey or the Monitoring the Future survey to verify that the reported victimizations actually occurred within the specified 1-year measurement period. These alternative surveys depended only on the respondents' memories for correct temporal location of events. Thus reports on the alternative victim surveys may have been subject to "forward telescoping" that inflated their victimization estimates. Events reported as occurring within the past year might actually have occurred some time before the measurement period. This problem does seem likely on the National Youth Survey and the Monitoring the Future survey. However, the inflation of incidence estimates from telescoping distortions will be modest and fractional, as well as offset by memory decay errors. O'Brien (1985, p. 51) suggested an inflation factor of 30% to 40% (cited from an unpublished Bureau of the Census memo), which is clearly not large enough to account for the fivefold increases observed in these data. Measures of victim prevalence will be even less affected by this problem, resulting in even smaller degrees of inflation.

In addition to the strong convergence between our two alternative data sources, the National Youth Survey and the Monitoring the Future survey results also correspond closely with the findings from other surveys that have estimated victimization. For instance, Koss et al. (1987) estimated sexual assault rates to be 10 to 15 times the number reported by the NCVS. Using the National Youth Survey, we estimated the incidence of sexual assault to be approximately 13 times the NCVS figure. Straus and Gelles (1990), using the 1985 National Family Violence Survey, reported that 2.1% of youths aged 15 to 17 experienced acts of "very severe violence" from their parents during the prior year. Our analysis of the National Youth Survey data estimated a yearly rate of assault by parents of 2.7%. Although none of these smaller surveys alone can definitely validate or invalidate NCVS results, together they make a much stronger case when there is such strong convergence among themselves despite their methodological differences.

In sum, the large discrepancies in estimated levels of criminal victimization of adolescents between the NCVS and alternative national surveys of adolescent experiences cannot be dismissed as mere technical deviations or explained as measurement or sampling error. Rather, they may reflect more substantial differences in the social dynamics of the interviews by which the survey data are elicited from adolescent respondents. For example, Koss (1992) has previously identified the importance for getting valid reports on sexual violence victimizations of establishing rapport with survey respondents, of assuring confidentiality of information, and of avoiding the contextual activation of stereotyped responses (which are prompted by official or legalistic labels and categories). Straus and Gelles (1990) have noted the importance of similar issues in valid and complete responding on family violence victimization questions.

To this point, similar considerations have not been applied to surveys of adolescent respondents as victims. It seems important, given the striking pattern of results reported here, to study more carefully the nature of the interview as a social event, to evaluate the differential validity of this procedure for adolescent respondents (as well as other special groups), and to consider development of alternative or supplemental surveys that will be less subject to such biases. The school crime supplement (Bastian and Taylor 1991) represents a move in this direction, but it provides only a slight expansion in the content of the questions (to specifically ask about school-related victimizations); it does not appreciably change the information-eliciting procedures used or the social dynamics of the interview.

Although the NCVS measures of victimization are quite useful for general estimates of criminal victimization, they provide uncertain estimates with adolescent respondents. Caution is required in making any overall estimates of the level of teenage victimization or of rate differentials between younger and older respondents. Additional efforts are needed to develop procedures more appropriate to this category of victims (who constitute the most frequently victimized segment of the population).

APPENDIX: VICTIMIZATION QUESTIONNAIRE ITEMS

Monitoring the Future survey

A20: During the last 12 months, how often

a. Has something of yours (worth under $50) been stolen? (THEFT)

b. Has something of yours (worth over $50) been stolen? (THEFT)

c. Has someone deliberately damaged your property (your car, clothing, etc.)? (VANDAL)

d. Has someone injured you with a weapon (like a knife, gun, or club)? (VIOLENT)

e. Has someone threatened you with a weapon, but not actually injured you? (THREAT)

f. Has someone injured you on purpose without using a weapon? (VIOLENT)

g. Has an unarmed person threatened you with injury, but not actually injured you? (THREAT)

Response categories

1. Not at all
2. Once
3. Twice
4. 3 or 4 times
5. 5 or more times

National Survey of Youth—1978

How many times in the last year ("from Christmas a year ago to the Christmas just past")

a. Has something been taken directly from you or an attempt made to do so by force or threatening to hurt? (ROB)(VIOLENT)

b. Have you been beaten up by your mother or father? (ASSAULT-PARENT)

c. Has your car, motorcycle, or bike been stolen or an attempt to do so? (THEFT)

d. Have things been taken from your car, motorcycle, or bike such as hub-caps, books or packages, or bike locks? (THEFT)

e. Have any of your things been damaged on purpose, such as car or bike tires slashed or books and clothing ripped up? (VANDALISM)

f. Have some of your things such as your jacket, notebooks, or sports equipment been stolen from a public place such as a school cafeteria, restaurant, or bowling alley? (THEFT)

g. Have you been sexually attacked or raped or an attempt to do so? (ASSAULT-SEX)

h. Have you been attacked with a weapon such as a gun, knife, bottle, or chair by someone other than your mother or father? (VIOLENT)

i. Have you been beaten up or threatened with being beaten up by someone other than your mother or father? (VIOLENT)

j. Has your pocket been picked or your purse or wallet snatched or an attempt to do so? (PICKPOCKET)

Response categories

Number is provided to indicate frequency (up to 3 digits)

National Crime Victimization Survey

During the past 6 months

a. Did you have your (pocket picked/purse snatched)? (PICKPOCKET)

b. Did anyone take something (else) directly from you by using force, such as by a stickup, mugging, or threat? (ROB)(VIOLENT)

c. Did anyone *try* to rob you by using force or threatening to harm you? (other than the incidents already mentioned) (ROB)(VIOLENT)

d. Did anyone beat you up, attack you, or hit you with something, such as a rock or bottle? (other than the incidents already mentioned) (VIOLENT)

e. Were you knifed, shot at, or attacked with some other weapon by anyone at all? (other than the incidents already mentioned) (VIOLENT)

f. Did anyone *try* to attack you in some other way? (other than any incidents already mentioned) (VIOLENT)

g. Did anyone steal things that belonged to you from inside *any* car or truck, such as packages or clothing? (THEFT)

h. Was anything stolen from you while you were away from home, for instance at work, in a theater or restaurant, or while traveling? (THEFT)

i. (Other than any incidents you've already mentioned) was anything (else) at all stolen from you during the last 6 months? (THEFT)

REFERENCES

Ageton, Suzanne S. 1983. *Sexual Assault Among Adolescents.* Lexington, MA: Lexington Books.

Bachman, Jerald, Patrick M. O'Malley, and Lloyd Johnston. 1978. *Monitoring the Future: A Continuing Study of the Lifestyles and Values of Youth.* Ann Arbor: University of Michigan, Institute for Social Research.

Bastian, Lisa D. and Bruce M. Taylor. 1991. *School Crime: A National Crime Victimization Survey Report.* Washington, DC: U.S. Department of Justice, Bureau of Justice Statistics.

Biderman, Albert D. and J. P. Lynch. 1991. *Understanding Crime Incidence Statistics: Why the UCR Diverges From the NCS.* New York: Springer-Verlag.

Biderman, Albert D. and Albert J. Reiss. 1967. "On Exploring the 'Dark Figure' of Crime." *Annals of the American Academy of Political and Social Science* 374:1–15.

Bureau of Justice Statistics. 1980. *Criminal Victimization in the United States 1978.* Washington, DC: U.S. Department of Justice.

———. 1994. *Technical Background on the Redesigned National Crime Victimization Survey* (Bulletin No. NCJ-151172). Washington, DC: U.S. Department of Justice.

Chappell, Duncan. 1989. "Sexual Criminal Violence." Pp. 68–108 in *Pathways to Criminal Violence,* edited by N. A. Weiner and M. E. Wolfgang. Newbury Park, CA: Sage.

Eigenberg, Helen M. 1990. "The National Crime Survey and Rape: The Case of the Missing Question." *Justice Quarterly* 7:655–71.

Elliott, Delbert S., David Huizinga, and Suzanne S. Ageton. 1985. *Explaining Delinquency and Drug Use.* Beverly Hills, CA: Sage.

Garofalo, James. 1990. "The National Crime Survey 1973–1986: Strengths and Limitations of a Very Large Data Set." Pp. 75–97 in *Measuring Crime: Large-Scale, Long-Range Efforts,* edited by D. L. MacKenzie, P. J. Baunach, and R. R. Roberg. Albany: State University of New York Press.

Gilbert, Neil. 1994. "Miscounting Social Ills." *Society* 32:18–26.

Gottfredson, Michael. 1986. "Substantive Contributions of Victimization Surveys." Pp. 251–87 in *Crime and Justice: Annual Review of Research,* Vol. 7, edited by M. Tonry and N. Morris. Chicago: University of Chicago Press.

Gove, Walter, M. Hughes, and Michael Geerken. 1985. "Are Uniform Crime Reports a Valid Indicator of the Index Crime? An Affirmative Answer With Minor Qualifications." *Criminology* 23:451–501.

Hall, Eleanor R. and Patricia J. Flannery. 1984. "Prevalence and Correlates of Sexual Assault Experiences in Adolescents." *Victimology* 9:398–406.

Jackson, Patrick G. 1990. "Sources of Data." Pp. 21–50 in *Measurement Issues in Criminology,* edited by K. L. Kempf. New York: Springer-Verlag.

Kilpatrick, Dean G., Connie L. Best, Lois J. Veronen, Angelynne E. Amick, Lorenz A. Villeponteaux, and Gary A. Ruff. 1985. "Mental Health Correlates of Criminal Victimization: A Random Community Survey." *Journal of Consulting and Clinical Psychology* 53:866–73.

Koss, Mary P. 1992. "Defending Date Rape." *Journal of Interpersonal Violence* 7:121–26.

Koss, Mary P., Thomas E. Dinero, and Cynthia A. Seibel. 1988. "Stranger and Acquaintance Rape." *Psychology of Women Quarterly* 12:1–24.

Koss, Mary P., Chris Gidycz, and Nadine Wisniewski. 1987. "The Scope of Rape: Incidence and Prevalence of Sexual Aggression and Victimization in a National Sample of Higher Education Students." *Journal of Consulting and Clinical Psychology* 55:162–70.

Lauritsen, Janet L., John H. Laub, and Robert J. Sampson. 1992. "Conventional and Delinquent Activities: Implications for Prevention of Violent Victimization Among Adolescents." *Violence and Victims* 7:91–108.

Lauritsen, Janet L., Robert J. Sampson, and John H. Laub. 1991. "The Link Between Offending and Victimization Among Adolescents." *Criminology* 29:265–91.

MacKenzie, Doris Layton, Phyllis J. Baunach, and Roy R. Roberg, eds. 1990. *Measuring Crime: Large-Scale, Long-Range Efforts.* Albany: State University of New York Press.

McDermott, Joan. 1983. "Crime in the School and in the Community: Offenders, Victims, and Fearful Youths." *Crime & Delinquency* 29:270–82.

O'Brien, Robert M.. 1985. *Crime and Victimization Data.* Beverly Hills, CA: Sage.

Skogan, Wesley G. 1977. "Dimensions of the 'Dark Figure' of Unreported Crime." *Crime & Delinquency* 23:41–50.

———. 1981. *Issues in the Measurement of Victimization.* Washington, DC: U.S. GPO, U.S. Department of Justice, Bureau of Justice Statistics.

———. 1984. "Reporting Crimes to the Police: The Status of World Research." *Journal of Research in Crime and Delinquency* 21:113–37.

Straus, Murray A. and Richard J. Gelles. 1990. "How Violent Are American Families? Estimates From the National Family Violence Resurvey and Other Studies." Pp. 95–112 in *Physical Violence in American Families,* edited by M. A. Straus and R. J. Gelles. New Brunswick, NJ: Transaction.

Turner, Anthony. 1981. "The San Jose Recall Study." Pp. 22–27 in *The National*

Crime Survey: Working Papers, Vol. 1, edited by R. Lehnen and W. Skogan. Washington, DC: U.S. Department of Justice.

Weis, Joseph. 1989. "Family Violence Research Methodology and Design." Pp. 117–62 in *Crime and Justice: Annual Review of Research,* Vol. 11, edited by L. Ohlin and M. Tonry. Chicago: University of Chicago Press.

Whitaker, Catherine J. and Lisa D. Bastian. 1991. *Teenage Victims: A National Crime Survey Report.* Washington, DC: U.S. Department of Justice, Bureau of Justice Statistics.

DISCUSSION QUESTIONS

1. What types of data were used by the authors in order to examine juvenile victimization?
2. Why do multiple measures of the same phenomena yield different results and estimates?
3. Why is it important to validate the instruments used in criminal justice research?
4. What did the authors conclude in this study?

14

Racial Prejudice and Support for the Death Penalty by Whites

STEVEN E. BARKAN, University of Maine
STEVEN F. COHN, University of Maine

COMMENTARY

Our article, "Racial Prejudice and Support for the Death Penalty by Whites," concludes that racial prejudice against African Americans contributes to support by whites in the United States for the death penalty. Our data come from the General Social Survey (GSS), a large, random sample of the English-speaking, noninstitutionalized U.S. population that has been conducted regularly since the early 1970s. Because this is a random sample of the national population, our results can be safely generalized from our sample to the whole country.

Our article is a good example, we believe, of *secondary data analysis.* Secondary data analysis occurs when scholars analyze data that they themselves have not gathered. The GSS is an example of one such data set. The data are collected by the National Opinion Research Center in Chicago and made available to scholars across the world. Several thousand articles using GSS data have been published in academic journals during the last three decades.

As an example of secondary data analysis, our article illustrates both the advantages and disadvantages of such an approach. Let's first discuss the advantages, the most important of which have to do with time and money. Simply put, secondary data analysis permits scholars to carry out their research much more quickly and much more inexpensively than would be the case if they had to gather the data themselves. If the GSS or another suitable data set had not existed, we would have needed to gather our own national data to study racial

Source: Journal of Research in Crime and Delinquency, Vol. 31, No. 2, May 1994, 202–209.
© 1994 Sage Publications, Inc. Reprinted by permission of Sage Publications, Inc.

prejudice and death penalty attitudes. Among other things, we would have had to come up with suitable questions to include in our survey, and then we would have had to find a qualified organization to gather the data (probably with a telephone poll of a random sample of the U.S. population) and to prepare them for computer use. This all would have been a time-consuming and relatively expensive process, especially for professors like ourselves who teach in a small, undergraduate department that lacks the resources of departments at much larger universities.

If our article illustrates the advantages of secondary data analysis for criminal justice research, it also illustrates the disadvantages. Simply put, we, and other scholars who do secondary data analysis, are prisoners of the measures included in the data sets we analyze. We ordinarily do not get to choose how the variables included in the data sets are measured. Usually the measures are fine, but sometimes they are not ideal.

In our own article, the way death penalty attitudes are measured in the GSS data set we used was not ideal. The GSS asks, "Do you favor or oppose the death penalty for persons convicted of murder?" The possible responses to this question were "favor" and "oppose." Although this is a standard measure of views on the death penalty in the GSS and other national surveys, several scholars (e.g., Bowers, 1993; Williams et al., 1988) have noted that it does not allow for alternatives, such as life in prison without parole, which many people might prefer over the death penalty. We would have thus favored a measure of death penalty opinion that took these critiques into account, but did not have one available because we had to use what the GSS provided.

Would our results have been any different had we been able to use a better measure of death penalty opinion? We do not know, and we cannot know until we or someone else replicates our study with a better measure. And the fact that we do not and cannot know illustrates a shortcoming of at least some research relying on secondary data analysis.

Having said all this, we wish to emphasize that the lack of an ideal measure of death penalty opinion does not necessarily invalidate our findings. The measure we used was indeed a good, if not perfect, measure of death penalty opinion, and we assume that racial prejudice would still increase support by whites for the death penalty even with a better measure of death penalty opinion. Whether our assumption turns out to be true, of course, must await a future research project with such a measure.

ABSTRACT Although many studies have found that Whites are more likely than Blacks to support the death penalty, little research has investigated the reasons for this difference. Using data from the 1990 General Social Survey, this study finds that White support for capital punishment is associated with prejudice against Blacks. Final remarks discuss the implications of the results for legislative and judicial decisions regarding capital punishment.

Capital punishment continues to be one of the most controversial issues in crime and criminal justice in the United States. Reflecting the attention it has received, a number of studies have examined public opinion on the death penalty. Investigations have focused on the extent of support for the death penalty, the reasons for this support, and methodological problems in studying death penalty attitudes (Bohm 1987, 1991, 1992; Bowers 1993; Ellsworth and Ross 1983; Harris 1986; Rankin 1979; Sarat and Vidmar 1976; Skovron, Scott, and Cullen 1989; Thomas and Foster 1976; Tyler and Weber 1982; Vidmar and Ellsworth 1974; Warr and Stafford 1984; Williams, Longmire, and Gulick 1988; Young 1991, 1992). With the wide public support of the death penalty influencing recent U.S. Supreme Court decisions on its constitutionality (Bohm 1991; Bowers 1993; Ellsworth and Ross 1976; Finckenauer 1988) and also, one presumes, calls by legislators for its imposition, such studies continue to be important.

In this regard, investigations of death penalty opinion have long indicated substantial racial differences in support for capital punishment, with Whites far more likely than Blacks to favor it (Bohm 1991; Smith 1975; Stinchcombe et al. 1980; Vidmar and Ellsworth 1974). Although, in attempting to explain this difference, some observers (e.g., Young 1991) have speculated that White support for the death penalty may be partly motivated by racial prejudice, no study has yet assessed this possibility. Given recent evidence that support by Whites for harsher treatment of criminals derives partly from racial prejudice (Cohn, Barkan, and Halteman 1991), it is important to determine whether racial prejudice also underlies White support for the death penalty. Evidence of such an influence may have important implications for judicial and legislative actions on the death penalty and for theoretical debates in criminology on the nature of public attitudes toward crime and punishment (Cohn et al. 1991; Thomas, Cage, and Foster 1976).

This study investigates whether White support for the death penalty is, in fact, associated with racial prejudice. It uses data from the 1990 General Social Survey (GSS; Davis and Smith), which included a special module of items on racial attitudes and perceptions. These and other items in the 1990 GSS permit a systematic examination of the influence of racial prejudice on White support for the death penalty.

THE STUDY

The GSS is a random sample of the adult, noninstitutionalized population of the United States and has been conducted almost annually since 1972. The 1990 GSS included 1,150 Whites, 159 Blacks, and 63 members of other races; only Whites are included in this analysis.

We identified several items in the racial attitudes module of the 1990 GSS that we thought measured racial prejudice and thus might predict White support for the death penalty. Two items asked respondents to indicate the degree to which they favored or opposed (*strongly favor* to *strongly oppose*) "living in a neighborhood where half your neighbors were Blacks," and "having a close relative or family member marry a Black person." These items measure a sense of personal antipathy to Blacks that we thought would be especially likely to predict death penalty support.

Six additional items asked respondents to indicate on 7-point scales the degree to which they thought Blacks were lazy, unintelligent, desirous of living off welfare, unpatriotic, violent, and poor. A factor analysis distinguished these items from the antipathy measures. We thus weighted the two antipathy items by their factor loadings and summed the weighted scores into an Antipathy to Blacks scale (alpha reliability = .67). We similarly constructed a Racial Stereotyping scale from the items on Blacks' laziness, unintelligence, preferences for welfare, and lack of patriotism (alpha reliability = .69); higher scores on both scales indicate increasing racial prejudice. We excluded from the latter scale the item asking whether Blacks are more likely to be poor, because we judged it as not clearly indicating racial prejudice and because its factor loading, .40, was substantially lower than those for the other items. We also excluded the item on Blacks' violence after a reliability analysis indicated that inclusion of this item lowered the overall reliability of the scale containing the other measures.

We included several additional variables as controls in our list of independent variables. The first, political conservatism, was suggested by previous work linking conservatism to support by Whites for the death penalty (Young 1992) and to punitive treatment of criminals (Langworthy and Whitehead 1986). Although the inclusion of conservatism might attenuate the association of racial prejudice with death penalty support, we agree with Young (1992) that it results in a "more rigorous test" (p. 82) of this association.

The next two variables, membership in a fundamentalist church (Smith 1990) and attendance at religious services, were suggested by previous work linking fundamentalism and low levels of religiosity to White support for the death penalty (Young 1992) and by other recent research on fundamentalism and retributive attitudes (Grasmick, Davenport, Chamlin, and Bursik 1992; Grasmick, Morgan, and Kennedy 1992; Ellison and Sherkat 1993). The other religion items Young (1992) used from the 1988 GSS either were not included in the 1990 GSS or were asked only of a split sample.

The next variable, fear of crime, has also been hypothesized to predict punitiveness (Sheley 1985). Although the evidence for fear's effect on punitiveness is inconsistent (Cohn et al. 1991; Cullen, Clark, Cullen, and Mathers 1985; Langworthy and Whitehead 1986), we deemed it advisable to include fear of crime in our list of predictor variables. Our fear of crime measure derives from the GSS's standard variable asking respondents whether there is "any area right around here—that is, within a mile—where you would be afraid to walk alone at night." Although this measure is not without its problems (Ferraro and LaGrange 1987), it has been used in many previous studies to indicate fear of crime (e.g., Ortega and Miles 1987) and is the only such measure in the GSS.

Three other variables, education, age, and gender, have been found in previous research to affect support for capital punishment (Bohm 1991; Stinchcombe et al. 1980; Young 1991, 1992); such support generally decreases with education and increases with age, and is greater for men than for women.

Two final variables, Southern residence and population size of the respondent's place of interview, addressed aspects of respondents' residence. Although neither variable has received extensive attention in the death penalty opinion literature (but see Bohm 1991), we thought it advisable to include southern residence in view of potentially greater racial prejudice in the South and population size in view of the higher levels of violent crime in more urban areas.

The dependent variable, support for the death penalty, is measured by a standard GSS item: "Do you favor or oppose the death penalty for persons convicted of murder?" Although this item, like that on fear of crime, is not ideal (Harris 1986; Williams et al. 1988), it has been used in many previous studies and is the only measure in the 1990 GSS of attitudes toward capital punishment. In the 1990 GSS, 82.8% of White respondents said they favored the death penalty, compared to only 55.5% of Black respondents.

RESULTS

The first column of Table 1 lists the bivariate correlations of the predictor variables with support for the death penalty. The results indicate that White support for the death penalty is, as hypothesized, associated with antipathy to Blacks and with racial stereotyping. Following Young (1992), political conservatism is also associated with death penalty support, whereas the association for membership in a fundamentalist church just misses statistical significance ($p < .052$). Replicating previous research, education negatively predicts support, and men are more supportive than women. Finally, southern Whites are also slightly more supportive, whereas the remaining variables show no relationship.

Although these results tentatively support our expectation for our indicators of racial prejudice, multivariate analysis is obviously necessary to test for spuriousness. Because the dependent variable is dichotomous, logistic regression (SPSS 4.0) is an appropriate statistical technique (Hanushek and Jackson 1977).

The second column of Table 1 reports the multivariate results; missing cases were handled through listwise deletion. Antipathy to Blacks and racial stereotyping continue to predict death penalty support, as does political conservatism. In addition, men continue to be more supportive than women.

Somewhat surprisingly, the relationship between membership in a fundamentalist church and White support for the death penalty is not significant. Thinking that fundamentalism might be linked to racial prejudice (Gorsuch and Aleshire 1974; McFarland 1989), in a separate analysis we excluded the two measures of racial prejudice. In their absence, the coefficient for fundamentalist membership rose from its original –.01 to .18 but still remained statistically insignificant ($p < .22$); further exclusion of the political conservatism variable resulted in yet a higher coefficient, .28, but one that was still statistically insig-

Table 1. Bivariate Correlations (Pearson's *r*) and Logistic Regression Coefficients of Independent Variables with Support for the Death Penalty (one-tailed tests)

Independent Variable	r	B
Antipathy to Blacks	.17***	.26***
Racial stereotyping	.10**	.08*
Political conservatism	.18***	.30***
Fear of crime	.03	.25
Fundamentalist church	.05	–.01
Religious attendance	–.03	–.03
Education	–.09**	–.03
Age	.00	–.01
Gender (1 = male)	.07*	.37*
Southern residence	.06*	.07
Population size	.03	.00
Constant		–1.45
Goodness of fit		903.22

*$p < .05$; **$p < .01$; ***$p < .001$

nificant ($p < .11$). Although these results are not conclusive, they do suggest that fundamentalism may be linked to death penalty support partly through its association with racial prejudice and political conservatism. Further research is needed to test this possibility; if confirmed, the causal sequence we suggest would extend Young's (1992) work by further explaining the association between fundamentalism and death penalty support among Whites and reinforce previous conclusions (Gorsuch and Aleshire 1974; McFarland 1989) that fundamentalism is related to a general tendency toward prejudice.

DISCUSSION AND CONCLUSIONS

Bohm (1991) recently pointed to the relative paucity of research on U.S. public opinion on the death penalty and called for additional studies to increase scholarly understanding of several issues. One important question for such research, Bohm (1991) suggested, is why Whites are more likely than Blacks to support the death penalty.

Attempting, like Young (1991, 1992), to answer this question, this study provides what we believe to be the first systematic evidence that White support for the death penalty is associated with racial prejudice. Simply put, many White people are both prejudiced against Blacks and are more likely to favor capital punishment. Although some scholars have attributed the racial difference in death penalty support to perceptions by Blacks of racial bias in its application (Smith 1975), our study suggests that racial prejudice by Whites is at least part of the explanation.

If this is true, the influence of public support for capital punishment on legislative and judicial policy making may be misguided. To the extent that such support derives from feelings of retribution and a desire for deterrence, it is perhaps appropriate that legislative and judicial officials consider the large public majority in favor of capital punishment. But, to the extent that public support is motivated by racial prejudice, it is unacceptable in a democratic society for officials to be guided by such support. If the reasons for supporting capital punishment are as relevant as the amount of support for "judging whether public sentiment is an acceptable indicator of evolving standards of decency" (Sarat and Vidmar 1976, p. 193), then our results suggest that public sentiment may be an unacceptable indicator of contemporary standards of appropriate punishment for persons convicted of homicide (see also Grasmick, Davenport et al. 1992; Young 1991). Along with recent evidence that methodological problems in surveys of death penalty opinion may artificially inflate public support for capital punishment (Bowers 1993; Harris 1986; Williams et al. 1988), our findings thus indicate that inferences from the overwhelming support for capital punishment found in such surveys must be drawn very cautiously.

That said, we must concede that although our results suggest a causal relationship between racial prejudice and death penalty support, they do not prove such a relationship because of the possibility of spuriousness. Although our analysis controlled statistically for the variables we thought most likely to cause spuriousness, there may be other variables that need to be controlled. It may also be argued that because the measures of prejudice and death penalty support are part of the same attitudinal cluster, they cannot be in a causal relationship. However, this argument overlooks the massive amount of research in social psychology showing that attitudes within the same cluster may indeed influence each other (McGuire 1985).

More theoretically, our results complement previous evidence of the role played by racial prejudice in White attitudes toward the punishment of criminals (Cohn et al. 1991). To the extent that White punitiveness derives from such prejudice, consensus perspectives on crime and society cannot be assumed.

Future research on the determination of death penalty attitudes would benefit from more adequate measures of support for the death penalty (Harris 1986; Williams et al. 1988) and of fear of crime (Ferraro and LaGrange 1987). Because of speculation that the large White-Black difference in death penalty support may be partly explained by beliefs among Blacks of racial bias in the death penalty's application (Smith 1975; Young 1991), it is particularly important for investigations of Black attitudes to include adequate measures of perceptions of procedural fairness in the criminal justice system (Hagan and Albonetti 1982), including perceptions of bias in the use of the death penalty. With capital punishment a continuing controversy of literally life and death importance, additional investigations of the bases for opinions on the death penalty will continue to be needed.

REFERENCES

Bohm, Robert M. 1987. "American Death Penalty Attitudes: A Critical Examination of Recent Evidence." *Criminal Justice and Behavior* 14:380–96.

———. 1991. "American Death Penalty Opinion, 1983–1986: A Critical Examination of the Gallup Polls." Pp. 113–45 in *The Death Penalty in America: Current Research,* edited by Robert M. Bohm. Cincinnati, OH: Anderson.

———. 1992. "Retribution and Capital Punishment: Toward a Better Understanding of Death Penalty Opinion." *Journal of Criminal Justice* 20:227–36.

Bowers, William. 1993. "Capital Punishment and Contemporary Values: People's Misgivings and the Court's Misperceptions." *Law and Society Review* 27:157–75.

Cohn, Steven F., Steven E. Barkan, and William A. Halteman. 1991. "Punitive Attitudes Toward Criminals: Racial Consensus or Racial Conflict?" *Social Problems* 38:287–96.

Cullen, Francis T., Gregory A. Clark, John B. Cullen, and Richard A. Mathers. 1985. "Attribution, Salience, and Attitudes Toward Criminal Sentencing." *Criminal Justice and Behavior* 12:305–31.

Davis, James Allan and Tom W. Smith. 1990. *General Social Survey, 1972–1990.* [MRDF]. Chicago: University of Chicago, National Opinion Research Center [producer]. Storrs: Roper Public Opinion Research Center, University of Connecticut [distributor].

Ellison, Christopher G. and Darren E. Sherkat. 1993. "Conservative Protestantism and Support for Corporal Punishment." *American Sociological Review* 58:131–44.

Ellsworth, Phoebe C. and Lee Ross. 1976. "Public Opinion and Judicial Decision Making: An Example From Research on Capital Punishment." Pp. 151–71 in *Capital Punishment in the United States,* edited by Hugo A. Bedau and Chester M. Pierce. New York: AMS Publications.

———. 1983. "Public Opinion and Capital Punishment: A Close Examination of the Views of Abolitionists and Retentionists." *Crime & Delinquency* 29:116–69.

Ferraro, Kenneth F. and Randy LaGrange. 1987. "The Measurement of Fear of Crime." *Sociological Quarterly* 57:71–101.

Finckenauer, James O. 1988. "Public Support for the Death Penalty: Retribution as Just Deserts or Retribution as Revenge?" *Justice Quarterly* 5:81–100.

Gorsuch, Richard L. and Daniel Aleshire. 1974. "Christian Faith and Ethnic Prejudice: A Review and Interpretation of Research." *Journal for the Scientific Study of Religion* 13:281–307.

Grasmick, Harold G., Elizabeth Davenport, Mitchell B. Chamlin, and Robert J. Bursik, Jr. 1992. "Protestant Fundamentalism and the Retributive Doctrine of Punishment." *Criminology* 30:21–45.

Grasmick, Harold G., Carolyn Stout Morgan, and Mary Baldwin Kennedy. 1992. "Support for Corporal Punishment in the Schools: A Comparison of the Effects of Socioeconomic Status and Religion." *Social Science Quarterly* 73:179–89.

Hagan, John and Celesta Albonetti. 1982. "Race, Class, and the Perception of Criminal Justice in America." *American Journal of Sociology* 88:329–55.

Hanushek, Eric A. and John E. Jackson. 1977. *Statistical Methods for Social Scientists.* New York: Academic Press.

Harris, Philip W. 1986. "Over-Simplification and Error in Public Opinion Surveys on Capital Punishment." *Justice Quarterly* 3:429–55.

Langworthy, Robert H. and John T. Whitehead. 1986. "Liberalism and Fear as Explanations of Punitiveness." *Criminology* 24:575–91.

McFarland, Sam. 1989. "Religious Orientations and the Targets of Discrimination." *Journal for the Scientific Study of Religion* 28:324–36.

McGuire, William J. 1985. "The Nature of Attitudes and Attitude Change." Pp. 233–346 in *The Handbook of Social*

Psychology, edited by Gardner Lindzey and Elliot Aronson. Reading, MA: Addison-Wesley.

Ortega, Suzanne T. and Jessie L. Miles. 1987. "Race and Gender Effects on Fear of Crime: An Interactive Model With Age." *Criminology* 25:133–52.

Rankin, Joseph H. 1979. "Changing Attitudes Toward Capital Punishment." *Social Forces* 58:194–211.

Sarat, Austin and Neil Vidmar. 1976. "Public Opinion, the Death Penalty, and the Eighth Amendment: Testing the Marshall Hypothesis." Pp. 190–223 in *Capital Punishment in the United States,* edited by Hugo A. Bedau and Chester M. Pierce. New York: AMS Publications.

Sheley, Joseph F. 1985. *America's "Crime Problem": An Introduction to Criminology.* Belmont, CA: Wadsworth.

Skovron, Sandra Evans, Joseph E. Scott, and Francis T. Cullen. 1989. "The Death Penalty for Juveniles: An Assessment of Public Support." *Crime and Delinquency* 35:546–61.

Smith, Tom W. 1975. "A Trend Analysis of Attitudes Toward Capital Punishment, 1936–1974." Pp. 257–318 in *Studies of Social Change Since 1948.* Vol. 2, edited by James E. Davis. Chicago: National Opinion Research Center.

———. 1990. "Classifying Protestant Denominations." *Review of Religious Research* 31:225–45.

Stinchcombe, Arthur L., Rebecca Adams, Carol A. Heimer, Kim Lane Scheppele, Tom W. Smith, and D. Garth Taylor. 1980. *Crime and Punishment: Changing Attitudes in America.* San Francisco: Jossey-Bass.

Thomas, Charles W., Robin J. Cage, and Samuel C. Foster. 1976. "Public Opinion on Criminal Law and Legal Sanctions: An Examination of Two Conceptual Models." *Journal of Criminal Law and Criminology* 67:110–16.

Thomas, Charles W. and Samuel C. Foster. 1976. "A Sociological Perspective on Public Support for Capital Punishment." Pp. 172–89 in *Capital Punishment in the United States,* edited by Hugo A. Bedau and Chester M. Pierce. New York: AMS Publications.

Tyler, Tom R. and Renee Weber. 1982. "Support for the Death Penalty: Instrumental Response to Crime, or Symbolic Attitude?" *Law and Society Review* 17:21–45.

Vidmar, Neil and Phoebe C. Ellsworth. 1974. "Public Opinion and the Death Penalty." *Stanford Law Review* 26:1245–70.

Warr, Mark and Mark Stafford. 1984. "Public Goals of Punishment and Support for the Death Penalty." *Journal of Research in Crime and Delinquency* 21:95–111.

Williams, Frank P., Dennis R. Longmire, and David B. Gulick. 1988. "The Public and the Death Penalty: Opinion as an Artifact of Question Type." *Criminal Justice Research Bulletin* 3:1–5.

Young, Robert L. 1991. "Race, Conceptions of Crime and Justice, and Support for the Death Penalty." *Social Psychology Quarterly* 54:67–75.

———. 1992. "Religious Orientation, Race and Support for the Death Penalty." *Journal for the Scientific Study of Religion* 31:76–87.

DISCUSSION QUESTIONS

1. As noted by the authors, what are some of the advantages and disadvantages of secondary data analysis?
2. What problems exist in research using data for something other than that for which it was intended?
3. What data did the authors use to examine this issue?
4. What did the authors conclude from this analysis, and what implications does it have for criminal justice?

15

A Badge and a Baccalaureate

Policies, Hypotheses, and Further Evidence

ROBERT E. WORDEN, University at Albany, SUNY

COMMENTARY

"A Badge and a Baccalaureate" was a spin-off study, much as *Frasier* is a spin-off television series. In 1985 I was conducting research on the relationships between patrol officers' attitudes and their behavior. At a colleague's invitation to present a conference paper on some aspect of police reform, and not wishing to stray very far from the focus of my current research, I analyzed the effect of college education on police officers' attitudes. Recommendations for raising educational standards for police had become a staple element of commission reports and other reform agendas, and one presumably important mechanism whereby higher education was expected to enhance police performance was in shaping officers' outlooks, but the empirical evidence on these questions was hardly conclusive.

"A Badge and a Baccalaureate," and the larger study of attitudes and behavior from which it stemmed, was a secondary analysis of data collected for the Police Services Study (PSS). The object of the PSS was to compare the delivery of police services under different institutional arrangements, testing theoretical expectations that patrol services would be more effectively and efficiently delivered on a smaller scale, and thereby following up on previous findings that small to medium-sized police departments perform better in some respects (see Whitaker, 1983). The PSS examined twenty-four different police departments, ranging in size from 13 sworn officers to over 2,000; this was—and remains—unusual for studies of police, which normally concentrate on one or a few medium-sized or larger departments, and thus the PSS forms a

Source: Justice Quarterly, Vol. 7, No. 3, September 1990, pp. 565-592.
© 1990. Reprinted by permission of Academy of Criminal Justice Sciences.

Previous versions of this paper were presented at the 1985 annual meeting of the American Society of Criminology, San Diego, November 13–17, and the 1988 annual meeting of the Midwestern Criminal Justice Association, Chicago, October 5–7. The author gratefully acknowledges the comments and suggestions of Francis T. Cullen, Stephen Mastrofski, George I. Miller, Gordon P. Whitaker, Alissa Pollitz Worden, and the anonymous *JQ* referees.

somewhat stronger basis for generalizations about American policing. The PSS provided for several different forms of data collection: 7,200 hours of systematic observation of officers on patrol; face-to-face interviews of officers; telephone interviews of residents; face-to-face or telephone interviews of citizens involved in observed encounters with officers; interviews with city officials, police managers, leaders of community organizations, and more.[1] Thus, the PSS data can be utilized to address a wide range of research questions, and many different studies have been based on analyses of these data: Whitaker's (1982) description of the nature of patrol work; Smith and Visher's (1981) analysis of the situational influences on officers' decisions to invoke the law; Worden's (1993) examination of gender-related differences in officers' attitudes; Percy's (1984) analysis of citizen participation in crime prevention activities; Mastrofski's (1988) study of oversight by public officials; as well as my study of attitudes and behavior (Worden, 1989). With the collection of comparable data in later years, in the same or different jurisdictions, PSS data may serve as the partial basis for a longitudinal analysis of policing (but with much caution regarding differences in measurement and sampling over time).

The first version of "A Badge and a Baccalaureate," which focused only on attitudes, inspired little interest. The findings—that education was weakly if at all related to attitudes—were consistent with those of several previous studies, and so to some the study seemed to add nothing new. The paper was initially rejected by the journal in which it was ultimately published; as the then-editor wrote to me, ". . . one [reviewer] felt your subject had been covered fully in various earlier writing. . . . We think your area of discussion and your results have appeared in papers published on this subject several years ago." A few years later, however, it occurred to me to exploit another set of PSS data to examine the effects of college education on performance—the "bottom line" issue—and to do so in a rather unusual way. Police performance is, as I point out in the article, a complex and multidimensional phenomenon, and many indicators of performance are ambiguous. Since the PSS had interviewed a sample of citizens with whom officers had encounters during observation, one could link survey information on officers—including their educational background—with citizens' satisfaction with officers' performance in individual incidents. Citizen satisfaction is not the only standard against which we would assess police performance, but it is one important metric, which had not been used in research on police officers' education.

One of the greatest pitfalls of secondary analysis is that one is constrained in measuring analytical constructs for purposes that were not originally envisioned. The PSS police officer survey was not designed with my purposes in mind. The attitudinal constructs that in the 1980s I distilled from extant ethnographic research on police (see Worden, 1995) did not inform the formulation of the survey instrument. Consequently, the reliabilities of multi-item indices

[1]These data are archived at and available through the ICPSR, although I acquired copies of the data as a graduate research assistant on the project.

were rather low, and for the measurement of some attitudes I had to rely on a single survey item; for some outlooks—for example, officers' beliefs about human nature—I had no measure at all. The best measure of officers' college education—highest earned degree—was fairly crude, and I had no information on officers' college majors or other qualitative dimensions of their educational experiences. The validity and reliability of measures is always a concern, but especially so when one finds null relationships—estimated relationships could be so attentuated due to measurement error that we reject true hypotheses.

Such problems notwithstanding, secondary analyses of Police Services Study data have been well worthwhile. The PSS data have some unique strengths, as they combine many forms of interlinked data over a number of different jurisdictions. Survey data on officers can be linked with observational data on those officers' encounters with citizens; observational data on police-citizen encounters can be linked with survey data on those citizens. The departments and the jurisdictions they serve vary in their structural attributes. The cost of collecting such data—a comparable study would cost over five million dollars to conduct today—makes efforts to exploit these data in creative ways, mindful of the limitations, more than justified. No one study by itself is conclusive; findings based on PSS data serve to confirm or refute previous findings, and later studies will confirm or refute findings based on PSS data.

ABSTRACT Arguments for and against measures intended to raise the educational levels of police officers turn partly on the hypothesized relationships between college education and officers' attitudes and behavior. The purpose of this analysis is to provide additional empirical evidence concerning these hypotheses. The results suggest that college education is weakly related to some attitudes and unrelated to others. The results also show that officers' performance in police-citizen encounters, measured in terms of citizens' evaluations, is largely unrelated to officers' educational backgrounds.

Upgrading police personnel by raising the educational levels of police officers has been—and remains—both an integral element of police professionalization (Fogelson 1977) and part of the conventional wisdom of police administration. Presidential commissions, academicians, and police executives have maintained that higher education is essential for anyone charged with such a complex and important task. Suppositions about the effects of education are embodied in policies that encourage or require officers to obtain a college education. The now-defunct Law Enforcement Education Program, through which educational grants and loans were made available to police personnel, is only one example of such policies, which is notable for the scale of its operation. Other policies, underwritten by state and local governments, work toward the same end. A recent survey of municipal, county, and state law enforcement agencies by the Police Executive Research Forum (PERF) reveals that more than half of the responding departments offer educational pay incentives and/or tuition assistance programs; all but a small fraction have policies of some kind that are intended to facilitate higher education for officers (Carter, Sapp, and Stephens 1989:59–65). Moreover, although formal requirements for entry or promotion do not normally include a college degree, informal practices often impose a de facto college requirement (Carter et al. 1989:54–56). Thus a commitment to raising the educational levels of police officers—a commitment backed by public resources—persists, even though federal support has been curtailed sharply.

When the movement to educate police gained momentum in the 1960s and early 1970s, advocates' arguments rested principally on intuitive propositions that connected college education to improved police performance. Little if any empirical evidence was—or could have been—marshaled in support of those propositions because so few officers at that time had attended college (Goldstein 1977:290; Sherman 1980:76). Since that time, many propositions have been subjected to empirical scrutiny, but the evidence is neither consistent nor compelling. The purpose of this paper is to bring additional empirical evidence to bear on some of the arguments surrounding higher education for police. In particular, this analysis tests hypotheses that link college education to officers' attitudes and to officers' performance in their encounters with citizens. Analyses of officers' attitudes—about how their jobs should be performed, and about the contexts in which they work—in some ways replicate previous research. The analyses of officers' performance add a new dimension to existing research, inasmuch as performance is measured in terms of citizens' (rather than, say, supervisors') evaluations. These analyses show that educational levels are related weakly (if at all) to officers' attitudes and performance.

THEORETICAL AND POLICY ISSUES

The arguments for and against measures intended to raise the educational levels of police officers have been advanced on several fronts. Hence it is necessary 1) to disentangle the hypotheses on which these arguments rest in order to evaluate them and 2) to specify the policy implications of these hypotheses.

Advocates of higher education for police maintain—implicitly or explicitly—that it will improve the quality of policing partly by shaping the attitudes and values of police officers, with concomitant effects on officers' behavior. According to this view, college-educated officers are more likely to appreciate the role of police in a democratic society and to be more tolerant of people different from themselves (L. Brown 1974:110–19; Lynch 1976; Saunders 1970; A. Smith, Locke, and Fenster 1970; see also Goldstein 1977:286–88). Thus they are more likely to believe that the job of policing is not limited to the crime-fighting function, but also extends to maintaining order and helping citizens. Such officers are more likely to recognize the need to operate within the parameters set by the rule of law, although they are also more likely to advocate flexibility in fashioning solutions to problems. Critics' arguments also turn partly on officers' attitudes. The critics posit that college-educated officers are more likely to become frustrated with their work, with the restrictions imposed by supervisors, and with limited opportunities for advancement. Therefore they are more likely to be disaffected from their jobs and the organizations in which they work, and less likely to remain in policing (see, e.g., Swanson 1977).

It is conceivable that *both* proponents and opponents of educational requirements and incentives could be largely correct in these respects, because their arguments are not mutually contradictory. Indeed, both sides of the issue seem to agree that college-educated officers, insofar as they need organizational latitude in order to be flexible, are likely to value autonomy over obedience to supervisors' directives. Otherwise the hypotheses are logically independent, and the postulated relationships could coincide empirically. Officers with a college degree, for example, might hold a broader conception of the police role than do officers without a degree, and they might also be more dissatisfied with promotional opportunities. If this is the case, even conclusive empirical research will have ambiguous policy implications.

Proponents of higher education also hold that it will affect officers' performance more directly, and not only by shaping their attitudes.[1] Whereas critics maintain that police tasks, which require common sense and/or street sense, are not performed better by college-educated officers, proponents hypothesize that college-educated officers are better able to analyze complex problems with which the police frequently are confronted, are more articulate, and for these reasons are able to choose more judiciously from a wider repertoire of responses (Cascio and Real 1976; Finckenauer 1975; Sterling 1974; see also Muir 1977:227–35). These expectations were echoed by the respondents to the recent PERF survey. Respondents tended to believe that college-educated officers communicate better with the citizenry, are better decision makers, are more "professional," and perform more effectively; some respondents volunteered that college-educated officers have better verbal and written skills (Carter et al. 1989:46–52).[2]

These propositions rest largely on more general expectations about attitudinal and behavioral changes that are caused by educational experiences; these expectations form the theoretical foundation for policies that encourage officers to go (or return) to college. Yet the hypothesized relationships might hold even if college education has no causal effect on students' attitudes or on their behavioral predispositions, as long as those who choose to go to college differ in important respects from those who choose not to go (A. Smith, Locke, and Walker 1967). That is, college-educated officers might tend to hold different attitudes or to perform more effectively not because they went to college but rather because of traits they possessed before attending college. Therefore, in assessing each of these hypotheses, it might be useful to draw a distinction between officers whose

---

[1]There are both theoretical and empirical reasons to suspect that officers' attitudes are *not* related strongly to their behavior (Worden 1989; see also Schuman and Johnson 1976); thus one cannot draw inferences about the impact of education on performance from findings about the relationship between education and attitudes.

[2]These survey items referred to officers with two or more years of education.

college experience precedes their entry into the occupation—i.e., pre-service graduates—and officers who pursue a college education after they begin their police careers. This distinction corresponds to different (but not mutually exclusive) policies—entry requirements and recruitment strategies on one hand, and policies regarding tuition assistance, salary incentives, duty scheduling, and the like on the other. Whether either or both sets of policies have the expected benefits is an empirical question that turns, of course, on whether the expected relationships hold within the respective subgroups of officers. In the case of the latter policies, however, which promote in-service education, the benefits also depend on whether attitudinal and behavioral differences are attributable to educational experiences or to other characteristics.

There are good reasons to expect little or no attitudinal or behavioral change in officers who undertake college studies as in-service students. These officers already have developed a set of occupational attitudes (Niederhoffer 1969) as well as a set of "operational styles" (M. Brown 1981). They also are subject to potentially powerful influences in their work environment. Police administrators can communicate—through the training they provide, the regulations they promulgate, the evaluative criteria they apply, and the infractions they punish, as well as through informal channels—an orientation to police work, or "a common definition of the situations [officers] are likely to encounter" (Wilson 1968:139). Furthermore, officers' peers, who collectively constitute a "police culture" (see, e.g., Reuss-Ianni 1983), usually are thought to exert an even greater influence on officers' attitudes and (to some extent) on their behavior (M. Brown 1981; Van Maanen 1974). In view of these forces, one might well expect to observe little attitudinal or behavioral change as a result of college education (Dalley 1975; Sherman and Bennis 1977).

One might expect to observe more marked differences when one examines officers who began their police careers with a college education. Such differences could be attributed to either or both of two factors. First, the effect of a college education on attitudes and behavioral predispositions may be greater for pre-service students than for in-service students because the former are not subject (as students) to administrative or peer group pressures. Second, pre-college differences in outlooks, intelligence, motivation, and the like might manifest themselves later in occupational attitudes and performance, even if college education per se has little or no observable effect. If college-educated recruits differ in the expected ways from other officers, the source of the differences is irrelevant for some policy purposes; whatever the reasons for the differences, it might be desirable to recruit college graduates.

Extant Evidence

A substantial literature (substantial at least by social science standards) has developed around the subject of higher education for police. Even so, one can draw only very tentative inferences from extant evidence. One reason is that studies of attitudes have focused on different attitudes or sets of attitudes (e.g., professionalism, cynicism); thus the findings are not cumulative. Another reason is that patrol officers' performance is a multidimensional theoretical construct, for some dimensions of which it is difficult to devise valid measures. Any one dimension of performance has been investigated in only a handful of studies; hence the findings are not cumulative. Moreover, previous research leaves some aspects of performance unexamined (or examined only in terms of questionable indicators).

Attitudes. Much of the available evidence provides weak or inconsistent (if any) support for the claim that college education has salutary effects on officers' attitudes. Miller and Fry (1976) found that education has no positive effect on officers' "public service orientation"; on the contrary, those with a degree displayed less of such an orientation than those without a degree. Hudzik's (1978) findings show that college-educated officers place less value on obedience to supervisors than do officers without a college education; Roberg's (1978) results indicate that college-educated officers are more "open-minded." Yet Smith and Ostrom (1974), Miller and Fry (1976), and Smith (1978) report that educational achievement bears no significant relationship to a preference for autonomy or to resistance to management control. Likewise, Weiner (1974) reports only a small and statistically insignificant relationship between education and beliefs concerning "obedience to law," which would seem on their face to reflect officers' inclinations toward flexibility or rigidity in enforcement. The principal exception to the rule of null findings concerns officers' attitudes toward legal restrictions on the use of police authority. College-educated officers appear to be more amenable (or less hostile) to restrictions imposed by the courts (Smith 1978; Smith and Ostrom 1974; Weiner 1974).

Other findings offer some support for the arguments of those who oppose educational requirements for police. Hudzik (1978) reports that education bears a negative and statistically significant relationship to job satisfaction; Miller and Fry (1976) also found a negative, albeit weak, relationship between education and job satisfaction (but cf. Barry 1978; Fischer, Golden, and Heininger 1985). As one thus would expect, college-educated officers are also more likely to express dissatisfaction with departmental administration and policies and to give their departments low evaluations as places to work (Hudzik 1978; cf. Regoli 1976 and Weiner 1974 on cynicism). The source of this dissatisfaction may be the presumed conflict between supervisors and independent-minded college graduates, but in this connection one should recall that the evidence is inconsistent on the relationship between education and resistance to supervisory restrictions. One alternative explanation is that college-educated officers are more frustrated by dim prospects for advancement (Barry 1978; Fischer, Golden, and Heininger 1985); they also might be more sensitive to (perceived) shortcomings in administrative practices generally.

Performance. Analyses of officers' performance also have yielded mixed results. Police performance, of course, is difficult to conceptualize and even more difficult to operationalize; police officers perform many different tasks, and information about how well they perform some of them is quite scarce. Moreover, no consensus exists about many aspects of performance: arresting one party to a domestic dispute, for example, might be regarded as good police work by some and as inept policing by others; conducting frequent field interrogations might be seen as good, aggressive police work by some and as harassment by others. Hence research on police officers' performance has been eclectic in measuring that performance. Some research is based on objective indicators, such as absenteeism. Other research is based on subjective indicators, such as supervisory ratings. Still other research is based on behaviorally oriented questionnaires administered to the officers. The findings of these studies generally give somewhat more—but not much more—support than do attitudinal studies to the arguments in favor of higher education.

Analyses of objective indicators of performance have found that college-educated officers are less likely to be the subjects of citizens' complaints, less likely to suffer injuries, and less likely to miss work (Cascio 1977; Cohen and Chaiken 1972; Sanderson 1977); these relationships generally are modest in magnitude, even if they are statistically significant. Moreover, the relationships between education and other objective indicators generally are equally modest but statistically insignificant. Nonetheless, these findings are remarkable for their consistency. Further, they are quite consistent with the interpretation that college-educated officers are better able to analyze problems and to devise non-coercive solutions.

Analyses of survey data reveal a more pronounced predisposition among college-educated officers to exercise their discretion. Finckenauer (1975) examined officers' responses to hypothetical incidents and found that college-educated officers are less likely to invoke the law in discretionary situations. Trojanowicz and Nicholson (1976) constructed scales of behavioral styles, on which the scores of college-educated officers reflected a stronger preference for variety in their work and a greater willingness to experiment with novel approaches to police tasks. Although one might question the validity of survey responses as measures of behavior,[3] these findings are compatible with—and might help to explain—the relationships found in objective data.

Analyses of subjective indicators of performance provide mixed evidence. In his analysis of officers in the Baltimore Police Department, Finnigan (1976) found that supervisors' ratings of officers' performance bore the hypothesized relationship to officers' educational backgrounds, even when he controlled for other factors such as age and IQ. Wycoff and Susmilch (1979) report similar findings among a sample of Dallas police officers. Furthermore, officers' education is related to their success in being promoted (Cohen and Chaiken 1972; Sanderson 1977), which usually reflects (to some degree) subjective evaluations of their performance. In his study of Dade County, however, Cascio (1977) found that supervisors' evaluations of officers' performance were unrelated to officers' education, despite his careful efforts to develop valid evaluative scales.

[3]See M. Brown (1981:248) on the validity of using hypothetical scenarios to measure police behavior.

None of these indicators of officers' performance is wholly valid, of course. Many objective indicators bear only a tenuous relationship to performance: many poor officers will never sustain an injury; many citizens who are justifiably dissatisfied with an officer's performance will never file complaints, whereas other citizens will file complaints even though their grievances are unwarranted. Subjective indicators capture only those aspects of officers' performance that are visible to supervisors; they also reflect departmental (and individual supervisors') priorities, making it difficult to compare the indicators across departments. Even so, to note the shortcomings of these indicators is not to condemn the research based on them, but rather to underscore the care with which results should be interpreted; many different indicators—each with its own flaws—should be examined, because conclusions can not be drawn confidently from any one of them.

METHODS

This study adds some pieces to the theoretical puzzle by examining further the relationships between officers' educational attaintment and selected occupational attitudes, and between educational attainment and performance. The analyses of officers' attitudes are of value principally as replications of previous research although earlier studies have conceived and/or operationalized the attitudinal dimensions somewhat differently from this study. The analyses of officers' performance represent a departure from previous research by measuring performance in terms of citizens' evaluations. Such evaluations represent one indicator in terms of which officers' performance can be measured; although it is not a wholly valid measure on its face, it suffers a different set of shortcomings from other indicators. This approach to measuring officers' performance complements previous research, and it might offer new insights.

Data

The data for this analysis were collected for the Police Services Study (PSS), which was designed to evaluate the impact of organizational arrangements on the delivery of police services.[4] The second phase of the PSS, which was conducted in 1977, provided for the collection of many different forms of data in each of 24 police departments in three metropolitan areas (Rochester, St. Louis, and Tampa-St. Petersburg) concentrating largely on 60 neighborhoods served by those departments. The sample of departments is not random, but it is a rough cross-section of organizational arrangements and service conditions for

[4]The PSS was a project conducted by Elinor Ostrom, Roger B. Parks, and Gordon P. Whitaker; it was funded by the National Science Foundation through grant GI43949. Information on the details of data collection can be obtained from the Workshop in Political Theory and Policy Analysis at Indiana University.

urban policing in the United States. Although the PSS was not designed specifically to examine hypotheses of concern here, some of the data collected for the PSS are singularly useful for this purpose.

I use two sources of data for this analysis. One is a survey of officers in each department. Interviewees were called to police headquarters while on duty for a private interview of approximately 30 minutes in length; officers were assured that their responses would remain confidential (cf. Wycoff and Susmilch 1979:28–29). The other source is a survey of citizens with whom some of the surveyed patrol officers recently had had contact. Citizens were interviewed by phone or, in some cases, face to face; each respondent was asked about the nature of his or her encounter with the police, and whether he or she was satisfied with the officer's performance.

Samples

Officers. Because the survey was intended to collect information relevant to the 60 study neighborhoods, selection procedures generally identified officers with responsibilities in those areas—for patrol, supervision, or administration. In the six largest departments, samples of officers and supervisors assigned to those areas were selected, in addition to command staff; in the smaller departments, all officers, supervisors, and command staff were selected.[5] The interviewed officers are fairly representative of sworn police personnel in urban areas at that time: 94 percent male; 88.5 percent white and 10.5 percent black; average age 33 years (cf. Flanagan, Hindelang, and Gottfredson 1979:51; U.S. Department of Justice 1978).

Citizens. Citizens were selected for "debriefing" interviews from PSS coding of calls for service and/or observed police-citizen encounters during samples of shifts (matched across neighborhoods by day of week and time of day). Selection criteria excluded some citizens: those who were arrested or suspected of a crime and those who were involved in certain types of incidents, such as homicides, rapes, or missing persons, and for whom an interview might have been traumatic. In addition, special procedures were used to contact and interview citizens involved in domestic disputes; those procedures made it less likely that interviews with those citizens would be completed. Thus the sample does not represent citizens (arrestees and other suspects) whose relationships to the police are the most antagonistic. Perhaps more important, the sample underrepresents citizens whose contacts with the police involved the more complex and/or emotionally stressful situations.

[5]In two departments, the seventh and eighth largest, samples of all officers were selected regardless of their assignments to study neighborhoods or to other areas. Overall, of the 1,435 officers selected, two refused to be interviewed, eight could not be contacted, and eight others were not interviewed for unidentified reasons.

Measures

The measurement of key theoretical constructs is seldom straightforward, but it is especially problematic for secondary analysis, and requires careful consideration. The discussion of measurement first addresses attitudes; I consider the content or objects of the attitudes in question, the nature of the expected relationships with education, and the scales on which the attitudes are measured.[6] The discussion then turns to the measure of officers' performance, namely citizens' evaluations. Finally, I describe the measures of the independent variable—educational background—and of control variables.

Attitudes. This analysis examines seven attitudes to which education might be expected to bear some relationship. Three attitude measures are based on single questionnaire items, and four are additive indices.[7] The items on which measures are based, however, were not developed specifically to measure the attitudinal dimensions described below; many of the items probably tap two or more attitudinal dimensions. Such shortcomings are characteristic especially of the multi-item scales: although each constituent item on its face is related to the more general attitudinal dimension, the items are not parallel, and the reliabilities of the scales fall short of conventional standards for attitude measures.

Some officers delimit the scope of the police role to fighting crime and enforcing the law; others include a wider range of functions in their definitions, some of which have little (if any) connection with fighting crime. One might hypothesize that college-educated officers define the police role more broadly, because by learning about social institutions and social problems they might develop a deeper appreciation of the social value of different police functions. The measure of officers' attitudes about the *scope of the police role* is an index formed by summing officers' coded responses to three questionnaire items: 1) Do you think police should help to quiet family disputes if they get out of hand? (1 = no, 2 = yes); 2) Do you think the police here should handle cases involving public nuisances, such as barking dogs and burning rubbish? (1 = no, 2 = yes); 3) Police should not have to handle calls that involve social or personal problems where no crime is involved (1 = strongly agree, 4 = strongly disagree). Higher values on the scale correspond to broader conceptions of the police role. The theta coefficient for this scale is .49.[8]

Some officers resent restrictions on police practices—on search and seizure, interrogation, the use of force—and are willing to violate legal and departmental injunctions when they conflict with the goal of crime control; other officers accept these restrictions as legitimate (see Broderick 1977; M. Brown 1981). By

[6]See Worden (1986:Ch. 4) for an extended discussion of these attitudes and measures thereof.

[7]These additive indices are statistically indistinguishable from factor scales derived from principal components factor analyses.

[8]See Carmines and Zeller (1979:59–62) for a discussion of the theta coefficient as a measure of reliability.

exposing officers to alternative viewpoints on these restrictions, a college education might be expected to engender greater respect for them; otherwise, officers often see only the drawbacks of such provisions. The measure of officers' attitudes toward *legal restrictions* is an additive index based on three items (all of which are coded 1 = strongly disagree, 4 = strongly agree): 1) Police officers here would be more effective if they didn't have to worry about "probable cause" requirements for searching citizens; 2) If police officers in tough neighborhoods had fewer restrictions on their use of force, many of the serious crime problems in those neighborhoods would be greatly reduced; 3) When a police officer is accused of using too much force, only other officers are qualified to judge such a case. Higher values on the factor scale reflect negative attitudes toward legal restrictions. The theta coefficient for this scale is .52.

White (1972:67–69) distinguishes between officers who are "discretion-control oriented" and those who are "command-control oriented." The former are satisfied only by following events to their conclusions, and therefore prefer wide latitude in order to bring about the outcomes that they deem desirable. The latter are "satisfied to perform discrete interventions into passing events" (White 1972:68), and they adopt the norms and standards established by administrators. This outlook concerns officers' "zones of acceptance" (Simon 1976)—their willingness to adhere to departmental regulations and supervisors' orders. College-educated officers are thought to be more discretion-control oriented, perhaps because a college education encourages independent and critical thought or because college-educated officers are more skeptical about the legitimacy of supervisors' authority. The measure of officers' attitudes toward *discretion* is an additive index based on two Likert items (both coded 1 = strongly agree, 4 = strongly disagree): 1) Police officers do a better job when they have clear, precise guidelines to follow in handling incidents; 2) A police officer does the best job by following the orders of superior officers. High values reflect a discretion-control orientation. The theta coefficient for this scale is .38.

College-educated officers are thought to be more flexible in enforcing the law. Because a college education is supposed to provide insights into human behavior and to foster a spirit of experimentation, college-educated officers are (hypothetically) less inclined to invoke the law to resolve problems, and correspondingly are inclined more strongly to develop extralegal solutions. The measure of officers' attitudes toward *rigid enforcement* is based on responses to a single questionnaire item: Patrol officers on the street are more effective if they are able to decide on their own when to enforce particular laws (1 = strongly agree, 4 = strongly disagree). Lower values on this measure reflect inclinations for greater flexibility.

Supervisors' demands—for "activity," for paperwork, for adherence to (seemingly counterproductive) regulations—are not generally welcomed by patrol officers, but college-educated officers are thought to be especially sensitive to (and resentful of) overseeing by supervisors. The measure of officers' perceptions of the restrictiveness of *supervision* is an additive index based on two items (coded 1 = strongly agree, 4 = strongly disagree): 1) Immediate supervisors in this department let each officer do his work the way that officer thinks best; 2) Most supervisors in this department are careful to fit rules and regulations to the situation rather than insisting that rules and regulations have to be followed regardless of the situation. Officers who perceive supervisors as restrictive score higher on the scale. The theta coefficient for the scale is .32.

College-educated officers also are thought to be less satisfied with the organizations in which they work, partly because of supervisory and administrative constraints on their professional autonomy and partly because of the limited opportunities for advancement. Officers' attitudes toward their *departments as places to work* are measured in terms of their responses to this question: Compared to other departments in the [metropolitan] area, would you say your department is (1) a much worse place to work, (2) a somewhat worse place, (3) about the same, (4) a somewhat better place, or (5) a much better place to work? Although this item provides no absolute basis for understanding officers' assessments, it does provide a single point of reference for college-educated and other officers in each metropolitan area, in terms of which officers can be compared.

Critics have hypothesized further that college-educated officers have lower morale, not only as a result of their frustration with restrictions imposed by superiors and with impediments to upward mobility, but also because they might find that police work is not sufficiently challenging or stimulating. Respondents' *morale* is based on interviewers' subjective assessments, coded on a trichotomous scale: low (1), neutral (2), and high (3). The drawbacks of this measure are obvious, and because each respondent was interviewed by only one researcher, no estimate of intercoder reliability can be computed.

Performance. Whether or not education is related to the above attitudes, college education might improve officers' performance in police–citizen encounters. If, as the advocates of educational requirements and incentives maintain, college-educated officers are better able to diagnose problems, to choose appropriate tactics, and to persuade and cajole (rather than threaten and coerce), one would expect their superior performance to be reflected in citizens' evaluations: citizens whose encounters are with college-educated officers should be more satisfied with their contact with the police, other things being equal. *Citizen satisfaction* is measured on a five-point scale—very satisfied (coded 5), satisfied, neutral, dissatisfied, and very dissatisfied (coded 1)—based on citizens' responses to the question, "How satisfied were you with what the police did?"

Citizens' evaluations have been criticized as invalid measures of the performance of public agencies, at least partly because many citizens have had no contact with the agencies which they could use as the basis for informed evaluations (see Beck et al. 1987; Stipak 1977, 1979; cf. Parks 1984). Obviously this criticism does not apply to the data analyzed here. Another point, however, on which survey data have been criticized is that respondents' evaluations are based to some extent on more general attitudes toward state authority. This is probably the case, albeit probably less so for citizens who have had contact with the agency in question than for citizens without such experience, and less so when citizens are asked for evaluations of specific experiences than when they are asked for more global assessments of agency performance. The more general attitudes toward government also are related to variables (such as race and income) for which the regression analyses control.

Educational Background. The PSS data make it possible to measure officers' educational backgrounds in three different ways: years of formal education, number of college credits earned, and highest earned degree. Years of formal education is probably the worst indicator of the three, partly because, as Sherman (1980:76) points out, there is no good reason to suppose that "a year of education is a fungible property at an interval level of measurement," and partly because respondents to the PSS survey apparently did not distinguish between part-time and full-time studies. The number of college credits earned is a better indicator, if only because it reflects more accurately the amount of officers' exposure to college coursework. A rather large number of officers (183), however, could not remember how many credits they had earned; others no doubt approximated the number. In any case, the number of credits fails to capture much about the quality of educational experiences. The highest earned degree is perhaps the best indicator of the three, for reasons explained below. One need not choose only one of these indicators for analysis, but to conserve space only the last—the highest earned degree—is used in tabular presentations of results. All three indicators lead to the same conclusions, with some exceptions, which are noted below.

College degrees reflect structure and coherence in educational experiences which may be lacking when officers merely accumulate credits.[9] An officer's highest degree also might provide a rough indication of the nature of the curriculum to which the officer was exposed. Vocational curricula, as a rule, fail to raise issues concerned with the performance of police functions; they concentrate instead on the mechanics of police activities. They do not stimulate valuative and ethical discourse that might lead to attitude change (cf. Rokeach 1968). Neither do they offer the kind of intellectual challenge that could be expected to promote the development of analytical and communication skills. Other curricula, by prompting officers to reflect on issues that they would not consider otherwise and to confront viewpoints to which otherwise they would not be exposed, are more likely to cause attitude change.[10] Two-year (AA) programs are more likely than baccalaureate programs to be vocational rather than academic (although there are numerous exceptions among both types of programs). Whether an officer has an associate's or a bachelor's degree is only a very rough indicator of curriculum type, however; stronger relationships might be found if one could isolate officers who graduated from more rigorously

[9]Many departments provide educational incentives without requiring that college courses lead to a degree (Carter et al. 1989:62).

[10]For useful treatments of variations in curricula, see Kuykendall (1977), Mathias (1976:380–81); Saunders (1970:95); and Sherman and National Advisory Commission (1978:67–82).

academic (two- or four-year) programs. In any case, whether associate's and bachelor's degree programs have similar or different effects, on average, is an empirical question about which no assumptions need be made for this analysis.

In addition, the data enable one to identify officers who earned degrees before they entered police work—pre-service associate's or bachelor's degrees. The attitudes and performance of these officers can be compared to those of other officers who earned degrees as in-service students, and with those of officers without degrees, in order to assess the likely benefits of selection policies that make a college degree a requirement.

None of the available indicators, however, captures adequately the qualitative aspects of officers' educational backgrounds. For example, the PSS data contain no information at all about the majors of college-educated officers. For some of the reasons noted above, one might expect to find stronger relationships among officers with certain majors (such as humanities or social sciences) than among officers with other majors (such as police science); certainly it would be desirable to test for such conditional effects. Because it fails to distinguish among officers whose educational backgrounds differ qualitatively, the analysis reported below might understate the effect of college education. Previous research, however, reports no direct relationship between officers' college majors and their performance (Cascio 1977; Finnigan 1976). More generally, Wycoff and Susmilch (1979:19–22) found that qualitative dimensions of educational programs are unrelated to officers' attitudes. For policy purposes, moreover, refined measures of the quality of educational experiences may be of little use despite any explanatory value they might have, inasmuch as policies are unlikely to make equally refined distinctions among educational programs and curricula.

Control Variables. Information about several potentially confounding factors is also available. For an analysis of officers' attitudes, confounding variables include the officer's rank, length of service, gender, and race.[11] Officers' rank also might mediate the effects of education; the effects of education on attitudes might be different for supervisory and command staff than for patrol officers (Wycoff and Susmilch 1979:30–31). In addition, characteristics of the organizational context might mediate the effect of education on attitudes; that is, education might have greater effects on officers' attitudes in departments that are more supportive of college education. Organizational support for college education is measured in two ways, each based on officers' attitudes toward college

[11]By virtue of their role, officers who hold supervisory positions might develop attitudes different from those they held as patrol officers (Carlson and Sutton 1975; see also Reuss-Ianni 1983). If they are also more highly educated, the failure to control for rank would lead to erroneous inferences. Similarly, officers with more experience tend to have less formal education, but they also may hold distinctive attitudes either because police officers' attitudes change over time or (more likely) because their attitudes were shaped early in their careers by cultural and subcultural forces that have changed since (Niederhoffer 1969).

Controlling for length of service also controls for age in these data; the correlation is .87. Unfortunately, data on intelligence are unavailable.

education: the proportion of respondents in each department who agreed 1) that college education should be required for hiring and 2) that college education should be required for promotion.

For an analysis of citizens' evaluations, potentially confounding variables include the citizen's race, sex, age, income,[12] role in the incident (as a principal or a third party), and evaluation of police response time, as well as the nature of the problem (see, e.g., Beck et al. 1987; Christenson and Taylor 1983; Durand 1976; Mastrofski 1981; Percy 1980). Within any one department, there is little reason to suppose that these variables would be related to officers' educational backgrounds, and that therefore they would confound the relationship between officers' education and citizens' evaluations. In this sample, however, one can expect to find interjurisdictional variation in officers' educational levels, which might bear some correspondence to interjurisdictional variation in the composition of the communities.

FINDINGS

Most of the findings are drawn from the results of ordinary least squares (OLS) regression analyses.[13] Several comments about the coding of the independent variables and the interpretation of the regression coefficients are in order. All but one of the characteristics of officers are dummy variables. Education (i.e., highest earned degree) is defined in terms of two dummy variables: whether an officer's highest degree is 1) a bachelor's degree or 2) an associate's degree; officers with no degree thus serve as the baseline against which college-educated officers are compared.[14] One-third of the officers had earned college degrees; half of those had earned baccalaureates. Whether officers earned their highest degree as pre-service students is also defined in terms of two dummy variables:

[12]Income is measured on a scale with five categories, ranging from "less than $5000" to "more than $20,000" in increments of $5000.

[13] Because the purpose of these analyses is to test hypotheses, and because there is no theoretical reason to specify a definite causal ordering among the independent variables, stepwise regression is inappropriate for this application; see Hanushek and Jackson (1977). In addition, because the purpose is to test hypotheses about the effects of college education, and not to explain officers' attitudes or citizens' evaluations, the small proportions of explained variance are of secondary concern. The focus is on the coefficients of the education variables, and they are unbiased estimates as long as potentially confounding variables (such as rank) are included in the regression models. Moreover, because the relationships in question are either null or small, one need consider principally whether omitted variables suppress the hypothesized relationships (and not whether the relationships are spurious). Finally, the regression results are not distorted by multicollinearity. The education variables in each model are related only weakly to other attributes of the officers (e.g., experience, rank); the largest correlation is .08.

[14]Twenty-nine officers in the sample had earned graduate degrees (22 of those were master's degrees), but these officers are not distinguished from other bachelor's degree holders for the purposes of these analyses.

one for pre-service bachelor's degrees and another for pre-service associate's degrees. Thus the estimated effect of college education for pre-service degree recipients is the sum of two regression coefficients: the coefficient associated with having a degree and the coefficient associated with having earned a degree as a pre-service student. The coefficients for pre-service degrees show whether and how much pre-service degree recipients differ from other officers who hold the same degree. Forty percent of the officers with degrees had earned them as pre-service students; half of those degrees also were baccalaureates. Officers' rank is defined in terms of three dummy variables—immediate supervisor, mid-level administrator, and top-level administrator—rather than as a single interval variable because it is not plausible to assume that the effects of increments in rank are equal. Officers' race is also a dummy variable; black officers, as well as the few Latino and Asian officers, are coded as minorities. Length of service, which is coded in years, is the only interval variable.

Attitudes

The correlations between officers' educational backgrounds and their attitudes are small. When the correlations are corrected for attenuation due to errors in measuring attitudes, they are uniformly larger (of course), but even then only two attitudes yield coefficients that exceed .10 across the measures of education. The regression results also show that the effects of college education on officers' attitudes are quite modest at best (see Table 1).

Officers' educational backgrounds are related to several attitudes. First, officers who earned baccalaureates as in-service students draw the boundaries of the police role somewhat more *narrowly* than do officers without a college degree. This difference does not reach a conventionally acceptable level of statistical significance in the aggregate, although it is statistically significant among patrol officers.[15] This finding is consistent with those of previous research if one can equate beliefs about the scope of the police role with a "public service orientation" (Miller and Fry 1976). One possible explanation is that in-service officers who choose to pursue their education are motivated partly by a desire to establish their status as "professionals," which for many officers implies a role circumscribed to law enforcement (Manning 1977; Walker 1977). Officers who earned baccalaureates as pre-service students appear not to have formed such an image of the police role; on the contrary, their conceptions of the police role are somewhat broader than those of officers with no college degree.

---

[15]Regression analyses that allow the estimated effects of education to vary for patrol officers, supervisors, and command officers, through the inclusion of slope dummy variables (Hanushek and Jackson 1977:127–28), show that all of the estimated effects across ranks are within the customary margin of sampling error, with four exceptions. One exception is that education has a negative and statistically significant affect on the attitude of patrol officers—but not of higher-ranking officers—toward the scope of the police role. Similar analyses using the other measures of education confirm the direction but not the statistical significance of this effect. (Other exceptions are noted below.)

Table 1. Regression Analyses of Officers' Attitudes

Regressors	Scope of Police Role	Legal Restrictions	Discretion	Rigid Enforcement	Department Rating	Morale	Supervision
Bachelor's degree	–.050 (–1.40)	–.150* (–4.44)	.105* (3.11)	–.019 (–0.55)	–.014 (–0.40)	–.014 (–0.39)	–.029 (–0.83)
Pre-service bachelor's	.081* (2.26)	.025 (0.73)	–.050 (–1.50)	–.009 (–0.25)	.036 (1.03)	.049 (1.41)	–.002 (–0.04)
Associate's degree	.019 (0.53)	–0.62** (–1.84)	.062** (1.88)	–.018 (–0.52)	–.004 (–0.12)	.006 (0.19)	–.075* (–2.16)
Pre-service associate's	–.047 (–1.35)	.020 (0.61)	–.023 (–0.70)	.009 (0.28)	–.031 (–0.88)	–.026 (–0.76)	.038 (1.09)
Immediate supervisor	.046 (1.44)	–.103* (–3.41)	–.124* (–4.10)	.086* (2.82)	.116* (3.67)	.098* (3.18)	–.047 (–1.48)
Mid-level administrator	.092* (2.70)	–.119* (–3.72)	–.171* (–5.36)	.135* (4.18)	.190* (5.64)	.167* (5.07)	–.043 (–1.28)
Top-level administrator	.076* (2.60)	–.147* (–5.36)	–.107* (–3.90)	.087* (3.12)	.077* (2.65)	.130* (4.57)	–.012 (–0.41)
Length of service	–.153* (–4.01)	–.018 (–0.49)	–.109* (–3.05)	.098* (2.70)	–.111* (–2.97)	–.065** (–1.75)	.083* (2.22)
Female	.011 (0.40)	.025 (0.92)	–.017 (–0.62)	.047** (1.74)	.006 (0.21)	.038 (1.36)	–.036 (–1.27)
Minority	–.003 (–0.10)	–.132* (–5.02)	–.007 (–0.25)	.073* (2.73)	–.056* (–2.03)	–.016 (–0.58)	.056* (2.05)
R^2	.022	.086	.088	.062	.033	.036	.013
N	1285	1362	1362	1361	1308	1361	1352

NB Entries are standardized coefficients (with t values in perentheses).

$*p < .05$ $**p < .10$

Second, officers with a college degree have more positive (or less negative) attitudes toward legal restrictions than do officers without a degree.[16] This result holds for both alternative measures of educational attainment, and also is consistent with previous research. The reason for this difference, which holds for both pre-service and in-service degree recipients, is not readily apparent in cross-sectional analysis, but it may be that education has the hypothesized effect on this attitude. This outcome is especially remarkable if, as the above results show, officers with (in-service) bachelor's degrees have a more restrictive conception of the police role; such a conception presumably would make legal restrictions more salient.

Third, college-educated officers generally display a greater preference for autonomy. Both officers with an associate's degree and those with a bachelor's degree are more discretion-control oriented; this finding too is corroborated by the other measures of education. Officers who earned their degrees as pre-service students, however, do not differ significantly on this dimension from officers with no college degrees. This finding suggests that the apparent effect of college education on attitudes toward discretion may in fact be a selection effect: in-service officers who undertake college studies may be more discretion-control oriented.

Fourth, education is related negatively to officers' attitudes toward rigid enforcement—i.e., college-educated officers are less inclined toward rigid enforcement. Although the relationship is statistically insignificant when education is measured in terms of either highest degree or years of education, it is statistically significant when education is measured in terms of college credits (beta = .076). Thus the analysis offers some support for the proposition that college-educated officers' attitudes predispose them to greater flexibility in applying the law. This relationship, too, may be an artifact of selection; that is, it might reflect pre-college differences in officers' attitudes.

Nevertheless, to dwell on the handful of statistically significant relationships that emerge from these analyses would be to overemphasize the impact of education on officers' attitudes. All of these relationships are quite small; only two of the 28 education-related coefficients in Table 1 exceed .10, and little of the variance in any attitude is explained by education (or by the control variables). Furthermore, all but (perhaps) one of the relationships could be attributed plausibly to selection rather than to the effects of college coursework. Thus insofar as officers' performance of police duties is shaped by their attitudes toward the scope of the police role, toward legal restrictions, toward discretion, and toward rigid enforcement, the indirect effects of police education on performance would appear to be very small indeed. This analysis gives little support to arguments that higher education will improve the quality of street-level policing by changing the attitudes of patrol officers.

By the same token, the analysis provides little or no support for the view that college-educated officers become frustrated or disaffected in the face of often

[16]This finding does not hold for command personnel with pre-service baccalaureates.

tedious work and/or organizational constraints on their behavior. They are no more likely than other officers to report that supervisors restrict their discretion (officers with an associate's degree report that they have more latitude rather than less). In addition, the morale and department ratings of college graduates are as high as (or no lower than) those of other officers, other things being equal.[17]

Neither is there evidence that the effects of education on attitudes are larger in police departments that exhibit greater support for higher education. Interactions between officers' educational levels and organizational support for education yield small and statistically insignificant coefficients, regardless of the threshold of agreement by which one defines "support." This finding perhaps should come as no surprise, because whether police departments are favorable or antipathetic to higher education, they nevertheless have rules, incentive systems, formal and informal priorities, training programs, and the like, to which officers must adapt. These and other features of the day-to-day work environment constitute the setting in which officers' occupational attitudes are formed.[18]

Performance

The performance of patrol officers, measured in terms of citizens' satisfaction, does not covary with officers' education. The bivariate relationship is virtually nil. A cross-tabulation (not presented here) reveals that citizens who encounter college-educated officers are 1) slightly less likely to be neutral in their evaluations and correspondingly more likely to be *either* satisfied *or* dissatisfied, and 2) if satisfied, slightly more likely to be very satisfied. Yet the differences are very small. Substantially the same results are obtained when one controls for other factors in a regression analysis. Table 2 reports the results of two analyses: one includes all of the incidents about which citizens were interviewed, and the other is restricted to selected incidents in which one might expect the effect of education to be more pronounced.[19] The results of the former analysis show that the effects of officers' characteristics generally, and of officers' educational levels particularly, are small and statistically insignificant. The results of the latter analysis are similar. One might expect that the impact of college education

---

[17]When educational levels are measured in terms of college credits, however, education bears a small, *positive,* and statistically significant relationship to morale; the standardized regression coefficient is .057. Further analysis, however, suggests that this relationship is attributable to outliers who have many college credits (i.e., more than 150 semester credits)—and who are generally higher-ranking officers with high morale. (Morale is unrelated to years of education.) The findings for department ratings also hold when the analysis includes dummy variables for the metropolitan areas. In addition, the morale and department ratings of command personnel with pre-service bachelor's degrees are *lower* than those of patrol officers with pre-service bachelor's degrees; this difference is statistically significant.

[18]More generally, see Jurik and Halemba's (1984) discussion of the "job model," which they apply to correctional officers.

[19]The same conclusions are reached when education is measured either by years of education or by number of college credits.

I excluded officers' rank from the analyses of citizens' evaluations because it displays almost no variation; all but a handful of the encounters involved patrol officers.

Table 2. Regression Analyses of Citizens' Satisfaction

	ALL INCIDENTS		SELECTED INCIDENTS	
	Beta	**t**	**Beta**	**t**
Officers' Characteristics				
Bachelor's degree	.032	0.58	.162	1.48
Pre-service bachelor's	.011	0.20	–.105	–0.94
Associate's degree	–.030	–0.64	–.088	–0.84
Pre-service associate's	–.011	–0.24	–.004	–0.03
Length of service	–.003	–0.06	–.065	–0.79
Minority	–.030	–0.76	.041	0.47
Female	.040	1.02	–.010	–0.12
Citizens' Characteristics				
Age	.062	1.59	.047	0.59
Female	–.070**	–1.81	–.012	–0.15
Minority	–.024	–0.60	–.027	–0.32
Income	.116*	2.95	.130**	1.65
Third Party	.078*	2.06	.075	0.95
Evaluation of police response:				
Faster than expected	.184**	4.65	.210*	2.57
Slower than expected	–.123*	–3.08	–.112	–1.38
Don't know	–.044	–1.15	–.075	–0.97
Type of problem				
Disturbance/assistance	.038	0.62	—	—
Victimization	–.012	–0.20	—	—
R^2	.12		.13	
N	644		168	

*p < .05
**p < .10

on officers' performance would be greater in situations that call for diagnostic and communication skills. The impact of education might even be obfuscated in an analysis that includes many routine cases, such as reports of "cold" crimes. Yet null findings also are obtained when the analysis is restricted to incidents that involve interpersonal conflicts and other disturbances. Citizens who were involved in such incidents expressed somewhat higher satisfaction with officers with bachelor's degrees, but the difference is not statistically significant.

Another approach to this question, which can be undertaken with the PSS data, is to examine why some citizens were dissatisfied. Most citizens were satisfied with their contact with the police, or at least neutral toward the experience; only 12 percent were dissatisfied. Those who were dissatisfied were asked why; each respondent was allowed to cite up to four sources of dissatisfaction. Six sources (beside an "other" category) were coded; all of these have been cross-tabulated with officers' education (see Table 3). The percentages in Table 3 are

Table 3. Cross-tabulation of Sources of Citizen Dissatisfaction by Officers' Education

	OFFICERS' EDUCATION		
	No College Degree	**Associate's Degree**	**Bachelor's Degree**
Source of Dissatisfaction			
Not courteous	20.4	5.0	31.2
Unable to solve problem	33.3	65.0	25.0
Incompetent	11.1	0.0	6.2
Used poor judgment, did the wrong thing	24.1	25.0	12.5
Didn't care, not understanding	38.9	40.0	37.5
Poor response time	18.5	10.0	12.5
N	54	20	16

Note: Entries are percentages of dissatisfied citizens who cited each source of dissatisfaction. Percentages exceed 100 because citizens could cite up to four sources.

generally based on rather small numbers, so they should be interpreted cautiously. Insofar as these responses are representative of dissatisfied citizens, however, they are strikingly consistent with the results of previous research. Dissatisfied citizens whose encounters involved officers with bachelor's degrees are less likely to cite poor judgment or an inability to solve their problems as the reasons for their dissatisfaction; one would expect to observe such a pattern if college-educated officers are better decision makers. The same respondents, however, are more likely to cite discourtesy as a source of their dissatisfaction. Perhaps because of the relative gravity of their concerns, these citizens were less likely to file a complaint: 25 percent told the interviewer that they had filed a complaint, compared to 32 percent of the dissatisfied citizens whose encounters involved officers with either no degree or an associate's degree.

In summary, most citizens are satisfied (or at least not dissatisfied) with their contacts with the police, and citizens are not generally more (or less) satisfied when their contacts are with college-educated officers. Although few citizens are dissatisfied, and although they are equally unlikely to be dissatisfied regardless of the officers' educational backgrounds, some evidence (albeit only suggestive evidence) shows that citizens are somewhat more likely to be dissatisfied with the decision-making and problem-solving abilities of less highly educated officers. These results are open to at least two plausible interpretations. One interpretation is that college-educated officers in fact are more tolerant of citizens who are different from themselves, are better able to analyze problems, make decisions, and apply verbal skills in effecting solutions, and for these reasons routinely perform more effectively in police-citizen encounters than do less highly educated officers; but the difference in performance in most cases cannot be detected by citizens. Another interpretation is that the superior analytical, decision-making, and communication skills that college-educated officers (presumably) possess have no observable effect on their performance except in a small proportion of the encounters in which they become involved; thus any observable differences in officers' performance are difficult for social scientists to detect in the aggregate. Therefore it would seem that the effect of college education on officers' performance in police-citizen encounters is small, or at best is limited to a restricted set of circumstances.[20]

CONCLUSIONS

The results of this study are by no means conclusive, but they are largely consistent with those of previous research, and thus lend added weight to their implications. The effects of college education on the attitudes of in-service police officers are small; the attitudes of officers who earn college degrees as preservice students do not differ substantially from those of their less highly educated colleagues. Furthermore, when officers' performance in police-citizen encounters is measured in terms of citizens' evaluations, little or no difference between college-educated and less highly educated officers can be detected. Thus although college-educated officers may be superior from the perspective of supervisors, who find that such officers are more reliable employees and better report writers, they are not superior from the perspective of police clientele, who are concerned principally with effective and courteous service in their contacts with police. Therefore this analysis suggests that patrol officers' performance and morale will be affected neither by policies that encourage in-service education nor by entry requirements that include college education.

The question of performance bears further scrutiny. Much of the research in this area has analyzed officers' attitudes with the implicit or explicit presumption that if education affects attitudes, then attitudes in turn would affect performance. Yet there are other equally compelling reasons to hypothesize that education affects officers' performance: education fosters the development of better judgment, analytical capacities, and communication skills, which in turn affect performance (Muir 1977:227–35). It may be, however, that the presumably superior judgment and skills of college-educated officers manifest themselves only in "critical incidents" (cf. Muir 1977:59 ff.)—complex situations in which desirable outcomes hinge less on the direct application of an officer's legal authority (or clerical skills) than on his or her insight into the dynamics of human problems and ability to communicate. If this is the case, future research on this subject should survey citizens rather than officers, and it should focus on types of incidents in which such personal skills could be expected to make a difference in performance. This research strategy represents a more direct approach to the question of performance, although officers' judgment, skills, tolerance, and so forth would remain subjects of inference rather than measurement,

[20]Cf. Bayley and Bittner, whose review of extant findings led them to speculate that "the situations police consider most problematic are not encountered often" (1984:38).

locked in a "black box" between the "input" of college education and the "output" of citizens' satisfaction.

Such research will not suffice to answer all of the empirical questions relevant to considerations of educational policies. Higher education might prepare candidates more thoroughly for supervisory and administrative positions,[21] and it might enhance the human resources on which innovative managerial practices (such as quality circles or problem-oriented policing) could draw. Stiffer educational requirements might serve to attract better recruits by raising the status of the occupation. Not all of these propositions, however, lend themselves to rigorous empirical analysis, and policy decisions cannot rest on empirical grounds alone. Even so, empirical research in this area can make a contribution to policy deliberations, if policy questions are formulated in terms of testable hypotheses.

REFERENCES

Barry, Donald M. (1978) "A Survey of Student and Agency Views on Higher Education in Criminal Justice." *Journal of Police Science and Administration* 6:345–54.

Bayley, David H. and Egon Bittner (1984) "Learning the Skills of Policing." *Law and Contemporary Problems* 47:35–59.

Beck, Paul Allen, Hal G. Rainey, Keith Nicholls, and Carol Traut (1987) "Citizen Views of Taxes and Services: A Tale of Three Cities." *Social Science Quarterly* 68:223–43.

Broderick, John J. (1977) *Police in a Time of Change.* Morristown, NJ: General Learning Press.

Brown, Lee P. (1974) "The Police and Higher Education: The Challenge of the Times." *Criminology* 12:114–24.

Brown, Michael K. (1981) *Working the Street: Police Discretion and the Dilemmas of Reform.* New York: Russell Sage Foundation.

Carlson, Helena and Markeley S. Sutton (1975) "The Effects of Different Police Roles on Attitudes and Values." *Journal of Psychology* 4:57–64.

Carmines, Edward G. and Richard A. Zeller (1979) *Reliability and Validity Assessment.* Beverly Hills: Sage.

Carter, David L., Allen D. Sapp, and Darrel W. Stephens (1989) *The State of Police Education: Policy Direction for the 21st Century.* Washington, DC: Police Executive Research Forum.

Cascio, Wayne F. (1977) "Formal Education and Police Officer Performance." *Journal of Police Science and Administration* 5:89–96.

Cascio, Wayne F. and Leslie J. Real (1976) "Educational Standards for Police Officer Personnel." *The Police Chief* 43 (August):54–55.

Christenson, James A. and Gregory S. Taylor (1983) "The Socially Constructed and Situational Context for Assessment of Public Services." *Social Science Quarterly* 64:264–74.

Cohen, Bernard and Jan M. Chaiken (1972) *Police Background Characteristics and Performance.* New York: Rand.

Dalley, A. F. (1975) "University Vs. Non-University Graduated Policeman: A Study of Police Attitudes." *Journal of*

[21]Advocates of professional education for police managers, however, should consider the potential implications for bureaucratic accountability; see Mosher (1982).

Police Science and Administration 3:458–68.

Durand, Roger (1976) "Some Dynamics of Urban Service Evaluations Among Blacks and Whites." *Social Science Quarterly* 56:698–706.

Finckenauer, James O. (1975) "Higher Education and Police Discretion." *Journal of Police Science and Administration* 3:450–57.

Finnigan, James C. (1976) "A Study of Relationships Between College Education and Police Performance in Baltimore, Maryland." *The Police Chief* 43 (August):60–62.

Fischer, Robert J., Kathryn M. Golden, and Bruce L. Heininger (1985) "Issues in Higher Education for Law Enforcement Officers: An Illinois Study." *Journal of Criminal Justice* 13:329–38.

Flanagan, Timothy J., Michael J. Hindelang, and Michael R. Gottfredson (1979) *Sourcebook of Criminal Justice Statistics—1979.* Washington, DC.: U.S. Government Printing Office.

Fogelson, Robert M. (1977) *Big-City Police.* Cambridge: Harvard University Press.

Goldstein, Herman (1977) *Policing a Free Society.* Cambridge: Ballinger.

Hanushek, Erik A. and John E. Jackson (1977) *Statistical Methods for Social Scientists.* New York: Academic Press.

Hudzik, John K. (1978) "College Education for Police: Problems In Measuring Component and Extraneous Variables." *Journal of Criminal Justice* 6:69–81.

Jurik, Nancy C. and Gregory J. Halemba (1984) "Gender, Working Conditions, and the Job Satisfaction of Women in a Non-Traditional Occupation: Female Correctional Officers in Men's Prisons." *Sociological Quarterly* 25:551–66.

Kuykendall, Jack L. (1977) "Criminal Justice Programs in Higher Education: Course and Curriculum Orientations." *Journal of Criminal Justice* 5:149–63.

Lynch, Gerald W. (1976) "The Contributions of Higher Education to Ethical Behavior in Law Enforcement." *Journal of Criminal Justice* 4:285–90.

Manning, Peter K. (1977) *Police Work: The Social Organization of Policing.* Cambridge: MIT Press.

Mastrofski, Stephen (1981) "Surveying Clients to Assess Police Performance." *Evaluation Review* 5:397–408.

Mathias, William J. (1976) "Higher Education and the Police." In Arthur Niederhoffer and Abraham S. Blumberg (eds.), *The Ambivalent Force: Perspectives on the Police.* 2nd Edition. Hinsdale, IL: Dryden, pp. 377–85.

Miller, Jon and Lincoln Fry (1976) "Reexamining Assumptions About Education and Professionalism in Law Enforcement." *Journal of Police Science and Administration* 4:187–98.

Mosher, Frederick C. (1982) *Democracy and the Public Service.* 2nd Edition. New York: Oxford University Press.

Muir, William Ker, Jr. (1977) *Police: Streetcorner Politicians.* Chicago: University of Chicago Press.

Niederhoffer, Arthur (1969) *Behind the Shield: The Police in Urban Society.* Garden City, NY: Anchor.

Parks, Roger B. (1984) "Linking Objective and Subjective Measures of Performance." *Public Administration Review* 44:118–27.

Percy, Stephen L. (1980) "Response Time and Citizen Evaluation of Police." *Journal of Police Science and Administration* 8:75-86.

Regoli, Robert M. (1976) "The Effects of College Education on the Maintenance of Police Cynicism." *Journal of Police Science and Administration* 4:340–45.

Reuss-Ianni, Elizabeth (1983) *Two Cultures of Policing.* New Brunswick, NJ: Transaction.

Roberg, Roy R. (1978) "An Analysis of the Relationships Among Higher Education, Belief Systems, and the Job Performance of Patrol Officers." *Journal of Police and Administration* 6:336–44.

Rokeach, Milton (1968) *Beliefs, Attitudes, and Values: A Theory of Organization and Change.* San Francisco: Jossey-Bass.

Sanderson, B. E. (1977) "Police Officers: The Relationship of College Education to Job Performance." *The Police Chief* 44 (August):62–63.

Saunders, Charles B., Jr. (1970) *Upgrading the American Police: Education and Training for Better Law Enforcement.* Washington, DC: Brookings Institution.

Schuman, Howard and Michael P. Johnson (1976) "Attitudes and Behavior." *Annual Review of Sociology* 2:161–207.

Sherman, Lawrence W. (1980) "Causes of Police Behavior: The Current State of Quantitative Research." *Journal of Research in Crime and Delinquency* 17:69–100.

Sherman, Lawrence W. and Warren Bennis (1977) "Higher Education for Police Officers: The Central Issues." *The Police Chief* 44 (August):32–34.

Sherman, Lawrence W. and the National Advisory Comission on Higher Education for Police Officers (1978) *The Quality of Police Education.* San Francisco: Jossey-Bass.

Simon, Herbert A. (1976) *Administrative Behavior.* 3rd edition. New York: Free Press.

Smith, Alexander, Bernard Locke, and Abe Fenster (1970) "Authoritarianism in Policemen Who Are College Graduates and Non-College Police." *Journal of Criminal Law, Criminology, and Police Science* 61:313–15.

Smith, Alexander, Bernard Locke, and William F. Walker (1967) "Authoritarianism in College and Non-College Oriented Police." *Journal of Criminal Law, Criminology, and Police Science* 58:128–32.

Smith, Dennis C. (1978) "Dangers of Police Professionalization: An Empirical Analysis." *Journal of Criminal Justice* 6:199–216.

Smith, Dennis C. and Elinor Ostrom (1974) "The Effects of Training and Education on Police Attitudes and Performance: A Preliminary Analysis." In Herbert Jacob (ed.), *The Potential for Reform of Criminal Justice.* Beverly Hills: Sage, pp. 45–81.

Sterling, J. W. (1974) "The College Level Entry Requirement: A Real or Imagined Cure-All?" *The Police Chief* 41 (August):28–31.

Stipak, Brian (1977) "Attitudes and Belief Systems Concerning Urban Services." *Public Opinion Quarterly* 41:41–55.

—— (1979) "Citizen Satisfaction with Urban Services: Potential Misuse as a Performance Indicator." *Public Administration Review* 39:46–52.

Swanson, Charles R. (1977) "An Uneasy Look at College Education and the Police Organization." *Journal of Criminal Justice* 5:311–20.

Trojanowicz, Robert C. and Thomas G. Nicholson (1976) "A Comparison of Behavioral Styles of College Graduate Police Officers V. Noncollege-Going Police Officers." *Police Chief* 43 (August):56–59.

U.S. Department of Justice (1978) *The National Manpower Survey of the Criminal Justice System.* Volume 2: *Law Enforcement.* Washington, DC: U.S. Government Printing Office.

Van Maanen, John (1974) "Working the Street: A Developmental View of Police Behavior." In Herbert Jacob (ed.), *The Potential for Reform of Criminal Justice.* Beverly Hills: Sage, pp. 83–130.

Walker, Samuel (1977) *A Critical History of Police Reform.* Lexington, MA: Heath.

Weiner, Norman L. (1974) "The Effect of Education on Police Attitudes." *Journal of Criminal Justice* 2:317–28.

White, Susan O. (1972) "A Perspective on Police Professionalization." *Law & Society Review* 7:61–85.

Wilson, James Q. (1968) *Varieties of Police Behavior: The Management of Law and Order in Eight Communities.* Cambridge: Harvard University Press.

Worden, Robert E. (1986) "The Premises of Police Work: What Policemen Believe and What Difference It Makes." Unpublished doctoral dissertation, University of North Carolina.

—— (1989) "Situational and Attitudinal Explanations of Police Behavior: A Theoretical Reappraisal and Empirical Assessment." *Law & Society Review* 23:667-711.

Wycoff, Mary Ann and Charles E. Susmilch (1979) "The Relevance of College Education for Policing: Continuing the Dialogue." In David M. Petersen (ed.), *Police Work: Strategies and Outcomes in Law Enforcement*. Beverly Hills: Sage, pp. 17–35.

DISCUSSION QUESTIONS

1. Under what circumstances would you be more likely to rely on secondary data?
2. What types of measures were used in this analysis?
3. What does the author conclude from this study?
4. Are there other ways in which this study could have been accomplished? If so, how?

PART VII

Other Methods

This part presents examples of research approaches that do not fall conveniently within the usual categories. Designs employing focus groups, content analysis, simulations, case studies, and combinations of differing methods are among those that do not fit elsewhere and, so, reside here. Each of these "other" methods has strengths and limitations. We discuss below those methods employed in the three articles that make up this section.

Mastrofski and Ritti, "You Can Lead a Horse to Water . . . ," conducted a case study using multiple methods. The researchers examined police reaction to changes in drunk driving, or driving-under-the-influence (DUI), laws in one Pennsylvania police department. As you will see, they combined in-depth interviews with use of a structured questionnaire, review of documents and records, and a telephone survey of local residents.

The drawback most often mentioned regarding case studies is limited or no ability to generalize findings. However, the primary advantage of a case study approach is the ability to remain flexible, follow leads, and generate in-depth data. Further, as did the researchers in this study, case study results may be examined in relation to what is known about other similar populations or sites to attempt to determine whether the empirical base is atypical. Mastrowski and

Ritti, interestingly, find that the department's responsiveness to the state's drunk driving law is not due to external political pressure or formal policy as might be expected. Rather, it is due to the inability of local authorities to impose their will on street-level practices. The case study approach afforded the opportunity to reach insights and a conclusion that may not have been possible using other approaches.

Durham, Elrod, and Kinkade, "Images of Crime and Justice: Murder and the 'True Crime' Genre," employ content analysis to examine the portrayal of homicide cases in "true crime" books. Comparing the content with official data on murders, they find the crime portrayals differ significantly from the full range of cases that typify murder in America. In other words, the true-crime portrayals are not typical.

Good content analysis is disciplined by theoretical considerations, starting, as do the researchers, with a theoretical problem rather than with the already existing data. It is the question that counts, not the count itself. The authors provide a good example of the selection of a working universe, the construction of analytic categories, and the operational definition of these categories.

Schneider, Ervin, and Snyder-Joy, "Further Exploration of the Flight from Discretion," combine historical analysis with in-depth interviews and a focus-group discussion to examine the implementation of risk/needs instruments, and perceptions of value of such instruments, among parole/probation officers in one jurisdiction. The combination of methods allowed the researchers to develop different types of data on the research questions. Besides allowing examination of differing dimensions of the questions, using a combination of methods brought flexibility. This allowed the researchers to identify important issues to follow, obtain difficult-to-develop insights to assist in interpreting quantitative data, and develop greater understanding of the subjects' language and meanings. Often quantitative data indicate where to look, while meaningful explanation is achieved through complementary qualitative approaches.

16

You Can Lead a Horse to Water . . .

A Case Study of a Police Department's Response to Stricter Drunk-Driving Laws

STEPHEN D. MASTROFSKI, The Pennsylvania State University
R. RICHARD RITTI, The Pennsylvania State University

COMMENTARY

We take this opportunity to write about our behind-the-scenes experiences conducting research for this article. We will comment on obtaining access to collect data, using a variety of data collection methods, and the rigors of fieldwork.

We enjoyed easy access to the Melville Police Department and other public and private organizations in Melville. We attribute that in large part to the sponsorship of our study by the Pennsylvania Department of Transportation, the state agency that solicited and funded our research proposal. This sponsorship legitimated our project, enabling us to secure the participation of an advisory board of police leaders from departments large and small around the state. Their advice and support, along with that of the Pennsylvania Police Chiefs' Association, made it possible to obtain a 79 percent response rate to our mail survey of police chiefs. They and the Association publicized our study and encouraged police agencies to participate. Having got our "foot in the door" with the mail survey, we selected a sample of nineteen departments for intensive fieldwork. Securing permission from the chief of each department, including Melville, required no more than a phone call to each.

Source: Justice Quarterly, Vol. 9, No. 3, September 1992, ©1992. Reprinted by permission of the Academy of Criminal Justice Sciences.

This work was sponsored by the Pennsylvania Department of Transportation. The contents of this report reflect the views of the authors who are responsible for the facts and the accuracy of the data presented herein. The contents do not necessarily reflect the official views or policies of the Commonwealth of Pennsylvania at the time of publication. This report does not constitute a standard, specification or regulation.

In Melville, we enjoyed the good offices of a precinct commander who was assigned by the chief as the department liaison to the project. He took special pains to prepare all of the department's middle managers for our site visit. A long-time member of the force, he also proved a valuable source of inside information, which we were pleased to cultivate over several meals and other social events tangential to our study. Community groups seemed eager to talk to us because our funding agency sponsored many statewide conferences and training sessions on drunk driving. We also credit our ease of access to our affiliation with Pennsylvania State University, an institution widely known throughout the state's law enforcement community. A continuing education institute associated with our academic department had for years provided training to police executives and supervisors around the state, so many had firsthand contact with our academic institution. Penn State was also highly visible to the police because of the success of its athletic teams. Many of our first conversations with police administrators and community leaders began and ended with casual discussion of the football team. Finally, we note that our study's topic was not the sort to register high in the concerns of most police or other public officials in Melville. Had we attempted a study of drug enforcement, the political salience of this topic would have undoubtedly made our task more challenging.

Field researchers who study organizations quickly learn that getting approval from the top administrator is no guarantee of access to the rank-and-file employees. Such access was particularly challenging in Melville, where the officers' bargaining unit and management had an adversarial relationship that could fairly be described as hostile. Thus, anointment by top administrators meant that we were immediately suspect by labor representatives. Because our study was funded by a state agency, the union was unlikely to oppose our presence formally, but many administrators cautioned us that we should expect informal resistance and lots of refusals to submit to surveys and interviews if the union leaders decided that it was in their interest to do so. We did not make special efforts to meet with the union's leaders, because management did not want us to formally acknowledge their influence. We also felt that we should not appear to be going "hat in hand" to ask for their endorsement, for doing so might encourage them to use us as a negotiating lever with management. We opted instead for a more informal, fait accompli approach.

The union president happened to be a shift commander in one of the precincts. We scheduled our interviews and surveys for that precinct late on the second day of precinct-level fieldwork—making sure that we began in another precinct on the first day. We conducted in-depth interviews first, and included the shift commander among those requested. We treated the shift commander like all other interviewees and did not mention the union. We made sure, however, to stress the importance of the study for a *complete* picture of the topic. We told him that we had spent several days talking to the "brass," and now we wanted to learn the views and experiences of the officers who actually did the work. This strategy seemed to work well. The shift commander said that he had heard through the grapevine what we were doing. He had been skeptical of the study's utility, but he thought it was a good idea for us to get the rank-and-file perspective. Not only did he participate in the interview, he later introduced us to the officers reporting to roll call, and before we handed out our questionnaire, he announced to his subordinates that "You don't have to fill out this survey and there will be no consequences if you decline, but I'm making out the form, and if you want to have *your* views heard, you should do it too." We later heard from some department administrators that this was absolutely the best endorsement for which we could hope. We experienced fewer than 5 percent refusals for our survey questionnaire, and none for our in-depth interviews.

Our access to the rank and file was also facilitated by other techniques used frequently by field researchers. Our open-ended in-depth interviews were flexible. They could be completed in 15–20 minutes, or they could take much longer, depending upon the inclination of the respondent. We tried to do these interviews *before* we handed out the structured questionnaires to all officers, because we wanted the word to get out that we were "OK," were not asking threatening questions, and we knew something about the topic. We found that this procedure sometimes worked "too well." Occasionally officers who were not on our sample list would seek us out because *they* wanted to be interviewed. We accommodated them whenever we could.

We kept the structured questionnaire short so that it could be administered at roll call, minimizing the amount of time that officers would be detained from their normal duties. We suspect that we were aided here by the cold winter weather, which made more appealing the prospect of staying a few more minutes in the warm station house to complete the survey. We also required that officers turn in the survey before leaving the roll-call room, making it much easier to retrieve all surveys.

Because of the need to do in-depth interviews and administer structured questionnaires at roll call, we ended up "hanging out" at each precinct station house. We were often introduced by officers we had just interviewed to other officers passing through. Casual conversations about the study's topic and invitations to "watch us handle a DUI arrestee" often followed. In fact, that is how we were approached by the "bounty hunter" who told us that his supervisors had tried to prevent him from seeing us.

Our access was also enhanced by our efforts to guarantee the confidentiality of those who granted interviews or completed the questionnaire. We emphasized these guarantees to our research subjects and made the questionnaires anonymous, so that even we could not link survey responses to individuals. We were careful in the kinds of personal characteristics questions we asked so that officers would not feel we were trying to trick them by learning their identities that way. Finally, although we did not promise or suggest that we would mask the department's identity in our published work, we decided to do so to protect public officials whose identity would be certain if the city were named.

Our multimethod approach to data collection produced many benefits, but it was labor-intensive. We have already mentioned how the in-depth interviews helped us gain higher response rates to our structured questionnaire. Gathering documents and perusing agency records while in the field also helped us ask more informed questions of our respondents, and our interviewees sometimes gave us leads that we were able to pursue through agency records while in the field. "Hanging out" enabled us to fit in a bit better, since desk officers, bored with their work, would strike up conversations and often revealed useful things about the organization indirectly that we would not have thought to ask them. This approach meant long work hours that began with day-shift roll call and did not end until well into the midnight shift. Short naps at the precinct station between interviews were important for getting enough sleep to keep this up for several days running. We also conducted a telephone survey of residents of Melville from our research offices at the university. We were assisted in our fieldwork by graduate students, and we employed undergraduates to conduct the telephone interviews. We were able to use these different methods of data collection because of the funding we received, but we have also done similar projects at a single site with little or no external funding.

In sum, our approach to fieldwork in this study was to plan carefully certain data collection activities (the interviews and roll-call questionnaires) but to remain flexible in how and when we carried them out. Doing so enabled us to collect a tremendous amount of information about the department and the community in a short time on-site.

ABSTRACT We present a case study illustrating the complexity of the process that determines how vigorously local police agencies enforce recent drunk-driving laws. Police enforcement practices are influenced most strongly by the play of local factors in a system of "games." The local forces exerting greatest influence are 1) the local demand for drunk-driving enforcement, 2) the police leadership's priority for DUI enforcement, 3) the police leadership's capacity for command and control of the organization, and 4) the disposition of the local police culture regarding drunk driving and related work issues. In "Melville," the study site, there is little external demand for drunk-driving enforcement, and police management tries to suppress it while making only symbolic gestures of support. Management's capacity to control street-level enforcement practices is limited, however, and a small cadre of officers generates a disproportionate number of arrests for personal financial gain (bounty), giving the department a much higher arrest rate than the department desires. Thus Melville's responsiveness to the state's drunk-driving law is not due to external political pressure or formal policy, but rather to the *inability* of local authorities to impose their will on street-level practices. Melville's case suggests that the degree to which police implement a new criminal law may be entirely independent of efforts to ensure political accountability and organizational control.

Glendower: I can call spirits from the vasty deep.
Hotspur: Why, so can I, or so can any man;
But will they come when you do call for them?

—Shakespeare, *Henry IV, Part I,* III.i (53)

From time to time legislatures struggle mightily to produce major changes in the criminal law in response to popular or professional pressures. Sometimes an act that once was legal is made criminal, such as the manufacture and distribution of alcoholic beverages (the Volstead Act). Sometimes the penalties for an existing crime are increased, such as the so-called "Rockefeller drug laws" in New York State in the early 1970s. And sometimes what once was criminal is decriminalized, or at least made a less serious offense (e.g., public drunkenness). Such enactments often represent the culmination of an important political drama, but one that is essentially symbolic, because the struggle to pass the law is a struggle about what shall be *written* into law. Like Glendower's summons, these laws evoke powerful forces—law enforcement agencies in this case, instead of demons. In the case of criminal laws passed by *states* for enforcement by *local* police, the metaphor of "vasty deep" seems apt because the latter are often far removed from the former, both geographically and in orientation to the issue at hand. Like Hotspur, then, we are led to wonder what police agencies will do when called to implement major changes in the criminal law.

In this paper we are concerned with the police reaction to changes in drunk-driving, or driving-under-the-influence (DUI), laws. Recent changes in drunk-driving laws around the nation have created an expectation of increased DUI enforcement. We argue that the police implementation of the new laws lacks uniformity because the organizations responsible for enforcement are local and are influenced heavily by local extralegal considerations. We briefly discuss the characteristics of local police organizations and their relationship to DUI enforcement levels. Then we illustrate the play between these characteristics and police DUI enforcement practices in a case study analysis of one police department.

DUI LEGAL REFORM IN THE 1980s

During the 1980s most states passed tougher drunk-driving laws following the "Scandinavian model": 1) a per se standard of evidence requiring only proof that the driver's blood alcohol level exceed a given threshold, 2) vigorous enforcement using breath and blood tests, and 3) severe sentences, including mandatory incarceration and loss of license (Jacobs 1989:123–26). Rationales for these changes included just deserts, deterrence, incapacitation, and even rehabilitation. Whatever the rationale, however, successful implementation requires higher drunk-driving arrest rates.

A number of scholars have pointed out that before the 1980s American criminal justice officials, reflecting widespread popular values, rarely treated drunk driving as a serious offense (Brown 1981; Gusfield 1981; Jacobs 1989; Reinarman 1988). Yet there are many reasons to expect police to respond dramatically after the flurry of drunk-driving legislation that swept the United States in the first half of the last decade. This issue achieved nationwide attention with astounding speed. Grass-roots campaigns by Mothers Against Drunk

Drivers (MADD), Remove Intoxicated Drivers (RID), Students Against Drunk Drivers (SADD), and other groups received a great deal of attention from the press. A 1982 Gallup national survey showed that 89 percent of respondents favored stricter DUI laws, and 77 percent favored a two-day jail term for first offenders (Flanagan and McLeod 1983:287). A 1987 National Punishment Survey showed that the public rated a drunk driver who killed someone as committing a crime slightly more serious than someone who raped a victim without causing other physical injury. Someone who drove drunk but did not cause an accident was rated as a slightly more serious offender than an unarmed robber who took $10 from a victim without causing bodily harm. In the case of death due to the DUI accident, 91 percent of respondents favored incarcerating the offender; in the case of the drunk driver who caused no accident, 54 percent favored incarceration (Flanagan and Jamieson 1988:150–51).

Not only have public attitudes shifted significantly, but the antidrunk-driving movement has been institutionalized in the proliferation of grass-roots citizen groups, state-supported anti-DUI programs, and federal interest in drunk driving as a national problem (Jacobs 1989:196). The availability of state and federal funds to undertake DUI enforcement is an incentive to local police departments to field special DUI enforcement programs; these programs endure despite fluctuations in the public's concern about drunk driving. Perhaps most important for local police, the rapid growth of citizens' antidrunk-driving groups means that local special interest groups are paying attention to drunk driving in their communities, thus increasing the likelihood that drunk driving remains on the local political and law enforcement agenda (Reinarman 1988).

Several features of the drunk driving offense itself should make rigorous enforcement attractive to police. Compared to other types of offenses, especially those occurring in private places, enforcement opportunities are plentiful and accessible to police (see Jacobs 1989:43–47 for estimates). The law affords police greater power to stop and question drivers of automobiles than to intervene with pedestrians and citizens in private places. Also, in view of the kind of evidence provided by breath and blood tests, a conviction is far more likely. In addition, because DUI arrests can be (and usually are) accomplished without a citizen complainant or a witness, the administrator can consider an officer's DUI arrests to be mostly the product of his or her own initiative and skill. Consequently, administrators who want to increase arrest rates presumably can exert some direct control over officers whose DUI activity is subpar. Thus police departments can use the DUI law to demonstrate their commitment to law enforcement in a manner that features organizational productivity.

Despite several indicators of a climate favoring DUI enforcement over the last decade, the police response appears to be quite variable. According to the Uniform Crime Reports, different types of communities show substantially different changes in DUI arrest rates. Between 1975 and 1985, for example, the DUI arrest rate per capita increased 69 percent in cities of 100,000 to 249,999 population, but only 38 percent in communities of fewer than 10,000 persons (U.S. Department of Justice 1989:169). In 1985 the DUI arrest rate per 100,000 population ranged from 78 in Delaware of 1,260 in California (Flanagan and Jamieson 1988:398).[1]

A Framework for Understanding the Implementation of DUI Laws

The enactment of legislation raises questions of implementation, and that implementation has been described metaphorically as a system of "games" involving a variety of players who have some stake in how the legislation is carried out (Bardach 1977). The stakes in the games associated with the implementation of any law will vary. Control of the implementation process is the principal object of these games, which consist of various tactics and strategies by stakeholders. Several types of games disrupt successful implementation: those involving the diversion of resources to carry out the law, the deflection of goals from the lawmakers' original intent, disruptions to effective administrative control of the implementation process, and the dissipation of energies in other games. Such an analytic framework invites a particular approach to analyzing the implementation of legislation:

> It directs us to look at the players, what they regard as the stakes, their strategies and tactics, their resources for playing, the rules of play (which stipulate the conditions for winning), the rules of "fair" play (which stipulate the boundaries beyond which lie fraud or illegitimacy), the nature of the communications (or lack of them) among the players, and the degree of uncertainty surrounding the possible outcomes. The game metaphor also directs our attention to who is not willing to play and for what reasons, and who insists on changes in some of the game's parameters as a condition for playing (Bardach, 1977:56).

Who are the players in the DUI enforcement games? State agencies are not irrelevant, but their impact is usually quite limited. States characteristically do *not* set up special agencies to monitor the local enforcement of criminal laws, as they often do with various civil and regulatory laws (e.g., equal employment, environmental, labor, antitrust).[2] Indeed, states rarely provide additional funds for the enforcement of new criminal laws (Casper and Brereton 1984).[3] Even

---

[1]Some of this disparity may accrue to differences in the laws, although surveys of current DUI laws show a rather consistent pattern across most states in the key elements of the Scandinavian model.

[2]States have set up antidrunk-driving task forces and agencies (Jacobs, 1984:197), but they, like the national drug "czar," characteristically lack the authority or power to establish implementation standards and monitor compliance.

[3]Federal legislation has linked highway funds to a state's *passage* of antidrunk-driving countermeasures, but the receipt of funds has not been tied to actual levels of DUI *enforcement*. Some states provide for the return of some portion of DUI fines to the government of the arresting police department, but no systematic data are available on the scope of this incentive system and on whether these funds are earmarked for future DUI enforcement.

though the nationalization of drunk driving as an issue and the passage of tougher laws undoubtedly have stimulated enforcement,[4] a great deal of scholarship on law enforcement in America, directs our attention to *local* players to predict DUI enforcement levels (Gardiner 1969; Goldstein 1977; Langworthy 1985; Ostrom, Parks, and Whitaker 1978; Slovak 1986; Wilson 1968; Wilson and Boland 1978). Local factors are the screen through which the effects of the broader trend must be filtered.

The "DUI enforcement game," then, is played on local turf and dominated by local players. Elsewhere we have argued that precisely who plays, how they play, and the consequences for DUI enforcement levels are determined largely by several environmental and organizational factors: 1) the local demand for drunk-driving enforcement, 2) the police administration's priority for DUI enforcement, 3) the police administration's capacity for command and control of the organization, and 4) the disposition of the local police culture regarding drunk driving and related work issues (Mastrofski, Ritti, and Hoffmaster 1987).

Demand for DUI Enforcement

The everyday work of police is determined mostly by the demands placed on the department by its citizens through "calls for service" (Goldstein 1990:20). Virtually every American police department places top priority on responding to calls for service; unless a routine crime comes to police attention through this mechanism, a special effort by the department's leader is required to divert resources for DUI enforcement. Drunk-driving offenses rarely come to police attention because of a citizen's complaint; *police*-initiated enforcement is needed to achieve arrest levels beyond the relatively few offenses made known to police from reported accidents (Jacobs 1989:110). Making a DUI arrest is time-consuming, however; sometimes it takes four hours to process. An officer can commit this kind of time only if resources are adequate to handle the calls for service workload or if the department is willing to reduce the level of response to calls for service. From the rational administrator's perspective, it seems risky to fail to respond to a specific request for service. Nonresponse produces a disgruntled citizen, whereas the failure to stop or arrest a potential drunk driver rarely generates a specific complaint about police service.

Because the police rarely experience demand for DUI enforcement through calls for service, the principal source of pressure, when it is experienced at all, is the demand for action by politically salient local "players." Characteristically, such pressure originates with citizens' groups, elected officials, candidates for local office, heads of human service agencies, and the press. The nature and the extent of external pressure for DUI enforcement establish the stakes of the DUI

[4]Between the mid-1970s and mid-1980s the nation's drunk-driving arrest rate increased 55 percent. It peaked in 1983 and has declined somewhat since then (Greenfield 1988:2).

enforcement game and determine the risks associated with the tactics employed by the players.[5] When these pressures are sufficiently high, the police chief ignores or opposes them only at great peril. Where the political pressures about drunk driving are not strong, the risks of ignoring the problem or assigning it a low priority are modest. A police administrator, however, may seize upon DUI in entrepreneurial fashion, crusading to create an issue, solve a problem, and help establish an identity for himself and the department (Bullington and Block 1990). In this way, someone in the police organization fashions a benefit from initiating DUI enforcement, even when the stakes (initially at least) are low. This strategy is risky, however, because the crusading chief must quickly develop community support or else face any opposition that arises without allies.

Priorities of the Police Administration

Setting agency priorities is one of the key functions of top administrators. Wilson (1968) argued that the selection of the chief is the most significant influence that local elected officials can exert on their police department. It is the chief who articulates the department's general goals, sets its operational priorities, and establishes an ethos for accomplishing them (e.g., through professionalism). Gardiner (1969) found that the principal determinant of traffic enforcement was management policy, but a number of subsequent analyses have called these findings into question. Managerial priorities appear not to play a dominating role in directing arrest patterns generally (Aaronson, Dienes, and Musheno 1984; Brown 1981; Klockars 1985; Manning 1977; Muir 1977) or in DUI arrest patterns specifically (Mastrofski et al. 1987). Still, a police administrator rarely states publicly that enforcement of *any* offense is a low priority, because such a statement would belie the convenient fiction that the law is being enforced fully (Klockars 1985).

Police Administrators' Command and Control Capacity

A chief who wishes to give drunk-driving enforcement a high priority must do so by shaping patrol officers' street-level discretion. Probably the most frequent management approach to persuading the rank and file is simply exhortation—arguing for a particular perspective and providing what the chief believes are compelling reasons for that view. For example, the chief may highlight the threat to highway safety posed by drunk drivers and may even invite citizen advocate groups to address officers, giving the victim's perspective on drunk driving.

The department also may influence the socialization of those people it selects as police by the way it trains them—both initially and throughout their careers. The amount and quality of recruit training devoted to DUI enforcement

[5]Although conceivably there could be external pressure *not* to enforce DUI laws (e.g., from bar and restaurant owners), we have not found this in the literature or in our own research. Visible pressure groups have coalesced to seek more enforcement, not less.

not only signals the department's commitment; it also provides the basic knowledge and skills necessary to do the job correctly and in a way that will not embarrass the officer in court. Assigning rookies to work with experienced officers who have a commitment to DUI enforcement is another way of reinforcing DUI efforts.

A third major way in which administrators shape their subordinates' behavior is to reward and punish them on the basis of their adherence to policies, rules, and priorities. The chief can issue policies and directives specifying the procedures for identifying, arresting, and processing drunk drivers, and he can order his subordinates to commit their efforts to this purpose. To make those policies meaningful, the chief must have the capacity to monitor officers' DUI arrest productivity, and he must have sufficient influence over factors that matter to officers, namely job benefits and career opportunities. The chief also must have control over disciplinary actions: He must be able to withhold significant work benefits and to censure, suspend, and even dismiss officers who fail to perform adequately or who misbehave. Few chiefs, however, especially in large departments, enjoy this kind of power.[6] Their capacity to offer positive reinforcement is typically limited to distributing desirable job assignments and training opportunities. The capacity to offer direct financial rewards for arrests is constrained severely by personnel rules, although administrators sometimes can offer *indirect* financial rewards by influencing the disbursement of overtime pay (often this is a factor in time-consuming DUI arrests). Yet because administrators' capacity to influence all of these factors is modest at best, the real power of the top administrator and the rest of the supervisory hierarchy is to make the officers' work environment the least onerous possible. They can do so by protecting officers from outside censure and internal discipline when their enforcement initiatives generate complaints (Muir 1977; Van Maanen 1983). They also can make it as easy and efficient as possible to process DUI arrests.

In view of the widely acknowledged importance of the street-level officer's discretion in determining actual enforcement practices, the police administrator's command and control capacity depends on his power to recruit and indoctrinate officers with his priorities and to reward and discipline them accordingly. The stronger the command and control capacity, the greater the likelihood that the administrator will secure enforcement practices consistent with his priority for DUI enforcement—whatever that priority might be. Some literature suggests that strong interaction effects sometimes exist between external pressure for police practice and the command and control capacity; police chiefs who are willing and able to take advantage of strong crisis-generated pressure to change practices controlling lethal force and corruption have enjoyed some success in reducing the level of undesired incidents (Sherman 1977; 1983; Fyfe 1979).

---

[6]Bardach (1977:139) calls this centralization of the administrator's power the "management game" and notes that despite recurring campaigns in government for "better management," this strategy cannot overcome the structural limitations of control of major programs and the agencies that must administer them.

Informal Social Control

In addition to the formal system of hierarchical control, police organizations have informal systems that influence the exercise of street-level discretion on matters such as DUI enforcement. A number of scholars have noted this bifurcation of control systems in police departments, and refer to the loosely structured informal system as a police subculture reflecting the values, beliefs, and orientations of the rank and file (Manning 1977; 1989; Reuss-Ianni, 1983; Rubinstein 1973; Skolnick 1966; Van Maanen 1974). Evidence suggests that the rank and file vary considerably in their law enforcement priorities (Broderick 1977; Brown 1981; Muir 1977; Worden 1989); patterns in these belief systems may reflect a particular *local* police culture, much as members of the courtroom work group have been found to vary in their local legal culture (Eisenstein, Flemming, and Nardulli 1988).

The tendency of the rank and file to be actively engaged in DUI enforcement has been found to influence the level of DUI arrests in departments, independent of management directives (Mastrofski et al. 1987). Particularly interesting is the prospect that increasingly heterogeneous police forces will not show a single, uniform orientation to a task such as DUI enforcement, but rather will demonstrate diversity through cliques that reinforce divergent enforcement perspectives (Mastrofski 1990:8–17). Perhaps strong support (or opposition) by a small group of officers will have a disproportionate effect on the department's performance in DUI enforcement.

Although the values, beliefs, and orientations of the rank and file are explicit objects of the police hierarchy's formal system of command and control, the local police culture clearly responds very slowly, if at all, if only because it is easier to change police administrators (by firing, hiring, and demotion) than the rank and file. The local police culture therefore is always a potential force in shaping a department's DUI enforcement practices, particularly when the formal command and control capacity is weak. This is the chronic state of police departments that Wilson characterized as having the "watchman" style (1968:ch.5).

We have suggested that several local factors determine how vigorously the new DUI laws will be enforced. Much of the literature on police organizations suggests that a causal chain links these factors, beginning with the political environment and ending with the performance of the rank and file, as reflected in patterns of arrest (Gardiner 1969; Langworthy 1985; Slovak 1986; Wilson 1968; Wilson and Boland 1978). In his volume on drunk driving in America, James Jacobs argued that this model indeed operates for DUI enforcement:

> [T]he police do respond to pressure; they do shape their priorities according to the wishes of the public; interest groups and public opinion have succeeded in making drunk driving enforcement a higher priority (1989:112).

Most research on policy implementation, however, suggests that the causal link between political climate, formal policy, and actual practice are very weak (Palumbo and Calista 1990). Therefore we are inclined to suspect that these factors interact in more complex, less predictable ways. Thus, even in the face of strong environmental pressure for vigorous implementation of laws such as the drunk driving reforms, the impetus for change will be dissipated. Where external pressure for more DUI enforcement is weak or nonexistent, such links would appear to be even more tenuous. These, in fact, are the conditions of the case study we will present; we suspect that the relatively low level of pressure for DUI enforcement in this case is typical of communities that account for the majority of the country's population. Under these conditions, we would expect the formal policies and actions of the government leaders and police administration to be less relevant to determining enforcement levels than the agency's less visible but more pervasive *informal* social system.

DRUNK-DRIVING ENFORCEMENT IN PENNSYLVANIA

In 1983 Pennsylvania instituted a DUI law similar to those being passed in other states in the early 1980s. It included a per se rule of evidence, mandatory jail sentences for convicted offenders,[7] a mandatory one-year license suspension, and severe restrictions on prosecutorial and judicial discretion to reduce charges (other than dismissal for cause).

The new law and the publicity surrounding its development seem to have stimulated DUI arrests in Pennsylvania: they increased 40 percent between 1981 and 1987. Yet except for a one-year decline following passage of the law, the number of alcohol-related fatal accidents has moved upward (Pennsylvania Commission on Crime and Delinquency 1988). In addition, comparison of DUI arrest rates to those of other northeastern states shows that Pennsylvania rates are among the lowest.

A 1989 survey of Pennsylvania police agencies with one or more full-time sworn officers revealed tremendous variation in the DUI arrest rate for that year.[8] Table 1 shows that on average, the arrest rate in departments in the smallest size category (one to five sworn) was more than three times that of the largest department (more than 100 sworn). The table also shows considerable within-category variation in the DUI arrest rate: some categories ranged from zero to 20 DUI arrests per officer. So it appears that Pennsylvania police organizations react in quite different ways when "summoned from the vasty deep" to enforce drunk-driving laws.

In the remainder of the paper we report the findings of a case study of Melville (a fictional name), one of these Pennsylvania police departments.

---

[7]A mandatory minimum of 48 hours was required for first offenders, 30 days for second offenders, 90 days for third offenders and one year for fourth offenders.

[8]We conducted a mail survey of Pennsylvania police departments with one or more full-time sworn officers drawn from the list of departments reporting Uniform Crime Statistics. The response rate was 79.2 percent. See Mastrofski and Ritti (1990:20) for survey details.

Table 1. Pennsylvania DUI Arrests per Officer, by Department Size, 1989

Number of Officers in Department	Number of Departments	Mean Number of Arrests	Standard Deviation
1–5	373	4.50	4.80
6–10	168	3.66	3.24
11–25	135	3.06	2.54
26–50	36	2.50	1.60
51–100	11	2.58	1.69
>100	12	1.31	.64
Entire Sample	735	3.86	3.99

Focusing on the organizational characteristics discussed earlier, our analysis will show that in order to understand Melville's response to Pennsylvania's DUI law, we must consider in detail the complex ways in which features of the police organization and its environment interact. In this case the interaction produces results that would not be predicted from a routine statistical analysis of organizational characteristics.

METHODS

We conducted intensive field research in Melville during late 1989 and early 1990. Two field researchers spent more than two weeks on site, during which they conducted in-depth interviews with department administrators, supervisors, police officers, court officials, representatives of citizens' groups, and the press. More than 30 such interviews were conducted, and varied in length from 20 minutes to two hours.[9] We also held casual discussions with police around the station house and observed officers at work, including the arrest and processing of drunk drivers. In addition, we administered an anonymous survey questionnaire to more than 100 uniformed officers to obtain their views and experiences regarding drunk driving.[10] The department provided a variety of

[9]We interviewed all administrators in the chain of command responsible for units with DUI enforcement, from the chief down to the patrol and traffic division levels. One supervisor in each patrol section and two supervisors in the traffic division were interviewed; we selected them on the basis of availability. We selected patrol-rank officers by asking line supervisors to identify two types of officers: those who were strongly committed to DUI enforcement and those who were not, but were highly regarded as good police officers (15 in all). Respondents provided information on their peers as well as about themselves during the interviews.

[10]To protect Melville's identity, we do not report the precise number of surveys completed. The survey was administered to patrol officers at roll call, and took about 10–15 minutes. All work shifts and stations were sampled; we returned to each shift more than once to reach officers who had had days off. More than 95 percent of the officers who were given a survey completed it. The sample is considered to be representative of the officers whose routine responsibilities include DUI enforcement.

documents, records, and reports. In 1990 we also conducted a telephone survey of 232 randomly selected licensed drivers over age 21.[11]

DUI ENFORCEMENT IN MELVILLE

Melville is one of a dozen Pennsylvania departments with 100 or more full-time police officers. From 1982 (the year before the state's new DUI law took effect) to 1985, DUI arrests per officer in Melville climbed from 1.3 to 1.6, an average annual increase of more than 7 percent. By 1988, however, the department's arrest rate had returned to 1.3. Melville, though well below the average for all departments in Pennsylvania, was average for its size category (1.3) and nearly three times greater than the line of best fit would predict from a regression of arrest rate on department size. The most intriguing finding is that Melville's DUI arrest rate is as *high* as it is, in view of the department's and certain other organizational and environmental features. Indeed, the analysis that follows suggests that a substantial number of drunk driving arrests in Melville were made *despite* a number of organizational policies and informal norms that conspired against it.

Melville's police appear to have ample opportunity to apprehend drunk drivers. Melville has a great variety of roadways: state and federal highways, commercial strips, a downtown, and residential neighborhoods. The city has a large number of public drinking establishments; its wine and spirit consumption is well above that of most counties in the state. Melville has a significant college student population in residence. The city also attracts many out-of-town visitors to various sports, cultural, and business events. The absolute number of alcohol-related fatalities reported is typically among the highest in the state.

DEMAND FOR DUI ENFORCEMENT

Melville feels little pressure from the state to pursue DUIs. In the 1970s the department had received state funds for overtime associated with DUI enforcement, but its administrators were unable to recall any such state or federal support in the years since the 1983 law. State law allows local jurisdictions to receive some of the funds generated by its DUI offenders' fines, but the department was

[11]We identified respondent households by using a modified random-digit-dialing method: we randomly selected telephone numbers from the directory and replaced the last two digits with random numbers to give unlisted numbers an equal chance of selection. Only residences were surveyed. We used a four-callback procedure. Respondents were informed that the survey was about traffic laws and enforcement of those laws. The topic of drunk driving was not mentioned until respondents had been asked open-ended questions about what the law enforcement priorities of their local police should be. The response rate was 52 percent. We considered this rate good, given the deterioration of response rates to telephone surveys over the years, especially in large cities such as Melville.

unable to point to any such funds in its treasury. The state Department of Transportation, the principal source of state DUI-related enforcement funds, does not routinely monitor individual police agencies' DUI arrest productivity. Indirectly the state makes a variety of DUI training programs available to Pennsylvania police, but each department may choose the extent of participation. The only state requirement for DUI training is found in the minimum requirements for municipal officers' recruit training, approximately 10 of the required 520 hours.

At the local level the demand for drunk-driving enforcement in Melville is not particularly strong. Other matters dominate the police-related political agenda: drugs, relations with poor and minority citizens, hiring practices, maintaining levels of service, and the distribution of services to various segments of the community. Drunk-driving enforcement has not been an issue in recent or earlier campaigns for local elected office. From time to time the local press discusses the subject in its editorials, and occasionally it features stories in which the courts seem to downplay the seriousness of a case.

Local court officials are proud of the county's high conviction rate in drunk-driving cases, but the district attorney pointedly avoids publicity campaigns to heighten citizens' concern about specific crimes. The DA prides himself on running a very "professional" office; his chief assistant stated, "We don't have a crime of the month or year!" The prosecutors pay attention mainly to technical issues. The prosecutor's office tries to be consistent in its decisions on individual cases: "We preach to our people not to get into a persecution mode. We don't want improper prosecutions." The office is very influential in determining who is offered pretrial diversion from the criminal process (for rehabilitative purposes) and on what terms. Most first offenders receive diversion; the restrictiveness of the terms is determined on a scale reflecting the blood-alcohol level of the offender. Thus the district attorney's office strives to provide a measured, deliberate, and professional climate for DUI enforcement, one that avoids inflaming public passions.

The most sharply focused support for DUI enforcement comes from a county chapter of Mothers Against Drunk Drivers (MADD). Formed in the early 1980s, this chapter spent its first few years publicizing the issue and lobbying state policy makers for changes in the law. By 1989 the membership had grown considerably and the organization's objectives became more diverse; victim assistance played an increasingly central role. Recently the organization had participated in a "red ribbon" public awareness campaign, in which drivers were urged to tie ribbons to their car door handles to signify their concern about the drunk driving problem and their support for vigorous enforcement of the DUI laws. Melville's mayor served as the chair of this campaign. The chapter also routinely provides lectures and presentations regarding drunk driving to schools, businesses, and civic groups.

The group's monitoring of DUI enforcement is focused on the court. The chapter does not attempt to monitor all cases, but relies on tips from callers that an offender may be receiving undue leniency or inattention. Volunteer members who specialize in this function then call the district attorney's office and ask about the status of the case. The MADD chapter and the DA's office report a good working relationship. The chapter rarely investigates police enforcement practices. Indeed, the group avoids any action that appears to be adversarial or confrontational with the police departments in the county; it prefers to nurture a "cooperative relationship" that emphasizes shared concern about drunk driving. A recent example is the chapter's purchase of video cameras for county area police departments, including Melville, to tape DUI arrests.

The quiescence of most of Melville's public about the need for drunk-driving enforcement was mentioned consistently in interviews with administrators, supervisors, and patrol officers. The need for increased DUI enforcement is hardly ever raised at community meetings and gripe sessions. Other issues appear to be more important to the public; most frequently they complain about violent crime, drugs, theft, vandalism, and minor disorders (e.g., unruly juveniles). Neighborhoods are more interested in obtaining foot patrols than in drunk driving enforcement. The telephone survey of Melville's licensed drivers reinforces the picture presented by police: only 5 percent stated that DUI enforcement was their top priority, compared to more than 50 percent who cited violent crime or drugs.[12]

The workload demand on the Melville police appears to be higher than in other departments in the state. The number of Part 1 and Part 2 UCR offenses per officer is among the highest in Pennsylvania. Administrators and officers repeatedly mention the difficulty of meeting a heavy citizen demand for a variety of services, many of which require special details that do not show up in calls-for-service statistics (e.g., regulating traffic for special events). The demand for these services is mentioned frequently by officers and administrators as a significant constraint on their capacity to look for, arrest, and process drunk drivers.

The Chief's Priorities

DUI enforcement is not a departmental priority in Melville. Violent crimes, burglary, auto theft, drug dealing, and simply keeping up with the demand for service are the leading concerns of top management. The principal issues for local elected officials are economic development and race relations. The police role is that of contributing to a safe, stable, and progressive environment for economic development and community harmony. Several officers in the patrol division suggested that the chief "took care of" the criminal investigations division (in which he himself had spent much of his career), and that the patrol function therefore received inadequate support. The criminal investigations division accounts for 13 percent of the sworn force and 33 percent of the full-time civilian employees. We did not attempt to determine whether that fact and other departmental policies constitute favoritism, but it is clear that drugs and the traditional major street crimes occupy the chief's mind.

---

[12]Respondents were asked, "Given the kinds of public safety problems faced by your community, please describe in your own words what should be the MOST IMPORTANT priority for your local police . . . that is, preventing what kind of crime?"

In the chief's words, DUI enforcement is "in the middle." That is, he believes DUI deserves police attention, but resources are simply inadequate in view of the need to respond to other, more serious problems:

> If I pull my guys off of answering calls for service to do more DUI, then the mayor has to answer all the citizens' complaints that we're not answering their demands for service. And then the mayor lets me know about it. I don't need that. So I keep those complaints from getting to the mayor by giving the citizens what they want.

The chief believes his officers would arrest a drunk driver if they observed something flagrant, but most would not be inclined to seek out DUI violations because of their heavy, citizen-initiated workload. Under the severe constraints on resources that the chief perceives to be hindering his department, he reluctantly finds this approach acceptable. Consequently the department has not used any special squads, blitzes, or sobriety checkpoints except for stepped-up traffic enforcement during the holidays. The chief would consider special measures only if external funding were made available.

One important factor of the city's perspective on its drunk-driving problem is how it handles court overtime for DUI arrests. The contract with the police union provides that officers who must go to court when not on regular duty will receive time-and-a-half pay; if an officer is in court more than 15 minutes, he or she will receive a minimum of three hours' overtime pay. Drunk-driving arrests frequently involve two or three court appearances, costing the city an extra $250 to $300 per arrest. In past years, enterprising offices could plan their arrests so that they had overtime nearly every day of the week. As a result, some of the most aggressive patrol-rank officers were bringing home larger paychecks than mid-level administrators. To reduce the expense of overtime pay, the city consolidated its DUI court cases into one day per week, thus restricting sharply the amount of overtime an officer could accumulate. In the following year the DUI arrest rate fell almost 13 percent, although a decline had begun two years earlier.

Another indicator is the lack of DUI enforcement training provided by the department. Indeed, the department provides only the state-required minimum for recruits. In-service training also is offered at the state-mandated minimum level. A few officers in the traffic division have been trained in the use of breath-testing equipment, but no effort has been made to train comprehensively in the new law. Further, the department provides no training in conducting field sobriety tests. A median time of one hour of DUI-related training was reported by the sample survey of officers since the new law had been passed. Only one-fourth of the officers rated their DUI training as excellent or good.

Other indicators also are revealing. The department places a low priority on traffic enforcement and on related services generally. The most important priority for the traffic division is in the *regulation* of traffic flow to ensure orderly and efficient entry and exit in the downtown area, especially during the city's many special events. The traffic division operates the department's only breath-testing machine but otherwise spends relatively little time on traffic enforcement. Training on traffic accident investigation is minimal. Consequently, many supervisors encourage officers not to assign blame when writing accident reports; this advice results in statements such as "Two cars collided." Traffic citations are issued infrequently. Homicide detectives conduct investigations of all fatal accidents, but they have no training in accident reconstruction. As a result, they produce reports based on witness interviews—"he-says-she-says" reports, as one officer wryly observed.

A final indicator of the administration's perspective on DUI enforcement is its relationship with the local MADD chapter, particularly its treatment of the video camera donated by the chapter. Administrators accepted the gift camera in a publicized ceremony, but it has not been put to its intended use, nor are there any plans to do so. Administrators feel that the camera will require extra time to use; will involve too much extra paperwork to document evidence, and will only provide defense attorneys with another means of attacking police procedures on technical grounds (a view supported by the district attorney's office). Leaders of the MADD chapter know that the department has not deployed the camera, but the group has exerted no pressure to use it. They prefer to emphasize the "positive," cooperative aspects of their relationship with the police rather than engage in confrontation. Thus the presentation of the camera fulfilled the symbolic function of demonstrating that the MADD group did something to further DUI enforcement and showed that the police are appreciative, but it has had no impact on actual police enforcement practices. In general, department administrators are positive about MADD and describe good relations with the group. They are pleased that MADD expends its energies on public awareness, education, and victim assistance projects, but they express some wariness of involvement by this or any citizen organization in matters relating directly to how the police do their work.

Command and Control Capacity

Melville's command and control capacity appears to be severely constrained by a number of factors. Its ability to shape officers' attitudes through selection processes is limited by the hiring restrictions of previous years. Between 1983 and 1988 the size of the sworn force decreased 17 percent and began to inch up again only in 1989. During the cutback period, officers with the greatest seniority were more likely to remain in the department, thus producing a force heavily skewed toward older officers. In the random-sample survey of uniformed officers, 56 percent have served more than 15 years and 79 percent have served nine or more years. Many officers and administrators note that older officers tend to be more tolerant toward drunk drivers because they themselves are more likely than the younger officers to come from the "shot-and-a-beer" crowd. Further, the older officers joined the force and formed their work habits long before the emergence of popular pressure to treat DUIs more seriously. The department is further constrained in its hiring practices by a court order establishing quotas for hiring females and members of racial minorities. Under these circumstances, hiring officers who might be aggressive in DUI enforcement is neither a priority nor feasible.

Policies on handling specific aspects of DUI enforcement do not seem to most officers to be well articulated. For example, only 12 percent of those surveyed stated that the department's policies and guidelines on when to pull over a potential drunk driver were "very helpful"; 11 percent gave this response about when to conduct field sobriety tests; 15 percent about when to take a driver into custody to determine the level of intoxication; and 9 percent about when to use an alternative to arrest in dealing with a drinking driver. In all cases, the largest proportion responded that the department has no policy (from 33 to 46% depending upon the policy).

The Melville department also is limited in its capacity to reward selectively those officers who pursue management priorities. Although the department has a significant number of supervisory and management positions, few of these have opened up because of financial cutbacks in past years. Written examination scores heavily affect prospects for promotion, although several officers believe that outside political influences occasionally have forced even a resistant chief to promote on other considerations. Patrol assignments to different parts of the city are determined by periodic bids; the more senior officers receive preference.

The rank-and-file bargaining unit is aggressive and is willing to challenge the administration in matters that traditionally have been viewed as management's prerogative. Further, many officers believe that the administration is cowed by external pressure regarding female and minority officers and subjects them less frequently to discipline for poor performance.

The major incentive at the chief's disposal is the assignment of officers to specialist duties and units. Almost one-third of the department works in specialist (nonpatrol) divisions. Assignment to the criminal investigations division, the largest of these, is particularly prized. Training and facilitating educational opportunities also are incentives within the control of department administrators, but are not used much. Another incentive available to the department hierarchy is the assignment of officers to "details," which are additional duties paid for by private organizations requiring police service.

The department's capacity to monitor officers' performance is not well developed. Centralized activity statistics on individual officers are not available, although some mid-level supervisors maintain their own records. Only one of these collects DUI arrests specifically, and he pays no special attention to them. The traffic division, which is responsible for maintaining the results of breath tests, finds it difficult to provide information on individual officers' productivity in DUI arrests because this record system is not computerized.

Local Police Culture

Overall, Melville police do not hold attitudes conducive to a high level of DUI enforcement. None of the officers who completed the anonymous survey said that drunk driving should be a top enforcement priority; only 6 percent said it should be the second priority; and 13 percent said it should be the third.

Forty-one percent of the sample agreed that "Police should concentrate on highly intoxicated drivers rather than those who are slightly over the legal limit." Although 83 percent of the officers reported an inclination to intervene when they spotted someone who *might* be driving while intoxicated, nearly 50 percent expressed a preference for an alternative to arrest.

According to the survey, about one officer in three believes that citizens of the community place a "high" or "very high" priority on DUI enforcement, and one in four perceives the same for the department's administrators. About one in five thinks that local elected officials want increased DUI enforcement, one in four states that officials are satisfied with the current enforcement level, and one in two says that local officials have expressed no opinion or that the respondent does not know that opinion.

Although a significant fraction of the department perceives a community climate of concern about DUI enforcement, very few translate that perception into personal views that DUI should be a high priority. This may be the case because very few officers regard pursuing DUI arrests as improving their chances for professional advancement. None indicate that it "greatly improves chances"; only 1 percent say that it "somewhat improves chances." Further, only about 7 percent of the officers anticipate receiving formal or informal recognition when they do a good job, again reinforcing the previous observation that the department's capacity (or willingness) to reward on the basis of performance is quite limited. Officers do not seem to perceive overwhelming peer pressure against officers who produce high arrest figures, but nearly half believe that at least some officers would resent such productivity.

Perhaps more revealing than the survey results are the comments of officers, supervisors, and administrators in interviews and casual conversation. The following section contains a distillation of comments made by these individuals.

Why Officers Avoid Making DUI Arrests

Incompetence and Laziness. Because of ineptitude or laziness, some officers simply try to avoid any police work that may increase their visibility in the department (e.g., having to go to court) or may require much time in dealing with citizens or handling paperwork. They view overtime as an intrusion on their time off, find going to court a hassle or intimidating, and allow their distaste or frustration in dealing with drunks to overpower any sense of the good that might derive from their intervention. This approach corresponds closely to the "avoider" style described by Muir (1977).

Opinion That Drunk Driving Is Not Serious. Some officers rank DUI as a low priority, either because of personal belief or on the basis of the perceived priorities of authoritative sources, such as community and department leaders. Acknowledging that they themselves occasionally committed this offense, some officers commented, "There but for the grace of God go I." Some suggest that the punishment for DUI is often too severe. Others believe that handling assigned calls should be the top priority and that there is little time for proactive work. Still others want to focus exclusively on more "glamorous" crimes: robbery, burglary, drugs, and auto theft.

Lack of Faith in the Utility of Arrest. Two views fall into this category. One is that the courts and correctional programs do not succeed, so there is no point in initiating a formal process. A second perspective is that arrest is not necessarily the most effective and most efficient police response. Officers holding this view will arrest the falling-down drunk, but they handle the less inebriated in alternative ways—following them home, providing them with alternative transportation, or taking their car keys. These officers regard arrest as *a means, not an end.* They are concerned about the amount of time they must spend "out of service" to process drunk-driver arrests, and define their leniency as a more efficient form of ensuring the public's safety.

Why Officers Make DUI Arrests

Professional Productivity. The opposite of the "avoider" mentioned above, this officer sees his or her role in terms of the amount of activity generated. Law enforcement, especially making arrests, is considered a key part of that role. Arrests are an end of police work, not the means. Drunk driving is just one of many violations that this officer, like Brown's (1981) "clean-sweep crime-fighter," is eager and willing to enforce.

DUI as Serious Crime. This officer, a moral specialist, takes two forms: the drunk hater and the utilitarian. The drunk hater is motivated by personal experience with a drunk driver or alcohol abusers. The utilitarian calculates what offenses cause the greatest harm and concludes that the loss of life, limb, and property to drunk drivers is too great.

DUI as Bounty. The bounty hunter engages in DUI enforcement strictly for the money it brings in overtime pay. These officers are few and are isolated from most of their colleagues, unless they find a like-minded partner. Administrators would like to keep them from tapping the city's budget for overtime pay, but they cannot denounce them formally for fear of appearing soft on drunk driving and opposed to full enforcement of the laws. Administrators and most rank-and-file officers say that bounty hunting is contrary to their image of police officers as professionals, who should be motivated by a spirit of public service rather than private gain. In Melville, the term "bounty hunter" is nearly always used disdainfully.

One of our field research experiences illustrates the intensity of feelings, both pro and con, about bounty hunting. While waiting to administer the survey to an oncoming shift, one of our researchers was approached by Officer Jones (a pseudonym). Jones said that he had received orders to stay away from us, but that he intended to talk to us anyway because he had heard that we wanted to talk to him and others who made a lot of DUI arrests. Officer Jones was known as a bounty hunter and readily admitted, "I am in it for the money. I have made more money than X [his boss, a mid-level administrator]. They even posted this fact with hopes of discouraging my activities." This tactic only spurred him on, however. He made a large number of arrests generally, and he caught many drunk drivers because he made stops frequently, hoping to discover some violation. First the department tried to suppress this effort by transferring Jones to areas offering less opportunity, but he just "sat on stop signs, stopping everyone who rolled through them" until he found his DUI for the day. Then the department transferred him to a desk job at the station house, but that did not stop him either. He arrested people who came in drunk to ask questions about someone's arrest or who simply wanted information. When they left, he followed them to their car; as soon as they started the engine, he arrested them. Finally, when Jones was ordered to remain in the station house, he arrested persons for trespassing or disorderly conduct when they "stumbled in."

Jones's antagonistic and defiant relationship with the department hierarchy was reiterated in various ways by other bounty hunters we interviewed. It is most remarkable that in the face of departmental discouragement and peer group scorn, this small group of officers accounts for a substantial share of the department's DUI arrests. In 1989 the leading bounty hunter (not Jones, by a long shot) made 41 DUI arrests and had 48 "assists," in which he was recorded as the second officer. The top 4.6 percent of the DUI arresters accounted for 42 percent of all DUI arrests. Nearly all of these officers were identified as bounty hunters by themselves or by others. At the other extreme, 58 percent of the officers made no DUI arrests, and 79 percent made two or fewer. The irony here is that the department's subcultural outcasts account for so substantial a share of the department's drunk driving arrests.

DISCUSSION

In some respects, Melville is close to the ideal type of department with a low DUI enforcement. Although the opportunity to arrest drunk drivers appears to be ample, the demand for this activity is quite low. The Melville community's political leaders find other concerns more pressing. Management's priorities too are elsewhere, and generally reflect the community's demands. The department actually has undertaken a number of strategies to *limit* drunk driving enforcement. The dominant local police culture reinforces this view for a variety of reasons—in part as a reaction to specific management policies, and in part because of the large proportion of "older" officers still on the force. The most interesting aspect is the hierarchy's rather limited and underdeveloped command and control capacity. This, in fact, probably accounts for management's inability to *restrict* drunk driving arrests even further. Bounty hunting as a police method is costly, unprofessional, and unpopular among police generally—yet it appears to produce results, and its proponents pursue it stubbornly in the face of formal and informal obstacles.

A theoretical perspective requires us to examine the department's reactions to the DUI law at three levels: outward appearances to the public, internal policies, and the reactions of the major street-level decision makers, namely the patrol officers.

Outward Appearances

Earlier we stated that the extent to which the new state law on drunk driving is enforced depends heavily on features of local police organizations and their local environments. Without some compelling external threat or incentive, police departments have great leeway in determining the scope of their enforcement efforts for particular violations. In this, the most common, situation, police administrators pay more attention to those laws which afford them the greatest opportunity to demonstrate their (and their organization's) worth to key local constituencies. In Melville, DUI enforcement does not present such opportunities. Further, police leaders see no benefit in making an issue of DUI to establish their identity as agents of change. Their priorities are simply elsewhere. Yet the administration does not care to antagonize the local MADD chapter, a small but active segment of the community concerned about drunk driving. Open acknowledgement of the department's low priority for DUI enforcement could bring unwanted publicity, expose the myth of full enforcement, and stimulate a more active and more broadly based citizens' movement that would try to influence department policies and practices, and might even become adversarial.

Consequently the department's administrators "play it safe" by resorting to symbolic responses to the DUI issue. Outward appearances are managed through several of what Manning (1977) calls "presentational strategies." A sizable traffic division operates the breath-testing machine, but has little time for traffic enforcement because its officers are too busy with special events. A symbiotic relationship with the local MADD chapter is established, in which each party exchanges symbolic gestures. The mayor's and the department's participation in MADD's red-ribbon campaign and video camera donation gives the citizen's group essential publicity and signals that it is doing something about the drunk-driving problem. By engaging in these activities the department signals that it, too, cares about this problem. Even more to the point, it placates a citizen's group *without really intruding on internal department policies and day-to-day practices.*

From the perspective of the police administrators, the department's legitimacy and value can be nurtured best by focusing on other issues: "serious street crime," drug dealing, and service delivery. The large number of police specialists available to address these problems provides ample opportunity to employ other presentational strategies that signify departmental effectiveness. Station houses, symbols of service distribution, also serve this purpose. Elaborate hierarchies and written rules and directives also provide the image of a department responsive to the chief and to the city's direction.

Internal Policies

At the second level, internal policies are implemented to allow the agency to deal with the nuts and bolts of administering the agency, which is dominated by the concern for providing services to a demanding public with limited resources. Undoubtedly the department could do more tc support drunk-driving enforcement: it could provide more training at relatively low cost, could press for more efficient allocation of personnel to shifts, and could require more productivity from officers on those shifts. Such tactics, however, are certain to generate stiff resistance from the union, thus forcing the administration to expend precious energy and political goodwill. All of this would result from pressing an enforcement initiative in an area for which there is currently no compelling external political demand. Thus, as bad as the situation in Melville may appear to advocates of strict drunk-driving enforcement, the department's policies seem perfectly rational from a practical administrator's perspective.

The Street-Level Decision Makers

Finally, the directives and policies of the administration seem to have had only limited impact on street-level practice. Because the formal hierarchy has a very limited capacity to alter patterns of street-level decision making, the administration has experienced only modest success in suppressing overtime (and thus DUI arrests). Many officers continue to make DUI arrests for reasons related to their view of the public interest, but a small core of "bounty hunters" does so for purely personal economic gain. Most of these officers persist in this activity despite the reduced opportunities for overtime. This street-level resistance to top-down influence is all the more remarkable because it requires that officers *take action* to be productive, thus reversing the traditional roles of management and labor. Ultimately this situation exacerbates the difficulty of inducing police officers to do what management wants.

CONCLUSION

A case study cannot test theory, but it can be used to suggest ways to develop it. Our study of Melville indicates that drunk driving is not a significant local political issue, that the police administration has no interest in pursuing it beyond symbolic gestures, and that the great majority of police officers also are not committed. The remarkable point about Melville is that in the face of all these forces conspiring against aggressive DUI enforcement, a few outcasts—bounty hunters–can generate a disproportionately high number of drunk driving arrests, making the department's DUI arrest rate much higher than would otherwise be expected. The irony is that this group, insulated from the formal hierarchy by the hierarchy's weak capacity for command and control, actually works aggressively to fulfill the ostensible objectives of the state's new DUI law. Another irony is that the impetus for this enforcement effort comes not from policy concerns about reducing a social problem, but from these officers' desire for pecuniary gain. Melville is the case of the horse led to water that drank in spite of itself. It demonstrates the risks of assuming that there is a rational progression from political environment to public policy, and ultimately to performance. It cautions us to examine closely cases of apparent implementation of state laws, because any success may be due to factors entirely independent of efforts to accomplish political and administrative accountability.

Future research might attempt to determine how frequently street-level police enforcement practices occur independent of, or in opposition to, formal policy. To what extent can small numbers of self-styled specialists in police departments determine how vigorously laws are enforced? For example, would we find this pattern of implementation in police enforcement practices where there was strong external pressure for DUI enforcement? Under such circumstances would the processes of accountability between the community, the police administration, and the rank and file be linked more strongly, or would there simply be greater pressure to produce even more dramatic symbolic responses?

REFERENCES

Aaronson, D. E., C. T. Dienes, and M. C. Musheno (1984). *Public Policy and Police Discretion: Processes of Decriminalization.* New York: Clark Boardman.

Bardach, E. (1977). *The Implementation Game: What Happens after a Bill Becomes a Law.* Cambridge, MA: MIT Press.

Broderick, J. J. (1977). *Police in a Time of Change.* Morristown, NJ: General Learning Press.

Brown, M. K. (1981). *Working the Street: Police Discretion and the Dilemmas of Reform.* New York: Russell Sage Foundation.

Bullington, B. and A. Block. (1990). "A Trojan Horse: Anti-Communism and the War on Drugs." *Contemporary Crises: Law, Crime and Social Policy* 14:39-55.

Casper, J. D. and D. Brereton. (1984). "Evaluating Criminal Justice Reforms." *Law and Society Review* 18:121–44.

Eisenstein, J., R. Flemming, and F. Nardulli. (1988). *The Contours of Justice: Communities and their Courts.* Boston: Little, Brown.

Flanagan, T. J., and K. M. Jamieson. (1988). *Sourcebook of Criminal Justice Statistics—1987.* Washington, D.C.: U.S. Department of Justice.

Flanagan, T. J. and M. McLeod. (1983). *Sourcebook of Criminal Justice Statistics—1982.* Washington, D.C.: U.S. Department of Justice.

Fyfe, J. J. (1979). "Administrative Interventions on Police Shooting Discretion: An Empirical Examination." *Journal of Criminal Justice* 7:300–23.

Gardiner, J. A. (1969). *Traffic and the Police: Variations in Law Enforcement Policy.* Cambridge, MA: Harvard University Press.

Goldstein, H. (1977). *Policing a Free Society.* Cambridge, MA: Ballinger.

———. (1990). *Problem-Oriented Policing.* New York: McGraw-Hill.

Greenfield, L. A. (1988). *Drunk Driving.* Bureau of Justice Statistics Special Report. Washington, D.C.: U.S. Department of Justice.

Gusfield, J. (1981). *The Culture of Public Problems: Drinking-Driving and the Symbolic Order.* Chicago: University of Chicago Press.

Jacobs, J. B. (1989). *Drunk Driving: An American Dilemma.* Chicago: University of Chicago Press.

Klockars, C. B. (1985). *The Idea of Police.* Beverly Hills: Sage.

Langworthy, R. H. (1985). "Wilson's Theory of Police Behavior: A Replication of the Constraint Theory." *Justice Quarterly* 2:89–98.

Ostrom, E., R. B. Parks, and G. P. Whitaker (1978). *Patterns of Metropolitan Policing.* Cambridge, MA: Ballinger.

Manning, P. K. (1977). *Police Work: The Social Organization of Policing.* Cambridge, MA: Ballinger.

———. (1989). "The Police Occupational Culture in Anglo-American Societies." In W. G. Bailey (ed.), *Encyclopedia of Police Science,* pp. 384–88. New York: Garland.

Mastrofski, S. D. (1990). "The Prospects of Change in Police Patrol: A Decade in Review." *American Journal of Police* 9:1–79.

Mastrofski, S. D. and R. Ritti. (1990). *More Effective DUI Enforcement in Pennsylvania: Final Report.* University Park, PA: Pennsylvania State University.

Mastrofski, S. D., R. Ritti, and D. Hoffmaster. (1987). "Organizational Determinants of Police Discretion: The Case of Drinking-Driving." *Journal of Criminal Justice* 15:387–402.

Muir. W. K., Jr. (1977). *Police: Streetcorner Politicians.* Chicago: University of Chicago Press.

Palumbo, D. J. and D. J. Calista. (1990). *Implementation and the Policy Process: Opening Up the Black Box.* New York: Greenwood.

Pennsylvania Commission on Crime and Delinquency. (1988). "The Effort to Reduce Drunken Driving in Pennsylvania: The Effects on the Criminal Justice System and Highway Safety." *The Justice Analyst* October.

Reinarman, C. (1988). "The Social Construction of an Alcohol Problem: The Case of Mothers Against Drunk Drivers and Social Control in the 1980s." *Theory and Society* 17:91–120.

Reuss-Ianni, E. (1983). *The Two Cultures of Policing: Street Cops and Management Cops.* New Brunswick, NJ: Transaction Books.

Rubinstein, J. (1973). *City Police.* New York: Farrar, Straus and Giroux.

Sherman, L. W. (1977). "Police Corruption Control: Environmental Context vs. Organizational Policy." In D. H. Bayley (ed.), *Police and Society,* pp. 107–26. Beverly Hills: Sage.

———. (1983). "Reducing Police Gun Use: Critical Events, Administrative Policy, and Organizational Change." In M. Punch (ed.), *Control in the Police Organization,* pp. 98–125. Cambridge, MA: MIT Press.

Skolnick, J. H. (1966). *Justice Without Trial: Law Enforcement in a Democratic Society.* New York: Wiley.

Slovak, J. S. (1986). *Styles of Urban Policing: Organization, Environment, and Police Styles in Selected American Cities.* New York: New York University Press.

U.S. Department of Justice. (1989). *Uniform Crime Reports—1987.* Washington, D.C.: U.S. Department of Justice.

Van Maanen, J. (1974). "Working the Street: A Developmental View of Police Behavior." In H. Jacob (ed.). *The Potential for Reform of Criminal Justice,* pp. 83–130. Beverly Hills: Sage.

———. (1983). "The Boss: First-Line Supervision in an American Police Agency." In M. Punch (ed.), *Control in the Police Organization,* pp. 275–317. Cambridge, MA: MIT Press.

Wilson, J. Q. (1968). *Varieties of Police Behavior: The Management of Law and Order in Eight Communities.* Cambridge, MA: Harvard University Press.

Wilson, J. Q. and B. Boland (1978). "The Effect of Police on Crime." *Law and Society Review* 12:267–390.

Worden, R. E. (1989). "Situational and Attitudinal Explanations of Police Behavior: A Theoretical Reappraisal and Empirical Assessment." *Law and Society Review* 23:663-711.

DISCUSSION QUESTIONS

1. What problems would you foresee in gaining access to data within police agencies?
2. Why is confidentiality of subjects so important?
3. Explain the researchers' comment that "getting approval from the top administrator is no guarantee of access to rank-and-file employees."
4. How did the researchers ensure that they collected a sufficient amount of data?

17

Images of Crime and Justice

Murder and the "True Crime" Genre

ALEXIS M. DURHAM, III, University of Tampa
H. PRESTON ELROD, University of North Carolina–Charlotte
PATRICK T. KINKADE, Texas Christian University

COMMENTARY

Contrary to what students often believe about how social science research originates, such research does not always come out of scholarly immersion in academic literature. The genesis of the project described in our article represents an excellent case in point. We were all employed at the same university when a particularly brutal murder was committed in the city in which we resided. A young woman had persuaded her boyfriend and another friend to break into the house where her father and stepmother lived, and to kill both of them. The young woman harbored bitter feelings toward her stepmother, and also anticipated that by killing both of them she would be the beneficiary of a million-dollar insurance policy. The murdered woman was a beautiful socialite who had devoted part of her life to involvement in charitable works throughout the city. The community was stunned by the murder, and the case made national headlines. It was profiled in newspapers across the country and on a number of television "news magazines."

The case captured our attention as well. Our initial thought was that the facts of the case were such as to merit a book-length depiction: brutal murder of a wealthy socialite plotted by the bitter young stepdaughter; revenge, violence, and money, the standard fare of True Crime. We put together a proposal to do a book on the case, and sent it off to the agent with whom we worked. The agent was not overwhelmed with the commercial prospects of a book about the case, and ultimately nothing came of our proposal.

But the experience set us to thinking more about the case, and about others like it. There are many, many murders annually in the Dallas–Fort Worth area, only a small fraction of which receive anything more than brief media attention. Virtually none of them are picked up by the national press.

Source: Journal of Criminal Justice, Vol 23, No. 2, pp. 143–152. Copyright © 1995, reprinted with permission from Elsevier Science.

What seemed clear to us was that the more unusual the case, the more likely it would receive extensive media attention. Moreover, the more likely a case is to receive significant media attention, the more likely that such attention will form part of the information citizens receive about crime and justice. Our concern was that such cases are simply not representative of crime in America. Citizens who develop an understanding of the crime problem as a result of exposure to media depictions of such "glamourous" cases are unlikely to have the kind of understanding that makes it possible for them to support sensible, rather than sensational, responses to the crime problem.

We decided to put together a research project to measure the extent to which True Crime depictions of real cases adequately represent crime in America. We conducted a content analysis of a sample of True Crime books and compared the crime events contained in those volumes with official data on crime compiled by the FBI. Our findings confirmed a number of the suspicions spawned by our observations of the media frenzy over the Texas murder case.

The research was not without its difficulties, but this is a normal part of the research process. For instance, it was not immediately clear whether our study ought to focus on the print or electronic media. We decided to examine books, then found ourselves unsure of which books to examine. Because the True Crime genre had not been the focus of other research, there was no generally accepted operational definition of the genre that we could use in determining which books to include in our sampling frame. Once this issue was resolved, we had to figure out how to obtain lists of all the books that would qualify for inclusion. Such implementation problems are typical of the kinds of obstacles that arise during the execution of a research project, and they do get resolved in due course.

Although this research represents only a small beginning to understanding the impact of True Crime on public perceptions of crime and justice, we found it exciting to be involved in the early stages of the study of a new aspect of criminology. Subsequent research will surely enhance, improve, and elaborate upon what we have accomplished. Part of the fun of research is watching to see what other researchers discover about a topic you have examined, even if subsequent work fails to confirm your results. Generally speaking, it is more fun if their findings agree with your own, but if they do not, this is not a problem. Divergent findings give you more to argue about, and as peculiar as it may seem, most researchers seem to feel that arguing about research is itself one of the joys of the profession.

ABSTRACT Crime has long been an important topic in the media. Researchers examining the relationship between beliefs about crime and exposure to the media have found evidence suggesting that such beliefs are influenced by both the form and content of media coverage of crime. Moreover, other research has discovered that the media often presents a seriously distorted picture of criminal activity. The study described in this article examines the question of whether a newly important form of crime coverage, the "true crime" genre, provides a distorted portrayal of homicide. True crime books are accounts of actual homicide cases which are presented in a style which often resembles fiction. A content analysis of true crime cases is compared with official data on murder, and the results indicate that, in accord with research on other media forms, the portrayal of homicide in the true crime realm is extremely narrow, and significantly differs from the full range of cases which typify murder in America.

INTRODUCTION

Research on the popular media has looked closely at the media's effect on public perceptions of crime and has made some very interesting discoveries. For instance, in the 1970s, England experienced a panic over street crimes, in particular, violent robberies. These crimes were defined by law as a violent attack and robbery of an individual during pedestrian activity. The British press and the police described mugging as "a frightening new strain of crime," despite the fact that it was a centuries-old form of English crime (Hall et al., 1978:3). In addition, mugging rates were actually stable during the entire period of the panic. Hall and his colleagues found that the labeling of the crime and press coverage of muggings resulted in a public outcry that motivated law enforcement officials to divert resources to respond to this "new" hazard to public safety. The increased police attention naturally resulted in a greater number of arrests, which, in turn, were reported in the press and ultimately used to further validate the concern about violent crime.

As the British mugging case illustrates, media accounts of crime do not always accurately represent actual levels of criminal activity. Criminologists and media analysts have long been interested in both the nature and the effect of media representations of crime. Television and newspapers have received significant attention from scholars, and numerous research studies have found that media portrayals of crime and criminals often deviate substantially from reality. Through a content analysis of true crime books, the research reported in this article details the findings of a study of the adequacy of the increasingly popular true crime genre as it depicts murder in the United States.

The true crime genre is an important, yet unstudied, aspect of popular representations of crime. This genre presents accounts of actual crime cases, often in narrative form. The appeal of the genre is that it purports to be about the real world, not merely the fictional world of the novel. Although true crime magazines, such as *True Detective,* have long captivated large readerships with the gruesome details of real crime cases, other media forms have recently become more heavily involved in portraying such cases. Movies, such as *Goodfellas,* and television miniseries, such as *To Catch a Killer,* have brought actual criminal cases to life before millions of viewers. Similarly, books such as *Bad Blood, Fatal Vision,* and *Human Harvest* offer detailed depictions of sensational homicide cases.

The genre has become enormously popular in recent years. *Bowker's Annual,* which is the publishing industry's handbook on book sales, does not have a separate true crime category, thus summary figures for such works are not available. A visit to any bookstore, however, will reveal special true crime sections. Such sections did not exist a few years ago. *Publisher's Weekly* devoted a recent article to the explosion of interest in the genre, documenting the increase in bookstore shelf space devoted to true crime (Weyr, 1993). Time-Life has now initiated a special twenty volume true crime series, and Doubleday established the first true crime book club in 1992.

In light of its growing popularity as a source of information about crime, it is appropriate that the genre be subjected to the kinds of scrutiny previously devoted to other forms of crime reporting. The objective of this exploratory study is to determine the extent to which true crime homicide cases resemble the typical homicide committed in the United States. In an effort to take an initial step toward development of a better understanding of the extent to which the genre reflects the reality of homicide in America, a comparison of the results of a content analysis of a sample of true crime books with homicide data from the Federal Bureau of Investigation's (FBI's) *Uniform Crime Reports* is presented.

LITERATURE REVIEW

During the past two decades, researchers have examined a broad range of media treatments of criminal activity. These examinations suggest that such treatments do have an impact on public understanding of crime. Newspaper accounts of crime have been an especially fruitful area for investigators, and studies of such accounts have routinely found that newspapers present a distorted picture of crime. Davis (1951) studied crime news in Colorado newspapers and found:

> a marked lack of association between the percentages change in total Colorado crime and in newspaper coverage . . . The findings of this study bear out the hypothesis that there is no consistent relationship between the amount of crime news in newspapers and the local crime rates. (Davis, 1951:327, 330)

Sheley and Ashkins (1981) found that New Orleans newspaper stories about murder and robbery accounted for 45 percent of newspaper crime stories, although such offenses accounted for only a little more than 12 percent of actual crimes. A Canadian study revealed a similar relationship in Canadian newspapers. Doob (1985) found that although about 55 percent of crime news stories in Canadian papers were about violent offenses, less than 6 percent of Canadian crimes were violent.

The disproportionate focus on violent crimes is not limited to newspaper crime coverage. A study of television news from 1974–1986 for the three major networks found that violent crime was disproportionately featured relative to property crime (Randall, Lee-Simmons, and Hagner, 1988). This is consistent with the previously noted New Orleans study which found that 80 percent of television newscast crime stories dealt with murder or robbery, compared to the actual 12 percent of crimes that murder and robbery constituted, according to police statistics (Sheley and Ashkins, 1981).

The misrepresentation of crime types, as well as of offender and victim characteristics, is important because large numbers of citizens obtain their information about crime from the mass media. Graber (1980) found that 95 percent of a panel of citizens indicated that the mass media was their *primary* source of crime information. If this is true, and if the media does affect the ways in which people think about crime-related issues, then inaccurate media portrayals of crime may well result in public perceptions that reflect significant misunderstandings of complex crime and justice issues.

Sutherland recognized this potential forty years ago in his observations on sex crimes. "Fear is seldom or never related to statistical trends in sex crimes . . . Ordinarily, from two to four spectacular sex crimes in a few weeks are sufficient to evoke the phrase 'sex crime wave' " (quoted in Kappeler, Blumberg, and Potter, 1993:10). More recently, Fishman's (1978) analysis of an alleged New York crime wave against the elderly in the mid-1970s provides an excellent example of how the media may create enormous public concern over matters unworthy of such elevated levels of attention. The local print and electronic media ran numerous stories on crimes against the elderly and concluded that the city was in the midst of a crime wave. This reporting resulted in both heightened public perceptions of the risks of crime and an increase in public fear, despite the fact that police data indicated that the crime wave had essentially been a fabrication of the media (Fishman, 1978).

Reinarman and Levine (1989) documented the explosion in media coverage of the drug problem in the 1980s. They showed that the media portrayed the crack problem as quickly reaching crisis and epidemic proportions, despite the fact that the official evidence on cocaine and crack available during the first three years of the crack crisis gave a rather different picture. As media attention to crack was burgeoning, the actual extent of crack use was virtually unknown, and almost all official measures of other cocaine use were actually decreasing. In fact, claims of a crack crisis actually preceded the spread of crack use, at least as measured by official data (Reinarman and Levine, 1989:550).

Although considerable research has been conducted on the character and consequences of media representations of crime, there has been little attention devoted to the true crime genre. In part, this may be due to the fact that until recently it has not been a major element in modern popular culture. As noted earlier, the emergence of exclusive true crime sections in bookstores is a recent phenomenon, and it appears that most large bookstores now have such sections. Moreover, conventional bookstores are not the only places where such books can be found. Examination of the holdings in bookstores at four large American airports revealed that a number of true crime titles could be purchased by travelers seeking diversion on their flights. Some of these volumes were featured in special display cases. Even grocery stores now carry true crime titles, some in separate true crime sections.

Public libraries also feature large numbers of true crime titles. A computer search of the Hillsborough County library system (Tampa, Florida) revealed more than 300 hardcover titles. This is a significant underestimate of total true crime titles in the system because the library's many soft-covered volumes are not cataloged in the computer data base.

Thus, it appears that the true crime genre has become an important source of information about crime for substantial numbers of American readers. Consequently, it is important to examine the genre to gain a better understanding of its nature and influence on public perceptions of crime. Concern with the accuracy of portrayals of crime in other media has already led to a variety of research initiatives. Examination of the body of research on newspaper and television handling of crime-related issues suggests a large number of research questions relevant to the study of the true crime genre.

Following the approach used to analyze television and newspaper depictions of crime, this project addresses the question of whether the homicides portrayed by the true crime genre are representative of the full distribution of homicides. More specifically, are homicide victims and offenders of various genders, ages, classes, and races proportionately represented in true crime homicide cases relative to their representation in all homicide cases? Are aggravating and mitigating circumstances, such as brutality, found in true crime cases in proportion to their representation in all homicide cases? Are true crime homicides more or less likely to involve firearms than typical cases? Are true crime homicides more likely to be felony murders or crimes of passion? Are they usually solved, and is the offender generally convicted? The content analysis that is the subject of the remainder of this article provides answers to these questions.

METHOD

To address the research questions of concern in this study, a content analysis was performed on a sample of true crime books. Computer searches were run in the public library system of a major metropolitan area (population in excess of one million inhabitants) and in a private college library consortium located in the same urban area. The two lists were merged and produced a total of 300 titles. The initial searches were conducted using the library categorization classification for true crime accounts of murder (364.1523).

Each of the titles was numbered, and a systematic random sample was drawn from the sampling frame, using a random start at item number 5, and a sampling interval of 7. This procedure was used to generate a sample of fifty volumes, 16.6 percent of the 300 items contained in the sampling frame. Six volumes could not be located (checked out or lost by library), and were replaced by six additional randomly selected titles. Please see the Appendix for the final list of books included in this study.

Relying primarily upon information published by the FBI (1991) in the annual *Uniform Crime Reports,* a coding template was created to facilitate extraction of information from the volumes in the sample. Coding proved to be largely unproblematic because the data collected required little interpretation (e.g., sex, age, race of offender and victim, murder weapon, conviction and sentence information). Nonetheless, intercode reliability was measured through a recoding of 30 percent of the sample of fifty volumes. This recoding revealed no coding disparities or errors.

Findings

Data from the FBI's (1991) *Uniform Crime Reports (UCR)* were compared to data produced by the content analysis of the true crime accounts of homicide cases. Although the volumes in this study covered murder cases, there also were other crimes described in the accounts of these homicides. For example, some cases involved rapes or thefts committed as part of the crime incident. Nonetheless, homicides account for almost 80 percent of the total crimes recounted in the true crime books. Moreover, the vast majority of the text of these volumes is committed to discussion of the homicides. Readers of such books thus spend virtually all of their reading time learning about murders. In contrast, official data reveal that homicides are quite rare. Of the fourteen million UCR Crime Index offenses committed annually, homicides account for less than 1 percent of the total (Federal Bureau of Investigation, 1991).

The data also make clear that the sociodemographic characteristics of both offenders and victims in the true crime sample differ from the UCR profile. As Table 1 shows, about 19 percent of victims were fifty-five or older in the true crime sample, more than twice as many as in the UCR group. In addition, more than twice as many victims were under fifteen in the true crime sample (11.6 percent versus 5.0 percent). True crime victims, thus, were more likely to be very young or very old compared to typical victims. Males accounted for about 70 percent of true crime victims, females 30 percent. UCR data indicate that females are victims somewhat less often than is the case for true crime. Data on race of victim revealed some striking disparities. Although only 47.1 percent of UCR victims were White, in the true crime sample almost all victims (95.6 percent) were Caucasian.

Examination of the gender and race data for offenders is equally interesting. Females are three times more likely to be offenders in the true crime data than they are in the UCR (24.2 percent versus 7.1 percent). It is important to note that for almost 30 percent of UCR cases, the gender of the offender is unknown. When only those UCR cases in which the gender of the offender is known are examined, 10 percent of UCR offenders are female, again compared to 24.2 percent in the true crime sample. Either way the figures are computed, females are significantly overrepresented as offenders in the true crime sample when compared to the UCR figures.

The data for true crime offender race diverges from the UCR data as sharply as was true for victim race. In UCR cases in which offender race was known (thus excluding the unknown category in Table 1), about 43 percent of offenders were White, compared to 90 percent of true crime offenders.

Table 1. Characteristics of Victims and Offenders

	UCR Index Data (%)	True Crime Data (%)
Gender of victim[a]		
Male	78.0	69.5
Female	21.8	29.5
Unknown*	.1	1.1
Age of victim[b]		
<15	5.0	11.6
15–24	30.9	23.2
25–34	29.1	21.1
35–44	16.9	13.7
45–55	7.6	11.6
55+	8.7	18.9
Unknown*	1.7	0.0
Race of victim[c]		
White	47.1	95.8
Black	49.6	1.1
Other	2.5	3.2
Unknown*	0.8	0.0
Gender of offender[d]		
Male	63.5	75.8
Female	7.1	24.2
Unknown*	29.6	0.0
Age of offender[e]		
<25	34.0	29.3
25–34	18.6	39.4
35–44	8.4	20.2
45–54	3.3	5.1
55+	2.3	5.0
Unknown*	33.7	1.0
Race of offender[f]		
White	30.0	90.4
Black	38.5	0.0
Other	1.3	9.6
Unknown	30.2	0.0

Note: percentages may not total 100% due to rounding.

[a]Chi-square = 2.57, $df = 1$, $p > .109$.

[b]Chi-square = 25.59, $df = 5$, $p < .001$.

[c]Chi-square = 91.83, $df = 2$, $p < .001$.

[d]Chi-square = 21.87, $df = 1$, $p < .001$.

[e]Chi-square = 18.87, $df = 4$, $p < .001$.

[f]Chi-square = 196.06, $df = 3$, $p < .001$.

*Chi-square calculations do not include unknown categories due to expected cell counts of less than 5.

Although almost 40 percent of UCR offenders were Black, not a single true crime offender was Black.

Comparisons also were made of various gender and racial victim/offender combinations (Table 2). Cases involving male victims and male offenders comprised 64.4 percent of the UCR cases, but only 51.1 percent of the true crime sample. About 19 percent of the true crime cases involved female offender/male victim, while the corresponding figure for the UCR data was less than 10 percent. The percentage of female victim/female offender cases in the true crime sample was more than twice that for the UCR group (6.4 percent versus 2.6 percent).

When victim/offender race combinations are considered, 91.6 percent of cases involved White offenders and White victims. This is more than twice the corresponding percentage in the UCR data (40.8 percent). Even more extraordinary is the fact that although 46.7 percent of UCR cases involved Black victims and offenders, the true crime sample did not contain one such case.

Further examination of the relationship between the victim and offender revealed far more cases in the true crime sample involving family members (Table 3). Approximately one-third (32.6 percent) of such cases involved family members, compared to only 12.5 percent of UCR cases. In addition, about 41 percent of true crime cases involved strangers, compared to only 15 percent of the UCR data. It appears that true crime victims are killed either by people they are related to or by people they do not know. UCR victims are far more likely to be killed by acquaintances. It must be noted, however, that almost 40 percent of UCR cases involved offenders with an unknown relationship to the victim. When only cases with known relationships are included in the analysis, some of the differences between the two data sources are diminished. For instance, the percentage of family-related cases rises from 12.5 percent to 20 percent. Even with this recomputation, however, the percentages of family and stranger homicide are still considerably higher for the true crime data.

Data on social class also are very interesting. Although no formal method of measuring social class was used in this research, it was possible to loosely classify most of the true crime cases. Occupation, education, and wealth were used as informal criteria for this classification. Principals working as professionals, who were college educated or wealthy, were classified as upper/middle class. Those working at trade occupations, lacking high school education, or who were unemployed and uneducated were classified as lower/working class. By and large, true crime cases involved middle- or upper-class victims. The true crime data reveal that 73 percent of victims and 61 percent of offenders were middle- or upper-class individuals. Twenty-seven percent of victims and 39 percent of offenders were lower- or working-class persons.

This contrasts sharply with the distribution of homicide victims and offenders described in the research literature. Beginning with Wolfgang's (1958) landmark analysis of homicide, studies "of homicide consistently find that lower-class contexts are correlated with this type of offense" (Brownfield, 1986: 422). Moreover, almost two-thirds (61 percent) of the true crime victim/offender combinations involved upper- or middle-class victims and offenders,

Table 2. Gender and Racial Relationship of Victims and Offenders

	UCR Index Data (%)	True Crime Data (%)
Gender (victim/offender)[a]		
Male/male	64.4	51.1
Male/female	9.7	19.1
Female/male	22.3	23.4
Female/female	2.6	6.4
Race (victim/offender)[b]		
White/white	40.8	91.6
White/black	6.4	0.0
White/other	0.5	4.2
Black/white	3.2	1.1
Black/black	46.7	0.0
Black/other	0.2	0.0
Other/white	0.7	2.0
Other/black	0.3	0.0
Other/other	1.2	1.1

Note: Percentages may not total 100% due to small percentages of cases with unknown victims and offenders.

[a]Chi-square = 16.52, $df = 3$, $p < .001$.

[b]Chi-square not calculated because of large number of cells with expected counts of less than 5.

Table 3. Personal Relationship of Victim to Offender

	UCR Index Data (%)	True Crime Data (%)
Family	12.5	32.6
Acquaintance	34.1	26.3
Stranger	15.0	41.1
Unknown	38.4	0.0

Note: Chi-square = 32.23, $df = 2$, $p < .001$.

while only 12 percent involved upper- or middle-class victims and lower- or working-class offenders. This is interesting in light of upper- and middle-class fear of being victimized by members of the lower classes. Slightly more than one-quarter (27 percent) of cases involved lower- or working-class offenders and victims, but there were no cases of lower- or working-class victims and upper- or middle-class offenders.[1] It may well be that at least some of the high level of public interest in these cases derives from the fact that relative to the real

Table 4. Weapons Used

	UCR Index Data (%)	True Crime Data (%)
Firearms	66.3	44.1
Knives	15.8	22.1
Blunt instruments	5.0	11.0
Personal weapons	5.6	4.4
Other/unknown	7.3	18.4

Note: Percentages may not total 100% due to rounding. Chi-square = 46.13, $df = 4$, $p < .001$.

distribution of homicides, the participants typically come from advantaged situations (almost three-quarters of the cases).

With regard to the murder weapons used, UCR data indicate that approximately two-thirds of homicides involve guns (Table 4). True crime offenders used a wider range of weapons; only 44.1 percent used firearms. True crime offenders were twice as likely as UCR offenders to kill with a blunt instrument (11 percent versus 5 percent), and about one-third more likely to kill with a knife (22 percent versus 15.8 percent). Of special interest is the fact that all of the true crime offenders under age eighteen used a gun while only about half of the UCR cases with youthful offenders involved guns. For older offenders, more UCR offenders used guns than in the true crime sample, but fewer used knives or blunt objects.

Scrutiny of the data for the circumstances associated with the murders revealed that most true crime cases did not involve robbery, while robbery was involved in 10.2 percent of UCR cases (Table 5). Although the magnitude of the percentages is small, rapes were six times more likely in true crime cases (3.3 percent versus 0.6 percent), and romantic triangles were involved three times as often in true crime cases (4.4 percent versus 1.5 percent). The "other/unknown" categories are large for both data sources, and a substantial number of true crime cases in this category involved killing to obtain inheritance money, assassination, and revenge (total of 33.4 percent). (Comparison of these circumstance categories to the UCR is not possible because such data are not included in the UCR figures.) Arguments accounted for 30.5 percent of UCR cases while the figure for true crime was only 8.8 percent. Finally, gangland killings were many times more prevalent in the true crime data than in the UCR statistics (3.3 percent versus .01 percent), though still relatively rare.

Finally, comparisons were obtained on case outcomes (Table 6). Similar figures emerged for both data sources on arrest (83 percent) and prosecution (more than 90 percent). Virtually all convicted true crime offenders were incarcerated (prison, jail, mental institution) subsequent to conviction, and the vast majority of these ultimately were sent to state prison (imprisoned). Some of the convicted were imprisoned while awaiting appeals on sentences to death. Although less than 2 percent of UCR homicide arrestees were ultimately sentenced to

Table 5. Circumstances of Homicide

	UCR Index Data (%)	True Crime Data (%)
Rape	0.6	3.3
Robbery	10.2	1.1
Burglary	0.9	1.1
Larceny-theft	0.15	1.1
Motor vehicle theft	0.24	0.0
Arson	0.63	0.0
Prostitution/vice	0.09	1.1
Other sex offenses	0.22	20.0
Narcotic drug laws	6.3	8.8
Gambling	0.15	1.1
Romantic triangle	1.5	4.4
Child killed by baby-sitter	0.14	0.0
Brawl due to alcohol	2.3	3.3
Brawl due to narcotics	1.2	2.2
Arguments over money or property	2.4	6.6
Other arguments	28.1	2.2
Gangland killings	0.1	3.3
Juvenile gang killings	3.8	0.0
Institutional killing	0.08	0.0
Sniper attack	0.01	1.1
Other/unknown	40	51.1

Note: Percentages in UCR column do not equal 100% due to rounding. True crime column percentages exceed 100% due to events with multiple circumstances.

Table 6. Case Outcome

	UCR Index Data[a] (%)	True Crime Data (%)
Arrested	83.0	83.3
Arrestees processed through the following stages		
Prosecuted	91.0	93.0
Convicted	69.0	73.0
Incarcerated	61.0	69.7
Imprisoned	50.0	66.6
Death penalty	1.4	16.1

[a]Source: Maguire and Flanagan (1991).

death, about 16 percent of true crime arrestees received capital punishment. Thus there is some evidence that true crime convicts received more severe sanctions than did their UCR counterparts. This may reflect differences in the brutality or heinousness of the murders for which they were sentenced.

DISCUSSION

Following the tradition of studies on other media forms, this research sought to determine whether true crime portrayals of murder provide a distorted picture of American homicide. Examination of the characteristics of the sample of true crime books generally confirms what has been discovered in studies of television and newspapers. Although such books depict actual murder cases, they fail to accurately represent the features of homicide as they typically occur in the United States.

In true crime, offenders tend more often to be female than is characteristic of the UCR homicide offender distribution. Although less than half (43 percent) of known UCR offenders are White, almost all true crime offenders (90 percent) are White. Female offender/male victim and female/female combinations are overrepresented in true crime. Although male/male combinations represented about two-thirds of all UCR cases, they are less than half of true crime cases. In addition, although only about half of all actual homicide victims are White, in the true crime world virtually all victims are White. A larger percentage of true crime than UCR victims were young; twice as many were under the age of fourteen. Moreover, in contrast to the real world, true crime victims are overwhelmingly middle or upper class. In fact, both victims and offenders at the lower end of the socioeconomic spectrum are not adequately represented in true crime.

In sum, true crime presents cases involving higher status White victims who are often killed by related middle- or upper-class White offenders, including females, using guns and a variety of other methods. Unlike many UCR homicides, the crimes did not occur subsequent to arguments and were often the result of a plot to inherit money or gain revenge on a family member. Offenders are generally caught and convicted and, when compared to the overall distribution of homicide case outcomes, significant numbers are sentenced to death.

The findings of this research are consistent with research looking at the accuracy of other kinds of depictions of criminal activity (e.g., Davis, 1951; Sheley and Ashkins, 1981; Doob, 1985). Readers cannot obtain an adequate understanding of homicide by reading true crime accounts of murder cases. Whether this is of any significance, of course, depends on matters beyond the scope of this research. One important concern involves the extent to which accounts of crime influence both public understanding of crime and, ultimately, public enthusiasm for various solutions to the crime problem. Some research has found that exposure to errant crime reporting does lead to inaccurate estimates to the relative distribution of crimes, overestimations of the likelihood of becoming a victim of violent crime, and perceptions that the sentencing of criminals is too lenient (Sheley and Ashkins, 1981; Gerbner and Gross, 1976; Roberts and Doob, 1990).

It may be, therefore, that exposure to true crime homicide cases results in a mistaken understanding of the homicide problem, as well as misinformed judgments regarding the steps that ought to be taken to address the problem. In light of the growing popularity of the genre, this possibility is especially disturbing. Before moving to accept such unhappy conclusions, however, several tasks still remain. First, additional research is needed to replicate the findings of this study. Larger studies derived from more extensive true crime data bases need to be conducted to assure that the results of this study are representative.

Second, studies examining the influence of exposure to true crime on perceptions of murder must be conducted. Even heavy true crime readers may be exposed to other kinds of information that mitigate the impact of the distorted view of homicide represented in the genre. In addition, readers may be able to recognize as anecdotal the cases about which they read. They may understand very well that the crimes which are the subject of such books are selected because they are unusual cases.

Finally, research is needed which examines the relationship between exposure to true crime, perceptions of murder, and judgments regarding the most appropriate methods to address the homicide problem. Although it may be discovered that exposure to true crime does indeed have an impact on perceptions of murder, these perceptions may not translate into preferences regarding public policy for responding to homicide. Research conducted on other forms of media representation of crime does suggest that there may be grounds to suspect such links, yet definitive answers must await further research. The findings of the research detailed in this study represent only the first step in specifying the role of the true crime genre in the continuing development of the public's understanding of homicide.

ACKNOWLEDGMENTS

The authors would like to express their appreciation to Marilyn Mulla and Joe Stines of the Hillsborough County Public Library System, and to Marlyn R. Pethe and Mickey Wells of the University of Tampa Library for their assistance in creating the data base utilized in this project.

NOTES

1. The overall figures for victims and offenders differ from the sum of the breakdown of victim/offender categories as a result of a number of cases lacking adequate information on class position.

REFERENCES

Brownfield, D. (1986). Social class and violent behavior. *Criminology* 24(3): 421–38.

Davis, F. (1951). Crime news in Colorado newspapers. *American Journal of Sociology* 57:325–30.

Doob, A. N. (1985). The many realities of crime. In *Perspectives in criminal law,* eds. E. Greenspan and A. Doob. Aurora: Canada Law Book.

Federal Bureau of Investigation. (1991). *Uniform crime reports.* Washington, DC: U.S. Department of Justice.

Fishman, M. (1978). Crime waves as ideology. *Social Problems* 25:531–43.

Gerbner, G., and Gross, L. (1976). Living with television: The violence profile. *Journal of Communication* 26:173–99.

Graber, D. (1980). *Crime news and the public.* New York: Praeger.

Hall, S., Critcher, C., Jefferson, P., Clarke, J., and Roberts, B. (1978). *Policing the crisis: Mugging, the state, and law and other.* London: MacMillan.

Kappeler, V. E., Blumberg, M., and Potter, G. W. (1993). *The mythology of crime and justice.* Prospect Heights, IL: Waveland Press.

Maguire, K., and Flanagan, T. (1991). Sourcebook of criminal justice statistics—1990. Washington, DC: U.S. Government Printing Office.

Randall, D., Lee-Simmons, L., and Hagner, P. (1988). Common versus elite crime coverage in network news. *Social Science Quarterly* 69:910–29.

Reinarman, C., and Levine, H. G. (1989). Crack in context: Politics and media in the making of a drug scare. *Contemporary Drug Problems* 16(4):535–77.

Roberts, J., and Doob, A. (1990). News media influences on public views of sentencing. *Law and Human Behavior* 14(5):451–68.

Sheley, J., and Ashkins, C. (1981). Crime, crime news, and crime views. *Public Opinion Quarterly* 45:492–506.

Weyr, T. (1993). Marketing America's psychos. *Publisher's Weekly* 240(15):38–41.

Wolfgang, M. (1958). *Patterns in criminal homicide.* Philadelphia: University of Pennsylvania Press.

APPENDIX

Angel of Darkness
Anyone's Sin
Aurora's Motive
Bad Blood
Bad Company
Bad Dreams
Best Evidence
Beyond Reason
Billionaire Boys Club
Blood Games
Blood Relations
Blood Warning
Burning Bed, The
Careless Whisper
Closing Time
Cold Kill
Counterfeit Man
Deadly Greed
Deadly Whisper
Death at White Bear Lake, A
Dominici Affair, The
Early Graves
Evil Intentions
Feed to Kill
Heater, The
Hell Ranch
Hot Toddy
Human Harvest
Incident at Big Sky
Innocence Lost
Kiss and Kill
Life for Death
Money to Burn
Murder in Little Egypt
Please Don't Kill Me

Plot to Kill the Pope, The
Precious Victims
Prophet of Death
Sins of the Father
St. Joseph's Children
Sunset Murders, The
Trial of the Fox
Ultimate Evil, The
Unholy Matrimony
Victorian Murderesses
White Mischief
Who Killed John Lennon
Woodchipper Murders, The
Yale Murder, The
Zodiac

DISCUSSION QUESTIONS

1. What prompted the initiation of this research study?
2. Discuss the researchers' decision to examine books as the focus of the study.
3. What issues are present in conducting a content analysis?
4. How did the researchers provide a basis for comparing content with empirical reality? What issues were present?

18

Further Exploration of the Flight from Discretion

The Role of Risk/Need Instruments in Probation Supervision Decisions

ANNE L. SCHNEIDER, Arizona State University
LAURIE ERVIN, Indiana University
ZOANN SNYDER-JOY, Western Michigan University

COMMENTARY

The idea for a study of how the Wisconsin risk/need instrument was being used by Oklahoma Probation and Parole was initiated by a Department of Corrections employee who had recently completed her degree in political science at Oklahoma State University. She thought it might be possible to obtain funding from the National Institute of Justice to conduct a study of the implementation of the Wisconsin risk/need instruments in Oklahoma. From that point, the project unfolded in several phases: qualitative research to understand the issues in the use of the risk/need instruments in Oklahoma; blending of the applied research questions gleaned from the qualitative study with theoretically interesting concepts that were then incorporated into a mailed survey of probation officers in the state; and a quantitative longitudinal study based on data drawn from probation files.

The choice of methodologies should be guided by the questions and topics that are being studied. In our situation, we decided to use three different methodologies because each brought its own particular strengths to the study. Qualitative research—including focus groups, in-depth interviews, and extensive examination of documents—is essential whenever previous research and theory yields scanty information about the topic and issues; when there are likely to be strong contextual effects (that is, the previous research and theory may not be a useful guide in the specific situation confronted by the researcher); and when researchers want to enhance the validity of their interpretations by

Source: Journal of Criminal Justice, Vol. 24, pp. 109–121. Copyright © 1996, reprinted with permission from Elsevier Science.

drawing on the experiences of those most involved in the research setting itself. In our case, we knew very little about the use of risk/need instruments generally (and there were only a handful of published studies on it), and nothing at all about how these were being used in Oklahoma. We began with exploratory discussions (interviews) with several DOC officials using no protocol at all other than to discern as much as we could about the history of probation decision making, why the risk/need instruments had been introduced, and what people in different roles thought about them. DOC also gathered up a large amount of documentary materials, including in-house studies and memoranda from which we could reconstruct (with their help) the history of probation decision making in the state. After this was complete, we conducted a group interview (today it would be called a focus group) with six DOC officials, and used that information to prepare an interview protocol from which additional in-depth interviews were conducted. We ceased the qualitative component when we thought we had covered the full range of issues, topics, and interpretations.

The survey research was needed to determine how widespread various perceptions and practices actually were. Although the qualitative work was essential to understand the issues, we could not rely on it to make statements such as whether most, many, some, or a few of the probation officers thought the risk/need instruments were helpful; nor could we provide any ideas on how much strategic manipulation of the points actually occurred, or how widespread various reasons for manipulation of the points might be.

The survey could have been done in person, by telephone, or with a mailed/telephone methodology (which is what we used). In-person interviews were not practical because the probation officers were all over the state and it would have been very expensive to send interviewers out to them. Further, the probation officers were skeptical and somewhat suspicious of this study, due to the involvement of the state DOC in it; yet, without state DOC approval they would not have been permitted to participate at all. Telephone interviews that come in "cold" to a professional group may not be well received, particularly when the call is at work. We also wanted the probation officers to have the opportunity to see what we were asking so that their answers could be thoughtful. Thus, we decided on a mailed survey. Since there were only about 200 probation officers in the state, we decided to interview the full population rather than a sample. Our goal for the response rate was 66 percent (we ended up with 60 percent).

We used fairly standard protocol for mailed surveys. A letter was sent in advance from DOC explaining the purposes of the study and granting the probation officers permission to participate in it. We sent a stamped envelope for them to return the questionnaire, and we guaranteed them confidentiality. For those not received within about a week, we called the officers and asked if they would like for us to take their answers over the telephone or whether they would return the completed questionnaire to us quickly. We coded the date of return on each questionnaire we received, along with the date of any telephone contacts. One of the first analyses was to examine whether there were significant differences between "early" and "late" respondents—fortunately, there were no systematic patterns in terms of the variables we were interested in.

In our study, it was important to do both the qualitative and the quantitative components. Without the first, we would have missed many of the most important and interesting topics. Without the second, we would have had some rather serious misperceptions about how widespread certain ideas were.

ABSTRACT Quantitative decision models increasingly are replacing human judgment and discretion in criminal justice decision making. Some view this change positively, as they believe discretion is arbitrary and introduces race, class, gender, and other forms of bias into decisions. Others equate the spread of quantitative decision models with the "scientification" of administration and contend that it detracts from professionalism, democracy, and participatory administration. This study examines the implementation process and the role of risk/need assessment instruments for decisions about the proper level of supervision in parole and probation situations. The findings indicate a generally negative or, at best, neutral view toward the instruments, although they were seen as having some value for management and legitimation purposes. Paradoxically, the respondents found it hard to envision a system without them, and a slight majority believed the system was better off with the instruments than with discretionary decisions. One of the intriguing findings is that those who had more confidence in the value of the instruments also were more likely to believe they were personally effective in reducing recidivism, rehabilitating offenders, and reducing the crime rate. In this sense, the scientific status of the risk/need instruments lends perceptual rationality and legitimation to the work of the probation officers.

INTRODUCTION

Decision making in the public sector has undergone extraordinary changes in the past several decades. While most decisions in public agencies were once based on case-by-case analysis, judgment, intuition, experience, patronage, and other personal or political considerations, decisions in the modern agency often are guided or determined by tests, quantitative criteria, or formal multivariate statistical decision models. Discretionary decision making has been widely criticized as being arbitrary, unfair, race or gender biased, too dependent on political power arrangements or social stereotyping, and ineffective in achieving policy goals (Walker, 1993; Petersilia and Turner, 1987; Gottfredson and Gottfredson, 1988). The attempt to control or eliminate discretion through reliance on quantitative decision models also has been criticized, however, and viewed as part of an inevitable and detrimental scientification of administration and politics (Stone, 1993; Fischer, 1980).

Formal decision models have been used in criminal justice to guide decisions regarding diversion, sentencing, bail, parole, intensity of probation supervision, and treatment modality (see Walker, 1993; Gottfredson and Gottfredson, 1988;

Gottfredson and Tonry, 1987; Pinkele and Louthan, 1985). In spite of the enormous increase in reliance on scientific decision aids, very little is known about how these instruments have been implemented, how they are actually used, and how they are viewed by those whose discretion is being curtailed.

The research reported here is a study of how a statistical decision system (the Wisconsin risk/need instruments) was implemented in the Oklahoma Probation and Parole Department, as well as a study of probation officers' perceptions of this innovation. Data are drawn from historical records, in-depth interviews, and a structured survey of probation officers throughout the state.

THEORY AND APPROACH

Two perspectives have dominated the debate about the use of technical and scientific analysis in administrative decision making. Some view the primary problems in administration as human irrationality, politics, and organizational dynamics that preclude achievement of the instrumental goals of policy. From this perspective, quantitative risk/need instruments that have been adequately validated and properly implemented should produce an improvement in agency performance.

Critics, however, place more confidence in human judgment and discretion guided by professional norms (Lipsky, 1980). Decentralized organizations, combined with grass roots learning models of organizational behavior are viewed as superior to rule oriented hierarchies and to scientific or pseudoscientific decision-making systems. The scientification of bureaucracy and government, from this point of view, is simply a mechanism for avoiding accountability and eschewing responsibility for policy failures. Better decisions would be made in more flexible, professionally oriented settings where service deliverers and clients come face to face and negotiate the conditions of their encounter. If quantitative decision models are used at all, they would be flexible guidelines easily overridden by the better judgment of the case worker. If the agency prohibited discretionary decisions, case workers would develop other schemes to bypass the advice from the instruments and rely on their own judgment.

Another much less explored possibility turns away from the issue of whether quantitative decision models or discretionary judgment is most effective, and examines the role and function of such decision models within the highly politicized, ideologically divisive, and critical environment within which probation officers carry out their responsibilities.

Anticipated Advantages of Formal Decision Models

Formal models usually are thought to be more consistent and uniform than discretionary decisions and are generally believed to predict risks and needs more accurately than human decision makers (Brennan, 1987a; Gottfredson and Gottfredson, 1988). Risk/need estimates are expected to improve efficiency by enabling agencies to concentrate resources on those persons with the greatest probability of failure (Wright, Clear, and Dickson, 1984; Sigler and Williams, 1994). Proponents emphasize the fallibility of human judgment, abuse of discretion, and the politicization of administration, any of which could produce errors in decisions (Walker, 1993). From the perspective of those who believe that increasing reliance on scientific analysis will improve policy and administration, the introduction of quantitative decision aids is a sign of progress and is expected to have the potential for increasing public safety by reducing recidivism rates, reducing costs, and increasing accountability.

Proponents of quantitative decision models draw heavily on the experimental research carried out on human decision making, which almost always finds that formal decision models outperform human judgment (Meehl, 1954; Dawes and Corrigan, 1974; Gottfredson and Gottfredson, 1986; Kahneman, Slovic, and Tversky, 1982). Dawes (1975), for example, has shown that formal models predicted graduate student success better than university professors, even when the models incorporated exactly the variables that the professors said were important, and when the models used the exact weights the professors claimed they were using.

A second reason for expecting formal decision models to outperform human judgment in criminal justice lies in the political and social nature of decision making within this policy context. Decisions by persons in public life have implications beyond those for which the decisions putatively are intended. When risky decisions are involved and outcomes are highly uncertain, it is reasonable to expect public officials to deviate from the presumably rational decision in the direction of increased protection against political or administrative criticism. Thus, probation officers may be inclined to overclassify cases and assess the risk at higher levels than is needed, thereby providing greater intensity of supervision (Brennan, 1987b), higher costs, and less efficiency.

The Limitations of Formal Decision Models

A number of criticisms have been advanced about the widespread adoption of quantitative decision models. From a technical perspective, concern has been expressed when decision models have been adopted by jurisdictions without sufficient validation of their predictive validity (Wright, Clear, and Dickson, 1984), or when they are used for purposes other than those for which they were developed (Gottfredson, 1987; Glaser, 1987; Brennan, 1987b; Gottfredson and Gottfredson, 1988). The presumed effectiveness of these instruments in increasing uniformity, effectiveness, or efficiency may be undermined by implementation problems, including the reluctance of professionals to permit quantitative prediction systems to replace their professional judgments. Almost nothing is known about whether the formal decision models are as objective as they appear, as the initial assignment of points to each of the attributes on some of the instruments may involve a measure of subjectivity. It is possible that those who score the attributes used in the decision system are able to produce the classification they subjectively determined was most appropriate. Formal decision models have been suspected of introducing race, ethnicity, or gender bias into decision outcomes, much in the same manner as discretionary decision systems, due to the intercorrelation of certain risk and need variables with the personal characteristics of the individual (Petersilia and Turner, 1987; Farrington and Tarling, 1983).

Critics of formal decision models defend discretionary decisions on the grounds that there is not a system of rules or scientific aids that can anticipate all of the possible contingencies and variances in human behavior that will actually be encountered (Pinkele and Louthan, 1985; Fischer, 1980; Dryzek, 1990). These models also cannot adequately handle complex decision situations characterized by multiple definitions of "good decisions," particularly when these vary widely in their predictors (such as the different variables that might produce fairness v. recidivism). Reliance on a limited set of variables with questionable validity to predict only one of many different desirable outcomes may introduce errors in decisions for which no one can be held accountable.

Critics also note that the proliferation of quantitative decision aids within criminal justice is an indication of the increasing scientification of administration that has occurred in virtually all areas of administration within the United States. Such trends are seen as inevitable in advanced, modern societies, but many scholars view them with alarm. Habermas (1975), for example, argues that governments faced with declining performance and increasing expectations from citizens will seek to define most problems as technical ones, and will seek to convince the public that they are searching for technically correct solutions rather than acknowledging the structural basis of the problems. Stone (1993) argues that "clinical reason" eliminates discourse and creates new elites thereby thwarting democratic participatory decisions. Thus, governments increasingly are not held accountable for policy failures, and the public is increasingly excluded from meaningful discourse about public issues.

Purpose of the Study

The purpose of this study is to fill some of the gaps in the literature regarding the implementation of risk/need instruments and perceptions about the value of such instruments, using data from probation and parole officers in the Oklahoma Department of Corrections (DOC). The first part of the study traces the evolution of parole and probation decision making regarding the intensity of supervision through six distinctive decision-making models over a fifteen-year time period. This historical analysis provides insight on how decisions about the appropriate level of supervision actually were made as well as the rationales for changes as they occurred. The specific characteristics of the Wisconsin risk/need instruments changed in intriguing ways during this time period, and there was considerable experimentation with different approaches, including experimentation with the Iowa risk/need instruments.

The second part of the study taps the attitudes, perceptions, and expectations about the risk/need instruments held by those persons whose discretion was being limited through their use. Probation and parole officers were asked about the usefulness of the instruments to probation/parole officers, to supervisors, to the system, and whether they believed the instruments actually were capable of making better decisions than they would have made relying on their discretion. They were asked why they used them at all and whether or how they manipulated them. The underlying themes for this part of the study were drawn from ideas about the role of expertise in administration and were intended to examine whether case workers will "buy into" the notion of scientific rationality as the superior decision model or whether they will resist the imposition of scientific rationality and find ways to avoid the loss of their professional judgment. The study tapped into the various ways that administrative systems may induce people to believe in scientific rationality, such as an ideology that scientific instruments can make better decisions and are more professional, or more specific tools, such as explicit positive and negative incentives for complying with the levels of supervision dictated by the instruments.

The third part of the study turns to a correlation analysis to assess the nature of relationships between confidence in the value of risk/need instruments and beliefs about one's own effectiveness and job satisfaction. Predictors of higher and lower levels of confidence in the risk/need instruments also were examined.

Methodology and Data

Data for the study were drawn from several sources. Much of the information for the fifteen-year history was drawn from a compilation of articles and memoranda edited by Robin Berry (1988) of the Department of Corrections. This information was supplemented with in-depth interviews and a focus group discussion involving a nonrandom sample of six persons from the Oklahoma Department of Corrections. The group included two senior probation officers who worked in the central office, a district supervisor with fifteen years of experience as a probation officer, a case supervisor with twelve years as a probation officer, a team supervisor with ten years of experience, and one additional probation officer. After the focus group discussion was complete, these persons were interviewed individually. The in-depth interviews and focus group discussion were used to gather qualitative information, identify issues regarding the risk/need instrument, obtain insights that would help interpret the survey results, and to sensitize the researchers to the nuances of language and meanings of the probation and parole officers who would be involved in the survey. After the qualitative information had been obtained, a questionnaire was constructed and sent to all probation and parole officers in the state (N = 296), with 179 (60 percent) responding. A letter from the Department of Corrections was sent in advance explaining the study and ensuring employees that they could participate in the study anonymously. The surveys were returned directly to the researchers, and telephone follow-ups were used to encourage additional participation. The questionnaires were used for the quantitative parts of the study.

The average age of the respondents was thirty-five years, the average length of employment was 5.5 years. Most of the respondents were men (63 percent), most were Caucasian (83 percent), and all had at least a bachelor's degree.

HISTORICAL CONTEXT

During the fifteen-year time period covered by the study, Oklahoma used six different decision-making systems for determining the level of supervision that should be given to persons serving sentences of probation or parole under the supervision of the State Department of Corrections (DOC) (Berry, 1988).

The Committee System

Before 1976, there was no formal assessment of risks or needs and no formal assignment of cases to levels of supervision intensity. The system was based on judgment and discretion, with both in the hands of the probation and parole officers and their supervisors. The gradual replacement of individual judgment with more structured decisions began in 1976 when decision making shifted to a three-person committee of probation and parole officers along with their supervisors. These individuals assessed the risks and needs of each person referred to probation and parole and assigned them to one of three different levels of supervision intensity: Level I (maximum supervision), Level II (moderate), or Level III (minimum supervision). These classification decisions were based on subjective assessments without benefit of formal decision aids (Collins, 1988). Two other levels of supervision (Levels IV and V) were specified, but both dealt with persons who could not be kept under direct supervision, such as mental commitments or absconders.

As was to be true until 1984, the contrast in required supervision intensity was surprisingly small. Levels I and II both required one contact per month, with the contact being out-of-the-office for Level I and in-office for Level II. Level III required one contact every ninety days (Berry, 1988). Other contacts were encouraged. Interviews with the six respondents from the nonrandom sample indicated there may not have been much actual difference in the amount of supervision probation officers provided to clients, or there may have been substantial differentiation that was not related to the point system.

Adoption of the Wisconsin Instruments

The committee system was abandoned in 1981, reportedly on the grounds that it was arbitrary and inconsistent (Berry, 1988), and the Wisconsin Client Classification instruments were adopted to replace the committee decision systems. The major impetus for shifting to a structured decision system was to gain accreditation from the American Correctional Association (ACA). Collins (1988) reported that the instrument adopted was the original Wisconsin instrument, although the scoring system used in it differs from the Wisconsin instruments studied by Wright, Clear, and Dickson (1984). There was no validation of the instrument in Oklahoma or on cases drawn from Oklahoma files.

Berry's (1988) historical account says that there were three major goals proposed for the shift to an objective client classification system: (a) to maintain the current level of client misbehavior (arrests, new convictions, technical violations); (b) to improve resource utilization; and (c) to minimize client involvement in formal supervision and minimize client contact with officers. The official statement of purpose was:

> A sound classification system is the most effective means to accomplish effective utilization of resources in probation and parole supervision efforts. The classification system must ensure service delivery in accordance with the needs of the client and safety of the community. The goal of our classification system is having clients progress to the point that services are no longer needed and our efforts may be redirected to those in need. (Berry, 1988)

The Assessment of Client Risk used ten variables, seven of which were verifiable items in the file: number of address changes, employment, age at first conviction, prior periods of supervision, prior revocations, prior felony convictions, and prior convictions for any offense. Three subjective factors were scored by the officials: alcohol use, drug use, and attitude. Alcohol and drug use were assessed in terms of no problem, moderate problem, or serious problem. Interestingly, serious alcohol problems were scored more heavily (4) than serious drug problems (2). Attitudes were scored from 0 to 5, using response categories of whether the person was "motivated to change" or "rationalizes behavior; negative, not motivated to change." The maximum score was unlimited, as the instrument counted all prior convictions toward the total. In fact, prior convictions could entirely dominate the scoring on this instrument. The second instrument, Assessment of Client Needs, was considerably more subjective and incorporated variables ranging from employment and financial management to sexual behavior.

Pilot Test of the Wisconsin System

A pilot test of Oklahoma's version of the Wisconsin instruments was conducted in 1981 by the Department of Corrections (Collins, 1988), in which two-thirds of the probation officers in each of the seven districts in the state were randomly selected to begin using the new risk classification instrument. Others continued with the committee approach. Officers participating in the experiment reclassified all clients on their case load.

Reanalysis of the 1,600 cases (see Table 1) showed a substantial difference in the proportion classified at each level. The Wisconsin classification system assessed only 3.9 percent of the cases as needing Level I supervision (the maximum level), compared with 11.3 percent of the cases assessed by the committee. The contrast at Level III is even more stark, as 75 percent of the cases were classified as Level III by the Wisconsin system, compared with 28 percent by the committee system. This finding is not entirely unexpected, given the contention that probation officers will overclassify as a strategy to protect them from political or agency criticism if a person on their case load reoffends. It is a completely different result than that found by Sigler and Williams (1994) whose study compared officers' classifications with those of four different screening instruments. In that study, the probation officer classifications put far fewer people into the maximum category (6 percent) than three of the instruments,

Table 1. Classification Decisions: Comparison of Committee Decisions and Formal Decision Model in Oklahoma

	SUPERVISION		
Classification Decisions	Level I (Maximum) %	Level II (Moderate) %	Level III (Minimum) %
Committee	11	60	28
Wisconsin model	4	21	75

Note: Data are recalculations from Collins (1988:11).

which ranged from 33 to 88 percent in the maximum category. The difference between the findings could reflect different political or agency contexts. As will be explained more fully below, the Oklahoma system was expected to be used to help determine statewide allocation of resources, so that allocations would not be based solely on the number of persons on probation, but also on the intensity of supervision that would be needed. This could provide an agency incentive to overclassify as a means of enhancing the agency budget.

Experimentation with the Iowa Instruments

In 1985, three districts were asked to test the Iowa risk instrument. The Iowa instrument initially was developed for parole release decisions. It did not contain a need assessment (although Oklahoma incorporated a need instrument in its implementation), and it relied almost exclusively on information about the number and type of prior offenses. In comparison with the Wisconsin instruments, the Iowa protocol was more sophisticated, complex, and time consuming to complete. It also required considerably more data and training. Respondents in the study reported that the instrument was less intuitively understandable, as well, because it is almost impossible to determine from a casual inspection how the various attributes were being weighted and combined to produce the final level of risk.

The Iowa instrument was used for about eighteen months and then dropped due to general dissatisfaction. Department of Corrections officials enumerated some of the problems: it required data that often were not available, it was being used in a manner different than that for which it was developed, staff did not trust the results, and it was time consuming and confusing to complete.

Changes in the Wisconsin System

The Wisconsin system was changed repeatedly during its use in Oklahoma. In 1984, there was an expansion in the number of levels from three to five, a change in the points assigned to the specific categories within the reassessment risk/need instruments, and an increase in the contrast among levels in the intensity of supervision. Maximum supervision cases (Level I) were changed to require two face-to-face contacts per month; Level II cases required one contact per month, and Level III cases were to have one contact every three months. Level IV, a new classification, was for persons assessed as low risk and low need who had been under supervision for at least six months. Contacts were to occur only as needed, and the client was expected only to submit a written monthly report. Level V was for clients on early termination, and the level of supervision was not specified.

More changes were made in the Wisconsin instrument in 1987: changes in the classification categories, changes in the intensity of supervision, changes in the items on the risk/need instruments, and changes in the points. Three face-to-face contacts were now required for the Level I cases, two for the Level II, one for the Level III, one per every three months for Level IV cases, and only a mail in report for persons classified at Level V.

Generally, the Oklahoma adaptation of the Wisconsin model can be characterized as a relatively flexible, somewhat judgmental, constantly changing yet highly structured decision system. In the early years, it prescribed very little differences in the level of supervision, but permitted probation officers to use heavier supervision for whichever cases they believed needed it. Over time, considerably greater differentiation was incorporated into the system, so that offenders in the maximum supervision category (Level I) received far more intensive supervision than those in the minimum category (Level V), and there was considerably less discretion available to officers to determine on the basis of their own judgment which offenders should receive heavier supervision.

ATTITUDES ABOUT THE RISK/NEED INSTRUMENTS

Qualitative Information

The qualitative data obtained from the six DOC officials through in-depth interviews and the focus group indicated considerable ambivalence about the purposes of the instruments and whether they were being used effectively. The respondents said the risk/need instruments were supposed to help probation officers understand the factors that make a person more likely to commit crimes, and to ensure that the officers carefully reviewed the person's file to determine their scores on these factors. As one person pointed out, the forms made it easy for a supervisor to determine whether the probation officer had studied the file.

The six officials agreed that the instruments were supposed to be used to ensure uniformity in allocating resources. Probation officers would know how much time they needed to spend on a case; supervisors would know how to allocate cases across officers to ensure equitable case loads; and state level officials would have a better idea how state-wide resource allocations should be distributed to take into account not only the number of persons on probation, but also the intensity of supervision needed. The officials, however, did not believe that these goals were being met because there were too many overrides and too much discretion in the way the instruments were being scored. One person noted:

> It [the scoring] is not uniform among districts. Some have more people in lower classifications; some in higher. This is a sign that the instrument has

> been manipulated. That is one of the dangers. Some districts override more than others, perhaps because they are more law-enforcement oriented. (Hatley, 1989)

Another doubted that probation officers actually were paying attention to the level of supervision that the instrument said should be used:

> As for classifying people to different levels of supervision, it is doing that; but I don't think it is meeting any of the purposes I've described. Most officers (I may be over generalizing) prefer the client to report in a routine way, and gives the officer contact with clients each month, even if they are on Level III or Level IV. It is easier for the officer to keep track of them if they report in every month. On 90 day supervision, for example, you lose track of them and then have to track them down. The instrument was designed to improve allocation of resources, but I don't think it is accomplishing those ends. (Hatley, 1989)

The persons in the focus group talked about the role of the instrument in holding probation officers accountable and ensuring that they were doing their job. One pointed out that "the instrument is the only measurement tool we have to judge an officer's performance. It is a quantitative measurement of how to maintain a case load. One of the effects is that the emphasis has shifted to quantity rather than quality time. Rather than concentrating on how many you need to see, you should be making a difference in their lives. Because of the instrument, more emphasis is placed on number of visits rather than quality of visits" (Hatley, 1989).

The instrument provided a specific record of how many contacts were to occur, and whether they were to occur in the probation officer's office or in the field. These were monitored monthly for compliance by the probation officer. Under a more discretionary system, there was no way to determine how often a contact was supposed to be made, as this was a discretionary decision by the officer; therefore, there was no way to determine whether the officer was meeting with the client as often as needed.

Assessments were not totally negative, however. When asked what would happen if the instruments were suddenly abandoned, one person said:

> If your clients are obnoxious, as most of the high risk clients are, you don't want to see them as often. But if you have the instrument reminding you that you have to see them, then you'll do it more often than you would otherwise be inclined to. If I didn't have the instrument, and a full case load, then those are the people I would not see. (Hatley, 1989)

Another said that abandoning the instruments would result in more clients being seen at the higher and medium levels, especially in the high crime areas of the state:

> In our district we see the clients more often to hold them more accountable. It is better to err by giving too much supervision than to give too little

and get burned by it later. This protects the officer and community. We have to oversupervise in this district. (Hatley, 1989)

Another said:

> I think we need some sort of structure. I am one of the few people left who used the unstructured approach. Judgment, however, was too subjective, appearances are a poor judge. Some of the areas on the instrument are good predictors. You need to combine the instrument with discretion. (Hatley, 1989)

The discussion of overrides indicated that most were upward—moving an offender into a higher level of supervision. The strategy for getting an offender into a less intensive supervision did not rely on overrides but on ignoring problems on the need instrument, or underestimating risk in some of the judgmental categories, so that the number of points would be low enough to ensure a lower classification. According to one of the probation officers, this was a way to organize a case load and ensure that you did not have too many high risk cases:

> Officers can manipulate the system by scoring the instrument however they want to. There are instructions about scoring, but I'm not sure if there is attention paid here or anywhere else as far as whether the forms are correct. (Hatley, 1989)

One of the reasons there were not more overrides is that these were a hassle:

> They [overrides] are not common, really, because they are a hassle. You have to talk to your supervisor. You never override to a lower level, always to a higher. Frequently an officer may feel a client's risk should be overridden but to avoid the hassle will see the client more often and leave the instrument showing a lower risk assignment. Overrides increase supervision. (Hatley, 1989)

The quantitative system was implemented without any officer input, as a strategy to help ensure ACA accreditation. Training was limited:

> There really wasn't any officer input at all. Some people went out and got trained; then came back and trained us. At that time, case loads were high. We didn't have much money or resources, so they pushed it as a way for the officer to reduce the case load. The instrument was supposed to make case load management easier. A lot of officers at that time resented the instrument for attempting to quantify human behavior. The officers felt they had a good feel for which clients were going to be bad and good. Some officers, early on, figured out that if they could get their clients to the lowest possible assessment, [requiring contact only every three months], and then see them once per month, they'd be heroes for seeing their clients more often than they were required to. (Hatley, 1989)

The Survey of Probation Officers

Attitudes toward the instruments from probation officers around the state were generally negative or neutral (Table 2). Slightly more than one-third (37 percent) believed that the risk/need instruments were appropriate for making decisions about the level of supervision, and less than one-half (47 percent) believed they were a helpful tool. Strong majorities of 76 percent and 61 percent believed the officers should have more discretion in selecting the level of supervision and that the officer's knowledge is better than the instruments.

On the various ways that the instruments were supposed to be useful, only one-fourth to one-third generally concurred with their presumed value. Twenty-six percent said the instruments were useful in identifying high risk offenders; 37 percent said they were useful in providing initial insight into the offender or in helping the officers allocate their time among different cases. More than one-half agreed that the instruments help ensure that high risk cases get more intensive supervision. Generally, less than one-half of the respondents believed that the instruments were useful in any of the specific tasks of the probation officer.

The instruments were not judged much better in terms of their usefulness to supervisors or to the system. More than one-half said that they were useful in providing uniformity of supervision state-wide, but most disagreed with assertions that the instruments helped supervisors evaluate probation officers, helped supervisors allocate case loads, and they emphatically rejected the notion that the instruments reduced the costs of probation and parole.

Less than a majority believed the instruments were useful in justifying the supervision level to the public or legislature, but they strongly rejected the notion that reliance on quantitative decision aids protected the employee from blame if an offender committed another offense while on supervision.

The survey posed questions regarding four different reasons for why the officers completed the instruments and used them in their decision making: (a) trust in expertise (i.e., they believe the instruments are scientific and are willing to yield their subjective judgment to it); (b) professionalism (i.e., professional norms work in favor of relying on the instruments); (c) positive incentives; and (d) expectations of supervisors within the hierarchical system of control, including negative evaluations.

Respondents strongly rejected the notion that the instruments reflect expertise. When asked whether the officer's knowledge is more accurate than the instrument, only 15 percent disagreed. Only 13 percent agreed with the statement that experienced officers find the instruments make better decisions than they would. Professionalism also was not viewed as the reason for using them, as only 20 percent agreed with the statement that they would use the instruments even if they were not required because it is the professional thing to do. About one-third said that positive rewards were provided for properly completing the instruments; while 83 percent said that negative evaluations were given for failure to complete the instruments positively and 78 percent said that supervisors look more favorably on those who properly complete the instruments.

Table 2. Perceptions of the Risk/Need Instruments

Item	Agree %	Neutral %	Disagree %
Are the risk/need instruments useful?			
The risk/need instruments are appropriate for making decisions about the level of supervision	37	31	33
The instruments are a helpful tool for the probation officer	47	26	28
Officers should have more discretion in selecting the level of supervision	76	18	6
The officer's knowledge is more accurate than the instrument	61	24	15
Instruments are useful to probation officers			
In identifying high risk offenders	26	29	45
In providing initial insight into the offender	37	31	31
In helping officer manage case load (i.e., allocate their time)	37	29	33
In making sure high risk cases get intensive supervision	53	23	24
In assisting the offender to get assistance needed for success	24	31	45
Instruments are useful to supervisors and the system			
In providing uniformity of supervision state wide	57	23	20
In helping supervisors evaluate probation officers	21	22	48
In reducing costs of probation and parole	10	27	63
The instruments are useful in protecting the employee from blame	19	18	63
They are useful in justifying the supervision level to the public or legislature	49	27	24
Reasons for using the risk/need instruments			
Research has shown these instruments to be effective	24	44	32
The instruments are more accurate than a subjective evaluation of an offender	27	31	42
The officer's knowledge is more accurate than the instrument	13	26	53
Experienced officers find it makes better decisions than they would	13	29	53
Using the instruments is the professional thing to do	20	26	42
Positive rewards are provided for properly completing the instruments	31	26	42
Negative evaluations are given for failure to properly complete the instruments	83	12	4
Supervisors look more favorably on those who properly complete the instruments	78	15	6
The system would be better off without the risk/need instruments	23	25	52

Table 3. Extent of Manipulation and Outside Influence

	Never/ Seldom %	Sometimes %	Often/ Always %
Problems are ignored and not recorded properly to lessen work load	46	42	12
Officers score the instruments incorrectly to manage their case loads	41	36	22
When officers believe an override is needed, they just see the client more often rather than getting an override	44	32	14
Do media and public opinions influence level of supervision?	53	32	14
Does the political agenda of the district attorney or sheriff influence the level assignments?	75	20	5

Several questions probed for information about whether the officers manipulated the point system and the ways in which this occurred (Table 3). One type of manipulation reported during the open-ended interviews was to ignore serious needs of the offender and not record his or her problems accurately in order to obtain a lower supervision level and lessen work load. Only 12 percent said that this happens often or always, but 42 percent said it happens sometimes (Table 3). The qualitative portion of the study also revealed the contention that officers score the instruments incorrectly in order to manage their case load within the time frame they have available—that is, they underestimate the level of supervision needed to ensure that they can actually provide the level called for in their case load. Only 22 percent said this happens often or always, and 36 percent said it happens sometimes. About the same results were obtained from a question about whether officers scored the instruments incorrectly to justify the level of supervision they believed was appropriate. Another type of manipulation reported during the qualitative phase was to ignore the classification level when it suggested a less intensive level of supervision and simply see the offender more often, rather than seek an override from the supervisor. This manipulation was noted as a way to let the officer exercise independent judgment without calling this to the attention of the supervisor. Fourteen percent said that this happens often or always, and 44 percent said it happens sometimes.

Two questions probed the extent of media and political influence. Fifty-three percent of the respondents indicated that media and public opinion seldom influenced the level of supervision, compared with 32 percent who said it happened sometimes and 14 percent who said it often or always influenced the level of supervision. The political agenda of the sheriff or district attorney was rejected as a factor influencing their decisions in scoring or using the instrument by 75 percent of the respondents, although 20 percent said it influenced them sometimes and 5 percent said it often or always was a factor in determining the levels assigned to probationers.

One of the paradoxes of the study is that, in spite of the generally negative views of the instruments, when asked whether the system would be better off without the risk/need instruments, only 23 percent agreed, 25 percent were neutral, and 52 percent disagreed.

Correlates of Belief in the Usefulness of the Instruments

The final part of the analysis probed for possible causes and consequences of perceptions that the risk/need instruments were useful. For this analysis, a thirteen-item scale of usefulness was constructed from the questions on the instrument. The specific items include all of those shown in the usefulness section of Table 2, except for the item on whether the instruments were useful in justifying the level of supervision to the public and legislature, which had a negative correlation with several of the other items. Cronbach's alpha was .93 for the thirteen-item usefulness scale.

It was expected that some correlation would be found between the background characteristics of the respondents and confidence in the instrument, particularly the contention that younger and less experienced officers would find the instruments more useful; however, there were no relationships of this type. The level of education, gender, age, and years of experience did not correlate with positive attitudes about the instruments. It also was expected that persons who had received more training would find them more useful, but there were no relationships here, either. Small but statistically significant correlations were found for three variables, however. These included those who believed that their level of training was adequate ($r = .15, s = .04$), those who were familiar with research on risk/need instruments ($r = .12, s = .10$), and those who were aware of local research that had been done to validate the instruments ($r = .18, s = .01$).

Two additional scales were developed to measure the respondents' perceptions of how effective they were in their jobs and their satisfaction with the job. The effectiveness scale was constructed from three five-point agree/disagree questions regarding the extent to which the probation officer believed he or she was: (a) effective in rehabilitating offenders, (b) effective in preventing recidivism, and (c) effective in contributing to a reduction in the crime rate. Cronbach's alpha was .78. The job satisfaction scale was constructed from nine agree/disagree items (using a five-point scale) pertaining to whether they like their duties, are satisfied with their job assignment, would not be interested in another job, enjoy their work, like their job better than the average person, are enthusiastic about their job, have a strong sense of accomplishment, have an opportunity to use their skills and abilities, and find the work interesting and challenging. Cronbach's alpha for this scale was .91. A correlation was not observed between the perceptions of the instrument's usefulness and the nine-point scale of job satisfaction.

There was a strong relationship between beliefs that the risk/need instruments were useful and the probation officers' perceptions of effectiveness ($r = .42, s = .001$). This study's interpretation of this finding is that the risk/need instruments serve a particular purpose—perhaps not the one intended, but, instead, one that enables probation officers to believe in the risk/need instruments as the product of a rational, scientific society that will enable them to be effective in their work. The risk/need instruments rationalize the work and grant renewed confidence that they can make a difference in the lives of persons who have violated the law.

CONCLUSIONS

The optimistic vision of increased rationality, professionalism, and efficiency in probation supervision decisions that would accompany the introduction of quantitative risk/need instruments was not borne out in the Oklahoma experiment. The paradox, however, was that even though most persons involved in this study recognized the limitations of the instruments and acknowledged that they were not being used as intended and were not having the effects that were promised, they were reluctant to abandon them. In practice, the use of the risk/need instruments mirrored the findings reported by Simon (1993:4) that "the risks and needs score was a constructive compromise that lent the aura of statistical prediction to the process without really taking away any power from the local case-by-case system or even accurately mirroring past experience."

More than just a constructive compromise, however, the findings from this study suggest that the risk/need instruments lend perceptual rationality and legitimation to the work carried out by probation officers. These instruments fit the model of a scientific profession and the style of decision making that modern correctional systems should adopt. Persons who believed in the instruments—in their logic, rationality, consistency with values—believed they were personally more effective in rehabilitating offenders, reducing recidivism, and reducing the crime rate.

ACKNOWLEDGMENT

This study was aided with grants from the National Institute of Justice and the Arizona State University College of Public Programs.

REFERENCES

Berry, R., ed. (1988). Department of Corrections Division of Probation and Parole, assessment history since 1976. Oklahoma City, OK: Oklahoma Department of Corrections.

Brennan, T. (1987a). Classification: An overview of selected methodological issues. In *Prediction and classification, crime and justice,* vol. 9, *A review of research,* eds. D. Gottfredson and M. Tonry. Chicago: University of Chicago Press.

Brennan, T. (1987b). Classification for control in jails and prisons. In *Prediction and Classification, Crime and Justice,* vol. 9, *A review of research,* eds. D. Gottfredson and M. Tonry. Chicago: University of Chicago Press.

Carroll, J. (1987). A psychological approach to deterrence: The evaluation of crime opportunities. *Journal of Personality and Social Psychology* 36:1512–20.

Collins, D. (1988). Analysis of the Wisconsin assessment of client risk as implemented in Oklahoma. In *Department of Corrections Division of Probation and Parole, assessment history since 1976,* ed. R. Berry. Oklahoma City, OK: Oklahoma Department of Corrections.

Cornish, D. B., and Clarke, R. V. (1986). *The reasoning criminal.* New York: Springer-Verlag.

Dawes, R. (1975). Case by case vs. rule-generated procedures for the allocation of scarce resources. In *Human judgement and decision processes in applied settings,* eds. M. Kaplan and S. Schwartz. New York: Academic Press.

Dawes, R., and Corrigan, B. (1974). Linear models in decision making. *Psychological Bulletin* 81:95–106.

Dryzek, J. (1990). *Discursive democracy.* London: Cambridge University Press.

Farrington, D. and Tarling, R. (1983). Criminal prediction. Albany, NY: State University of New York Press.

Fischer, F. (1980). *Values and public policy: The problem of methodology.* Boulder, CO: Westview Press.

Glaser, D. (1987). Classification for risk. In *Prediction and classification, crime and justice,* vol. 9, *A review of research,* eds. D. Gottfredson and M. Tonry. Chicago: University of Chicago Press.

Gottfredson, D. M., and Tonry, M., eds. (1987). *Prediction and classification, crime and justice,* vol. 9, *A review of research.* Chicago: University of Chicago Press.

Gottfredson, M. R., and Gottfredson, D. M. (1988). *Decision making in criminal justice.* New York: Plenum Press.

Gottfredson, S. D. (1987). Prediction: An overview of selected methodological issues. In *Prediction and classification, crime and justice,* vol. 9, *A review of research,* eds. D. M. Gottfredson and M. Tonry. Chicago: University of Chicago Press.

Gottfredson, S. D., and Gottfredson, D. M. (1986). The accuracy of prediction. In *Criminal careers and "career criminals",* eds. A. Blumstein, J. Cohen, J. Roth, and C. Visher. Washington, DC: National Academy of Sciences.

Habermas, J. (1975). *Legitimation crisis.* Translated by T. McCarthy. Boston: Beacon Press.

Hatley, E. (1989). Interviews with Oklahoma Correctional Personnel, Oklahoma City, Oklahoma.

Kahneman, D., Slovic, P., and Tversky, A. (1982). *Judgement under uncertainty: Heuristics and biases.* Cambridge, MA: Cambridge University Press.

Lipsky, M. (1980). *Street level bureaucracy: Dilemmas of the individual in public service.* New York: Russell Sage.

Meehl, P. (1954). *Clinical versus statistical prediction.* Minneapolis, MN: University of Minnesota Press.

Petersilia, J., and Turner, S. (1987). Guideline-based justice: Prediction and racial minorities. In *Prediction and classification, crime and justice,* vol. 9, *A review of research,* eds. D. M. Gottfredson and M. Tonry. Chicago: University of Chicago Press.

Pinkele, C. F., and Louthan, W. C. (1985). *Discretion, justice, and democracy.* Ames, IA: Iowa State University Press.

Sigler, R., and Williams, J. J. (1994). A study of the outcomes of probation officers and risk-screening instruments classifications. *Journal of Criminal Justice* 22:495–502.

Simon, J. (1993). *Poor discipline.* Chicago: University of Chicago Press.

Stone, D. (1993). Clinical authority in the construction of citizenship. In *Public policy and democracy,* eds. H. Ingram and S. R. Smith. Washington, DC: Brookings.

Walker, S. (1993). *Taming the system: The control of discretion in criminal justice, 1950–1990.* New York: Oxford University Press.

Wright, G. (1984). *Behavioral decision theory.* Beverly Hills, CA: Sage Publications.

Wright, K., Clear, T., and Dickson, P. (1984). Universal applicability of probation risk-assessment instruments: A critique. *Criminology* 22:113–34.

DISCUSSION QUESTIONS

1. Why did the researchers employ multiple methods? Why were the specific ones chosen?
2. How did the researchers address the initial skepticism of potential survey respondents?
3. Discuss the protocols used by the researchers in conducting the survey portion of the research.
4. Discuss the advantages and limitations of using research information to structure formal decision models.

Epilogue

Policy and Utilization Issues in Criminal Justice Research

KNOWLEDGE FOR WHAT?

Sixty years ago Robert S. Lynd (1939) posed the question "Knowledge for What?" By now, you have spent a good deal of time and effort learning about criminal justice research methods. Much of your attention has been directed toward fundamentals and issues related to *conducting* research, learning about various strategies and techniques, their strengths and their limitations. In this final section, we direct your attention to the use of research findings.

As Maxfield and Babbie (1994: 39) point out, "Because crime is an important social problem, rather than simply a social artifact of interest to researchers, much research in criminal justice is closely linked to public policy." Over the past thirty years there has been increasing interest in the use of research information to serve as a significant input, if not the predominant basis, for policy development and decision making in criminal justice organizations and agencies (Lovell, 1988, 1996). But, as LoBiondo-Wood and Haber (1998: 468) point out, "[i]ncorporation of research findings into practice (. . .) is a difficult and challenging process," [and may present] "more challenges to overcome than does conduct of research." In considering the challenges, several questions emerge. For example, what is the role and potential for research information in policy development and criminal justice practice? Further, what factors facilitate or inhibit the use of research information for policy development and decision making in real-life organizations? Or what conditions offer the most promising opportunities for the use of research information? Such questions are merely a starting place.

The following discussion centers on the use of research findings for policy development in criminal justice. We present an overview of *research utilization;* the policy context(s) in which research information may be used (or, perhaps, may be disregarded); factors that may facilitate or inhibit the use of research information in the context(s) of policy development; and, related to conditions that may foster use, several notions concerning planning for research utilization.

RESEARCH INFORMATION

For our present purposes, the term *research information* refers to empirical findings, and resulting conclusions or recommendations, produced using scientific methodologies. Research may be initiated and conducted for a variety of purposes. The anticipated payoff may be contribution to an existing body of knowledge, as is the case with *basic research.* As well, the impetus and intent may be to inform policy or practice directly through *applied research,* in which research results address specific questions.

A large amount of both basic and applied research information, covering many aspects of crime and criminal justice, already has been produced. Decision makers and others addressing policy or program questions may choose to identify, acquire, and consider relevant research information already available. Or, depending on the questions, resources, and other important factors, they may initiate new applied studies designed to provide information for their use. Of course, we must also keep in mind that (1) relevant empirical information may not be available regarding particular questions and that (2) policy makers may choose not to include research information as an input to a given decision or set of decisions.

DEFINING RESEARCH UTILIZATION

Rich (1981) points out that *utilization* refers to the process by which research information (or any information) enters policy making. Decision makers receive the information, review and assimilate it, and use the information in policy making.

The literature concerning research utilization presents a range of possible uses in this process. First, decision makers may find specific research findings to be so definitive or compelling that they base changes in programs or policies directly on the research information. When this occurs, the research information is said to have *impact,* directly and significantly affecting a particular decision or set of decisions. And the decision makers have made *instrumental use* of the information (see Lovell, 1988).

Second, although the information supplied by an empirical study or studies may not be sufficiently definitive or compelling as to dictate or drive a decision, it may nonetheless influence the thinking of the decision maker(s). In this situation, the decision maker(s) may engage in *conceptual use* of the information: to sort out assumptions, clarify logic, generate new hypotheses, reduce their own uncertainties, or arrive at a better understanding of the range of activities and constraints involved in a given decision (see Rich, in Lovell, 1988; LoBiondo-Wood and Haber, 1998). In other words, the decision maker(s) may use the research information to guide and clarify policy making, even though they do not base specific changes in programs or policies on the information.

Third, decision makers may put research information to *persuasive use.* Here again, the decision maker(s) do not base specific changes in programs or policies directly on research findings. Rather, the decision maker(s) use research results to substantiate or legitimize a position or decision already arrived at, to refute or cast doubt on propositions advanced by others, to persuade or neutralize others, to buttress a request for funding, or other similar purposes. In such instances, "the research findings may not change the decision discernibly from what it otherwise would have been (. . .)," but, "(. . .) such uses may have significant effect in ensuring adoption of a contested course of action" (Weiss and Bucuvalas, 1980: 11).

Finally, decision makers may choose to disregard research information, even if it is available and relevant to a greater or lesser degree to particular policy or program questions. Scholars and experts term this *nonuse* of research information.

These are not the only possibilities regarding decision makers and potential uses of research information. Other conceptualizations may apply. Our point is that research information may be used by policy makers in a number of ways, for a number of purposes.

THE CONTEXT FOR POLICY DEVELOPMENT

We encounter the term *policy* frequently. This term carries many connotations. Policy may refer to a guiding expression—a statement or set of statements set forth by designated decision makers concerning what they want to achieve, how to get from here to there, what values to espouse and internalize or reflect, and so forth. As expressions, policies may be more or less specific, may vary in scope and application, may originate from differing realms of jurisdiction (e.g., those enacted by persons at a national level of government, state level of government, local level of government; those enacted by leaders of specific public organizations; those enacted by leaders of specific private organizations), among other permutations and possibilities.

The term *policy* also may refer to the strategies leaders enact to achieve intended purposes (e.g., building additional prisons may be an overall strategy enacted by the leaders of a state to affect crime, and many persons will think of this as a policy). Sometimes persons refer to the standard operating procedures (SOPs) developed to guide specific actions in a given organization as policies.

The context for policy development obviously may vary. We could be considering a legislative committee engaged in deciding what should be done statewide about sentencing violent offenders. We could be considering the efforts of the leaders of a federal agency, such as the U.S. Justice Department's Office of Juvenile Justice and Delinquency Prevention (OJJDP) as they attempt to devise a national approach to the issue of disproportionate representation of minorities in secure confinement. We could be considering the efforts by the leadership of a municipal police department to develop a definitive policy concerning high-speed police pursuits. There are endless examples, and each context clearly would have unique aspects. Nonetheless, there are some concerns common to the context for policy development, and these are important to consideration of research utilization.

First, policy making most often involves the collective action of a number of decision makers and "will usually involve multiple stakeholders—people who have some direct or indirect interest in the (. . .) results" (Rossi and Freeman, in Maxfield and Babbie, 1995: 327). For example, imagine the case of the municipal police department whose leaders confront the issue of developing a definitive policy concerning high-speed pursuit. In that situation, we could expect the department's chief and a number of the upper-level leaders to be directly involved. Beyond this, we could expect a set of interested others, some of whom might lobby to be directly involved, others of whom might attempt to exert influence indirectly. The interested others certainly could include the leaders of a patrol officers' union, the leaders of a supervisors' union, the city attorney, the mayor, members of a city council, members of interested citizens' groups, and others.

Some policy issues will draw more attention than others, but we can expect multiple stakeholders on most policy issues. And differing stakeholder interests may produce conflicting perspectives, which result in the need to resolve questions of value or preference.

Second, policy making often involves decision makers who not only have differing interests but also have unequal influence. Following Allison (1971), where questions of value or preference must be resolved, policy makers engage in a form of bargaining, bringing their influence to the decision-making table, to have their policy preferences reflected in the resulting decision. This may have a large effect on the nature of the information decision makers may choose to consider, the sources from which they gather information, and the uses they may individually or collectively make of it.

Third, policy makers confront their issues in the midst of other ongoing efforts and enterprises. Seldom would a policy issue or question be so unique that there would not already be policies, strategies, and programs that would be affected by or would themselves affect yet another effort. The impetus of previous or existing policies, strategies, and programs, and the investments already made in these, may shape the way in which problems or issues will be defined as well as the way(s) in which these will be addressed. Again, this may have a large effect on the nature of the information decision makers choose to consider, the sources from which they gather information, and the uses they individually or collectively make of it.

Finally, policy makers conduct most of their work in and through organizations, most of which are best characterized as bureaucratic. In the language of organizations, *bureaucracy* is not a dirty word; rather, it refers to a ubiquitous form of organization. What this means for our present discussion is that the rules and repertoires for action, the practices, and traditions that make up the ways of doing business in given organizations may greatly affect decision makers' orientations with respect to the use of information for policy decisions—when, how, and where they will search for information (see Rich, 1981). As Rich (1981: 13) points out, "Information is only one of several resources which policy makers use in making a decision."

These observations about the context for policy development only scratch the surface. But as a step toward additional consideration, they suggest the complexity of the policy arena and the policy-making process in which research information may be one potential resource.

FACTORS AFFECTING RESEARCH UTILIZATION

Scholars have employed varying perspectives in seeking to understand research utilization and identify factors that are important in the use or nonuse of research information for policy making. This means the literature on research utilization contains an array of factors of potential importance, with one or another set of factors emphasized as more important depending on the perspective of the writer. There is not an adequate theory that integrates the various perspectives to completely explain or predict the use of research information for policy making.

From consideration of the initiation of the research to consideration of the decision to use or not use research information, experts have viewed the route as "strewn with competing and conflicting influences" (Weiss and Bucuvalas, 1980: 16). Experts have conceptualized factors of importance arising from several realms, including differences in the orientations of researchers and of policy makers; other factors related to the production of research information; factors associated with the transmission of research results; factors arising from the nature of the policy context and the nature of doing business in policy making; politics; factors stemming from the nature of organizational decision making and the processes though which use of research information may occur in complex, bureaucratic organizations; and more. At first glance, the overall picture may appear mind-boggling. But, to simplify somewhat, sort things, and attain a basic understanding of what the experts are addressing, let us briefly visit two realms of importance, highlighting some of the major avenues to travel.

Related to the Research

Remember that policy makers facing particular issues may choose to consider available information resulting from basic research or from applied research conducted elsewhere or at another time. They also may initiate or commission new applied research for their potential use. This means that some factors of potential importance to research use may vary depending on whether or not the research is specifically tailored to a given policy decision. For example, the research questions or the formulations of the problems for study may differ. Obviously, as you have learned, this affects all of the conduct of the research and the direction of the results. Researchers' formulations may not match decision makers' definitions of problems, they may focus on different facets of the issues, and they may consider different sets of conditions as fixed and subject to change (Weiss and Bucuvalas, 1980: 17). This would be of great importance in whether policy makers view certain research as relevant, whether they even consider the research, and whether they ultimately use the research—even research they commission.

Weiss and Bucuvalas (1980: 17–19) have compiled a lengthy summary of potential obstacles to the effective application of research information in decision making arising from the realm of research production. These are as applicable at present as they were when Weiss and Bucuvalas compiled them. We present a portion of the listing to provide a place of departure for further thought along this avenue. Among other observations concerning sources of potential discontinuity in the utilization process, Weiss and Bucuvalas point out:

1. Research takes time, and results may not be ready when an issue must be resolved.
2. [With basic research] social scientists (. . .), because of the system of rewards (. . .) to which they respond, tend to pursue lines of investigation that grow out of the core issues in their disciplines. These may be remote from concerns in councils of action.
3. Researchers simplify problems in order to make them amenable to study. Decision makers must deal with problems in their multifaceted complexity.
4. Social science has few theories or "laws" of wide generality that can provide a framework for policy research. (. . .) A good deal of research proceeds on a trial and error basis, and the results do not cumulate.
5. There are important limitations in social science methodology. Data sources are limited and sometimes inaccurate.
6. Researchers often conceptualize problems to fit the methodologies in which they are expert rather than to fit the nature of the question or the needs of the decision makers.
7. Much social science research examines the effects of variables, such as race or socioeconomic status, that decision makers can do little about. It does not concentrate on studying manipulable variables over which agencies can exercise some control.

8. Much research concludes with inconsistent findings. There is on-the-one-hand, but there is also on-the-other. Such conclusions offer little direction for action.
9. Some research conclusions are repetitions of the obvious. They indicate again what direct experience or previous research had led decision makers to expect. They seem to make little new contribution.
10. Some social science research studies conclude that things are not going well. People are in need; programs are not working. But there is often little in such reports to give guidance for effective corrective action.
11. In all applied research, to go from data to recommendations involves a "leap." The leap may be guided by the researchers' ideological predilections, practical lore, assessment of political feasibilities, judgements of clients' preferences and biases, or ignorance. Or researchers may not develop recommendations at all and let the decision maker determine the implications from the research. In any case interpretations of what the data "mean" for action can vary within wide limits. Interpretations are heavily influenced by the values of the researchers and decision makers.
12. The results of a series of studies in the same substantive area do not necessarily converge and cumulate. Often they provide divergent and even contradictory conclusions. As more studies are undertaken to resolve the discrepancies, a range of new issues emerges and a more complex picture of reality appears. The decision maker is faced not with answers to what seemed like a straightforward question but rather with more questions and more problems than he [or she] had recognized at the outset.

A general expectation that specific research findings provide specific answers and that responsible policy makers implement those answers in policy or practice sometimes is met. In the most practical sense, policy makers want to know what research studies can do for them. They want to know whether research findings can make a difference. At the very least, factors of importance include (a) whether research relevant to particular questions is available or can be produced, (b) whether the research is sufficiently conclusive as to offer guidance or direction, (c) whether the research can be made available for decision makers to consider in time to make a decision, and (d) whether the research results are presented in a form that decision makers can understand and use.

Related to the Policy-Making/Decision-Making Arena

We already have introduced several concerns linking the context for policy making to consideration of research utilization. Experts often address such concerns under the rubric of *political factors.* Keep in mind the potential importance of multiple stakeholders, decision makers with differing interests and unequal influence, and the possibility of variation based on the locus of the policy decision(s) under examination (national, state, local, etc.). Seldom would a single set of research results resolve the issues of all groups participating in a given policy decision or be persuasive to all (Weiss and Bucuvalas, 1980).

Previous decisions, policies, investments, and actions form the base upon which current and proposed policies are argued, expressed, and implemented. "Decision makers have to deal with much of the world as given. They [may have to] accept many aspects of social structure, agency organization, and social services as fixed, rather than as 'variables' open to investigation" (Weiss and Bucuvalas, 1980: 20). This may be very important in their decisions to consider and use research results that cast the "givens" as problematic.

Some experts have focused specifically on the nature of organizational decision making and on the processes through which use of research information may occur in complex, bureaucratic organizations to locate factors of importance. For example, the California Department of Corrections is a large, complex organization, with a yearly budget of $4.4 billion, more than 47,000 employees, a headquarters division with many staff units, an institutions division operating 33 prisons plus other facilities incarcerating more than 170,000 people on any given day, and a parole division supervising more than 100,000 persons on any given day. Important policy questions of many sorts are constantly addressed by the leaders of this organization.

Experts have proposed a number of factors relating research utilization and the process of decision making. Among others, we note the following:

1. An organization's policy makers may need to be "successful," while at the same time responding to powerful external elites (e.g., a governor, a mayor, legislators or other members of governing bodies, the judiciary, and other significant parties). There may be multiple, perhaps conflicting expectations. The "need to respond" may take precedence over the need to consider research (Lovell, 1988, 1996).
2. "Many decision makers may have been immersed in the substance of program and policy issues for decades. They have rich firsthand experience and many sources of direct information [e.g., expertise of staff, regular compilation of data by staff]. The contribution that (. . .) research [results] can make [may] seem marginal at best" (Weiss and Bucuvalas, 1980: 21).
3. Research information must compete "with a mountain of ordinary information [conventional wisdom, staff expertise, regularly compiled information] which it cannot replace but only reshape here and there" (Lindblom and Cohen, 1979: 32).
4. "Crisis management" may characterize the approach to decision making and policy making in an organization. Deadlines and immediate response may force the attention of policy makers. Initiating research, even reviewing research, may be seen as a luxury (Allison, 1971; Lovell, 1988).
5. Internal "bureaucratic politics" may affect the use of information. Competing, perhaps conflicting interests among organizational leaders, union leaders, and others may force political compromise (Allison, 1971; Rich, 1981; Stojkovic and Lovell, 1997).

6. Perceptions of organizational needs, together with time and resource constraints, may shape the regular search patterns of an organization. The search for information related to decision making may be limited to the inventory of information available within an organization or to review of information from similar or related organizations (Simon, 1976, 1967; Allison, 1971; Rich 1991; among a host of others).
7. The quality or conclusiveness of research information [or any information] and its appropriateness to a policy decision or problem may establish a necessary but not a sufficient condition for its use. For decision makers, enhancing bureaucratic interests may be more a determinant of use and/or type of use than quality or applicability of information (Rich 1981, 1991).

Criminal justice leaders operate within the political, ideological, procedural, and structural contexts of complex organizations. "As individuals, they may avoid exposure to research, find it unintelligible, misunderstand it, consider it unreliable, or reject that which is antipathetic to their own interests" (Weiss and Bucuvalas, 1980: 19). But most do understand scientific methodologies, most do understand well the strengths and limitations of research and research results, and most are sophisticated consumers of policy-related information.

As we have stated, our aim is to present a basic map of the territory to be explored—to provide you with concepts, language, and ideas for thinking about the use of research information for policy making. The picture that emerges is complex and there is no unifying theoretical framework. But life for policy makers concerned with criminal justice and criminal justice organizations is complex. Think once again of the municipal police department leaders confronting the situation of developing a definitive high-speed-pursuit policy. There have been research studies of good quality on high-speed pursuit. Research information is available. The department leaders could initiate a study specifically to determine the extent and nature of issues concerning high-speed pursuits in their jurisdiction, perhaps to find out when these occur, who is involved, when these are appropriately undertaken, when these are appropriately terminated, and when these result in favorable or unfavorable consequences. Think again of the potential set of interested parties. Now imagine what factors might be important in whether or not the department leaders choose to include research information as part of their consideration. Further, think about how you would design a study to investigate research use regarding such a policy development effort.

RESEARCH USE IN PERSPECTIVE

There is a growing body of knowledge on research utilization, not much specific to criminal justice. Much of the literature appears to be shaped by the expectation of research information having direct and immediate effects on policy and practice. As we have seen, decision makers may use research information in various ways. Research information may have direct effect on specific decisions, but it also may have indirect effects. Certainly, research-based knowledge may have a cumulative effect, becoming a part of what we and decision makers know, shaping perspectives, and so on.

Considering the array of factors that may inhibit research utilization, it may seem that use must seldom occur. But that is not the case. A great deal of quality basic and applied research has been and continues to be conducted in criminal justice. For example, the research conducted by Sherman and Berk (1984) concerning domestic violence and police practices was used in several states to develop mandatory arrest policies. Many agencies, such as the federal Office of Juvenile Justice and Delinquency Prevention, continuously fund research on issues of importance, disseminate the results, and use the results in various ways to guide and clarify large-scale policy development. Persons designing determinate sentencing guidelines and parole decision-making guidelines adopted by many jurisdictions utilize research and research methods as a basis for their efforts. We could go on and on. Our experience is that responsible policy makers want to be informed, and they want the best information they can get. There are well-established roles for research information and there is much potential.

References

Aiken, Leona S. and Stephen G. West (1991) *Multiple Regression: Testing and Interpreting Interactions.* Newbury Park, CA: Sage.

Allison, G. (1971) *Essence of Decision.* Boston: Little, Brown.

Babbie, Earl (1998) *The Practice of Social Research,* Eighth Edition. Belmont, CA: Wadsworth.

Barich, William (1986) A Reporter at Large: The Crazy Life. *New Yorker,* November 3: 97–130.

Barkin, Steven E. and Steven F. Cohn (1994) Racial Prejudice and Support for the Death Penalty by Whites. *Journal of Research in Crime and Delinquency* 32: 202–9.

Bowers, William (1993) Capital Punishment and Contemporary Values: Peoples' Misgivings and the Courts' Misperceptions. *Law and Society Review* 27: 157–75.

Brandl, Steven G. (1996) In the Line of Duty: A Descriptive Analysis of Police Assaults and Accidents. *Journal of Criminal Justice* 24: 255–64.

Crutchfield, Robert D., George S. Bridges, and Susan R. Pitchford (1994) Analytical and Aggregation Bias in Analysis of Imprisonment: Reconciling Discrepancies in Studies of Racial Disparity. *Journal of Research in Crime and Delinquency* 31: 166–82.

Decker, Scott (1996) Collective and Normative Features of Gang Violence. *Justice Quarterly* 13: 243–64.

Decker, Scott and Richard Rosenfeld (1995) "My Wife Is Married and So Is My Girlfriend": Adaptations to the Threat of AIDS in an Arrestee Population. *Crime and Delinquency* 41: 37–53.

Durham, Alexis M., H. Preston Elrod, and Patrick T. Kinkade (1995) Images of Crime and Justice: Murder and the "True Crime" Genre. *Journal of Criminal Justice* 23: 143–52.

Frank, James, Steven G. Brandl, Francis T. Cullen, and Amy Stichman (1996) Reassessing the Impact of Race on Citizens' Attitudes Toward the Police: A Research Note. *Justice Quarterly* 13: 321–34.

Gold, R. L. (1958) Roles in Sociological Field Observations. *Social Forces* 36: 217–33.

Leiber, Michael J. and Tina L. Mawhorr (1995) Evaluating the Use of Social Skills Training and Employment with Delinquent Youth. *Journal of Criminal Justice* 23: 127–41.

Lindblom, C. and D. Cohen (1979) *Usable Knowledge.* New Haven: Yale University Press.

LoBiondo-Wood, G. and J. Haber (1998) *Nursing Research: Methods, Critical Appraisal, and Research Utilization.* St. Louis: Mosby.

Lovell, R. (1988) Research Utilization in Complex Organizations: A Case Study in Corrections. *Justice Quarterly* 5: 257–80.

Lovell, R. (1996) Research in Prison. In M. McShane and F. Williams III (eds.), *Encyclopedia of American Prisons.* New York: Garland.

Lynd, R. (1939) *Knowledge for What?* Princeton: Princeton University Press.

MacKenzie, Doris Layton and James W. Shaw (1990) Inmate Adjustment and Change During Shock Incarceration: The Impact of Correctional Boot Camp Programs. *Justice Quarterly* 7: 125–47.

Mastrofski, Stephen D. (1988) Varieties of Police Governance in Metropolitan America. *Politics and Policy* 8: 12–31.

Mastrofski, Stephen D. and R. Richard Ritti (1992) You Can Lead a Horse to Water . . . : A Case Study of a Police Department's Response to Stricter Drunk-Driving Laws. *Justice Quarterly* 9: 465–91.

Maxfield, Michael G. and Earl Babbie (1994) *Research Methods for Criminal Justice and Criminology.* Belmont, CA: Wadsworth.

Maxfield, Michael G. and Earl Babbie (1998) *Research Methods for Criminal Justice and Criminology,* Second Edition. Belmont, CA: Wadsworth.

Percy, Stephen L. (1984) Citizen Participation in the Coproduction of Urban Services. *Urban Affairs Quarterly* 19: 431–46.

Pope, Carl E. (1980) Patterns in Burglary: An Empirical Examination of Offense and Offender Characteristics. *Journal of Criminal Justice* 8: 39–52.

Pope, Carl E., Stan Stojkovic, and William Feyerherm (1987) Confinement Patterns in the Milwaukee County House of Correction. *Journal of Criminal Justice* 15: 301–16.

Pope, Carl E. and Darnell Hawkins (1993) Race and Juvenile/Criminal Justice Processing: Implications of Site Specific Research. Paper presented at the annual meetings of the Western Society of Criminology, Monterey, CA.

Pope, Carl E., Rick Lovell, Stan Stojkovic, and Harold Rose (1996) Minority Phase II Study: Final Report. Wisconsin Office of Justice Assistance and the Governor's Commission on Juvenile Justice.

Rich, R. (1981) *Social Science Information and Public Policy Making.* San Francisco: Jossey-Bass.

Rich, R. (1991) Knowledge Creation, Diffusion, and Utilization: Perspectives of the Founding Editor. *Knowledge: Creation, Diffusion, and Utilization* 12: 319–37.

Roe, Keith (1985) Swedish Youth and Music: Listening Patterns and Motivations. *Communication Research* 12: 353–62.

Royse, David (1991) *Research Methods in Social Work.* Chicago: Nelson-Hall.

Schmid, Thomas J. and Richard S. Jones (1993) Ambivalent Actions: Prison Adaptation Strategies of First-Time, Short-Term Inmates. *Journal of Contemporary Ethnography* 21: 439–63.

Schneider, A., L. Ervin, and Z. Snyder-Joy (1996) Further Exploration of the Flight from Discretion: The Role of Risk/Need Instruments in Probation Supervision Decisions. *Journal of Criminal Justice* 24: 109–21.

Shaw, C. R. and H. McKay (1942) *Juvenile Delinquency and Urban Areas.* Chicago: University of Chicago Press.

Sherman, Lawrence W. (1992) *Policing Domestic Violence: Experiments and Dilemmas.* New York: Free Press.

Sherman, Lawrence W. and Richard A. Berk (1984) The Specific Deterrent Effects of Arrest for Domestic Assault. *American Sociological Review* 49: 261–72.

Sherman, Lawrence W. and David Weisburd (1995) General Deterrent Effects of Police Patrol in Crime "Hot Spots": A Randomized, Controlled Trial. *Justice Quarterly* 12: 625–48.

Silberman, M. (1995) *Corrections in America.* Belmont, CA: Wadsworth.

Simon, H. (1976) *Administrative Behavior,* Third Edition. New York: Free Press.

Singer, Simon I., Murray Levine, and Susyan Jou (1993) Heavy Metal Music Preference, Delinquent Friends, Social Control, and Delinquency. *Journal of Research in Crime and Delinquency* 30: 317–29.

Smith, Douglas A. and Christy A. Visher (1981) Street-Level Justice: Situational Determinants of Police Arrest Decisions. *Social Problems* 29: 167–77.

Smith, H. W. (1975) *Strategies of Social Research: The Methodological Imagination.* Englewood Cliffs, NJ: Prentice Hall.

Stojkovic, S. and R. Lovell (1997) *Corrections: An Introduction,* Second Edition. Cincinnati: Anderson.

Suttles, G. D. (1968) *The Social Order of the Slum.* Chicago: University of Chicago Press.

Taylor, Ralph B. (1994) *Research Methods in Criminal Justice.* New York: McGraw-Hill.

Taxman, Faye S. and Alex Piquero (1998) On Preventing Drunk Driving Recidivism: An Examination of Rehabilitation and Punishment Approaches. *Journal of Criminal Justice* 26: 129–43.

Vander Ven, Thomas M. (1998) Fear of Victimization and the Interactional Construction of Harassment in a Latino Neighborhood. *Journal of Contemporary Ethnography* 27: 374–98.

Weiss, C. and M. Bucuvalas (1980) *Social Science Research and Decision Making.* New York: Columbia University Press.

Wells, L. Edward and Joseph H. Rankin (1995) Juvenile Victimization: Convergent Validation of Alternative Measurements. *Journal of Research in Crime and Delinquency* 32: 287–307.

Whitaker, Gordon P. (1982) What Is Patrol Work? *Police Studies* 4: 13–22.

Whitaker, Gordon P. (1983) Police Department Size and the Quality and Costs of Police Services. In Stuart Nagel, Erika Fairchild, and Anthony Champagne (eds.), *The Political Science of Criminal Justice.* Springfield, IL: Thomas.

Williams, Frank P., David R. Longmire, and David B. Gulick (1998) The Public and the Death Penalty: Opinion as an Artifact of Question Type. *Criminal Justice Research Bulletin* 3: 1–5.

Worden, Alissa P. (1993) The Attitudes of Women and Men in Policing: Testing Conventional and Contemporary Wisdom. *Criminology* 31: 203–41.

Worden, Robert E. (1989) Situational and Attitudinal Explanations of Police Behavior: A Theoretical Reappraisal and Empirical Assessment. *Law and Society Review* 23: 667–711.

Worden, Robert E. (1990) A Badge and a Baccalaureate: Policies, Hypotheses and Further Evidence. *Justice Quarterly* 7: 565–92.

Worden, Robert E. (1995) Police Officers' Belief Systems: A Framework for Analysis. *American Journal of Police* 14: 49–81.

Zwerman, G. and G. Gardner (1986) Obstacles to Research in a State Prison. *Qualitative Sociology* 0(3): 293–300.

Index